Partial Evaluation and
Automatic Program Generation

C. A. R. Hoare, Series Editor

BACKHOUSE, R. C., *Program Construction and Verification*
DEBAKKER, J. W., *Mathematical Theory of Program Correctness*
BARR, M. and WELLS, C., *Category Theory for Computing Science*
BEN-ARI, M., *Principles of Concurrent and Distributed Programming*
BIRD, R. and WADLER, P., *Introduction to Functional Programming*
BORNAT, R., *Programming from First Principles*
BUSTARD, D., ELDER, J. and WELSSH, J., *Concurrent Program Structures*
CLARK, K. and McCABE, F. G., *Micro-Prolog: Programming in Logic*
CROOKES, D., *Introduction to Programming in Prolog*
DAHL, O.-J., *Verifiable Programming*
DROMEY, R. G., *How to Solve it by Computer*
DUNCAN, E., *Microprocessor Programming and Software Development*
ELDER, J., *Construction of Data Processing Software*
ELLIOTT, R. J. and HOARE, C. A. R. (eds), *Scientific Applications of Multiprocessors*
FREEMAN, T. L. and PHILLIPS, R. C., *Parallel Numerical Algorithms*
GOLDSCHLAGER, L. and LISTER, A., *Computer Science: A modern introduction (2nd edn)*
GORDON, M. J. C., *Programming Language Theory and its Implementation*
GRAY, P. M. D., KULKARNI, K. G. and PATON, N. W., *Object-Oriented Databases*
HAYES, I. (ed), *Specification Case Studies*
HEHNER, E. C. R., *The Logic of Programming*
HENDERSON, P., *Functional Programming: Application and implementation*
HOARE, C. A. R., *Communicating Sequential Processes*
HOARE, C. A. R. and GORDON, M. J. C. (eds), *Mechanized Reasoning and Hardware Design*
HOARE, C. A. R. and JONES, C. B. (eds), *Essays in Computing Science*
HOARE, C. A. R. and SHEPHERDSON, J. C. (eds), *Mathematical Logic and Programming Languages*
HUGHES, J. G., *Database Technology: A software engineering approach*
HUGHES, J. G., *Object-oriented Databases*
INMOS LTD, *Occam 2 Reference Manual*
JACKSON, M. A., *System Development*
JOHNSTON, H., *Learning to Program*
JONES, C. B., *Systematic Software Development using VDM (2nd edn)*
JONES, C. B. and SHAW, R. C. F. (eds), *Case Studies in Systematic Software Development*
JONES, G., *Programming in Occam*
JONES, G. and GOLDSMITH, M., *Programming in Occam 2*
JOSEPH, M., PRASAD, V. R. and NATARAJAN, N., *A Multiprocessor Operating System*
KALDEWAIJ, A., *Programming: The derivation of algorithms*
KING, P. J. B., *Computer and Communications Systems Performance Modelling*
LEW, A., *Computer Science: A mathematical introduction*
MARTIN, J. J., *Data Types and Data Structures*
McCABE, F. G., *High-Level Programmer's Guide to the 68000*
MEYER, B., *Introduction to the Theory of Programming Languages*
MEYER, B., *Object-oriented Software Construction*
MILNER, R., *Communication and Concurrency*
MITCHELL, R., *Abstract Data Types and Modula 2*
MORGAN, C., *Programming from Specifications*
PEYTON JONES, S. L., *The Implementation of Functional Programming Languages*
PEYTON JONES, S. and LESTER, D., *Implementing Function Languages*
POMBERGER, G., *Software Engineering and Modula-2*
POTTER, B., SINCLAIR, J. and TILL, D., *An Introduction to Formal Specification and Z*
REYNOLDS, J. C., *The Craft of Programming*
RYDEHEARD, D. E. and BURSTALL, R. M., *Computational Category Theory*
SLOMAN, M. and KRAMER, J., *Distributed Systems and Computer Networks*
SPIVEY, J. M., *The Z Notation: A reference manual (second edition)*
TENNENT, R. D., *Principles of Programming Languages*
TENNENT, R. D., *Semantics of Programming Languages*
WATT, D. A., *Programming Language Concepts and Paradigms*
WATT, D. A., *Programming Language Processors*
WATT, D. A., WICHMANN, B. A. and FINDLAY, W., *ADA: Language and methodology*
WELSH, J. and ELDER, J., *Introduction to Modula 2*
WELSH, J. and ELDER, J., *Introduction to Pascal (3rd edn)*
WELSH, J., ELDER, J. and BUSTARD, D., *Sequential Program Structures*
WELSH, J. and HAY, A., *A Model Implementation of Standard Pascal*
WELSH, J. and McKEAG, M., *Structured System Programming*
WIKSTRÖM, Å., *Functional Programming using Standard ML*

Partial Evaluation and Automatic Program Generation

Neil D. Jones
University of Copenhagen, Denmark

Carsten K. Gomard
DIKU and Computer Resources International A/S, Denmark

Peter Sestoft
Technical University of Denmark, Denmark

with chapters by

Lars Ole Andersen and Torben Mogensen
University of Copenhagen, Denmark

Prentice Hall
New York London Toronto Sydney Tokyo Singapore

First published 1993 by
Prentice Hall International (UK) Limited
Campus 400, Maylands Avenue
Hemel Hempstead
Hertfordshire HP2 7EZ
A division of
Simon & Schuster International Group

Printed and bound in Great Britain at
the University Press, Cambridge

Library of Congress Cataloging-in-Publication Data

Jones, Neil D.
    Partial evaluation and automatic program generation / Neil D.
Jones, Carsten K. Gomard, Peter Sestoft ; with chapters by Lars Ole
Andersen and Torben Mogensen.
        p.   cm.
    Includes bibliographical references and index.
    ISBN 0-13-020249-5
    1. Electronic digital computers–Programming.   2. Generators
(Computer programs)   I. Gomard, Carsten K.   II. Sestoft, Peter.
III. Title.
QA76.6.J666   1993
005.4'5–dc20   93–16674
                                                          CIP

British Library Cataloguing in Publication Data

A catalogue record for this book is available
from the British Library

ISBN 0–13–020249-5 (pbk)

---

1 2 3 4 5   97 96 95 94 93

Contents

Preface

This book is about *partial evaluation*, a program optimization technique also known as *program specialization*. It presents general principles for constructing partial evaluators for a variety of programming languages; and it gives examples, applications, and numerous references to the literature.

Partial evaluation

It is well known that a one-argument function can be obtained from a two-argument function by specialization, i.e. by fixing one input to a particular value. In analysis this is called restriction or projection, and in logic it is called currying. Partial evaluation, however, works with *program texts* rather than mathematical functions.

A partial evaluator is an algorithm which, when given a program and some of its input data, produces a so-called residual or specialized program. Running the residual program on the remaining input data will yield the same result as running the original program on all of its input data.

The theoretical possibility of partial evaluation was established many years ago in recursive function theory as Kleene's 's-m-n theorem'. This book concerns its practical realization and application.

Partial evaluation sheds new light on techniques for program optimization, compilation, interpretation, and the generation of program generators. Further, it gives insight into the properties of the programming languages themselves.

Partial evaluation can be thought of as a special case of program transformation, but emphasizes *full automation* and generation of *program generators* as well as transformation of single programs.

Partial evaluation and compilation

Partial evaluation gives a remarkable approach to compilation and compiler generation. For example, partial evaluation of an interpreter with respect to a source program yields a target program. Thus compilation can be achieved without a compiler, and a target program can be thought of as a specialized interpreter.

Compiler generation

Moreover, provided the partial evaluator is *self-applicable, compiler generation* is possible: specializing the partial evaluator itself with respect to a fixed interpreter yields a compiler. Thus a compiler can be thought of as a specialized partial evaluator: one which can specialize only an interpreter for a particular language.

Finally, specializing the partial evaluator with respect to itself yields a compiler generator. Thus a compiler generator can be thought of as a specialized partial evaluator: one which can specialize only itself.

Other applications

The application of partial evaluation is not restricted to compiling and compiler generation. If a program takes more than one input, and one of the inputs varies more slowly than the others, then specialization of the program with respect to that input gives a faster specialized program. Moreover, very many real-life programs exhibit interpretive behaviour. For instance they may be parametrized with configuration files, etc., which seldom vary, and therefore they may be profitably specialized.

The range of potential applications is extremely large, as shown by the list of examples below. All have been implemented on the computer, by researchers from Copenhagen, MIT, Princeton, and Stanford universities; and INRIA (France) and ECRC (Germany). All have been seen to give significant speedups.

- Pattern recognition

- Computer graphics by 'ray tracing'

- Neural network training

- Answering database queries

- Spreadsheet computations

- Scientific computing

- Discrete hardware simulation

This book

We give several examples of such applications, but the main emphasis of the book is on principles and methods for partial evaluation of a variety of programming languages: functional (the lambda calculus and Scheme), imperative (a flowchart language and a subset of C), and logical (Prolog). We explain the techniques necessary for construction of partial evaluators, for instance program flow analysis, in sufficient detail to allow their implementation. Many of these techniques are applicable also in other advanced programming tasks.

The book is structured as follows. The first chapter gives an overview of partial evaluation and some applications. Then Part I introduces fundamental programming language concepts, defines three mini-languages, and presents interpreters for them. Part II describes the principles of self-applicable partial evaluation, illustrated using two of the mini-languages: flow charts and first-order recursion equations. Part III shows how these principles apply to stronger languages: the lambda calculus, and large subsets of the Prolog, Scheme, and C programming languages. Part IV discusses practical aspects of partial evaluation, and presents a wide range of applications. Part V presents more a theoretical view and a number of advanced techniques, and provides extensive references to other research.

The book should be accessible even to beginning graduate students, and thus useful for beginners and researchers in partial evaluation alike.

The perspective on partial evaluation and the selection of material reflect the experience of our group with construction of several partial evaluators. These include the first non-trivial self-applicable partial evaluators for a functional language, an imperative language, the lambda calculus, a Prolog subset, and a subset of C. This work has been carried out at the University of Copenhagen.

Acknowledgements

Many have contributed to both the substance and the ideas appearing in this book. In particular we want to thank Lars Ole Andersen and Torben Mogensen who wrote two specialist chapters, and Olivier Danvy who provided numerous constructive comments and suggestions. More broadly we would like to express our thanks to: Peter Holst Andersen, Henk Barendregt, Job Baretta, Anders Bondorf, Hans Bruun, Mikhail Bulyonkov, Charles Consel, Robert Glück, Chris Hankin, Reinhold Heckmann, Fritz Henglein, Carsten Kehler Holst, Paul Hudak, John Hughes, Kristian Damm Jensen, Jesper Jørgensen, John Launchbury, Alan Mycroft, Hanne and Flemming Nielson, Patrick O'Keefe, Sergei Romanenko, Bill Scherlis, David A. Schmidt, Harald Søndergaard, Morten Heine Sørensen, Carolyn Talcott, Valentin Turchin, Phil Wadler, Daniel Weise, and last but not least, Lisa Wiese.

Parts of the research reported here were supported by DIKU (the Department of Computer Science, University of Copenhagen) by the Danish Natural Sciences Research Council, and by ESPRIT Basic Research Action 3124, 'Semantique'.

Chapter 1

Introduction

Partial evaluation has been the subject of rapidly increasing activity over the past decade since it provides a unifying paradigm for a broad spectrum of work in program optimization, interpretation, compiling, other forms of program generation, and even the generation of automatic program generators [19,24,79,101,141].

Many applications to date have concerned compiling and compiler generation from interpretive programming language definitions, but partial evaluation also has important applications to scientific computing, logic programming, metaprogramming, and expert systems.

It is a program optimization technique, perhaps better called *program specialization*. *Full automation* and the *generation of program generators*, as well as transforming single programs, are central themes and have been achieved. In comparison with program transformation work such as [43,141], partial evaluation has less dramatic speedups (typically linear) but greater automation.

1.1   Partial evaluation = program specialization

What is the essence of partial evaluation?
A one-argument function can be obtained from one with two arguments by *specialization*, i.e. by 'freezing' one input to a fixed value. In analysis[1] this is called 'restriction' or 'projection', and in logic it is called 'currying'. Partial evaluation, however, deals with *programs* rather than functions.

The idea of specializing programs is also far from new. It was first formulated and proven as Kleene's s-m-n theorem more than 40 years ago [149], and is an important building block of the theory of recursive functions. However, efficiency matters were quite irrelevant to Kleene's investigations of the boundary between computability and noncomputability, and Kleene's construction gave specialized programs that were *slower* than the originals.

---

[1]The branch of mathematics.

1

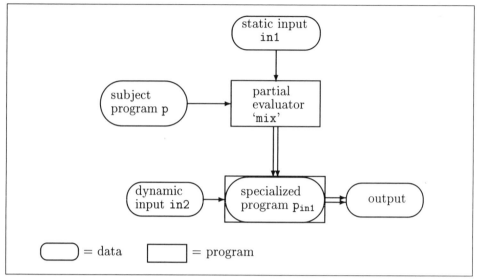

Figure 1.1: A partial evaluator.

A *partial evaluator* is given a *subject program* together with part of its input data, in1. Its effect is to construct a new program p_{in1} which, when given p's remaining input in2, will yield the same result that p would have produced given both inputs. In other words a partial evaluator is a program specializer. In Figure 1.1 the partial evaluator is called mix.[2]

Figure 1.2 shows a two-input program to compute x^n, and a faster program p_5 resulting from specialization to $n = 5$. The technique is to *precompute* all expressions involving n, to *unfold* the recursive calls to function f, and to *reduce* x*1 to x. This optimization was possible because the program's control is completely determined by n. If on the other hand $x = 5$ but n is unknown, specialization gives no significant speedup.

Our goal is to generate efficient programs from general ones by completely automatic methods. On the whole the general program will be simpler but less efficient than the specialized versions a partial evaluator produces. A telling catch phrase is *binding-time engineering* — making computation faster by changing the times at which subcomputations are done.

How is partial evaluation done?
Intuitively, specialization is done by performing those of p's calculations that depend only on in1, and by generating code for those calculations that depend on

---

[2]Notation: data values are in ovals, and programs are in boxes. The specialized program p_{in1} is first considered as data and then considered as code, whence it is enclosed in both. Further, single arrows indicate program input data, and double arrows indicate outputs. Thus mix has two inputs while p_{in1} has only one; and p_{in1} is the output of mix.

A two-
input $p =$
program

```
f(n,x) =if n = 0 then 1
            else if even(n) then f(n/2,x)↑2
            else x * f(n-1,x)
```

Program p, specialized to static input n = 5:

$p_5 =$ `f5(x) = x * ((x↑2)↑2)`

Figure 1.2: Specialization of a program to compute x^n.

the as yet unavailable input in2. A partial evaluator performs a mixture of execution and code generation actions — the reason Ershov called the process 'mixed
computation' [79], hence the name `mix`.

Three main partial evaluation techniques are well known from program transformation [43]: *symbolic computation, unfolding* function calls, and *program point
specialization*. The latter is a combination of *definition* and *folding*, amounting to
memoization. Figure 1.2 applied the first two techniques; the third was unnecessary since the specialized program had no function calls. The idea of program
point specialization is that a single function or label in program p may appear in
the specialized program p_{in1} in several specialized versions, each corresponding to
data determined at partial evaluation time.

1.1.1   Program data and behaviour

Programs are both input to and output from other programs. Since we shall be
discussing several languages, we assume given a fixed set D of first-order data
values including *all* program texts. A suitable choice of D is the set of Lisp's
'list' data as defined by $D = LispAtom + D^*$, e.g. (1 (2 3) 4) is a list of three
elements, whose second element is also a list. An example of a Lisp-like program
is p =

```
(define (length x)
  (case x of
  ()              => 0
  (x1 . xrest)    => (add 1 (length xrest)))))
```

We use the `typewriter` font for programs and for their input and output. If p is
a program in language L, then $[\![p]\!]_L$ denotes its meaning — often an input/output
function. To minimize notation, we use the same font both for concrete programs
and for variables denoting programs.

The subscript L indicates how p is to be interpreted. When only one language is being discussed we often omit the subscript so $[\![p]\!]_L = [\![p]\!]$. Standard languages used in the remainder of this article are:

L = implementation language

S = source language

T = target language

The program meaning function $[\![\_]\!]_L$ is of type $D \to D^* \to D$. Thus for $n \geq 0$,

$$\mathtt{output} = [\![\mathtt{p}]\!]_L \ [\mathtt{in}_1, \mathtt{in}_2, \ldots, \mathtt{in}_n]$$

results from running p on input values $\mathtt{in}_1$, $\mathtt{in}_2, \ldots$, $\mathtt{in}_n$, and output is undefined if p goes into an infinite loop.

1.1.2   An equational definition of partial evaluation

The essential property of mix is now formulated more precisely. Suppose p is a source program, in1 is the data known at stage one (static), and in2 is data known at stage two (dynamic). Then computation in one stage is described by

$$\mathtt{out} = [\![\mathtt{p}]\!] \ [\mathtt{in1}, \mathtt{in2}]$$

Computation in two stages using specializer mix is described by

$$\begin{aligned} \mathtt{p_{in1}} &= [\![\mathtt{mix}]\!] \ [\mathtt{p}, \mathtt{in1}] \\ \mathtt{out} &= [\![\mathtt{p_{in1}}]\!] \ \mathtt{in2} \end{aligned}$$

Combining these two we obtain an equational definition of mix:

$$[\![\mathtt{p}]\!] \ [\mathtt{in1}, \mathtt{in2}] = [\![\underbrace{[\![\mathtt{mix}]\!] \ [\mathtt{p}, \mathtt{in1}]}_{\substack{\text{specialized} \\ \text{program}}}]\!] \ \mathtt{in2}$$

where if one side of the equation is defined, the other is also defined and has the same value. This is easily generalizable to various numbers of static and dynamic inputs at the cost of a more complex notation[3].

Partial evaluation with different input, output, and implementation languages is also meaningful. An example is AMIX, a partial evaluator with a functional language as input and implementation language, and stack code as output [120].

$$[\![\mathtt{p}]\!]_S \ \mathtt{in1} \ \mathtt{in2} = [\![\underbrace{[\![\mathtt{mix}]\!]_L \ [\mathtt{p}, \mathtt{in1}]}_{\substack{\text{specialized} \\ \text{program}}}]\!]_T \ \mathtt{in2}$$

---

[3]Exactly the same idea applies to Prolog, except that inputs are given by partially instanted queries. In this case in1 is the part of a query known at stage one, and in2 instantiates this further.

1.2 Why do partial evaluation?

1.2.1 Speedups by partial evaluation

The chief motivation for doing partial evaluation is speed: program $\mathtt{p_{in1}}$ is often faster than p. To describe this more precisely, for any p, $\mathtt{d_1}$, ..., $\mathtt{d_n} \in D$, let $t_\mathtt{p}(\mathtt{d_1},\ldots,\mathtt{d_n})$ be the time to compute $[\![\mathtt{p}]\!]_{\mathrm{L}} [\mathtt{d_1},\ldots,\mathtt{d_n}]$. This could, for example, be the number of machine cycles to execute p on a concrete computer, or one could approximate by counting 1 for every elementary operation.

Specialization is clearly advantageous if in2 changes more frequently than in1. To exploit this, each time in1 changes one can construct a new specialized $\mathtt{p_{in1}}$, faster than p, and then run it on various in2 until in1 changes again. Partial evaluation can even be advantageous in a *single run*, since it often happens that

$$t_\mathtt{mix}(\mathtt{p}, \mathtt{in1}) + t_\mathtt{p_{in1}}(\mathtt{in2}) < t_\mathtt{p}(\mathtt{in1}, \mathtt{in2})$$

An analogy is that compilation *plus* target run time is often faster than interpretation in Lisp: $t_\mathtt{compiler}(\mathtt{source}) + t_\mathtt{target}(\mathtt{d}) < t_\mathtt{int}(\mathtt{source}, \mathtt{d})$.

1.2.2 Efficiency versus generality and modularity?

One often has a class of similar problems which all must be solved efficiently. One solution is to write many small and efficient programs, one for each. Two disadvantages are that much programming is needed, and maintenance is difficult: a change in outside specifications can require every program to be modified.

Alternatively, one may write a single highly parametrized program able to solve any problem in the class. This has a different disadvantage: *inefficiency*. A highly parametrized program can spend most of its time testing and interpreting parameters, and relatively little in carrying out the computations it is intended to do.

Similar problems arise with highly modular programming. While excellent for documentation, modification, and human usage, inordinately much computation time can be spent passing data back and forth and converting among various internal representations at module interfaces.

To get the best of both worlds: write only one highly parametrized and perhaps inefficient program; and *use a partial evaluator to specialize* it to each interesting setting of the parameters, automatically obtaining as many customized versions as desired. All are faithful to the general program, and the customized versions are often much more efficient. Similarly, partial evaluation can remove most or all the interface code from modularly written programs.

1.2.3   A sampler of applications

Because of its generality and conceptual simplicity, partial evaluation is applicable to a wide range of problems. The essence of applying partial evaluation is to solve a problem indirectly, using some relatively static information to generate a faster *special-purpose program*, which is then run on various data supplied more dynamically. Many applications begin with general and rather 'interpretive' algorithms.

First, we give some examples which follow this line of thought, but do not use a partial evaluator as such. An early example is a 'symbolic' solution method for sparse systems of linear equations [107]. Another is speeding up execution of functional programs by 're-opening closures' [13]; and gaining significant parser speedups by compiling LR parsing tables into machine code [216]. A recent application is a very fast operating system kernel which uses on-the-fly code generation [221].

Related problems and a variety of others have been solved using general-purpose partial evaluators. Applications include circuit simulation [14], computer graphics [186], neural net training [126], numerical computations [22], optimizing hard real-time systems [205], and scientific computing of several sorts [21].

The most developed area, programming language processors and especially compiling, will be discussed in detail in several later chapters and thus are not mentioned here. Related applications include pattern matching in general [54], and as applied to a lazy language [138] or constraint logic programming [252]; efficiently implementing term rewriting systems [250]; and Lafont's interaction nets [18].

The following sketches give something of the flavor of problem-solving by program specialization.

Computer graphics. 'Ray tracing' repeatedly recomputes information about the ways light rays traverse a given scene from different origins and in different directions. Specializing a general ray tracer to a fixed scene to transform the scene into a specialized tracer, only good for tracing rays through that one scene, gives a much faster algorithm.

Database queries. Partial evaluation can compile a query into a special-purpose search program, whose task is only to answer the given query. The generated program may be discarded afterwards. Here the input to the program generator is a general query answerer, and the output is a 'compiler' from queries into search programs.

Neural networks. Training a neural network typically uses much computer time, but can be improved by specializing a general simulator to a fixed network topology.

Scientific computing. General programs for several diverse applications including orbit calculations (the n-body problem) and computations for electrical circuits have been sped up by specialization to particular planetary systems and circuits.

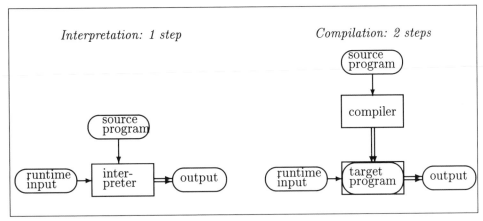

Figure 1.3: Compilation in two steps, interpretation in one.

1.3   Computation in one stage or more

Computational problems can be solved either by single stage computations, or by multistage solutions using program generation. Partial evaluation provides a way to go automatically from the first to the second. To clarify the problems and payoffs involved we first describe two familiar multistage examples:

1. a *compiler*, which generates a target (= object) program in some target language from a source program in a source language;

2. a *parser generator*, which generates a parser from a context free grammar.

Compilers and parser generators first transform their input into an executable program and then run the generated program, on runtime inputs for a compiler or on a character string to be parsed. Efficiency is vital: the target program should run as quickly as possible, and the parser should use as little time per input character as possible. Figure 1.3 compares two-step compilative program execution with one-step interpretive execution. Similar diagrams describe two-step parser generation and one-step general parsing.

1.3.1   Interpreters

A source program can be run in one step using an *interpreter*: an L-program we call int that executes S-programs. This has as input the S-program to be executed, together with *its* runtime inputs. Symbolically,

$$\texttt{output} = [\![\texttt{source}]\!]_{\text{S}} \; [\texttt{in}_1, \ldots, \texttt{in}_n] = [\![\texttt{int}]\!]_{\text{L}} \; [\texttt{source}, \texttt{in}_1, \ldots, \texttt{in}_n]$$

Assuming only one input for notational simplicity, we define program int to be an *interpreter for* S *written in* L if for all source, d $\in$ D

$$[\![\texttt{source}]\!]_S \ d = [\![\texttt{int}]\!]_L \ [\texttt{source, d}]$$

1.3.2   Compilers

A compiler generates a target (object) program in target language T from a source program source in language S. The compiler is itself a program, say compiler, written in implementation language L. The effect of running source on input in_1, in_2,..., in_n is realized by first compiling source into target form:

$$\texttt{target} = [\![\texttt{compiler}]\!]_L \ \texttt{source}$$

and then running the result:

$$\texttt{output} = [\![\texttt{source}]\!]_S \ [in_1,\dots,in_n] = [\![\texttt{target}]\!]_T \ [in_1,\dots,in_n]$$

Formally, compiler is an S-*to*-T-*compiler written in* L if for all source, d $\in$ D,

$$[\![\texttt{source}]\!]_S \ d = [\![\ [\![\texttt{compiler}]\!]_L \ \texttt{source}]\!]_T \ d$$

Comparison
Interpreters are usually smaller and easier to write than compilers. One reason is that the implementer thinks only of *one time* (the execution time), whereas a compiler must perform actions to generate code to achieve a desired effect at run time. Another is that the implementer only thinks of *one language* (the source language), while a compiler writer also has to think of the target language. Further, an interpreter, if written in a sufficiently abstract, concise, and high-level language, can serve as a language definition: an *operational semantics* for the interpreted language.

However compilers are here to stay. The overwhelming reason is *efficiency*: compiled target programs usually run an order of magnitude (and sometimes two) faster than when interpreting a source program.

Parsing
One can parse by first generating a parser from an input context-free grammar:

$$\texttt{parser} = [\![\texttt{parse-gen}]\!]_L \ \texttt{grammar}$$

and then applying the result to an input character string:

$$\texttt{parse-tree} = [\![\texttt{parser}]\!]_L \ \texttt{char-string}$$

On the other hand, there exist one-step general parsers, e.g. Earley's parser [72]. Similar tradeoffs arise — a general parser is usually smaller and easier to write than a parser generator, but a parser generated from a fixed context-free grammar runs *much* faster.

1.3.3   Semantics-directed compiler generation

By this we mean more than just a tool to help humans write compilers. Given a specification of a programming language, for example a formal semantics or an interpreter, our goal is *automatically* and *correctly* to transform it into a compiler from the specified 'source' language into another 'target' language [195,215].

Traditional compiler writing tools such as parser generators and attribute grammar evaluators are not semantics-directed, even though they can and do produce compilers as output. These systems are extremely useful in practice — but it is entirely up to their users to ensure generation of correct target code.

The motivation for automatic compiler generation is evident: thousands of person-years have been spent constructing compilers by hand; and many of these are not correct with respect to the intended semantics of the language they compile. Automatic transformation of a semantic specification into a compiler faithful to that semantics eliminates such consistency errors.

The three jobs of writing the language specification, writing the compiler, and showing the compiler to be correct (or debugging it) are reduced to one: writing the language specification in a form suitable as input to the compiler generator.

There has been rapid progress towards this research goal in the past few years, with more and more sophisticated practical systems and mathematical theories for the semantics-based manipulation of programs, including compiler generation. One of the most promising is partial evaluation.

1.3.4   Executable specifications

A still broader goal is *efficient implementation of executable specifications*. Examples include compiler generation and parser generation, and others will be mentioned later. One can naturally think of programs int and parser above as *specification executers*: the interpreter executes a source program on its inputs, and the parser applies a grammar to a character string. In each case the value of the first input determines how the remaining inputs are to be interpreted. Symbolically:

$$[\![\texttt{spec-exec}]\!]_{\text{L}} \ [\texttt{spec},\texttt{in}_1,\ldots,\texttt{in}_n] = \texttt{output}$$

The interpreter's source program input determines what is to be computed. The interpreter thus executes a specification, namely a source S-program that is to be run in language L. The first input to a general parser is a grammar that defines the structure of a certain set of character strings. The specification input is thus a grammar defining a parsing task.

A reservation is that one can of course also commit errors (sometimes the most serious ones!) when writing specifications. Achieving our goal does not eliminate all errors, but it again reduces the places they can occur to one, namely the specification. For example, a semantics-directed compiler generator allows quick tests of

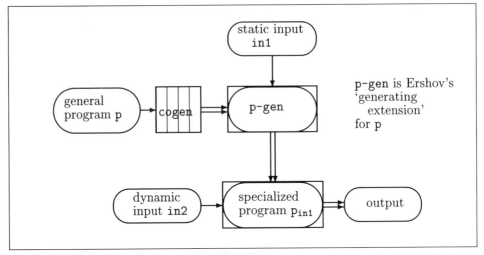

Figure 1.4: A generator of program generators.

a new language design to see whether it is in accordance with the designers' intentions regarding program behaviour, computational effects, freedom from runtime type errors, storage usage, efficiency etc.

1.3.5   Generating program generators

In practice one rarely uses specification executers to run S-programs or to parse strings — since experience shows them to be much slower than the specialized programs generated by a compiler or parser generator. Wouldn't it be nice to have the best of both worlds — the simplicity and directness of executable specifications, and the efficiency of programs produced by program generators? This goal is illustrated in Figure 1.4:

- Program cogen accepts a two-input program p as input and generates a *program generator* (p-gen in the diagram).

- The task of p-gen is to generate a specialized program p_{in1}, given known value in1 for p's first input.

- Program p_{in1} computes the same output when given p's remaining input in2 that p would compute if given both in1 and in2.

Andrei Ershov gave the appealing name *generating extension* to p-gen. We shall see that partial evaluation can realize this goal, both in theory and in practice on the computer.

Parser and compiler generation

Assuming cogen exists, compiler generation can be done by letting p be the interpreter int, and letting in1 be source. The result of specializing int to source is a program written in the specializer's output language, but with the same input/output function as the source program. In other words, the source program has been compiled from S into cogen's output language. The effect is that int-gen is a compiler.

If we let p be program parser, with a given grammar as its known input in1, by the description above parser-gen is a parser generator, meaning that parser-gen transforms its input grammar into a specialized parser. This application has been realized in practice at Copenhagen (unpublished as yet), and yields essentially the well-known LR(k) parsers, in program form.

Efficiency is desirable at three different times:

1. The specialized program p_{in1} should be fast. Analogy: *a fast target program.*

2. The program specializer p-gen should quickly construct p_{in1}. Analogy: *a fast compiler.*

3. cogen should quickly construct p-gen from p. Analogy: *fast compiler generation.*

It would be wonderful to have a program generator generator, but it is far from clear how to construct one. Polya's advice on solving hard problems: solve a simpler problem similar to the ultimate goal, and then generalize. Following this approach, we can clump boxes cogen and p-gen in Figure 1.4 together into a single program with two inputs, the program p to be specialized, and its first argument in1. This is just the mix of Figure 1.1, so we already have a weaker version of the multiphase cogen.

We will see how cogen can be constructed from mix. This has been done in practice for several different programming languages, and efficiency criteria 1, 2 and 3 have all been met. Surprisingly, criteria 2 and 3 are achieved by *self-application* — applying the partial evaluator to itself as input.

1.4   Partial evaluation and compilation

One may compile by specializing an interpreter to execute only one fixed-source program, yielding a target program in the partial evaluator's output language so target = [[mix]] [int, source]. Program target can be expected to be faster than interpreting source since many interpreter actions depend only on source and so can be precomputed.

In general, program target will be a mixture of int and source, containing parts derived from both. A common pattern is that the target program's *control structure* and *computations* resemble those of the source program, while its *appearance* resembles that of the interpreter, both in its language and the names of its specialized functions.

The cost of interpretation

A typical interpreter's basic cycle is first, syntax analysis; then evaluation of subexpressions by recursive calls; and finally, actions to perform the main operator, e.g. to subtract 1 or to look up a variable value. In general, running time of interpreter int on inputs p and d satisfies $a_p \cdot t_p(d) \leq t_{int}(p, d)$ for all d, where a_p is a constant. (In this context, 'constant' means that a_p is independent of d, but may depend on source program p.) In experiments a_p is often around 10 for simple interpreters run on small source programs, and larger for more sophisticated languages. Clever use of data structures such as hash tables or binary trees can make a_p grow slowly as a function of p's size.

Optimality

The 'best possible' mix should remove *all computational overhead* caused by interpretation. This criterion has been satisfied for several partial evaluators for various languages, using natural self-interpreters.

1.4.1   Partial evaluation versus traditional compiling

Does partial evaluation eliminate the need to write compilers? Yes and no... *Pro*: when given a language definition in the form of an operational semantics, a partial evaluator eliminates the *first and largest* order of magnitude: the interpretation overhead. A virtue is that the method yields target programs that are *always correct* with respect to the interpreter. Thus the problem of compiler correctness seems to have vanished. This approach is clearly suitable for prototype implementation of new languages from interpretive definitions (known as *metaprogramming* in the Prolog community).

Contra: the generated target code is in the partial evaluator's output language, typically the language the interpreter is written in. Thus partial evaluation will not devise a target language suitable for the source language, e.g. P-code for Pascal. It won't invent *new runtime data structures* either, so human creativity seems necessary to gain the full handwritten compiler efficiency. Recent work by Wand, and Hannan and Miller, however, suggests the possibility of deriving target machine architectures from the text of an interpreter [277,110].

Finally, partial evaluation is *automatic and general*, so its generated code may not be as good as handwritten target code. In particular we have not mentioned classical optimization techniques such as common subexpression elimination, exploiting available expressions, and register allocation. Some of these depend on specific machine models or intermediate languages and so are hard to generalize;

but there is no reason why many well-known techniques could not be incorporated into the next generation of partial evaluators.

1.5   Automatic program generation

This section shows the sometimes surprising capabilities of partial evaluation for generating program generators.

1.5.1   The first Futamura projection

Compiling by partial evaluation always yields correct target programs, verified as follows:

$$
\begin{aligned}
\texttt{out} \quad &= \quad [\![\,\texttt{source}\,]\!]_S \ \texttt{input} \\
&= \quad [\![\texttt{int}]\!] \ [\texttt{source}, \texttt{input}] \\
&= \quad [\![\,[\![\texttt{mix}]\!] \ [\texttt{int}, \texttt{source}]\,]\!] \ \texttt{input} \\
&= \quad [\![\texttt{target}]\!] \ \texttt{input}
\end{aligned}
$$

The last three equalities follow respectively by the definitions of an interpreter, $\texttt{mix}$, and $\texttt{target}$. The net effect has thus been to translate from S to L. Equation $\texttt{target}$ $= [\![\texttt{mix}]\!]$ $\texttt{int}\,\texttt{source}$ is often called the *first Futamura projection*, first reported in [92].

1.5.2   Compiler generation by self-application

We now show that $\texttt{mix}$ can also generate a stand-alone compiler:

$$\texttt{compiler} = [\![\texttt{mix}]\!] \ [\texttt{mix}, \texttt{int}]$$

This is an L-program which, when applied to $\texttt{source}$, yields $\texttt{target}$, and is thus a compiler from S to L, written in L. Verification is straightforward from the $\texttt{mix}$ equation:

$$
\begin{aligned}
\texttt{target} \quad &= \quad [\![\texttt{mix}]\!] \ [\texttt{int} \ , \texttt{source}] \\
&= \quad [\![\,[\![\texttt{mix}]\!] \ [\texttt{mix}, \texttt{int}]\,]\!] \ \texttt{source} \\
&= \quad [\![\texttt{compiler}]\!] \ \texttt{source}
\end{aligned}
$$

Equation $\texttt{compiler} = [\![\texttt{mix}]\!]$ $[\texttt{mix}, \texttt{int}]$ is called the second Futamura projection. The compiler generates specialized versions of interpreter $\texttt{int}$, and so is in effect $\texttt{int-gen}$ as discussed in Section 1.3.5. Operationally, constructing a compiler this way is hard to understand because it involves self-application — using $\texttt{mix}$ to specialize itself. But it gives good results in practice, as we shall see.

Remark. This way of doing compiler generation requires that mix be written in its own input language, e.g. that S = L. This restricts the possibility of multiple language partial evaluation as discussed in Section 1.1.2[4].

1.5.3   The third Futamura projection

By precisely parallel reasoning, cogen = $[\![$mix$]\!]$ [mix, mix] is a *compiler generator*: a program that transforms interpreters into compilers. The compilers it produces are versions of mix itself, specialized to various interpreters. This projection is even harder to understand intuitively than the second, but also gives good results in practice. Verification of Figure 1.4 is again straightforward from the mix equation:

$$[\![\text{p}]\!] \text{ [in1, in2]} = [\![[\![\text{mix}]\!] \text{ [p, in1]}]\!] \text{ in2} = \ldots = [\![[\![[\![\text{cogen}]\!] \text{ p}]\!] \text{ in1}]\!] \text{ in2}$$

While easily verified from the definitions of mix and interpretation, it is far from clear what the pragmatic consequences of these equations are. What is the effect in practice of applying programs to themselves as inputs? Isn't self-application most often used to show problems *impossible to solve* on the computer, as in the proof of the unsolvability of the halting problem? And even assuming that these equations can be realized on the computer, how does a compiler generated mechanically as above compare in efficiency and structure with handmade compilers?

Answers to these questions form the bulk of this book.

1.5.4   Speedups from self-application

A variety of partial evaluators satisfying all the above equations have been constructed. Compilation, compiler generation, and compiler generator generation can each be done in two different ways:

target   = $[\![$mix$]\!]$ [int, source] = $[\![$compiler$]\!]$ source

compiler = $[\![$mix$]\!]$ [mix, int] = $[\![$cogen$]\!]$ int

cogen   = $[\![$mix$]\!]$ [mix, mix] = $[\![$cogen$]\!]$ mix

The exact timings vary according to the design of mix and int, and with the implementation language L. Nonetheless, we have often observed that *in each case the second way is about 10 times faster than the first.* Moral: self-application can generate programs that run faster!

---

[4]The output language of mix may, however, be different from its input and implementation languages.

1.5.5   Hierarchies of metalanguages

A modern approach to solving a wide-spectrum problem is to devise a *user-oriented language* to express computational requests, viz. the widespread interest in expert systems. A processor for such a language usually works interpretively, alternating between reading and deciphering the user's requests, consulting databases, and doing problem-related computing — an obvious opportunity to optimize by partial evaluation.

Such systems are often constructed using a *hierarchy* of metalanguages, each controlling the sequence and choice of operations at the next lower level [234]. Here, efficiency problems are yet more serious since each interpretation layer multiplies computation time by a significant factor. We shall see that partial evaluation allows one to use metaprogramming without order-of-magnitude loss of efficiency.

1.6   Critical assessment

Partial evaluation and self-application have many promising applications, and work well in practice for generating program generators, e.g. compilers and compiler generators, and other program transformers, for example style changers and instrumenters. They are, however, still far from perfectly understood in either theory or practice. Significant problems remain, and we conclude by listing some of them.

Greater automation and user convenience
The user should not need to give advice on *unfolding* or on *generalization*, that is to say, where statically computable values should be regarded as dynamic. (Such advice is required in some current systems to avoid constructing large or infinite output programs.)

The user should not be forced to *understand the logic* of a program resulting from specialization. An analogy is that one almost never looks at a compiler-generated target program, or a Yacc-generated parser.

Further, users shouldn't need to understand *how the partial evaluator works*. If partial evaluation is to be used by non-specialists in the field, it is essential that the user thinks as much as possible about the problem he or she is trying to solve, and as little as possible about the tool being used to aid its solution. A consequence is that debugging facilities and interfaces that give feedback about the *subject program's binding-time separation* are essential for use by non-specialists.

Analogy with parser generation
In several respects, using a partial evaluator is rather like using a parser generator such as Yacc. First, if Yacc accepts a grammar, then one can be certain that the parser it generates assigns the right parse tree to *any* syntactically correct input string, and detects any incorrect string. Analogously, a correct partial evaluator

always yields specialized programs faithful to the input program. For instance, a target program will be faithful to its source, and a generated compiler will always be correct with respect to the interpreter from which it was derived.

Second, when a user constructs a context-free grammar, he or she is mainly interested in what strings it generates. But use of Yacc forces the user to think from a new perspective: possible *left-to-right ambiguity*. If Yacc rejects a grammar, the user may have to modify it several times, until it is free of left-to-right ambiguity.

Analogously, a partial evaluator user may have to think about his or her program from a new perspective: how clear is its *binding-time separation*? If specialized programs are too slow, it will be necessary to modify the program and retry until it has better binding-time properties.

Partial evaluation is no panacea

Not *all* programs benefit from specialization. Knowing the value of x will not significantly aid computing x^n as in Figure 1.2, since no actual operation on x can be done by the partial evaluator. Further, the efficiency of `mix`-generated target programs depend crucially on how the interpreter is written. For example, if the interpreter uses *dynamic name binding*, then generated target programs will have runtime variable name searches; and if it uses *dynamic code creation* then generated target programs will contain runtime source language text.

Some recurring problems in partial evaluation

Rapid progress has occurred, but there are often problems with termination of the partial evaluator, and sometimes with semantic faithfulness of the specialized program to the input program (termination, backtracking, correct answers, etc.). Further, it can be hard to predict how much (if any) speedup will be achieved by specialization, and hard to see how to modify the program to improve the speedup.

An increasing understanding is evolving of how to construct partial evaluators for various languages, of how to tame termination problems, and of the mathematical foundations of partial evaluation. On the other hand, we need to be able to

- make it easier to use a partial evaluator;

- understand how much speedup is possible;

- predict the speedup and space usage from the program *before* specialization

- deal with typed languages;

- generate machine architectures tailor-made to a source language defined by an interpreter.

1.7   Overview of the book

Prerequisites

Our presentation style is semiformal. On the one hand, the various terms and algorithms used are precisely defined. For example, the programs we present may be unambiguously executed by hand. On the other hand, we do not use advanced mathematical concepts and terminology (domains, algebras, categories, etc.); ordinary discrete mathematics is sufficient.

We assume the reader to be familiar with a Pascal-like programming language. Prior knowledge of a functional language such as Lisp, Scheme, ML, Miranda, or Haskell would make some parts easier to follow, but is not a prerequisite. Finally, some experience with compilers (e.g. an undergraduate compiler construction course) would be desirable.

Outline

Part I introduces concepts and notation of programming languages.

Chapter 2 introduces functions, recursion, and data types, and the distinction between a program (text) and the function it defines.

Chapter 3 defines the concepts of interpreter and compiler and discusses program running times and interpretation overhead. Then three mini-languages are presented: the lambda calculus, first-order recursion equations, and a flow chart language. Interpreters for executing them are given also, to introduce the concepts of abstract syntax, environment, and closure, which will be used in the partial evaluators presented later.

Part II presents partial evaluators for two of the mini-languages introduced in Chapter 3. This introduces a variety of techniques for partial evaluation, useful also in the partial evaluation of stronger languages.

Chapter 4 concerns the flow chart language. A partial evaluator is developed in considerable detail, emphasizing concrete examples and carefully motivating the various design decisions that are taken. Enough details are given to allow the reader to implement the partial evaluator and generate compilers on his or her own computer. It is shown by examples that partial evaluation can compile, generate compilers, and even generate a compiler generator. The key to the latter two is self-application as in the Futamura projections of Section 1.5. It may come as a surprise that self-application leads to considerable improvements in compiler running times. Program texts illustrating all of these are included.

The important topic of *binding-time analysis* is introduced, and a variety of technical problems are identified, analysed, and solved.

Chapter 5 describes a self-applicable partial evaluator for a first-order language of recursive equations. Many of the principles of Chapter 4 can be adapted to this stronger programming language.

Chapter 6 presents one way to recognize a good partial evaluator, and shows that there is a theoretical limit to the amount of speed-up that can in general be expected from partial evaluation.

Chapter 7 compares *offline* partial evaluation (using a separate binding-time analysis phase) to *online* partial evaluation. The offline approach appears beneficial to self-application, and all partial evaluators presented in this book are offline. Finally, some advice on constructing a self-applicable partial evaluator for a new programming language is given.

Part III   presents partial evaluators for four languages which are stronger in various respects than the flow chart and recursion equation language.

Chapter 8 describes a self-applicable partial evaluator for the untyped lambda calculus, stronger than the previous partial evaluator in that it can deal with higher-order functions. It is seen that type inference provides a simple and elegant way to do binding-time analysis for higher-order partial evaluation.

Chapter 9 describes a self-applicable partial evaluator for a Prolog subset, emphasizing problems not seen in the earlier chapters.

Chapter 10 presents a partial evaluator 'Similix', which handles a substantial subset of Scheme including both higher-order functions and restricted side effects. Scheme is interesting because it is a realistic language.

Chapter 11 presents some techniques required to deal with languages (C, Pascal, etc.) where the programming style relies on both (recursive) function calls and a global, mutable state, including arrays and pointers.

Part IV   discusses practical problems frequently encountered when using partial evaluation, and gives several examples of its practical application.

Chapter 12 shows that some subject programs are less amenable to speed-up by partial evaluation than others, and presents some transformation that improve the results of partial evaluation while preserving the meaning of the subject program.

Chapter 13 describes several applications of partial evaluation and demonstrates that the utility of partial evaluation is not limited to compiler generation.

Part V   presents advanced topics, more briefly than the previous subjects and with references to current literature.

Chapter 14 contains a discussion of termination in partial evaluation. An algorithm sufficient to guarantee that program specialization terminates (in the absence of infinite static loops) is presented and justified, for the simple flow chart language of Chapter 4.

Chapter 15 explains the program analysis method called abstract interpretation, presents a so-called closure analysis which is useful for doing analysis of higher-order programs, and applies this to produce a higher-order binding-time analysis for the partial evaluator in Chapter 10. Finally, it presents a projection-based approach to binding-time analysis of partially static data structures.

Chapter 16 relates partial evaluation to recursive function theory, gives a more abstract view of program specialization, and discusses the types of program-processing programs: interpreters, compilers, and partial evaluators.

Chapter 17 explains the relation between partial evaluation and classical program transformation methods such as Burstall and Darlington's fold/unfold technique.

Finally, Chapter 18 gives an overview of the literature on partial evaluation and closely related topics, and serves as a guide to further studies in the field.

Part I

Fundamental Concepts in Programming Languages

Chapter 2

Functions, Types, and Expressions

In this chapter we relate *mathematical* functions to the functions that can be defined in a programming language such as Pascal, Lisp, Scheme, ML or Miranda. We also introduce relevant mathematical ideas in a way that is independent of algorithmic or programming concepts.

It is important to understand that *programs* and *functions* are two distinct domains. One is a syntactic world of program texts containing symbols, commands, expressions, etc. These can be interpreted in quite arbitrary ways, according to the whims of a programming language designer (for example '+' can mean addition, set union, a tab skip, or string concatenation). The other is the relatively well-understood world of mathematical functions, sets, etc.

There are, however, connections between the two worlds. In one direction, mathematical concepts can be used to explicate program meanings, as is done in denotational semantics [241,256]. In the other direction, some programming languages have been designed to model mathematical concepts. For instance, two of the miniature programming languages introduced in Chapter 3 are based on lambda notation and recursion equations. Chapter 3 also introduces a simple imperative language, not directly based on mathematical ideas.

2.1 Functions

Informally, a mathematical function is a relation between the elements of two sets: a relation that relates each element of the first set to exactly one element of the second. More formally, recall that the *Cartesian product* $A \times B$ of two sets A and B is the set

$$A \times B = \{(a, b) \mid a \in A \text{ and } b \in B\}$$

A *total function* f from A to B (written as $f : A \xrightarrow{t} B$) is formally a subset of $A \times B$ with the properties:

23

1. $\forall a \in A\ \forall b, b' \in B :\ (a, b) \in f$ and $(a, b') \in f$ implies $b = b'$.

2. $\forall a \in A\ \exists b \in B$ such that $(a, b) \in f$.

Property 1 says f is *single-valued*, meaning that each a in A is mapped to at most one b in B. This b is usually written $f(a)$ or just fa. Property 2 says f is *total*, meaning that each a in A is mapped to at least one b in B. In other words, $f(a)$ is defined for every a in A.

In computer science we often meet functions which are undefined for some arguments. A *partial function* f from A to B (written $f : A{\rightarrow}B$) is a subset f of $A \times B$ that satisfies 1, but not necessarily 2. A natural example is the function that maps a program's input to the corresponding output. This function is undefined for any input that causes the program to go into an infinite loop. We shall use the notation

$$f(a) = \perp$$

(where $\perp$ is called *bottom*) to indicate that $f(a)$ is undefined, i.e. that f contains no pair of form (a, b). Sometimes $\perp$ will be treated as if it were a special value. Thus it is possible to consider a partial function $f : A{\rightarrow}B$ as a total function which may yield the undefined value $\perp$, that is, $f : A \xrightarrow{t} (B + \{\perp\})$.

Note that every total function is also a partial function, whereas the converse is not true.

Examples
Suppose sets X and Y have x and y elements, respectively. It is easy to see that there are in all y^x different total functions from X to Y. Further, there must be $(y+1)^x$ different partial functions from X to Y (to see this, think of 'undefined' as the special value $\perp$). If, for example, $X = \{red, green\}$ and $Y = \{red, blue\}$ then

- the set of total functions from X to Y is: $\{f_1, f_2, f_3, f_4\}$;

- the set of partial functions from X to Y is: $\{f_1, f_2, f_3, f_4, f_5, f_6, f_7, f_8, f_9\}$;

where the functions $f_1, \ldots, f_9$ are defined as follows:

f_1	$f_1(\text{red}) = \text{red}$	$f_1(\text{green}) = \text{red}$
f_2	$f_2(\text{red}) = \text{red}$	$f_2(\text{green}) = \text{blue}$
f_3	$f_3(\text{red}) = \text{blue}$	$f_3(\text{green}) = \text{red}$
f_4	$f_4(\text{red}) = \text{blue}$	$f_4(\text{green}) = \text{blue}$
f_5	$f_5(\text{red}) = \text{red}$	$f_5(\text{green}) = \perp$
f_6	$f_6(\text{red}) = \text{blue}$	$f_6(\text{green}) = \perp$
f_7	$f_7(\text{red}) = \perp$	$f_7(\text{green}) = \text{red}$
f_8	$f_8(\text{red}) = \perp$	$f_8(\text{green}) = \text{blue}$
f_9	$f_9(\text{red}) = \perp$	$f_9(\text{green}) = \perp$

Equality of functions

Two functions $f, g : A{\rightarrow}B$ are *equal*, written $f = g$, if

$$\forall a \in A. \ f(a) = g(a)$$

Note that for partial functions f and g, and $a \in A$, this means that either both $f(a)$ and $g(a)$ are undefined ($\bot$), or both are defined and equal.

Composition of functions

The *composition* of two functions $f : A{\rightarrow}B$ and $g : B{\rightarrow}C$ is the function $g \circ f : A{\rightarrow}C$ such that $(g \circ f)(a) = g(f(a))$ for any $a \in A$.

Finite functions and updating

When $a_1, \ldots, a_n \in A$ and $b_1, \ldots, b_n \in B$, the notation $[a_1 \mapsto b_1, \ldots, a_n \mapsto b_n]$ denotes the partial function $g : A{\rightarrow}B$ such that

$$g(x) = \begin{cases} b_i & \text{if } x = a_i \text{ for some } i \\ \bot & \text{if } x \neq a_i \text{ for all } i \end{cases}$$

When $f : A{\rightarrow}B$ is a partial function, the notation $f[a_1 \mapsto b_1, \ldots, a_n \mapsto b_n]$ denotes the partial function $g : A{\rightarrow}B$ such that

$$g(x) = \begin{cases} b_i & \text{if } x = a_i \text{ for some } i \\ f(x) & \text{if } x \neq a_i \text{ for all } i \end{cases}$$

and is called the result of *updating* f by $[a_i \mapsto b_i]$ (also called *overriding*).

Functions and algorithms

The term 'function' as used in programming languages like Pascal, Lisp, Scheme, or ML, is not the same as the mathematical concept. The first reason is that a Pascal 'function declaration' specifies an *algorithm*, i.e. a recipe for computing the declared function. An example algorithm to compute the factorial $n!$ of n, programmed in Pascal:

```
function fac(n:integer):integer;
begin
     if n = 0 then fac := 1 else fac := n * fac(n - 1)
end
```

On the other hand, a mathematical function f is just a set of ordered pairs. For instance,

$f(n) = $ the nth digit of π's decimal expansion

specifies a well-defined function on the natural numbers even though it does not say *how* to compute $f(n)$ for a given natural number n.

A second difference is that a Pascal-defined 'function' need not even be single-valued. For example, consider the following function declaration:

```
var global:integer;
function f(a:integer):integer;
begin
    global := global + 1;
    f := a + global
end
```

Repeated execution of the call `f(1)` may return different values every time, since every call changes the value of the variable `global`.

2.2   Types in programming languages

For the purpose of this book, a *type* can be considered *a set of values.* The concept is non-trivial due to the many ways that new values can be built up from old, and the next few sections will discuss several of them. A more sophisticated treatment of types involves partial orders and domain theory as in denotational semantics; but the view of types as sets of values will be sufficient for the greater part of this book, except briefly in some of the last chapters.

2.2.1   Product and function types

If f is a partial function from A to B we write $f : A{\to}B$, and say f has *type* $A{\to}B$. For example, $f(n) = n!$ has type $\mathcal{N}{\to}\mathcal{N}$ where $\mathcal{N} = \{0, 1, 2, \ldots\}$ is the set of natural numbers. More generally we can form some simple *type expressions.* Each of these denotes a set of values, obtained by the following rules:

1. The names of various standard sets are type expressions, including

   - $\mathcal{N} = \{0, 1, 2, \ldots\}$, the set of *natural numbers*;
   - $\mathcal{Z} = \{\ldots, -2, -1, 0, 1, 2, \ldots\}$, the set of *integers*;
   - $\mathcal{B} = \{true, false\}$, the set of *booleans*, also called *truth values*;
   - $\mathcal{ID}$, the set of all *identifiers* (finite strings of letters or digits that begin with a letter).

2. If $A_1, \ldots, A_n$ are types (sets), then $A_1 \times \cdots \times A_n$ is the *Cartesian product* of $A_1, A_2, \ldots,$ and A_n.

3. If A and B are types (sets), then

   - $A{\to}B$ is the set of *partial functions* from A to B;
   - $A\xrightarrow{t}B$ is the set of *total functions* from A to B.

A function $f : A{\to}B$ is *higher-order* if either A or B is a function type. If neither A nor B is a function type, then f is *first-order.*

Some examples of function definitions and their types

Following are several examples of function definitions with appropriate types. Note that the same definition may be compatible with several types, for example *square* below could be assigned types $\mathcal{Z} \to \mathcal{Z}$, $\mathcal{N} \to \mathcal{N}$, or $\mathcal{N} \xrightarrow{t} \mathcal{N}$.

Function definition	Type
$square(x) = x^2$	$square : \mathcal{N} \xrightarrow{t} \mathcal{N}$
$g(n) = $ if $n = 0$ then 1 else $n * g(n-1)$	$g : \mathcal{N} \xrightarrow{t} \mathcal{N}$
$h(m, n) = m + n$	$h : \mathcal{N} \times \mathcal{N} \xrightarrow{t} \mathcal{N}$
$k(m, n) = (m + n, m - n)$	$k : \mathcal{Z} \times \mathcal{Z} \xrightarrow{t} \mathcal{Z} \times \mathcal{Z}$
$sum(f, x) = f(0) + f(1) + \cdots + f(x)$	$sum : (\mathcal{N} \xrightarrow{t} \mathcal{N}) \times \mathcal{N} \xrightarrow{t} \mathcal{N}$
$add(n) = p, \text{where } p(x) = x + n$	$add : \mathcal{N} \xrightarrow{t} (\mathcal{N} \xrightarrow{t} \mathcal{N})$
$power(n) = q, \text{where } q(x) = x^n$	$power : \mathcal{N} \xrightarrow{t} (\mathcal{N} \xrightarrow{t} \mathcal{N})$
$twice(f)(x) = f(f(x))$	$twice : (\mathcal{N} \to \mathcal{N}) \xrightarrow{t} (\mathcal{N} \to \mathcal{N})$

The list above contains:

1. a recursively defined function g (note that $g(n)$ is n factorial);

2. functions h, k with structured data as arguments and results;

3. a function *sum*, which takes a function as an argument.

The function arrow associates to the right, so $A \to (B \to C)$ can be abbreviated $A \to B \to C$. If $f : A \to B \to C$ then $f(a) : B \to C$ for any $a \in A$, so f is a function-producing function. Function application associates to the left, so $f\,a\,b$ means $(f(a))(b)$, assuming $f : A \to B \to C$, and $a \in A$, $b \in B$.

Higher-order functions

A *higher-order* function is a function which takes a function as argument or returns a function as its result (when applied). The functions *sum*, *add*, *power*, and *twice* defined above are higher-order. For instance, $add(1)$ is the function which, given any argument x, returns $x + 1$; and $power(2)$ is the 'squaring function', so

$$add(1)(7) \quad = \quad 8 \quad \text{and}$$
$$power(2)(7) \quad = \quad 49$$

The higher-order function *twice* takes a function as its first argument and yields a function as its result. For example, *twice(square)* is the function j which raises its argument to the fourth power:

$$twice(square) = j, \text{ where } j(x) = (x^2)^2 = x^4$$

Curried functions

Compare the function *add* above with the familiar addition function $plus(x, y) = x + y$. They are related as follows:

$$plus : (\mathcal{N} \times \mathcal{N}) \xrightarrow{t} \mathcal{N} \quad \text{and} \quad add : \mathcal{N} \xrightarrow{t} (\mathcal{N} \xrightarrow{t} \mathcal{N})$$
$$add \; x \; y = plus(x, y)$$

The difference is that *plus* takes both its arguments at the same time, whereas *add* can be applied to a single argument and so is a function-producing function. We say that *add* is a *curried* version of *plus*. The term 'curry' stems from the name of H.B. Curry, a mathematical logician. The idea is attributed also to M. Schönfinkel (1924).

Programming notations for product and function types

We have discussed functions as mathematical objects, and the type notation used to describe them. We now see how they are realized in two programming languages.

Pascal

Pascal is a statically typed imperative programming language [127], and has built-in product types. The declaration

```
var T: record
            a:A; b:B
        end
```

declares variable T to be a pair of a and b; its type is the Cartesian product of types A and B. The components of T are referred to in Pascal by *selectors* as T.a and T.b.

Pascal also has built-in function types and function calls. The declaration

```
function f(a1:A1, a2:A2,..., an:An) : B;
    ...
    a1 := f1(x+1,3);       (* call f1 *)
    ...
    f := ...               (* return value of f *)
end
```

defines a function $f : A_1 \times \cdots \times A_n \to B$. The arguments a1,..., an may be of any definable type, including functions, so *sum* as seen above may be programmed directly in Pascal. However, the result type B is severely restricted by Pascal (to pointer or scalar types). Consequently, function k (whose result is a pair), and the functions *add* and *power* (whose results are functions) cannot be directly expressed in Pascal, but *sum* and *twice* can.

ML

Standard ML is a statically typed functional programming language [185]. ML makes much use of *pattern matching* for manipulating structured values such as pairs or lists. The declaration

```
fun f (x: int, y: int) = abs(x - y) < 2
```

declares a function f whose (single) argument is a pair of integers and whose result is a boolean. Function f's argument has product type int * int, corresponding to $\mathcal{Z} \times \mathcal{Z}$ above. Function f's result type is bool, corresponding to $\mathcal{B}$ above. This result type is not given explicitly in the program but can be inferred automatically.

ML allows expressions that evaluate to a pair, which cannot be done in Pascal. An example expression is: (x-1,x+1).

ML treats functions as any other kind of values, and there are no restrictions on the argument and result types of a function. Thus all the example functions above can be directly defined in ML. The function-producing function *add* is defined in ML by

```
fun add (x: int) (y: int) = x + y
```

and then add(1) denotes the 'add one' function.

Scheme

Scheme is a functional language [49], related to Lisp, and is dynamically typed. Thus in general the type of an expression cannot be determined until run time. The atomic values in Scheme are numbers 4.5 and atoms 'foo. So-called *S-expressions* are used to build composite data structures. A pair (a, b) can be represented as the S-expression '(a . b), or alternatively as '(a b).

Scheme has function definitions, but no pattern matching. Application of a function (or operator) f to an argument a is written prefix as (f a). Thus function f shown above is defined in Scheme by:

```
(define (f x y) (< (abs (- x y)) 2))
```

2.2.2   Type inference

When x is a variable and t a type, we write $x : t$ to indicate that the value of x belongs to type t.

We say that an expression is *well-typed* if all operators and functions in the expression are applied to arguments of a suitable type. When e is an expression, we write $e : t$ to indicate that e is well-typed *and* that the value of e has type t. For instance, $3 + 5 : \mathcal{N}$.

Now suppose e is an expression, such as $x + x$, which contains occurrences of the variable x. Then the type e can be determined only under some *assumptions* about the type of x. Such assumptions are represented by a *type environment* $\tau = [x \mapsto t, \ldots]$, which maps x to its type, so $\tau x = t$.

The assertion that 'whenever $x : \mathcal{N}$, then $x + x : \mathcal{N}$' is written as follows:

$$[x \mapsto \mathcal{N}] \vdash x + x : \mathcal{N}$$

More generally, the notation $\tau \vdash e : t$ is called a *judgement* and means that 'in type environment τ, expression e is well-typed and has type t'.

Type inference is often based on a set of *type inference rules*, one for each form of expression in the language. For an expression which is a variable occurrence, we have the assertion:

$$\tau[x \mapsto t] \vdash x : t$$

since the type of a variable occurrence is determined by the type environment. (Recall that $\tau[x \mapsto t]$ is the same function as τ, except that it maps x to t.)

Now consider an expression *not e* whose value is the negation of the value of its subexpression e. If subexpression e is well-typed and has type $\mathcal{B}$, then the entire expression is well-typed and has type $\mathcal{B}$. This is expressed by the inference rule, where the part above the line is called the *premise*:

$$\frac{\tau \vdash e : \mathcal{B}}{\tau \vdash not\ e : \mathcal{B}}$$

Now consider an expression $e_1 + e_2$, which is the sum of two subexpressions e_1 and e_2. If each subexpression is well-typed and has type $\mathcal{Z}$, then the entire expression is well-typed and has type $\mathcal{Z}$. This is expressed by a two-premise inference rule:

$$\frac{\tau \vdash e_1 : \mathcal{Z} \qquad \tau \vdash e_2 : \mathcal{Z}}{\tau \vdash e_1 + e_2 : \mathcal{Z}}$$

Now consider an expression (e_1, e_2) which builds a pair. If e_1 has type t_1 and e_2 has type t_2, and both are well-typed, then the pair (e_1, e_2) is well-typed and has type $t_1 \times t_2$:

$$\frac{\tau \vdash e_1 : t_1 \qquad \tau \vdash e_2 : t_2}{\tau \vdash (e_1, e_2) : t_1 \times t_2}$$

When f is a function of type $t \rightarrow t'$, and e is an (argument) expression of type t, and both are well-typed, then the application $f(e)$ is well-typed and has type t':

$$\frac{\tau \vdash f : t \rightarrow t' \qquad \tau \vdash e : t}{\tau \vdash f(e) : t'}$$

Using type inference rules, the type of a complex expression can be inferred from the assumptions (about the types of variables) held in the type environment τ. For instance, when $\tau = [m \mapsto \mathcal{Z}, n \mapsto \mathcal{Z}]$, then the inference

$$\frac{\dfrac{\tau \vdash m : \mathcal{Z} \quad \tau \vdash n : \mathcal{Z}}{\tau \vdash m + n : \mathcal{Z}} \qquad \dfrac{\tau \vdash m : \mathcal{Z} \quad \tau \vdash n : \mathcal{Z}}{\tau \vdash m - n : \mathcal{Z}}}{\tau \vdash (m + n, m - n) : \mathcal{Z} \times \mathcal{Z}}$$

shows that $(m + n, m - n)$ has type $\mathcal{Z} \times \mathcal{Z}$. The nodes in the inference tree are obtained from the inference rules by instantiating the types t, t_1, and t_2 to $\mathcal{Z}$.

For another example, when $\tau = [f \mapsto \mathcal{N} \rightarrow \mathcal{N}, x \mapsto \mathcal{N}]$, the following inference

$$\frac{\tau \vdash f : \mathcal{N} \rightarrow \mathcal{N} \quad \dfrac{\tau \vdash f : \mathcal{N} \rightarrow \mathcal{N} \quad \tau \vdash x : \mathcal{N}}{\tau \vdash f(x) : \mathcal{N}}}{\tau \vdash f(f(x)) : \mathcal{N}}$$

shows that $f(f(x))$ has type $\mathcal{N}$. Thus if the arguments of function *twice* above have type $\mathcal{N} \rightarrow \mathcal{N}$ and $\mathcal{N}$, then its result has type $\mathcal{N}$.

2.2.3   Sum types

The sum of two or more sets is a set of tagged values. A *tagged value* is written as a *tag* applied to a value. For instance, if *Inttag* and *Booltag* are tags, then the *Inttag*(17) and *Booltag*(*false*) are values belonging to the sum type

> *Inttag* $\mathcal{Z}$ | *Booltag* $\mathcal{B}$

The tags are also called *constructors*.

A general sum type has the following form, where the C_i are the tags (or constructors):

> $C_1 \, t_{11} \times \ldots \times t_{1k_1} \mid \cdots \mid C_n \, t_{n1} \times \ldots \times t_{nk_n}$

where $n \geq 1$, all $k_i \geq 0$, and all constructors C_i must be distinct. A value belonging to this type is a *construction* of form $C_i(v_{i1}, \ldots, v_{ik_i})$, where $v_{i1} : t_{i1}, \ldots, v_{ik_i} : t_{ik_i}$. The above sum type denotes the following set of values:

$$\bigcup_{i=1}^{n} \{\, C_i(v_1, \ldots, v_{k_i}) \mid v_j : t_{ij} \text{ for } j = 1, \ldots, k_i \,\}$$

Note that while all values belonging to a product type such as $\mathcal{N} \times (\mathcal{B} \times \mathcal{B})$ must have the same structure, namely $(n, (b_1, b_2))$, the values of a sum type may have different structures. However, all values with the same constructor must have the same structure.

Programming notations for sum types

In Pascal, sum types can be expressed by *variant records*, using an enumerated type to hold the tags (such as *Inttag* and *Booltag* above). The first example could be written:

```
type tag = (Inttag, Booltag);
     sum = record
              case t : tag of
                  Inttag  : ( N : integer);
                  Booltag : ( B : boolean)
              end
```

In ML, the notation is closer to that shown above:

```
datatype sum = Inttag of int | Booltag of bool

fun f1 (Inttag (n))  =  Inttag(1 - n)
  |   f1 (Booltag (b)) =  Booltag(not b)
```

Since the programming language Scheme is dynamically typed, it has no notation for defining sum types. However, in Section 2.3.4 we show an encoding of sum types in Scheme.

2.3   Recursive data types

Our last way to define types is by recursive type equations. The collection of values defined this way is called a *data type*. An equation defines a type T as a sum type

$$T = C_1 \, t_{11} \times \ldots \times t_{1k_1} \mid \cdots \mid C_n \, t_{n1} \times \ldots \times t_{nk_n}$$

where the type expressions t_{ij} may contain T and names of other types. As before, all constructors must be distinct.

Since a data type is essentially a sum type, its values need not all have the same form. Since it may be recursive, its values may be arbitrarily large.

Familiar examples of data types include search trees, game trees, and expressions in a programming language. We begin with a simple and widely used special case: the type of lists, i.e. finite sequences of elements from a given base type.

2.3.1   List types

When describing programming languages, one often needs sequences of values whose length is not statically determined. Typical examples are the input files and output files of a program, and program texts. For such applications the *list type* is useful.

Let A be a type (set). Then the set of *finite lists* of elements of A is the data type As defined by:

$$As = nil \mid cons \, A \times As \tag{2.1}$$

where *nil* and *cons* are constructors. The definition says that an element of *As* is either *nil*, or has form *cons*(*a*, *as*), where *a* has type *A* and *as* has type *As*. That is, a finite list is either the empty list *nil*, or is non-empty and has a first element (head) *a* of type *A*, and a tail *as*, which must in turn be a list of *A* elements.

The type of finite lists of elements of *A* is often called A^*. For example, the list containing 9 and 13 is written *cons*(7, *cons*(9, *cons*(13, *nil*))), and has type $\mathcal{Z}^*$. Usually the more convenient notation [7, 9, 13] is used:

1. The list containing $a_1, a_2, \ldots, a_n$ in that order is written

   $$[a_1, a_2, \ldots, a_n]$$

   instead of *cons*(a_1, *cons*(a_2, ..., *cons*(a_n, *nil*)...)) for $n \geq 0$, when all $a_i : A$.

2. The empty list is written [] instead of *nil*.

3. The constructor '*cons*' can be written infix as '::', such that

   $$a :: [a_1, a_2, \ldots, a_n]) = [a, a_1, a_2, \ldots, a_n]$$

4. The infix constructor '::' associates to the right, so that

   $$a_1 :: (a_2 :: (\cdots :: (a_n :: nil) \cdots)) = a_1 :: a_2 :: \cdots :: a_n :: nil$$

5. The operators $hd : A^* \rightarrow A$ and $tl : A^* \rightarrow A^*$ are defined by:

   $$\begin{aligned} hd([a_1, a_2, \ldots, a_n]) &= a_1, & \text{provided } n \neq 0 \\ tl([a_1, a_2, \ldots, a_n]) &= [a_2, \ldots, a_n], & \text{provided } n \neq 0 \end{aligned}$$

Programming notations for list types

Since Pascal has no built-in declarations or operations for manipulating lists, they must be encoded using pointers, which requires great care.

ML uses essentially the infix :: notation and the bracket list notation [7,9,13] above. The type A^* is written as A list, where ML type A denotes set *A*. The use of pattern matching allows simple and compact programs. For example, the length of a list is computed by:

```
fun length nil      = 0
  | length (_ :: xs) = 1 + length xs
```

Scheme uses S-expressions to represent lists, writing the empty list *nil* as (), and the example list above above as '(7 9 13). The functions *hd* and *tl* are called car and cdr in Scheme.

In fact, Scheme S-expressions roughly correspond to the recursive datatype:

$$Se = () \mid cons\ Se \times Se \mid atom\ Basetype \tag{2.2}$$

except that the constructor *atom* on *Basetype* values is omitted. Application of a constructor C to a value a is written as function application (C a), so the list shown above is actually an abbreviation for (cons 7 (cons 9 (cons 13 nil))).

2.3.2   The meaning of recursive data type definitions

It is important to agree on the meaning (or semantics) of type equation such as equation (2.1), defining the type of lists. If we regard a type as a set of values, it is natural to interpret | as set union $\cup$, and *nil* as the one-element set $\{nil\}$. The equation then asserts the equality of two sets:

$$As = \{nil\} \cup \{ \, cons(a, as) \mid a \in A \text{ and } as \in As \, \} \qquad (2.3)$$

We define that the set As specified by type equation (2.1) is the least set which is a solution to equation (2.3).

The least set solving equation (2.3) can be constructed iteratively, starting with the empty set $As_0 = \{\}$. For example, if A denotes the set $\{1, 2\}$, then

$$
\begin{aligned}
As_0 &= \{\} \\
As_1 &= \{[]\} \cup \{a :: as \mid a \in A \text{ and } as \in As_0\} \\
&= \{[]\} \\
As_2 &= \{[]\} \cup \{a :: as \mid a \in A \text{ and } as \in As_1\} \\
&= \{[], [1], [2]\} \\
As_3 &= \{[]\} \cup \{a :: as \mid a \in A \text{ and } as \in As_2\} \\
&= \{[], [1], [2], [1, 1], [1, 2], [2, 1], [2, 2]\} \\
As_4 &= \ldots
\end{aligned}
$$

Note that As_1 contains all lists of length less than 1, As_2 contains all lists of length less than 2, etc. The set As of all finite lists is clearly the union of all these: $As = As_0 \cup As_1 \cup As_2 \cup \ldots$.

2.3.3   Syntax trees

Recursive data types are often used for representing program fragments, such as arithmetic expressions. For instance, the set of arithmetic expressions built from integer constants and the operators *Add* and *Mul* (for addition and multiplication) can be represented by the data type *Nexp*:

$$Nexp = Int \; \mathcal{N} \mid Add \; Nexp \times Nexp \mid Mul \; Nexp \; \times Nexp$$

For example, the arithmetic expression 5+(6*7) can be represented by the *Nexp*-value $Add(Int(5), \; Mul(Int(6), \; Int(7)))$. Drawing this value as a tree makes its structure more obvious:

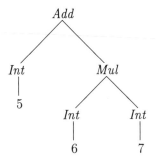

This is called an *abstract syntax tree* (or just a *syntax tree*) for the expression
5+(6*7). Also, a recursive data type used for representing program fragments is
often called an *abstract syntax*.

Recursive data type definitions resemble the production rules of a context-free
grammar. However, a grammar describes a set of linear strings of symbols, whereas
a recursive data type definition describes a set of trees, where each subtree is
labelled by a constructor.

Programming notations for syntax trees
Pascal has no recursive declarations in the sense just given, so all structure manipulation must be done by means of pointers.

ML has a notion of data type very similar to the one above. The type of arithmetic expressions can be defined as follows, together with a function to evaluate
the expressions:

```
datatype nexp =
     Int of int          (* Constant       *)
   | Add of nexp * nexp  (* Addition        *)
   | Mul of nexp * nexp  (* Multiplication *)

fun neval (Int n)        = n
   | neval (Add(e1, e2)) = (neval e1) + (neval e2)
   | neval (Mul(e1, e2)) = (neval e1) * (neval e2)
```

The *Nexp* element above, written in ML as an element of the nexp datatype, would
be Add(Int 5, Mul(Int 6, Int 7)).

2.3.4   Encoding recursive data types in Scheme

In Scheme, one cannot declare recursive data types. However, there is a standard
way to encode them using Scheme's (dynamically typed) lists.

A tagged value $C(v_1, \ldots, v_n)$ is represented as a Scheme list (C v_1' ... v_n'). The first element of the list is a Scheme atom C representing the constructor, and the remaining elements v_i' are representations of the constructor's arguments v_i.

For example, *Inttag*(17) is represented as (Inttag 17). Also, the *Nexp* value shown above is encoded in Scheme as

```
(Add (Int 5) (Mul (Int 6) (Int 7)))
```

Pattern matching on a tagged value v is encoded as a sequence of tests on its tag. Since the tag is the first element in the encoding, it can be extracted by (car v). The first and second constructor arguments can be extracted by (car (cdr v)) and (car (cdr (cdr v))), which can be abbreviated (cadr v) and (caddr v).

Using this encoding, the neval function shown in ML above can be written in Scheme as follows:

```
(define (neval v)
   (if (equal? (car v) 'Int)
       (cadr v)
       (if (equal? (car v) 'Add)
           (+ (neval (cadr v)) (neval (caddr v)))
           (if (equal? (car v) 'Mul)
               (* (neval (cadr v)) (neval (caddr v)))
               (error)
)))))
```

In practice the tags on numbers are usually left out, writing 5 instead of (Int 5). Then pattern matching exploits the fact that there is a predicate number? in Scheme which distinguishes numbers from all other values. Similarly, a source program variable x is usually represented just as the Scheme atom x instead of (Var x), say. Then pattern matching exploits the Scheme predicate atom?.

We use this encoding of recursive data types and pattern matching frequently in later chapters. However, since pattern matching improves the readability and reduces the length of programs, we shall allow ourselves to use it freely in pseudo-Scheme programs, although this introduces some ambiguity. The intention is that a knowledgeable programmer can convert pseudo-Scheme programs into real Scheme programs by replacing pattern matching with a sequence of tests as above.

2.4   Summary

In this chapter we have introduced the following concepts and terminology for future use:

- algorithms and programs, and their differences from functions;

- the Cartesian product $A \times B$ of two sets;

- the set $A \xrightarrow{t} B$ of total functions from set A to set B;

- the set $A \rightarrow B$ of partial functions from set A to set B;

- notations for finite functions and updating $(f[x \mapsto v])$;

- types as sets of possible data values;

- sum data types with constructors;

- recursively defined data types with constructors;

- abstract syntax as a special case of recursively defined data types;

- an encoding of recursive data types in Scheme.

2.5   Exercises

Exercise 2.1 Discuss the relations between a mathematical function $f : A \rightarrow B$ and the following concepts from programming:

1. an array in Pascal;

2. a relation in a database;

3. a function in Pascal.

$\square$

Exercise 2.2 Give an example illustrating the difference between the type $A \rightarrow (B \rightarrow C)$ and the type $(A \rightarrow B) \rightarrow C$. $\square$

Exercise 2.3 The types $A \rightarrow (B \rightarrow C)$ and $A \times B \rightarrow C$ are similar but not identical. Give an intuitive explanation of the similarity. Can you define an ML function uncurry, such that whenever f is a function of type $(A \rightarrow (B \rightarrow C))$, then uncurry f is the corresponding function of type $A \times B \rightarrow C$? $\square$

Exercise 2.4 Use the type inference rules to show that when arguments m and n k both have type $\mathcal{Z}$, then expression $k(m, n)$ has type $\mathcal{Z} \times \mathcal{Z}$. $\square$

Exercise 2.5 Define a recursive data type Bintree of binary trees whose leaves are integers. Define a function add of type Bintree $\rightarrow \mathcal{Z}$, such that add(tree) calculates the sum of all the leaves in tree. $\square$

Exercise 2.6 Which set has most members:

$$\begin{aligned} \text{Fun} &= \{f \mid f \text{ is a partial function: } \mathcal{N} \rightarrow \mathcal{N}\} \\ \text{Prog} &= \{p \mid p \text{ is a Pascal program, defining a function: } \mathcal{N} \rightarrow \mathcal{N}\} \end{aligned}$$

$\square$

Chapter 3

Programming Languages and Interpreters

3.1 Interpreters, compilers, and running times

To give a semantics for a programming language is to assign systematically a meaning to every program in the language.

3.1.1 Operational semantics

Here we define the meaning of programs in a language S by giving an *interpreter* for S-programs, that is, a program for executing S-programs. This provides a very concrete computer-oriented semantics. Interpreters have been used for language definition for many years, e.g. for Lisp [181], the lambda calculus [162], and as a general formalism for language definitions [25].

More abstract versions of operational semantics exist, notably Plotkin's *structural operational semantics* [220], and Kahn's *natural semantics* [142]. In these systems a language definition is a set of axioms and inference rules sufficient to execute programs. They have some advantages over interpreters as language definitions: they are more compact; they are less dependent on current computer architectures (for example, arbitrary decisions due to the sequential nature of most computers can be avoided); their mathematical properties are easier to analyse; and they seem better suited to describing communication among parallel processes.

On the other hand, it is still not clear how to implement structural operational semantics or natural semantics efficiently on current computers, although progress has recently been made [142,110]. Axiomatic and algebraic semantics seem less well suited to automation, although both have been used as guidelines for writing correct compilers.

3.1.2 Programming languages

Let L-programs denote the set of syntactically correct programs in language L. As in Chapter 1, we define the meaning of program p ∈ L-programs to be

$$[\![p]\!]_L: \texttt{input} \rightarrow \texttt{output}$$

That is, the meaning of program p is the input–output function it computes.

3.1.3 Interpreters

Let L be an (implementation) language and S be a (source) language. An interpreter **int** ∈ L-programs for a language S has two inputs: a *source program* p ∈ S-programs to be executed, and the source program's input data d ∈ D. Running the interpreter with inputs p and d on an L-machine must produce the same result as running p with input d on an S-machine.

More precisely, the L-program **int** is an *interpreter* for S if for every p ∈ S-programs and every d ∈ D,

$$[\![p]\!]_S \, d = [\![\texttt{int}]\!]_L \, [p,d]$$

We use the symbol

$$\boxed{\begin{array}{c} S \\ L \end{array}} \;=\; \{ \; \texttt{int} \; | \; \forall p, d. \; [\![p]\!]_S \, d = [\![\texttt{int}]\!]_L \, [p,d] \; \}$$

to denote the set of all interpreters for S written in L.

3.1.4 Compilers

Now let T be a (target) language. A compiler **comp** ∈ L-programs from S to T has one input: a *source program* p ∈ S-programs to be compiled. Running the compiler with input p (on an L-machine) must produce a **target**, such that running **target** on a T-machine has the same effect as running p on an S-machine.

More precisely, the L-program **comp** is a *compiler* from S to T if for every p ∈ S-programs and every d ∈ D,

$$[\![p]\!]_S \, d = [\![[\![\texttt{comp}]\!]_L \; p]\!]_T \, d$$

We use the symbol

$$\boxed{\begin{array}{c} \text{S} \longrightarrow \text{T} \\ \boxed{\text{L}} \end{array}} = \{\ \text{comp}\ \mid\ \forall p, d.\ [\![p]\!]_S\, d\ =\ [\![\,[\![\text{comp}]\!]_L\, p\,]\!]_T\, d\ \}$$

to denote the set of compilers from S to T written in L.

3.1.5   Compilation

Suppose we are given a collection of S-programs, nature unspecified. This set can be denoted by

Suppose we also have a compiler `comp` from source language S to target language T, written in L. We can then perform translations (assuming L-programs can be executed). This situation can be described by the diagram

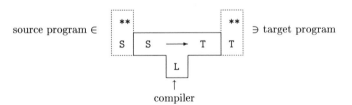

3.1.6   Layers of interpretation

Diagrams such as these can be thought of as describing 'computer runs'. For example, suppose a Lisp system (called L) is processed interpretively by an interpreter written in Sun RISC machine code (call this M). The machine code itself is processed by the central processor (call this C) so two levels of interpretation are involved, as described by the following figure:

The major problem with implementing languages interpretively is that the 'natural' running time of the interpreted program must be multiplied by the basic cycle time used by the interpreter. This cost of one level of interpretation may well be an acceptable price to pay to have a powerful, expressive language (as was the case with Lisp since its beginnings). On the other hand, if one uses several layers of interpreters, each new level of interpretation multiplies the time by a significant constant factor, so the total time may be excessive. Compilation is clearly preferable if there are too many interpreters, each interpreting the next.

3.1.7   Program running times

We study the time difference between executing a program directly on a machine and executing it with the aid of an interpreter. That is, we study the cost of interpretation.

For many programming languages one can predict the actual running time on the computer with reasonable precision. For example, the *number* of elementary operations (required to execute the program) is a good time estimate.

To make this more concrete, suppose that arithmetic expression **exp** contains c constants, v variables, and m additions or multiplications. A measure of the time to evaluate **exp** is $c + v + m$, since every constant, variable, or operator needs to be accessed once. By this measure, evaluation of x+2*y would take 5 time units.

In fact, $c + v + m$ is roughly proportional to the time that would be taken by machine code instructions to evaluate the expression. Since we are mainly interested in the rate of growth of execution time, the difference between, say, time $10n + 5$ and $10n + 8$ is immaterial, whereas the difference between $10n$ and $11n$ will be considered significant.

Considering a whole program p rather than just an expression, we count one for each variable access, function call, pattern match, arithmetical operation, and logical operation performed.

Definition 3.1 For program p and inputs $d_1, \ldots, d_n$, let $t_{\mathbf{p}}(d_1, \ldots, d_n)$ represent the *running time* of p on $d_1, \ldots, d_n$. □

3.1.8 Interpreter running times

Suppose we are given a programming language S. To define the effect of S-program execution we write an interpreter for S using some existing implementation language, say L. The interpreter is thus an L-program. Its input consists of the S-program s (usually in the form of an abstract syntax tree), together with the input data for s. We now exemplify this using an interpreter (written in ML) for an extremely simple expression language.

Evaluating expressions in contexts

The value of the expression $x + 2 \times y$ clearly depends on the current values of x and y. More generally, an expression e can only be evaluated if the current values of all variables in it are known. These values can be represented by a so-called *environment*, namely a function $env : Variable \rightarrow Value$. If, for example, $env(x) = 5$ and $env(y) = 7$ the value of $x+2\times y$ in environment env is $5+2\times7 = 19$.

An appropriate evaluation function for expressions with variables thus has type

> eval : $Expression \times Environment \rightarrow Value$
> env   : $Environment = Variable \rightarrow Value$

One way to evaluate an expression is by *substitution*. For example, one could first substitute for every variable the value bound to it in env, and then apply function neval of Section 2.3 to evaluate the resulting constant expression. An alternative is to do the substitution only when needed during evaluation, using env to the current value of variables. This approach is seen in the following ML program, where eval is defined by recursion on the expression's syntax.

```
datatype exp =
     Num of int        (* Constant       *)
   | Var of string     (* Variable       *)
   | Add of exp * exp  (* Addition       *)
   | Mul of exp * exp  (* Multiplication *)

fun eval (Num n,      env) = n
   | eval (Var v,      env) = env(v)
   | eval (Add(e1, e2), env) = eval (e1, env) + eval (e2, env)
   | eval (Mul(e1, e2), env) = eval (e1, env) * eval (e2, env)
```

For example, if $env = [x \mapsto 5, y \mapsto 7]$ then evaluation of $x + 2 \times y$ proceeds as follows:

```
eval(Add (Var "x", Mul (Num 2, Var "y")), env)
  = eval(Var "x", env) + eval(Mul (Num 2, Var "y"), env)
  = env("x") + eval(Num 2, env) * eval(Var "y", env)
  = 5 + 2 * env("y")
  = 5 + 2 * 7
  = 19
```

The running time of the interpreter

Now consider the running time of the interpreter `eval`. It exceeds the running time $t_{\mathtt{exp}} = c + v + m$ for direct evaluation because of the 'interpretation overhead': the extra book-keeping time needed for `eval` to decompose `exp` into its subexpressions and to find variable values in `env`.

The interpreter's running time with inputs p and $d_1, \ldots, d_n$ is approximately

$$t_{\mathtt{int}}(\mathtt{p}, d_1, \ldots, d_n) = \alpha \cdot t_{\mathtt{p}}(d_1, \ldots, d_n)$$

where α is a factor depending only on the program p being interpreted.

Interpretation overhead

Such overhead is typical for a wide range of interpreters. We shall see below that for `eval` above the factor α is between 3 and 5, which thus is the overhead for the 'interpretation loop' in `eval`. For realistic interpreters the interpretation overhead can be substantially larger (factors from 3 to 200 have been reported in the literature), depending on the language being implemented.

Detailed time analysis

In the interpreter `eval`, an access to a source program variable v is done by an application (`env v`). Suppose, a little optimistically, that such an application takes 1 time unit. Then a source program variable access involves a call, a match, an access to variable `env`, an access to variable v, and an application, totalling 5 time units.

Then the total time is 3 for constants (a call, a match, and an access to variable n), 5 for a source program variable (a call, a match, two variable accesses, and an application), and 5 for an addition or multiplication (call, match, two variable accesses, and either + or ×) plus the time to evaluate the arguments. The total interpretation time thus is:

$$t_{\mathtt{int}}(\mathtt{exp}) = 3c + 5v + 5m$$

Thus we can relate the maximum evaluation time for the interpreter to the 'natural' evaluation time $t_{\mathtt{exp}}$:

$$3 \times t_{\mathtt{exp}} \leq t_{\mathtt{int}}(\mathtt{exp}) \leq 5 \times t_{\mathtt{exp}}$$

3.2   The untyped lambda calculus: syntax and semantics

Lambda notation was developed in the 1930s by Alonzo Church [47,48] as a way to write expressions denoting functions and as a medium for studying an important question: what functions can be computed by mechanical devices? (His answer was: those that can be specified by lambda expressions.) Since then *lambda calculus* has been studied extensively within the field of mathematical logic. It is widely

used in computer science, and is the core of Lisp, Scheme, and most other functional
programming languages, including ML, Miranda, and Haskell.

3.2.1   Lambda notation for functions

A starting point is the observation that arithmetic expressions alone are not suitable for defining functions. For example, it is not clear whether the expression $n!$
denotes the factorial function itself (of type $n! : \mathcal{N} \to \mathcal{N}$) or its value given the
current value of n (of type $n! : \mathcal{N}$). Another problem: if $y^2 + x$ is regarded as
a function of two variables, should $(y^2 + x)(3, 4)$ have the value $13 = 3^2 + 4$ or
$19 = 4^2 + 3$?

These problems are solved by using the notation $\lambda x.exp$ to denote a function of
one variable. The 'λ' is the Greek letter 'lambda', x is the *formal parameter*, and
exp is the *body* of the function. An application $(\lambda x.exp)(5)$ of this function to the
value 5, say, is evaluated by first substituting 5 for all free occurrences of x in exp,
then evaluating the resulting expression. A definition of 'free occurrence' appears
in the next section.

A function of several variables can be defined by writing $\lambda(x_1, \dots, x_n).exp$. Using
this notation we can define the two different interpretations of $y^2 + x$ by

$$(\lambda(y, x).y^2 + x)(3, 4) \quad = \quad 13$$
$$(\lambda(x, y).y^2 + x)(3, 4) \quad = \quad 19$$

The notation can be augmented by writing $\lambda x : A.exp$ to give the type A of x.
If exp has type B, then $\lambda x : A.exp$ will have type $A \to B$. A function of several
arguments can be written as

$$\lambda(x_1 : A_1, \dots, x_n : A_n) . exp$$

which has type $A_1 \times \cdots \times A_n \to B$, provided exp has type B.

Note that according to these rules $\lambda(x : A, y : B).exp : C$ has type $(A \times B) \to C$
while the expression $\lambda x : A.\lambda y : B.exp : C$ has type $A \to (B \to C)$. The latter is
a curried version of the former.

From now on we consider only the untyped lambda calculus, and therefore do
not add types to the expressions. We now give some examples from Section 2.2.1
rewritten as lambda expressions:

$$\begin{array}{l}
square = \lambda x.x^2 \\
h = \lambda(m, n).m + n \\
k = \lambda(m, n).(m + n, m - n) \\
twice = \lambda f.\lambda x.f(f(x)) \\
add = \lambda n.\lambda x.x + n
\end{array}$$

The untyped pure lambda calculus, containing only variables, abstraction, and
application, has been studied at length in mathematical logic by Church [48] and

Barendregt [16]. We choose for our mini-language a dialect which is extended with data values (typically numbers or lists) and a conditional expression. Our treatment has different goals and thus is less formal than that of Church and Barendregt.

3.2.2 Syntax of the lambda calculus

The abstract syntax of our variant of the untyped lambda calculus is defined by the grammar below. For the sake of generality the set ⟨Constant⟩ of possible constant values and the set ⟨Op⟩ of operations on them have not been specified: various dialects will have their own data domains. In our examples, ⟨Const⟩ will be the natural numbers and ⟨Op⟩ the arithmetic operations.

⟨Lam⟩	::=	⟨Constant⟩	Constants
	|	⟨Var⟩	Variables
	|	⟨Lam⟩⟨Lam⟩	Application
	|	λ⟨Var⟩.⟨Lam⟩	Abstraction
	|	if ⟨Lam⟩ then ⟨Lam⟩ else ⟨Lam⟩	Conditional
	|	⟨Op⟩⟨Lam⟩...⟨Lam⟩	Base application

Examples
As in the earlier discussion we shall only parenthesize when necessary to remove ambiguity, and shall write, for example, `f x` for `f(x)` and `f x y` for `(f(x))(y)`. Note that an operator such as `+` by itself is a lambda expression. Thus `(5+6)` should formally be written as `(+ 5 6)`, but we shall use ordinary infix notation where it clarifies the examples. In an expression `---λx.---` the part λx is understood to apply to the *longest* complete expression to the right of the 'dot'.

```
x
5
+ 5 x                        (or 5 + x in ordinary notation)
λx.x + 1
(λy.(λx.x/y)6)2
if x=y then x+y else x-y
```

3.2.3 Evaluating lambda expressions

Evaluating a lambda expression is simple: the expression is repeatedly rewritten by a series of *reductions* until the final answer is reached, if ever. We write M⇒P to mean that lambda expression M can be reduced (or rewritten) to lambda expression P.

An *occurrence* of variable x in a lambda expression is *bound* if it is inside a subexpression of form λx..... For instance, the occurrence of x is bound in λx.x but not in λy.x.

An *occurrence* of variable x in a lambda expression is *free* if it is not bound. For instance, the occurrence of x is free in λy.x but not in λx.x.

A *variable* x is *free* in a lambda expression if it has a free occurrence. For instance, x is free in λy.x(λx.x), but not in λy.λx.x.

We use a special notation for *substitution*. When N and M are lambda expressions, [N/x]M is the result of substituting N for all free occurrences of x in M.

3.2.4   Lambda calculus reduction rules

α-conversion: λx.M $\Rightarrow$ λy.[y/x]M

> Renaming the bound variable x to y. Restriction: y must not be free in M.

β-reduction: $(\lambda$x.M$)($N$)$ $\Rightarrow$ [N/x]M

> Function application. A function λx.M is applied to argument N by substituting N for every free occurrence of x in M. Restriction: no free variable in N may become bound as a result of the substitution [N/x]M. This problem can be avoided by first renaming bound variables in M.

δ-reduction: op $a_1 \ldots a_n$ $\Rightarrow$ b
> whenever b is the result of applying op to constants $a_1, \ldots, a_n$

> Computation with data values. For example, (+ 5 6) can be reduced to 11. Restriction: the arguments $a_1, \ldots, a_n$ must be data constants.

reduction of conditional: if `true` then M else N $\Rightarrow$ M
> if `false` then M else N $\Rightarrow$ N

reduction in context: ...M... $\Rightarrow$ ...N...
> whenever M $\Rightarrow$ N

> A subexpression of a lambda expression may be reduced without changing the rest of the expression.

repeated reduction: M_1 $\Rightarrow$ M_3
> whenever M_1 $\Rightarrow$ M_2 and M_2 $\Rightarrow$ M_3

> A computation consists of a series of the above reductions. For instance, a conditional (if B then M else N) may be reduced by first reducing B to an atomic value b; then if b is `true`, the conditional reduces to M, else if b is `false`, the conditional reduces to N.

Examples

+ 5 6	⇒	11	by δ-reduction
(5 + 6) = 11	⇒	true	by two δ-reductions
λa.a + 5	⇒	λb.b + 5	by α-conversion
(λa.a + 5)6	⇒	6 + 5	by β-reduction
(λa.a + 5)6	⇒	11	by repeated reductions
(λx.(λy.x+y)6)7	⇒	(λx.x+6)7	by reduction in context
if true then 13 else 14	⇒	13	by conditional
if 5+6=11 then 13 else 14	⇒	13	by δ and conditional
(λx.((λx.x+x)5)+x+(λx.x*x)3)4	⇒	23	by repeated reductions

A *redex* is an expression which can be reduced by a β-, δ-, or conditional reduction. A *top-level redex* is a redex not inside a lambda abstraction. Functional programming languages restrict the use of β-, δ-, and conditional reductions to top-level redexes.

A lambda expression is in *weak head normal form* (or *whnf*) if it is a constant, such as 17, or a function λx.M, or a free variable x, or an application x e_1 ... e_n of a free variable x, where $n \geq 1$. If a lambda expression is in whnf, it has no top-level redex.

All of the above expressions can be reduced to whnf. However, some lambda expressions cannot. For example, (λy.y y)(λy.y y) can be β-reduced, but it reduces to itself, which can again be β-reduced, and so on indefinitely:

    (λy.y y)(λy.y y)
    ⇒ (λy.y y)(λy.y y)
    ⇒ (λy.y y)(λy.y y)
    ⇒ ...

A restriction on substitution

In α-conversion and β-reduction, the substitution [N/x]M may only be done if no free variable in N becomes bound as a result of the substitution. A free variable that becomes bound is said to be *captured*.

For example, let y be a free variable of the argument N in:

$$\underbrace{(λx.2+(λy.x+y)5)}_{M}\underbrace{(y+1)}_{N}$$

Blindly applying β-reduction and substitution would yield the lambda expression 2+(λy.(y+1)+y)5, in which the free variable y in N has become captured: bound by the lambda abstraction λy. in M.

This is clearly wrong, since the y's of M and N have nothing to do with each other, and luckily the restriction on substitution prevents β-reduction in this case. However, (λx.M)N can always be reduced if we first rename M's bound variable y to z by an α-conversion.

Functional programming languages

In functional programming languages, considered as implementations of the lambda calculus, renaming is not needed. Such implementations do not allow free variables in the 'program' (the top-most lambda expression), and they do not perform reductions inside lambda abstractions $\lambda x.M$. Because of these restrictions, the expressions considered in reduction rules have no free variables. In particular, there are no free variables in the argument N of an application $(\lambda x.M)N$, and therefore no variables can be captured.

Also, because of the restrictions, every whnf at top-level is a constant or a function.

3.2.5   Call-by-value and call-by-name

Even with this restriction, the reductions on a lambda expression may be done in many different orders. For example, we may β-reduce a top-level application $(\lambda x.M)N$ right away, *or* we may require the argument N to be evaluated to a whnf *before* β-reduction of the application. These alternatives are known as call-by-name reduction and call-by-value reduction, or normal order reduction and applicative order reduction.

The *call-by-name* reduction order does not impose further restrictions. Thus the application $(\lambda x.M)N$ can be reduced immediately by a β-reduction.

The *call-by-value* reduction order further restricts the use of β-reduction to top-level redexes $(\lambda x.M)P$ where the argument P is a whnf (that is, a constant or a function). Thus with call-by-value, a (top-level) application $(\lambda x.M)N$ must be reduced by *first* reducing the argument N to a whnf P; then $(\lambda x.M)P$ is reduced by a β-reduction.

In principle, call-by-name is preferable to call-by-value because of the *completeness property*: namely, if M can be reduced to a constant c, then the call-by-name reduction order will reduce M to c.

In other words, if there is *any* way to reduce an expression to a constant, then call-by-name will do it. This does *not* hold for call-by-value, as shown by the example:

   $(\lambda x.1+2)$ $((\lambda y.y\ y)(\lambda y.y\ y))$

Call-by-name reduces this expression to 3, since x does not occur in the body $1+2$. However, call-by-value attempts to reduce the argument $((\lambda y.y\ y)(\lambda y.y\ y))$ to a whnf, which is impossible as shown above.

An obvious question is: can different reduction sequences produce different final unreducible answers (in the form of constant values)? The answer is 'no' as a consequence of the *Church–Rosser theorem* [115].

3.2.6 Recursion in the lambda calculus

The pure lambda calculus has no explicit way of expressing recursion. An extension often seen is the so-called *Y constant*, with δ reduction rule

Fix-point reduction: Y M $\Rightarrow$ M(Y M)

Clearly this allows application of M as many times as desired by reductions:

Y M $\Rightarrow$ M(Y M) $\Rightarrow$ M(M(Y M)) $\Rightarrow$ M(M(M(Y M))) $\Rightarrow$ ...

For example, let M be (λf.λn.if n=0 then 1 else n*f(n-1)). Then define the factorial function by:

    fac = Y M

Now 3!, say, can be computed as follows:

    fac(3) = Y(M)(3)
    ⇒ M(Y M)(3)
    ⇒ (λn.if n=0 then 1 else n * (Y M)(n-1)) (3)
    ⇒ 3*(Y M)(2)
    ⇒ 3*M(Y M)(2)
    ⇒ 3*(λn.if n=0 then 1 else n * (Y M)(n-1))(2)
    ⇒ 3*2*(Y M)(1)
    ⇒ 3*2*M(Y M)(1)
    ⇒ 3*2*(λn.if n=0 then 1 else n * (Y M)(n-1))(1)
    ⇒ 3*2*1*(Y M)(0)
    ⇒ 3*2*1*M(Y M)(0)
    ⇒ 3*2*1*(λn.if n=0 then 1 else n * (Y M)(n-1))(0)
    ⇒ 3*2*1*1
    ⇒ ... ⇒ 6

This gives a *syntactical* view of recursion; the fix-point constant Y explicates recursion by unfolding a formula as often as needed to obtain the desired result. This view resembles the interpretation of recursive type equations as seen in Section 2.3.

Surprisingly, the fix-point constant is not really necessary. It can be expressed in the untyped lambda calculus by the following lambda expression, called the *Y combinator*:

Y_n = λh.(λx.h(x x))(λx.h(x x))

To see this, let M be any lambda expression. Then we have

Y_n M = (λh.(λx.h(x x))(λx.h(x x)))M
$\Rightarrow$ (λx.M(x x))(λx.M(x x))
$\Rightarrow$ M((λx.M(x x))(λx.M(x x)))

Denoting the lambda expression (λx.M(x x))(λx.M(x x)) by C, we observe that

Y_n M $\Rightarrow$ C and also C $\Rightarrow$ M C. Thus C behaves as Y M above, so the lambda expression called Y_n faithfully simulates the Y constant.

A call-by-value version of the Y combinator
The expression called C is not in whnf, and β-reducing it gives an application M C whose argument is C. Call-by-value reduction will attempt to reduce the argument C to a whnf first, producing M(M C), then M(M(M C)), and so on. This process will not terminate. Thus Y_n is useless with call-by-value reduction order.

However, the lambda expression Y_v below encodes recursion under call-by-value:

$$Y_v = \lambda h.(\lambda x.h(\lambda a.(x\ x)a))(\lambda x.h(\lambda a.(x\ x)a))$$

3.3   Three mini-languages

We now present three simple languages and interpreters for them.

Section 3.3.1 presents an interpreter for the untyped call-by-value lambda calculus. A program is simply a lambda expression, and the computed value is an expression also. The lambda calculus is especially interesting because of its simplicity, its computational power, and its notable differences from conventional languages. Further, it illustrates some fundamental concepts in a simple context:

- Binding of variables to values.

- Call-by-name and call-by-value argument evaluation.

- First-order representation of functions by closures.

Section 3.3.2 presents the language of first-order *recursion equations*. This is also a functional, expression-oriented language. Unlike the lambda calculus, the concepts of 'program' and 'computed value' are separated. The programming languages Lisp, Scheme, ML, and Miranda (among others) resemble a combination of the lambda calculus and recursion equations.

Section 3.3.3 presents the language of traditional imperative flow charts with assignments and jumps, and gives an interpreter for it. Moreover, a mathematical semantics for flow charts is given in Section 3.3.4.

Later in the book we present partial evaluators for each of the three mini-languages, showing a range of partial evaluation techniques necessary to handle the various features.

3.3.1   An interpreter for the call-by-value lambda calculus

We now develop an interpreter for untyped call-by-value lambda expressions — an executable ML program, shown in Figure 3.1.

```
datatype lambda =
    Int of int                        (* Constant       *)
  | Var of string                     (* Variable       *)
  | Abs of string * lambda            (* Abstraction    *)
  | Apply of lambda * lambda          (* Application    *)
  | Op of string * lambda list        (* Base application *)
  | If of lambda * lambda * lambda    (* Conditional    *)
and value =
    Numb of int
  | Closure of lambda * (string list * value list)

fun lookup (x, (n::ns, v::vs)) = if n = x then v
                                 else lookup(x, (ns, vs))

fun eval (Int n,            env) = Numb n
  | eval (Var x,            env) = lookup(x, env)
  | eval (Abs(x,e),         env) = Closure(Abs(x,e), env)
  | eval (Apply(e,f),       env) =
    let val f1 = eval(f, env)
        val Closure(Abs(x,e1), (ns, vs)) = eval(e, env)
    in  eval (e1, (x::ns, f1::vs)) end
  | eval (Op("+",[e1, e2]), env) =
    let val Numb v1 = eval (e1, env)
        val Numb v2 = eval (e2, env)
    in  Numb (v1 + v2) end
  | eval (If (e,f,g),       env) =
    case eval(e, env) of
        (Numb 1) => eval(f, env)     (* 1 is true      *)
      | (Numb _) => eval(g, env)     (* non-1 is false *)

fun interpret e = eval (e, ([], []))
```

Figure 3.1: Interpreter for call-by-value lambda calculus.

Environments represent delayed substitution

An obvious approach would be to program the reduction rules and substitution directly in ML, but this is rather inefficient. Computing [N/x]M by substituting N into M at every β-reduction is impractical, since it may build extremely large expressions by repeatedly copying N.

A better alternative is to use an *environment* to map the free variables of an expression to their values. This amounts to a 'delayed' substitution: instead of computing [N/x]M explicitly, we represent it by a pair

(M, env[x↦N])

where the updated environment env[x↦N] records the fact that x will, when referenced, be replaced by N. Such a pair of an expression and an environment is called a *closure*, and is widely used in practical implementations of functional languages. Note that the substitution is not actually done; but the environment remembers that it is to be effectuated when variable x is used in M.

As a consequence the interpreter will manipulate two types of values: numbers and closures. Whenever a β reduction $(\lambda x.M)(N) \Rightarrow [N/x]M$ is to be performed, the evaluator updates the environment and then evaluates M in the new environment. All references to x within M are looked up in the environment.

The environment is represented by a pair of a name list and a value list, such that $value_i$ is the value of the variable called $name_i$:

$$([name_1,\ldots,name_n],[value_1,\ldots,value_n])$$

The interpreter written in ML is shown in Figure 3.1. In the conditional, 1 is used for 'true' and all other numbers for 'false'. The interpreter performs call-by-value reduction of the lambda calculus; namely, in the Apply branch, ML evaluates the binding let val f1 = eval(f, env) of the argument f1 *before* the lambda body e1.

The interpreter will fail with an error on a lambda expression which attempts to apply a number, or add a closure to something, or determine the truth value of a closure. This is a kind of graceless dynamic typechecking. Also, it will fail (in lookup) if an unbound variable is referenced, so it works only for programs which are *closed* lambda expressions: those without free variables.

3.3.2   An interpreter for first-order recursion equations

Syntax

Here we describe a language of call-by-value recursion equation systems. The function defined by the equation system is the one given by the first equation.

⟨Program⟩	::=	⟨Equation⟩, ..., ⟨Equation⟩	Function definitions
⟨Equation⟩	::=	⟨FuncName⟩ (⟨Varlist⟩) = ⟨Expr⟩	
⟨Varlist⟩	::=	⟨Var⟩, ..., ⟨Var⟩	Formal parameters
⟨Expr⟩	::=	⟨Constant⟩	Constant
	|	⟨Var⟩	Variable
	|	if ⟨Expr⟩ then ⟨Expr⟩ else ⟨Expr⟩	
	|	⟨FuncName⟩ (⟨Arglist⟩)	Function application
	|	⟨Op⟩ ⟨Expr⟩ ... ⟨Expr⟩	Base application
⟨Arglist⟩	::=	⟨Expr⟩, ..., ⟨Expr⟩	Argument expressions

As in the lambda calculus, we leave unspecified the set of possible constant values ⟨Constant⟩ and the base functions ⟨Op⟩ operating on them. However, note that the interpreter in Figure 3.2 implements only integer constants. We allow expressions to be written using customary precedence and associative rules, infix notation, etc.

```
datatype expr =
    Int of int                 (* Constant          *)
  | Var of string              (* Variable          *)
  | If of expr * expr * expr   (* Conditional       *)
  | Call of string * expr list (* Function call     *)
  | Op of string * expr list   (* Base application  *)

fun lookup (x, (n::ns, v::vs)) =
    if x = n then v else lookup(x, (ns, vs))

fun eval (Int n,             env, pgm) = n
  | eval (Var x,             env, pgm) = lookup(x, env)
  | eval (Call(f, exps),     env, pgm) =
    let val vals = evlist(exps,env,pgm)
        val (vars, exp) = lookup(f, pgm)
    in  eval(exp, (vars, vals), pgm) end
  | eval (Op("+",[e1,e2]), env, pgm) =    (* similar for *,-,... *)
    eval(e1,env,pgm) + eval(e2,env,pgm)
  | eval (If(e,f,g),         env, pgm) =
    case eval(e, env, pgm) of
        1 => eval(f, env, pgm)            (* 1 is true       *)
      | _ => eval(g, env, pgm)            (* non-1 is false *)
and evlist ([],              _,  _)  = []
  | evlist (e::es,           env, pgm) =
    eval(e, env, pgm) :: evlist(es, env, pgm)

fun interpret (pgm, args) =
    let val (_, (vars, exp)::_) = pgm
    in  eval(exp, (vars, args), pgm) end
```

Figure 3.2: Interpreter for call-by-value recursion equations.

Scope

In an equation

```
f(x₁,...,xₙ) = expression
```

the *scope* of $x_1,\ldots,x_n$ is the expression. This means that variables $x_1,\ldots,x_n$ bound on the left hand side can be used only inside the expression. Moreover, these are the only variables that can be used in the expression. The variables $x_1,\ldots,x_n$ must all be distinct.

Call-by-name and call-by-value in recursion equations

The distinction between call-by-value and call-by-name (see Section 3.2.5) applies to recursion equations as well as to the lambda expressions. An example where termination behaviour differs is:

```
h(x,y) = if y ≤ 1 then y else h(h(x+1,y),y-2)
```

Using call-by-name, h(1,2) evaluates to 0, but using call-by-value it is undefined.

Operational semantics

Figure 3.2 shows an interpreter for recursion equations, written in ML. A program is represented as a pair of lists. The first is a list of function names $[f_1, \ldots, f_n]$ and the second is a list of corresponding pairs $([x_{i1}, \ldots, x_{ia_i}], \text{body}_i)$, where $[x_{i1}, \ldots, x_{ia_i}]$ are the parameters of function f_i and body_i is its body.

In ML the type of a program can be described by

```
type funcname = string
type var = string
type program = (funcname list) * ((var list * expr) list)
```

The interpreter passes round the entire program in parameter pgm; this allows to find the definition of a called function. The interpreter uses an environment env just as the previous interpreter did.

Remarks

1. A function arguments are evaluated by call-by-value. Namely, in the Call branch, ML evaluates the binding let val vals = evlist(exps,env,pgm) of the argument values *before* the function body exp. A call-by-name semantics can also be defined, by letting the environment bind variables to closures that contain unevaluated argument expressions; these (sometimes called *thunks* or *suspensions*) are evaluated when needed, e.g. to perform a test or as arguments of a base function that demands evaluated arguments (e.g. addition).

2. We have not allowed functions as expression values or function arguments, but this is easily accommodated using closures, as in Section 3.3.1.

3. The interpreter fails if an unbound variable is referenced.

3.3.3   An interpreter for flow chart programs

Flow charts form a simple imperative language much closer to traditional machine architectures than the functional languages just discussed. Their essential characteristic is that computation proceeds sequentially by execution of a series of commands, each of which updates some component of an implicit *program state*. This state usually consists of the values of certain registers (accumulators, index registers, etc.) together with a *store* or *memory* which maps variables or their corresponding storage locations to the values currently stored in them.

Syntax

Following is a grammar for flow chart programs:

$$
\begin{array}{lll}
\langle\text{Program}\rangle & ::= & \textbf{read }\langle\text{Var}\rangle, \ldots, \langle\text{Var}\rangle; \langle\text{BasicBlock}\rangle^{+} \\
\langle\text{BasicBlock}\rangle & ::= & \langle\text{Label}\rangle: \langle\text{Assignment}\rangle^{*} \langle\text{Jump}\rangle \\
\langle\text{Assignment}\rangle & ::= & \langle\text{Var}\rangle := \langle\text{Expr}\rangle; \\
\langle\text{Jump}\rangle & ::= & \textbf{goto }\langle\text{Label}\rangle; \\
& | & \textbf{if }\langle\text{Expr}\rangle\textbf{ goto }\langle\text{Label}\rangle\textbf{ else }\langle\text{Label}\rangle; \\
& | & \textbf{return }\langle\text{Expr}\rangle; \\
\langle\text{Expr}\rangle & ::= & \langle\text{Constant}\rangle \\
& | & \langle\text{Op}\rangle \langle\text{Expr}\rangle \ldots \langle\text{Expr}\rangle \\
\langle\text{Label}\rangle & ::= & \text{any identifier or number}
\end{array}
$$

The set $\langle\text{Constant}\rangle$ of constants and the set $\langle\text{Op}\rangle$ of base functions are left unspecified, and again the interpreter in Figure 3.3 implements only integer constants. The values of the variables mentioned in the initial **read** statement are supplied by the input. The values of all other (numeric) variables are initially zero.

Example

A program to compute the greatest common divisor of natural numbers x and y:

```
read x, y;
1: if x = y goto 7 else 2
2: if x < y goto 5 else 3
3: x := x - y
   goto 1
5: y := y - x
   goto 1
7: return x
```

Operational semantics

As for the previous two languages we give the semantics for flow chart programs operationally by an interpreter written in ML. As before we use an abstract program syntax. The store behaves much like the environment in the previous interpreter, but with a difference: it must also be possible to change the value bound to a variable, i.e. to update an existing store. Equivalence with the mathematical semantics given in the next section can be proven by induction on the length of a computation.

The kernel of the interpreter in Figure 3.3 is the command execution function **run**, which returns the program's final answer, provided it terminates. The first argument is the current 'point of control', and the second argument is the command to be executed. If control is not transferred, then the command is performed, the store is updated, and the instruction counter is incremented. In all cases, the function **nth** is used to find the next command to be executed.

As seen in function **lookup**, the initial value of a non-input variable is 0. The

```
datatype expr =
    Int of int                  (* Integer constant     *)
  | Var of string               (* Variable             *)
  | Op of string * expr list    (* Base application     *)
and command =
    Goto of int                 (* Goto command         *)
  | Assign of string * expr     (* Assignment command   *)
  | If of expr * int * int      (* If-then-else command *)
  | Return of expr              (* Return command       *)
and program = Read of string list * command list

fun nth (c::cs, 1) = c
  | nth (c::cs, n) = nth(cs, n-1)

fun lookup (x, ([], []))        = 0     (* Initial value *)
  | lookup (x, (n::ns, v::vs)) =
    if x = n then v else lookup(x, (ns, vs))

fun update (([], []), x, w)       = ([x], [w])
  | update ((n::ns, v::vs), x, w) =
    if x = n then (n::ns, w::vs)
    else let val (ns1, vs1) = update((ns,vs), x, w)
         in (n::ns1, v::vs1) end

fun eval (Int n,            s) = n
  | eval (Var x,            s) = lookup(x, s)
  | eval (Op("+",[e1,e2]), s) = eval(e1, s) + eval(e2, s)

fun run (l, Goto n,       s, p) = run(n, nth (p, n), s, p)
  | run (l, Assign(x, e), s, p) =
    let val s1 = update(s, x, eval(e, s))
    in  run(l+1, nth(p, l+1), s1, p) end
  | run (l, If(e,m,n),    s, p) =
    if eval(e, s) = 0
    then run(m, nth(p, m), s, p)
    else run(n, nth(p, n), s, p)
  | run (l, Return e,     s, p) = eval(e, s)

fun interpret (pgm, args) =
    let val Read (vars, cmds) = pgm
        val (c1 :: _)         = cmds
        val store             = (vars, args)
    in  run(1, c1, store, cmds) end
```

Figure 3.3: Interpreter for flow chart language.

interpreter fails if a jump to an undefined address is attempted.

The intention is that the value of `run(lab, cmd, s, program)` is the final output resulting from executing `program` with store `s`, beginning at command `cmd` which has label `lab`.

3.3.4 Mathematical semantics of flow charts

Suppose one is given a flow chart program p with input variables $x_1 \ldots x_k$. It consists of a `read`-statement `read` $x_1 \ldots x_k$; followed by a sequence of labelled basic blocks: $l_0:bb_0 \ l_1:bb_1 \ldots l_n:bb_n$. If the program has variables $x_1, \ldots, x_m$ ($m \geq k$) then a *store* $\bar{v}$ can be represented by an m-tuple of values $\bar{v} = (v_1, \ldots, v_m)$.

The program's store (memory) is a mapping from variables to their current values. Input to a program p is a list of values $d = (v_1 \ldots v_k)$, initially bound to $x_1 \ldots x_k$. All the non-input variables $x_{k+1}, \ldots, x_m$ have initial value 0, so the initial store is the tuple: $(v_1, \ldots, v_k, 0, \ldots, 0)$.

Base functions must have no side effects. Assignments, conditionals, and jumps are executed in the usual way, and `return exp` terminates execution, yielding the value of `exp` as the value of the program execution $[\![p]\!]_L d$.

The meaning of each basic block bb_ℓ is a *store transformer* w_ℓ: $\text{Value}^m \rightarrow \text{Value}^m$ computing the effect of assignments on the store. If $bb_\ell = a_1; \ldots; a_n;$ `<Jump>`, the store transformer w_ℓ is defined by:

$$w_\ell(\bar{v}) = (t[\![a_n]\!] \circ \ldots \circ t[\![a_1]\!]) \, \bar{v}$$

$$t[\![x_j := e]\!] \, \bar{v} = (v_1, \ldots, v_{j-1}, \text{eval}[\![e]\!]\bar{v}, v_{j+1}, \ldots, v_m)$$
$$\text{where } \bar{v} = (v_1, \ldots, v_m)$$

The *control function* c_ℓ: $\text{Value}^m \rightarrow \{l_0, \ldots, l_n\} \cup \text{Value}$ returns either the label of the basic block to be executed after bb_ℓ, or the program's final result in case a `return`-statement is executed. The function c_ℓ is defined by:

$$
\begin{aligned}
c_\ell(\bar{v}) &= \text{eval}[\![e]\!](w_\ell(\bar{v})) && \text{if } bb_\ell = \ldots; \text{ return e} \\
&= l_j && \text{if } bb_\ell = \ldots; \text{ goto } l_j \\
&= l_j && \text{if } bb_\ell = \ldots; \text{ if e goto } l_j \text{ else } l_k \\
& && \text{and eval}[\![e]\!](w_\ell(\bar{v})) = \text{true} \\
&= l_k && \text{if } bb_\ell = \ldots; \text{ if e goto } l_j \text{ else } l_k \\
& && \text{and eval}[\![e]\!](w_\ell(\bar{v})) = \text{false}
\end{aligned}
$$

A *(finite) computation* is a (finite) sequence

$$(pp_0, \bar{v}_0) \rightarrow (pp_1, \bar{v}_1) \rightarrow \ldots \rightarrow (pp_i, \bar{v}_i) \rightarrow (pp_{i+1}, \bar{v}_{i+1}) \rightarrow$$

where $\bar{v}_0$ holds the values d of the input variables $x_1, \ldots, x_k$, and $pp_0 = l_0$. If $pp_i = l_\ell$, then $\bar{v}_{i+1} = w_\ell(\bar{v}_i)$, and $pp_{i+1} = c_\ell(\bar{v}_i)$. Finite computations end with $pp_t \in \text{Value}$ for some t.

This defines the standard evaluation of a flow chart program. If it terminates, the value computed is $[\![p]\!]_L\, d\ =\ pp_t$, else $[\![p]\!]_L\, d\ =\ \perp$.

3.4   Compiling compilers

3.4.1   Compiler bootstrapping, an example of self-application

The term *bootstrapping* comes from the phrase 'to pull oneself up by one's bootstraps' and refers to the use of compilers to compile themselves. The technique is widely used in practice, including industrial applications. Suppose we have extended a known language S to a larger one called S', such that S-programs ⊆ S'-programs. Suppose also that the extension is conservative, so every S program has the same semantics in both languages. Finally, assume that we already have a compiler from source language S to target language T, and that the compiler is available both in source form h ∈ S-programs and in target form t ∈ T-programs:

high-level compiler h ∈ | S   ⟶   T / S

low-level compiler t ∈ | S   ⟶   T / T

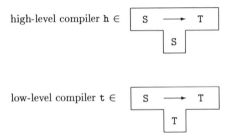

The two versions of the compiler must agree, that is, $[\![h]\!]_S = [\![t]\!]_T$. Then h and t can be used to create a compiler from S' to T as follows:

1. Extend the existing compiler h into a compiler h' ∈ S-programs for S'. This must be a conservative extension of h, so that $[\![\,[\![h]\!]_S\, p\,]\!]_T = [\![\,[\![h']\!]_S\, p\,]\!]_T$ for all S-programs p:

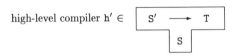

high-level compiler h' ∈ | S'   ⟶   T / S

2. Now use t on h' to obtain an S' compiler t1' in target language form:

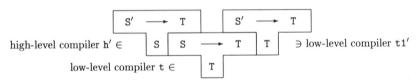

high-level compiler h' ∈ ... low-level compiler t ∈ ... ∋ low-level compiler t1'

3. Use t1′ to obtain an S′ compiler t2′ in target language form:

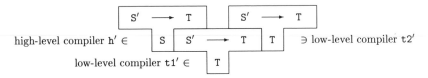

4. Finally, use t2′ to obtain an S′ compiler t3′ in target language form:

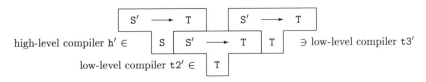

These runs can be written more concisely in the notation for program execution introduced in Chapter 1:

$$t1' = [\![t]\!]_T h'$$
$$t2' = [\![t1']\!]_T h'$$
$$t3' = [\![t2']\!]_T h'$$

Now t1′ and t2′ (and t3′) are semantically equivalent since they are all obtained from the same source program, h′.

$$
\begin{aligned}
[\![t1']\!]_T &= [\![[\![h]\!]_S h']\!]_T && \text{by definition of } t1' \\
&= [\![[\![h']\!]_S h']\!]_T && \text{since } h' \text{ is a conservative extension of } h \\
&= [\![[\![[\![t]\!]_T h']\!]_T h']\!]_T && \text{since } t \text{ is a compiler from } S \text{ to } T \\
&= [\![[\![t1']\!]_T h']\!]_T && \text{by definition of } t1' \\
&= [\![t2']\!]_T && \text{by definition of } t2'
\end{aligned}
$$

Note that t1′ and t2′ may not be *textually* identical since they were produced by two different compilers, t and t1′, and it is quite possible that the extended language S′ may require different target code than S.

However, it should be clear that t2′ and t3′ *are* textually identical since the compilers used to compile them are semantically equivalent — at least, if one assumes the extended compiler h′ to be correct. If they are not textually identical, then h′ (or, less likely, t) must be wrong.

Note that bootstrapping involves self-application in the sense that (compiled versions of) h′ are used to compile h′ itself. Moreover, self-application is useful: it gives a simple way to prove h′ wrong.

3.4.2 Compiler generation from interpreters

Later in this book we shall see that it is possible to convert an interpreter into a compiler:

by partial evaluation. As already argued in the introduction, this is interesting for several reasons:

- In practice, interpreters are smaller, easier to understand, and easier to debug than compilers.

- An interpreter is a (low-level form of) operational semantics, and so can serve as a definition of a programming language.

- The question of compiler correctness is completely avoided, since the compiler will always be faithful to the interpreter from which it was generated.

3.5 The central problems of compilation

Above we have seen how to interpret, that is, evaluate, programs in three rather different mini-languages. The remainder of this book shows how to specialize, that is, partially evaluate, programs in these and more complex languages.

Specialization of an *interpreter* with respect to a source program amounts to *compilation*, as already argued in Chapter 1. While a very promising direction for automating compilation, partial evaluation has not yet successfully accomplished all the tasks done by traditional handwritten compilers. Those that have been achieved with considerable success include:

1. Removal of as much interpretation overhead as possible.

2. Generation of target code in which as little computation as possible is done at run-time. Ideally, one wishes to execute at run-time only those computations 'that the programmer ordered when he wrote the program'.

3. Going from an interpreter's *general-purpose implementation mechanisms* to target code that is tailored to execute only *one particular source program*.

Some achievements of traditional handwritten compilers are, even though generally well-understood, as yet not fully automated. Following are some challenges on which work is currently being done:

1. Changing language style, for example from non-linear, value-oriented *expressions* to linear, command-oriented *machine code*.

2. Sequentializing naturally non-sequential processes, e.g. devising a stack to remember temporary results obtained while evaluating the parts of an arithmetic expression in a particular sequence.

3. Lowering the level of abstraction from source level (e.g. 'higher-level language') to a target code level tailored to that particular source code, e.g. P-code for implementing Pascal.

4. Devising data structures at the machine code level suitable for implementing higher-level data (products, sums, recursively defined data, functions as values, etc.), all implemented in a linear storage space.

5. Implementing value management, e.g. going from implicit last-in first-out scope rules to stacked activation blocks containing environment bindings.

3.6 Summary

This chapter concerned interpreters: operational semantics for programming languages in a directly executable form. Important topics included the following:

- interpreted programs usually run slower than directly executed ones;

- the speed difference is often a practically significant factor;

- the interpretation overhead is nearly constant for a given source program being interpreted — the constant depends on the program but not the input;

- the lambda calculus is a useful notation for defining functions;

- computation in the lambda calculus can be defined by reduction relations;

- evaluation strategies used in functional languages are restrictions of these relations;

- call-by-name evaluation terminates more often than call-by-value.

We also presented interpreters written in ML for three mini-languages: the call-by-value lambda calculus, first-order recursion equations, and a simple imperative flow chart language.

Finally, we summarized the achievements and non-achievements of compilation by automatic program specialization.

3.7   Exercises

Exercise 3.1 Identify the free and bound variable occurrences in the following lambda expressions. For each bound occurrence, point out the binding lambda.

1. (x (λx.λx.x x) x)
2. (x (λx.(λx.x) x) x)
3. λh.(λx.h (x x)) (λx.h (x x))

□

Exercise 3.2 Use the α and β reduction rules to reduce the following lambda expressions:

1. x ((λy.x) z)
2. (λx.x y) (λz.z)
3. (λy.λz.z y) (λk.z)
4. (λx.(λy.x y) x) (λx.z)
5. (λf.λg.λx.f x (g x)) (λx.λy.x) (λx.λy.x) a

□

Exercise 3.3 Find two λ-expression M and N such that

1. M is evaluated faster with call-by-value than with call-by-name
2. N is evaluated faster with call-by-name than with call-by-value

□

Exercise 3.4 Let M be any lambda expression. Show that there is a lambda expression D such that Y_v M ⇒ D and D ⇒ M(λa.M D a), using the call-by-value reduction order:

$$Y_v = λh.(λx.h(λa.(x x)a))(λx.h(λa.(x x)a))$$

□

Exercise 3.5 A lambda expression is said to be in *normal form* when no β-, δ-, or conditional reduction can be applied to any subexpression.

Find a λ-expression P without free variables, such that reduction of P to normal form requires renaming by α-reduction.   □

Exercise 3.6 Show every step in the call-by-name reduction of the expression: Y_n(M)(1), where Y_n and M are defined as follows:

```
Y_n = λh.(λx.h(x x))(λx.h(x x))
M   = λf.λn.if n=0 then 1 else n*f(n-1)
```

Repeat the exercise, using call-by-value and the Y_v combinator. □

Exercise 3.7 Reduce the expression fib(4) with call-by-name, where fib is defined as:

$$\text{fib} = Y_n \underbrace{\left(\lambda\text{f.}\lambda\text{n.if (n=1 or n=2) then 1 else f(n-1)+f(n-2)}\right)}_{M}$$

Repeat the exercise, using call-by-value and the Y_v combinator. □

Exercise 3.8 * Write an interpreter for the call-by-name lambda calculus. □

Exercise 3.9 * Write an interpreter for call-by-name recursion equations. □

Exercise 3.10 * Consider a tiny imperative language. A program has only one variable X, whose value is a list. Programs have the following syntax:

program	::=	read X;	Initialize X from input
		cmd;	Program body
		write X	Output X
cmd	::=	X := expr	Assignment to X
	|	cmd ; cmd	Sequence of commands
	|	while expr do cmd	While loop
expr	::=	X	Variable X
	|	hd expr	First element of expr
	|	tl expr	Remaining elements of expr

The informal semantics is straightforward. An expression e evaluates to a list. For example, X evaluates to its current value. If e evaluates to ["A","B","C"], then expression hd e evaluates to ["A"], and tl e evaluates to ["B","C"].

An assignment X := e evaluates e to obtain a value v, then makes v the new current value of X. A sequencing c1;c2 executes c1, then c2. A while loop while e do c first evaluates e to a value v. If v is ["nil"] then the loop has no further effect; otherwise it has the same effect as c; while e do c.

Consider the example program pgm:

```
read X;
while hd X do X := tl X;
write X
```

This program outputs the longest suffix of its input starting with "nil", if any. For instance, if the input is ["A","nil","B"], then the output is ["nil","B"].

1. The running time $t_p(\text{inp})$ of a program p on input inp is the number of operations that p performs when executed with input inp. The operations counted are: assignment, test (in the while loop), hd, tl, and fetching the value of X. For instance,

$$t_{\text{pgm}}(["A","nil","B"]) = 9$$

Assume the input to pgm is a list inp = $[A_1, \ldots, A_n, "nil"]$, where $A_i \neq$ "nil". Describe the running time $t_{\text{pgm}}(\text{inp})$ as a function of n.

2. Write an interpreter int for the tiny imperative language. The interpreter should be in the same language, extended as desired with constants and other list manipulation operations and/or command forms as desired. It *may not*, however, use recursive or other function calls.

   Hint: use a 'control stack', whose top contains the expression or command currently being executed, and whose lower elements can contain expressions or commands to be executed later, together with 'flags', each describing what is to be done when the expressions or commands above it are finished.

3. The running time $t_{\text{int}}(\text{p}, \text{inp})$ of the interpreter is the number of operations that int performs when executing p on inp.

   How large is $t_{\text{int}}(\text{pgm}, ["A","nil","B"])$?

4. Assume again that the input is a list inp = $[A_1, \ldots, A_n, "nil"]$, where $A_i \neq$ "nil". Describe the running time $t_{\text{int}}(\text{pgm}, \text{inp})$ as a function of n.

5. What is the relation between $t_{\text{int}}(\text{pgm}, \text{inp})$ and $t_{\text{pgm}}(\text{inp})$ for large n?

□

Part II

Principles of Partial Evaluation

Chapter 4

Partial Evaluation for a Flow Chart Language

It was known as long ago as 1971 [92] that the program transformation principle called *partial evaluation* or *program specialization* is closely connected with compilation. In particular, a program specializer can be used to compile, given an interpretative definition of a programming language as input data. Further, a program specializer can generate a compiler and even a compiler generator, provided it is self-applicable. The purpose of this chapter is to show using a concrete example, that certain rather simple techniques are sufficient to construct a fully automatic and non–trivial program specializer for a simple imperative language. Further, the specializer is self-applicable, with the consequence that it can both compile and generate stand-alone compilers.

To introduce the basic principles of partial evaluation we use the simple imperative language that was introduced in Section 3.3.3. Compared to a real programming language this language is ridiculously small and it can seem doubtful what can be learned from studying such a language. Years of work in partial evaluation have led to the following reasons:

- The semantics of the language is so easy to understand that it does not distract focus from the problems of partial evaluation.

- This language was the first imperative language for which self-applicable partial evaluation was successfully implemented. A key to success was indeed the simplicity of the language. Subsequent experiments with partial evaluation of stronger imperative languages have all used the techniques presented here as a stepping stone (as we shall see in later chapters).

- Partial evaluation of the flow chart language also serves as a stepping stone to partial evaluation of languages as diverse as Scheme and Prolog. Despite the different natures of the languages, the core techniques carry over and serve as a natural starting point (see later chapters).

- Many of the usual complications in partial evaluation arise, but due to the simplicity of the language they appear in a very clean form. Solving the problems for the miminal imperative language first and then moving the solutions to more complex frameworks has been shown to be fruitful.

4.1   Introduction

We show that certain basic techniques are sufficient to construct a nontrivial and self-applicable program specializer for a very simple imperative language. The result, called `mix`, is only 65 lines long.

We present one approach to program specialization, namely *polyvariant specialization*, also called *polyvariant mixed computation* [40] (others exist, e.g. *supercompilation* [265,267]). Successive concepts and techniques will be brought in only on the basis of need, so as to distinguish necessary from arbitrary design decisions and reduce the inevitable complexity problems that occur when documenting an existing system. To make our `mix` as simple and readable as possible we have assumed 'library' functions as needed; we let these functions do some cumbersome work not central to the concepts of program specialization.

Three fundamental assumptions dominate this chapter, and differentiate it from much other work in program transformation. The first is that we are only interested in methods that are *completely automatic,* with no need at all for user advice while program transformation is taking place. The second is that our methods must be strong enough to compile by specializing an interpreter with respect to a fixed source program. Third, we must be able automatically to generate stand-alone compilers. To do this we must be able to *self-apply* the specializer, i.e., to specialize the specializer itself with respect to a fixed interpreter.

Thesis

Our main thesis is that program specialization can be done by three steps, all essentially independent of the particular programming language being transformed. The underlying ideas are not new, having been seen implicitly in several earlier works including [19,76,175,265,267] and more explicitly in [40].

We consider only deterministic languages, and suppose that any program has a set of *program points* which include the 'current control point' at any instant during program execution. Examples include labels in a flow chart language, function names in a functional language, and procedure (predicate) names in a logic programming language. The three steps of the program specialization algorithm are as follows:

1. Given the value of part of the program's input, obtain a description of all computational states reachable when running the program on all possible

input values.

2. Redefine the program's control by incorporating parts of the data state into the control state, yielding perhaps several specialized versions of each of the program's control points (0, 1 or more; hence the term *polyvariant* specialization).

3. The resulting program usually contains many trivial transitions. Optimize it by traditional techniques, yielding the specialized (or *residual*) program.

A note on termination

In some places this chapter is not completely precise with respect to termination properties. These problems are in general ignored, so certain equations describing computer executions may be formally incorrect because of the possibility that one side is undefined when the other is not. The purpose of this chapter is to communicate certain programming concepts; a more formalistic treatment might make it harder to understand the basic algorithms. We defer the discussion of problems and solutions concerning termination to Chapter 14. Hence we simply ignore the problem, just ensuring that the programs we deal with terminate 'often enough'.

4.2 What is partial evaluation?

Given a program and its input data, an interpreter can execute the program producing a final answer. Given a program and only part of this program's input data, a program specializer will attempt to execute the given program as far as possible yielding as result a *residual program* that will perform the rest of the computation when the rest of the input data is supplied.

To define program specialization more precisely we need a concise notation describing the effect of running a program. Suppose p is a program written in the language L. Recall from Section 3.1.2 that we denote the result of running the program p on some input data d (if it terminates) by

$$\llbracket \mathtt{p} \rrbracket_\mathtt{L} \, \mathtt{d} \; = \; \mathtt{result}$$

Since program specializers accept both programs and data as input, we assume that both p and d are drawn from a common set D of data values. A well-known notation allowing programs to be treated as data is Lisp's list notation, hence we take D to be the set of Lisp S-expressions. We shall represent programs as Lisp lists as described in Section 2.3.4.

4.2.1   The flow chart language

In this chapter, L is a simple flow chart language with variables, assignment statements, `gotos` and tests. The syntax is shown in Figure 4.1. This is almost the
language described in Section 3.3.3, but the syntax has been changed to make
single-entry blocks explicit. The main modification to the language is that the set
of constants is that of Lisp S-expressions, and operations work on S-expressions.
For brevity we shall write the constant expression (`quote value`) as `'value`.

⟨Program⟩	::=	`read` ⟨Var⟩, ..., ⟨Var⟩; ⟨BasicBlock⟩⁺
⟨BasicBlock⟩	::=	⟨Label⟩: ⟨Assignment⟩* ⟨Jump⟩
⟨Assignment⟩	::=	⟨Var⟩ := ⟨Expr⟩;
⟨Jump⟩	::=	`goto` ⟨Label⟩;
	|	`if` ⟨Expr⟩ `goto` ⟨Label⟩ `else` ⟨Label⟩;
	|	`return` ⟨Expr⟩;
⟨Expr⟩	::=	⟨Constant⟩
	|	⟨Var⟩
	|	⟨Op⟩ ⟨Expr⟩ ... ⟨Expr⟩
⟨Constant⟩	::=	`quote` ⟨Val⟩
⟨Op⟩	::=	`hd` | `tl` | `cons` | ...
		plus any others needed for writing
		interpreters or program specializers
⟨Label⟩	::=	any identifier or number

Figure 4.1: Syntax of L-programs.

The program's store (memory) is a function from the program's variables into
their current values. Input to a program p is a list of values d = (v_1 ... v_n), initially bound to var_1, ..., var_n. All the non–input variables var_{n+1}, ..., var_{n+k}
have as initial values the empty list (), so the initial store is the finite function:

$$[var_1 \mapsto v_1, \ldots, var_n \mapsto v_n, var_{n+1} \mapsto (), \ldots, var_{n+k} \mapsto ()]$$

Base functions are assumed free of side effects on the values of the variables.
Assignments, conditionals, and `goto` are executed in the usual way, and `return`
expression terminates execution, yielding the value of **expression** as the value
of the program execution $[\![p]\!]_L$ d.

Syntactic sugar

For the sake of readability we shall write programs freely using Pascal-like constructs such as `begin` ...`end`, `while` ...`do` ... and `repeat` ...`until` ... to be
regarded as structured ways of writing programs in the syntax given above.

4.2.2   Residual programs and program specialization

Definition 4.1 Let p be an L-program taking as input a two-element list, and let d1 ∈ D. Then an L-program r is a *residual program for* p *with respect to* d1 iff

$$\llbracket p \rrbracket_L \, [\texttt{d1, d2}] = \llbracket r \rrbracket_L \, \texttt{d2}$$

for all d2 ∈ D. □

The equation expresses that running r on d2 yields the same result as running p on both d1 and d2. Intuitively, the input d1 is already incorporated in the residual program r. We now define a (correct) program specializer to be a program which given p and d1 yields as result a residual program r, such that the above equation holds.

Definition 4.2 An L-program mix is a *program specializer* iff for every p, d1 ∈ D, the program r = $\llbracket p \rrbracket_L$ d1 is a residual L-program for p with respect to d1. Expressed symbolically we get the *mix equation*:

$$\llbracket p \rrbracket_L \, [\texttt{d1, d2}] = \llbracket (\llbracket \texttt{mix} \rrbracket_L \, [\texttt{p, d1}]) \rrbracket_L \, \texttt{d2}$$

for all d2 ∈ D. □

The program p is called the *subject program*. Note that the right hand side of the mix equation involves two program executions. First, a residual program r = $\llbracket \texttt{mix} \rrbracket_L$ [p, d1] is generated. Second, the residual program r is run on data d2.

The equations can be generalized to the situation where p takes a fixed number n pieces of input data, of which m are given to the program specializer, $0 \leq m \leq n$. In the equations above, $n = 2$ and $m = 1$.

Example 4.1 Consider the program fragment in Figure 4.2. It might occur inside an interpreter which represents the runtime store of an interpreted program by a list namelist of names of variables, and a parallel list valuelist of their values. The 'input data' to the program fragment are the three variables name, namelist, and valuelist, that is, $n = 3$.

```
while name ≠ hd (namelist) do
begin
    valuelist := tl (valuelist);
    namelist  := tl (namelist)
end;
value := hd (valuelist);
```

Figure 4.2: An L-program program fragment to look up a name.

Suppose the program specializer is given the initial values of the variables name and namelist, for example name = z and namelist = (x y z) but that valuelist is unknown, that is, $m = 2$. Since the program's control is entirely determined by `name` and `namelist` it can be symbolically executed, yielding as a residual program fragment:

```
valuelist := tl (valuelist);
valuelist := tl (valuelist);
value     := hd (valuelist);
```

Note that the `while`-loop has disappeared, and the residual program fragment contains only those commands from the subject program whose effect can not be computed at program specialization time. Note also that the command

```
valuelist := tl (valuelist)
```

appears twice in the residual program, once for each iteration of the loop, even though it appeared only once in the subject program. The two iterations stem from the fact that we had to take `tl` of `namelist` twice before its `hd` was equal to `name`.   □

Three remarks in relation to the definition of program specialization:

Further optimization: Since variable `valuelist` will not be used after the program fragment, it is tempting to optimize the resulting program to: `value := hd (tl (tl (valuelist)))`. An appropriate technique for doing such transformations is to use 'dags' [4]. Since the optimization is not essential to program specialization, we shall not pursue the idea further here.

The existence of residual programs: The general possibility of partially evaluating a program is known as Kleene's *s-m-n theorem* in recursive function theory. This, however, only states the existence of a residual program; nothing is said about efficiency. The usual proof of the s-m-n theorem involves generating a trivial residual program such as:

```
name := 'z;  namelist := '(x y z);
while name ≠ hd(namelist) do
begin
    valuelist := tl (valuelist);
    namelist  := tl (namelist)
end;
value := hd(valuelist);
```

This residual program clearly satisfies the defining equation, but it is of no practical interest.

The language of the residual program: Note that the program specializer is assumed to generate residual programs, `r`, written in the same language as the input program `p`. This makes it much easier to understand the transformations `mix` performs as long as the aim is to understand principles and gain experience with program specialization. If the goal were maximal efficiency it would be natural to let `mix` generate programs in a lower-level language [120].

4.3   Partial evaluation and compilation

In this section we first show by a concrete example that a partial evaluator can be used to compile, given an interpreter and a source program. We then show that this remarkable fact is a simple consequence of the mix equation as presented above and from the definitions of interpreters and compilers from Section 3.1. This result is known as *the first Futamura projection*.

4.3.1   An interpreter for Turing machine programs

This section presents a concrete program that will be used to illustrate several points later in the chapter. The program is an interpreter for a Turing machine (Post's variant) with tape alphabet $A = \{0,1,B\}$, where B stands for 'blank'. A Turing program Q is a list $(I_0\ I_1\ \ldots I_n)$ of instructions each of form

> `right, left, write a, goto i, or if a goto i`

A computational state consists of a current instruction I_i about to be executed, and an infinite tape of squares a_i:

> $\ldots a_{-2}\ a_{-1}\ a_0\ a_1\ a_2\ \ldots$

Only finitely many of the squares contain symbols a_i not equal to B; a_0 is called the *scanned square*. Instruction effects: `write a` changes a_0 to a, `right` and `left` change the scanning point, and `if a goto i` causes the next control point to be I_i in case $a_0 = a$; in all other cases the next control point is the following instruction (if any).

An example program Q in the Turing language is given in Figure 4.3. The input to this program is $a_0 a_1\ \ldots a_n \in \{0,1\}*$, and the initial tape contains B in all other positions, that is, a_{n+1}, $a_{n+2},\ldots$, and a_{-1}, $a_{-2},\ldots$. Program output is the final value of $a_0\ a_1\ \ldots$ (at least up to and including the last non–blank symbol) and is produced when there is no next instruction to be executed. Note that a different square may be scanned on termination than at the beginning.

```
0: if 0 goto 3
1: right
2: goto 0
3: write  1
```

Figure 4.3: A Turing machine program.

The program finds the first 0 to the right on the initial tape and converts it to 1 (and goes into an infinite loop if none is found). If the input to Q is 110101, the output will be 1101.

The Turing interpreter in Figure 4.4 has a variable Q for the whole Turing program, and the control point is represented via a suffix Qtail of Q (the list of instructions remaining to be executed). The tape is represented by variables Left, Right with values in A*, where Right equals a_0 a_1 a_2 ... (up to and including the last non–blank symbol) and Left similarly represents a_{-1} a_{-2} a_{-3} .... Note that the order is reversed.

```
read (Q, Right);
init:      Qtail := Q;  Left := '();

loop:      if Qtail = '() goto stop else cont;
cont:      Instruction  :=  first_instruction(Qtail);
           Qtail        :=  rest(Qtail);
           Operator     :=  hd(tl(Instruction));

           if Operator = 'right goto do-right else cont1;
cont1:     if Operator = 'left  goto do-left  else cont2;
cont2:     if Operator = 'write goto do-write else cont3;
cont3:     if Operator = 'goto  goto do-goto  else cont4;
cont4:     if Operator = 'if    goto do-if     else error;

do-right: Left      := cons(firstsym(Right), Left);
          Right     := tl(Right); goto loop;
do-left:  Right     := cons(firstsym(Left), Right);
          Left      := tl(Left); goto loop;
do-write: Symbol    := hd(tl(tl(Instruction)));
          Right     := cons(Symbol,tl(Right)); goto loop;
do-goto:  Nextlabel := hd(tl(tl(Instruction)));
          Qtail     := new_tail(Nextlabel, Q); goto loop;
do-if:    Symbol    := hd(tl(tl(Instruction)));
          Nextlabel := hd(tl(tl(tl(tl(Instruction)))));
          if Symbol = firstsym(Right) goto jump else loop;

jump:     Qtail     := new_tail(Nextlabel,Q); goto loop;

error:    return ('syntax-error: Instruction);

stop:     return right;
```

Figure 4.4: Turing machine interpreter written in L.

The interpreter uses some special base functions. These are new_tail, which takes a label lab and the program Q as arguments and returns the part (suffix) of the program beginning with label `lab`; `first_instruction`, which returns the first instruction from an instruction sequence; and `rest`, which returns all but the first instruction from an instruction sequence. Moreover, we need a special version `firstsym` of `hd` for which `firstsym () = B`, and we assume that `tl () is ()`.

Example 4.2 Let `Q` be (`0: if 0 goto 3  1: right  2: goto 0  3: write 1`). Then

$$
\begin{aligned}
&\llbracket\text{int}\rrbracket_{\text{L}}\,[\text{Q, 110101}] &&=&& \text{1101} \\
&\text{new\_tail(2, Q)} &&=&& \text{(2: goto 0 3: write 1)} \\
&\text{first\_instruction(Q)} &&=&& \text{(0: if 0 goto 3)} \\
&\text{rest(Q)} &&=&& \text{(1: right 2: goto 0 3: write 1)}
\end{aligned}
$$

are some typical values of these auxiliary functions.   □

Time analysis. The Turing interpreter in Figure 4.4 executes between 15 and 28 operations per executed command of `Q`, where we count one operation for each assignment, `goto` or base function call.

4.3.2   The Futamura projections

Futamura was the first researcher to realize that self-application of a partial evaluator can in principle achieve compiler generation [92]. Therefore the equations describing compilation, compiler generation, and compiler generation are now called the *Futamura projections*.

$$
\begin{aligned}
\text{target} &= \llbracket\text{mix}\rrbracket_{\text{L}}\,[\text{int, source program}] \\
\text{compiler} &= \llbracket\text{mix}\rrbracket_{\text{L}}\,[\text{mix, int}] \\
\text{cogen} &= \llbracket\text{mix}\rrbracket_{\text{L}}\,[\text{mix, mix}]
\end{aligned}
$$

Although easy to verify, it must be admitted that the intuitive significance of these equations is hard to see. In the remainder of this chapter we shall give some example target programs, and a compiler derived from the interpreter just given.

4.3.3   Compilation by the first Futamura projection

In this section we shall show how we can compile programs using only an interpreter and the program specializer. We start by verifying the *first Futamura projection*, which states that specializing an interpreter with respect to a source program has the effect of compiling the source program. Let `int` be an S-interpreter written in L, let `s` be an S-program, and `d` its input data. The equation is proved by:

$$\llbracket s \rrbracket_S \, d \;=\; \llbracket int \rrbracket_L \, [s,d] \qquad \text{by the definition of}$$
an interpreter

$$=\; \llbracket (\, \llbracket mix \rrbracket_L \, [int,s]\,)\, \rrbracket_L \, d \quad \text{by the mix equation}$$

$$=\; \llbracket target \rrbracket_L \, d \qquad\qquad \text{by naming the residual}$$
program: target

These equations state nothing about the quality of the target program, but in practice it can be quite good. Figure 4.5 shows a target program generated from the above interpreter (Figure 4.4) and the source program s = (0: if 0 goto 3   1: right   2: goto 0   3: write 1). Here we just present the result; a later section will show how it was obtained.

```
read (Right);
lab0: Left := '();
      if '0 = firstsym(Right) goto lab2 else lab1;
lab1: Left := cons(firstsym(Right), Left);
      Right := tl(Right);
      if '0 = firstsym(Right) goto lab2 else lab1;
lab2: Right := cons('1, tl(Right));
      return(Right);
```

Figure 4.5: A mix-*generated target program.*

Notice that the target program is written in the same language as the interpreter; this comes immediately from the mix equation. On the other hand, this target program's *structure* more closely resembles that of the source program from which it was derived than that of the interpreter. Further, it is composed from bits and pieces of the interpreter, for example Left := cons(firstsym(Right), Left). Some of these are *specialized* with respect to data from the source program, e.g. if '0 = firstsym(Right) goto lab2 else lab1. This is characteristic of mix-produced target programs.

Time analysis.   We see that the target program (Figure 4.5) has a quite natural structure. The main loop in the target program takes 8 operations while the interpreter takes 61 operations to interpret the main loop of the source program, so the target program is nearly 8 times faster than the interpreter when run on this source program.

4.4   Program specialization techniques

We now describe basic principles sufficient for program specialization; a concrete algorithm will be given in a later section.

4.4.1 States, program points, and divisions

A *computational state* at any instant during execution of a program in our simple imperative language is a pair (pp, store), where pp is a program point indicating the current point of control and store contains the current values of all program variables. A store containing the current values of variables $X_1, \ldots, X_n$ will be represented by a list of the form $(v_1 \ldots v_n)$. When an assignment is executed, the store is updated and pp reset to the next program point; when a conditional or a goto is executed, only the control point is updated.

Suppose now that only part of the input data is at hand. Then we cannot execute the program but we can specialize it with respect to the known input. In this case the initial and subsequent stores will be incomplete (at specialization time), hence we cannot expect to be able to evaluate at specialization time all expressions in the subject program.

What form should such an incomplete store take? A simple method is to classify every variable independently as *static* if its values can be determined at program specialization time, and as *dynamic* if not static. A *partial computational state* is thus a pair of form (pp, vs), where vs is a list of the values of the static variables, and the values of the dynamic variables are unknown.

Such a static/dynamic classification is called a *division* in [130], where more general versions are also considered. Where the opposite is not explicitly stated, we shall assume throughout this chapter that the same division is valid at all program points. Call such a division *uniform*. This assumption, which simplifies matters without being essential, often holds in practice although counterexamples may easily be found, e.g., it would be convenient to violate the assumption for a program that swaps two variables, one initially static and the other dynamic.

An essential requirement for use in program specialization is that the division is *(uniformly) congruent*. This means that in any transition from computational state (pp, store) to (pp', store'), the values of the static variables at program point pp' must be computable from the values of the static variables at pp. Expressed concisely: *any variable that depends on a dynamic variable must itself be dynamic.*

An expression exclusively built from constants and static variables is also called static, while it is called dynamic if it contains a dynamic variable. Suppose that the subject program contains the assignment

    X := exp

If exp is dynamic then by the congruence condition X must also be dynamic.

Consider the program fragment in Figure 4.2 and assume, as there, that name and namelist are static, while value and valuelist are dynamic:

```
while name ≠ hd (namelist) do
begin
    valuelist := tl (valuelist);
    namelist  := tl (namelist)
end;
value := hd (valuelist);
```

We see that none of the assignments violates the congruence condition.

4.4.2 Program point specialization

The idea of program point specialization is to incorporate the values of the static variables into the control point. Suppose that at program specialization time we discover that if the program had been executed normally with all input data supplied, the computation might eventually be in a state with control at point pp and with vs as the values of the static variables. Then the pair (pp, vs) is made a program point in the residual program. The code that (pp, vs) labels in the residual program is an optimized version of the code at pp in the subject program. The potential for optimization is because we know the values of the static variables. As hinted by the examples, this means that a program point pp may appear in several residual versions, each with different values of the static variables.

Let us continue the above example. Since we need explicitly named program points, this time we use a desugared version of the program fragment.

```
search: if name = hd(namelist) goto found else cont;
cont:   valuelist := tl(valuelist);
        namelist  := tl(namelist);
        goto search;
found:  value := hd(valuelist);
```

Assume our task is to specialize this fragment beginning at search, and that initially name is z and namelist is (x y z). Thus initially the value of vs in the specializer is the pair:

```
vs = (z, (x y z))
```

Now consider program execution on this initial vs and unknown variables value and valuelist. The list vs can assume three different values at search, namely: (z, (x y z)), (z, (y z)), and (z, (z)). At label cont, vs can assume the two first of the listed values, and at point found, vs has (z, (z)) as its only value.

Definition 4.3 A *specialized program point* is a tuple (pp, vs) where pp is a program point from the subject program and vs is a set of values of the static variables. □

A specialized program point (pp, vs) represents a set of states of the subject program's computation — all those with control point pp and static variable values vs. In the residual program the value of vs is 'built in' to the specialized program point (pp, vs), and not explicit as it is at program specialization time.

Definition 4.4 The set of all specialized program points (pp, vs) that are reachable during program execution is called poly. □

Note that poly thus represents the set of points of control in the residual program; in our example:

```
poly = { (search, (z,(x y z))),(search,(z,(y z))),(search,(z,(z))),
         (cont,   (z,(x y z))),(cont,  (z,(y z))),
         (found,  (z,(z)))                                          }
```

In the next sections we show how to compute poly and how to generate a residual program given poly. We address the latter question first.

4.4.3 Generating code for the various commands

Suppose we are given a specialized program point (pp, vs). In the subject program the label pp is attached to a basic block consisting of a sequence of commands. The generated code for a basic block is the concatenation of the code generated for the commands.

In the following we assume a rich library of basic functions. In particular, suppose exp is an expression and vs is a list of values of the program's static variables. We need two functions: eval(exp, vs), which returns the value of a static expression exp; and reduce(exp, vs), which performs constant folding [4] of static parts of a dynamic expression. If vs, for example, says that b = 2, the expression b * b + a can be replaced by 4 + a.

Command	*Done at specialization time*	*Generated code*
X := exp (if X is dynamic)	reduced_exp := reduce(exp, vs)	X := reduced_exp
X := exp (if X is static)	val := eval(exp, vs); vs := vs[X ↦ val]	
return exp	reduced_exp := reduce(exp, vs)	return reduced_exp
goto pp′	goto (pp′, vs)	

Code generation for a conditional: `if exp goto pp' else pp''`		
	Done at specialization time	*Generated code*

(if `exp` is dynamic)	`reduced_exp := reduce(exp,vs)`	`if reduced_exp`
		`goto(pp',vs)`
		`else(pp'',vs)`

(if `exp` is static and `val = true`)	`val := eval(exp,vs)`	`goto (pp', vs)`
(if `exp` is static and `val = false`)	`val := eval(exp,vs)`	`goto (pp'',vs)`

Computing poly

Let pp_0 be the first label in the program and let vs_0 be the initial values of the static data. It is clear that (pp_0, vs_0) should be in `poly`. Moreover, if any specialized program point (`pp`, `vs`) is in `poly`, all specialized program points reachable from (`pp`, `vs`) should be there. That is, `poly` is the closure of vs_0 under the relation 'reachable from'.

We now address this more carefully. Consider specialized program point (`pp`, `vs`), where `pp` is attached to a basic block of commands in the subject program: a sequence of assignments ended by a 'passing of control'. Some assignments might reassign static variables, thus forcing the entry list of statically known values, `vs`, to be updated, so a new specialized program point has form (`pp'`, `vs'`). The set of successors naturally depends on the form of control passage. Let us write `successors(pp, vs)` for the set of possible successors (it has two elements for a dynamic conditional, none for a return and otherwise one). In the earlier example,

```
successors(search,(z, (x y z)))  =  { (cont,   (z, (x y z))) }
successors(search,(z, (z)))      =  { (found,  (z, (z))) }
successors(cont,   (z, (x y z)))  =  { (search,(z, (y z))) }
```

and so on. A first approximation to the overall structure of `mix` can now be given (Figure 4.6).

```
poly := { (pp_0, vs_0) };
while poly contains an unmarked (pp, vs) do
begin
    mark (pp, vs);
    generate code for the basic block starting at pp using the values in vs;
    poly := poly ∪ successors(pp, vs)
end
```

Figure 4.6: A simple specialization algorithm.

Rules for computing successors are easily given. If the basic block labelled by `pp` transforms the static store vs into vs′, then use:

Code generation for a conditional: if exp goto pp′ else pp″		
control component of pp	*successors(*pp, vs*)*	
return	{}	
goto pp′	{(pp′, vs′)}	
if exp goto pp′ else pp″	{(pp′, vs′)} {(pp″, vs′)} {(pp′, vs′), (pp″, vs′)}	if exp evaluates to true if exp evaluates to false if exp is dynamic

4.4.4   Transition compression

When the subject program in Figure 4.2 is slavishly specialized using the algorithm in Figure 4.6, the following residual program is produced:

```
(search, (z, (x y z))): goto (cont, (z, (x y z)));
(cont,   (z, (x y z))): valuelist := tl (valuelist);
                        goto (search, (z, (y z)));
(search, (z, (y z)))  : goto (cont, (z, (y z)));
(cont,   (z, (y z)))  : valuelist := tl (valuelist);
                        goto (search, (z, (z)));
(search, (z, (z)))    : goto (found, (z, (z)));
(found,  (z, (z)))    : value := hd (valuelist);
```

Though correct this result is not very pleasing. We therefore apply the technique called *transition compression* to eliminate the redundant gotos.

Definition 4.5 Let pp be a label occurring in program p, and consider a jump goto pp. The replacement of this goto by a copy of the basic block labelled pp is called *transition compression.*   □

When we compress the above program to remove superfluous jumps, we obtain the natural residual program, except that the composite label (search, (z, (x y z))) should be replaced by a simple one (a number or an identifier):

```
(search, (z, (x y z))): valuelist := tl (valuelist);
                        valuelist := tl (valuelist);
                        value     := hd (valuelist);
```

The benefits of the compression are evident: the code becomes neater and more efficient. However, indiscriminate use of transition compression offers two pitfalls: code duplication and infinite compression. Code duplication can occur when two distinct transitions to the same program point are both compressed. When the residual program contains a loop, the compression can even be continued infinitely.

When should transition compression be done?

Transition compression can be performed as a separate phase after the whole residual program has been generated, making it easy to avoid the above–mentioned problems. A program flow chart can then be built and analysed to see which transitions can safely be compressed. It is, however, desirable in practice to do the compressions along with the code generation since this may be more efficient than generating a whole program containing superfluous `gotos` just to compress many of the `gotos` afterwards. Doing compression on the fly makes it more complicated to ensure safe compression. One solution is to annotate some `gotos` as 'residual', and let `mix` compress transitions from all the remaining ones. (We elaborate on this approach in Chapter 5.)

In this chapter we use a simpler strategy which does not involve annotating `gotos`. We compress *all* transitions that are not a part of a residual conditional. Note that the language does not permit more extensive compressing than directed by our strategy, since the branches of an if-statement may only contain jumps and *not* any other commands. The strategy causes some code duplication, but experience indicates that it is a minor problem. More important is that the compression strategy will not cause the program specializer to loop infinitely unless the subject program (with the given initial static data) contains a potential 'bomb', that is, a sequence of instructions that will certainly loop infinitely whenever executed, no matter what (dynamic) input data is supplied.

Doing transition compression and code generation at the same time improves the results of self-application significantly. The explanation of this phenomenon is a little subtle, and since the issue is not, for now, important, we postpone the treatment to a later section.

4.4.5   Choosing the right division is tricky

The task of classifying variables as static or dynamic is more difficult than it might appear at first sight. A natural strategy would be to denote as static all variables that are assigned values computed from constants and static input data. As the following program fragment demonstrates, this strategy might cause the program specializer to loop infinitely.

```
iterate: if Y ≠ 0 then begin
             X := X + 1;  Y := Y - 1; goto iterate;
         end;
```

This seemingly innocent program has two variables, X and Y. If the initial value of X is known to be 0 and Y is unknown, it seems natural to classify X as static and Y as dynamic. The reason is that the only value assigned to X is X + 1, which can be computed at program specialization time since X is known. But this does not work, as the following shows.

As is usually done in practice we intermingle the computation of `poly` and the code generation. Initially `poly` contains the specialized program point (`iterate`, 0). The code generation yields

```
(iterate, 0): if Y ≠ 0 then begin
                    Y := Y - 1; goto (iterate, 1);
             end;
```

We see that (`iterate`, 1) should be added to `poly`, hence we should add to the residual program

```
(iterate, 1): if Y ≠ 0 then begin
                    Y := Y - 1; goto (iterate, 2);
             end;
```

and so forth *ad nauseam*. The problem is that `poly` becomes infinite:

$$\text{poly} = \{(\text{iterate, 0}), (\text{iterate, 1}), (\text{iterate, 2}), \ldots\}$$

This happens because the value of X, though known, is unbounded since its values are computed under dynamic control. The problem did not arise when we specialized the example programs of this chapter (an interpreter and `mix` itself). The problem is handled by classifying the unbounded variable(s) as dynamic. A division which ensures finiteness of `poly` is itself called *finite*.

In this example, X should be classified as dynamic to prevent the program specializer from making use of its value, disregarding that it could have be computed at partial evaluation time. The process of classifying of a variable X as dynamic, when congruence would have allowed X to be static, is called *generalization*. As just witnessed, generalization can be necessary to avoid non-terminating partial evaluation. Another purpose of generalization is to avoid useless specialization (see Section 4.9.2).

To classify a sufficient number of the variables as dynamic to ensure finiteness of `poly`, always avoiding classifying an unnecessarily large number, is not computable. We treat the problem and how to find an acceptable approximate solution in Chapter 14.

4.4.6 Simple binding-time analysis

By assuming that the same division is applicable for each program point and ignoring the problem of ensuring finiteness, it is easy to compute the division of all program variables given a division of the input variables. This process is called *binding-time analysis*, often abbreviated *BTA*, since it determines at what time the value of a variable can be computed, that is, the time when the value can be bound to the variable.

Call the program variables X_1, X_2, ..., X_N and assume that the input variables are X_1, ..., X_n, where $0 \leq n \leq N$. Assume that we are given the binding times

$\bar{b}_1, \ldots, \bar{b}_n$ for the input variables, where each $\bar{b}_j$ is either S (for static) or D (for dynamic). The task is now to compute a congruent division (Section 4.4.1) for *all* the program variables: $B = (b_1, \ldots, b_N)$ which satisfies $\bar{b}_i = D \Rightarrow b_i = D$ for the input variables. This is done by the following algorithm:

1. Construct the initial division $\bar{B} = (\bar{b}_1, \ldots, \bar{b}_n, S, \ldots, S)$ and set $B = \bar{B}$

2. If the program contains an assignment

   $$X_k = \texttt{exp}$$

   where variable X_j appears in $\texttt{exp}$ and $b_j = D$ in B then set $b_k = D$ in B.

3. Repeat step 2 until B does not change any longer. Then the algorithm terminates with congruent division B.

4.4.7   Online and offline partial evaluation

Above we have described partial evaluation as a process which has two (or more) stages. *First* compute a division B from the program and the initial division $\bar{B}$, *without* making use of the concrete values of the static input variables. *Then* the actual program specialization takes place, making use of the static inputs to the extent determined *by the division*, not by the concrete values computed during specialization. This approach is called *offline partial evaluation*, as opposed to *online partial evaluation*.

A partial evaluator makes (at least) two kinds of decisions: which available values should be used for specialization and which transitions should be compressed. Each decision is made according to a *strategy* employed by the partial evaluator.

Definition 4.6 A strategy is said to be *online* if the concrete values computed during program specialization can affect the choice of action taken. Otherwise the strategy is *offline*. □

Almost all offline strategies, including those to be presented in this book, base their decisions on the results of a preprocess, the binding-time analysis.

Many partial evaluators mix online and offline methods, since both kinds of strategies have their advantages. The main advantage of online partial evaluation is that it can sometimes exploit more static information during specialization than offline, thus yielding better residual programs. Offline techniques make generation of compilers, etc., by self-application feasible and yield faster systems using a simpler specialization algorithm.

Chapter 7 contains a more detailed comparison of online and offline partial evaluation.

4.4.8 Compiling without a compiler

We now return to compilation by specializing the Turing interpreter from Figure 4.4. The first task is to determine a division of the interpreter's variables, given that the program to be interpreted (Q) is static while its initial input tape (Right) is dynamic. It is fairly easy to see that the following variables

Q, Qtail, Instruction, Operator, Symbol and Nextlabel

may be static (S) whereas Right and Left must be dynamic (D) in the division. This information is given to the program specializer along with the interpreter text. Suppose mix is given the Turing interpreter text, a division of the interpreter variables and the Turing program in Figure 4.3

Q = (0: if 0 goto 3   1: right   2: goto 0   3: write 1)

Then the residual program shown in Figure 4.5 is generated. All assignments X := exp, where X is static, and tests if exp ..., where exp is static, have been reduced away; they were performed at program specialization time. The labels lab0, lab1, and lab2 seen in Figure 4.5 are in fact aliases for specialized program points (pp, vs), where pp is an interpreter label and vs holds the values of the static interpreter variables. In the table below we show the correspondence between the labels in the target program and the specialized program points. (Since the interpreter variable Q holds the whole Turing program as its value at every program point, it is omitted from the table. The variable Operator is omitted for space.) The ()'s are the values of uninitialized variables.

Target label	Interpreter label	Static interpreter variables (vs): Instruction	Qtail	Symbol	Nextlabel
lab0	init	( )	( )	( )	( )
lab1	cont	right	(2:goto 0 3:write 1)	0	3
lab2	jump	if 0 goto 3	(1:right 2:goto 0 3:write 1)	0	3

4.5   Algorithms used in mix

We have described techniques that together form program specialization. They were presented one at a time, and it is possible to build a program specializer that applies these techniques in sequence, yielding an algorithm like this:

> *Input:*   A subject program, a division of its variables into static and dynamic, and some of the program's input.
> *Output:* A residual program.

Algorithm:

- Compute `poly` and generate code for all the specialized program points in `poly`;

- Apply transition compression to shorten the code;

- Relabel the specialized program points to use natural numbers as labels.

This structure reflects the principles of program specialization well, but we have found it inefficient in practice since it involves first building up a large residual program, and then cutting it down to form the final version.

A more efficient algorithm

We now present the algorithm we implemented, where the phases mentioned above are intermingled. Along with the computation of poly, we generate code and apply transition compression. Variable `pending` holds a set of specialized program points for which code has not yet been generated, while `marked` holds the set of specialized program points for which code has already been generated. The algorithm is shown in Figure 4.7.

For simplicity we have omitted the relabelling of the specialized program point (`pp`, `vs`).

4.6   The second Futamura projection: compiler generation

We have seen how specializing an interpreter with respect to a source program gave a compiled version of the source program. In this section we examine how a stand-alone compiler can be generated by specializing `mix` with respect to the interpreter. The theoretical basis for this is the *second Futamura projection*:

$$\texttt{compiler} = [\![\texttt{mix}]\!]_L \, [\texttt{mix}, \texttt{int}]$$

This equation states that when `mix` is specialized with respect to an interpreter, the residual program will be a compiler. (Our `mix` has in fact an extra argument, `division`, not made explicit in the Futamura projections to avoid cluttering up the equations.) For the proof, let `int` be an S-interpreter written in L and let `s` be an S-program.

$$
\begin{aligned}
[\![s]\!]_S \, d \;&=\; [\![\texttt{int}]\!]_L \, [s, d] && \text{by definition of interpreter} \\
&=\; [\![([\![\texttt{mix}]\!]_L \, [\texttt{int}, \texttt{s}])]\!]_L \, d && \text{by the mix equation} \\
&=\; [\![([\![([\![\texttt{mix}]\!]_L \, [\texttt{mix},\texttt{int}])]\!]_L \, s)]\!]_L \, d && \text{by the mix equation} \\
&=\; [\![([\![\texttt{compiler}]\!]_L \, s)]\!]_L \, d && \text{by naming the residual program}
\end{aligned}
$$

This establishes `compiler` as an S-to-L-compiler written in L.

```
    read(program, division, vs₀);
1    pending := { (pp₀, vs₀) };       (* pp₀ is program's initial program point        *)
2    marked   := {};
3    while pending ≠ {} do
4    begin
5      Pick an element (pp, vs) ∈ pending and remove it;
6      marked := marked ∪ {(pp, vs)};
7      bb := lookup (pp, program);   (* Find the basic block labeled by pp in program*)
                                     (* Now generate residual code for bb given vs   *)
8      code := initial_code(pp, vs);(* An empty basic block with label (pp, vs) :  *)

9      while bb is not empty do
10     begin
11,12    command := first_command(bb); bb := rest (bb);
13       case command of
14       X := exp:
15         if X is classified as static by division
16         then vs := vs [X ↦ eval(exp, vs)];
                                          (* Static assignment                 *)
17         else code := extend(code, X := reduce(exp, vs));
                                          (* Dynamic assignment                *)
18       goto pp':
19         bb := lookup (pp', program);        (* Compress the transition      *)
20       if exp then goto pp' else goto pp'':
           if exp is static by division
           then begin                         (* Static conditional           *)
21             if eval (exp, vs) = true
22             then bb := lookup (pp', program);
                                              (* Compress the transition       *)
23             else bb := lookup (pp'', program);
                                              (* Compress the transition       *)
           end
24         else begin                         (* Dynamic conditional           *)
25             pending := pending ∪ ( {(pp', vs)} \ marked );
26             pending := pending ∪ ( {(pp'', vs)} \ marked );
27             code    := extend (code,  if reduce(exp, vs)
                                         goto (pp', vs)
                                         else (pp'', vs) );
           end
         return exp:
           code := extend(code, return reduce(exp, vs));
         otherwise error;
28     end; (* while bb is not empty *)

29     residual := extend(residual, code);       (* add new residual basic block   *)
30   end     (* while pending ≠ {} *)
```

Figure 4.7: The mix *algorithm.*

4.6.1   Specializing mix

When we want to specialize `mix` with respect to `int` we have to determine a division of the variables of `mix`. We do not address this in full detail as we did with the Turing interpreter since `mix` is a somewhat larger program. In the following discussion we will refer to the `mix` algorithm as presented in Figure 4.7.

The question to ask now is: what information will be available to mix_1 when the following run, the compiler generation, is performed (for accuracy we show also the arguments div_{mix} and div_{int}, which were left out above)?

$$\text{compiler} = [\![mix_1]\!]_L \ [mix_2, \ div_{mix}, \ [int, \ div_{int}]]$$

In this run mix_1 is the active specializer that is actually run on its three arguments. The first argument is the program text of mix_2 which is identical to mix_1. The second argument is a division of mix_2's variables. The third argument is the initial values of mix_2's static input variables. Two of mix_2's three input variables are static, namely **program**, whose value is the interpreter, and **division**, whose value is the division div_{int}. Thus mix_2 is given the interpreter text and a division of the interpreter's variables but *not* the initial values of the interpreter's input variables.

Recall that `mix` applied to an interpreter and a source program yields a target program. When $[\![mix_1]\!]_L \ [mix_2, div_{int}, int]$ is run, only the interpreter is available to mix_2, so it can only perform those actions that depend only on the interpreter text and not on the source program. It is vital for the efficiency of the generated compiler that mix_2 can perform some of its computation at compiler generation time.

We shall now examine the most important mix_2 variables to see which have values at hand during compiler generation time and so can be classified as static by the division.

To begin with, the variables **program** and **division** are static. Variables vs and vs_0 are intended to hold the values of some interpreter variables: this information is not available before the source program is supplied, hence they are dynamic. The congruence principle now forces **pending**, **marked**, **code**, and **residual** to be classified as dynamic. These variables will thus not be reduced away by mix_1, and so will appear in the residual program corresponding to `int`, namely, the compiler.

Now consider lines 5–7 in the algorithm. The variable pp gets its value from **pending** and is hence dynamic. The variable bb gets its value by looking up pp in **program** (= the interpreter). Even though the source program is clearly static and bb always a part of it, the congruence principle implies that bb must be dynamic since pp is dynamic. It would be quite unfortunate if it were so. The dependency principle would now classify **command** as dynamic, with the consequence that hardly any computation at all could be done at compiler generation time.

Variable pp can be said to be of *bounded static variation*, meaning that it can only assume one of finitely values; and that its possible value set is statically computable. Here pp must be one of the labels in the interpreter, enabling us to employ a programming 'trick' with the effect that bb, and thereby command, become static. The trick is seen so often in program specialization that we devote a later section (4.8.3) to an explicit treatment. For now, the reader is asked to accept without explanation that bb and command are static variables.

4.6.2 The structure of a generated compiler

It turns out that the structure of the generated stand-alone compiler is close to that of a traditional recursive descent compiler. We have already seen an example of target code generated by specializing the interpreter, and by the mix equation the generated compiler works in exactly the same way. Our present concern is the structure and efficiency of the compiler.

Figure 4.8 shows the compiler generated from the Turing interpreter. (The compiler is syntactically sugared for readability.)

The generated compiler represents an interesting 'mix' of the partial evaluator mix and the Turing interpreter. The inner while-loop, line 10–23, closely resembles the interpretation loop. The conditionals that perform the syntactic dispatch stem directly from the interpreter. The intervening code generating instructions are, of course, not like in the interpreter but the connection is tight; the code *generated* here is exactly the instructions that the interpreter would have *performed*.

The inner while-loop containing syntactic dispatch and code generation looks quite natural, save perhaps the actions for compiling if-statements. This differs from a handwritten compiler using pure predictive parsing, which would be likely to perform one linear scan of the source program and generate code on the fly, followed by backpatching.

This compiler is, on the other hand, derived automatically from an interpreter, and it has thus inherited some of the interpreter's characteristics. An interpreter does not perform a linear scan of the source program; it follows the flow of control as determined by the semantics. The compiler does the same. As long as control can be determined from the source program alone a linear code sequence is generated.

When an if-statement is encountered this is no longer possible, since code must be generated for both of the branches. The compiler uses pending and marked to keep track of which source program fragments have to be compiled. After compiling an if-statement, compilation has to go on from two different points. One (to be executed on a false condition) is characterized by Qtail, the other (to be executed when a jump is made) is characterized by lbl, the target of the conditional jump. Therefore the two tuples (cont, Qtail) and (jump, lbl) are added to pending provided they are not already there and that they have not already been processed (that is, they are not in marked).

One point needs further explanation: the pairs (init, Q), (cont, Qtail), and (jump, lbl) are claimed to be of form (pp, vs). This does not seem reasonable at first sight since vs should contain the values of *all* of the interpreter's static

```
read(Q);
1     pending := { ('init, Q) };
2     marked := {};
3     while pending ≠ '() do
4     begin
5       Pick an element (pp, vs) ∈ pending and remove it;
6       marked := marked ∪ {(pp, vs)};
7       case pp of
8       init:Qtail := Q;                              (* vs = Q *)
9             generate initializing code;
10            while Qtail ≠ '()' do
11            begin
12              Instruction := hd(Qtail); Qtail := tl(Qtail);
13              case Instruction of
14              right:      code := extend(code,
                                          left := cons(firstsym(right),left),
                                          right := tl(right))
15              left:       code := extend(code,
                                          right:= cons(firstsym(left),right),
                                          left := tl(left))
16              write s:    code :=
                            extend(code, right := cons(s, tl(right)))
17              goto lbl:   Qtail := new_tail(lbl, Q);
18              if s goto lbl:pending := pending ∪ {('cont, Qtail)} \ marked;
19                          pending := pending ∪ {('jump, lbl)} \ marked;
20                          code := extend(code,   if s = firstsym(right)
                                                  goto ('jump, lbl)
                                                  else ('cont, Qtail));
21,22           otherwise:  error
23            end;
24      cont:if Qtail ≠ '() goto line 11              (* vs = Qtail *)
25      jump:Qtail := new_tail(lbl, Q); if Qtail ≠ '() goto line 11
                                                      (* vs = lbl *)
26      otherwise:  error;
27      residual := extend(residual, code)
28    end;
```

Figure 4.8: A mix-*generated compiler.*

variables. The point is that the only static variables whose values can be referenced after the program points init, cont, and jump are Q, Qtail, and lbl. This is detected by a simple live static variable analysis described later on.

The variables **pending** and **marked** have two roles. First, **pending** keeps track of the advance of the compilation, in a way corresponding to the recursion stack in a recursive descent compiler. Secondly, **pending** and **marked** take care of the correspondence between labels in the source and target programs, as the symbol table does in a traditional compiler.

As to efficiency, computer runs show that $\texttt{target} = [\![\text{compiler}]\!]_L \ \texttt{source}$ is computed about 9 times as fast as $\texttt{target} = [\![\text{mix}]\!]_L \ [\texttt{mix, source}]$.

4.7   Generating a compiler generator: mix³

We have seen how to use `mix` to generate a stand-alone compiler. In this section we shall demonstrate how a stand-alone compiler generator, cogen, is generated. The *third Futamura projection* is

$$\text{cogen} = [\![\text{mix}]\!]_L \ [\text{mix, mix}]$$

We claim that `cogen` is a compiler generator, that is, `cogen` applied to an interpreter yields a compiler. The claim is verified by

$$
\begin{aligned}
[\![\text{cogen}]\!]_L \, \text{int} \ &= \ [\![\, ([\![\text{mix}]\!]_L \, [\text{mix, mix}] \,) \,]\!]_L \, \text{int} \quad &\text{by definition of cogen} \\
&= \ [\![\text{mix}]\!]_L \, [\text{mix, int}] &\text{by the mix equation}
\end{aligned}
$$

since we already know that $[\![\text{mix}]\!]_L \, [\text{mix, int}]$ yields a compiler. Furthermore, `cogen` has the interesting property that it is self-generating.

$$
\begin{aligned}
[\![\text{cogen}]\!]_L \, \text{mix} \ &= \ [\![\, ([\![\text{mix}]\!]_L \, [\text{mix, mix}] \,) \,]\!]_L \, \text{mix} \quad &\text{by definition of cogen} \\
&= \ [\![\text{mix}]\!]_L \, [\text{mix, mix}] &\text{by the mix equation} \\
&= \ \text{cogen} &\text{by definition of cogen}
\end{aligned}
$$

We shall not describe `cogen` here, but its size and speed measures are given in Section 4.10 at the end of the chapter.

4.8   The tricks under the carpet

4.8.1   Successful self-application: binding-time analysis

For self-application to be successful it is essential to use a prephase called binding-time analysis. Its output is a division: a classification of each program variable as static or dynamic. The program specializer uses the division to determine the static parts of the subject program in advance, instead of analysing the subject program on-line at program specialization time. As a consequence the results of self-application are much smaller and more efficient.

The important point is that the static parts of the subject program are determined prior to the specialization phase, and that the program specializer can use this information when it is run. We have found that supplying a division of the subject program's variables was the simplest way of communicating the necessary insight to `mix`.

Experiments have shown that specialization can be made still more efficient by annotating the subject program: all assignments and conditionals are marked as either *eliminable* or *residual*. This allows the program specializer to determine its actions at a very low cost. The subject will not be pursued here, but we will return to it in Chapter 7.

4.8.2   The use of base functions

We included plenty of base functions to make `mix` more readable and keep focus on the principles of program specialization. Base functions have been used to perform computation in places where it did not matter how the job was done; examples include lookup of variables, store updates, etc. Using base functions has made programming in L less cumbersome and program execution more efficient since a base function written in the underlying implementation language, Chez Scheme, runs faster than the corresponding interpreted L-instructions.

Partial evaluation of base function calls is done by another base function, `reduce`, which uses a trivial strategy: if all arguments in a base function call are static, evaluate the call completely. If some are dynamic then leave the base function call untouched, and replace the static argument expressions, if any, by their values. This approach works well when a base function is usually called with all arguments either static or dynamic, but when both static and dynamic arguments are present, useful information is likely to be wasted. One situation where it would *not* be beneficial to use this simple strategy is the lookup of a dynamic label in a static program, as described in the next section.

4.8.3   Variables of bounded static variation

It often happens in partial evaluation that a variable seems dynamic since it depends on dynamic input, but only takes on finitely many values. In such cases a bit of reprogramming can yield much better results from partial evaluation. This kind of reprogramming, or program transformation, which does not alter the standard meaning of the program but leads to better residual programs is called a *binding-time improvement*. The term 'improvement' of binding times refers to the goal of the transformation: that more computations can be classified as static to be reduced by the partial evaluator. The following shows a classical example seen in `mix` itself, and Chapter 12 gives a survey of the most common binding-time improvement techniques.

Consider the following line from the `mix` algorithm, which finds the basic block labelled by `pp`:

```
bb := lookup (pp, program);
```

Recall that `pp` is taken from `pending` and hence is dynamic. If `lookup` were implemented by a base function then `bb` would also be dynamic. However, since `pp` can only assume one of finitely many values (the labels that appear in the program), there is an alternative. We implement the lookup by the following loop:

```
pp' := pp₀;                    (* first label (static)    *)
while pp ≠ pp' do
  pp' := next label after pp';  (* pp' remains static      *)
  bb := basic block at label pp'; (* bb is static too       *)
<computations involving bb>
```

Intuitively, `mix` compares the dynamic pp to all possible values it can assume (pp_0, pp_1 ...), and specializes code with respect to the corresponding outcome of the lookup (bb_0, bb_1 ...). The point is that the choice between the labels is done at run-time, but their range of values can be known at compile-time.

In the residual program of `mix` (e.g. the compiler) the flow chart equivalent (a lot of nested conditionals) of this appears:

```
case pp of
        pp₀: < code specialized with respect to bb₀ >
        pp₁: < code specialized with respect to bb₁ >
        ...
        ppₙ: < code specialized with respect to bbₙ >
    end case
```

In fact the trick of exploiting 'statically bounded values' is necessary to avoid trivial self-application in the `mix` described above. In partial evaluators for more complex languages it is common for this to occur in several places, although here we apply the technique only to labels.

This trick is so common that it has been named *The Trick*.

4.8.4 Transition compression on the fly revisited

The size of the generated case-statement naturally depends on how well the value of pp can be approximated, that is, the size of the set of possible values $\{pp_0, ..., pp_n\}$. A program point pp_i should only be in the set, and thus contribute to the case-statement, if pp can assume the value pp_i. We now address an important question: which values can pp (which is taken from `pending`) assume? A first answer is: any label that appears in the subject program. This answer is definitely safe but a smaller set also suffices. Since we initialize `pending` to $\{(pp_0, vs_0)\}$, the approximating set must contain pp_0, which is assumed to be the first label in the program. When `mix` encounters a residual if-statement: if exp goto pp' else pp'', the algorithm adds specialized program points containing pp', respectively pp''. This implies that all program points pp' and pp'' appearing in the branches of a conditional should also be in the set approximating pp. Due to our simple transition compression strategy which compresses all other `goto`s, no others need appear in the approximating set.

As a consequence we use a base function `find-blocks-in-pending` to compute the set of basic blocks labelled by those program points pp that can appear in pending. The result is stored in `blocks-in-pending`. When `mix` takes a program point `pp` from `pending` and looks it up, it does not scan the whole program, only `blocks-in-pending`. (Romanenko gives the first description of this idea [227]).

The reader might want to re-examine the interpreter in Figure 4.4 and the structure of the generated compiler in Figure 4.8 to see that the generated case-statement contains one branch for each program point among `init`, `cont`, `jump` that is either initial (`init`) or the target of a conditional jump with a dynamic condition (`cont`, `jump`).

The underlying reason why only three of the interpreter's 15 labels contribute to the case-statement is that transition compressing is done on the fly. If `mix` had generated all the trivial `goto`s, and compressed them afterwards, many specialized program points, namely the targets of all `goto`s (and not only the targets of residual conditionals), would be added to `pending` during program specialization. This would mean that every program point `pp'`, being the target of a `goto` in the subject program, would be in the set $\{pp_0, \ldots, pp_n\}$. This advantage of compressing on the fly is certainly not evident at first sight: smaller residual programs are produced when `mix` is self-applied.

4.9 The granularity of binding-time analysis

Until now we have assumed that task of binding-time analysis is to compute *one* division, valid at all program points. For most small programs it has turned out to be a very reasonable assumption that one division could be used to classify the status of a variable throughout the whole program. There are, however, a series of objections to this simplified view of BTA.

4.9.1 Pointwise divisions

Consider the following program fragment where the initial division is (S, D):

```
read (X Y);
init: X := X + 1;
      Y := Y - 1;
      goto cont;
cont: Y := 3;
next: ...
```

Obviously a congruent, uniform division would have to be (S, D), but (judging from the shown fragment alone) a more detailed division init:(S, D), cont:(S, D), next:(S, S) would be safe. We shall call such a division *pointwise*.

As opposed to the simplest possible binding-time analysis computing uniform divisions (Section 4.4.6), an analysis to compute pointwise divisions will have to consider the control flow of the program. Constructing the algorithm is not hard and is left as an exercise.

The `mix` algorithm (Figure 4.7) needs a slight extension to handle pointwise divisions. The `division` argument should be replaced by a `division-table` and each time a specialized program point (`pp, vs`) has been fetched from `pending` the relevant division should be computed by `division = lookup(pp,division-table)`. We have claimed that it is crucial for getting good results from self-application that the division is kept static. Since `pp` is static (Section 4.8.3), the use of pointwise divisions does not destroy this property.

4.9.2   Live and dead static variables

The use of an imperative language introduces a serious problem: specialization with respect to dead static data. This problem is not directly caused by self-application, but it appears at every program specialization of 'non–toy programs', that is, programs beyond a certain size. Consider a specialized program point (`pp, vs`) where, as usual, `vs` contains the values of those of the program values that are static. Some of these static values might be completely irrelevant for the computations to be performed at the program point `pp`. For a simple example, consider the program fragment:

```
start: if ⟨dynamic condition⟩
          then a := 1; ⟨commands using a⟩; goto next
          else a := 2; ⟨commands using a⟩; goto next
next:  ⟨commands not referring to a⟩;
```

As far as this program fragment is concerned the variable a is static, hence its value is in `vs`, even though that value is completely irrelevant to further computations. The unfortunate effect is that the specialized program point (`start, ...`) has two successors: (`next, ..1..`) and (`next, ..2..`), even though the code pieces generated for these two successors are clearly identical.

Fortunately, this problem can be avoided by doing a *live variable analysis* [4] to recognize which static variables can affect future computation or control flow, and by specializing program points only with respect to such variables. This analysis is performed by the base function `find-projections` which given the program text and the division computes the set of live static variables for each program point that can appear in pending. When `find-projections` is applied to the interpreter text and the corresponding division, the result is

```
(jump  Nextlabel Q)
(cont  Qtail Q)
```

showing that when the interpreter's control is at point `jump`, the only static variables that will be referenced (before they are redefined) are `Nextlabel` and `Q`.

In the programs used as examples in this chapter we did not need to compute pointwise divisions as discussed in Section 4.9.1, but it was essential to the successful specialization of the larger programs (such as `mix` itself) to reclassify dead static variables as dynamic. We started out by computing a uniform division and the subsequent reclassification of the dead variables transformed the uniform division into a pointwise one.

4.9.3   Polyvariant divisions

Even pointwise divisions can be accused of being overly restrictive, namely in the case where the S/D-status of a variable depends not only on the program point but also on *how* the program point was reached. An example (assume initial division (S, D)):

```
read (X Y);
init: if Y > 42 goto xsd else dyn
dyn:  X := Y;
      goto xsd;
xsd:  X := X + 17;
      ...
```

A congruent, pointwise division would have to rule `xsd`:(D, D). A *polyvariant division* assigns to each label a *set* of divisions. For the above program, a congruent, polyvariant division would be: `init`:$\{(S, D)\}$, `dyn`:$\{(D, D)\}$, `xsd`:$\{(S, D),(D, D)\}$. A division which is not polyvariant is called *monovariant*.

Computing a polyvariant division is not hard, but how should `mix` exploit the more detailed information? When generating code for (`pp`, `vs`), there is a set of possible divisions for `pp` to choose from. Unless (`pp`, `vs`) is the initial specialized program point, there exists a (`pp`$_1$, `vs`$_1$) such that (`pp`, `vs`) $\in$ `successors`((`pp`$_1$, `vs`$_1$)) and the proper division for `vs` depends on the division used for `vs1`. A way of keeping track of the divisions would be to extend the definition of a specialized program point to include a division component. Then, by employing the trick from Section 4.8.3, the division would be static by self-application (ensuring good results).

A tempting alternative is to transform the source program prior to partial evaluation by duplicating the blocks that have more than one possible division. The above example is transformed into:

```
read (X Y);
init:  if Y > 42 goto xsd-s else dyn
dyn:   X := Y;
       goto xsd-d;
xsd-s: X := X + 17;
       ...
xsd-d: X := X + 17;
       ...
```

The duplication would otherwise have been done during specialization by `mix` itself, so the pre-transformation introduces no 'extra' code duplication. The transformation can be regarded as specialization of the source program with respect to binding-time information, and its chief advantage is that the mix algorithm is kept simple (that is, no modification is needed).

In the programs in this chapter (including mix itself) we have not needed polyvariant divisions. The absence of functions, procedures, and subroutines does not encourage the modular programming style where one piece of code can be used in many different contexts, and that eliminates much of the need for polyvariance. The later chapters will contain examples where the need for a polyvariant division arises naturally.

4.10 Overview of mix performance

Following are some program sizes and running times for a preliminary version of mix. Int is the Turing interpreter from Figure 4.4, source is the Turing program from Figure 4.3, and target is the result of compiling source from the Turing language to our language L (Figure 4.5). The run times are measured in Sun 3/50 cpu seconds using Chez Scheme, and include garbage collection.

Program	Size (#lines)	Ratio	Size (bytes)	Ratio
source	4		57	
target	7	1.75	265	4.6
int	31		1.1 K	
compiler	60	1.94	4.5 K	4.1
mix	65		2.8 K	
compiler generator	126	1.94	15.0 K	5.4

Run		Time	Ratio
output	$= [\![\text{int}]\!]_L$ [source, data]	0.085	
	$= [\![\text{target}]\!]_L$ data	0.010	8.5
target	$= [\![\text{mix}]\!]_L$ [int, source]	2.63	
	$= [\![\text{compiler}]\!]_L$ source	0.27	9.7
compiler	$= [\![\text{mix}]\!]_L$ [mix, int]	28.90	
	$= [\![\text{cogen}]\!]_L$ int	3.37	8.6
cogen	$= [\![\text{mix}]\!]_L$ [mix, mix]	59.30	
	$= [\![\text{cogen}]\!]_L$ mix	7.13	8.3

4.11   Summary and a more abstract perspective

This chapter discussed self-applicable partial evaluation of a flow chart language. In spite of the simplicity of this language, we shall see that almost all the concepts introduced here are also central to partial evaluation of more complex languages: functional languages, logic programming languages, imperative languages with recursive procedures, etc. Furthermore, essentially the same methods suffice for partial evaluation of such seemingly rather different languages.

The essence of program specialization
The previous sections were intentionally concrete and detailed. We now reduce the ideas involved to their essential core, as a preliminary to partial evaluation of more complex languages.

Almost all programming languages involve some form of *state*, which may be a pair *(pp, store)* as in the flow chart language; or *(fname, environment)* in a functional language, where *fname* is the name of the function currently being evaluated and *environment* binds actual parameters to their values; or *(pname, argumentlist)* in Prolog where *pname* is the name of the current procedure (predicate) and *argumentlist* is a list of terms, perhaps containing uninstantiated (free) variables.

Equally central is the concept of a *state transition*, effected by a goto, a function call, or a predicate call. Each changes the state and control point, described symbolically by

$$(pp, v) \Rightarrow (pp', v'),$$

where p, p' are control points and v, v' are data such as stores or argument lists.

Suppose there is a way to decompose or factor a data value v into static and dynamic parts without loss of information. Such a *data division* can be thought of as a triple of functions $(stat, dyn, pair)$, each mapping the set V of data values to itself. The ability to deompose and recompose without information loss can be expressed by three equations:

$$
\begin{aligned}
pair(stat(v), dyn(v)) &= v \\
stat(pair(v_s, v_d)) &= v_s \\
dyn(pair(v_s, v_d)) &= v_d
\end{aligned}
$$

Remarks. In this chapter a division was specified by an $S - D$ vector, for instance $SDSD$ specified the division of $V = D^4$ where $pair((a, c), (b, d)) = (a, b, c, d)$, $stat((a, b, c, d)) = (a, c)$, and $dyn((a, b, c, d)) = (b, d)$. More generally, offline specializers as used in this chapter will use a single, predefined division, whereas an online specializer will decide static and dynamic projections more dynamically.

Using the division, the transition can be decomposed into:

$$(pp, v) \Rightarrow (pp', v') = (pp, pair(v_s, v_d)) \Rightarrow (pp', pair(v'_s, v'_d))$$

This transition can be specialized by reassociating to get

$$((pp, v_s), v_d) \Rightarrow ((pp', v_s'), v_d')$$

This is also a transition, but one with *specialized control points* (pp, v_s) and (pp', v_s'), each incorporating some static data. The runtime data are v_d, v_d', the result of the dynamic projections.

Fundamental concepts revisited
Residual code generation amounts to finding commands or a function or procedure call which syntactically specifies the transition from v_d to v_d'. If $v_d = v_d'$ then *transition compression* may be possible since no residual code beyond at most a control transfer need be generated. (For flow charts, this happens if the basic block begun by pp contains no dynamic expressions or commands.) Finally, we have seen the congruence condition to be needed for code generation. In the current context this becomes: v_s' must be functionally determined by v_s in every transition.

4.12 Exercises

Exercise 4.1 Write a program and choose a division such that partial evaluation without transition compression terminates, and partial evaluation with transition compression on the fly (as described in this chapter) loops. □

Exercise 4.2 The purpose of this exercise is to investigate how much certain extensions to the flow chart language would complicate partial evaluation. For each construction, analyse possible problems and show the specialization time computations and the code generation

1. for loop,
2. while loop,
3. case/switch conditional,
4. computed goto, cgoto ⟨Expr⟩, where Expr evaluates to a natural number = a label,
5. gosub ... return.

Do any of the above constructions complicate the binding-time analysis? □

Exercise 4.3 At the end of Section 4.2.2 it is mentioned that mix could generate residual programs in a low-level language, e.g. machine code.

1. Write the mix equation for a mix that generates machine code.
2. Do the Futamura projections still hold?
3. What are the consequences for compiler generation?

□

Exercise 4.4 Consider the mix-generated program in Figure 4.5. The program is suboptimal in two ways; discuss how to revise the partial evaluation strategy to obtain an optimal residual program in this particular example.

1. The same conditional statement appears twice.

2. The assignments to the variable Left do not contribute to the final answer.

Would the proposed revisions have any adverse effects?   □

Exercise 4.5 Specialize the Turing interpreter with respect to to following program:

```
0: if B goto 3
1: right
2: goto 0
3: write 1
4: if B goto 7
5: left
6: goto 4
7: write 1
```

□

Exercise 4.6 The mix equation and the Futamura projections as presented in this chapter gloss over the fact that partial evaluation (here) consists of a binding-time analysis phase and a specialization phase. Refine the mix-equation and the Futamura projections to reflect this two-phase approach.   □

Exercise 4.7 Will specialization of the Turing interpreter (Figure 4.4) with respect a program p terminate for all Turing programs p?   □

Exercise 4.8 Use the algorithm in Section 4.4.6 to determine a congruent division for the Turing interpreter when the division for the input variables (Q, Right) is

1. (S, D),

2. (D, S).

□

Exercise 4.9 Write a binding time analysis algorithm that computes a pointwise division.   □

Exercise 4.10 Write a binding time analysis algorithm that computes a polyvariant division.   □

Exercise 4.11 The binding time analysis algorithm from Section 4.4.6 is not likely to be very efficient in practice. Construct an efficient algorithm to do the same job.   □

Chapter 5

Partial Evaluation for a First-Order Functional Language

This chapter presents self-applicable partial evaluation for a first-order functional language. Many of the ideas and principles that worked for the simple flow chart language in Chapter 4 adapt smoothly to this stronger programming language.

In fact the language used below is very similar to that used in the very first self-applicable partial evaluator (constructed by Jones, Sestoft, and Søndergaard [135,136]).

In a flow chart, a program point is a label; in a first-order functional language, a program point is a function definition. Labelled statements were specialized with respect to static global variables, and function definitions will be specialized with respect to static function parameters. The strong similarity between the techniques for the two languages means that the core algorithm for polyvariant program point specialization carries over to this new language with little modification.

5.1 From flow charts to functions

This section examines the basic concepts of partial evaluation as presented in Chapter 4, and shows their counterparts in a first-order functional language.

As an example language we will use a first-order subset of Scheme, here called 'Scheme0'. Indeed, most work in partial evaluation of functional languages has been done in a Lisp or Scheme framework, because it is trivial to parse such programs, that is, to convert them from concrete to abstract syntax. Concrete syntax (a string of characters) is convenient for writing example programs, but abstract syntax (a tree data structure) is required for symbolic manipulation; the simple Lisp or Scheme notation offers a good compromise. Another reason for using a Scheme subset here is to pave the way for Chapter 10, which describes a publicly available partial evaluator for a higher-order subset of Scheme.

Figure 5.1 gives the syntax of Scheme0. Note that a Scheme0 program is very similar to a system of recursion equations as presented in Section 3.3.2. A Scheme0 program takes its input through the (formal) parameters of the first function. It has call-by-value semantics and is statically scoped. Partial function applications are not allowed, and the language contains no nameless functions (that is, lambda abstractions). There is no assignment operation, and base function applications (Op ...) have no side-effects, so Scheme0 programs are purely applicative. The expression ⟨Expr⟩ in a function definition ⟨Equation⟩ is called the function *body*. The first function in a program is called its *goal function*.

⟨Program⟩	::=	(⟨Equation⟩ ... ⟨Equation⟩)	Function definitions
⟨Equation⟩	::=	(define ((⟨FuncName⟩ ⟨Varlist⟩)) ⟨Expr⟩)	
⟨Varlist⟩	::=	⟨Var⟩ ... ⟨Var⟩	Formal parameters
⟨Expr⟩	::=	⟨Constant⟩	Constant
	|	⟨Var⟩	Variable
	|	(if ⟨Expr⟩ ⟨Expr⟩ ⟨Expr⟩)	Conditional
	|	(call ⟨FuncName⟩ ⟨Arglist⟩)	Function application
	|	(⟨Op⟩ ⟨Expr⟩ ... ⟨Expr⟩)	Base application
⟨Arglist⟩	::=	⟨Expr⟩ ... ⟨Expr⟩	Argument expressions
⟨Constant⟩	::=	⟨Numeral⟩	
	|	(quote ⟨Value⟩)	
⟨Op⟩	::=	car | cdr | cons | = | + | ...	

Figure 5.1: Syntax of Scheme0, a first-order functional language.

Programs and program points. A flow chart program (Chapter 4) is a collection of labelled basic blocks; a Scheme0 program is a collection of named function definitions. In the flow chart program, a program point is the label of a basic block; in a Scheme0 program, a program point is the name of the defined function. During ordinary program execution, control passes from program point to program point; by jumps in a flow chart program and by function calls in Scheme0.

Global variables versus function parameters. In the flow chart language, values are bound to global, mutable variables. The bindings are created or changed by assignments, and the language has a notion of current state. In Scheme0, values are bound to function parameters. The bindings are created by function application and cannot be modified; they are immutable and the language has no notion of current state.

Divisions. In the flow chart language, each global variable is classified as static or dynamic; such a classification is called a division. Similarly, in Scheme0 a *division* is a classification of each function parameter as static or dynamic. During specialization, a *static* parameter can never be bound to a residual expression, only to ordinary values; a *dynamic* parameter may be bound to residual expressions as well as ordinary values.

A *monovariant division* for a Scheme0 program maps each function to a single classification of its variables. This corresponds roughly to a pointwise division in the flow chart language, namely, one giving a classification for each individual program point. A *polyvariant division* maps each function to a finite set of classifications of its variables.

In a functional language the added flexibility of polyvariant divisions is often useful. One may write a general library function and call it from several places with different combinations of static and dynamic arguments, without one argument combination affecting the others.

Existing partial evaluators handle polyvariant binding times by creating several (monovariant) copies of function definitions. This copying is done prior to specialization, as described in Section 4.9.3. Therefore we shall assume from now on that divisions are monovariant.

Congruence. A division is *congruent* if the value of every static parameter is determined by the values of other static parameters (and thus ultimately by the available input). Equivalently, a parameter whose value depends on a dynamic parameter must itself be dynamic. This means that a static parameter cannot be bound to a residual expression during specialization.

In the flow chart language, congruence is formulated as a requirement on assignment statements: it is these that create and modify variable bindings. In Scheme0, congruence is formulated as a similar requirement on function applications (`call f ... e`$_j$` ...`). If the j'th argument expression e$_j$ depends on a dynamic variable, then the corresponding parameter x$_j$ in (`define (f ... x`$_j$` ...) ...`) must also be dynamic.

Specialized program points. In the flow chart language, the specialization of a program point `pp` is a specialized basic block, labelled with a specialized label (`pp,vs`). This specialized label is a pair of an original label `pp` (from the subject program) and values `vs` of the static variables in the global state. A specialized flow chart program is a collection of such specialized basic blocks.

Similarly, in Scheme0 a *specialized program point* is a specialized function definition whose name is a specialized function name. A specialized function name is a pair (`f,vs`) of an original function name `f` and values `vs` of the static parameters of `f`. A specialized Scheme0 program is a collection of such specialized function definitions.

However, choosing specialization points other than function definitions may give more 'natural' residual programs. For example, introducing a specialization point at each conditional (`if e`$_1$` e`$_2$` e`$_3$`) in which the condition e$_1$ is dynamic, may give a more reasonable and compact branching structure in the residual program. Such new specialization points can be introduced by defining a new function for each dynamic conditional before specialization takes place. The new function's body will consist of the conditional expression (`if e`$_1$` e`$_2$` e`$_3$`), and the conditional expression must be replaced by a call to the new function. This idea is used in the partial evaluator Similix (Chapter 10).

Transition compression.   In the flow chart language, transition compression is used to improve residual programs by removing superfluous jumps, such as a jump to a trivial basic block consisting only of a jump, etc. Transition compression may be done during specialization, or after. These alternatives are also called *on the fly compression* and *postphase compression*. It was argued that on the fly compression is preferable.

The Scheme0 notion corresponding to transition compression is *unfolding* of a function application. Unfolding replaces a function call (call f ... e_j ...) by a copy of f's body, where every argument expression e_j is substituted for the corresponding formal parameter x_j.

A trivial basic block corresponds to a function which does nothing but call another function; calls to such functions can be eliminated by unfolding. Unfolding is more complicated than (flow chart) transition compression, as it involves substitution of argument expressions for formal parameters in addition to plain inlining of code. This substitution introduces the risk of computation duplication, which is even worse than code duplication: it wastes run time in addition to space.

Like transition compression, unfolding may be done *on the fly* or in a *postphase*. As for the flow chart language, unfolding on the fly greatly improves the residual programs generated by specialization, and in particular compilers generated by self-application. A strategy for unfolding on the fly must (1) avoid infinite unfolding, (2) avoid duplication of code and computation, and (3) produce as few residual calls as possible. Several strategies have been suggested that attempt to satisfy these requirements.

The most conservative strategy would do no unfolding on the fly. Then during specialization, a function application would always reduce to a residual function application, never to a value. But then the result of the function application would be dynamic, even when all its arguments were static, which means that the static data would be exploited badly, and very little specialization is achieved.

The second-most conservative strategy is to unfold on the fly precisely those applications which have *only* static parameters. This introduces a risk of infinite unfolding, but only if there is already a potential infinite loop in the subject program, controlled only by static conditionals (or none at all).

We choose for now to unfold precisely those calls without dynamic parameters, but in Section 5.5.6 we consider an even more liberal strategy for on the fly unfolding. In both cases we must accept the risk of infinite unfolding.

Binding-time analysis.   In the flow chart language, a congruent division was found by a simple program flow analysis. There are two ways to find a congruent division for a given Scheme0 program. One method is abstract interpretation, described in more detail in Chapter 15. This is the functional counterpart of classical program flow analysis as done by compilers: the program is evaluated over the abstract value domain $\{S, D\}$, where S abstracts all ordinary values (static results) and D

abstracts all residual expressions and values (dynamic results). This is the method we shall use here. It was used also in the very first self-applicable partial evaluator [135] and is used in the partial evaluator Similix (see Chapter 10).

The other method employs a type inference system to build a set of constraints on the binding times of all variables. A *constraint* is an inequality on the binding times of variables. For instance, if x depends on y, we want to express the congruence requirement 'if y is dynamic, then x must be dynamic too'. With the ordering $S < D$ on the binding-time values, and writing bt(x) for the binding time of x, the requirement is the constraint $bt(y) \leq bt(x)$. The constraint set can be solved subsequently, giving the binding times for each variable. Variants of this method are used in partial evaluators for the lambda calculus (Chapter 8), and for a subset of C (Chapter 11).

Annotations for expressing divisions.   A program division div can be given to the specializer in two ways: separately as a mapping from function names to variable classifications, or integrated into the subject program as *annotation*.

Divisions and annotations provide the same information in slightly different ways. A division describes the binding time of a variable or expression, whereas an annotation tells how to handle program phrases at specialization time. Annotations can be conveniently represented in a *two-level syntax*, which has a static and a dynamic version of each construct of the language (conditional, function application, and base function application). In general, reduction of the static version (at specialization time) will produce a value, whereas reduction of the dynamic version will not change its form, only reduce its subexpressions.

Annotations are not necessary in principle — the relevant information can always be computed from the division — but they greatly simplify the symbolic reduction of expressions in the specialization algorithm. Thus we shall use annotations to represent divisions in the Scheme0 specializer.

We require divisions to be congruent. Similarly, annotations should be *consistent*. For instance, a static base function must be applied only to static argument expressions; and an argument expression in the static argument list of a function call must be static. Consistency rules for annotations are shown in the form of type inference rules in Section 5.7 below. The type rules for annotations are related to the type inference approach to binding-time analysis mentioned above.

Specialization algorithm.   The specialization algorithm for Scheme0 is very similar to that for flow charts. It has a set **pending** of functions yet to be specialized, and a set **marked** of those already specialized. As long as **pending** is non-empty, it repeatedly selects and removes a member (f . vs) from **pending**, and constructs a version of function f, specialized to the values vs of its static parameters. The specialization of f's body with respect to vs may require new functions to be added to **pending**, namely those called from the specialized body. As in the flow chart specializer, the residual program is complete when **pending** is empty.

A Scheme0 function body is specialized by reducing it symbolically, using the values of static variables. Since Scheme0 has no statements and all program fragments are expressions, a single function reduce suffices for this purpose. Compare this with the flow chart specializer, which has different mechanisms for reduction of statements and reduction of expressions.

The Scheme0 reduction function works on the annotated syntax for Scheme0, using the annotations to decide whether to evaluate or reduce expressions.

Example 5.1 Figure 5.2 below first shows the append function for list concatenation, written as a Scheme0 program. Second, it gives an annotated version (in the two-level Scheme0 syntax) corresponding to input xs being static and input ys being dynamic. Third, the specialization of the annotated program with respect to the list xs = '(a b) is shown. Finally, this specialized program is improved by transition compression: unfolding of the calls to the rather trivial functions app-b and app-().

The result is the specialized function app-ab, with the property that (app-ab ys) equals (app '(a b) ys) for all lists ys. □

5.2 Binding-time analysis by abstract interpretation

Binding-time analysis of a Scheme0 subject program computes a division: a classification of each function parameter x_{ij} as static (S) or dynamic (D). This classification can be found by an *abstract interpretation* of the program over the abstract value domain $\{S, D\}$. Here we show the details of this for *monovariant binding-time analysis*; polyvariant analysis is quite similar.

The binding-time analysis is *safe* if the division it computes is congruent: a parameter may be classified as static (S) only if it cannot be bound to a residual expression. Consequently it is always safe to classify a parameter dynamic: D is a safe approximation of S. Therefore the binding-time analysis may well be *approximate*, classifying a parameter dynamic even when it cannot be bound to a residual expression.

Assume henceforth we are given a Scheme0 subject program pgm of form

```
(define (f₁ x₁₁ ... x₁ₐ₁) e₁)
    ⋮
(define (fₙ xₙ₁ ... xₙₐₙ) eₙ)
```

and a binding-time classification τ_1 for the program's input parameters (that is, the parameters of its first function f_1).

The analysis computes a congruent monovariant division for pgm. A division div maps a function name f to a binding-time environment τ, which is a tuple of binding-time values. The binding-time environment $\tau = (t_1, \ldots, t_a)$ maps a variable x_j to its binding time t_j.

A program implementing the append function:

```
(define (app xs ys)
    (if (null? xs)
        ys
        (cons (car xs) (call app (cdr xs) ys))))
```

Assuming `xs` is static, the annotated append function is as shown below. The `lift` operation embeds the static expression `(cars xs)` in a dynamic context:

```
(define (app (xs) (ys))
    (ifs (null?s xs)
        ys
        (consd (lift (cars xs))
               (calld app ((cdrs xs)) (ys)))))
```

The append function specialized with respect to `xs = '(a b)`:

```
(define (app-ab ys) (cons 'a (app-b ys)))
```

```
(define (app-b ys) (cons 'b (app-() ys)))
```

```
(define (app-() ys) ys)
```

The above residual program can be improved by unfolding the calls to `app-b` and `app-()`, giving:

```
(define (app-ab ys) (cons 'a (cons 'b ys)))
```

Figure 5.2: Example specialization of the append function in Scheme0.

$$
\begin{array}{llll}
t & \in & \text{BindingTime} & = & \{S, D\} \\
\tau & \in & \text{BTEnv} & = & \text{BindingTime}^* \\
\text{div} & \in & \text{Monodivision} & = & \text{FuncName} \rightarrow \text{BTEnv}
\end{array}
$$

We impose the ordering $S < D$ on the set BindingTime:

$$t \leq t' \quad \text{iff} \quad t = S \text{ or } t = t'$$

That is, '$\leq$' means 'is less dynamic than'. This ordering extends pointwise to binding-time environments in BTEnv and divisions in Monodivision, as follows. Division div_1 is smaller than division div_2 if div_1 classifies no more variables as dynamic. More precisely, for binding-time environments $\tau = (t_1, \ldots, t_a)$ and $\tau' = (t_1', \ldots, t_a')$:

$$(t_1, \ldots, t_a) \leq (t_1', \ldots, t_a') \quad \text{iff} \quad t_j \leq t_j' \text{ for } j \in \{1, \ldots, a\}$$

and for divisions

$$\texttt{div}_1 \leq \texttt{div}_2 \quad \text{iff} \quad \texttt{div}_1(\texttt{f}_k) \leq \texttt{div}_2(\texttt{f}_k) \text{ for all functions } \texttt{f}_k$$

The division $\texttt{div}$ computed by the analysis should respect the given classification τ_1 of the input parameters. Thus if input parameter $\texttt{x}$ is D according to τ_1, then it must be dynamic according to $\texttt{div}(\texttt{f}_1)$ too. This requirement on $\texttt{div}$ can now be expressed by the inequality $\texttt{div}(\texttt{f}_1) \geq \tau_1$.

In the analysis we need to find the best (least dynamic) common description of two or more elements of BTEnv or Monodivision. The *least upper bound*, often abbreviated *lub*, of τ and τ' is written $\tau \sqcup \tau'$ and is the smallest τ'' which is greater than or equal to both τ and τ'. It is easy to see that the least upper bound $\tau \sqcup \tau'$ is the smallest (least dynamic) binding-time environment which is at least as dynamic as both τ and τ'. For instance, $(S, S, D, D) \sqcup (S, D, S, D) = (S, D, D, D)$. Compare $\sqcup$ with set union: the union $A \cup B$ of two sets A and B is the least set which is greater than or equal to both A and B.

5.2.1   Analysis functions

The core of the binding-time analysis is the analysis functions $\mathcal{B}_e$ and $\mathcal{B}_v$ defined below. The first analysis function $\mathcal{B}_e$ is applied to an expression $\texttt{e}$ and a binding-time environment τ, and the result $\mathcal{B}_e[\![\texttt{e}]\!]\tau \in \{S, D\}$ is the binding time of $\texttt{e}$ in binding-time environment τ. The $\mathcal{B}_e$ function is defined in Figure 5.3.

$\mathcal{B}_e[\![\texttt{e}]\!]$: BTEnv $\rightarrow$ BindingTime		
$\mathcal{B}_e[\![\texttt{c}]\!]\tau$	$=$	S
$\mathcal{B}_e[\![\texttt{x}_j]\!]\tau$	$=$	t_j where $\tau = (t_1, \dots, t_a)$
$\mathcal{B}_e[\![(\texttt{if } \texttt{e}_1 \texttt{ e}_2 \texttt{ e}_3)]\!]\tau$	$=$	$\mathcal{B}_e[\![\texttt{e}_1]\!]\tau \sqcup \mathcal{B}_e[\![\texttt{e}_2]\!]\tau \sqcup \mathcal{B}_e[\![\texttt{e}_3]\!]\tau$
$\mathcal{B}_e[\![(\texttt{call f } \texttt{e}_1 \ \dots \ \texttt{e}_a)]\!]\tau$	$=$	$\bigsqcup_{j=1}^{a} \mathcal{B}_e[\![\texttt{e}_j]\!]\tau$
$\mathcal{B}_e[\![(\texttt{op } \texttt{e}_1 \ \dots \ \texttt{e}_a)]\!]\tau$	$=$	$\bigsqcup_{j=1}^{a} \mathcal{B}_e[\![\texttt{e}_j]\!]\tau$

Figure 5.3: The Scheme0 binding-time analysis function $\mathcal{B}_e$.

The definition of $\mathcal{B}_e$ can be explained as follows. The binding time of a constant $\texttt{c}$ is always static (S). The binding time of variable $\texttt{x}_j$ is determined by the binding-time environment. The result of a conditional $(\texttt{if } \texttt{e}_1 \texttt{ e}_2 \texttt{ e}_3)$ is static if all subexpressions are static, otherwise dynamic — recall that the least upper bound $D \sqcup S$ is D. Note that the result is dynamic if the condition is dynamic, even if both branches are static. Function application and base function application are similar to conditional.

The second analysis function $\mathcal{B}_v$ is applied to an expression $\texttt{e}$, binding-time environment τ, and the name $\texttt{g}$ of a function in the subject program $\texttt{pgm}$. The result $\mathcal{B}_v[\![\texttt{e}]\!]\tau\texttt{g} \in$ BTEnv is the least upper bound of the argument binding times in all calls to g in expression e. Thus $\mathcal{B}_v[\![e]\!]\tau g$ gives the binding-time context of g in e. The $\mathcal{B}_v$ function is defined in Figure 5.4.

$$\mathcal{B}_v[\![e]\!] : \text{BTEnv} \rightarrow \text{FuncName} \rightarrow \text{BTEnv}$$

$$\mathcal{B}_v[\![c]\!]\tau g \qquad\qquad = \quad (S,\ldots,S)$$

$$\mathcal{B}_v[\![x_j]\!]\tau g \qquad\qquad = \quad (S,\ldots,S)$$

$$\mathcal{B}_v[\![(\text{if } e_1\ e_2\ e_3)]\!]\tau g \quad = \quad \mathcal{B}_v[\![e_1]\!]\tau g \sqcup \mathcal{B}_v[\![e_2]\!]\tau g \sqcup \mathcal{B}_v[\![e_3]\!]\tau g$$

$$\mathcal{B}_v[\![(\text{call } f\ e_1\ \ldots\ e_a)]\!]\tau g \; = \quad t \sqcup (\mathcal{B}_e[\![e_1]\!]\tau,\ldots,\mathcal{B}_e[\![e_a]\!]\tau) \quad \text{if } f = g$$
$$= \quad t \qquad\qquad\qquad\qquad\qquad \text{if } f \neq g$$
$$\text{where } t = \textstyle\bigsqcup_{j=1}^{a} \mathcal{B}_v[\![e_j]\!]\tau g$$

$$\mathcal{B}_v[\![(\text{op } e_1\ \ldots\ e_a)]\!]\tau g \quad = \quad \textstyle\bigsqcup_{j=1}^{a} \mathcal{B}_v[\![e_j]\!]\tau g$$

Figure 5.4: The Scheme0 binding-time propagation function $\mathcal{B}_v$.

This definition is explained as follows. A constant c contains no call to function g, so the least upper bound of the argument binding times is $(S,\ldots,S)$, namely the identity for $\sqcup$. (Compare with the sum of a set of numbers. If the set is empty, the sum is 0, which is the identity for $+$.) A variable x_j also contains no calls to g. A conditional (if e_1 e_2 e_3) contains those calls to g which are contained in e_1, e_2, or e_3. A function call (call f e_1 ... e_a) possibly contains calls to g in the subexpressions e_j. Moreover, if f is g, then the call itself is to g, and we must use the first analysis function $\mathcal{B}_e$ to find the binding times of the arguments expressions e_1 ... e_a. Finally, a base function application contains only those calls to g which are in the subexpressions e_j.

5.2.2   The congruence requirement

We can now express the congruence requirement by equations involving $\mathcal{B}_v$ (which in turn uses $\mathcal{B}_e$). The congruence requirement for a monovariant division says: if there is some call of function g where the j'th argument expression is dynamic, then the j'th parameter of g must be described as dynamic. In other words, the binding time of the j'th parameter of g must be equal to or greater than that of the j'th argument expression of every application of g.

Function $\mathcal{B}_v$ was defined such that $\mathcal{B}_v[\![e]\!]\tau g$ is equal to or greater than (at least as dynamic as) the binding times of all argument patterns of function g in e. Taking the least upper bound of these values over all expressions in the program gives congruent binding times for g's arguments. Thus g's binding-time environment (div g) should satisfy:

$$(\text{div } g) \quad = \quad \textstyle\bigsqcup_{i=1}^{n} \mathcal{B}_v[\![e_i]\!](\text{div } f_i)\ g$$

where f_1 ... f_n are all functions in program pgm, and e_1 ... e_n are the corresponding function bodies. Extending this idea from g to all functions $\mathbf{f}_k$, we have that division div is congruent if it solves the equation system:

$$(\text{div } \mathbf{f}_k) \;=\; \bigsqcup_{i=1}^{n} \mathcal{B}_v[\![\mathbf{e}_i]\!](\text{div } \mathbf{f}_i) \; \mathbf{f}_k \text{ for } k = 1, \ldots, n$$

Note that div appears on both sides of the equations. Because of the way $\mathcal{B}_e$ and $\mathcal{B}_v$ were defined, the equation system always has one or more solutions. Below we show how to compute the best (least dynamic) one.

5.2.3   Finding the best division

In general we want as much specialization as possible, that is, as many static expressions as possible. In other words, we are interested in as small a division as possible, so the goal of our analysis is to find the smallest (or least dynamic) congruent division. This division is the smallest solution to the equations shown above which also satisfies $(\text{div } \mathbf{f}_1) \geq \tau_1$, that is, which respects the input classification τ_1.

This smallest solution can be computed by starting with the very least division

$$\text{div}_0 = [\mathbf{f}_1 \mapsto \tau_1, \mathbf{f}_2 \mapsto (S, \ldots, S), \; \ldots, \; \mathbf{f}_n \mapsto (S, \ldots, S)]$$

which classifies every parameter as static, except that the binding-time environment of the goal function $\mathbf{f}_1$ is τ_1. To possibly find a new value for $(\text{div } \mathbf{f}_k)$, we repeatedly compute $\bigsqcup_{i=1}^{n} \mathcal{B}_v[\![\mathbf{e}_i]\!](\text{div } \mathbf{f}_i) \; \mathbf{f}_k$, for all $k \in \{1, \ldots, n\}$. If the new value is greater than the old one, we update div and recompute again. If the new value is not greater for any k, we stop, and we have found the smallest solution div to the congruence equations. (Because the analysis function $\mathcal{B}_v$ is monotonic, the new value will always be equal to or greater than the old one.)

The recomputation terminates, since a change in div must change the binding time of some value from S to D, which can happen only finitely many times.

5.3   Adding annotations

Annotation of subject programs is a convenient way to represent the divisions found by binding-time analysis. For this purpose we introduce a *two-level syntax* for Scheme0. Two-level languages are studied in depth by Nielson in [201].

5.3.1   Two-level syntax for Scheme0

In the two-level syntax, conditional expressions, function calls, and base function applications appear in a static as well as a dynamic version, such as ifs and ifd, cars and card, etc. During partial evaluation, a static expression e evaluates to some *value* v, whereas a dynamic expression evaluates to a *residual expression* e'.

Moreover, the parameter list of a function definition or function application is split into two: a list of the static parameters and a list of the dynamic parameters. Constants are always static, so it is not necessary to annotate them.

A new construct (lift e) marks a static expression e that occurs in a *dynamic context*. During partial evaluation, a static expression e evaluates to some value v, but if it is in a dynamic context, it should really result in a residual *expression*. This is achieved by turning v into the constant expression (quote v). The lift mark tells the specializer to do this [187,227]. The two-level syntax is shown in Figure 5.5. The nonterminals ⟨Arglist⟩, ⟨Constant⟩, and ⟨Op⟩ were defined in Figure 5.1.

⟨Expr⟩	::=	⟨Constant⟩	Constant
	|	⟨Var⟩	Variable
	|	(ifs ⟨Expr⟩ ⟨Expr⟩ ⟨Expr⟩)	Static conditional
	|	(ifd ⟨Expr⟩ ⟨Expr⟩ ⟨Expr⟩)	Dynamic conditional
	|	(calls ⟨FuncName⟩ ⟨SDArgs⟩)	Static function appl.
	|	(calld ⟨FuncName⟩ ⟨SDArgs⟩)	Dynamic function appl.
	|	(⟨Op⟩s ⟨Expr⟩ ... ⟨Expr⟩)	Static base appl.
	|	(⟨Op⟩d ⟨Expr⟩ ... ⟨Expr⟩)	Dynamic base appl.
	|	(lift ⟨Expr⟩)	Lifting a static expr.
⟨SDArgs⟩	::=	(⟨Arglist⟩) (⟨Arglist⟩)	Argument lists

Figure 5.5: Syntax of two-level (annotated) Scheme0 expressions.

For a two-level Scheme0 program to be well-formed, every application of a function f must agree with the definition of f, in particular as concerns the number of static and dynamic parameters. This requirement corresponds to the congruence requirement for monovariant divisions.

5.3.2 From division to annotations

Let a division div be given, and consider a function definition

    (define (f x_1 ... x_a) e)

Assume that $x_{s_1} ... x_{s_m}$ are the static parameters, and $x_{d_1} ... x_{d_k}$ the dynamic parameters of f, according to div. The corresponding annotated definition is:

$$(\text{define (f } \underbrace{(x_{s_1} ... x_{s_m})}_{\text{static}} \; \underbrace{(x_{d_1} ... x_{d_k})}_{\text{dynamic}}) \; e^{ann})$$

The body e^{ann} is the annotated version of e, obtained as follows. Consider a function call in e:

```
(call g e₁ ... eₐ)
```

and assume $e_{s_1} \ldots e_{s_m}$ are the static parameters of g according to div, and $e_{d_1} \ldots e_{d_k}$ are the dynamic ones. We must split the argument list into two, and we must make the call a calls or a calld. If there are no dynamic arguments (that is, if $m = a$ and $k = 0$), then the call is static (should be unfolded during specialization) and is transformed to

```
(calls g (e_{s_1} ... e_{s_a}) ())
```

If there are dynamic arguments (that is, $m < a$ and $k > 0$), then the call is dynamic (should not be unfolded during specialization) and is transformed to

```
(calld g (e_{s_1} ... e_{s_m}) (e_{d_1} ... e_{d_k}))
```

This annotation of the call corresponds to the second-most conservative call unfolding (or transition compression) strategy mentioned on page 104. We shall discuss more liberal unfolding techniques in Section 5.5 below. Note that with a monovariant division div it may well happen that an argument expression e_j is static according to the binding-time analysis, yet it is in the dynamic argument list because the jth parameter of f is dynamic according to the division div.

Conditionals and base function applications are marked as static or dynamic, depending on the binding times of their arguments. A conditional (if e₁ e₂ e₃) is annotated as (ifs e₁ e₂ e₃) if e₁ is static, and as (ifd e₁ e₂ e₃) if e₁ is dynamic. A base function application (op e₁ ... eₐ) is annotated as (ops e₁ ... eₐ) if all e_j are static, and as (opd e₁ ... eₐ) if some e_j is dynamic.

Every expression e which is static according to the binding-time analysis, but appears in a dynamic context, must be marked as (lift e). The *dynamic contexts* are: dynamic argument lists, the argument list of an opd, a subexpression of an ifd, the branches of an ifs which is itself in a dynamic context, the body of the goal function, and the body of a function definition having at least one dynamic parameter.

As noted previously, *polyvariant binding times* can be dealt with by inventing sufficiently many versions of each function. For instance, assume that a two-argument function f is called at one point with static arguments only (S, S), and at another point with one static and one dynamic argument (S, D). Then we first construct two versions f_{SS} and f_{SD} of f, then annotate the program as above. Thus a simple way to handle polyvariant binding times is to introduce a sufficient set of binding-time variants and apply the essentially monovariant annotation procedure. The specialization algorithm shown below can be used in both cases.

5.4   Specialization algorithm for Scheme0

The Scheme0 specializer is outlined in Figures 5.6 and 5.7 below. The specializer is rather similar to that for flow charts shown in Figure 4.7, and the reader is encouraged to compare the two as we proceed.

5.4.1   Specializing function definitions

The main function `specialize` in Figure 5.6 takes as input an annotated subject program `program` and a list vs_0 of the values of the first function's static parameters, and returns a specialized program. A specialized program is a list of specialized function definitions. Since the subject program is annotated, a `division` argument is not needed.

Function `complete` implements the specialization loop. As in the flow chart specializer in Figure 4.7, `pending` holds the set of functions (that is, program points) yet to be specialized, and `marked` holds those already specialized. While `pending` is non-empty, function `complete` repeatedly selects a member (`f . vs`) of `pending`, then constructs the definition of a new specialized function called (`f . vs`), where `f` is an original function name and `vs` is the values for its static parameters. When `pending` becomes empty, the list of specialized function definitions is returned. This list corresponds to `code` in the flow chart specializer.

The auxiliary functions `lookup` and `successors` (not shown in the figure) are similar to those in the flow chart specializer. The application (`lookup f program`) finds the definition of function `f` in `program`, and the application (`successors` e_{vs}) finds the set of residual calls in expression e_{vs}.

The function `reduce`, which constructs the specialized function body e_{vs}, is shown in the next section. It is called with the original function's body `e`, a list of the function's parameters ($x_1 \ldots x_m x_{m+1} \ldots x_a$), which may occur in `e`, and a list ($vs_1 \ldots vs_m x_{m+1} \ldots x_a$) of the corresponding values and expressions: values vs_j for the static parameters and the trivial expressions x_j for the dynamic parameters x_j. (The intention is that dynamic parameter reduces to itself when `e` is specialized.)

Note that the specializer functions are themselves written in Scheme0 but with syntactic sugar, such as `if-then-else`, `let-in`, infix cons ':::', `case-of`, and simple pattern matching.

5.4.2   Reducing Scheme0 expressions

The core of the Scheme0 specializer is the function `reduce` for symbolic reduction of expressions, shown in Figure 5.7 below, again using syntactically sugared Scheme0. It corresponds partly to the large `case` statement (lines 13–28 of Figure 4.7) and

```
(define (specialize program vs₀)
   let ((define (f₁ _ _ ) _ ) . _ ) = program
   in  (complete (list (f₁ :: vs₀)) () program)
)


(define (complete pending marked program)
   if pending is empty then
      ()
   else
      let (f . vs) ∈ pending
      let (define (f (x₁...xₘ) (xₘ₊₁...xₐ)) e) = (lookup f program)
      let (vs₁ ... vsₘ) = vs
      let eᵥₛ = (reduce e (x₁...xₘ xₘ₊₁...xₐ) (vs₁...vsₘ xₘ₊₁...xₐ))
      let newmarked  = marked ∪ {(f . vs)}
      let newpending = (pending ∪ (successors eᵥₛ)) \ newmarked
      let newdef     = (list 'define (list (f . vs) xₘ₊₁...xₐ) eᵥₛ)
      in (newdef :: (complete newpending newmarked program))
)
```

Figure 5.6: Main loop of Scheme0 specialization algorithm.

partly to the base functions **eval** and **reduce** for expression evaluation and reduction in the flow chart specializer. In Scheme0 there are no statements, only
expressions, so a single reduction function suffices. On the other hand, reduction
is now more complicated, mainly due to the presence of function calls.

The **reduce** function takes as arguments an annotated Scheme0 expression e, a
list $vn = (y_1 \ ... \ y_k)$ of variables that may occur in e, and a list $vv = (v_1 \ ... \ v_k)$ of corresponding variable values. Function **reduce** returns either a value (a
number or S-expression) or a reduced residual expression, according to whether e
is static or dynamic.

The **vn** and **vv** together constitute the specialization environment which maps y_j
to v_j. Here v_j is either a value (a number or S-expression) or a Scheme0 expression,
according to whether y_j is static or dynamic. A dynamic variable **y** will typically be
mapped to itself: the expression **y**. In the flow chart specializer, the environment
vs maps only static variables, and so corresponds only to the static part of **vn** and
vv.

The cases of function **reduce** can be explained as follows. A number or a constant
is static and reduces to a value. A variable y_j reduces to the value or expression
v_j found in **vv**. The conditional expression e_1 of a static **ifs** must be static and
reduce to a value. Depending on this value the entire **ifs** reduces to the reduction
of its **then** or **else** branch. A dynamic **ifd** reduces to an **if** expression.

A static function call (**calls**) is reduced by reducing the called function's body,
in an environment which binds the function's parameters to the reduced argument
expressions. This amounts to unfolding the call. The result is a value if the function

The environment is represented by a list $\text{vn} = (\text{y}_1 \ \ldots \ \text{y}_k)$ of the names of the variables that may occur in e, and a list $\text{vv} = (\text{v}_1 \ \ldots \ \text{v}_k)$ of corresponding values.

```
(define (reduce e vn vv)
    case e of
        number n         => n
        (quote c)        => c
        yⱼ               => vⱼ where (y₁ ... yⱼ ... yₖ) = vn
                                     (v₁ ... vⱼ ... vₖ) = vv
        (ifs e₁ e₂ e₃)   => if (reduce e₁ vn vv)
                              then (reduce e₂ vn vv)
                              else (reduce e₃ vn vv)
        (ifd e₁ e₂ e₃)   => (list 'if (reduce e₁ vn vv)
                                       (reduce e₂ vn vv)
                                       (reduce e₃ vn vv))
        (calls f (e₁ ... eₘ) (eₘ₊₁ ... eₐ)) =>
                            (reduce e_f (x₁ ... xₐ) (e'₁ ... e'ₐ))
                            where e'ⱼ = (reduce eⱼ vn vv) for j = 1,...,a
                                  (define (f (x₁...xₘ) (xₘ₊₁...xₐ)) e_f)
                                         = (lookup f program)
        (calld f (e₁ ... eₘ) (eₘ₊₁ ... eₐ)) =>
                            (list 'call (f :: (e'₁ ... e'ₘ)) e'ₘ₊₁ ... e'ₐ)
                            where e'ⱼ = (reduce eⱼ vn vv) for j = 1,...,a
        (ops e₁ ... eₐ) => (op (reduce e₁ vn vv) ... (reduce eₐ vn vv))
        (opd e₁ ... eₐ) => (list 'op (reduce e₁ vn vv) ...
                                     (reduce eₐ vn vv))
        (lift e)        => (list 'quote (reduce e vn vv)))
```

Figure 5.7: Reduction of Scheme0 expressions.

body reduces to a value, otherwise it is a residual expression. Note that with the call annotation strategy used until now, the dynamic argument list $(\text{e}_{m+1} \ \ldots \ \text{e}_a)$ of a calls is always empty. In Section 5.5 below this will no longer be the case.

A dynamic function call (calld) reduces to a call (call (f . vs) ...) of a new specialized function (f . vs). The arguments of the residual call are the reduced dynamic argument expressions, and vs is the list of values of the static argument expressions.

An application of a static base function ops reduces to the result of applying op to the values of its (necessarily static) argument expressions. An application of a dynamic base function opd reduces to a base function application whose arguments are the reduced argument expressions.

The expression (lift e) reduces to the constant expression (quote v) where v is the value of the expression e.

5.4.3   Self-application of the specializer

Values of bounded static variation

The Scheme0 specializer shown in Figure 5.6 has the same drawback as the flow chart specializer in Chapter 4: when self-applied it would produce very bad results. The reason is the same as previously. Assume we specialize function specialize with the program being static and vs_0 dynamic. Then in function complete, the parameter pending is dynamic, and since the argument f in (lookup f program) comes from pending, the result of the look-up is also dynamic. But then the expression e to be reduced is dynamic too, so function reduce cannot decompose e at specialization time.

For instance, if we attempt to generate a compiler by specializing the specializer with respect to an interpreter int, then the expressions e will be subexpressions of int. Thus the interpreter would not be decomposed by this process, the generated compiler would contain the entire unmodified interpreter, and compilation would simply proceed by general partial evaluation — clearly an unsatisfactory result.

The solution to this problem is 'the trick', exactly as used for the flow chart specializer. We have to write and unfold lookup to obtain a binding-time improvement, exploiting the fact that the argument f is of bounded static variation (cf. Section 4.8.3). Namely, the value of f must be one of the finitely many function names fv in the program, which is static. Figure 5.8 shows how to obtain this effect in Scheme0. This solution is slightly more complicated than in the flow chart language.

The new function generate serves the same purpose as that part of the old complete which begins with the call to lookup.

Assume again that we specialize the function specialize with the program being static and vs_0 dynamic. Then in function generate, the parameters program and defs are static, and so is the expression e extracted from defs. Thus *now* the e parameter of function reduce is static too, so reduce can decompose e, and the results of specializing the specializer will be far better.

In a sense, that part of the old complete function which depends on the result of lookup has been moved into the body of lookup (giving the function generate). This transformation can be understood as a special case of the transformation to *continuation passing style*. The transformation was used already in the very first self-applicable partial evaluator [135], but the understanding in terms of continuations is more recent [56,139].

Separating static and dynamic data

It is also worth noting that splitting reduce's environment into a variable list vn and a value list vv is very beneficial for self-application of the specializer. Namely, when specializing the specializer (and thus the reduce function) with respect to a known subject program but unknown inputs, vn will be static and vv will be dynamic. Had these two lists been merged into one, then the resulting list would

```
(define (specialize program vs₀)
   let ((define (f₁ _ _ ) _ ) . _ ) = program
   in  (complete (list (f₁ :: vs₀)) () program)
)


(define (complete pending marked program)
   if pending  is empty then
      ()
   else
      let (f . vs) ∈ pending
      in (generate f vs program pending marked program)
)


(define (generate f vs defs pending marked program)
   if defs = () then
      (error-undefined-function f)
   else
      let ((define (fv (x₁...xₘ) (xₘ₊₁...xₐ)) e) . restdefs) = defs
      let (vs₁ ... vsₘ) = vs
      in
      if f = fv then
         let eᵥₛ = (reduce e (x₁...xₘ xₘ₊₁...xₐ)(vs₁...vsₘ xₘ₊₁...xₐ))
         let newmarked  = marked ∪ {(f . vs)}
         let newpending = (pending ∪ (successors eᵥₛ)) \ newmarked
         let newdef = (list 'define (list (f . vs) xₘ₊₁...xₐ) eᵥₛ)
         in (newdef :: (complete newpending newmarked program))
      else
         (generate f vs restdefs pending marked program)
)
```

Figure 5.8: Self-applicable version of Scheme0 specialization algorithm.

be dynamic, since we do not handle partially static structures at this point (see Section 15.4).

When specializing the specializer with respect to an interpreter (to obtain a compiler), this means that the variable names used in the interpreter would still be present in the compiler. During compilation, the syntactic analysis of the source program would proceed by interpretation of the interpreter's syntactic analysis. In particular, instead of just accessing a component of the source program, the compiler would do a lookup in a list of interpreter data structures, to find the data structure corresponding to a certain interpreter variable.

Binding-time improvements

The use of the two binding-time improvements discussed above is by no means confined to self-application of partial evaluators. In fact, they have proven themselves highly useful many other contexts, such as specialization of interpreters, pattern matchers, etc. The challenge in writing a self-applicable partial evaluator is that one has to be conscious not only of *what* the partial evaluators does, but also *how* it does it.

5.5   Call unfolding on the fly

So far we have done a minimum of call unfolding on the fly (during specialization). That is, we unfolded only calls having no dynamic arguments. More unfolding is often desirable as witnessed by the first residual program in Figure 5.2, for example. To do more unfolding on the fly, one needs an *unfolding strategy*. Such a strategy must (1) avoid infinite unfolding, and (2) avoid duplication of code and computation, and still eliminate as many calls as possible.

5.5.1   Avoiding infinite unfolding

To avoid infinite unfolding, a strategy may unfold a recursive call only if the value of some static argument gets smaller in a well-founded ordering (or if all arguments are static). Then unfolding must stop in finitely many steps, unless there is a potential *infinite static loop*: a loop not involving any dynamic tests. This strategy was used by Sestoft [246].

In the Scheme0 specializer we use a simple strategy resembling the transition compression strategy used in flow chart `mix`, namely, a call is unfolded precisely if it is not in a branch of a dynamic conditional. Thus a call in a branch of a dynamic conditional is made dynamic (`calld`), and all other calls are made static (`calls`). This strategy ensures finite unfolding as long as the subject program contains no infinite static loops.

Consider the `append` function from Figure 5.2, and suppose for a change that `ys` is static and `xs` is dynamic. The annotated program now is:

```
(define (app (ys) (xs))
   (ifd (null?d xs)
        (lift ys)
        (consd (card xs) (calld app (ys) ((cdrd xs))))))
```

The condition (`null? xs`) now becomes dynamic, so the recursive call to `app` appears in a branch of a dynamic conditional (`ifd`) and must be made dynamic (`calld`). It will not be unfolded, and with good reason: the unfolding would not be stopped by a static conditional.

This strategy ensures that a function will be unfolded twice only if no dynamic conditional has been passed between the two unfoldings. However, a 'harmless' call, such as a non-recursive call which just happens to be in the branch of a dynamic conditional, will not be unfolded either. Thus our strategy avoids infinite unfolding but is slightly more conservative than necessary.

5.5.2 Avoiding duplication of code and computations

An unfolding strategy must also avoid *duplication* of code and computation, so we need to refine our strategy. Recall that when unfolding a call (calls (f (...) (...e_j...))), the reduced form of dynamic argument expression e_j is substituted for the corresponding dynamic variable x_j in the reduced body of function f. Thus duplication happens if the variable x_j occurs several times in the reduced body of f. In this case we shall say that e_j is *duplicable*.

The number of occurrences of x_j in a reduced function body can be *approximated* by analysing the annotated Scheme0 program. For example, x_j occurs twice in the reduced form of (consd x_j x_j), and twice in the reduced form of (ifd ... x_j x_j), since these dynamic expressions reduce to themselves. Counting the occurrences of x_j in other expressions is similar, with one exception: a static conditional reduces to exactly one of its branches, so x_j occurs only once in the reduced form of:

```
(ifs ...
    (... x_j ...)
    (... x_j ...))
```

For a static conditional it is safe to take the maximum (instead of the sum) of the number of occurrence in the branches. Thus we can approximate the number occurrences of x_j by an analysis done when annotating the program.

Code duplication will sometimes lead to computation duplication. In this example a very moderate code duplication gives exponential computation duplication:

```
(define (f n) (if (= n 0) 1 (g (f (- n 1)))))
(define (g m) (+ m m))
```

Unfolding of the call to g would give:

```
(define (f n) (if (= n 0) 1 (+ (f (- n 1)) (f (- n 1)))))
```

The unfolded program has run time exponential in n where the original has linear run time.

Code duplication without computation duplication occurs when x_j occurs (once) in both branches of a dynamic conditional.

5.5.3 Unfolding and side-effects

Scheme0 does not allow *side-effects*, such as incrementing a global variable X, or outputting a message to a printer. However, for completeness it should be noted that side-effects would create new problems for unfolding, since side-effects should never be *duplicated, reordered,* or *discarded*.

Imagine a call (call g e_1) where the (dynamic) argument expression e_1 has a side-effect. First, unfolding the call may duplicate e_1 if the corresponding formal parameter appears twice in g. Secondly, unfolding may reorder side-effects, since it postpones the evaluation of e_1. Third, unfolding may discard e_1 if the formal parameter does not appear in all branches of g.

Even in the absence of side-effects, unfolding may change the termination properties of a program by discarding an argument expression whose evaluation would not terminate.

5.5.4   Program transformations to assist unfolding

Until now an unfolding strategy has been described as a procedure to decide which calls to unfold, and we have seen that many problems must be taken into account. To simplify the unfolding strategy and improve the results of unfolding, one may automatically transform the subject program before specialization. This is done in the Similix partial evaluator (Chapter 10).

Insertion of let-expressions
Automatic introduction of a let-binding for each duplicable variable allows to separate the problems of code duplication from those of finite call unfolding. Consider the example program from Section 5.5.2. Insertion of let-bindings would give

```
(define (f n) (let (x n) (if (= x 0) 1 (g (f (- x 1))))))
(define (g m) (let (y m) (+ y y)))
```

Now the unfolding strategy need not be concerned with code duplication at all, only with ensuring finite unfolding. Unfolding the call to g cannot lead to infinite unfolding, and we get

```
(define (f n)
        (let (x n) (if (= x 0) 1 (let (y (f (- x 1))) (+ y y)))))
```

This is far better than the result above, although the outer let-binding is superfluous. For functions of more than one argument, lets need only be inserted for the duplicable arguments.

Also, in a strict language let-expressions provide a simple way to avoid reordering and discarding computations with side-effects. The partial evaluator Similix inserts let-expressions prior to program specialization to separate the problem of infinite unfolding from those of duplication, reordering, and discarding.

Insertion of function calls
Until now, a specialized program point is a pair of a program point (a label or a function name) *present in the subject program* and the static data values. Similix replaces each dynamic conditional (ifd ...) with a call to a new function f whose definition (define (f ...) (ifd ...)) is added to the subject program.

The parameters to f are the free variables of (ifd ...). The inserted calls are annotated as dynamic to appear in the residual program and *all* other calls are unfolded. This strategy is a slight variant of the compression strategy of Chapter 4 and the Scheme0 strategy of Section 5.5.1 and its termination properties are the same: unfolding will loop infinitely only if the subject program contains an infinite static loop.

The 'moving' of the cut points for unfolding to the dynamic conditionals has reduced code duplication in many practical applications. For an example, suppose that function f has a static parameter x (possible values 2 and 3) and dynamic parameter y.

```
(define (f x y) (+d (*s x x) (ifd (=d y 0) 1 (calld g y))))
```

The Scheme0 strategy would duplicate the conditional and deliver specialized functions

```
(define (f-2 y) (+ 4 (if (= y 0) 1 (call g y))))
(define (f-3 y) (+ 9 (if (= y 0) 1 (call g y))))
```

Instead we could introduce a new function h and transform the subject program into:

```
(define (f x y) (+d (*s x x) (calld h y)))
(define (h y) (ifd (=d y 0) 1 (calls g y)))
```

which partially evaluates to:

```
(define (f-2 y) (+ 4 (call h y)))
(define (f-3 y) (+ 9 (call h y)))
```

where the conditional is not duplicated.

The compression strategy from Chapter 4 has a tendency to duplicate conditionals since the cut points for unfolding are in the branches instead of *before* the conditional. See for example the residual program in Figure 4.5.

5.5.5   Harmless duplication

Consider unfolding a call (calls (f (...) (...e_j...))) where e_j is duplicable. The duplication is *harmless* if the reduced form e_j' of e_j is just a variable. Substituting one variable for another will make the resulting expression neither larger nor more expensive to evaluate. Thus before annotating the calls, we would like to detect when e_j' *must* be a variable. Unfortunately, we can detect only when it *cannot* be a variable.

Let e_j be a dynamic expression. If e_j is not a variable, then its reduced form e_j' will also not be a variable. When e_j is a variable w, then e_j' is not necessarily a variable, since w may be bound (by an unfolded call) to a non-variable dynamic expression:

```
(define (f () (v)) (calls g () ((consd v v))))
(define (g () (w)) (calls h () (w)))
(define (h () (z)) (consd z z))
```

Here w will be bound to the residual expression (consd v v); unfolding the call to h would duplicate that expression.

Before annotating a call we cannot detect when e_j *must* reduce to a variable. However, during specialization we can easily detect whether the reduced form of e_j is a variable. This suggests a call unfolding strategy which does not require insertion of lets, and which works in two stages: during annotation, and during specialization.

5.5.6   A two-stage call unfolding strategy

When annotating the program, we count the occurrences of dynamic variables, then annotate function calls as follows. A call is made static (calls) if it has no dynamic arguments, or if it is not in a branch of a dynamic conditional and all its duplicable dynamic arguments *are* variables. The call is made dynamic (calld) in all other cases, that is, if it has a dynamic argument, and either appears in a branch of a dynamic conditional or has a duplicable non-variable dynamic argument.

When specializing the program, a dynamic call will never be unfolded. This is sufficient to avoid infinite unfolding (disregarding infinite static loops). To avoid code duplication, a static call may be unfolded if all of its duplicable dynamic argument expressions *reduce* to variables. For a static call without dynamic arguments this requirement is trivially satisfied, so it will always be unfolded.

Note that the meaning of static call has changed: a static call will *possibly* but not necessarily be unfolded. The two-stage call unfolding strategy therefore requires a change to the reduce function in the specializer. The calls case must check that each dynamic argument expression either is not duplicable or reduces to a variable. The necessary changes are shown in Figure 5.9. Note that this unfolding strategy, as opposed to those presented previously, is partially but not exclusively steered by the annotations. Thus the strategy combines online and offline techniques (see Section 4.4.7 and Chapter 7).

5.6   Implementation

An implementation of the Scheme0 specializer using the ideas described so far in this chapter is given in Appendix A. The implementation includes monovariant and polyvariant binding-time analysis, annotation, and the specializer.

The implementation can be obtained electronically (via the Internet) by anonymous ftp from ftp.diku.dk as file pub/diku/dists/jones-book/Scheme0.tar.Z.

```
    case e of
        ⋮

    (calls f (e₁ ... e_m) (e_{m+1} ... e_a)) =>
            let e'_j = (reduce e_j vn vv)  for j = 1,...,a
            let (define (f (x₁...x_m) (x_{m+1}...x_a)) e_f)
                    = (lookup f program)
            in if e'_j is a variable or x_j is not duplicable, j = m + 1,...,a
                then (reduce e_f (x₁ ... x_a) (e'₁ ... e'_a))
                else (list 'call (f :: (e'₁ ... e'_m)) e'_{m+1} ... e'_a)
        ⋮
```

Figure 5.9: On the fly call unfolding with online 'variable test'.

On a Unix system, proceed as follows:

1. Type 'ftp ftp.diku.dk' on your terminal.

2. In response to 'Name (freja.diku.dk:...):', type 'ftp'

3. In response to 'Password:', type your own e-mail address.

4. Type 'binary'

5. Type 'cd pub/diku/dists/jones-book'

6. Type 'get Scheme0.tar.Z' to get the packed Scheme0 files.

7. Type 'bye' to terminate the ftp session.

8. Type 'zcat Scheme0.tar.Z | tar xf -' to unpack the files.

5.7   Using type rules for binding-time checking

Section 5.2 presented binding-time analysis as an interpretation of the subject program over the abstract value domain $\{S,D\}$. This section applies the notion of *type inference* rules (see Section 2.2.2) to annotated (two-level) Scheme0 expressions. The type inference rules can immediately be used for *checking* the correctness of binding-time annotations. In Chapter 8 we show how to use such rules for *inferring* binding-time annotations. Type inference methods can profitably be used for binding-time analysis, especially for languages such as the lambda calculus which are more powerful than Scheme0.

The set of binding-time checking rules for two-level Scheme0 are shown in Figure 5.10. The *judgement* $\tau \vdash e : t$ asserts that the annotations of expression e are *consistent* and that its binding time is t, given that the variables in e have the binding times determined by environment τ.

In a judgement $\tau \vdash$ e $: t$, the parameter τ is a binding-time environment, e is a two-level Scheme0 expression, and $t \in \{S, D\}$ is the binding time of e in binding-time environment τ.

$$\tau \vdash \text{c} : S$$

$$\tau[\text{x} \mapsto t] \vdash \text{x} : t$$

$$\frac{\tau \vdash \text{e}_1 : S \ldots \tau \vdash \text{e}_a : S}{\tau \vdash (\text{ops } \text{e}_1 \ \ldots \ \text{e}_a) : S}$$

$$\frac{\tau \vdash \text{e}_1 : D \ \ldots \ \tau \vdash \text{e}_a : D}{\tau \vdash (\text{opd } \text{e}_1 \ \ldots \ \text{e}_a) : D}$$

$$\frac{\tau \vdash \text{e}_1 : S \quad \tau \vdash \text{e}_2 : t \quad \tau \vdash \text{e}_3 : t}{\tau \vdash (\text{ifs } \text{e}_1 \ \text{e}_2 \ \text{e}_3) : t}$$

$$\frac{\tau \vdash \text{e}_1 : D \qquad \tau \vdash \text{e}_2 : D \qquad \tau \vdash \text{e}_3 : D}{\tau \vdash (\text{ifd } \text{e}_1 \ \text{e}_2 \ \text{e}_3) : D}$$

$$\frac{\tau \vdash \text{e}_1 : S \ldots \tau \vdash \text{e}_a : S}{\tau \vdash (\text{calls f } (\text{e}_1 \ \ldots \ \text{e}_a) \ ()) : S}$$

$$\frac{\tau \vdash \text{e}_1 : S \ldots \tau \vdash \text{e}_m : S \qquad \tau \vdash \text{e}_{m+1} : D \ldots \tau \vdash \text{e}_a : D \qquad m < a}{\tau \vdash (\text{calls f } (\text{e}_1 \ \ldots \ \text{e}_m) \ (\text{e}_{m+1} \ \ldots \ \text{e}_a)) : D}$$

$$\frac{\tau \vdash \text{e}_1 : S \ldots \tau \vdash \text{e}_m : S \qquad \tau \vdash \text{e}_{m+1} : D \ldots \tau \vdash \text{e}_a : D \qquad m < a}{\tau \vdash (\text{calld f } (\text{e}_1 \ \ldots \ \text{e}_m) \ (\text{e}_{m+1} \ \ldots \ \text{e}_a)) : D}$$

$$\frac{\tau \vdash \text{e} : S}{\tau \vdash (\text{lift e}) : D}$$

Figure 5.10: Binding-time checking rules for annotated Scheme0.

The rules can be read as follows. A constant c is static in any binding-time environment. Variable x has binding time t if the environment maps x to t. An application of a static base function ops must have static arguments and its result is static. An application of a dynamic base function opd must have dynamic arguments and its result is dynamic. A static conditional ifs must have a static first argument e_1, its branches must both have the same binding time t, and this is the binding time of the result. A dynamic conditional ifd must have all three subexpressions dynamic, and its result is dynamic. The result of a function call without dynamic arguments is static. The result of a function call with dynamic arguments is dynamic. Finally, if the result of expression e is static, then the result of (lift e) is dynamic.

An annotated Scheme0 program ($\text{def}_1 \ \ldots \ \text{def}_n$) is checked by checking each function definition def_i as follows. Assume the definition has the form:

```
(define (f (x₁ ... xₘ) (xₘ₊₁ ... xₐ)) e)
```

The two parameter lists show that the relevant binding-time environment is $\tau = [x_1 \mapsto S, \ldots, x_m \mapsto S, x_{m+1} \mapsto D, \ldots, x_a \mapsto D]$. Then we must check that $\tau \vdash e : t$, where $t = S$ if the function has no dynamic arguments (that is, if $m = a$), and $t = D$ if it has a dynamic argument (that is, if $m < a$).

Together with the well-formedness requirements on two-level Scheme0 programs, this suffices to ensure binding-time safety. If the annotated subject program is correct with respect to these rules, the specializer will not fail: it will never attempt to add one to a residual expression, or mistake a value (such as a data structure) for an expression. However, the specializer may well loop, attempting to produce an infinite residual program or unfolding a function infinitely often. Handling this *finiteness* aspect of specializer safety is addressed in Chapter 14.

5.8   Constructing the generating extension

Let a Scheme0 program **pgm** be given, and let **pgma** be a two-level (annotated) version of **pgm**, the first parameter of which is static, and the second one dynamic. A *generating extension* of **pgma** is a program **pgmgen** for which

$$[\![[\![pgmgen]\!]\ in1\,]\!]\ in2\ =\ [\![pgm]\!]\ [in1, in2]$$

for all inputs **in1** and **in2**. That is, the result of applying **pgmgen** to an argument **in1** is a version of **pgm** specialized to the value **in1** of its first argument.

As seen in Section 1.5.3, the program **pgmgen** can be generated by **cogen** or **mix**:

$$pgmgen\ =\ [\![cogen]\!]\ pgma\ =\ [\![mix]\!]\ [mix, pgma]$$

Sergei Romanenko noticed that the machine-generated **cogen** contains a rather natural function **gex**, shown in Figure 5.11, which transforms the two-level Scheme0 expressions of **pgma** into the Scheme0 expressions in **pgmgen** [227, p. 460].

Holst and Launchbury suggest that for strongly typed languages, it is easier to hand-code **cogen** (including **gex**) than to generate it by partial evaluation, because types make self-application more complicated (see Section 11.7 and [69,169]).

5.9   Exercises

Exercise 5.1 Specialize the Scheme0 function **power** with x dynamic and n static:

```
(define (power x n)
  (if (= n 0)
      1
      (* x (power x (- n 1))))))
```

```
(define (gex e)
   case e of
      number n      => n
      (quote c)     => (list 'quote c)
      variable y    => y
      (ifs e₁ e₂ e₃)  => (list 'if e₁ (gex e₂) (gex e₃))
      (ifd e₁ e₂ e₃)  => (list 'list ''if (gex e₁) (gex e₂) (gex e₃))
      (calls f (e₁ ... eₘ) (eₘ₊₁ ... eₐ)) =>
                    (list 'call f e₁ ... eₘ (gex eₘ₊₁) ... (gex eₐ))
      (calld f (e₁ ... eₘ) (eₘ₊₁ ... eₐ)) =>
                    (list 'list ''call (list 'quote f)
                          (list 'quote e₁) ... (list 'quote eₘ)
                          (gex eₘ₊₁) ... (gex eₐ))
      (ops e₁ ... eₐ) => (list op e₁ ... eₐ)
      (opd e₁ ... eₐ) => (list 'list (list 'quote op)(gex e₁)...(gex eₐ))
      (lift e)       => (list 'list ''quote e)
)
```

Figure 5.11: Constructing the generating extension.

1. Perform the binding-time analysis as described in Section 5.2 and annotate the program accordingly.

2. Do the specialization by hand with respect to n = 3.   □

Exercise 5.2 Partially evaluate Ackermann's function ack with m static and n dynamic:

```
(define (ack m n)
   (if (= m 0)
       (+ n 1)
       (if (= n 0)
           (ack (- m 1) 1)
           (ack (- m 1) (ack m (- n 1)))))))
```

1. Perform the binding-time analysis as described in Section 5.2 and annotate the program accordingly.

2. Do the specialization (without call unfolding) by hand with m = 2.

3. How would a reasonable call unfolding strategy lead to a better residual program than the one generated in step 2? Starting from Ackermann's function discuss (at least) two different unfolding strategies. Choose a strategy and specialize ack again with m = 2.

4. Suppose you wish to specialize ack with m dynamic and n static. Explain why the monovariant binding-time analysis gives an unnecessarily bad result, and sketch an automatic solution to the problem.   □

Chapter 6

Efficiency, Speedup, and Optimality

The motivation for studying partial evaluation is efficiency, and a partial evaluator has pragmatic success if it runs fast and produces fast residual programs. A
clear and machine-independent way to measure the quality of a partial evaluator
would be most useful to both users and writers of partial evaluators. When is a
partial evaluator 'strong enough' and what is the theoretical limit for the speedup
obtainable by partial evaluation?

The chapter begins with an analysis of comparative running times in a partial evaluation context. An argument is given that standard partial evaluation
techniques cannot accomplish *superlinear speedup*, and we outline a method that
automatically estimates how much speedup will be accomplished, given a program
with explicit binding time information.

Finally, the time overhead incurred by language interpretation is discussed. An
optimal partial evaluator is defined as one able to remove all such overhead; and a
technique is given to allow multiple levels of interpretation without the usual and
problematic multiplication of interpretational overhead.

6.1 Defining and measuring speedup

Suppose we are given a program p with two inputs: static s, known at specialization
time; and dynamic d. As in Section 3.1.7 we write $t_p(s, d)$ for the time to compute
$[\![p]\!]$ [s,d]. Let p_s be the result of specializing p to s, and let $|s|, |d|$ be the sizes
of s, d (for example the number of symbols required to write them). For the sake
of non-triviality we assume that for any fixed choice of s or d, computation time
$t_p(s, d)$ grows unboundedly in the size of the other input.

Our goal is to make meaningful, useful, and reliable statements about the relation
between run time $t_p(s, d)$ of the unspecialized program, and the time $t_{ps}(d)$ of its
specialized version. Doing this can be tricky because comparison of multi-argument
functions is not entirely straightforward, and because sometimes the time to run

the specializer itself is a significant factor.

6.1.1   Quantifying speedup

Let $\mathcal{R}^{\infty} = \{x \in \mathcal{R} \mid x \geq 1\} \cup \{\infty\}^1$. Define $\lim(A)$, where $A = \{a_0, a_1, a_2, \ldots\}$ is a set of reals, to be the maximum element of A if finite, else the smallest number b such that $b \geq a_i$ for all but a finitely many indices i. Note that $b = \infty$ is possible.

One may compare run times for *single input* programs by relating their asymptotic run time growth rates on larger and larger inputs from value set D. For example, program p is twice as fast as program q in the limit if

$$2 = \lim_{|x| \to \infty} \frac{t_q(x)}{t_p(x)}$$

The situation is more complex for multi-argument programs.

Definition 6.1   1. For a fixed two-input program p and static input s, define the *speedup function* $su_s(\_)$ by

$$su_s(d) = \frac{t_p(s, d)}{t_{ps}(d)}$$

2. The *speedup bound* $sb(s)$ is

$$sb(s) = \lim_{|d| \to \infty} su_s(d)$$

3. Partial evaluator mix gives *linear speedup* if $sb(s)$ is finite for every s in D.

□

A *largest* $su_s(d)$ does not always exist, even when s is fixed. Consider a program with a dynamically controlled loop with equally time consuming static and dynamic computations, and assume that *outside* the loop there is one dynamic and no static statements. Any $a < 2$ bounds $su_s(d)$ for all but finitely many d, but not $a = 2$. Still, $sb(s) = 2$ seems the right choice for the speedup, since the computations outside the loop contribute little to the total run time when the loop is iterated many times.

---

[1]For addition involving ∞ we use $x + \infty = \infty + x = \infty$ for all $x \in \mathcal{R} \cup \{\infty\}$.

6.1.2   A range of examples

Specialization is advantageous if $su_s(d) > 1$ for all s and d, and if d changes more frequently than s. To exploit it, each time s changes one may construct a new specialized p_s. This will be faster than p, and may be run on various d until s changes again.

If s and d both change frequently, the time to do specialization must also be accounted for. Partial evaluation will be advantageous in a *single run* if

$$t_{\mathtt{mix}}(p, s) + t_{\mathtt{ps}}(d) < t_{\mathtt{p}}(s, d)$$

A correct analogy is that compilation *plus* target run time can be faster than interpretation in Lisp:

$$t_{\mathtt{compiler}}(\mathtt{source}) + t_{\mathtt{target}}(d) < t_{\mathtt{interpreter}}(\mathtt{source}, d)$$

We investigate the growth of $su_s(d)$ as a function of d, for various values of s. The speedup function is often nearly independent of s; for instance speedups resulting from specializing an interpreter p to various source programs s are not strongly dependent on s. On the other hand, some algorithms, e.g. pattern matching programs, have a speedup strongly dependent on s.

Change of algorithm
Spectacular speedups can be achieved by changing p's computational method. The field of program transformation [43] has many examples; a typical example is to optimize the Fibonacci function by *memoizing*, decreasing its computation time from exponential to linear (or even logarithmic).

Use of non-uniform methods seems not to be in the spirit of full automation; it is more like artificial intelligence. In practice, program transformation systems are not yet as fully automated as partial evaluators.

The trivial partial evaluator
This achieves no speedup: $t_{\mathtt{p}}(s, d) \doteq t_{\mathtt{ps}}(d)$ so in the limit $su_s(d)$ approaches 1 for each s. (This holds even if we take into account the time to specialize p to s since this is independent of dynamic inputs.)

Additive running times
Suppose p's running time is an additive function of static and dynamic input sizes: $t_{\mathtt{p}}(s, d) = f(|s|) + g(|d|)$. Then specialization does not help much, even if we assume all static computations can be done at specialization time. The reason is that for any s, unboundedness of $g(n)$ implies

$$sb(s) = \lim_{|d| \to \infty} su_s(d) = \lim_{|d| \to \infty} \frac{f(|s|) + g(|d|)}{constant + g(|d|)} = 1$$

Interpreter speedups

We saw in Section 3.1.8 that a typical interpreter `int`'s running time on inputs p and d satisfies

$$\alpha_{\mathrm{p}} \cdot t_{\mathrm{p}}(\mathrm{d}) \leq t_{\mathtt{int}}(\mathrm{p}, \ \mathrm{d})$$

for all d. Here α_{p} is independent of d, but it may depend on static source program p. Often $\alpha_{\mathrm{p}} \doteq c + f(\mathrm{p})$, where constant c represents the time taken for 'dispatch on syntax' and recursive calls of the evaluation or command execution functions; and $f(\mathrm{p})$ represents the time for variable access. In experiments c is often around 10 for simple interpreters run on small source programs, and larger for more sophisticated interpreters. Clever use of data structures such as hash tables, binary trees, etc. can make α_{p} grow slowly as a function of p's size.

Interpreters thus typically give linear speedup, with the value of $sb(\mathrm{p}) \geq c$ large enough to be worth reducing. The speedup is not, however, strongly dependent on static data p.

String matching

A rather different example is Consel and Danvy's algorithm [54] to match a *pattern* string s against a *subject* string d. It has multiplicative time complexity $\mathcal{O}(m \cdot n)$ where $m = |\mathsf{s}|$ is the pattern length, and $n = |\mathsf{d}|$ is the subject length.

Specializing their algorithm with respect to the pattern eliminated the multiplicative overhead, giving a specialized matcher running in time $\mathcal{O}(n)$, as good as possibly can be expected, assuming that the whole subject string is to be read (see Section 12.1 for details).

The fact that $sb(\mathsf{s})$ can grow unboundedly as s varies can make the speedup obtained by partial evaluation falsely 'seem' superlinear. Consel and Danvy specialized an $\mathcal{O}(m \cdot n)$ algorithm to yield an $\mathcal{O}(n)$ matcher for the fixed pattern s. This gives a speedup bound $sb(\mathsf{s}) = m = |\mathsf{s}|$, which is still linear, although strongly dependent on s.

A final remark: the generated matchers are just as fast as the ones obtained by the well-known KMP (Knuth, Morris, and Pratt) technique [150]. On the other hand, the KMP technique generates a matching program in time $\mathcal{O}(|\mathsf{s}|)$. This is faster than partial evaluation in general, so the KMP technique is to be preferred if both pattern and subject change frequently.

6.2   Flow chart mix gives linear speedup

If `mix` uses reductions such as `(car (cons e1 e2))` $\Longrightarrow$ `e1` that discard 'unnecessary' computations[2], introduces memoization, or eliminates repeated subexpressions `(e + e)` $\Longrightarrow$ `(let v = e in (v + v))`, then it is easy to conceive examples of superlinear speedup (especially in the presence of recursion). But the partial

---

[2]Unsafe since discarded computations may have caused non-termination.

evaluators we have heretofore seen do not use these techniques, leading to the following question.

Jones posed the following in [131]: 'If *mix* uses only these techniques [program point specialization, constant folding, transition compression, and unfolding] do there exist programs p on which *mix* accomplishes superlinear speedups?' Equivalently: do there exist p, s for which $sb(s)$ is not finite?

In this section we show that partial evaluation of flow chart programs as in Chapter 4 gives, at most, linear speedups. The key point is that the assumption that partial evaluation terminates can be used to place a bound on $sb(s)$, thus excluding superlinear speedups. The theorem below is from Andersen and Gomard [11], but Yuri Gurevich independently came up with similar reasoning.

We use the flow chart framework of Section 3.3.3, where $\bar{v}$ is a vector of variable values. Given a program p and input $\bar{v}_0$, a (finite) computation $p(\bar{v}_0)$ is a (finite) sequence

$$p(\bar{v}_0) = (pp_0, \bar{v}_0) \rightarrow (pp_1, \bar{v}_1) \rightarrow \ldots$$

where pp_0 is the initial program point and $\bar{v}_0$ is the program input. We assume the cost in terms of time is the same for all transitions (not outrageous due to the absence of user-defined function calls). Thus it is reasonable to define the *running time* for a computation to be the length of the sequence (possibly infinite). To avoid subscripted subscripts, we henceforth write this as $|p(\bar{v}_0)|$, rather than $t_p(\bar{v}_0)$ as used before.

As before we assume the input $\bar{v}_0 = (s, d)$ to consist of a static part s and a dynamic part d.

Theorem 6.1 Partial evaluation by flow chart mix never accomplishes superlinear speedup.

Proof Assume that partial evaluation terminates. As usual, we call those computations that *are* performed at partial evaluation time *static* and those that are postponed *dynamic*.

Consider a finite computation $p(\bar{v}_0)$ for program p on input $\bar{v}_0$:

$$(pp_0, \bar{v}_0) \rightarrow (pp_1, \bar{v}_1) \rightarrow \ldots \rightarrow (pp_h, \bar{v}_h)$$

Assume that each $\bar{v}_i$ has form (s_i, d_i) where s_i depends only on static input s_0. Input to the program is thus $\bar{v}_0 = (s_0, d_0)$. Each step $(pp_i, \bar{v}_i) \rightarrow (pp_{i+1}, \bar{v}_{i+1})$ in the computation involves computing variable values $\bar{v}_{i+1}$ and a new control point pp_{i+1}. Variable values depending only on pp_i and s_i can be computed at partial evaluation time (= constant folding), and so can the shift of control to pp_{i+1} (= transition compression or unfolding) when it is uniquely determined by pp_i and s_i.

To compute the speedup gained by partial evaluation for p, s_0, and d_0, consider the computation $(pp_0, \bar{v}_0) \rightarrow \ldots$ above and simply sum the time spent on static respectively dynamic computations, calling the sums (t_{s_0}) and (t_{d_0}). We stress that we consider a standard computation and imagine: *if* this program had been partially evaluated with respect to s, *then* this part would have been static and this part would have been dynamic.

The speedup (a function of $\bar{v}_0 = (s_0, d_0)$):

$$su_{s_0}(d_0) = \frac{t_{s_0} + t_{d_0}}{t_{d_0}}$$

Assume that partial evaluation of p on s terminates in K steps. Then in the standard computation there can be at most $K - 1$ static steps *with no intervening dynamic computations* since mix is no faster than direct execution. This means that $(t_{s_0}) \leq (K - 1) \cdot (t_{d_0})$, and so the speedup for p, s_0, and d_0 is bounded by the same K. This bound is independent of d_0, which rules out superlinear speedup. Moreover, the bound is safe: in any computation there can be at most $K - 1$ consecutive static steps and the computation must end with a dynamic printing of the result.   □

Clearly, this bound is far larger than what is usually seen in practice.

Hansen [111] proves in the setting of logic programming that fold/unfold transformations at most can give rise to linear speedup. Note that unification is daringly assumed to run in constant time.

6.3   Speedup analysis

An *estimate* of the obtainable speedup, available before the specialization is done, would be valuable information. On the basis of a speedup estimate, the user could decide to rewrite the program in order to improve the prospective speedup (or just forget about it!). It would be logical to combine the speedup analysis with a *binding time debugger* as supplied with, for example, the Similix [28] and the Schism [60] systems. Another perspective would be to let the partial evaluator automatically reclassify as dynamic those static computations which are found not to contribute to a good speedup, the objective being faster specialization and smaller residual programs.

A user without detailed knowledge of partial evaluation is usually unable to predict how much can be gained by specialization. The question: 'is specialization of this program worthwhile?' can be answered using three different approaches.

1. Apply mix to p and s to get p_s. Then run the original and specialized programs to compute $su_s(d)$ for various values of d.

2. Apply mix to p and s to get p_s. Then approximate the speedup bound $sb(s)$ by a *speedup interval* $[u, v] \subseteq \mathcal{R}^\infty$. A speedup interval for p_s should characterize speedups for all possible d in a sense to be made precise below.

3. Approximate the speedup for *all* s *and for all* d similarly, by a speedup interval $[u, v] \subseteq \mathcal{R}^\infty$.

Clearly the first approach gives precise results, but only gives one speedup at a time, so the user will have to think for himself or herself how $su_s(\mathsf{d})$ varies as a function of d. It is undesirable when partial evaluation is applied to computationally heavy problems where experimenting is time-consuming.

The second must give an approximate answer due to the absence of d, and the third a still less precise approximation due to the absence of both s and d. In this section we will describe approach 3 in some detail, and sketch approach 2.

Precise estimation of speedup is clearly undecidable, and approximate estimation of speedup is still in its infancy. Here we show a simple *speedup analysis* which, when given a flow chart program with explicit binding time information (conveyed by annotations or a division), approximates the speedup to be gained by partial evaluation by a speedup interval $[l, h] \subseteq \mathcal{R}^\infty$. The interpretation is: the specialized version of the program will run at most h but at least l times faster than the original program. If h is ∞, an unbounded speedup is possible. For example, this can happen if the program contains a completely static loop where the number of iterations is determined by the static input.

6.3.1 Safety of speedup intervals

A speedup interval $[u, v]$ is safe for p if the speedup $su_s(\mathsf{d})$ 'converges' to values in the interval as (s,d) are chosen such that $|\mathsf{p}(\mathsf{s},\mathsf{d})| \to \infty$. Consider again the scenario at the end of Section 6.1 and assume the speedup achievable for that particular program is independent of the choice of s (that assumption does not hold in general). Then a safe (and precise) speedup interval is $[2,2]$.

In general, the speedup may not converge to one fixed x as $|\mathsf{p}(\mathsf{s},\mathsf{d})| \to \infty$, but we shall require that all programs that run 'long enough' shall exhibit a speedup arbitrarily close to the interval.

Definition 6.2 A speedup interval $[u, v]$ is safe for p if for all sequences $(\mathsf{s}_i, \mathsf{d}_i)$: $|\mathsf{p}(\mathsf{s}_i, \mathsf{d}_i)| \to \infty$ implies

$$\forall \varepsilon > 0 : \exists k : \forall j > k : \frac{|\mathsf{p}(\mathsf{s}_j, \mathsf{d}_j)|}{|\mathsf{p}_{\mathsf{s}_j}(\mathsf{d}_j)|} \in [u - \varepsilon, v + \varepsilon]$$

$\square$

6.3.2 Simple loops and speedup

Let a flow chart program with nodes n_i be given. A *loop* is a sequence of program points

$$\mathsf{pp}_1 \to \mathsf{pp}_2 \to \cdots \to \mathsf{pp}_k, \quad \text{for } k \in \mathcal{N}$$

where $pp_1 = pp_k$ and the program contains a (perhaps conditional) jump from pp_i to pp_{i+1} for $1 \leq i < k$. A *simple loop* is a loop $pp_1 \rightarrow \cdots \rightarrow pp_k$ where $pp_i \neq pp_j$ if $1 \leq i < j \leq k$.

Define for a node pp_i the *cost* $C(pp_i)$ as the sum of the running times of the basic block labelled pp_i. We write $C_s(pp_i)$ for the cost of the *static* statements in basic block pp_i, and $C_d(pp_i)$ for the dynamic statements. Speedup can be defined for a single basic block in the obvious way.

Definition 6.3 Let $l = pp_1 \rightarrow \cdots \rightarrow pp_k$ be a simple loop. The *speedup* $SU(l)$ in l is then defined by:

$$SU(l) = \begin{cases} \frac{C_s(l) + C_d(l)}{C_d(l)} & \text{if } C_d(l) \neq 0 \\ \infty & \text{otherwise} \end{cases}$$

where $C_s(l) = \sum_{i=1}^{k-1} C_s(pp_i)$ and $C_d(l) = \sum_{i=1}^{k-1} C_d(pp_i)$. □

The speedup of a loop is a number in $\mathcal{R}^\infty$, and is independent of variable values.

6.3.3   Doing speedup analysis

Let a flow chart program p with simple loops $\mathcal{L}$ be given. The basic idea behind the analysis is the observation that the speedup of the whole program is determined by the speedups of the loops. If the program runs for a sufficiently long time, it will spend most of its time inside loops.

Algorithm   For all simple loops $l \in \mathcal{L}$ in p, compute the speedup $SU(l)$. The *speedup interval* for p is the smallest interval $[u, v] \subseteq \mathcal{R}^\infty$ such that $\forall l \in \mathcal{L}$: $SU(l) \in [u, v]$. □

To see that the speedups for non-simple loops are also in the interval, it suffices to see that if $[u, v]$ is safe for loops l_1 and l_2 then it is also safe for a loop l composed from one instance of each of l_1 and l_2. Assuming without loss of generality that $SU(l_1) \leq SU(l_2) < \infty$, a little algebra yields:

$$SU(l_1) \leq SU(l) = \frac{C_s(l) + C_d(l)}{C_d(l)} \leq SU(l_2)$$

The speedup analysis does not take basic blocks outside loops into account. Clearly, the speedup of the loops will dominate the speedup of the whole program provided the running time is large. However, the analysis can easily be modified to handle the remaining basic blocks by accumulating speedups for all paths through the program without loops. Without the revision, the analysis will have nothing meaningful to say about programs without loops.

Example 6.1 The following program implements addition of natural numbers using a sequence of tests for zero, increments, and decrements. Assume m to be static and n to be dynamic.

```
read (m, n);
1: sum := n;
2: if (zero? m) goto 3 else 4;
3: sum := sum+1;  m := m-1;  goto 2;
4: return sum;
```

Counting one time unit for each statement for simplicity, the (unique) simple loop $2 \to 3 \to 2$ exhibits a speedup of 4. Hence, the approximated speedup of the whole program is $[4, 4]$. By the theorem below, this approximates the actual speedup arbitrarily well when the loop is iterated 'enough', that is, for large values of m. □

Theorem 6.2 Assume speedup analysis computes the speedup interval $[u, v]$ for program p. Then $[u, v]$ is safe for p.

Proof An upper bound $v = \infty$ is trivially safe, so we assume $v \neq \infty$.

Consider the sequence c of program points pp_i visited during a terminating computation p(s,d):

$$c = pp_1 \to pp_2 \to \cdots \to pp_k$$

To *delete* a simple loop $pp_i \to pp_{i+1} \to \cdots \to pp_{i+j} = pp_i$ from c is to replace c by:

$$pp_1 \to \cdots pp_i \to pp_{i+j+1} \cdots \to pp_k$$

Now delete as many simple loops as possible from c (the order is immaterial). Denote the multiset of deleted loops by $\mathcal{L}$. The program points remaining in c now occur only once. The total number of program points in p provides a uniform bound on the number of remaining program points, independent of the choice of (s,d). Denote the set of remaining nodes by NL and define $nlstat = \sum_{n \in NL} \mathcal{C}_s(n)$ and $nldyn = \sum_{n \in NL} \mathcal{C}_d(n)$. Define the cost functions $\mathcal{C}_s$ and $\mathcal{C}_d$ on the multiset $\mathcal{L}$ of loops to be the sum of the costs for each loop $l \in \mathcal{L}$.

We now calculate the speedup for p, s, d:

$$\frac{\mathcal{C}_s(\mathcal{L}) + nlstat + \mathcal{C}_d(\mathcal{L}) + nldyn}{\mathcal{C}_d(\mathcal{L}) + nldyn}$$

This expression can be rewritten to:

$$SU = \frac{\left(\frac{\mathcal{C}_s(\mathcal{L}) + \mathcal{C}_d(\mathcal{L})}{\mathcal{C}_d(\mathcal{L})}\right)}{\left(\frac{\mathcal{C}_d(\mathcal{L}) + nldyn}{\mathcal{C}_d(\mathcal{L})}\right)} + \frac{\left(\frac{nlstat + nldyn}{nldyn}\right)}{\left(\frac{\mathcal{C}_d(\mathcal{L}) + nldyn}{nldyn}\right)}$$

Now we will argue that for all $\varepsilon > 0$ there exists a K such that $SU \in [u - \varepsilon, v + \varepsilon]$ if $|p(s,d)| > K$. Choose a sequence of (s_i, d_i) such that $|p(s_i, d_i)| \to \infty$ and examine the fractions.

To the right of the +, the numerator $\frac{nlstat+nldyn}{nldyn}$ is uniformly bounded and the denominator $\frac{C_d(\mathcal{L})+nldyn}{nldyn} \to \infty$. (Recall that $C_d(\mathcal{L}) \to \infty$ since we assumed $v \neq \infty$. Intuitively, looping in fully static loops is excluded.)

To the left of the +, the denominator $\frac{C_d(\mathcal{L})+nldyn}{C_d(\mathcal{L})} \to 1$ so we conclude $SU \to \frac{C_s(\mathcal{L})+C_d(\mathcal{L})}{C_d(\mathcal{L})}$.

Since $\mathcal{L}$ is a multiset of simple loops, $\frac{C_s(\mathcal{L})+C_d(\mathcal{L})}{C_d(\mathcal{L})} \in [u, v]$ which concludes the proof. $\qquad\square$

6.3.4   Experiments

The speedup analysis has been implemented as a part of the C-Mix system, a partial evaluator for a subset of C (see Chapter 11 and [6]). The analysis is implemented as described above except that it has a differentiated cost function for statements and expressions.

In the table below the measured and estimated speedups for three different programs are shown. The **Add** program is given in Example 6.1 above. The **Int** program is an interpreter for a 'polish-form' language taken from [213]. In this example, the static input was a program computing the first n primes, and the dynamic input was $n = 500$. The program **Scanner** is a general lexical analysis taking as input a scanner table (static input) and a stream of characters (dynamic input). In the test run, it was given a specification of 8 different tokens which appeared 30 000 times in the input stream.

Example	Run-time (sec.)		Speedup (ratio)	
	Src	Res	Measured	Estimated
Add	12.2	4.6	2.7	$[2.7, 2.7]$
Scanner	1.5	0.9	1.7	$[1.5, 4.1]$
Int	59.1	8.7	6.8	$[5.1, \infty]$

For the **Add** program the speedup factor is *independent* of the dynamic input and converges to 2.7 as the static input grows. Hence the very tight interval.

The interval for the **Scanner** is quite satisfactory. If a specification of unambiguous tokens is given, very litle can be done at **mix**-time, and hence the speedup is near the lower bound (approached in the example). On the other hand, if the supplied table contains many 'fail and backtrack' actions, the upper bound can be approached (not shown).

The upper bound for **Int** is correctly ∞ as the interpreter's code for handling unconditional jumps is completely static:

```
while (program[pp] ≠ HALT)
    switch (program[pp])
        {
        case ...
        case JUMP:  pp := program[pp+1]; break;
        case ...
        }
```

Thus, an unboundedly high speedup can be obtained by specializing Int with respect to a program with 'sufficiently' many unconditional, consecutive jumps. To provide some practical justification that the seemingly non-tight speedup intervals computed by the analysis are indeed reasonable, we have applied Int to three different programs, i.e. three different static inputs. Each program exploits different parts of the interpreter. Primes is the program computing the first *n* primes. The Addp program is equivalent to the program Add in Example 6.1, but in 'polish-form'. The Jump program consists of a single loop with ten unconditional, consecutive jumps. The measured speedups are as follows.

Example	Run-time		Speedup
	Source	Residual	Measured
Primes	59.1	8.7	6.8
Addp	51.5	5.5	9.2
Jump	60.7	3.0	20.3

A limitation: loops are not related

Even though the speedup analysis demonstrated some pragmatic success above, it does have its limitations. Consider for example the program fragments below.

```
n := N;                      n := N;
while (n≠0)                   while (n≠0)
    { S1; S2; n := n-1; }         { S1; n := n-1; }
                             n := N;
                             while (n≠0)
                                 { S2; n := n-1; }
```

Suppose that S1 (fully static) and S2 (fully dynamic) do not interfere, meaning the two programs have the same effect. For the program on the left, the estimated speedup interval is $[4, 4]$ (counting 1 for all kinds of statements). The corresponding interval for the program on the right is $[3, \infty]$, where ∞ is due to the completely static loop. The latter result is still *safe* but certainly less tight than the former. The problem is that the analysis considers loops in isolation, and fails to recognize that the two loops iterate the same number of times.

6.3.5 Accounting for static data

In case both p and s are known (approach 2 from the beginning of this section), more precise results can be obtained. For example, the interpreter speedups shown above are concrete speedups for specific values of d. Now suppose we wish a speedup interval holding for *all* d. To estimate this, note that every residual transition pp → pp' in p_s corresponds to a *sequence of transitions* pp_0 → pp_1 → ... → pp_n in p. Recording the relationships between transitions in p_s and those in p can give the desired speedup information.

More concretely but still informally: consider the flow chart specializer of Figure 4.7. All program points in p_s come from the set pending. This contains the initial program point, and all others are of form (pp, vs), where pp is the target of a dynamic conditional statement in p.

Thus any residual basic block in p_s is generated as the result of a computation by Figure 4.7 of the following form: lines 5 through 8 begin at one of p's basic blocks; then the while loop starting at line 9 is repeated some number of times, until a dynamic conditional or the end of a basic block is encountered. (Static conditionals cause the current basic block to be extended, so a residual basic block may be much longer than any basic block in p.)

To estimate speedup, modify Figure 4.7 by adding two counters, both initialized to zero before line 9. One records the number of dynamic statements generated in a residual basic block, and the other counts the number of static *or* dynamic statements encountered. Generation of the the residual basic block is ended when a dynamic conditional or the end of a source basic block is encountered. At that time, the ratio of the two counters gives the speedup for the residual block that was generated.

Finally, once the speedup has been calculated for each basic block, the technique of the previous section can be applied to all loops in p_s to get a speedup interval for the entire program.

6.4 Optimality of mix

Interpreted programs are typically executed more slowly than those which are compiled (or executed directly, which amounts to being interpreted by hardware). The difference is often large enough to be worth reducing for practical reasons, and may depend on the size of the program being interpreted.

For practical purposes a trivial partial evaluator, e.g. as given by Kleene's original s-m-n construction [149], is uninteresting since in effect it yields target programs of the form 'apply the interpreter to the source program and its input'. On the other hand, mix should ideally remove all *interpretational overhead*.

How can we meaningfully assert that a partial evaluator is 'good enough'? Perhaps surprisingly, a machine-independent answer can be given. This answer involves the mix equation and a *self-interpreter* sint — an interpreter for L which is written in L, as was McCarthy's first Lisp definition. As argued above, the running time of self-interpreter sint will be around $\alpha_p \cdot t_p(d)$; and α_p will be large enough to be worth reducing.

For any program p and input d we have:

$$[\![p]\!]\, d \;=\; [\![\text{sint}]\!]\, p\ d \;=\; [\![[\![\text{mix}]\!]\, \text{sint}\ p]\!]\, d$$

so $p' = [\![\text{mix}]\!]$ sint p is an L-program equivalent to p. This suggests a natural goal: that p′ be at least as efficient as p. Achieving this goal implies that all overhead caused by sint's interpretation has been removed by mix, i.e. α_p has been reduced to 1.

Definition 6.4 mix is *optimal* provided

$$t_{p'}(d) \leq t_p(d)$$

for all p, $d \in D$, where sint is a self-interpreter and

$$p' = [\![\text{mix}]\!]\ \text{sint}\ p$$

□

Although it may seem quite strict, this criterion *has been satisfied* for several partial evaluators for various languages, using natural self-interpreters. In each case, p′ is identical to p up to variable renaming and reordering. An optimal mix will be seen in Chapter 8. On the other hand, the flow chart mix seen earlier is nearly but not quite optimal; see Exercise 6.12.

Note that the definition is not perfect because it can be 'cheated': if mix always outputs its second argument unaltered when its first argument is equal to sint, and performs trivial partial evaluation for all other values of the first argument, then mix is ruled optimal by the definition (and the mix equation still holds).

6.5 Hierarchies of meta-languages

Instead of solving a wide-spectrum problem by writing many special-purpose programs, one may devise a *user-oriented language* to express computational requests. An example is the current interest in developing expert systems.

A user-oriented language needs a processor, and these processors usually work interpretively, alternating between reading and deciphering the user's requests, consulting databases, and doing problem-related computing. Considerable time may be spent interpreting rather than computing or searching, giving obvious opportunities to optimize by partial evaluation. The possibility of alleviating these problems by partial evaluation has been described in several places [62,123,172,234, 260].

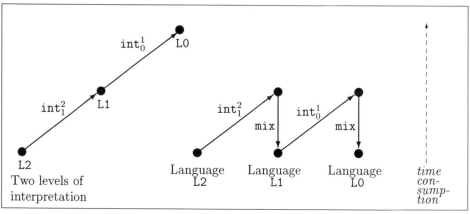

Figure 6.1: Overhead introduction and elimination.

Further, programming systems are often constructed with a hierarchy of meta-languages, each controlling the sequence and choice of operations at the next lower level [234]. In this context, efficiency problems are yet more serious due to the risk of multiple interpretation layers, each multiplying computation time by a significant factor. Assume L2 is executed by an interpreter written in language L1, and that L1 is itself executed by an interpreter written in implementation language L0.

The left hand side of Figure 6.1 depicts the time blowup occurring when running programs in language L2, where using earlier notation the time blowup is $\alpha_1^2 \cdot \alpha_0^1$.

Metaprogramming without order-of-magnitude loss of efficiency

The right side of Figure 6.1 illustrates graphically that partial evaluation can substantially reduce the cost of multiple levels of interpretation. This can be done in at least two ways.

1. A literal interpretation of Figure 6.1 would involve writing two partial evaluators, one for L1 and one for L0. This seems besides the point, which is to execute programs written in language L2 efficiently and with as little effort as possible. Fortunately there is an alternative approach using only *one* partial evaluator, for L0.

2. For concreteness let p2 be an L2-program, and let in, out be representative input and output data. Then

$$\text{out} = [\![\text{int}_0^1]\!]_{\text{L0}} \, [\text{int}_1^2, \, [\text{p2, in}]]$$

3. One may construct an interpreter for L2 written in L0 as follows:

$$\text{int}_0^2 := [\![\text{mix}]\!]_{L0} \, [\text{int}_0^1, \, \text{int}_1^2] \quad \text{satisfying}$$
$$\text{out} = [\![\text{int}_0^2]\!]_{L0} \, [\text{p2, in}]$$

4. By partial evaluation of int_0^2, L2-programs can be compiled to L0-programs. Better still, one may construct a compiler from L2 into L0 by

$$\text{comp}_0^2 := [\![\text{cogen}]\!]_{L0} \, \text{int}_0^2$$

The net effect is that metaprogramming may be used without order-of-magnitude loss of efficiency.

The development above, though conceptually complex, has actually been realized in practice by partial evaluation [71,138,139]. The first two describe how Jørgensen began with an interpreter for denotational semantics, and used partial evaluation to transform denotational definitions into interpreters written in Scheme. An application was to a denotational definition of a Miranda-like lazy programming language with pattern matching. The interpreter generated as in step 3 above was then converted to a compiler as in step 4. The target programs it produces run faster than those produced by a commercial Miranda compiler.

More theoretically, a thesis by Dybkjær concerns the use of category theory as a very general framework for designing programming languages [71]. The framework is constructive but extremely slow to implement directly. Dybkjær used exactly the technique above — partial evaluation of machine-produced programs — to obtain substantial speedups and to allow experiments that would not otherwise have been possible.

6.6   Exercises

Exercise 6.1 Consider a program p that has one input variable x and assume that x is dynamic.

1. Can partial evaluation optimize p?

2. Now assume that the input to p is known to be a one-digit prime number. Describe how this knowledge can be used to achieve better results from partial evaluation and show the structure of the residual program.

3. Could the weaker knowledge that the input would be prime have been exploited in a similar way?

□

Exercise 6.2 Use the algorithm in Section 6.3.3 to determine the speedup interval for the program in Figure 4.2.   □

Exercise 6.3

1. Use the algorithm in Section 6.3.3 to determine the speedup interval for the Turing interpreter in Figure 4.4.

2. What Turing programs bring the actual speedups as close to the upper and lower bounds as possible?

□

Exercise 6.4 Theorem 6.1 places an upper bound on the speedup that can be obtained by partial evaluation. State and prove a theorem about the lower bound. Hint: A 'no slowdown' theorem.   □

Exercise 6.5

1. Is Theorem 6.1 valid for the partial evaluator for Scheme0 as presented in Chapter 5? If not, can supplementary restrictions make it valid?

2. Same question, but for the 'no slowdown' theorem from Exercise 6.4.

□

Exercise 6.6 Formulate the algorithm in Section 6.3.3 for Scheme0 programs.   □

Exercise 6.7 Find an example program which shows that in Definition 6.2 the condition

$$\forall \varepsilon > 0 : \exists k : \forall j > k : \frac{|p(s_j, d_j)|}{|ps_j(d_j)|} \in [u - \varepsilon, v + \varepsilon]$$

is preferable to the simpler

$$\exists k : \forall j > k : \frac{|p(s_j, d_j)|}{|ps_j(d_j)|} \in [u, v]$$

□

Exercise 6.8 In Section 6.3.3 it is stated that $\mathcal{SU}(l_1) \le \mathcal{SU}(l_2) < \infty$, implies:

$$\mathcal{SU}(l_1) \le \mathcal{SU}(l) = \frac{C_s(l) + C_d(l)}{C_d(l)} \le \mathcal{SU}(l_2)$$

Prove it.   □

Exercise 6.9 A meta-interpreter `mint` is a program that takes as input: a specification `spec` for a language S, an S-program `p`, and input data `d`. Then `mint` returns the value of `p` on input `d`.

1. Write the defining equation for `mint`.

2. Demonstrate compiler generation using `mix`, `mint` and `spec`.

3. Demonstrate generation of a program `mcogen` that generates an S-compiler when applied to `spec`.

□

Exercise 6.10 Write a self-interpreter `sint` for the flow chart language (hint: just remove the code generation parts from `mix`, and the division input). □

Exercise 6.11 Annotate this to obtain $sint^{ann}$, assuming the program input is static and the data input is dynamic. Specialize $sint^{ann}$ with respect to a small source program using the flow chart `mix`. □

Exercise 6.12 Is the flow chart `mix` optimal? Explain your answer, and what is lacking if it is not optimal. □

Chapter 7

Online, Offline, and Self-application

This chapter concerns the definition, use, and comparison of online and offline partial evaluation techniques, as described in the next paragraph. All early partial evaluators were online, but offline techniques seem necessary to allow self-application and the generation of program generators (compilers, parser generators, etc.). Both online and offline partial evaluation are still being actively researched, with no conclusion that either one is the best approach.

The partial evaluators seen heretofore are all *offline* as described in Section 4.4.7. This means that they treat their static data in a rather uniform way, based on preprocessing the subject program. The general pattern is that given program p and knowledge of which of its inputs are to be static but *not their values*, an annotated program p^{ann} is constructed (or a division is computed, which amounts to the same thing). Once static data values are available, specialization proceeds by obeying the annotations (e.g. 'compute this', 'generate code for that'). In effect p^{ann} is a program-generating program, and the static data is its input (just this viewpoint is seen in Chapters 5 and 8).

Even though the static data determines the code that is generated, the particular static values computed during partial evaluation have no effect on the choice of actions made by the partial evaluator. Thus an expression x+y, in which x, y have been classified respectively as static and dynamic, will *always* generate code to perform the addition at run time, even in circumstances where y has a known constant as value. In contrast, *online* partial evaluators typically have no preprocessing, make more decisions on the fly, and so are better able to exploit computational opportunities such as the one just given.

In the following we shall mostly use the framework and terminology from Chapter 5, but the content of this chapter applies equally well to other languages.

7.1 Decision making as a prephase?

A partial evaluator typically has to choose an action in the following situations:

1. For each operator (+, if, ...), should/can the operator be reduced at partial evaluation time or should residual code be generated?

2. For each variable/parameter at each program point, should/can it be considered static or should it be dynamic?

3. For each function call/jump should it be unfolded/compressed or should it be residualized?

All offline specializers (to our knowledge) rely on a *prephase* (see Figure 7.1), including binding-time analysis and possibly other analyses, to resolve the problem of choosing the proper actions independently of the concrete static values. (An exception which we will not discuss here is by Glück [98].) Not shown in the figure is the *postphase*, often used by both online and offline specializers to perform last-minute reductions, unfoldings, or other transformations.

Chapters 4 & 5 presented typical offline program specializers. Static and dynamic computations were distinguished by a division or by program annotations constructed independently of the concrete values. Transition compression (Section 4.4.4) was applied everywhere except in the branches of a dynamic conditional statement (dynamic by the division, that is). In Section 5.5 a similar offline unfolding strategy was proposed for Scheme0. Section 5.5.6 suggested a hybrid strategy. The offline part: a call was annotated as 'definitely dynamic' (calld) if it appeared in a branch of a dynamic conditional or if it had a duplicable, non-variable, dynamic actual parameter. The online part: for calls annotated 'perhaps static' (calls) it was tested during specialization whether all duplicable, dynamic parameters would by bound to variables by a possible unfolding. If so, the unfolding would be performed.

Many partial evaluators use a combination of online and offline techniques. Almost all specializers called 'offline' (including those in the previous chapters; Chapter 8 presents an exception) use an online technique to ensure that multiple appearances of the same specialized program point share residual code. Concretely, the manipulation of the sets pending and marked involves comparison of values, and the choice of action depends on the outcome.

7.2 Online and offline expression reduction

In this section we compare the reduction of expressions as performed by online and offline specializers. We compare typical online and offline reduction algorithms and give examples of the advantages of the respective methods. The offline expression

Online partial evaluation is (usually) a one-phase process:

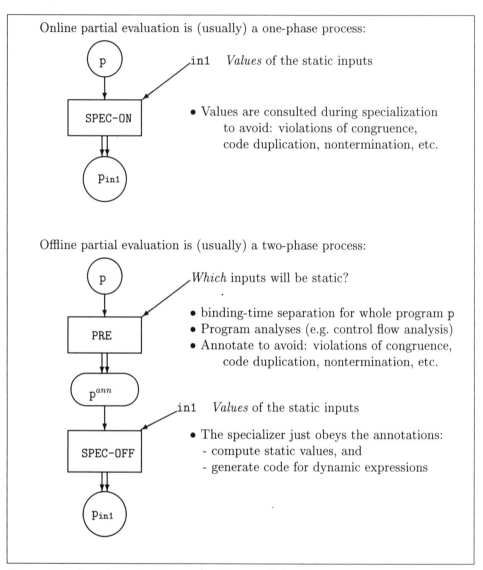

Figure 7.1: Structure of online and offline partial evaluators.

reducer, OffPE, takes an annotated expression (two-level Scheme0, Figure 5.5) as input and is in essence identical to the reduce-function defined in Section 5.4.2. The online expression reducer, OnPE, takes a plain Scheme0 expression as input and reduces it as much as possible.

In OffPE both values and residual expressions are represented as Scheme lists. There is no risk of confusion since the annotated syntax, as opposed to inspection of generated values/expressions, controls the actions of OffPE. This does not hold for OnPE: it is impossible to tell whether the three-element list (+ x y) represents an expression to be reduced or a final value (which could occur if the program to be specialized was a symbolic equation solver). The solution is to introduce *coding* or *tagging* of the data manipulated by OnPE such that the tag distinguishes between values and expressions.

Figure 7.2 shows the functions OnPE and OffPE. For clarity, the specializers are written using syntactic sugar, so to be self-applied they would have to be translated into Scheme0. We use case-expressions with simple pattern matching, double brackets ⟦·⟧ around syntactic objects, and sum injections inVal(...) and inExp(...) as in Section 2.2.3 to tag values and expressions as such in the sum domain On-Value.

The auxiliary function build-cst constructs a residual constant expression from a value ('adds a quote'). The functions build-car, build-cons, etc., construct compound residual expressions, and the functions car, cons, etc., perform the usual computations on ordinary values. Below are the domains of values used in OnPE and OffPE. Again, note that input expressions to OffPE are annotated and that the values computed by OnPE are tagged:

Expression	=	Scheme0 expressions (Figure 5.1)
2Expression	=	Two-level Scheme0 expressions (Figure 5.5)
On-Value	=	inVal Value + inExp Expression
Off-Value	=	Value ∪ Expression
On-Env	=	Var → On-Value
Off-Env	=	Var → Off-Value

Now consult Figure 7.2 to see the fundamental difference: OnPE chooses its action on the basis of input syntax *and* computed values, OffPE only examines input syntax.

7.2.1 Advantages of online methods

The main advantages of online over offline methods stem from their non-approximative distinction between static and dynamic calues.

A safe (offline) binding-time analysis always produces a congruent division, ensuring that there is sufficient information to do static computations. Binding-time improvements allow improvements in binding-time separation as in Chapter 12, but BTA still has to do a 'worst-case' analysis *before* the static input is given. For computability reasons it will inevitably classify some expressions as dynamic even though they may sometimes assume values computable by the specializer.

Online partial evaluators have more information available to inspect for staticness during specialization, to exploit for better binding-time determination. Online partial evaluators can thus perform some static computations which offline strategies would rule dynamic. Below we shall show a couple of examples (for more see

---

Online expression reduction:

```
OnPE: Expression → On-Env → On-Value

OnPE⟦x⟧ρ      = lookup ⟦x⟧ ρ
OnPE⟦car e⟧ρ  = case (OnPE⟦e⟧ρ) of
                           inVal(val): inVal(car val)
                           inExp(re): inExp(build-car re)
OnPE⟦cons e₁ e₂⟧ρ =
  case (OnPE⟦e₁⟧ρ),(OnPE⟦e₂⟧ρ) of
     inVal(v₁),inVal(v₂)  : inVal(cons v₁ v₂)
     inVal(v₁),inExp(re₂) : inExp(build-cons (build-cst v₁) re₂)
     inExp(re₁),inVal(v₂) : inExp(build-cons re₁ (build-cst v₂))
     inExp(re₁),inExp(re₂): inExp(build-cons re₁ re₂)

OnPE⟦if e₁ e₂ e₃⟧ρ =
  case (OnPE⟦e₁⟧ρ) of
     inVal(true) : (OnPE⟦e₂⟧ρ)
     inVal(false): (OnPE⟦e₃⟧ρ)
     inExp(re₁): (build-if re₁ (resid(OnPE⟦e₂⟧ρ))(resid(OnPE⟦e₃⟧ρ)))

resid pv = case pv of
                   inVal(v) : build-cst v
                   inExp(re): re
```

Offline expression reduction:

```
OffPE: 2Expression → Off-Env → Off-Value

OffPE⟦x⟧ρ           = lookup ⟦x⟧ ρ
OffPE⟦card e⟧ρ      = build-car (OffPE⟦e⟧ρ)
OffPE⟦cars e⟧ρ      = car (OffPE⟦e⟧ρ)
OffPE⟦consd e₁ e₂⟧ρ = build-cons (OffPE⟦e₁⟧ρ) (OffPE⟦e₂⟧ρ)
OffPE⟦conss e₁ e₂⟧ρ = cons (OffPE⟦e₁⟧ρ) (OffPE⟦e₂⟧ρ)
OffPE⟦ifd e₁ e₂ e₃⟧ρ = build-if(OffPE⟦e₁⟧ρ)(OffPE⟦e₂⟧ρ) (OffPE⟦e₃⟧ρ)
OffPE⟦ifs e₁ e₂ e₃⟧ρ = if(OffPE⟦e₁⟧ρ)(OffPE⟦e₂⟧ρ)(OffPE⟦e₃⟧ρ)
```

Figure 7.2: Fragments of online and offline partial evaluators

Ruf and Weise [230]).

Greater opportunities for static computation correspondingly increase the risk of non-termination or useless specialization. Examples are given in the literature, explaining the sometimes conservative and usually complex online methods used to avoid infinite unfolding. This should not be held against the online approach, because solution of these problems using an approximative BTA can be even more conservative. The real solution appears to be more powerful program analyses which, although exploited at different times, can improve the results of both online and offline partial evaluators.

Conditionals with mixed binding times

With monovariant BTA an expression must be classified as 'always dynamic' or 'always static'. This can lead to undesired generalization if, say, a function is sometimes called with static and sometimes with dynamic arguments. A polyvariant BTA can often handle this particular problem for offline methods, but other instances of mixed binding times are harder to deal with.

Consider a conditional expression e = (if e_1 e_2 e_3) where e_1 and e_2 are static and e_3 is dynamic. BTA must classify e as dynamic but an online test would discover that e is static if e_1 evaluates to true. If expression e was the argument to a function f, an online partial evaluator could apply the function whenever e_1 was true, but it would take more than just polyvariance to make an offline specializer do that.

In the expression (f (if e_1 e_2 e_3)), polyvariant analysis of function f is of no use because the argument is ruled dynamic by BTA. A transformation to (if e_1 (f e_2) (f e_3)) with subsequent polyvariant analysis would solve the problem. Another possibility is to convert the program to continuation passing style [56].

Static knowledge about 'dynamic' conditionals/calls

Consider a conditional expression e = (if e_1 e_2 e_3) and assume that e_1 is dynamic. Hence the conditional is dynamic and must appear in the residual program. In general, neither offline nor online specializers can infer any static information about the result of the dynamic conditional, but online methods can do this in a special case: when both e_2 and e_3 are static and have common characteristics. The extreme case where e_2 and e_3 have the same value is perhaps uncommon, but the values may have a common structure [230,281]. For example, suppose an interpreter for a language with dynamic typing is to be specialized with respect to a well-typed source program. Tagged values are pairs of type tags and 'raw' values, dynamic choices between tagged values with identical tags are not uncommon. An offline specializer cannot detect this in general because the equality of the tags depends on the well-typedness of the source program.

Very similar remarks apply to dynamic function calls. It can be possible to infer static information about the return value of a function call even though the call is dynamic. In an interpreter for an imperative language with recursive procedures, it could be that the evaluation function for recursive calls should not be unfolded for termination reasons. Still, it is very likely that the return value, an updated store, would have the same *structure* (an array, an association list, etc.) for all possible dynamic inputs. This would be easier to detect in an online specializer.

For offline specializers the pattern is the usual one: there exist binding-time improvements to reclaim some of the lost territory. For an example of tag elimination by offline partial evaluation, see Consel and Danvy [57].

Generating optimizing compilers

Section 7.3 gives detailed reasoning why offline methods lead to efficient self-application, and reading that section might help to clarify the claims below.

The introduction of offline methods made it possible to self-apply partial evaluators, and *compiler generation* has been by far the favourite application for self-applicable partial evaluators. To our knowledge, the generated compilers seen in the literature have in common the fact that they do not perform compile-time optimizations such as constant folding. This is due to the offline strategy: prior to compiler generation by self-application all interpreter actions are classified as either compile-time (= static) or run-time (= dynamic). The classification is done at compiler generation time and is thus source program independent. This contradicts the idea of constant folding which is to evaluate expressions which are *variable independent*, a property which holds for some source programs and not for others.

Switching to pure online techniques is no real solution because compilers generated by self-application of an online specializer are large and slow. We believe that the solution is to find a compromise between offline and online methods, as suggested by,for example, Bondorf [26]. Ruf and Weise [230] have taken a step in another direction and used a *strong and large* online specializer to specialize a *weaker and simpler* online specializer with respect to an interpreter thus obtaining compiler generation [230].

7.2.2   Advantages of offline methods

Offline partial evaluation was invented in 1984 and made self-application of partial evaluators feasible in practice [135]. It was realized as early as 1971 that it would in principle be possible to generate compilers by self-application, but all computer experiments achieved little apart from using enormous amounts of memory and disk space. Section 7.3 shows in detail why the offline technique leads to compact and efficient compilers; here we will review other advantages of offline partial evaluation.

Problem factorization

The component of an offline partial evaluator that performs the reduction of the annotated program (= function OffPE in Figure 7.2) is often called the *specialization kernel*. The other principal component in an offline partial evaluator is the BTA. The splitting of partial evaluation into two separate phases has proven helpful in both the design and implementation phases of several partial evaluation projects. (Section 7.4 presents a recipe which has been successfully followed a number of times.)

Much research in the field has been concentrated on the phases *one at a time*, and this has contributed to a better understanding of central problems in partial evaluation. A specialization kernel can be tested without BTA by supplying suitable annotations manually, and the results of a new BTA can be evaluated by inspecting the annotations it produces.

Efficiency
Given recent developments in BTA technology (work by Henglein, see [114] and Chapter 8), the offline approach BTA + specialization kernel is also more efficient than online. The reason is obvious by inspection of Figure 7.2: for each reduction or code generation step OnPE does twice as much testing as OffPE in addition to the overhead introduced by tagging all values.

Fast multistage specialization
Specializing the specializer can speed up the partial evaluation process. (An analogy: compilation followed by target code execution can be faster than interpretation.) If the specialized specializer is used several times, the gain can be substantial.

Fast multistage specialization follows the scheme below. BTA is the binding-time analyser, SPEC is the annotated specialization kernel.

1.	p^{ann}	:=	$[\![\text{BTA}]\!]\ \text{p}$	Preprocessing time
2.	p-gen	:=	$[\![\text{mix}]\!]\,[\,\text{SPEC},\ \text{p}^{ann}\,]$	
3.	p_{in1}	:=	$[\![\text{p-gen}]\!]\ \text{in1}$	Specialization time
4.	output	:=	$[\![\text{p}_{in1}]\!]\ \text{in2}$	Run time

The main goal is to make stage 4 fast, i.e. to generate a good specialized program. The second goal is to make stage 3 fast, i.e. to specialize fast. It is not a problem if Stages 1 and 2 are slow, if that speeds up stage 3: the result is slow generation of a good specializer, and the generation is performed only once.

As the table indicates, the automatically generated specializer p-gen contains no preprocessing. A special case is generation of a compiler comp = int-gen from an interpreter int.

Binding-time annotations as a user interface
Explicit binding times in the form of divisions or annotations have been used in several tools that are useful to the user of a partial evaluator. The binding-time analyser itself can be considered such a tool because the annotations allow the user to see whether the program has the desired binding-time properties. If the analysed program were an interpreter, something is probably rotten if the interpreter's program argument is classified as dynamic. This would be *much* easier to detect by inspection of an annotated interpreter than by inspection of a residual program produced by a partial evaluator.

A refinement of this idea is the *binding-time debugger*, which is roughly a stepwise binding-time analysis, allowing the user to see more clearly when things 'go wrong' [60,196].

Annotated programs can also be used to estimate the feasibility of partial evaluation. One example is the automatic speedup analysis presented in Section 6.3. In Chapter 13 the classes of 'oblivious' and 'weakly oblivious' programs are defined in terms of binding-time properties of programs (restrictions on the dynamic conditionals). The class of oblivious programs will be seen to yield compact, linear residual programs.

Program analysis

Binding-time analysis is often combined with other program analyses to satisfy other requirements than just congruence. Typical goals are to achieve finiteness, to avoid computation duplication, and to avoid specialization with respect to dead static variables. Though it is natural to combine these analyses with plain binding-time analysis, they are not all dependent on the availability of binding-time information. An example is liveness analysis, which can be used by online partial evaluators as well. The online partial evaluator then uses the rule: 'dead variables are definitely dynamic and live variables are checked online as usual', which achieves the same beneficial generalization as the offline partial evaluator without sacrificing the online potential.

On the other hand, some analyses do depend on binding-time information. An example is Holst's *poor man's generalization*, which is a refinement of liveness analysis: a variable should be generalized if no control decisions depend on its value [116]. This is clearly a combination of liveness and binding-time analysis.

Online partial evaluators often test a large part of the computation history to determine whether the partial evaluator is possibly entering an infinite loop. If a certain 'danger criterion' (e.g. a growing parameter in a recursive function) is observed, then an online generalization is performed [235,281]. Offline partial evaluators cannot, by definition, do this. At best the binding-time analysis can be refined to classify, *in advance*, enough variables as dynamic to ensure finiteness. This requires a more complicated program analysis (see Chapter 14).

In general, the use of various program analyses is much more widespread in the offline than in the online community. This must be so by definition for certain kinds of analyses (BTA, poor man's generalization [116]), but the differences in culture seem to matter too. We feel that there is good use for program analysis in online partial evaluators.

7.2.3   Which 'line' is better?

Clearly, it is impossible to say which is best: online or offline partial evaluation. Above we listed a number of advantages of the respective methods, but it depends greatly on the concrete problem to solve by partial evaluation how the advantages should be weighted. It would be hard to make general statements about this, and it would be more fruitful to study how the two schools of partial evaluation can learn from each other.

A compromise strategy, *mixline partial evaluation*, results from augmenting the usual binding-time domain, $\{S,D\}$, with a third binding time M. Now S should be interpreted as 'always static' as usual, D should mean 'always dynamic' as opposed to the usual 'sometimes dynamic', and the new binding time M means 'mixed binding times' to be tested online. This idea is not new (e.g. [26,53]), but large scale experiments have not been reported.

As briefly mentioned above we feel that many of the program analyses often used in offline partial evaluators would also be useful in the online world. Examples include: liveness, duplication, control flow, and termination.

7.3   BTA and the taming of self-application

In this section we argue that it is no accident that only offline specializers have been successfully self-applied. By 'successfully' we mean that the resulting program generators (typically compilers) have been reasonably *small* and *efficient*. Self-application of online specializers is of course possible in principle, but all such experiments have yielded large and slow program generators. For example, Lars Ole Andersen changed the offline partial evaluator described in [136] into being online. The generated compilers then became around 2 to 3 times larger in code size and 2 to 6 times slower.

In this section we make a case study of compilation and compiler generation by online partial evaluation. We find that result of compiler generation is not satisfactory and show how offline partial evaluation provides a simple solution.

7.3.1   Compilation by online partial evaluation

Let us compile program `source` by computing `target` $= [\![\mathtt{mix}]\!]_\mathrm{L}$ `[int, source]`, where `int` interprets an imperative language. We use the online partial evaluator `OnPE` as our `mix`-program. Assume that the following expression appears in the interpreter `int`:

```
E = (cons (car names) (car values))
```

The role of this part of the interpreter is to bind a source program name to its run time value, where `names` and `values` are interpreter variables: `names` is a list of variable names from `source` and `values` is a list of values bound to these. The important thing to note is that `names` and `values` have *different* binding times. The value of `names` can be computed given `source` alone, but the value of `values` cannot.

At specialization time the symbolic environment ρ in the `OnPE` may bind the interpreter's variable `names` to the On-Value `inVal((a b c))`, say, and the interpreter's variable `values` to the `On-Value inExp(exp)`, where `exp` is some residual expression. Here `a`, `b`, and `c` correspond to variable names from the interpreted program `source`.

The value of $\text{OnPE}[\![E]\!]\rho$ is the specialized version of the interpreter fragment E = `(cons (car names) (car values))`. In concrete residual syntax this could be written:

```
(cons (quote a) (car exp))
```

7.3.2 Self-application of an online partial evaluator

By the second Futamura projection, $\text{mix}_{int} = [\![\text{mix}]\!]_{L}$ [mix,int] is a compiler from the language interpreted by `int` into L. We shall consider operationally what happens when we apply the program specializer `mix` to itself in this manner, with `int` being the interpreter discussed above.

Consider again the expression E = `(cons (car names) (car values))`. This expression is part of `int`, and function `OnPE` in `mix` deals with expressions, so the compiler mix_{int} contains the result of specializing the function `OnPE` with respect to E. This compiler fragment is shown in Figure 7.3[1]. Compare this specialized `OnPE` with the original `OnPE` shown in Figure 7.2. The dispatch on the input expression syntax has been reduced away by the program specialization, but the `case`-expressions testing for staticness have completely dynamic arguments and hence they appear in the specialized `OnPE`.

We make two observations on this compiler. The first observation is the lack of distinction between binding times. The compiler treats all parts of the expression from the interpreter alike, although some parts are always 'compile time' and others always 'run time'. This behaviour is inherited from the online `mix` program, which handles both static and dynamic expressions by the `OnPE` function. This function can return both values and residual expressions, injected into the domain `On-Value`: values (`inVal(...)`) for static arguments and residual expressions (`inExp(...)`) for dynamic arguments. However, in the running compiler, the value of lookup_{names} will actually always have the form `inVal(v)`. Hence (`reduce-car` (lookup_{names} ρ)) will always evaluate to a constant value `inVal(...)`. This can be inferred at compiler generation time — and that is precisely the goal of using explicit binding-time information.

The second observation concerns excessive generality. The compiler fragment above can be used to specialize `int` in at least two ways. First, it can generate the usual target program `target` when given a source program but not the source program's input. Second, it could generate a strange 'target' program `crazy` when given as static data the input data to the source program, but not the source

---

[1]Many immaterial details, e.g. unfolding strategy, are left unspecified about the online partial evaluator used here. For readability, we have introduced two functions `reduce-car` and `reduce-cons` in the generated compiler.

```
OnPE(cons (car names) (car values)): On-Env → On-Value

OnPE(cons (car names) (car values)) ρ =
    reduce-cons (reduce-car (lookupnames ρ)) (reduce-car (lookupvalues ρ))

reduce-car: On-Value → On-Value
reduce-car pv =
    case pv of
        inVal(v): inVal(car v)
        inExp(e): inExp(build-car(e))

reduce-cons: On-Value → On-Value → On-Value
reduce-cons pv1 pv2 =
    case pv1,pv2 of
        inVal(v1),inVal(v2)  : inVal(cons v1 v2)
        inVal(v1),inExp(re2) : inExp(build-cons (build-cst v1) re2)
        inExp(re1),inVal(v2) : inExp(build-cons re1 (build-cst v2))
        inExp(re1),inExp(re2): inExp(build-cons re1 re2)
```

Figure 7.3: A fragment of an overly general compiler.

program itself! The resulting program would take a source program and produce the result of running the source program on the given input data:

$$[\![\text{crazy}]\!]_L \text{ source} = [\![\text{int}]\!]_L [\text{source},\text{data}] = [\![\text{source}]\!]_S \text{ data} = \text{output}$$

This compiler feature is a very useless one. Conclusion: the compiler mix_{int} is *much more general* than necessary.

The generality of the compiler mix_{int} is due to the lack of distinction between interpreter actions traditionally done at compile time (syntax analysis, environment manipulation, etc.) and those traditionally done at run time (evaluating source program expressions, etc.). Each time mix meets a cons operator, for example, it will decide online whether it is doing a compile time action or a run time action, and the compiler generated from the online mix inherits this behaviour.

To get the efficiency of traditional compilation, the expression (car names) in the interpreter fragment should be evaluated directly by the compiler since this is an instance of environment manipulation. On the other hand, residual code for (car values) should be generated directly by the compiler. In neither case should it bother to check whether or not the values are constant.

7.3.3 Removing generality by annotations

Below mix_1 and mix_2 may or may not be identical. The indexes are introduced for easier reference only.

During compiler generation

$$comp = [\![mix_1]\!]_L \, [mix_2, int]$$

mix_2 is partially evaluated with respect to incomplete input, int. Recall that mix_2 constantly tests whether the partial values are constants inVal(...) or residual expressions inExp(...), and that these tests are dynamic and appear in the generated compiler. This is *intuitively* wrong because it should be known *at compiler generation time* that the syntactic dispatch in the interpreter will be static at *compilation time*. To make these tests static in mix_2, extra information must be supplied because there is no way a priory that mix_2 can infer that comp should produce *only* normal target programs and no crazy programs as shown above.

The interpreter int has two arguments, source and data, and mix_2 must know that the compiler is *only* intended for application to source. One convenient way to communicate this information to mix_2 is to *annotate* the actions of int as either static or dynamic. This makes the binding times of int apparent as *syntax*,[2] and the syntactic dispatch in mix_2 is certainly reduced by mix_1.

The claim is thus that mix_2 should be an offline partial evaluator and that accordingly int should be annotated. In the annotated interpreter, int^{ann}, the annotated version of the subexpression E considered above, would be:

```
(consd (lift (cars names)) (card values))
```

Recall from the beginning of Section 7.2 that the Off-Values handled by OffPE are untagged. It is the correctness of the annotations ensures that lookup returns a constant value when applied to names and a residual expression when applied to names.

Let offmix be an offline partial evaluator which uses OffPE to reduce expressions. Consider generation of a compiler from the annotated interpreter int^{ann} by computing $[\![offmix]\!]_L \, [offmix^{ann}, int^{ann}]$. The decisions in $offmix^{ann}$ whether to do evaluation or to generate code will *not* depend on $offmix^{ann}$'s unavailable input (the source program source), but only on the annotations in the interpreter. Thus the decision can be made when the compiler is generated and need not be made anew every time the compiler is applied to a source program.

A fragment of the compiler is given in Figure 7.4. We see that it simply generates code, as expected of a compiler. It does not contain any tests on residual expressions as did the corresponding fragment of the mix-generated compiler in Figure 7.3; it is definitely shorter and quite a lot faster. So the use of binding-time annotations is indeed be very beneficial.

---

[2]Equipping the interpreter with an explicit division for each function would have the same effect.

OffPE$_{(\text{cons (car names) (car values)})}$: 2Environment $\rightarrow$ Exp

OffPE$_{(\text{cons (car names) (car values)})}$ ρ =
   build-cons(build-cst(car(lookup$_{\text{names}}$ ρ)))(build-car(lookup$_{\text{values}}$ ρ))

Figure 7.4: A fragment of a compiler generated by offline partial evaluation.

One might note that OffPE does not always produce exactly the same residual expressions as OnPE does. Given another interpreter fragment, OffPE might produce a residual expression such as (build-+ (build-cst 1) (build-cst 2)) — if the + expression leading to this were a run time action according to the annotations. The function OnPE would reduce this to (build-cst 3), but the experiments performed so far have shown that this rarely occurs when OffPE is used for compiling. Furthermore, since most operations in an interpreter are compile time actions, extending OffPE by adding reductions on dynamic data would not increase the size (or decrease the speed) of the compiler dramatically, and it would then give the same result as OnPE, as also mentioned in Section 7.2.3.

Compiler generation is just one application where binding-time information gives a speedup in self-application. The essential point is that self-application *stages* programs. Self-application is analogous to applying cogen. Annotations attached to a program expression contain information on how to stage the expression: when the annotation says 'static', cogen produces a program piece which, when executed, evaluates the expression. When the annotation says 'dynamic', cogen produces an expression which, when executed, generates residual code.

7.4 A recipe for self-application

Constructing a self-applicable partial evaluator for a new language is a tricky task and one that may require several iterations, both to refine the subject language and to develop methods sufficient to specialize it well. Following is a pattern that we have found to work well in practice, using offline specialization. There are, however, always unexpected complications for each new language.

The recipe suggests that a self-interpreter is written as the first programming step. We first explain why this starting point is so very appropriate for constructing program generators by the second Futamura projection:

   p-gen = [[mix]] mix p

The reasoning, well supported by practical experience, is as follows.

- Getting [[mix]] mix p to give good results, or any at all, is very tricky.

- Advice by Polya: to solve a hard problem, first solve a *similar but simpler* problem. Then generalize the simpler problem's solution.

- Related observation: in order to be able to perform its static computations, a non-trivial mix must contain a self-interpreter. Call this sint.

- Thus a simple problem similar to obtaining p-gen = $[\![\,\text{mix}\,]\!]$ mix p is to compute

$$\text{p}' = [\![\,\text{mix}\,]\!] \text{ sint p}$$

- An good solution to this problem is the 'optimality' criterion of Section 6.4, that p′ should essentially be identical to p. If one cannot at least make p′ very similar to p, an efficient $[\![\,\text{mix}\,]\!]$ mix p will be hard or impossible to construct.

The recipe

1. Think carefully through general questions, particularly:

   - What is known data, and what is unknown?
   - Can each variable be thought of as completely static or completely dynamic, or are partially static and dynamic values needed?
   - What is a specialized program point?

2. Write a clean self-interpreter sint, perhaps for a small subset of the language.

3. Use *ad hoc* hand methods to see how it could be specialized to some *very* simple program p.

4. Devise a set of annotations, such as the s/d annotations used in Chapter 5 or the underlines from Chapter 8. These give extra information attached to parts of a subject program, so specialization can be done as follows:

   - **do** (perform, evaluate, execute) those parts annotated as mix-time (e.g. evaluate static expressions, unfold function calls, etc.);
   - **generate code** for those parts annotated as run-time.

5. See whether you can annotate the program p of step 3 and get the right specialized program (again by hand).

6. Annotate the self-interpreter.

7. Program a specializer to behave as in step 4, not necessarily written in the same language.

8. Use it to specialize the annotated self-interpreter to various simple programs; and then to itself. If the optimality criterion is not violated too much, all the hardest hurdles have been cleared.

9. Program a specializer to behave as in step 4, in the language being specialized.

10. Introspect on the way the annotations were added, and devise a way to do as much as possible of it by machine.

11. Try ⟦mix⟧ mix p for various p.

Warning: high-level control constructs such as while loops, pattern matching, and some deeply nested constructions can give problems. It is important to cut the language down to the bare bones before beginning, otherwise much time will be wasted on problems that distract attention from the hard central core of the exercise, especially steps 2 to 6. In our experience, many of these problems are easily cleared up in retrospect after the core is working, and many more can be dealt with by liberal usage of 'syntactic sugaring' and 'desugaring', done using the computer to translate into and out of a rudimentary core language.

Final Comment. This approach provides a very convenient factorization of the problem:

1. What should the annotations be? This is a problem of *expressiveness* — they must contain sufficient information to be able to do specialization. The solution is often a two-level syntax, e.g. as used in Chapters 4, 5, 8, and in [202] by Nielson and Nielson.

2. How can one find appropriate annotations? This is a *program analysis* problem, solvable by abstract interpretation or type inference. Consult the material on binding-time analysis found in this book.

7.5   Exercises

Exercise 7.1 Write a simple online partial evaluator for Scheme0. Compare it to the offline partial evaluator in Chapter 5 in the following areas: quality of residual programs, partial evaluation-time efficiency, termination properties, and unfolding strategy.   □

Exercise 7.2 Write a simple online partial evaluator for flow charts, as done in Chapter 4. Compare it to the offline partial evaluator in Chapter 4 in the following areas: quality of residual programs, partial evaluation-time efficiency, termination properties, unfolding strategy.   □

Exercise 7.3 In Section 7.2.3 mixline, a compromise between offline and online, is suggested. Define the domains to be used by a mixline expression reducer and then define the mixline expression reducer itself.   □

Exercise 7.4 Consider the residual program in Figure 4.5. What residual program would be generated by a simple online partial evaluator which reduces and unfolds whenever possible?   □

Exercise 7.5 A general parser gen-parser is a program that, given a grammar and a character string, returns a parse tree:

parse-tree = [[gen-parser]]$_L$ grammar char-string

1. Show how to use a partial evaluator mix to generate a parser and a parser generator.

2. Will it make a difference to the structures of the parser and the parser generator whether mix is offline or online?

□

Part III

Partial Evaluation for Stronger Languages

Chapter 8

Partial Evaluation for the Lambda Calculus

This chapter describes partial evaluation for the lambda calculus (Section 3.2), augmented with an explicit fixed-point operator. The techniques used here diverge from those used in Chapters 4 and 5 in that they are not based on specialization of *named* program points. The algorithm essentially leaves some operators (applications, lambdas, etc.) untouched and reduces others as standard evaluation would do it. This simple scheme is able to handle programs that rely heavily on higher-order facilities. The requirements on binding-time analysis are formulated via a type system and an efficient binding-time analysis via constraint solving is outlined. The partial evaluator is proven correct.

History and recent developments
Self-applicable partial evaluation was first achieved in 1984 for a simple first-order functional language. This promising result was not immediately extendable to a higher-order language, the reason being that a specializer, given incomplete input data, in effect traces all possible program control flow paths and computes as many static values as possible. This seemed hard to do, since flow analysis of programs that manipulate functions as data values is non–trivial.

Breakthroughs occurred independently in 1989 by Bondorf (then at Dortmund) and by Gomard and Jones (Copenhagen). The latter, called *Lambdamix* and the subject of this chapter, is conceptually simpler, theoretically motivated, and has been proven correct. Bondorf's work is more pragmatically oriented, led to the now widely distributed system Similix, and is the subject of Chapter 10.

In common with the partial evaluators of earlier chapters, Lambdamix represents the concrete syntax of programs as constants (in fact Lisp S-expressions are used, though this is not essential). The natural question of whether partial evaluation is meaningful and possible in the classical *pure* lambda calculus without constants has recently been answered affirmatively.

Briefly: Mogensen devised a quite efficient self-interpreter for the pure lambda calculus, using 'higher-order abstract syntax' to encode lambda expressions as normal form lambda expressions. These are not difficult to interpret and even to specialize, although they are rather hard for humans to decipher. The ideas were later extended to give a self-applicable partial evaluator for the same language, using essentially the two level type system to be seen in this chapter. The partial evaluator was implemented, self-application gave the usual speedups, and it has since been proven correct by Wand using the technique of 'logical relations' [191,279].

8.1   The lambda calculus and self-interpretation

The classical lambda calculus (extended with constants, conditionals, and a fixpoint operator) is used here for simplicity and to allow a more complete treatment than would be possible for a larger and more practical language.

A lambda calculus program is an *expression*, e, together with an initial *environment*, ρ, which is a function from identifiers to values. The program takes its input through its free variables. The expression syntax given below differs from that of Section 3.2 in that we have introduced an explicit fixed-point operator.

⟨Lam⟩	::=	⟨Constant⟩	Constants
	|	⟨Var⟩	Variables
	|	λ⟨Var⟩.⟨Lam⟩	Abstraction
	|	⟨Lam⟩ ⟨Lam⟩	Application
	|	fix ⟨Lam⟩	Fixed point operator
	|	if ⟨Lam⟩ then ⟨Lam⟩ else ⟨Lam⟩	Conditional
	|	⟨Op⟩ ⟨Lam⟩ ... ⟨Lam⟩	Base application
⟨Var⟩	::=	any identifier	

Examples of relevant base functions include =, *, cons, etc. The fixed-point operator fix computes the least fixed point of its argument and is used to define recursive functions. For example, a program computing x^n can be defined by

```
(fix λp.λn'.λx'.
   if (= n' 0)
   then 1
   else (* x' (p (- n' 1) x'))) n x
```

Note that fix λf.e is equivalent to the Scheme constructs (rec f e) and (letrec ((f e)) f). Why introduce an explicit fixed-point operator instead of using the Y-combinator written as a lambda expression (Section 3.2.6) to express recursion? This is because an explicit fix allows a simpler binding-time analysis.

As a first step towards partial evaluation we show a self-interpreter for the lambda calculus in Figure 8.1. Below we explain the notation used in Figure 8.1 and the remainder the chapter.

Value domains

$$
\begin{aligned}
v : Val &= Const + Funval \\
Funval &= Val \rightarrow Val \\
\rho : Env &= Var \rightarrow Val
\end{aligned}
$$

$\mathcal{E}$: *Expression* $\rightarrow$ *Env* $\rightarrow$ *Val*

$$
\begin{aligned}
\mathcal{E}[\![\texttt{c}]\!]\rho &= \mathcal{V}[\![\texttt{c}]\!]\uparrow Const \\
\mathcal{E}[\![\texttt{var}]\!]\rho &= \rho(\texttt{var}) \\
\mathcal{E}[\![\lambda\texttt{var.e}]\!]\rho &= (\lambda value.(\mathcal{E}[\![\texttt{e}]\!]\rho[\texttt{var} \mapsto value]))\uparrow Funval \\
\mathcal{E}[\![\texttt{e}_1\ \texttt{e}_2]\!]\rho &= (\mathcal{E}[\![\texttt{e}_1]\!]\rho{\downarrow}Funval)\ (\mathcal{E}[\![\texttt{e}_2]\!]\rho) \\
\mathcal{E}[\![\texttt{fix e}]\!]\rho &= fix\ (\mathcal{E}[\![\texttt{e}]\!]\rho{\downarrow}Funval) \\
\mathcal{E}[\![\texttt{if e}_1\ \texttt{then e}_2\ \texttt{else e}_3]\!]\rho &= (\mathcal{E}[\![\texttt{e}_1]\!]\rho{\downarrow}Const) \rightarrow \mathcal{E}[\![\texttt{e}_2]\!]\rho,\ \mathcal{E}[\![\texttt{e}_3]\!]\rho \\
\mathcal{E}[\![\texttt{op e}_1\ldots\ \texttt{e}_n]\!] &= (\mathcal{O}[\![\texttt{op}]\!]\ (\mathcal{E}[\![\texttt{e}_1]\!]\rho{\downarrow}Const) \\
&\qquad \ldots\ (\mathcal{E}[\![\texttt{e}_n]\!]\rho{\downarrow}Const))\uparrow Const
\end{aligned}
$$

Figure 8.1: Lambda calculus self-interpreter.

Notation
Const is a 'flat' domain of constants large enough to include concrete syntax representations of lambda expressions (as input to and output from mix) and booleans for use in conditionals. As in earlier chapters (and in our implementation) a suitable choice is the set of Lisp S-expressions. Further, we assume there are enough base functions to test equality, and to compose and decompose abstract syntax.

The separated sum of domains *Const* and *Funval* is written *Val* = *Const* + *Funval*. Given an element $b \in Const$, $v = b{\uparrow}Const \in Val$ is tagged as originating from *Const*. In SML or Miranda this would be written $v = Const\ b$. We have introduced the $\uparrow$ notation for symmetry with $v{\downarrow}Const$. This strips off the tag yielding an element in *Const* if v is tagged as originating from *Const*. If v has any other tag, then $v{\downarrow}Const$ produces an error.

We assume that all operations are strict in the error value but omit details. The domain *Funval* = *Val* $\rightarrow$ *Val* contains partial functions from *Val* to *Val*. Function $\mathcal{V}$ computes the value (in *Const*) of a constant expression (in *Exp*). Function $\mathcal{O}$ links names to base functions. The notation $\rho[\texttt{var} \mapsto value]$ is, as in Section 2.1, a shorthand for $\lambda \texttt{x.if}\ (\texttt{x=var})\ \texttt{then}\ value\ \texttt{else}\ (\rho\ \texttt{x})$ and is used to update environments. Expression $v_1 \rightarrow v_2,\ v_3$ has the value v_2 if v_1 equals *true* and value v_3 if v_1 equals *false*, else the error value.

Since we use lambda calculus both as an object level programming language and as a meta-language, we distinguish notationally between the two for clarity. Object level lambda expressions are written in `typewriter` style: `e e`, `λvar.e`, `fix e` etc., and the meta-language is in *italics*: *e e*, $\lambda var.e$, *fix e* etc.

The self-interpreter

The structure of the self-interpreter is not much different from that of the lambda calculus interpreter written in ML and presented in Section 3.3.1. First-order structures have been replaced by functions in two places:

- The environment is implemented by a *function* from variables to values. Looking up the value of a variable var thus amounts to applying the environment ρ. This replaces the parallel lists of names and values seen in the interpreters from earlier chapters.

- The value of an abstraction λvar.e is a *function* which, when applied to an argument value, evaluates e in an extended environment binding var to the value. The value of an application e_1 e_2 is found by applying the value of e_1, which must be a function, to the value of e_2. This mechanism replaces the use of explicit closures.

It should be clear that, despite the extensive use of syntactic sugar, Figure 8.1 does define a self-interpreter, as the function $\mathcal{E}$ can easily be transformed into a lambda expression: fix $\lambda\mathcal{E}.\lambda e.\lambda\rho.\text{if } \dots$.

8.2   Partial evaluation using a two-level lambda calculus

As in the previous chapters we divide the task of partial evaluation into two phases: *first* we apply binding-time analysis, which yields a suitably annotated program, *then* reduce the static parts, blindly obeying the annotations. An annotated program is a two-level lambda expression. The two-level lambda calculus has two different versions of each of the following constructions: application, abstraction, conditionals, fixed points, and base function applications. One version is *dynamic*, the other is *static*. The static operators are those of the standard lambda calculus: if, fix, λ, etc. and the dynamic operators are underlined: $\underline{\text{if}}$, $\underline{\text{fix}}$, $\underline{\lambda}$, $\underline{@}$. ($\underline{@}$ denotes a dynamic application.) The abstract syntax of two-level expressions is given in Figure 8.2.

Intuitively, all static operators λ, $@$, $\dots$ are treated by the partial evaluator as they were treated by the self-interpreter. The result of evaluating a dynamic operator ($\underline{\lambda}$, $\underline{@}$, $\dots$) is to produce a piece of *code* for execution at run-time — a constant which is the concrete syntax representation of a residual one-level lambda expression, perhaps with free variables.

The lift operator also builds code — a constant expression with the same value as lift's argument. The operator lift is applied to static subexpressions of a dynamic expression.

A two-level *program* is a two-level expression te together with an initial environment ρ_s which maps the free variables of te to constants, functions, or code pieces. We shall assume that free dynamic variables are mapped to distinct, new variable

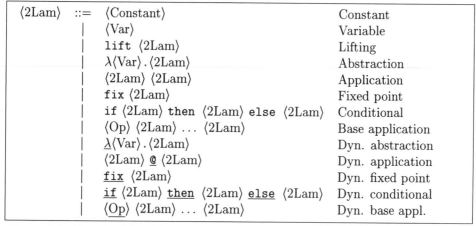

⟨2Lam⟩	::=	⟨Constant⟩	Constant
	|	⟨Var⟩	Variable
	|	lift ⟨2Lam⟩	Lifting
	|	λ⟨Var⟩.⟨2Lam⟩	Abstraction
	|	⟨2Lam⟩ ⟨2Lam⟩	Application
	|	fix ⟨2Lam⟩	Fixed point
	|	if ⟨2Lam⟩ then ⟨2Lam⟩ else ⟨2Lam⟩	Conditional
	|	⟨Op⟩ ⟨2Lam⟩ ... ⟨2Lam⟩	Base application
	|	λ̲⟨Var⟩.⟨2Lam⟩	Dyn. abstraction
	|	⟨2Lam⟩ @̲ ⟨2Lam⟩	Dyn. application
	|	fix̲ ⟨2Lam⟩	Dyn. fixed point
	|	if̲ ⟨2Lam⟩ then̲ ⟨2Lam⟩ else̲ ⟨2Lam⟩	Dyn. conditional
	|	⟨Op̲⟩ ⟨2Lam⟩ ... ⟨2Lam⟩	Dyn. base appl.

Figure 8.2: Two-level lambda calculus syntax.

names. The $\mathcal{T}$-rules (Figure 8.3) then ensure that these new variables become the free variables of the residual program.

Variables bound by $\underline{\lambda}$, will also (eventually) generate fresh variable names in the residual program, whereas variables bound by λ can be bound at specialization time to all kinds of values: constants, functions, or code pieces.

The $\mathcal{T}$-rule for a dynamic application is

$$\mathcal{T}[\![te_1 \ \underline{@} \ te_2]\!]\rho = \textit{build-@}(\mathcal{T}[\![te_1]\!]\rho{\downarrow}\textit{Code}, \mathcal{T}[\![te_2]\!]\rho{\downarrow}\textit{Code}){\uparrow}\textit{Code}$$

The recursive calls $\mathcal{T}[\![te_1]\!]\rho$ and $\mathcal{T}[\![te_2]\!]\rho$ produce the code for residual operator and operand expressions, and the function *build-@* 'glues' them together to form an application to appear in the residual program (concretely, an expression of the form (te$_1$' te$_2$')). All the *build*-functions are strict.

The projections ($\downarrow$*Code*) check that both operator and operand reduce to code pieces, to avoid applying specialization time operations (e.g. boolean tests) to residual program pieces. Finally, the newly composed expression is tagged ($\uparrow$*Code*) as being a piece of code.

The $\mathcal{T}$-rule for variables is

$$\mathcal{T}[\![var]\!]\rho = \rho(var)$$

The environment ρ is expected to hold the values of all variables regardless of whether they are predefined constants, functions, or code pieces. The environment is updated in the usual way in the rule for static λ, and in the rule for $\underline{\lambda}$, the formal parameter is bound to an as yet unused variable name, which we assume available whenever needed:

$$\mathcal{T}[\![\underline{\lambda}var.te]\!]\rho = \textbf{let } nvar = \textit{newname}(var)$$
$$\textbf{in } \textit{build-}\underline{\lambda}(nvar, \mathcal{T}[\![te]\!]\rho[var \mapsto nvar]{\downarrow}\textit{Code}){\uparrow}\textit{Code}$$

Two-level value domains

$$
\begin{aligned}
\mathit{2Val} &= \mathit{Const} + \mathit{2Funval} + \mathit{Code} \\
\mathit{2Funval} &= \mathit{2Val} \rightarrow \mathit{2Val} \\
\mathit{Code} &= \mathit{Expression} \\
\mathit{2Env} &= \mathit{Var} \rightarrow \mathit{2Val}
\end{aligned}
$$

$\mathcal{T}: \mathit{2Expression} \rightarrow \mathit{2Env} \rightarrow \mathit{2Val}$

$$
\begin{aligned}
\mathcal{T}[\![c]\!]\rho &= \mathcal{V}[\![c]\!]\!\uparrow\! \mathit{Const} \\
\mathcal{T}[\![\texttt{var}]\!]\rho &= \rho(\texttt{var}) \\
\mathcal{T}[\![\texttt{lift te}]\!]\rho &= \textit{build-const}(\mathcal{T}[\![\texttt{te}]\!]\rho\!\downarrow\! \mathit{Const})\!\uparrow\! \mathit{Code}
\end{aligned}
$$

$$
\begin{aligned}
\mathcal{T}[\![\lambda\texttt{var.te}]\!]\rho &= (\lambda \mathit{value}.(\mathcal{T}[\![\texttt{te}]\!]\ \rho[\texttt{var} \mapsto \mathit{value}]))\!\uparrow\! \mathit{2Funval} \\
\mathcal{T}[\![\texttt{te}_1\ \texttt{te}_2]\!]\rho &= \mathcal{T}[\![\texttt{te}_1]\!]\rho\!\downarrow\! \mathit{2Funval}\ (\mathcal{T}[\![\texttt{te}_2]\!]\rho) \\
\mathcal{T}[\![\texttt{fix te}]\!]\rho &= \mathit{fix}\ (\mathcal{T}[\![\texttt{te}]\!]\rho\!\downarrow\! \mathit{2Funval}) \\
\mathcal{T}[\![\texttt{if te}_1\ \texttt{then te}_2\ \texttt{else te}_3]\!]\rho & \\
&= \mathcal{T}[\![\texttt{te}_1]\!]\rho\!\downarrow\! \mathit{Const} \rightarrow \mathcal{T}[\![\texttt{te}_2]\!]\rho,\ \mathcal{T}[\![\texttt{te}_3]\!]\rho \\
\mathcal{T}[\![\texttt{op e}_1\ldots\ \texttt{e}_n]\!]\rho &= (\mathcal{O}[\![\texttt{op}]\!]\ (\mathcal{T}[\![\texttt{e}_1]\!]\rho\!\downarrow\! \mathit{Const}) \ldots (\mathcal{T}[\![\texttt{e}_n]\!]\rho\!\downarrow\! \mathit{Const}))\!\uparrow\! \mathit{Const}
\end{aligned}
$$

$$
\begin{aligned}
\mathcal{T}[\![\underline{\lambda}\texttt{var.te}]\!]\rho &= \textbf{let}\ \texttt{nvar} = \mathit{newname}(\texttt{var}) \\
&\quad\ \textbf{in}\ \ \textit{build-}\underline{\lambda}(\texttt{nvar}, \mathcal{T}[\![\texttt{te}]\!]\ \rho[\texttt{var} \mapsto \texttt{nvar}]\!\downarrow\! \mathit{Code})\!\uparrow\! \mathit{Code} \\
\mathcal{T}[\![\texttt{te}_1\ \underline{@}\ \texttt{te}_2]\!]\rho &= \textit{build-}\underline{@}(\mathcal{T}[\![\texttt{te}_1]\!]\rho\!\downarrow\! \mathit{Code},\ \mathcal{T}[\![\texttt{te}_2]\!]\rho\!\downarrow\! \mathit{Code})\!\uparrow\! \mathit{Code} \\
\mathcal{T}[\![\underline{\texttt{fix}}\ \texttt{te}]\!]\rho &= \textit{build-}\underline{\textit{fix}}(\mathcal{T}[\![\texttt{te}]\!]\rho\!\downarrow\! \mathit{Code})\!\uparrow\! \mathit{Code} \\
\mathcal{T}[\![\underline{\texttt{if}}\ \texttt{te}_1\ \underline{\texttt{then}}\ \texttt{te}_2\ \underline{\texttt{else}}\ \texttt{te}_3]\!]\rho & \\
&= \textit{build-}\underline{\textit{if}}(\mathcal{T}[\![\texttt{te}_1]\!]\rho\!\downarrow\! \mathit{Code} \\
&\qquad \mathcal{T}[\![\texttt{te}_2]\!]\rho\!\downarrow\! \mathit{Code},\ \mathcal{T}[\![\texttt{te}_3]\!]\rho\!\downarrow\! \mathit{Code})\!\uparrow\! \mathit{Code} \\
\mathcal{T}[\![\underline{\texttt{op}}\ \texttt{e}_1\ldots\ \texttt{e}_n]\!] &= \textit{build-}\underline{\textit{op}}((\mathcal{T}[\![\texttt{e}_1]\!]\rho\!\downarrow\! \mathit{Code}) \ldots (\mathcal{T}[\![\texttt{e}_n]\!]\rho\!\downarrow\! \mathit{Code}))\!\uparrow\! \mathit{Code}
\end{aligned}
$$

Figure 8.3: Two-level lambda calculus interpreter.

Each occurrence of var in te will then be looked up in $\rho[\texttt{var} \mapsto \texttt{nvar}]$, causing var to be replaced by the fresh variable nvar. Since $\underline{\lambda}\texttt{var.te}$ might be duplicated, and thus become the 'father' of many λ-abstractions in the residual program, this renaming is necessary to avoid name confusion in residual programs. Any free dynamic variables must be bound to their new names in the initial static environment ρ_s. The generation of new variable names relies on a side effect on a global state (a name counter). In principle this could be avoided by adding an extra parameter to $\mathcal{T}$, but for the sake of notational simplicity we have used a less formal solution.

The valuation functions for two-level lambda calculus programs are given in Figure 8.3. The rules contain explicit tagging and untagging with $\uparrow$ and $\downarrow$; Section 8.3 will discuss sufficient criteria for avoiding the need to perform them.

Example 8.1 Consider again the power program:

```
(fix λp.λn'.λx'.
    if (= n' 0)
    then 1
    else (* x' (p (- n' 1) x'))) n x
```

and suppose that n is known and x is not. A suitably annotated power program, power-ann, would be:

```
(fix λp.λn'.λx'.
    if (= n' 0)
    then (lift 1)
    else (* x' (p (- n' 1) x'))) n x
```

Partial evaluation of power (that is, two-level evaluation of power-ann) in environment $\rho_s = [\text{n} \mapsto 2\uparrow Const, \text{x} \mapsto \text{xnew}\uparrow Code]$ yields:

$$\mathcal{T}[\![\text{power-ann}]\!]\rho_s$$
$$= \mathcal{T}[\![(\text{fix } \lambda p.\lambda n'.\lambda x'.\text{if} \ldots) \text{ n x}]\!]\rho_s$$
$$= * \text{ xnew } (* \text{ xnew } 1)$$

In the power example it is quite clear that for all $d2$, $\rho = [\text{n} \mapsto 2, \text{x} \mapsto d2]$, $\rho_s = [\text{n} \mapsto 2, \text{x} \mapsto \text{xnew}]$, and $\rho_d = [\text{xnew} \mapsto d2]$ (omitting injections for brevity) it holds that

$$\mathcal{E}[\![\text{power}]\!]\rho = \mathcal{E}[\![\mathcal{T}[\![\text{power-ann}]\!]\rho_s]\!]\rho_d$$

This is the mix equation (see Section 4.2.2) for the lambda calculus. Section 8.8 contains a general correctness theorem for two-level evaluation. □

8.3 Congruence and consistency of annotations

The semantic rules of Figure 8.3 check explicitly that the values of subexpressions are in the appropriate summands of the value domain, in the same way that a type-checking interpreter for a dynamically typed language would. Type-checking on the fly is clearly necessary to prevent partial evaluation from committing type errors itself on a poorly annotated program.

Doing type checks on the fly is not very satisfactory for practical reasons. Mix is supposed to be a general and automatic program generation tool, and one wishes for obvious reasons for it to be impossible for an automatically generated compiler to go down with an error message.

Note that it is in principle possible — but unacceptably inefficient in practice — to avoid partial evaluation-time errors by annotating as dynamic all operators

(Const)	$\tau \vdash c : S$

(Var)	$\tau[x \mapsto t] \vdash x : t$

(Lift)
$$\frac{\tau \vdash te : S}{\tau \vdash \texttt{lift } te : D}$$

(Abstr)
$$\frac{\tau[x \mapsto t_2] \vdash te : t_1}{\tau \vdash \lambda x.te : t_2 \rightarrow t_1}$$

(Apply)
$$\frac{\tau \vdash te_1 : t_2 \rightarrow t_1 \quad \tau \vdash te_2 : t_2}{\tau \vdash te_1 \; te_2 : t_1}$$

(Fix)
$$\frac{\tau \vdash te : (t_1 \rightarrow t_2) \rightarrow (t_1 \rightarrow t_2)}{\tau \vdash \texttt{fix } te : t_1 \rightarrow t_2}$$

(If)
$$\frac{\tau \vdash te_1 : S \quad \tau \vdash te_2 : t \quad \tau \vdash te_3 : t}{\tau \vdash \texttt{if } te_1 \texttt{ then } te_2 \texttt{ else } te_3 : t}$$

(Op)
$$\frac{\tau \vdash te_1 : S \; \dots \; \tau \vdash te_n : S}{\tau \vdash \texttt{op } te_1 \; \dots \; te_n : S}$$

(Abstr-dyn)
$$\frac{\tau[x \mapsto D] \vdash te : D}{\tau \vdash \underline{\lambda}x.te : D}$$

(Apply-dyn)
$$\frac{\tau \vdash te_1 : D \quad \tau \vdash te_2 : D}{\tau \vdash te_1 \; \underline{@} \; te_2 : D}$$

(Fix-dyn)
$$\frac{\tau \vdash te : D}{\tau \vdash \underline{\texttt{fix}} \; te : D}$$

(If-dyn)
$$\frac{\tau \vdash te_1 : D \quad \tau \vdash te_2 : D \quad \tau \vdash te_3 : D}{\tau \vdash \underline{\texttt{if}} \; te_1 \; \underline{\texttt{then}} \; te_2 \; \underline{\texttt{else}} \; te_3 : D}$$

(Op-dyn)
$$\frac{\tau \vdash te_1 : D \; \dots \; \tau \vdash te_n : D}{\tau \vdash \underline{\texttt{op}} \; te_1 \; \dots \; te_n : D}$$

Figure 8.4: Type rules checking well-annotatedness.

in the subject program. This would place all values in the code summand so all type checks would succeed; but the residual program would always be isomorphic to the source program, so it would not be optimized at all.

The aim of this section is to develop a more efficient strategy, ensuring before specialization starts that the partial evaluator *cannot* commit a type error. This strategy was seen in Chapters 4 & 5. The main difference now is that in a higher-order language it is less obvious *what* congruence is and *how* to ensure it.

8.3.1 Well-annotated expressions

A simple and traditional way to preclude type check errors is to devise a type system. In typed functional languages, a type inference algorithm such as algorithm W checks that a program is well-typed prior to program execution [184]. If it is, then no run-time summand tags or checks are needed. Type checking is quite well understood and can be used to get a nice formulation of the problem to be solved by binding-time analysis [104,202].

We saw in Section 5.7 that type rules can be used to check well-annotatedness, and we now apply similar reasoning to the lambda calculus.

Definition 8.1 The *two-level types* t are as follows, where α ranges over type variables:

$$t ::= \alpha \mid S \mid D \mid t \to t$$

A *type environment* τ is a mapping from program variables to types. □

Definition 8.2 Let τ be a type environment mapping the free variables of a two-level expression te to their types. Then te is *well-annotated* if $\tau \vdash$ te $: t$ can be deduced from the inference rules in Figure 8.4 for some type t. □

For example, the two-level expression **power-ann** of Example 8.1 is well-annotated in type environment $\tau = [\text{n} \mapsto S, \text{x} \mapsto D]$. The whole expression has type D, and the part (**fix p** ...) has type $S \to D \to D$.

Our lambda calculus is basically untyped, but the well-annotatedness ensures that all program parts evaluated at partial evaluation time will be well-typed, thus ensuring specialization against type errors. The well-annotatedness criterion is, however, completely permissive concerning the run-time part of a two-level expression. Thus a lambda expression without static operators is trivially well-typed — *at partial evaluation time.*

Two-level expressions of type S evaluate (completely) to *first-order* constants, and expressions of type $t_1 \to t_2$ evaluate to a function applicable *only at partial evaluation time.* The value by $\mathcal{T}$ of a two-level expression te of type D is a one-level expression e. For partial evaluation we are only interested in fully annotated programs **p-ann** that have type D. In that case, $\mathcal{T}[\![\text{p-ann}]\!]\rho_s$ (if defined) will be a piece of code, namely the residual program.

In our context, the result about error freedom of well-typed programs can be formulated as follows. Proof is omitted since the result is well-known.

Definition 8.3 Let t be a two-level type and v be a two-level value. We say that t *suits* v iff one of the following holds:

1. $t = S$ and $v = ct\!\uparrow Const$ for some $ct \in Const.$
2. $t = D$ and $v = cd\!\uparrow Code$ for some $cd \in Code.$

3. (a) $t = t_1 \rightarrow t_2$, $v = f {\uparrow} \mathit{2Funval}$ for some $f \in \mathit{2Funval}$, and

   (b) $\forall\, v \in \mathit{2Val}$: t_1 suits v implies t_2 suits $f(v)$.

A type environment τ suits an environment ρ if for all variables x bound by ρ, $\tau(\mathbf{x})$ suits $\rho(\mathbf{x})$. □

The following is a non-standard application of a standard result [184].

Proposition 8.1 ('Well-annotated programs do not go wrong') If $\tau \vdash$ te : t, and τ suits ρ_s, then $\mathcal{T}[\![\mathbf{te}]\!]\rho_s$ does not yield a projection error. □

Of course $\mathcal{T}$ can 'go wrong' in other ways than by committing type errors. Reduction might proceed infinitely (so $\mathcal{T}[\![\mathbf{p\text{-}ann}]\!]\rho_s$ is not defined) or residual code might be duplicated. We shall not discuss these problems here.

8.4   Binding-time analysis

Definition 8.4 The *annotation-forgetting function* ϕ: $\mathit{2Exp} \rightarrow \mathit{Exp}$, when applied to a two-level expression te, returns a one-level expression e which differs from te only in that all annotations (underlines) and lift operators are removed. □

Definition 8.5 Given two-level expressions, te and $\mathbf{te}_1$, define te $\sqsubseteq$ $\mathbf{te}_1$ by

1. $\phi(\mathbf{te}) = \phi(\mathbf{te}_1)$

2. All operators underlined in te are also underlined in $\mathbf{te}_1$

□

Thus $\sqsubseteq$ is a preorder on the set of two-level expressions. Given a λ-expression e, let a *binding-time assumption* for e be a type environment τ mapping each free variable of e to either S or D.

Definition 8.6 Given an expression e and a binding-time assumption τ, a *completion* of e for τ is a two-level expression $\mathbf{te}_1$ with $\phi(\mathbf{te}_1) = $ e and $\tau \vdash \mathbf{te}_1 : t$ for some type t. A *minimal completion* is an expression $\mathbf{te}_2$ which is a completion of te fulfilling $\mathbf{te}_2 \sqsubseteq \mathbf{te}_1$ for all completions $\mathbf{te}_1$ of e. □

Minimal completions are in general not unique. Assume $\tau = [\mathbf{y} \mapsto D]$, and e = $(\lambda\mathbf{x}.\mathbf{x}{+}\mathbf{y})$ 4. There are two minimal completions, $\mathbf{te}_1 = (\lambda\mathbf{x}.\mathbf{x}\underline{+}\mathbf{y})$ (lift 4) and $\mathbf{te}_2 = (\lambda\mathbf{x}.(\mathtt{lift}\ \mathbf{x})\underline{+}\mathbf{y})$ 4 which yield identical residual programs when partially evaluated. The definition of $\sqsubseteq$ does not distinguish between (minimal) completions which differ only in the choice of lift-points. Residual programs are identical for completions $\mathbf{te}_1$ and $\mathbf{te}_2$ if $\mathbf{te}_1 \sqsubseteq \mathbf{te}_2$ and $\mathbf{te}_2 \sqsubseteq \mathbf{te}_1$, and the impact of different choices on efficiency of the partial evaluation process itself is of little importance.

The requirement that τ be a binding-time assumption implies that all free variables are first-order. This ensures the existence of a completion. Note that a λ-bound variable x can get any type in completions, in particular a functional type. Possible conflicts can be resolved by annotating the abstraction(s) and application(s) that force x to have a functional type.

The task of binding-time analysis in the λ-calculus is briefly stated: given an expression e and a binding-time assumption τ find a minimal completion of e for τ. In Section 8.6 we show by example that this can be done by type inference, and in Section 8.7 we show how to do it in a much more efficient way.

Proposition 8.2 Given an expression e and a binding-time assumption τ there exist(s) minimal completion(s) of e for τ.

Proof Follows from the properties of the constraint-based binding-time analysis algorithm in Section 8.7 $\qquad\qquad\square$

8.5 Simplicity versus power in Lambdamix

A value of type $t \neq D$ can only be bound to a variable by applying a function of type $t \rightarrow t'$. The partial evaluation time result of such a statically performed application is found by evaluating the function body, no matter what the type of the argument or the result is. This corresponds closely to unfolding on the fly of *all* static function calls (see Section 5.5).

Lambdamix does not perform specialization of *named* program points. Rather, generation of multiple variants of a source expression can be accomplished as an implicit result of unfolding a `fix` operator, since static variables may be bound to different values in the different unfoldings.

The only way to prevent a function call from being unfolded is to annotate the function as dynamic: $\underline{\lambda}$. All applications of that function must accordingly be annotated as dynamic. Dynamic functions $\underline{\lambda}\ldots$ can only have dynamic arguments (Figure 8.4). Note that this restriction does not exist in Chapter 5 where named functions are specialized. As an example, consider the append function, app, written as a lambda expression:

```
(fix λapp.λxs.λys.
      if   (null? xs)
      then ys
      else (cons (car xs) (app (cdr xs) ys))) xs0 ys0
```

Partial evaluation with xs0 = '(a b) and dynamic ys0 yields (cons 'a (cons 'b ys0)), a result similar to that produced by the Scheme0 specializer from Chapter 5 (with any reasonable unfolding strategy). Lambdamix handles this example well because the recursive calls to app should be unfolded to produce the optimal residual program. Unfolding the calls allows Lambdamix to exploit the static argument, (cdr xs).

Now assume that `xs0` is dynamic and that `ys0` is static with value `'(c d)`. When applied to a corresponding problem, the techniques from Chapter 5 would produce the residual Scheme0 program

```
(define (app-cd xs)
   (if (null? xs)
       '(c d)
       (cons (car xs) (app-cd (cdr xs)))))
```

where the recursive call to `app-cd` is not unfolded. Now consider this problem in the Lambdamix framework. With dynamic `ys0`, a minimal completion of the append program is:

```
(fix λapp.λxs.λys.
      if   (null? xs)
      then (lift ys)
      else (cons (car xs) (app (cdr xs) ys))) xs0 ys0
```

Note that even though `xs0` and `xs` are dynamic the function λxs.λys.... is still static in the minimal completion. Lambdamix will loop infinitely by unfolding the recursive applications of `app`. To avoid infinite unfolding, the recursive application `(app (cdr xs) ys)` must be annotated as dynamic, which forces the whole expression `fix λapp....` to be annotated as dynamic. This means that no computation can be done by terminating partial evaluation.

In this particular example, specialization of the named function `app` with respect to first-order data `ys0 = '(c d)` could be obtained by simple methods but to get a general solution to this class of problems we must also consider specialization with respect to higher-order values, i.e., functions. We shall return to this in Chapter 10.

8.5.1 Optimality of Lambdamix

Lambdamix has been tested on several interpreters derived from denotational language definitions [106]. Such interpreters are compositional in the program argument, which means that recursive calls in the interpreter can be safely unfolded when the interpreter is specialized with respect to a concrete source program. Lambdamix often performs well on interpreters fulfilling compositionality, and is often able to specialize away interpretive overhead such as syntactic dispatch, environment lookups, etc.

A compelling example: when the self-interpreter from Figure 8.1 (after removing all tagging and untagging operations) is specialized with respect to a lambda expression e, the residual program is an expression e' which is *identical* to e modulo renaming of variables and insignificant coding of base function applications. Thus Lambdamix is nearly optimal as defined in Chapter 6. (A small difference: the call: $(+ e_1 e_2)$ is transformed into $(apply '+ e_1 e_2)$, etc. The problem can be fully eliminated by treating base functions as free variables, bound in the initial environment [106] or by a simple post processing like in Chapter 11.)

8.6   Binding-time analysis by type inference

An intuitively natural approach to binding-time analysis for the lambda calculus uses a variant of the classical Algorithm W for polymorphic type inference [106, 185,202]. The guiding principle is that the static parts of an annotated program must be well-typed. This naturally leads to an algorithm that tries to type a given program in its given type environment.

If this succeeds, all is well and specialization can proceed. If type inference fails, the application of a user-defined or base function that led to the type conflict is made dynamic (i.e. an underline is added), and the process is repeated. Eventually, enough underlines will be added to make the whole well-typed and so suitable for specialization.

We only give an example for brevity, since the next section contains a much more efficient algorithm. Recall the power program of Example 8.1:

```
(fix λp.λn'.λx'.
    if (= n' 0) then 1
    else (* x' (p (- n' 1) x')))) n x
```

with initial type environment $\tau = [n \mapsto S, x \mapsto D]$. At the if, Algorithm W works with the type environment:

$$[p \mapsto (S \rightarrow D \rightarrow \alpha), n' \mapsto S, x' \mapsto D, n \mapsto S, x \mapsto D]$$

where α is an as yet unbound type variable. Thus expression (p (- n' 1) x') has type α, which is no problem. This leads, however, to a type conflict in expression (* x' (p (- n' 1) x')) since static operator * has type $S \times S \rightarrow S$, in conflict with x', which has type D.

The problem is resolvable by changing * to <u>*</u>, with type $D \times D \rightarrow D$. This forces $\alpha = D$ so the else expression has type D. The single remaining conflict, that 1 has type $S \neq D$, is easily resolved by changing the 1 to lift 1, or by underlining it. The first solution leads to the annotation of Example 8.1.

8.7   BTA by solving constraints

In this section we shall show an elegant and efficient solution to the problem of binding-time analysis for the lambda calculus. The key observation is that the requirement that a two-level expression is well-annotated can be formulated as a set of constraints on the types of the individual subexpressions. These constraints can be efficiently reduced to a normal form from which the minimal completion is easily computed. The description is adapted from a paper by Fritz Henglein [114]. That paper also gives the details of the efficient constraint reduction and proofs of the stated propositions.

The definition of completions places no restriction on the insertion of `lifts` (apart from the obvious demand that the expression must be well-annotated). To simplify the exposition, we shall assume for now that *no* `lifts` are allowed. Once the basic concepts are treated we present the modifications needed to account for `lift`-insertion (Section 8.7.3).

8.7.1   Combining static and dynamic type rules

Consider the type rules for λ and $\underline{\lambda}$:

$$(\text{Abstr}) \qquad \frac{\tau[\mathbf{x} \mapsto t_2] \vdash \mathbf{te} : t_1}{\tau \vdash \lambda\mathbf{x}.\mathbf{te} : t_2 \to t_1}$$

$$(\text{Abstr-dyn}) \qquad \frac{\tau[\mathbf{x} \mapsto D] \vdash \mathbf{te} : D}{\tau \vdash \underline{\lambda}\mathbf{x}.\mathbf{te} : D}$$

Compare these rules with a combined rule, which we call Abstr-comb:

$$(\text{Abstr-comb}) \qquad \frac{\tau[\mathbf{x} \mapsto t_2] \vdash \mathbf{e} : t_1 \quad ((t_2 \to t_1) = t \ \lor \ t = t_1 = t_2 = D)}{\tau \vdash \lambda\mathbf{x}.\mathbf{e} : t}$$

An application of rule (Abstr-comb) corresponds exactly to an application of either (Abstr) or (Abstr-dyn), depending on which disjuncts hold in $(t_2 \to t_1 = t \lor t = t_1 = t_2 = D)$. By making combined rules for the other operators that have both static and dynamic versions we get a type system, TypeComb, in which an expression e is typable if and only if e has completions. Given the type of all subexpressions of e in TypeComb, we immediately have the corresponding completion of e. For example, if a subexpression of form $\lambda\mathbf{x}.\mathbf{e}_1$ has type D, then in the corresponding completion the lambda will be annotated $\underline{\lambda}$. We find completions for an expression e by finding typings of e in TypeComb.

8.7.2   Constraints on expression types

Let e be a λ-expression and τ a binding-time environment for e. We associate a unique type variable α_x with every λ-bound variable x occurring in e and a unique type variable α_{e_1} with every subexpression $\mathbf{e}_1$ in e. We assume that all λ-bound variables are distinct.

As an informal example consider the expression $(\lambda\mathbf{x}.\mathbf{x} \ \mathbf{y}) \ \mathbf{z}$ and assume binding-time environment $\tau = [\mathbf{y} \mapsto D, \mathbf{z} \mapsto D]$. Let α be the type variable associated with $(\lambda\mathbf{x}.\mathbf{x} \ \mathbf{y})$. All other expressions must have type D, but both $\alpha = D$ and $\alpha = D \to D$ would give correct typings. The corresponding completions are respectively

$(\lambda x . x @ y) @ z$ and $(\lambda x . x @ y)\ z$.

Our strategy is to translate the inference rules of the system TypeComb into constraints on the type variables α associated with the subexpressions and bound variables of a given e to be analysed. The next step is to find the most general substitution of type terms for type variables such that all constraints are satisfied. This substitution characterizes all possible completions of e, and among these we choose a minimal completion.

We define $\leq_b$ and $\leq_f$ to be the 'flat' partial orders on type terms whose only strict inequalities are

$$S \quad <_b \quad D$$
$$D \to D \quad <_f \quad D$$

Note that $(t_2 \to t_1 = t \vee t = t_1 = t_2 = D) \Leftrightarrow t_2 \to t_1 \leq_f t$.

A *constraint system* C is a multiset[1] of constraints of the form

- $\alpha' \to \alpha'' \leq_f \alpha$,

- $\beta \leq_b \alpha$,

- $\alpha = \alpha'$, and

- $\alpha \rhd \alpha'$.

where $\alpha, \alpha', \alpha'', \beta$ are type variables or a type constant S or D. A substitution V (of ground type expressions for type variables) is a *solution* of C if the following two conditions are fulfilled:

1. For every constraint of form $\quad\quad\quad\quad\quad$ V fulfils

$\alpha' \to \alpha'' \leq_f \alpha$	$V(\alpha' \to \alpha'') \leq_f V(\alpha)$
$\beta \leq_b \alpha$	$V(\beta) \leq_b V(\alpha)$
$\alpha = \alpha'$	$V(\alpha) = V(\alpha')$
$\alpha \rhd \alpha'$	$V(\alpha) = D \Rightarrow V(\alpha') = D$

2. For every type variable α not occurring in C we have $V(\alpha) = \alpha$.[2]

We write $\mathrm{Sol}(C)$ for the set of all solutions of C.

We define the constraint system $C_\tau(\mathbf{e})$ by induction as follows.

---

[1] Using *multisets* instead of *sets* leads to a simpler formulation and faster implementation of the constraint transformations rules

[2] This condition guarantees that solutions V and V' are equal whenever their restrictions to the variables occurring in C are equal.

Form of e	$C_\tau(e) =$
$\lambda \mathtt{x}.\mathtt{e}_1$	$\{\ \alpha_x \to \alpha_{e_1} \leq_f \alpha_e\ \} \cup C_\tau(\mathtt{e}_1)$
$\mathtt{e}_1\ \mathtt{e}_2$	$\{\ \alpha_{e_2} \to \alpha_e \leq_f \alpha_{e_1}\ \} \cup C_\tau(\mathtt{e}_1) \cup C_\tau(\mathtt{e}_2)$
$\mathtt{fix}\ \mathtt{e}_1$	$\{\ \alpha_e \to \alpha_e \leq_f \alpha_{e_1}\ \} \cup C_\tau(\mathtt{e}_1)$
$\mathtt{if}\ \mathtt{e}_1\ \mathtt{then}\ \mathtt{e}_2\ \mathtt{else}\ \mathtt{e}_3$	$\{\ S \leq_b \alpha_{e_1},\ \alpha_e = \alpha_{e_2},\ \alpha_e = \alpha_{e_3},\ \alpha_{e_1} \rhd \alpha_e\ \}$ $\cup\ C_\tau(\mathtt{e}_1) \cup C_\tau(\mathtt{e}_2) \cup C_\tau(\mathtt{e}_3)$
c	$\{\ S = \alpha_e\ \}$
$\mathtt{op}\ \mathtt{e}_1\ \mathtt{e}_2$	$\{\ S \leq_b \alpha_{e_1},\ \alpha_{e_1} = \alpha_{e_2},\ \alpha_{e_2} = \alpha_e\ \} \cup C_\tau(\mathtt{e}_1) \cup C_\tau(\mathtt{e}_2)$
A λ-bound variable x	$\{\ \alpha_x = \alpha_e\ \}$
Free x with $\tau(\mathtt{x}) = t$	$\{\ t = \alpha_e\ \}$

Every type derivation for a λ-expression e corresponds uniquely to a *type labelling* of the syntax tree of e; that is, to a mapping of (λ-expression) occurrences in e into type expressions. A type labelling that arises from a type derivation in this fashion can, however, equally well be viewed as a mapping from the canonical type variables associated above with the occurrences in e to type expressions. Consequently every (implicit) type derivation for a λ-expression e determines uniquely a *substitution* on these type variables by mapping every other type variable to itself. By induction on the syntax of λ-expressions e it can be shown that such a substitution is a solution of the constraint system $C_\tau(e)$ and vice versa — every solution of $C_\tau(e)$ is a substitution determined by a type derivation for e. Since every implicit type derivation of e corresponds to a unique completion of e we have the following proposition.

Proposition 8.3 For every λ-expression e and binding-time assumption τ for e there is a one-to-one correspondence between the completions of e and the solutions of $C_\tau(e)$. $\square$

8.7.3   Inserting lift expressions

The definition of a completion allows any subexpression e of type S to be replaced by `lift` e of type D. When given an unannotated expression e there is no obvious *a priori* way to determine where to insert `lift`s to obtain completions. Our solution is to associate *two* type variables α_{e_1} *and* $\bar{\alpha}_{e_1}$ with each subexpression $\mathtt{e}_1$ of e. As above, α_{e_1} represents the 'immediate' type of $\mathtt{e}_1$, and $\bar{\alpha}_{e_1}$ represents its type after possible lifting. Given a solution V, the relation between the two variables must be $V(\alpha_{e_1}) \leq_b V(\bar{\alpha}_{e_1})$, where equality means 'no `lift` inserted' and $<_b$ indicates insertion of a `lift`. Below is the revised definition of $C_\tau(e)$.

It could be argued that it would be conceptually cleaner to introduce a separate class of constraints, say $\leq_l$, to control lift insertion instead of using $\leq_b$ which was introduced for other purposes. Running the risk of unnecessary confusion, we have chosen to use $\leq_b$ anyway because its properties also capture lift insertion. Leaving out a separate $\leq_l$ makes the presentation shorter.

Form of e	$C_\tau(e) =$
$\lambda x.e_1$	$\{\ \alpha_x \to \bar{\alpha}_{e_1} \leq_f \alpha_e,\ \alpha_e \leq_b \bar{\alpha}_e\ \} \cup C_\tau(e_1)$
$e_1\ e_2$	$\{\ \bar{\alpha}_{e_2} \to \alpha_e \leq_f \bar{\alpha}_{e_1},\ \alpha_e \leq_b \bar{\alpha}_e\ \} \cup C_\tau(e_1) \cup C_\tau(e_2)$
$\texttt{fix}\ e_1$	$\{\ \alpha_e \to \alpha_e \leq_f \bar{\alpha}_{e_1},\ \alpha_e \leq_b \bar{\alpha}_e\ \} \cup C_\tau(e_1)$
$\texttt{if}\ e_1\ \texttt{then}\ e_2\ \texttt{else}\ e_3$	$\{\ S \leq_b \bar{\alpha}_{e_1},\ \alpha_e = \bar{\alpha}_{e_2},\ \alpha_e = \bar{\alpha}_{e_3},\ \bar{\alpha}_{e_1} \triangleright \alpha_e,\ \alpha_e \leq_b \bar{\alpha}_e\ \}$ $\cup\ C_\tau(e_1) \cup C_\tau(e_2) \cup C_\tau(e_3)$
c	$\{\ S = \alpha_e,\ \alpha_e \leq_b \bar{\alpha}_e\ \}$
$\texttt{op}\ e_1\ e_2$	$\{\ S \leq_b \bar{\alpha}_{e_1},\ \bar{\alpha}_{e_1} = \bar{\alpha}_{e_2},\ \bar{\alpha}_{e_2} = \alpha_e,\ \alpha_e \leq_b \bar{\alpha}_e\ \}$ $\cup\ C_\tau(e_1) \cup C_\tau(e_2)$
A λ-bound variable x	$\{\ \alpha_x \leq_b \bar{\alpha}_e\ \}$
Free x with $\tau(x) = t$	$\{\ t = \alpha_e,\ \alpha_e \leq_b \bar{\alpha}_e\ \}$

Note that an abstraction $\lambda x.e$ can never get type S and thus never be lifted. This insight could yield a small 'optimization' of the constraint set generated above.

8.7.4 Normalization of type constraints

In Section 8.7.2 we have seen that the type derivations for a λ-expression e under binding-time assumption τ — and thus its completions — can be characterized by the solutions of a constraint system $C_\tau(e)$. In this section we present transformations that preserve the set of solutions of such a constraint system. A constraint system in normal form with respect to these transformations (i.e., cannot be transformed any further) will have the property that it directly defines a minimal solution.

Our transformation rules define a labelled reduction relation $C \overset{V}{\Rightarrow} C'$, where C and C' are constraint systems and V is a substitution. If the substitution is the identity substitution we simply write $C \Rightarrow C'$. For substitution V and constraint system C, the result of the application of V to all type expressions in C is written $V(C)$. Let $G(C)$ be the directed graph, where the nodes are the variables appearing in constraint system C and where the edge (α, β) is included if and only if there is an inequality constraint of the form $\alpha \to \alpha' \leq_f \beta$ or $\alpha' \to \alpha \leq_f \beta$ in C. If $G(C)$ contains a cycle we say C is *cyclic*; *acyclic* otherwise.[3] The transformation rules are given in Figure 8.5. The first two inequality constraint rules show how inequality constraints with *identical* right-hand sides are eliminated: if the left-hand sides have the *same* type constructor then these left-hand sides are equated

---

[3]Constraints of the form $\alpha = \alpha'$ and $\alpha \leq_b \alpha'$ need not be considered in the definition of cyclicity since our transformation rules eliminate all equational constraints, and $\leq_b$-inequality constraints remaining in a normal form constraint system are irrelevant.

in the 'reduced' system (Rule 1a); if the left-hand sides have *different* left-hand side type constructors then the right-hand side is equated with D (Rule 1b) and the inequalities are eventually eliminated by Rules 1g and 1h.

The transitive closure of the transformation rules is defined by: $C \overset{V}{\Rightarrow}+ C'$ if $C \overset{V}{\Rightarrow} C'$ and $C \overset{V' \circ V}{\Rightarrow}+ C'$ if $C \overset{V}{\Rightarrow}+ C'$, $C' \overset{V'}{\Rightarrow}+ C'$ for some C', where $V' \circ V$ denotes the composition of V' and V. We say C is a *normal form* (or *normalized*) constraint system if there is no C' such that $C \overset{V}{\Rightarrow} C'$ for any V. We say C *has* a normal form if there is a normal form C' such that $C \overset{V}{\Rightarrow}+ C'$ for some substitution V. The correctness of the transformations is captured in the following proposition, which is easily proved by induction on the length of transformation sequences and by case analysis of the individual rules using elementary properties of $\leq_b, \leq_f$.

Proposition 8.4 (Soundness and completeness of transformations)

Let $C \overset{V}{\Rightarrow}+ C'$. Then $\mathrm{Sol}(C) = \{(V' \circ V) \mid V' \in \mathrm{Sol}(C')\}$.   □

The transformations can be used to derive an algorithm for normalizing constraint systems based on the following proposition.

Proposition 8.5 (Normalization of constraint systems)

1. The transformations of Figure 8.5 are weakly normalizing; that is, every C has a normal form.

2. If C' is a normal form constraint system then

   (a) it has no equational constraints;

   (b) it is acyclic;

   (c) its constraints are of the form $\beta \to \beta' \leq_f \alpha$, $\gamma \leq_b \alpha$ or $\alpha \rhd \alpha'$ where α, α' are type variables; β is a type variable or the type constant D; and γ is a type variable or the type constant S.

   (d) for every inequality constraint of the form $\beta \to \beta' \leq_f \alpha$ the type variable α does not occur on the right-hand side of other $\leq_f$-inequalities or on the left-hand side of $\leq_b$-inequalities;

   (e) for every inequality constraint of the form $S \leq_b \alpha$ the type variable α does not occur on the right-hand side of $\leq_f$-inequalities or on either side of $\leq_b$-inequalities.

3. If C contains no constraints of the form $\alpha \leq_b \alpha'$ where α is a type variable and $C \overset{S}{\Rightarrow}+ C'$ then C' contains no constraint of that form either.

---

1. (inequality constraint rules)

   (a) $C \cup \{ \alpha \to \alpha' \leq_f \gamma, \beta \to \beta' \leq_f \gamma\}$
       $\Rightarrow C \cup \{ \alpha \to \alpha' \leq_f \gamma, \alpha = \beta, \alpha' = \beta' \}$ if γ is a type variable

   (b) $C \cup \{ \alpha \to \alpha' \leq_f \gamma, S \leq_b \gamma\}$
       $\Rightarrow C \cup \{ \alpha \to \alpha' \leq_f \gamma, S\leq_b \gamma, \gamma = D\}$ if γ is a type variable

   (c) $C \cup \{ \alpha \to \alpha' \leq_f \beta, \beta \leq_b \beta' \}$
       $\Rightarrow C \cup \{ \alpha \to \alpha' \leq_f \beta, \beta = \beta' \}$

   (d) $C \cup \{ S \leq_b \alpha, \alpha \leq_b \alpha' \}$
       $\Rightarrow C \cup \{ S \leq_b \alpha, S \leq_b \alpha', \alpha \rhd \alpha' \}$ if α, α' are type variables

   (e) $C \cup \{ S \leq_b \alpha', \alpha \leq_b \alpha' \}$
       $\Rightarrow C \cup \{ S \leq_b \alpha, S\leq_b \alpha', \alpha \rhd \alpha' \}$ if α, α' are type variables

   (f) $C \cup \{ S \leq_b \alpha, S \leq_b \alpha \} \Rightarrow C \cup \{ S \leq_b \alpha \}$

   (g) $C \cup \{ \alpha \to \alpha' \leq_f D \} \Rightarrow C \cup \{ \alpha = D, \alpha' = D \}$

   (h) $C \cup \{ S \leq_b D \} \Rightarrow C$

   (i) $C \cup \{ S \leq_b S \} \Rightarrow C$

   (j) $C \cup \{ D \leq_b \alpha \} \Rightarrow C \cup \{ D = \alpha \}$

   (k) $C \cup \{ \alpha \leq_b D \} \Rightarrow C \cup \{ S \leq_b \alpha \}$ if α is a type variable

2. (equational constraint rules)

   (a) $C \cup \{ \alpha = \alpha \} \Rightarrow C$

   (b) $C \cup \{ \alpha = \alpha' \} \overset{V}{\Rightarrow} V(C)$ if α is a type variable and $V = \{ \alpha \mapsto \alpha' \}$

   (c) $C \cup \{ \alpha' = \alpha \} \overset{V}{\Rightarrow} V(C)$ if α is a type variable and $V = \{ \alpha \mapsto \alpha' \}$

3. (dependency constraint rules)

   (a) $C \cup \{ \alpha \rhd D \} \Rightarrow C$

   (b) $C \cup \{ S \rhd \alpha \} \Rightarrow C$

   (c) $C \cup \{ D \rhd \alpha \} \Rightarrow C \cup \{ \alpha = D \}$

4. (occurs check rule)

   (a) $C \Rightarrow C \cup \{ \alpha = D \}$ if C is cyclic and α is on a cycle in $G(C)$.

Figure 8.5: Transformation rules for constraint systems.

Proof

1. Define a *megastep* as follows: apply any applicable rule and then apply the equational constraint transformation rules exhaustively. It is easy to see that every megastep terminates and that after it terminates all equational constraints have been eliminated. Let c be the number of constraints; n the number of variables occurring in them; and v the number of inequality constraints with a variable on the left-hand side. It is easy to check that every megastep decreases the sum $c + n + 2v$ by at least one. Consequently every sequence of megasteps terminates.

2. By definition of normal form.

3. None of the rules introduce $\leq_b$-inequalities with a variable on the left-hand side.

$\square$

From a constraint system C in normal form we can find a solution that characterizes a minimal completion of the original expression e. Consider two completions te_1 and te_2. If an operator is static in te_1 and dynamic in te_2, then there will be at least one subexpression of type D in te_2, where the corresponding subexpression in te_1 has a type $t \neq D$.

Now let C be a normal form constraint system. The normalization process can have forced subexpressions to have type D, but these subexpressions must be dynamic in *all* completions (cf. Proposition 8.4). To ensure that no other subexpressions get type D, we interpret all inequalities in C as equations. Since C is a normal form constraint system, by Proposition 8.5, part 2, these equations have a most general unifier U [163]. Let BS be the substitution that maps every type variable occurring in $U(C)$ to S. Since neither U nor BS substitutes D for any type variable, all the dependency constraints in C are trivially satisfied.

Note that there may be other ways of choosing a minimal completion, since *some* substitutions of D for a type variable correspond to moving a lift-expression (see Section 8.4). Avoiding type D whenever possible is a simple way to choose *one* minimal completion.

8.7.5   Binding-time analysis algorithm

Given an expression e and a binding-time assumption τ, do the following:

1. Generate the constraint system $C = C_\tau(e)$ (Section 8.7.3).

2. Compute normal form constraint system C_{nf} such that $C \overset{V}{\Rightarrow}+ C_{nf}$ (Section 8.7.4).

3. Solve C_{nf} equationally with most general unifier U and map 'remaining' type variables to S with substitution BS (Section 8.7.4).

4. The substitution $BS \circ U \circ V$ is a mapping from the type variables $\alpha_{e'}$ and $\bar{\alpha}_{e'}$ used to decorate e to ground types. $BS \circ U \circ V$ characterizes a minimal completion.

8.8 Correctness of Lambdamix

This section is devoted to the formulation and proof of a correctness theorem for Lambdamix. The existence of a correctness theorem guarantees that the specializer-generated target programs, compilers etc., are all faithful to their specifications. For readability we assume well-annotatedness, and so omit domain injections and projections in this section. (The equations are hard enough to read without them.)

For readers who are not interested in technical details we sketch the correctness result before we state formally and prove the 'real' theorem. Suppose we are given

1. a two-level expression te;

2. an environment ρ mapping the free variables of te to values;

3. an environment ρ_s, mapping the free variables of te to their specialization-time values (constants, functions, or fresh variable names);

4. an environment ρ_d, mapping these fresh variables to values;

5. $\tau \vdash$ te $: D$ whenever τ suits ρ_s.

Suppose furthermore that for variables x of type S: $\rho_s(\mathbf{x}) = \rho(\mathbf{x})$, that for variables y of type D: $\rho_d(\rho_s(\mathbf{y})) = \rho(\mathbf{y})$, and that base functions and higher-order values bound in the environments are handled 'correctly' (the formalization of this is in Definitions 8.7 and 8.8). It then holds that if both $\mathcal{E}[\![\mathcal{T}[\![\mathbf{te}]\!]\rho_d]\!]\rho_s$ and $\mathcal{E}[\![\phi(\mathbf{te})]\!]\rho$ are defined then

$$\mathcal{E}[\![\mathcal{T}[\![\mathbf{te}]\!]\rho_s]\!]\rho_d = \mathcal{E}[\![\phi(\mathbf{te})]\!]\rho$$

What we prove is thus that our partial evaluator fulfils the mix equation.

8.8.1 Correctness and termination properties

Non-trivial partial evaluators often have problems with the termination properties of the partial evaluator itself or with the generated residual programs. This partial evaluator is no exception. Consider again the equation

$$\mathcal{E}[\![\mathcal{T}[\![\mathtt{te}]\!]\rho_s]\!]\rho_d = \mathcal{E}[\![\phi(\mathtt{te})]\!]\rho$$

There may be two reasons why one side is defined while the other is not.

1. If a call-by-value strategy is used then the right side may be undefined while the left side is defined. This is because unfolding can discard non-terminating expressions (Section 5.5.2). Suppose we have

   $(\lambda\mathtt{x}.2)$ bomb

   where bomb is a non-terminating expression *made residual* thus trivially terminating *at partial evaluation time*. Partial evaluation will discard the bomb, but evaluation of $\phi((\lambda\mathtt{x}.2)$ bomb$)$ will loop under call-by-value. What has been said elsewhere in the chapter does not rely on any specific evaluation strategy, but the correctness result does rely on our lambda calculus being non-strict. For a strict language, a weaker result holds: *if* both sides are defined, they are equal.

2. As often mentioned it is hard to guarantee termination for a non-trivial partial evaluator as Lambdamix, and it is easy to construct an example where $\mathcal{T}$ loops on te where normal evaluation of $\phi(\mathtt{te})$ would terminate. When proving $\mathcal{E}[\![\mathcal{T}[\![\mathtt{te}]\!]\rho_s]\!]\rho_d = \mathcal{E}[\![\phi(\mathtt{te})]\!]\rho$ we shall assume that $\mathcal{T}$ is well-defined on all subexpressions of te. To get a smoother proof we shall make an even stronger assumption, namely that the binding-time analysis ensures that $\mathcal{T}$ is *total*. (Given any one concrete program to partially evaluate the two assumptions are identical.) If we lift this restriction our correctness result will be weakened to: *if* both sides are defined, they are equal. To get such a non-trivial binding-time analysis ensuring termination of Lambdamix, the techniques from Chapter 14 must be generalized to a higher-order language and this has not yet been done.

The rest of the section is devoted to the formalization and proof of the correctness result outlined above. Readers who are not interested may go straight to the next section without loss of continuity.

8.8.2   The correctness theorem

The relation $\mathcal{R}$ to be defined below (Definition 8.7) is central to the correctness proof. Intuitively, the relation $\mathcal{R}$ expresses that the function $\mathcal{T}$ handles a given two-level expression te correctly. For an expression of type S, let the initial environment ρ be split into a specialization-time part ρ_s and a run-time part ρ_d. Relation $\mathcal{R}$ implies that the result of partial evaluation must be the right answer:

$$\mathcal{T}[\![\mathtt{te}]\!]\rho_s = \mathcal{E}[\![\phi(\mathtt{te})]\!]\rho$$

expressing that if te has type S then normal evaluation of the unannotated expression yields the same result as partial evaluation of the annotated expression. For an expression of type D, relation $\mathcal{R}$ implies that the result of partial evaluation must be an expression, the residual program, which when evaluated yields the right answer:

$$\mathcal{E}[\![\mathcal{T}[\![\text{te}]\!]\rho_s]\!]\rho_d = \mathcal{E}[\![\phi(\text{te})]\!]\rho$$

For expressions of a function type, $\mathcal{R}$ expresses that the result of applying the function to a proper argument yields a proper answer.

Definition 8.7 The relation $\mathcal{R}$ holds for (te, ρ_s, ρ_d, ρ, t) $\in$ *2Exp* $\times$ *2Env* $\times$ *Env* $\times$ *Env* $\times$ *Type* iff

1. $\tau \vdash \text{te} : t$ if τ suits ρ_s,

2. One of the following holds

    (a) te has type S and $\mathcal{T}[\![\text{te}]\!]\rho_s = \mathcal{E}[\![\phi(\text{te})]\!]\rho$

    (b) te has type D and $\mathcal{E}[\![\mathcal{T}[\![\text{te}]\!]\rho_s]\!]\rho_d = \mathcal{E}[\![\phi(\text{te})]\!]\rho$

    (c) te has type $t = t_1 \rightarrow t_2$ and for all te$_1$: $\mathcal{R}(\text{te}_1, \rho_s, \rho_d, \rho, t_1)$ implies $\mathcal{R}(\text{te te}_1, \rho_s, \rho_d, \rho, t_2)$

    □

Note that the recursive definition of $\mathcal{R}$ has finite depth since in the definition of $\mathcal{R}(\text{te}, \rho_s, \rho_d, \rho, t)$, the recursive applications of $\mathcal{R}$, concern tuples (te', ρ_s', ρ_d', ρ', t') where t' has fewer type constructors than t.

Since an expression may have free variables, the environments involved ρ_s, ρ_d, ρ must in some sense be well-behaved. It turns out that the condition on the environments can also be formulated in terms of $\mathcal{R}$.

Definition 8.8 Given a set of identifiers, VarSet, and three environments, ρ, ρ_s, ρ_d and a type environment τ that suits ρ_s, we say that ρ_s, ρ_d, ρ *agree on* VarSet iff for all var $\in$ VarSet: $\mathcal{R}(\text{var}, \rho_s, \rho_d, \rho, \tau(\text{var}))$. □

Suppose ρ_s, ρ_d, ρ *agree* on VarSet. Then for all variables of type S: $\rho_s(x) = \rho(x)$, and for variables y of type D: $\rho_d(\rho_s(y)) = \rho(y)$. For a higher-order example: Suppose ρ_s maps identifier f to a function of type $S \rightarrow S$. By expanding the definitions of 'agreement' and $\mathcal{R}$ we find that $\forall$ te$_1$: $\mathcal{T}[\![\text{te}_1]\!]\rho_s = \mathcal{E}[\![\text{te}_1]\!]\rho$ implies $\mathcal{T}[\![\text{f te}_1]\!]\rho_s = \mathcal{E}[\![\text{f te}_1]\!]\rho$.

Theorem 8.1 (Main Correctness Theorem) Assuming that binding-time analysis ensures that $\mathcal{T}$ is defined on all arguments to which it is applied, the following holds:

For all ρ_s, ρ_d, ρ, τ, simultaneous fulfilment of the following three conditions

1. τ suits ρ_s,

2. ρ_s, ρ_d, ρ agree on FreeVars(te),

3. $\tau \vdash$ te : t for some type t,

implies that $\mathcal{R}($te, ρ_s, ρ_d, ρ, $t)$ also holds.

Proof The proof proceeds by induction on the structure of te. The proofs for the most interesting cases are found below. The remaining cases are proven elsewhere [105]. □

Corollary 8.1 Assume te, ρ_s, ρ_d, ρ, τ given such that τ suits ρ_s, and ρ_s, ρ_d, ρ agree on FreeVars(te).

1. If $\tau \vdash$ te : S then $\mathcal{T}[\![$te$]\!]\rho_s = \mathcal{E}[\![\phi(te)]\!]\rho$

2. If $\tau \vdash$ te : D then $\mathcal{E}[\![\mathcal{T}[\![te]\!]\rho_s]\!]\rho_d = \mathcal{E}[\![\phi(te)]\!]\rho$

□

We now introduce a name, $\mathcal{H}$, for the property expressed by Theorem 8.1. $\mathcal{H}$ is also used as induction hypothesis in the proof. $\mathcal{H}$ expresses that if environments agree on the free variables of a well-annotated two-level expression then the relation $\mathcal{R}$ will hold for the expression, the environments, and the type.

Definition 8.9 Given a two-level expression te, $\mathcal{H}($te$)$ holds if $\forall$ ρ_s, ρ_d, ρ, τ the following three conditions

1. τ suits ρ_s,

2. ρ_s, ρ_d, ρ agree on FreeVars(te),

3. $\tau \vdash$ te : t for some type t,

imply that $\mathcal{R}($te, ρ_s, ρ_d, ρ, $t)$ also holds. □

The proofs of the different cases all proceed in the same way. Assume te, ρ_s, ρ_d, ρ, τ are given such that the three conditions of Definition 8.9 are fulfilled. The inductive assumption gives that $\mathcal{H}($te$')$ for the subexpressions of te. Except in the case of abstraction the free variables of te are exactly those of the largest proper subexpressions of te. Thus ρ_s, ρ_d, ρ agree on the free variables of these expressions too (in the case of abstraction we have to construct some new environments ρ'_s, ρ'_d, ρ'). By well-annotatedness of te the subexpressions are also well-annotated and the inference rules of Figure 8.4 give us types for the subexpressions. This gives us some facts of the form $\mathcal{R}($sub-texp, ρ_s, ρ_d, ρ, $t')$ which then leads (with more or less trouble) to the goal: $\mathcal{R}($te, ρ_s, ρ_d, ρ, $t)$.

Case: λx.te
Proof Assume ρ_s, ρ_d, ρ, τ are given satisfying the conditions in Definition 8.9. It thus holds that $\tau \vdash \lambda$x.te : t'' where t'' must have the form $t' \rightarrow t$. Assume furthermore that te$'$ is given such that $\mathcal{R}($te$'$, ρ_s, ρ_d, ρ, $t')$. By alpha conversion of λx.te we can assume without loss of generality that x does not occur in any expressions other than the subexpressions of λx.te.

Define $\rho'_s = \rho_s[x \mapsto \mathcal{T}[\![te']\!]\rho_s]$ and
$\qquad \rho' = \rho[x \mapsto \mathcal{E}[\![\phi(te')]\!]\rho]$ and
$\qquad \tau' = \tau[x \mapsto t']$

and observe that $\forall$ id $\in$ FreeVars(te): $\mathcal{R}(\text{id}, \rho'_s, \rho_d, \rho', \tau'(\text{id}))$ since $\forall$ id $\in$ FreeVars(λx.te): $\mathcal{R}(\text{id}, \rho_s, \rho_d, \rho, \tau(\text{id}))$ and $\mathcal{R}(\text{x}, \rho'_s, \rho_d, \rho', t')$ where $\mathcal{R}(\text{x}, \rho'_s, \rho_d, \rho', t')$ follows from the assumption that $\mathcal{R}(\text{te}', \rho_s, \rho_d, \rho, t')$. We now have that ρ'_s, ρ_d, ρ' agree on FreeVars(te), that τ' suits ρ'_s (clear), and that $\tau' \vdash \text{te} : t$. Hence $\mathcal{R}(\text{te}, \rho'_s, \rho_d, \rho', t)$ by the induction hypothesis.

We are now close to the desired conclusion: $\mathcal{R}((\lambda\text{x}.\text{te})\ \text{te}', \rho_s, \rho_d, \rho, t)$. The last step is Lemma 8.1. □

Lemma 8.1 Assume, with the above definitions and assumptions, that $\mathcal{R}(\text{te}, \rho'_s, \rho_d, \rho', t)$ holds. Then $\mathcal{R}((\lambda\text{x}.\text{te})\ \text{te}', \rho_s, \rho_d, \rho, t)$ also holds.
Proof The type t must either have form $t_1 \to \ldots \to t_n \to S$ or $t_1 \to \ldots \to t_n \to D$. We assume that $t = t_1 \to \ldots \to t_n \to S$. (The opposite assumption leads to a very similar development.) Now $\mathcal{R}(\text{te}, \rho'_s, \rho_d, \rho', t)$ may be written:

$\forall$ te$_1$, ..., te$_n$: ($\forall$ i $\in$ [1..n]: $\tau \vdash$ te$_i$: t_i and $\mathcal{R}(\text{te}_i, \rho'_s, \rho_d, \rho', t_i)$)
implies

$$\mathcal{E}[\![\phi(\text{te te}_1\ \ldots\ \text{te}_n)]\!]\ \rho'$$
$$=\quad \mathcal{T}[\![\text{te te}_1\ \ldots\ \text{te}_n]\!]\ \rho'_s$$

where the equation may be rewritten to

$$(\mathcal{E}[\![\phi(\text{te})]\!]\rho')\ (\mathcal{E}[\![\phi(\text{te}_1)]\!]\rho')\ \ldots\ (\mathcal{E}[\![\phi(\text{te}_n)]\!]\rho')$$
$$=\quad (\mathcal{T}[\![\text{te}]\!]\rho'_s)\ (\mathcal{T}[\![\text{te}_1]\!]\rho'_s)\ \ldots\ (\mathcal{T}[\![\text{te}_n]\!]\rho'_s)$$

Since x is not free in te$_i$ we may again rewrite to get

$$(\mathcal{E}[\![\phi(\text{te})]\!]\rho')\ (\mathcal{E}[\![\phi(\text{te}_1)]\!]\rho)\ \ldots\ (\mathcal{E}[\![\phi(\text{te}_n)]\!]\rho)$$
$$=\quad (\mathcal{T}[\![\text{te}]\!]\rho'_s)\ (\mathcal{T}[\![\text{te}_1]\!]\rho_s)\ \ldots\ (\mathcal{T}[\![\text{te}_n]\!]\rho_s)$$

Now use the definitions of ρ'_s and ρ' and the application rules for $\mathcal{T}$ and $\mathcal{E}$ to get

$$(\mathcal{E}[\![\phi((\lambda\text{x}.\text{te})\ \text{te}')]\!]\rho)\ (\mathcal{E}[\![\phi(\text{te}_1)]\!]\rho)\ \ldots\ (\mathcal{E}[\![\phi(\text{te}_n)]\!]\rho)$$
$$=\quad (\mathcal{T}[\![(\lambda\text{x}.\text{te})\ \text{te}']\!]\rho_s)\ (\mathcal{T}[\![\text{te}_1]\!]\rho_s)\ \ldots\ (\mathcal{T}[\![\text{te}_n]\!]\rho_s)$$

More uses of the application rules yield

$$\mathcal{E}[\![\phi((\lambda\text{x}.\text{te})\ \text{te}'\ \text{te}_1\ \ldots\ \text{te}_n)]\!]\ \rho_s$$
$$=\quad \mathcal{T}[\![(\lambda\text{x}.\text{te})\ \text{te}'\ \text{te}_1\ \ldots\ \text{te}_n]\!]\ \rho$$

Now step back and see that the property which we want to establish, $\mathcal{R}((\lambda\text{x}.\text{te})\ \text{te}', \rho_s, \rho_d, \rho, t)$, may be written:

$$\forall \; te_1, \; \dots, \; te_n: \; (\forall \; i \in [1..n]: \; \tau \vdash te_i : t_i \; \text{and} \; \mathcal{R}(te_i, \; \rho_s, \; \rho_d, \; \rho, \; t_i))$$
implies

$$\mathcal{E}[\![\phi((\lambda \mathtt{x}.\mathtt{te}) \; \mathtt{te'} \; \mathtt{te_1} \; \dots \; \mathtt{te_n})]\!] \; \rho_s$$
$$= \; \mathcal{T}[\![(\lambda \mathtt{x}.\mathtt{te}) \; \mathtt{te'} \; \mathtt{te_1} \; \dots \; \mathtt{te_n}]\!] \; \rho$$

Since x does not appear free in te_i, $\mathcal{R}(te_i, \rho_s, \rho_d, \rho, t_i)$ is equivalent to $\mathcal{R}(te_i, \rho'_s, \rho_d, \rho', t_i)$ and the claim follows from the above development. $\qquad\square$

Case: $\lambda \mathtt{x}.\mathtt{te}$
Proof Let ρ_s, ρ_d, ρ, τ be given, and assume they satisfy the conditions in Definition 8.9. Then it holds that $\tau \vdash \lambda \mathtt{x}.\mathtt{te} : D$, and by the inference rules it holds also that $\tau[\mathtt{x} \mapsto D] \vdash \mathtt{te} : D$.

We shall assume that we have at hand an infinite list of variable names which have not previously been used, and when we write $\mathtt{x}_{new}$ we refer to an arbitrary variable from this list.

Lemma 8.2 For all $w \in Val$ it holds that

$$\forall \; id \in \text{FreeVars}(\mathtt{te}): \; \mathcal{R}(id, \; \rho_s[\mathtt{x} \mapsto \mathtt{x}_{new}], \; \rho_d[\mathtt{x}_{new} \mapsto w], \; \rho[\mathtt{x} \mapsto w],$$
$$\tau[\mathtt{x} \mapsto D](id))$$

since $\forall \; id \in \text{FreeVars}(\lambda \mathtt{x}.\mathtt{te}): \; \mathcal{R}(id, \; \rho_s, \; \rho_d, \; \rho, \; \tau(id))$ and $\mathcal{R}(\mathtt{x}, \; \rho_s[\mathtt{x} \mapsto \mathtt{x}_{new}], \; \rho_d[\mathtt{x}_{new} \mapsto w], \; \rho[\mathtt{x} \mapsto w], \; D)$. $\qquad\square$

Since $\tau[\mathtt{x} \mapsto D]$ clearly suits $\rho_s[\mathtt{x} \mapsto \mathtt{x}_{new}]$ and $\tau[\mathtt{x} \mapsto D] \vdash \mathtt{te} : D$ we may conclude from Lemma 8.2 and the induction hypothesis that $\forall \; w \in Val: \; \mathcal{R}(\mathtt{te}, \; \rho_s[\mathtt{x} \mapsto \mathtt{x}_{new}], \; \rho_d[\mathtt{x}_{new} \mapsto w], \; \rho[\mathtt{x} \mapsto w], \; D)$. To finish the proof for this case we must show that

$$\mathcal{E}[\![\mathcal{T}[\![\lambda \mathtt{x}.\mathtt{te}]\!]\rho_s]\!]\rho_d = \mathcal{E}[\![\phi(\lambda \mathtt{x}.\mathtt{te})]\!]\rho$$

We rewrite the left-hand side of the equation:

$$\mathcal{E}[\![\mathcal{T}[\![\lambda \mathtt{x}.\mathtt{te}]\!]\rho_s]\!]\rho_d$$
$$= \; \mathcal{E}[\![\lambda \mathtt{x}_{new}.(\mathcal{T}[\![\mathtt{te}]\!]\rho_s[\mathtt{x} \mapsto \mathtt{x}_{new}])]\!]\rho_d$$
$$= \; \lambda v.\mathcal{E}[\![\mathcal{T}[\![\mathtt{te}]\!]\rho_s[\mathtt{x} \mapsto \mathtt{x}_{new}]]\!]\rho_d[\mathtt{x}_{new} \mapsto v]$$

and the right-hand side:

$$\mathcal{E}[\![\phi(\lambda \mathtt{x}.\mathtt{te})]\!]\rho$$
$$= \; \mathcal{E}[\![\lambda \mathtt{x}.\phi(\mathtt{te})]\!]\rho$$
$$= \; \lambda v.\mathcal{E}[\![\phi(\mathtt{te})]\!]\rho[\mathtt{x} \mapsto v]$$

It now remains to show that

$$\lambda v.\mathcal{E}[\![\mathcal{T}[\![\mathtt{te}]\!]\rho_s[\mathtt{x} \mapsto \mathtt{x}_{new}]]\!]\rho_d[\mathtt{x}_{new} \mapsto v] = \lambda v.\mathcal{E}[\![\phi(\mathtt{te})]\!]\rho[\mathtt{x} \mapsto v]$$

When the two functions are applied to the same (arbitrary) $w \in Val$ the equality to be shown is

$$\mathcal{E}[\![\mathcal{T}[\![\texttt{te}]\!]\rho_s[\texttt{x} \mapsto \texttt{x}_{new}]]\!]\rho_d[\texttt{x}_{new} \mapsto w] = \mathcal{E}[\![\phi(\texttt{te})]\!]\rho[\texttt{x} \mapsto w]$$

which follows directly from $\forall\, w \in Val$: $\mathcal{R}(\texttt{te}, \rho_s[\texttt{x} \mapsto \texttt{x}_{new}], \rho_d[\texttt{x}_{new} \mapsto w], \rho[\texttt{x} \mapsto w], D)$. $\qquad\qquad\qquad\qquad\qquad\qquad\qquad\qquad\qquad\qquad\qquad\qquad\qquad\qquad\qquad\qquad\square$

Case: `fix te`

Proof The proof is by fixpoint induction. The basic idea is to use the structural induction hypothesis $\mathcal{H}(\texttt{te})$ to show the induction step in the fixpoint induction.

Assume ρ_s, ρ_d, ρ, τ are given satisfying the conditions in Definition 8.9. It thus holds that $\tau \vdash \texttt{fix te} : t$ and $\tau \vdash \texttt{te} : t \to t$. Since FreeVars(`fix te`) = FreeVars(`te`) it follows from the induction hypothesis that $\mathcal{R}(\texttt{te}, \rho_s, \rho_d, \rho, t \to t)$.

By the inference rules of Figure 8.4 t is of form $t_1 \to \ldots \to t_n \to S$, $n > 0$ or $t_1 \to \ldots \to t_n \to D$, $n > 0$. For now we shall assume that $t = t_1 \to \ldots \to t_n \to S$.

We will take $\texttt{te}_{t\perp}$ to be an (arbitrary) closed two-level expression of type t such that

$$\mathcal{T}[\![\texttt{te}_{t\perp}]\!]\rho_s = \lambda x_1.\ldots.\lambda x_n.\perp = \mathcal{E}[\![\phi(\texttt{te}_{t\perp})]\!]\rho$$

Thus $\mathcal{R}(\texttt{te}_{t\perp}, \rho_s, \rho_d, \rho, t_1 \to \ldots \to t_n \to S)$ holds. By induction on m, repeatedly using $\mathcal{R}(\texttt{te}, \rho_s, \rho_d, \rho, t \to t)$ we see that $\mathcal{R}(\texttt{te (te } (\ldots \texttt{te}_{t\perp})), \rho_s, \rho_d, \rho, t)$ where there are m applications of of `te` holds for any m.

Since t is of form $t_1 \to \ldots \to t_n \to S$, $\mathcal{R}(\texttt{fix te}, \rho_s, \rho_d, \rho, t)$ may also be written: $\forall\, \texttt{te}_1, \ldots, \texttt{te}_n$: $(\forall i \in [1..n]: \tau \vdash \texttt{te}_i : t_i$ and $\mathcal{R}(\texttt{te}_i, \rho_s, \rho_d, \rho, t_i))$ implies

$$\begin{aligned} &\mathcal{T}[\![(\texttt{fix te) te}_1 \ \ldots \ \texttt{te}_n]\!]\rho_s \\ = \ &\mathcal{E}[\![\phi((\texttt{fix te) te}_1 \ \ldots \ \texttt{te}_n)]\!]\rho \end{aligned}$$

This equation is shown by

$$\begin{aligned} &\mathcal{T}[\![(\texttt{fix te) te}_1 \ \ldots \ \texttt{te}_n]\!]\rho_s \\ = \ &(\mathcal{T}[\![\texttt{fix te}]\!]\rho_s)\,(\mathcal{T}[\![\texttt{te}_1]\!]\rho_s)\ \ldots\ (\mathcal{T}[\![\texttt{te}_n]\!]\rho_s) \\ = \ &\sqcup\underbrace{(\mathcal{T}[\![\texttt{te}]\!]\rho_s)((\mathcal{T}[\![\texttt{te}]\!]\rho_s)\ldots(\mathcal{T}[\![\texttt{te}_{t\perp}]\!]\rho_s))}_{\text{m te's}}\,(\mathcal{T}[\![\texttt{te}_1]\!]\rho_s)\ \ldots\ (\mathcal{T}[\![\texttt{te}_n]\!]\rho_s) \end{aligned}$$

Distribute applications over $\sqcup$, and use $\mathcal{T}$'s rule for application

$$= \ \sqcup(\mathcal{T}[\![(\texttt{te (te } (\ldots \ \texttt{te}_{t\perp})))\ \texttt{te}_1 \ \ldots \ \texttt{te}_n]\!]\rho_s)$$

Use that for all m

$$\mathcal{R}(\texttt{te (te } (\ldots \ \texttt{te}_{t\perp}))\ \texttt{te}_1 \ \ldots \ \texttt{te}_n, \rho_s, \rho_d, \rho, t)$$

$$\begin{aligned} = \ &\sqcup(\mathcal{E}[\![\phi(\texttt{te (te } (\ldots \ \texttt{te}_{t\perp})))\ \texttt{te}_1 \ \ldots \ \texttt{te}_n]\!]\rho) \\ = \ &\sqcup\,(\mathcal{E}[\![\phi(\texttt{te})]\!]\rho)\,((\mathcal{E}[\![\phi(\texttt{te})]\!]\rho)\ldots(\mathcal{E}[\![\phi(\texttt{te}_{t\perp})]\!]\rho)\,) \\ &\qquad (\mathcal{E}[\![\phi(\texttt{te}_1)]\!]\rho)\ \ldots\ (\mathcal{E}[\![\phi(\texttt{te}_n)]\!]\rho) \\ = \ &(\mathcal{E}[\![\phi(\texttt{fix te})]\!]\rho)\,(\mathcal{E}[\![\phi(\texttt{te}_1)]\!]\rho)\ \ldots\ (\mathcal{E}[\![\phi(\texttt{te}_n)]\!]\rho) \\ = \ &\mathcal{E}[\![\phi((\texttt{fix te) te}_1 \ \ldots \ \texttt{te}_n)]\!]\rho \end{aligned}$$

If t is of form $t_1 \to \ldots \to t_n \to D$, the proof proceeds in a very similar manner and we omit the calculation. □

8.9   Exercises

Some of the exercises involve finding a minimal completion. The formal algorithm to do this is targeted for an efficient implementation and is not suited to be executed by hand (for other than very small examples). So if not otherwise stated just use good sense for finding minimal completions.

Exercise 8.1 Find a minimal completion for the lambda expression listed below given the binding-time assumptions $\tau = [\text{m0} \mapsto S,\ \text{n0} \mapsto D]$. Specialize the program with respect to m0 = 42.

```
(λm.λn.+ m n) m0 n0
```
□

Exercise 8.2 Find a minimal completion for the lambda expression listed below given the binding-time assumptions $\tau = [\text{x0} \mapsto S,\ \text{xs0} \mapsto S,\ \text{vs0} \mapsto D]$. Specialize the program with respect to x0 = c and xs0 = (a b c d).

```
(fix λlookup.λx.λxs.λvs.
  if (null? xs)
  then 'error
  else if (equal? x (car xs))
      then (car vs)
      else (lookup x (cdr xs) (cdr vs))) x0 xs0 vs0
```
□

Exercise 8.3 In previous chapters, a self-interpreter sint has been defined by

$$[\![\text{sint}]\!]_{\text{L}}\ \text{p}\ \text{d} = [\![\text{p}]\!]_{\text{L}}\ \text{d}$$

Define sint, basing it on $\mathcal{E}$ for instance, such that this equation holds for the lambda calculus. □

Exercise 8.4

1. Write a self-interpreter sint for the lambda calculus by transforming the function $\mathcal{E}$ into a lambda expression fix $\lambda\mathcal{E}.\lambda\text{e}.\lambda\rho.\text{if}\ \ldots\ \text{e'}\ \rho'$ with free variables e' and ρ'.

2. Find a minimal completion for sint given binding-time assumptions $\tau = [\text{env'} \mapsto S,\ \rho' \mapsto D]$.

3. Find a minimal completion for sint given binding-time assumptions $\tau = [\text{env'} \mapsto S,\ \rho' \mapsto (S \to D)]$.

4. Specialize `sint` with respect to the power program in Section 8.1. The free variables e' and ρ' of `sint` shall have the following static values:
e' = ((fix λp.λn'.λx'....) n x) and ρ' = [n $\mapsto$ n, x $\mapsto$ x].

□

Exercise 8.5 Implement the partial evaluator from Figure 8.3 in a programming language of your own choice.
□

Exercise 8.6 * Implement the partial evaluator from Figure 8.3 in the lambda calculus. It might be a good idea to implement the self-interpreter first and then extend it to handle the two-level expressions. Use the partial evaluator to specialize `sint` with respect to various lambda expressions. Is the partial evaluator optimal? Try self-application of the partial evaluator.
□

Exercise 8.7 Given the expression (λx.x) y with $\tau(y) = S$, generate constraints, normalize the constraint set, and then give a minimal completion for the expression. Repeat the process for the same expression but with $\tau(y) = D$.
□

Exercise 8.8 * Implement the binding time analysis for the lambda calculus by constraint solving as described in Section 8.7. The 'sledgehammer' approach for normalizing the constraint set is perfectly suited for a prototype implementation. Just note that it can be done in almost-linear time, $O(n\alpha(n, n))$, where α is an inverse of Ackermann's function [114].
□

Exercise 8.9

1. At the end of Section 8.1 is listed how the lambda calculus interpreter in Section 3.1 has been revised to obtain that in Figure 8.1. How do these revisions affect the residual programs produced by partial evaluation of these interpreters?

2. What further revisions would be necessary to achieve optimality?

□

Exercise 8.10 Assume that a self-interpreter `op-sint` is available with the property that Lambdamix is ruled optimal when this particular self-interpreter is used in the Definition 6.4. Does it follow from this optimality property and Theorem 8.1 that `op-sint` is a correct self-interpreter when $\mathcal{E}$ is used as the canonical semantics for lambda expressions?
□

Exercise 8.11 Elaborate the proof for Theorem 8.1 by proving the cases for static and dynamic applications, static and dynamic conditionals, and dynamic fixed-point operators.
□

Exercise 8.12 Prove that residual programs are identical for completions te_1 and te_2 if $te_1 \sqsubseteq te_2$ and $te_2 \sqsubseteq te_1$. Discuss the impact of different choices on efficiency of the partial evaluation process itself.
□

Chapter 9

Partial Evaluation for Prolog

Torben Mogensen

Prolog was developed as an implementation of a formal logical system (first-order Horn clauses) on a computer. Programming in this logic language was supposed to consist of stating the relevant facts and laws about a given subject as logical formulae, which would allow the computer to answer similarly formulated questions about the subject by using logical inference. As with Lisp, the pure mathematical formalism was seen as too limited for 'real programming' and various features were added to the language, including control operators, side-effects, and the ability to make self-modifying programs. It is, however, considered bad style to overuse these features, so to a large extent Prolog programs will have the properties of the logic formalism.

One of the most pleasing aspects of Prolog is the ability to run programs 'backwards' or with incomplete input. The program defines a relation among query variables with no clear indication of which are considered input and which are output. When running the program, values are provided for some of these variables and the computer will attempt to find values of the other variables such that the relation holds. If no values are given *a priori*, the computer will attempt to enumerate all combinations of values that satisfy the relation. An example of this is shown below. The predicate ap specifies that the third argument is the list concatenation of the two first arguments. Calling ap with all parameters instantiated simply tests whether the third argument is the concatenation of the first two. Calling with the first two parameters instantiated to lists results in a solution where the third parameter gets bound to the concatenation of these. Calling with only the last parameter instantiated causes Prolog to enumerate all combinations of values for the first two parameters that satisfy the relation. Note that Prolog answers 'no' when no further solutions exist.

```
ap([],L,L).
ap([A|L],M,[A|N]) :- ap(L,M,N).
```

```
?- ap([1,2],[3,4],[1,2,3,4]).
yes

?- ap([1,2],[3,4],N).

N = [1,2,3,4] ? ;
no

?- ap(L,M,[1,2,3]).

L = [],
M = [1,2,3] ? ;

L = [1],
M = [2,3] ? ;

L = [1,2],
M = [3] ? ;

L = [1,2,3],
M = [] ? ;
no
```

On the surface, partial evaluation of Prolog seems almost trivial, as Prolog has this ability to run programs with 'unknown' input: any parameter can be replaced with a variable and the program can be run anyway.

There are, however, several problems with this approach. One is that Prolog programs with insufficiently instantiated parameters tend to go into infinite loops; and even when they terminate, the result is not a residual program, but a list of answer substitutions[1]. A partial evaluation strategy different from normal resolution is thus needed. Another problem is that in full Prolog the presence of meta-logical predicates, control operators, and 'negation by failure' makes execution with some input replaced by variables incorrect with respect to execution with full input. A simple example of this is the program

```
p(X,Y) :- var(X), X=7, Y=3.
p(7,5).
```

If we run this with the input goal p(A,B) we get the answers A=7, B=3 and A=7, B=5. This could lead us to believe that running with the goal p(7,B) would yield B=3 and B=5. This is not the case, as the first clause fails, making the only solution B=5. Often this problem is side-stepped by considering only pure Horn clauses.

---

[1]These can, however, be seen as equivalent to a list of Prolog facts.

In the previous chapters we have generated specialized function names for residual functions, using the static parameters to generate them. There is not as much need for the generation of specialized predicate names in Prolog, as the static parameters to a clause can become patterns in the specialized clauses, distinguishing these as easily as different names can. Renaming specialized clauses with respect to their static arguments can, however, reduce the size and the time requirement of the residual programs.

The earliest example of partial evaluation of Prolog was given by Jan Komorowski in the early 1980s [151]. The subject has been investigated by several people since then, for making the use of meta-interpreters more efficient, in essence compiling programs by partially evaluating the meta-interpreters with respect to them. As such, the early attempts at partial evaluation were influenced by the style of the meta-interpreters, both in the way the partial evaluators are written and in the programs that they are able to handle well.

An example of this is Fujita and Furukawa's work [88], which extends the classical three-line meta-interpreter to perform partial evaluation, yielding a very short partial evaluator. It is claimed to be self-applicable, but as noted in a paper by Bondorf, Frauendorf, and Richter, the operational semantics are not always preserved when self-application is attempted [33]. The main problem is that values in the partial evaluator that is running and the partial evaluator that is being specialized are not kept sufficiently separate.

Fuller uses a different approach [89]: the source program is represented as a ground term, which is given as input to the partial evaluator. The language is restricted to pure logic but care is taken to preserve semantics when self-application is performed. Run-time terms with variables are represented by ground terms in the partial evaluator and unification is simulated by meta-unification on these. Though self-application is successful, it is very inefficient and the resulting compilers are very large and slow.

The first efficiently self-applicable and semantically safe partial evaluator for Prolog appears to be the one reported in the paper by Bondorf *et al.* [33]. Source program and values are represented as ground terms, as in Fuller's work. By using *binding-time annotations* as in Section 5.3, efficient self-application is achieved: compiling by using a stand-alone compiler generated by self-application is several times faster than by specializing an interpreter. The language is extended to include meta-logical predicates and limited side-effects. The operational semantics is preserved, even at self-application.

Logimix [192] improves on this by refraining from representing values as ground terms (though the program still is). This speeds up the execution by simulating unification meta-circularly by unification in the underlying system. This gives significant efficiency improvements. Also, more of Prolog's control and meta-logical features are treated.

Fujita and Furukawa's partial evaluator [88] requires the input program to be stored in the data base. To avoid the scope problems this gives at self-application time and to make effective use of polyvariant specialization (see Section 4.4.2),

Fuller's partial evaluator, the one by Bondorf *et al.*, and Logimix all require the input program as a parameter in the goal of the partial evaluator [89,33,192].

Most work on partial evaluation of Prolog has not addressed self-application at all, either because it has not been considered relevant or because of the practical problems involved. Sahlin's Mixtus system [236] is a powerful partial evaluator for almost all of Prolog, but it is not clear whether it could be made self-applicable without major rewriting.

A theory of partial evaluation of Prolog is presented by Lloyd and Shepherdson [174]. They define partial evaluation to be an incomplete SLD resolution of a goal with respect to a set of clauses: a partial resolution tree is generated by unfolding selected subgoals repeatedly. At the end, the goal at the root of the tree is replaced by the sequence of the goals at the leaves. The clauses for these goals can then be partially evaluated in a similar fashion. No strategy for how to decide unfolding is given, nor is there any concept of specialization of predicates to some of their arguments. Negation is considered, but no other meta-logical or control features. As a consequence, few existing implementations of partial evaluators are covered by this theory.

9.1   An example

Let us illustrate some points by an example: compiling regular expressions into deterministic finite automata by partial evaluation. The partial evaluation was done using Logimix.

The program in Figure 9.1 takes as input a regular expression and a string (a list of characters) and tests whether the string is generated by the regular expression. The program uses the predicates `generate_empty`, `first`, and `next`.

The predicate `generate_empty` tests whether a regular expression generates the empty string. The predicate `first(R,S)` tests whether a particular symbol S can begin some string which is generated by the regular expression R. Predicate `next(R,S,R1)` is used to move one step forward in a regular expression: R1 is a regular expression that generates the string S1 ... Sn if and only if R generates the complete string S S1 ... Sn. Predicate `next(R,S,R1)` thus tests whether the strings generated by the regular expression R1 are exactly the tails of the strings that R generates, which begin with the symbol S.

Figure 9.2 shows the result of using Logimix to specialize the program in Figure 9.1 with respect to the regular expression (a|b)*aba. The predicate `generate` occurs in four different specialized versions, `generate_0` ... `generate_3`. This illustrates polyvariant specialization: each predicate is specialized according to different values of the static (known) input (the regular expression). The remaining parameter (the string) is dynamic (not known at partial evaluation time), and is thus still present as a parameter in the residual program. All calls to `generate_empty`, `first`, and `next` have been fully evaluated and are thus not present in the residual program. The use of ; ('or' in Prolog) in the residual rules stems from different results of calls to first. The residual program is equivalent to a deterministic finite automaton, and is in fact identical to the automaton derived for the same regular expression in [4].

```
generate(R,[]) :- generate_empty(R).
generate(R,[S|Ss]) :- first(R,S1),S=S1,next(R,S1,R1),generate(R1,Ss).
```

Figure 9.1: Testing whether a string is generated by a regular expression.

```
generate_0([]) :- fail.
generate_0([S|Ss]) :- S=a, generate_1(Ss) ; S=b, generate_0(Ss).

generate_1([]) :- fail.
generate_1([S|Ss]) :- S=a, generate_1(Ss) ; S=b, generate_2(Ss).

generate_2([]) :- fail.
generate_2([S|Ss]) :- S=a, generate_3(Ss) ; S=b, generate_0(Ss).

generate_3([]).
generate_3([S|Ss]) :- S=a, generate_1(Ss) ; S=b, generate_2(Ss).
```

Figure 9.2: Residual program.

9.2   The structure of Logimix

The Logimix partial evaluator consists of two parts: a meta-circular self-interpreter to perform the static parts of the program, and a specializer that unfolds dynamic goals or specializes them with respect to their static arguments. The specializer calls the interpreter to execute the static subgoals. This division of the partial evaluator reflects the different behaviours of interpretation and specialization: interpretation can fail or return multiple solutions, whereas specialization should always succeed with exactly one specialized goal.

9.2.1   The interpreter

The meta-circular interpreter has the program as a ground parameter, but simulates unification, backtracking, and other control directly by the same constructs in the underlying Prolog system. Only those control features that are possible to interpret in this way are included, that is (_,_), (_;_), (not_), (_->_;_),..., but not ! (cut). Predicates not defined in the program are assumed to be basic (predefined) predicates.

9.2.2   The specializer

The specializer requires annotation of variables and goals as *static* or *dynamic* and annotation of whether or not to unfold calls to user-defined predicates. During partial evaluation, static variables will be neither *more* nor *less* bound than they would be during normal (full) evaluation. This ensures that even meta-logical predicates (like `var/1`) have the same behaviour at specialization time as during a normal evaluation. Goals are considered static if they can be fully evaluated at partial evaluation time while preserving semantics. This means that they contain only static variables and that they neither have side-effects, nor depend on a state that can be modified by side-effects. Dynamic goals are specialized with respect to the values of the static variables. This involves evaluating static subgoals and unfolding some user-defined predicates (depending on their annotation) and creating specialized predicates for the calls that are not unfolded. Calls to primitives are executed only if they are static.

Binding of static variables happens only when evaluating static goals, and these bindings will be visible only to later static goals (which may be parts of dynamic goals). This means that backwards unification is not possible. Such backwards unification could change the behaviour of non-logical predicates like `var/1` as we saw in the example at the start of this chapter. Evaluation of a static goal will return a list of possible solutions, each consisting of values for the variables in the goal. Each element of this list is used to generate a specialized version of the goals following the static goal. These are then combined with ; to produce a single residual goal. This is seen in the residual program from the regular expression example, where residual goals corresponding to `S1 = a` and `S1 = b` are combined with a ;.

Additionally, static goals are annotated by the potential number of solutions ('at most one' or 'any number'). This is not essential, but allows the cases with at most one solution to be handled by a simpler procedure.

Due to unfolding, the residual programs can contain long chains of explicit unifications, e.g.

```
X=[A|B], B=[C|D], D=[E|F], F=[].
```

These are folded to single unifications in a post-processing stage. When this will not change the semantics of the program, the chains are folded, even across predicate calls. The example above becomes

```
X=[A,C,E].
```

The binding-time analysis is a combination of a dependency analysis, a groundness analysis, a determinacy analysis, and a side-effect analysis. The dependency analysis is used to trace which variables will depend on others by unification. Combined with groundness analysis this is used to determine in which cases the unification of a static and a dynamic variable should cause the static variable to be reclassified as dynamic, i.e. when the static variable can be non-ground. The determinacy analysis is used to find out whether a static goal has at most one solution, or possibly more than one. The side-effect analysis is used to classify goals containing side-effecting primitives as dynamic. All this information is used when annotating the program. At partial evaluation time the annotations are used to guide the actions of the partial evaluator, as sketched above.

The regular expression program in Figure 9.1 is annotated with the regular expression classified as static and the string dynamic, to yield the annotated program in Figure 9.3, which is used as input to Logimix to make the residual program in Figure 9.2. Dynamic variables and patterns and predicate calls that are not to be unfolded are underlined. In addition to this, static goals that can return at most one solution are marked with a superscript '1'.

```
generate(R,[]) :- generate_empty¹(R).
generate(R,[S|Ss]) :- first(R,S1), S=S1, next¹(R,S1,R1),
                      generate(R1,Ss).
```

Figure 9.3: Annotated regular expression program.

The variable S1 in the last clause seems superfluous, as it will be equal to S. However, if S were used in place of S1 in the call to first/2, the goal would no longer be static (due to the presence of the dynamic variable S). As it is, S1 is static and unbound when calling first/2, and static and ground after the call. This means that the unification of S and S1 will not make S1 dynamic. Thus S1 is a static parameter to next/3, which makes this a static goal. This again makes R1 a static parameter to the recursive call to generate/2, which is specialized with respect to it. Using S1 has no effect on the semantics of the program, and it will make normal execution somewhat slower due to unnecessary backtracking, but it improves the result of partially evaluating the program by making more things static. Modifications of programs to improve the results of partial evaluation are called *binding-time improvements* and are discussed in more detail in Chapter 12.

9.2.3   Specialization of goals

Figure 9.4 shows the kinds of goals that Logimix allows in the subset of Prolog that it handles. If a list of terms is empty, the parentheses are omitted. The keywords `basic` and `call` will be shown only where it is necessary to distinguish calls to predefined and user-defined predicates. Figures 9.5 and 9.6 show specialization

$$
\begin{array}{lll}
\textit{Goal} & \rightarrow & \texttt{basic } \textit{Name}(\textit{Term},\dots,\textit{Term}) \qquad \text{— call predefined predicate} \\
 & | & \texttt{call } \textit{Name}(\textit{Term},\dots,\textit{Term}) \qquad \text{— call user-defined predicate} \\
 & | & \texttt{true } | \texttt{ fail} \\
 & | & \textit{Goal} \texttt{ , } \textit{Goal} \; | \texttt{ not } \textit{Goal} \\
 & | & \textit{Goal} \texttt{ ; } \textit{Goal} \\
 & | & (\textit{Goal} \texttt{ -> } \textit{Goal} \texttt{ ; } \textit{Goal}) \\
 & | & \texttt{if}(\textit{Goal},\textit{Goal},\textit{Goal}) \\
\textit{Term} & \rightarrow & \textit{Variable} \; | \; \textit{Name}(\textit{Term},\dots,\textit{Term})
\end{array}
$$

Figure 9.4: Syntax for Prolog goals.

of dynamic goals. The static goals are executed normally. Evaluation rules are called from the specialization rules when static subgoals are encountered. The specialization rules do not address the annotation (shown with superscript 1) of single versus multiple solutions to static subgoals. These annotations merely cause application of simplified instances of the general rules, and are mostly interesting in self-application, where the simplified rules are easier to specialize.

The notation $\Theta \vdash G \rightarrow G'$ states that, with the substitution Θ, the dynamic goal G specializes to the residual goal G'. $\Theta \vdash G \Rightarrow \Theta_1,\dots\Theta_n$ states that the static goal G evaluates to a list of possible answer substitutions $\Theta_1,\dots\Theta_n$. If this list is empty (ϵ) the goal failed. $S \sqcup T \succ \Theta$ states that S and T unify with Θ as the most general unifier. The rules for evaluation of static goals are not shown here.

Since all completely static goals are handled by the first two rules, the remaining rules only handle goals with some static part. Hence, the rule for calls to basic predicates doesn't try to evaluate the calls. The control structures that have several subgoals may treat some combinations of static and dynamic subgoals differently. This is the case for $\_,\_$, where the substitutions for the first subgoal are passed on to the second subgoal when the first is static. Note that the difference between the two conditionals $\_->\_;\_$ and $\texttt{if}(\_,\_,\_)$ is reflected in the treatment of these when their first argument is static. In the rules for calls to user-defined predicates, it is assumed that the static parameters are the first n parameters. This is not required in Logimix, but it makes the notation in the description easier. When a call is unfolded the variables in the clause definition are renamed to new distinct names. This corresponds to the mechanism used in normal Prolog execution. When a goal is not unfolded, a call to a residual predicate is generated. The residual predicate is renamed as a function of the values of the static parameters. In the rule this is shown by having the static parameters as a subscript to the predicate name.

After the rules have been applied some local reductions, not described here, are applied to the residual goal.

$$\frac{\Theta \vdash G \;\Rightarrow\; \Theta_1, \ldots, \Theta_n}{\Theta \vdash G \;\rightarrow\; \texttt{true} \; ; \; \ldots \; ; \; \texttt{true}} \quad \text{If } G \text{ is static. } \texttt{true} \text{ occurs } n \text{ times}$$

$$\frac{\Theta \vdash G \;\Rightarrow\; \epsilon}{\Theta \vdash G \;\rightarrow\; \texttt{fail}} \quad \text{If } G \text{ is static}$$

$$\overline{\Theta \vdash \underline{\texttt{basic}}\ N(T_1, \ldots, T_n) \;\rightarrow\; \texttt{basic}\ N(\Theta(T_1), \ldots, \Theta(T_n))}$$

$$\frac{\begin{array}{ccc} \Theta((S_1, \ldots, S_n)) \sqcup (P_{11}, \ldots, P_{1n}) \succ \Theta_1 & \Theta'_1 = \Theta \circ \Theta_1 & \Theta'_1 \vdash R_1 \;\rightarrow\; R'_1 \\ \ldots & \ldots & \ldots \\ \Theta((S_1, \ldots, S_n)) \sqcup (P_{k1}, \ldots, P_{kn}) \succ \Theta_k & \Theta'_k = \Theta \circ \Theta_k & \Theta'_k \vdash R_k \;\rightarrow\; R'_k \end{array}}{\begin{array}{l} \Theta \vdash \texttt{call}\ N(S_1, \ldots, S_n, \underline{D_1}, \ldots, \underline{D_m}) \;\rightarrow\; (P_{1n+1}{=}\Theta'_1(D_1), \ldots, P_{1n+m}{=}\Theta'_1(D_m), R'_1) \\ \qquad\qquad\qquad\qquad\qquad\qquad\qquad\qquad\quad ; \ldots ; \\ \qquad\qquad\qquad\qquad\qquad\qquad\qquad\qquad\quad (P_{kn+1}{=}\Theta'_k(D_1), \ldots, P_{kn+m}{=}\Theta'_k(D_m), R'_k) \end{array}}$$

where S_i are the static parameters, D_i are the dynamic parameters and

$$N(P_{11}, \ldots, P_{1n}, \underline{P_{1n+1}}, \ldots, \underline{P_{1n+m}}) \text{:} -R_1$$
$$\ldots$$
$$N(P_{k1}, \ldots, P_{kn}, \underline{P_{kn+1}}, \ldots, \underline{P_{kn+m}}) \text{:} -R_k$$

are the clauses for N that unify with static parameters of the call.

$$\overline{\Theta \vdash \texttt{call}\ N(S_1, \ldots, S_n, \underline{D_1}, \ldots, \underline{D_m}) \;\rightarrow\; \texttt{fail}}$$

If no clauses for N unify with the call

$$\overline{\Theta \vdash \underline{\texttt{call}}\ N(S_1, \ldots, S_n, \underline{D_1}, \ldots, \underline{D_m}) \;\rightarrow\; \texttt{call}\ N_{(\Theta(S_1), \ldots, \Theta(S_n))}(\Theta(D_1), \ldots, \Theta(D_m))}$$

where S_i are the static parameters and D_i are the dynamic parameters. A definition of the residual predicate $N_{(\Theta(S_1), \ldots, \Theta(S_n))}$ is added to the residual program.

Figure 9.5: Specialization of Prolog goals (part I).

9.3   Conclusion

Logimix has been successfully applied to interpreters, yielding compiled programs where virtually all interpretation overhead is removed. Self-application of Logimix yields stand-alone compilers and compiler generators (see the table below). The figures are for execution under SICStus Prolog version 0.6 on a SPARCstation 2. Here sint is the self interpreter used in Logimix to execute static subgoals, used as a stand-alone program, and mix is Logimix itself. The size of the generated compiler generator cogen is approximately 30KB of non-pretty-printed Prolog source.

$$\frac{\Theta \vdash G_1 \;\Rightarrow\; \Theta_1, \ldots \Theta_n \quad \Theta_1 \vdash G_2 \;\rightarrow\; G_{21} \ldots \Theta_n \vdash G_2 \;\rightarrow\; G_{2n}}{\Theta \vdash G_1 \,,\, G_2 \;\rightarrow\; G_{21} \;;\; \ldots \;;\; G_{2n}} \quad \text{if } G_1 \text{ is static}$$

$$\frac{\Theta \vdash G_1 \;\Rightarrow\; \epsilon}{\Theta \vdash G_1 \,,\, G_2 \;\rightarrow\; \texttt{fail}} \quad \text{if } G_1 \text{ is static}$$

$$\frac{\Theta \vdash \underline{G_1} \;\rightarrow\; G_1' \quad \Theta \vdash G_2 \;\rightarrow\; G_2'}{\Theta \vdash \underline{G_1} \,,\, G_2 \;\rightarrow\; G_1' \,,\, G_2'}$$

$$\frac{\Theta \vdash G \;\rightarrow\; G'}{\Theta \vdash \underline{\text{not }} G \;\rightarrow\; \text{not } G'}$$

$$\frac{\Theta \vdash G_1 \;\rightarrow\; G_1' \quad \Theta \vdash G_2 \;\rightarrow\; G_2'}{\Theta \vdash G_1 \;\underline{;}\; G_2 \;\rightarrow\; G_1' \;;\; G_2'}$$

$$\frac{\Theta \vdash G_1 \;\Rightarrow\; \Theta_1, \ldots \Theta_n \quad \Theta_1 \vdash G_2 \;\rightarrow\; G_{21}}{\Theta \vdash G_1 \;\underline{\texttt{->}}\; G_2 \;\underline{;}\; G_3 \;\rightarrow\; G_{21}} \quad \text{if } G_1 \text{ is static}$$

$$\frac{\Theta \vdash G_1 \;\Rightarrow\; \epsilon \quad \Theta \vdash G_3 \;\rightarrow\; G_3'}{\Theta \vdash G_1 \;\underline{\texttt{->}}\; G_2 \;\underline{;}\; G_3 \;\rightarrow\; G_3'} \quad \text{if } G_1 \text{ is static}$$

$$\frac{\Theta \vdash \underline{G_1} \;\rightarrow\; G_1' \quad \Theta \vdash G_2 \;\rightarrow\; G_2' \quad \vdash G_3 \;\rightarrow\; G_3'}{\Theta \vdash \underline{G_1} \;\underline{\texttt{->}}\; G_2 \;\underline{;}\; G_3 \;\rightarrow\; G_1' \;\texttt{->}\; G_2' \;;\; G_3'}$$

$$\frac{\Theta \vdash G_1 \;\Rightarrow\; \Theta_1, \ldots \Theta_n \quad \Theta_1 \vdash G_2 \;\rightarrow\; G_{21} \ldots \Theta_n \vdash G_2 \;\rightarrow\; G_{2n}}{\Theta \vdash \underline{\texttt{if}}(G_1, G_2, G_3) \;\rightarrow\; G_{21}; \ldots; G_{2n}} \quad \text{if } G_1 \text{ is static}$$

$$\frac{\Theta \vdash G_1 \;\Rightarrow\; \epsilon \quad \Theta \vdash G_3 \;\rightarrow\; G_3'}{\Theta \vdash \underline{\texttt{if}}(G_1, G_2, G_3) \;\rightarrow\; G_3'} \quad \text{if } G_1 \text{ is static}$$

$$\frac{\Theta \vdash \underline{G_1} \;\rightarrow\; G_1' \quad \Theta \vdash G_2 \;\rightarrow\; G_2' \quad \vdash G_3 \;\rightarrow\; G_3'}{\Theta \vdash \underline{\texttt{if}}(G_1, G_2, G_3) \;\rightarrow\; \texttt{if}(G_1', G_2', G_3')}$$

Figure 9.6: Specialization of Prolog goals (part II).

job	time/s	speedup
output = sint(sint, data)	2.25	13.7
output = target(data)	0.16	
target = mix(sint[ann], sint)	19.2	1.78
target = comp(sint)	10.8	
comp = mix(mix[ann], sint[ann])	19.3	1.35
comp = cogen(sint[ann])	14.4	
cogen = mix(mix[ann], mix[ann])	172.0	1.14
cogen = cogen(mix[ann])	152.0	

The speedup gained from compilation by partial evaluation is of the same order as for functional languages, but the speedup from self-application is relatively small. This is because a large part of the operations in the specializer are dynamic at self-application time. The main culprits are the folding of sequences of dynamic unifications into single unifications (which, as described above, is a completely dynamic postprocess) and comparison of static values (which is static at partial evaluation time but dynamic at self-application time).

Improving Logimix

In general, Logimix is fairly sensitive to how a program is written. The regular expression example showed one example of this, but the fact that values are not propagated from dynamic goals to static goals also plays a part. As an example, consider the goal (s1,(d,s2)), where s1 and s2 are static subgoals and d is a dynamic subgoal. The binding of static variables in s1 are propagated to the second subgoal (d,s2), and through this to s2. If we instead write ((s1,d),s2), the binding of static variables in s1 are still propagated to d, but since the subgoal (s1,d) is dynamic, no static bindings are propagated from this to s2. This is normally not a problem, as one usually omits parentheses and writes s1,d,s2, which is parsed the 'right' way.

When unfolding a call to a dynamic predicate, the bindings that occur in its static subgoals are not propagated out to later goals in the clause where it was called from. Essentially, there are parentheses around the unfolded goal that prohibit the propagation of static bindings. Solving this problem either requires thought when writing the programs that are to be specialized, or alternatively rewriting Logimix to be less restrictive. The requirement that specialization returns exactly one specialized goal (and no bindings) will have to be lifted, so specialization instead returns a list of pairs (residual goal, static bindings). The static bindings can then be used to produce specialized versions of the subsequent subgoals. An alternative approach that achieves the same effect is to pass the following goals as a parameter to the procedure that specializes a goal, specifying a kind of continuation. Whenever a static binding occurs, it will have an affect on the entire continuation. This is similar to the strategy used for improving the results of Similix [31,28].

9.4   Exercises

Exercise 9.1 Consider the ap predicate for appending lists:

```
ap([],L,L).
ap([A|L],M,[A|N]) :- ap(L,M,N).
```

Assume that the intended call pattern to ap is with the first two parameters instantiated and the third possibly (but not always) uninstantiated.

1. Given that we want to specialize **ap** with respect to a static first parameter, annotate the predicate by underlining dynamic variables. Use the rule that static variables must have *exactly* the same value during normal evaluation and partial evaluation.

2. Consider whether it is safe (with respect to termination of specialization) to unfold the recursive call during specialization, using the assumptions above. Annotate the call accordingly, underlining it if it should not be unfolded.

3. By hand, specialize **ap** to the static first parameter [1,2,3]. Use the rules in Figures 9.5 and 9.6.

4. The specialized program will contain superfluous chains of unifications. Reduce these by using forwards unification only.

$\square$

Exercise 9.2 As Exercise 9.1, but specializing with the *second* parameter static and equal to [1,2,3]. $\square$

Exercise 9.3 As Exercise 9.1, but specializing the predicate **generates** shown below with the second parameter static and equal to [a,b,b]. It can be assumed that the basic predicates **generates_empty**, **first** and **next** don't use side-effects.

```
generates(R,[]) :- generates_empty(R).
generates(R,[S|Ss]) :- first(R,S),next(R,S,R1),generates(R1,Ss).
```

$\square$

Exercise 9.4 Assuming that the operations **generates_empty**, **first**, and **next** are relatively expensive, estimate the speedup of the residual program from Exercise 9.3 over the original. Would a binding-time improving reformulation of the program (as discussed in the example in the text) improve the result? $\square$

Chapter 10

Aspects of Similix: A Partial Evaluator for a Subset of Scheme

This chapter describes partial evaluation of a subset of the dynamically typed functional language Scheme, including higher-order functions and limited side effects. The presentation is based on the approach taken by Bondorf and Danvy in the partial evaluator Similix, but we focus here on the principles and do not give a completely faithful description of the actual Similix system. Similix uses polyvariant specialization of named functions and is an off-line partial evaluator, as is the Scheme0 specializer from Chapter 5. However, in addition to handling a more complex language, Similix also handles the problems of infinite unfolding and duplication in a new and illuminating way, and emphasizes preserving the termination properties of programs.

The binding-time analysis handles higher-order functions, using the closure analysis described in Chapter 15.

The Similix partial evaluator is rather more practical than those described in the preceding chapters. For instance, the set of basic functions is extensible, basic functions can be classified according to their effects, side effects are handled correctly, and the termination properties of residual programs are better. Moreover, the Similix system contains a binding-time debugger which provides useful feedback concerning the binding-time properties of programs. The result is a partial evaluator which is more complicated than those described earlier, but one which has had many practical applications.

Similix was initially developed by Bondorf and Danvy; the recent versions are due mainly to Bondorf. This chapter is based on their papers [28,30,31,32] and on Bondorf's thesis [27].

10.1 An overview of Similix

Our version of the Similix subject language is called Scheme1. It extends Scheme0 from Chapter 5 with lambda abstractions (higher-order functions) and `let` bindings. Lambda abstractions require some changes to the binding-time analysis and specialization, mainly because they may be *partially static*. Specialization with respect to higher-order values and partially static lambdas is explained in Section 10.2. Handling `let`-expressions requires a new *occurrence counting!analysis* to decide whether the `let` may be unfolded without risk of duplication.

In addition, the real Similix has a flexible way to define new base functions, and allows limited side effects in base functions. All side effects must be dynamic (that is, they must take place after specialization). Moreover, expressions with side effects cannot be discarded, nor duplicated, nor reordered. Base functions and side effects will not be further discussed in this chapter.

Recent versions of Similix use continuation-based reduction, which improves the binding times of many programs. It is explained in Section 10.5. Continuation-based reduction also allows the handling of partially static data structures without duplicating or discarding expressions (see Section 10.6).

10.1.1   The structure of Similix

Similix works in three main phases: preprocessing, specialization, and postprocessing. The *preprocessing* phase analyses, transforms, and annotates the subject program, based on a description of its input only. The *specialization* phase specializes the annotated subject program with respect to the given static input. The *postprocessing* phase unfolds calls to trivial residual functions.

1. Preprocessing The preprocessing is done in four main steps.

   1.1 Insert an identity `let`-binding `(let (x x) ...)` around the body of each function and lambda, for every variable `x`. The purpose is to isolate the problem of duplication from that of infinite unfolding.

   1.2 Do binding-time analysis, including detection of lambdas that may appear in dynamic contexts. Such lambdas must have dynamic parameters and body, and cannot be applied at specialization time.

   1.3 Create a new named function, called an *sp-function*, for each dynamic `if` and for each dynamic lambda. All sp-functions (and the goal function) are called by dynamic calls (`calld`); all other functions are called by static ones (`calls`).

   1.4 Analyse the number of occurrences of dynamic `let`-bound variables; annotate `let` expressions as dynamic (`letd`) or static (`lets`).

2. Specialization Starting with the program point (`g, vs0`) where `g` is the goal function and `vs0` is the static input, repeatedly construct specialized functions until the program is complete (if ever), as for Scheme0.

Specializing a function with respect to static base values (non-closures) works as for Scheme0. Specializing a function f with respect to a static lambda abstraction, the residual function must have a new parameter for each dynamic free variable in the lambda, and for each dynamic free variable of static lambdas bound in static free variables of the lambda, and so on, recursively.

3. Postprocessing Unfold the call to every residual function which is called at most one place (except the goal function). This eliminates trivial unshared functions.

10.1.2   The higher-order language Scheme1

The subject language Scheme1 which we use is similar to but simpler than the subject language of Similix. It is just Scheme0 from Figure 5.1 extended with let-bindings and lambda abstraction and application, that is, a dynamically typed functional language with call-by-value. For notational simplicity, the lambda abstractions are restricted to one argument.

As for Scheme0, a Scheme1 program **pgm** is a list of definitions of named functions $f_1, \ldots, f_n$:

```
(define (f₁ x₁₁ ... x₁ₐ₁)  body₁)
        ⋮
(define (fₙ xₙ₁ ... xₙₐₙ) bodyₙ)
```

$\langle Expr \rangle$	::=	$\langle Constant \rangle$	Constant
	|	$\langle Var \rangle$	Variable
	|	(if $\langle Expr \rangle$ $\langle Expr \rangle$ $\langle Expr \rangle$)	Conditional
	|	(call $\langle FuncName \rangle$ $\langle Arglist \rangle$)	Function application
	|	($\langle Op \rangle$ $\langle Expr \rangle$ ... $\langle Expr \rangle$)	Base application
	|	(lambda$^\ell$ ($\langle Var \rangle$) $\langle Expr \rangle$)	Lambda abstraction
	|	($\langle Expr \rangle$ $\langle Expr \rangle$)	Lambda application
	|	(let (($\langle Var \rangle$ $\langle Expr \rangle$)) $\langle Expr \rangle$)	Let-binding
$\langle Arglist \rangle$	::=	$\langle Expr \rangle$ ... $\langle Expr \rangle$	Argument expressions
$\langle Constant \rangle$	::=	$\langle Numeral \rangle$	
	|	(quote $\langle Value \rangle$)	

Figure 10.1: Syntax of Scheme1, a higher-order functional language.

Each function body $body_i$ is a Scheme1 expression. The syntax of expressions is shown in Figure 10.1. We distinguish *named functions* such as f_1 from labelled *lambda abstractions* such as (lambda$^\ell$ (x) e). Named functions must always be fully applied. For a given lambda (lambda$^\ell$ (x) e), FreeVars(ℓ) denotes its free variables, listed in some fixed order (e.g. alphabetically sorted).

10.1.3 Two-level Scheme1 expressions

As usual partial evaluation is done in phases. The preprocessing phase yields an annotated two-level Scheme1 program which is then submitted to the specialization phase. The annotations follow the pattern from Chapters 5 and 8 in that every operator if, call, ⟨Op⟩, lambda, application, and let, comes in a static and a dynamic version in the two-level Scheme1 syntax. In addition it has lift-expressions (Figure 10.2).

⟨Expr⟩	::=	⟨Constant⟩	Constant
	|	⟨Var⟩	Variable
	|	(ifs ⟨Expr⟩ ⟨Expr⟩ ⟨Expr⟩)	Static conditional
	|	(ifd ⟨Expr⟩ ⟨Expr⟩ ⟨Expr⟩)	Dynamic conditional
	|	(calls ⟨FuncName⟩ ⟨SDArgs⟩)	Static function appl.
	|	(calld ⟨FuncName⟩ ⟨SDArgs⟩)	Dynamic function appl.
	|	(⟨Op⟩s ⟨Expr⟩ ... ⟨Expr⟩)	Static base appl.
	|	(⟨Op⟩d ⟨Expr⟩ ... ⟨Expr⟩)	Dynamic base appl.
	|	(lift ⟨Expr⟩)	Lifting a static expr.
	|	(lambdas$^\ell$ (⟨Var⟩) ⟨Expr⟩)	Static lambda
	|	(lambdad$^\ell$ (⟨Var⟩) ⟨Expr⟩)	Dynamic lambda
	|	(⟨Expr⟩ ⟨Expr⟩)	Static lambda applic.
	|	(⟨Expr⟩ @d ⟨Expr⟩)	Dynamic lambda appl.
	|	(lets (⟨Var⟩ ⟨Expr⟩) ⟨Expr⟩)	Static let-binding
	|	(letd (⟨Var⟩ ⟨Expr⟩) ⟨Expr⟩)	Dynamic let-binding
⟨SDArgs⟩	::=	(⟨Arglist⟩) (⟨Arglist⟩)	Argument lists

Figure 10.2: Syntax of two-level Scheme1 expressions.

10.1.4 Binding-time analysis for Scheme1

The Scheme1 binding-time analysis is an extension of the Scheme0 binding-time analysis $\mathcal{B}_e$ given in Section 5.2. However, there are three new problems: (1) higher-order applications (e_0 e_1), (2) static lambda abstractions in dynamic contexts, and (3) let-expressions.

(1) Higher-order applications
When analysing a higher-order application (e_0 e_1) it is useful to know which function is applied, or more generally, which functions may be applied. The closure analysis presented in Section 15.2 provides such information: the possible values of e_0. Using this information, binding-time analysis of higher-order applications is basically rather similar to that of first-order applications. The binding-time analysis will be presented in Section 15.3, after the closure analysis.

(2) Lambdas in dynamic contexts

In Scheme0, all values were base values, and therefore a static value v could always be converted into a dynamic value, namely the expression (quote v). This conversion is called *lifting* and was indicated in the two-level Scheme0 syntax by the operator lift. Lifting is necessary when the static value appears in a *dynamic context*. A branch of a dynamic ifd is a typical example of a dynamic context: we must generate code for the if expression and therefore also for each branch, even when its value v is static.

It is far more complicated to lift functional values. In fact, such values are never lifted *during* specialization. Instead, all lambda abstractions that might need to be lifted are classified as dynamic lambdad *before* specialization. The reason is that lifting influences the binding times of other functions in the program.

To see this, consider lifting a functional value. The lifting should result in a lambda expression (lambda (x) e), that is, a piece of Scheme1 code. But then the lambda variable x must be dynamic: it will not be bound to a static value during specialization. Furthermore, if e contains a call (f x) of a named function, then (re)classifying x as dynamic will influence the binding times of function f and thus the rest of the program. Therefore the binding-time analysis must detect all lambdas that need to be lifted, and must reclassify their bound variables as dynamic, before specialization.

A lambda needs to be lifted if it appears in a dynamic context. A lambda is in a *dynamic context* if it is a possible value of: a (sub)expression whose binding time is dynamic, a dynamic variable (whether function-, lambda- or let-bound), the argument of a dynamic lambda application, or the body of a dynamic lambda.

(3) Binding-time analysis of let-expressions

It is tempting to think that the result of (let (x e_1) e) is static when the result of e is, even if e_1 is dynamic (for instance, when x does not appear in e). However, this is not safe, as it would require the specializer to discard the dynamic expression e_1. If the evaluation of e_1 is non-terminating, then discarding it would change the termination properties of the program. Therefore the binding-time analysis must assume that the result of (let (x e_1) e) is dynamic if e_1 is dynamic, even when e is static.

Thus $\mathcal{B}_e[\![$(let (x e_1) e)$]\!]\psi\tau\delta$ equals $\mathcal{B}_e[\![e_1]\!]\psi\tau\delta \sqcup \mathcal{B}_e[\![e]\!]\psi\tau\delta$ in the Scheme1 binding-time analysis to be presented in Section 15.3. However, Section 10.5 shows one way to improve the handling of let-expressions.

10.1.5   Specialization of Scheme1 programs

As in Scheme0, the named program points are the named functions, and a specialized program point is a pair (f . vs) of a named function and values for its static parameters. We generate a residual function for each specialized program point as in the Scheme0 specializer (Chapter 5). Lambda abstraction and application are treated as in Lambdamix (Chapter 8) with one exception: a named function f can now be specialized with respect to a static functional value.

When no static lambda (lambdas (x) ...) has any free dynamic variables, the Scheme1 specializer can reuse the main loop of the Scheme0 specializer (Figure 5.6) with no modification.

When a static lambda may have free dynamic variables, function specialization becomes more complicated. This is explained in Section 10.2.2 below.

10.1.6 Representation and equality of functional values

To generate a reasonable program with polyvariant program point specialization it is necessary to compare the values of static parameters. The Scheme0 specializer does this comparison when computing newpending in Figure 5.6.

In Similix and in this chapter, the value of a static parameter may be a function, so we need to compare *functions* for equality. Therefore we shall represent functional values by closures, essentially as in Section 3.3.1. Here, a *closure* (closure ℓ vv) contains the label ℓ of a lambda abstraction, and values vv of the lambda's free variables. Values of variables not free in the lambda could also be included in vv, but such variables would be dead and cause code duplication, as in Section 4.9.2.

Note that the Lambdamix specializer (Chapter 8) did not use polyvariant specialization and thus never had to compare functional values: the only operations on functions were definition and application. Therefore in Lambdamix it was sufficient to represent functions in the subject program by functions in the specializer.

Let the map function be defined in Scheme1 as follows:

```
(define (map f xs)
  (if (null? xs)
      '()
      (cons (f (car xs)) (map f (cdr xs)))))
```

Consider specializing the call (calld map (lambda (x) (+ 1 x)) xs) where xs is dynamic. Naming the specialized function map1+, the residual program should include a definition of form:

```
(define (map1+ xs)
  (if (null? xs)
      '()
      (cons (+ 1 (car xs)) (...))))
```

To generate the proper code for (...), namely a recursive call (map1+ (cdr xs)), we must discover that the functional argument f has the same value as in the previous call to map.

Two functions f and g are *extensionally equal* if and only if $\forall x : f(x) = g(x)$. Extensional equality is undecidable, so we must settle for an approximation: closure equality. Two closures are equal when (1) their labels ℓ are equal and (2) their environment components vv are equal. Equal closures define extensionally equal functions. The converse does not hold.

10.1.7   Reduction of two-level Scheme1 expressions

Reduction of two-level Scheme1 expressions is almost as simple as that for Scheme0 (Figure 5.7). The only complicated case is dynamic function application (calld), which involves function specialization. Since we may need to specialize with respect to higher-order values, we discuss calld separately in Section 10.2 below.

The function reduce for reduction of Scheme1 expressions is shown in Figure 10.3. The auxiliary function successors (not shown) must be extended to traverse Scheme1 expressions. The new cases of reduce are explained as follows.

A static lambda (lambdas$^\ell$ (x) e) reduces to a closure (closure ℓ vv) where vv is a list of the (static and dynamic) values of the variables free in the lambda.

A dynamic lambda (lambdad$^\ell$ (x) e) reduces to a residual lambda expression (lambda (z) e$'$) where the body e$'$ is the reduced form of e, and z is a fresh variable.

A static lambda application (e$_0$ e$_1$) is reduced by reducing e$_0$ to a closure (closure ℓ vv), then reducing the corresponding lambda body e$^\ell$ in an environment where x is bound to the reduced form e$'_1$ of e.

A dynamic lambda application (e$_0$ @d e$_1$) reduces to the residual application (e$'_0$ e$'_1$) where e$'_0$ is the reduced form of e$_0$ and e$'_1$ is the reduced form of e$_1$.

A static let-binding (lets (x e$_1$) e) reduces to the result of reducing e in an environment where variable x is bound to the reduced form e$'_1$ of e$_1$.

A dynamic let-binding (letd (x e$_1$) e) reduces to the residual let-binding (let (z e$'_1$) e$'$) where e$'_1$ and e$'$ are the reduced forms of e$_1$ and e, respectively, and z is a fresh variable.

10.2   Specialization with respect to functional values

10.2.1   Specialization with respect to fully static functions

Let us first consider the simple case where no static lambda (lambdas$^\ell$ (x) ...) has any free dynamic variables. Then every static lambda reduces to a static closure, consisting of a label ℓ and values for its free variables (which are all static by assumption). For example, consider the program

```
(define (f b)
    (g (lambda¹ (z) (+ z b))))
(define (g h)
    (h 3))
```

and assume that b, z, and h are static. The superscript 1 is a label. Further assume

The environment is represented by a list $vn = (y_1 \ldots y_k)$ of the variables that may occur in e, and a list $vv = (v_1 \ldots v_k)$ of corresponding values.

```
(define (reduce e vn vv)
   case e of
      number n        => n
      (quote c)       => c
      yⱼ              => vⱼ
                         where (y₁ ... yⱼ ... yₖ) = vn
                               (v₁ ... vⱼ ... vₖ) = vv
      (ifs e₁ e₂ e₃)  => if (reduce e₁ vn vv)
                         then (reduce e₂ vn vv)
                         else (reduce e₃ vn vv)
      (ifd e₁ e₂ e₃)  => (list 'if (reduce e₁ vn vv)
                                    (reduce e₂ vn vv)
                                    (reduce e₃ vn vv))
      (calls f (e₁ ... eₘ) (eₘ₊₁ ... eₐ)) =>
                         (reduce e_f (x₁ ... xₐ) (e'₁ ... e'ₐ))
                         where e'ⱼ = (reduce eⱼ vn vv)  for j = 1,...,a
                               (define (f (x₁...xₘ) (xₘ₊₁...xₐ)) e_f)
                                      = (lookup f program)
      (calld f (e₁ ... eₘ) (eₘ₊₁ ... eₐ)) =>
                         (list 'call (f :: (e'₁ ... e'ₘ)) e'ₘ₊₁ ... e'ₐ)
                         where e'ⱼ = (reduce eⱼ vn vv)  for j = 1,...,a
      (ops e₁ ... eₐ) => (op (reduce e₁ vn vv) ... (reduce eₐ vn vv))
      (opd e₁ ... eₐ) => (list 'op (reduce e₁ vn vv)...(reduce eₐ vn vv))
      (lift e)        => (list 'quote (reduce e vn vv)))
      (lambdasˡ (x) e)=> (list 'closure ℓ (v_{i₁} ... v_{iⱼ}))
                         where (y_{i₁} ... y_{iⱼ}) = FreeVars(ℓ)
                               (y₁ ... yₖ) = vn
                               (v₁ ... vₖ) = vv
      (lambdadˡ (x) e)=> (list 'lambda (z) (reduce e (x::vn) (z::vv)))
                         where z  is a fresh identifier
      (e₀ e₁)         => (reduce eˡ (x y₁ ... yᵢ) (e'₁ v₁ ... vᵢ))
                         where (closure ℓ (v₁...vᵢ)) = (reduce e₀ vn vv)
                               (y₁ ... yᵢ) = FreeVars(ℓ)
                               (lambdasˡ (x) eˡ) = (lookup ℓ program)
                               e'₁ = (reduce e₁ vn vv)
      (e₀ @d e₁)      => (list (reduce e₀ vn vv) (reduce e₁ vn vv))
      (lets (x e₁) e) => (reduce e (x :: vn) (e'₁ :: vv))
                         where e'₁ = (reduce e₁ vn vv)
      (letd (x e₁) e) => (list 'let (z e'₁) e')
                         where e'₁ = (reduce e₁ vn vv)
                               e' = (reduce e (x :: vn) (z :: vv))
                               z  is a fresh identifier
```

Figure 10.3: Reduction of Scheme1 expressions.

for the sake of argument that **g** is to be specialized with respect to the *fully static function* (lambda^1 (z) (+ z b)). If the static value of **b** is 10, then the residual program could be:

```
(define (f x)
   (g₁))
(define (g₁)
   13)
```

In this case code generation for specialized functions can proceed exactly as for Scheme0. All static parameters are removed from the called function's parameter list, no matter whether their values are first-order or higher-order.

10.2.2   Specialization with respect to partially static functions

Specialization with respect to a partially static lambda (one having free dynamic variables) is more involved. Consider again the program

```
(define (f x)
   (g (lambda¹ (z) (+ z x))))
(define (g h)
   (h 3))
```

but now assume that **x** is dynamic, while **z** and **h** are still static. Then **g**'s argument (lambda^1 (z) (+ z x)) is a *partially static function*, and reducing the application (h 3) in the body of **g** would give the residual expression (+ 3 x). The dynamic variable **x** appears in the specialized version g_1 of **g**, and therefore **x** must be passed to g_1 in the residual program.

The residual program could be:

```
(define (f x)
   (g₁ x))
(define (g₁ x)
   (+ 3 x))
```

For a slightly more complicated example, consider

```
(define (f x)
   (g (let (w (* x x)) (lambda² (z) (+ z w))))
)
(define (g h)
   (h 3))
```

Assume that **x** and **w** are dynamic and that **z** and **h** are static. The **let** binds **w** to the dynamic expression (* x x), and returns a closure (closure 2 (* x x)) in which **w** is a free dynamic variable, bound to (* x x).

Specializing **g** with respect to the closure (closure 2 (* x x)), we have to pass the dynamic value (* x x) of **w** to the residual version of **g**:

```
(define (f x)
   (g₂ (* x x)))
(define (g₂ w)
   (+ 3 w))
```

10.2.3 Finding the free dynamic variables

When specializing a function g with respect to a static closure (closure ℓ vv) as above, every free dynamic variable w of lambda ℓ gives rise to a new formal parameter of the specialized function. The corresponding new argument expression is the dynamic value bound to w in the closure's environment vv.

Observe that the *static* variables in vv may bind other static closures. These in turn may have dynamic free variables, and (partially) static closures, which in turn have dynamic free variables, and so on. Thus the closure's environment vv must be traversed recursively to find all dynamic free variables and their values. In general, fresh names must be used for the new formal parameters to avoid name clashes. This is because a function may take as arguments (via different parameters) two closures (closure ℓ vv) and (closure ℓ vv′) generated by the same lambda. Also, a closure (closure ℓ vv) may contain in vv another closure (closure ℓ vv′) generated by the same lambda abstraction, and thus having the same (dynamic) variable names.

The recursive traversal (and renaming) of partially static closures is done by the auxiliary functions **new-names** and **get-dynamic** below. The parameter newx is used in the generation of fresh names. The fresh names themselves are not important, but they must be generated systematically, and must be the same as those used by function **get-static** when constructing the static skeleton of a closure (see next section).

```
(define (new-names v newx)
   case v of
      ⟨A static base value⟩      => ()
      ⟨A dynamic value⟩          => (list newx)
      (closure ℓ (v₁ ... vₖ))  =>
               (append (new-names v₁ (cons x₁ newx))
                          ... (new-names vₖ (cons xₖ newx))))
            where (x₁ ... xₖ) = FreeVars(ℓ)
(define (get-dynamic v)
   case v of
      ⟨A static base value⟩      => ()
      ⟨A dynamic value⟩          => (list v)
      (closure ℓ (v₁ ... vₖ))  =>
               (append (get-dynamic v₁) ... (get-dynamic vₖ)))
```

Function **new-names** returns the list of (renamed) dynamic free variables that are to become new formal parameters of the specialized function. Function `get-dynamic` returns the corresponding list of dynamic values that become new arguments in the residual call.

When specializing a call (`calls f ...`) the fresh variable names returned by **new-names** have the general form $(z_h \; . \; ... \; (z_2 \; . \; (z_1 \; . \; z_0)) \; ...), h \geq 1$. Here z_0 is a static formal parameter (of `f`), whose value is a partially static closure (`closure` ℓ_0 vv$_0$). For $j = 1, ..., h - 1$, variable z_j is a static free variable of closure ℓ_{j-1} and its value is a partially static closure (`closure` ℓ_j vv$_j$). Finally, z_h is a dynamic free variable of ℓ_{h-1}.

10.2.4   Finding the static skeleton

A specialized program point (`f . vs`) is a pair of a function name `f` and values `vs` of its static parameters. A specialized program point should contain only static information that can actually be used (cf. Section 4.9.2).

Only the static 'skeleton' of a partially static closure (`closure` ℓ vv) is useful for specialization. More precisely, the label ℓ is useful, as are the values of fully static variables in vv. The dynamic value of a dynamic variable in vv is not useful during specialization. For partially static closures in vv, the useful parts are found recursively as for the top-level closure.

The recursive extraction of the static skeleton of a closure is done by function `get-static`:

```
(define (get-static v newx)
   case v of
       ⟨A static base value⟩        => v
       ⟨A dynamic value⟩            => newx
       (closure ℓ (v₁ ... vₖ))  =>
                  (list 'closure ℓ
                        (get-static v₁ (cons x₁ newx))
                        ... (get-static vₖ (cons xₖ newx)))
                  where (x₁ ... xₖ) = FreeVars(ℓ))
```

Function `get-static` extracts the static 'skeleton' of a closure, recursively replacing every dynamic value in the closure's environment component vv with a fresh variable. The resulting new environment maps a static base-type variable to its value, maps a dynamic variable to its fresh name, and maps a static closure-type variable to the static skeleton of its value. The fresh variables used by `get-static` are precisely those returned by **new-names**.

Note that `get-dynamic` extracts all dynamic values bound in the closure's environment component vv, whereas `get-static` throws them away. Thus their results are complementary.

10.2.5   Revised handling of function specialization

Function specialization has two aspects: the generation of a call to the specialized function (in the `calld` case of `reduce`), and the generation of a residual function definition (in the main loop of the specializer). To handle specialization with respect to partially static lambdas, changes are needed in those two places.

The revised treatment of a dynamic call `calld` in `reduce` is shown below. The function `get-dynamic` is used to build a list (a_1 ... a_k) of the new dynamic arguments to the specialized function. The function `get-static` returns the static parts of partially static closures.

```
(define (reduce e vn vv)
    case e of
        ...
        (calld f_i (e_1 ... e_m) (e_{m+1} ... e_a)) =>
                (list 'call (f_i::(e''_1...e''_m)) a_1...a_k e'_{m+1}...e'_a)
                where e'_j = (reduce e_j vn vv)  for j = 1,...,a
                      e''_j = (get-static e'_j x_{ij})  for j = 1,...,m
                and   (a_1 ... a_k) = (append (get-dynamic e'_1)
                                               ... (get-dynamic e'_m))
        ... )
```

The revised generation of residual functions (the revised main specialization loop) is shown in Figure 10.4. The only changes from the main loop of the Scheme0 specializer (Figure 5.6) are that `new-names` finds the new formal parameters (y_1 ... y_k), and that they are added to the specialized function (`f . vs`). The new formal parameters (y_1 ... y_k) correspond to the new arguments (a_1 ... a_k) found by `get-dynamic` in `reduce` above.

To obtain good results when self-applying the Scheme1 specializer, the revised main loop in Figure 10.4 still has to be rewritten in the manner of the self-applicable Scheme0 specializer in Figure 5.8.

10.3   Avoiding duplication

Duplication is avoided as outlined in Section 5.5.4. For every free variable `x`, an identity let-binding (`let (x x) body`) is inserted around every function body and every lambda body. Then these `let`-bindings are annotated as static 'lets' (unfoldable) or dynamic 'letd' (residual) after an occurrence counting analysis.

The *occurrence counting* analysis finds an upper limit on the number of times the `let`-bound variable `x` may occur in the *residual* expression. This can be done by analysing the *subject* program, because the occurrence counting is done after binding-time analysis, so it is known which parts of the program are static and which are dynamic. Using the results of the occurrence counting analysis, a `let`

```
The modified lines are marked with an asterisk * below.

(define (specialize program vs₀)
   let ((define (f₁ _ _ ) _ ) . _ ) = program
   in (complete (list (f₁ :: vs₀)) () program)
)


(define (complete pending marked program)
   if pending is empty then
      ()
   else
      let (f . vs) ∈ pending
      let (define (f (x₁...xₘ) (xₘ₊₁...xₐ)) e) = (lookup f program)
      let (vs₁ ... vsₘ) = vs
*     let (y₁...yₖ) = (append (new-names vs₁ x₁)...(new-names vsₘ xₘ))
      let eᵥₛ = (reduce e (x₁...xₘ xₘ₊₁...xₐ) (vs₁...vsₘ xₘ₊₁...xₐ))
      let newmarked = marked ∪ {(f . vs)}
      let newpending = (pending ∪ (successors eᵥₛ)) \ newmarked
*     let newdef = (list 'define (list (f . vs) y₁...yₖ xₘ₊₁...xₐ) eᵥₛ)
      in (newdef :: (complete newpending newmarked program))
)
```

Figure 10.4: Main loop of Scheme1 specialization algorithm.

is *annotated* as `lets` if the bound value x is static or occurs at most once in the residual code, otherwise it is annotated as `letd`.

The insertion of `let`-bindings means that a function call can be unfolded without risk of duplication: the function parameter is always used exactly once, namely in the `let`-binding. The annotation on the `let`-binding governs unfolding of the `let`, and unfolds only if no code duplication is possible.

The classification of a `let` as static or dynamic does not affect its binding time. In particular, making it `letd` does not mean that its body changes from a static to a dynamic context. To see this, note that a `let` expression can be classified as a dynamic `letd` only if the bound variable is dynamic. In this case the binding-time analysis has already deemed the result of the entire `let` expression dynamic (cf. Section 10.1.4), so its body is in a dynamic context already.

For an example, consider `(let (x e₁) (lambda (x) e))`. Assume that e_1 (and thus x) is dynamic, so the binding-time analysis classifies the result of the entire `let` as dynamic. The lambda in the `let` body is a possible result of the entire `let` expression, and therefore is in a dynamic context. Classifying the `let` as `lets` or `letd` does not change this.

10.4   Call unfolding on the fly

Similix uses a new strategy for call unfolding on the fly, creating a so-called *specialization point* for each dynamic conditional and for each dynamic lambda. The specialization point is a new named function (here called an *sp-function*) whose parameters are the free variables of the conditional or lambda, and whose body is the entire conditional or lambda.

A call to an sp-function (or to the goal function) is never unfolded: it must be a `calld`. A call to an existing function (except the goal function) is always unfolded: it must be a `calls`. If the subject program does not contain any loop which is controlled only by static data (or not controlled at all), then this approach avoids infinite unfolding; namely, in this case an infinite unfolding loop must involve a dynamic conditional or recursion via the Y combinator (or similar), which must involve a dynamic lambda.

The insertion of specialization points corresponds to the insertion of specialization points around dynamic conditionals in Scheme0 (cf. Section 5.5.4). In Scheme0, if we do not unfold dynamic conditionals, then infinite unfolding can happen only because of static infinite loops. In Scheme1 (but not in Scheme0), recursion can be expressed using the Y combinator (written as a lambda abstraction), and the truth values (`true` and `false`), and conditionals can be encoded as lambda expressions also:

`true`	as	`(lambda (x) (lambda (y) x))`
`false`	as	`(lambda (x) (lambda (y) y))`
`(if e`$_1$ `e`$_2$ `e`$_3$`)`	as	`(((e`$_1$ `(lambda (z) e`$_2$`)) (lambda (z) e`$_3$`)) ())`

The new variable `z` must not occur in e_2 and e_3. Thus controlled recursion need not involve any conditionals, but a dynamic truth value is now represented by a dynamic lambda. By specializing also at every dynamic lambda we therefore avoid infinite unfolding except when it corresponds to a static infinite loop.

In the residual program generated by the specializer, conditionals and lambda abstractions can appear only outermost in residual function bodies. However, after the residual program has been generated, a postprocessing phase unfolds the call to every residual function (except the goal function) which is called *exactly one place*, thus eliminating many trivial functions. The postunfolding must stop, as shown by the following argument. All infinite unfolding involves a cycle of functions (possibly just one function) calling each other cyclically. Consider such a cycle. If the goal function is on the cycle, then the unfolding stops there. If the goal function is not on the cycle, then there is a function on the cycle which can be called from outside the cycle. Thus there are at least two calls to that function, and none of them is unfolded, thus stopping the unfolding at that function.

10.5   Continuation-based reduction

The goal of continuation-based reduction is to exploit static subexpressions of dynamic expressions.

Example 10.1 Consider the expression

```
(+ 3 (let (x e) 10))
```

and assume that e is dynamic. Then the result of the entire let-expression will be considered dynamic by the binding-time analysis, even though the body is static. With the ordinary **reduce** function above, the residual program will be

```
(+ 3 (let (x e') 10))
```

where e' is the reduced form of e. That is, the addition of 3 and 10 has not been done. However, if the context '(+ 3 ...)' were propagated to the static expression 10, a better residual expression could be obtained:

```
(let (x e') 13)
```

The context was propagated to a static subexpression, resulting in a *binding-time improvement*.   □

Expression reduction with context propagation is called *continuation-based reduction*. However, the example is very simple, and the same improvement could be obtained just by *local* (intraprocedural) transformation of the let-expression to (let (x e') (+ 3 10)) before reduction.

General continuation-based reduction allows context propagation also across unfoldable (static) function calls. This may improve the binding times of a program considerably, and cannot be achieved by local transformations.

Consel and Danvy have shown that general continuation-based reduction can be obtained by a global transformation of the subject program: converting the subject program to *continuation passing style* (*CPS*) before reduction [56]. For a presentation of the CPS conversion itself, see Fischer [87], Plotkin [219], or Danvy and Filinski [68].

Consel and Danvy's technique allows propagation of contexts under dynamic conditionals as well as under dynamic let-bindings. In this case the residual programs will also be in CPS, which is sometimes not desirable. However, Danvy has shown that, subject to certain restrictions, programs in continuation passing style can systematically be converted back to direct style, thus eliminating the continuation parameters [67].

Bondorf has shown that some benefits of continuation-based reduction can be obtained by modifying the specializer, thus avoiding the transformation to CPS [31]. When applying the **reduce** function to an expression e, the context K of the reduced value is also passed to **reduce**. Modifying the handling of dynamic letd then propagates the context K to the (possibly static) body of the let. This is built into recent versions of Similix, but (currently) does not allow propagation of contexts under dynamic conditionals. The reason is that Similix encapsulates dynamic conditionals in sp-functions and hence in dynamic function calls, and contexts cannot be propagated across dynamic function calls.

The remainder of this section presents the idea in more detail. It is based on Bondorf's paper, which gives precise definitions, theorems, and proofs [31]. In the remainder of this section, keep in mind that Scheme1 has call-by-value semantics.

10.5.1   Continuation passing style

In continuation passing style (CPS) every function takes an extra argument: a *continuation*. The continuation is a function which consumes the result of the function and produces the final result of the computation. Thus the continuation represents the remainder of the current computation, or the context of the current subexpression reduction.

For example, the ordinary factorial function

```
(define (fac n)
    (if (zero? n)
        1
        (* n (fac (- n 1)))))
```

has the following form in CPS:

```
(define (faccps n K)
    (if (zero? n)
        (K 1)
        (faccps (- n 1) (lambda (r) (K (* n r))))))
```

The K argument is the continuation. It is applied to the result of the function call, as seen in the first branch (K 1). In the second branch, the continuation of the recursive call is (lambda (r) (K (* n r))). This continuation will take the result r of the recursive call, multiply it by n, and pass the result to the original continuation K. Note that the program in CPS has the same operational behaviour as the original one.

The relation between fac and faccps is the following for every function (continuation) K and non-negative integer n:

```
(K (fac n)) = (faccps n K)
```

In particular, (fac n) = (faccps n id), where id denotes the identity function (lambda (r) r). It also follows that (faccps n K) = (K (faccps n id)).

Continuations were invented in the late 1960s and used for transformation, proof, and mathematical description of programming languages; see e.g. [223]. Continuations are used also in implementations of functional programming languages such as Scheme and Standard ML.

10.5.2   Continuation-based reduction of Scheme1

The idea in continuation-based reduction of Scheme1 is to replace function `reduce` from Figure 10.3 in continuation-passing style. This in itself achieves nothing, but it allows us later to improve the handling of dynamic `letd`; this will be done in Section 10.5.4 below.

The continuation-based version `redcps` of `reduce` is shown in Figure 10.5. In the figure, `id` denotes the identity function `(lambda (r) r)`. For brevity, the cases for dynamic function call, dynamic base function, static lambda abstraction, and lambda application have been left out, as they present no new problems.

The main loop of the specializer in Figure 10.4 must be changed to call function `redcps` as $(\text{redcps e } (x_1 \ldots x_m \ x_{m+1} \ldots x_a) \ (vs_1 \ldots vs_m \ x_{m+1} \ldots x_a) \ \text{id})$ where `id` is the identity function `(lambda (r) r)`. This achieves the same as the old call to `reduce`, since `(redcps e vn vv id) = (reduce e vn vv)`.

10.5.3   Well-behaved continuations

It holds that

    (redcps e vn vv K) = (K (redcps e vn vv id))

for every function K. This equivalence has been used in the cases for `ifd`, `lambdad`, and `letd` to make the continuations of the recursive calls well-behaved. Roughly, a continuation K is *well-behaved* if whenever `(K r)` is an expression, then (1) K embeds its argument `r` in a strict position, that is, the evaluation of `(K r)` implies the evaluation of `r`; and (2) K does not introduce new variable bindings visible to `r`. The precise definition can be found in [31, Section 4].

The importance of well-behaved continuations will be clear in the improved handling of `let` shown in Section 10.5.4.

In the 'natural' CPS version of the `ifd` case, there would be a continuation K of form $(\text{lambda } (r_3) \ (K' \ (\text{list 'if } r_1 \ r_2 \ r_3)))$ which would embed the argument expression r_3 in a branch of an `if` expression. Since that branch may not be evaluated when the `if` is, K would not be well-behaved.

Likewise, in the 'natural' CPS version of the `letd` case, there would be a continuation K of form $(\text{lambda } (r) \ (K' \ (\text{list 'let } (x \ r_1) \ r)))$ which would embed the argument expression `r` in a `let`-expression. Since that makes the binding of `x` visible to `r`, K would not be well-behaved.

In the 'natural' CPS version of the `lambdad` case, there would be a continuation which would embed its argument `r` in a non-strict position, *and* introduce new variable bindings visible to `r`, thus violating requirement (1) as well as (2).

Using the equivalence shown above, all ill-behaved continuations have been avoided.

```
(define (redcps e vn vv K)
   case e of
      number n           => (K n)
      (quote c)          => (K c)
      yⱼ                 => (K vⱼ) where (y₁ ... yⱼ ... yₖ) = vn
                                        (v₁ ... vⱼ ... vₖ) = vv
      (ifs e₁ e₂ e₃)   =>
          (redcps e₁ vn vv
                  (lambda (r₁) (if r₁ (redcps e₂ vn vv K)
                                      (redcps e₃ vn vv K))))
      (ifd e₁ e₂ e₃)   =>
          (redcps e₁ vn vv
                  (lambda (r₁)
                        (K (list 'if r₁ (redcps e₂ vn vv id)
                                        (redcps e₃ vn vv id)))))
      (calls f (e₁ ... eₘ) (eₘ₊₁ ... eₐ)) =>
          (redcps e₁ vn vv
                  (lambda (r₁) ...
                        (redcps eₐ vn vv
                                (lambda (rₐ)
                                        (redcps e_f (x₁...xₐ)(r₁...rₐ) K)))
                        ...))
               where (define (f (x₁...xₘ)(xₘ₊₁...xₐ)) e_f)=(lookup f program)
      (calld f (e₁ ... eₘ) (eₘ₊₁ ... eₐ)) => ...
      (ops e₁ ... eₐ)  =>
          (redcps e₁ vn vv
                  (lambda (r₁) ...
                        (redcps eₐ vn vv
                                (lambda (rₐ)
                                        (K (op r₁ ... rₐ)))) ...))
      (opd e₁ ... eₐ)  => ...
      (lift e)         => (redcps e vn vv
                                  (lambda (r) (K (list 'quote r))))
      (lambdasˡ (x) e) => ...
      (lambdadˡ (x) e) =>
          (K (list 'lambda (z) (redcps e (x :: vn) (z :: vv) id)))
          where z  is a fresh identifier
      (e₀ e₁)          => ...
      (e₀ @d e₁)       => ...
      (lets (x e₁) e)  =>
          (redcps e₁ vn vv
                  (lambda (r₁) (redcps e (x :: vn) (r₁ :: vv) K)))
      (letd (x e₁) e)  =>
          (redcps e₁ vn vv
                  (lambda (r₁) (K (list 'let (z r₁)
                                        (redcps e (x::vn) (z::vv) id)))))
          where z  is a fresh identifier
```

Figure 10.5: Continuation-based reduction of Scheme1 expressions.

10.5.4   Extracting static information from a dynamic let

So far, nothing has been achieved by constructing the CPS version `redcps` of `reduce`; the two functions are equivalent. However, now we can improve the treatment of `letd` by using the equivalence

$$(\text{K (let (x } r_1) \text{ r)}) = (\text{let (x } r_1) \text{ (K r)})$$

which holds only when K is well-behaved. It does not hold for ill-behaved K, because (1) if r_1 is undefined, then the right hand side is undefined, yet if K does not embed its argument in a strict position, then the left hand side might be defined; and (2) if K could introduce new bindings, then these would be visible to r_1 on the left hand side but not on the right hand side.

Using the equivalence, we replace the right hand side of the `letd` case by

```
(redcps e₁ vn vv
        (lambda (r₁)
                (list 'let (z r₁)
                      (K (redcps e (x :: vn) (z :: vv) id)))))
```

Then we use the equivalence (K (redcps e vn vv id)) = (redcps e vn vv K) to transform it again, and obtain the following right hand side for the `letd` case of `redcps`:

```
(redcps e₁ vn vv
        (lambda (r₁)
                (list 'let (z r₁) (redcps e (x::vn) (z::vv) K))))
```

Note that the continuation K of the entire dynamic expression (letd (x e_1) e) is propagated to the body e. This is advantageous when e is static and e_1 is dynamic. Propagating K to e in this case allows the exploitation of the static information from e when reducing the context of the let-expression, as illustrated in Example 10.1.

It is significant that the context K of a static function call (calls) is propagated to the body of the called function when it is being reduced with `redcps` in Figure 10.5. This means that the context may propagate to a let-expression in another function, and in practice this turns out to greatly improve the binding times of programs. This cannot be achieved with local (intraprocedural) transformations of the source program.

10.5.5   Improved binding-time analysis for Scheme1

The binding-time analysis must reflect the improved handling of (let (x e_1) e). So far, the result of the let-expression has been deemed dynamic when either e_1 or e were dynamic (cf. Section 10.1.4). However, now the result of the let-expression is deemed dynamic precisely when e is, regardless of e_1, so now $\mathcal{B}_e[\![(\text{let (x } e_1)$

e)$]\!]\psi\tau\delta = \mathcal{B}_e[\![e]\!]\psi\tau\delta$ in the Scheme1 binding-time analysis.

10.6   Handling partially static structures

Assume that e_1 is static and e_2 is dynamic in the expression

```
(let (z (cons e₁ e₂)) (car z))
```

In the Scheme1 specializer as presented above, the expression (cons e_1 e_2) would be considered dynamic because e_2 is dynamic. Hence z would be dynamic, the expression (car z) would be dynamic, and so would the result of the entire let-expression. This is because base values must either be completely static, or else dynamic.

10.6.1   Partially static structures

If we allow *partially static* base values, then the value of z would be a pair whose first component is static, and whose second component is dynamic. Hence (car z) would be static, and if the value of e_1 were 10, say, then the entire let-expression could be reduced to 10.

Clearly, handling partially static base values will require considerable changes to the binding-time analysis as well as the specializer. Recursive partially static structures are particularly interesting. For example, consider the function mkenv that builds an environment association list from a (static) list of variable names and a dynamic list of corresponding values (the superscripts on cons are labels, called cons points):

```
(define (mkenv names values)
    (if (null? names)
        ()
        (cons¹ (cons² (car names) (car values))
                (mkenv (cdr names) (cdr values)))))
```

Function mkenv returns a list of pairs, whose first components are all static and whose second components are all dynamic. The function is likely to be used this way in an interpreter being specialized with respect to a source program but without its input. The example is due to Mogensen, who used grammars to describe partially static binding times in an untyped language [187]. The result of mkenv could be described by the grammar

$$\begin{array}{lcl}
\text{mkenv} & \to & \text{S} \mid \text{cons}^1 \\
\text{cons}^1 & \to & \text{P}(\text{cons}^2, \text{mkenv}) \\
\text{cons}^2 & \to & \text{P}(\text{S, D})
\end{array}$$

Here S denotes a static value, D denotes a dynamic value, and P denotes a pair of values. Nonterminal `mkenv` describes all possible results of the function, nonterminal `cons`[1] describes all structures built by the `cons` operator labelled 1, etc. Thus the grammar says that a result of `mkenv` is either completely static (namely, ()) or a result of `cons`[1]. A result of `cons`[1] is a pair of a value built by `cons`[2] and a result of `mkenv`. A result of `cons`[2] is a pair of a static and a dynamic value.

Using grammars of this form, Mogensen designed the first binding-time analysis with partially static binding times. Consel used a *cons point analysis* to collect essentially the same information for an untyped higher-order language [53]. Launchbury used projections to analyse a typed language [165,167]. In Section 15.4 we shall explain Launchbury's approach.

Mogensen also showed how to preprocess a subject program, using (partially static) binding-time information to separate static and dynamic computations. Every function parameter whose value is a partially static structure is split into (essentially) one static and one dynamic parameter. Every function returning a partially static result is split into two functions, one returning the static part, and one returning the dynamic part. The static part depends only on static arguments and thus can be fully computed at specialization time. After this preprocessing a simple specializer (not handling partially static structures) can be used [190].

10.6.2   Arity raising

Specialization of a program with partially static structures implies arity raising. With *arity raising*, one dynamic (or partially static) function parameter in the subject program may give rise to several function parameters in the residual program. For example, if a dynamic function parameter in the subject program is always a list of three elements, then it may be replaced by three simple parameters in the residual program, possibly raising the arity of the function.

Arity raising was originally done with hand annotations which guided the splitting of a dynamic variable according to the value of a static variable [245]. Then Sergei Romanenko gave an automatic forwards analysis of the structure of dynamic variables, and a backwards analysis of their use, for an untyped functional language [228]. Using a closure analysis (Section 15.2), Steensgaard and Marquard extended Romanenko's work to a higher-order language [253].

10.6.3   Safe specialization of partially static structures

Recall the expression (`let` (`z` (`cons` e_1 e_2)) (`car` `z`)) from above. If the value of e_1 is 10, say, then it could be reduced to 10. However, this would discard the dynamic expression e_2 entirely, which is undesirable: it might change the termination properties of the program.

Similarly, the expression

```
(let (z (cons e₁ e₂)) (+ (cdr z) (cdr z)))
```

is a dynamic expression which could reduce to the residual expression (+ e'_2 e'_2), where e'_2 is the reduced form of e_2. However, this would duplicate the dynamic expression e_2, which is also undesirable.

The problem can be solved by binding every dynamic `cons` argument in a dynamic (non-unfoldable) `letd`, as in:

```
(let (z (letd (y e₂) (cons e₁ y))) (car z))
```

Using an ordinary specializer, this would achieve little, as the `letd` expression will give rise to a residual `let`, so z and hence (car z) would be dynamic.

Using the new continuation-based `redcps` function from Section 10.5, the modification makes sense. Now the context (let (z ...) (car z)) will be propagated to the expression (cons e_1 y), *as if* the expression had been written

```
(letd (y e₂) (let (z (cons e₁ y)) (car z)))
```

Then reduction gives (let (y e'_2) 10), assuming that e_1 reduces to 10. The dynamic expression e_2 has not been discarded. Note that with continuation-based reduction it is *not* necessary to actually transform the source expression this way. Also, with continuation-based reduction this works even if the expression (letd (y e_2) ...) were hidden in the body of a function called by a static call (`calls`).

Similarly, the second expression above would reduce to (let (y e'_2) (+ y y)), in which e_2 has not been duplicated.

Recent versions of Bondorf's Similix include safe handling of partially static structures.

10.7 The Similix implementation

Bondorf's partial evaluator Similix (version 5.0 at the time of writing), including user manual, can be obtained by anonymous ftp from `ftp.diku.dk` as file `pub/diku/dists/jones-book/Similix-5.0.tar.Z` — see page 123 of this book.

Similix version 5.0 is written in Scheme and complies to the (unofficial) 'R4RS' standard [49], and so is highly portable. It has been tested under Unix with Aubrey Jaffer's free 'scm' system (which is available for Unix, VMS, MS-DOS, and MacOS), and with R. Kent Dybvig's commercial 'Chez Scheme' system.

10.8 Exercises

Exercise 10.1 For each higher-order application in the following program (the two applications of g in h) identify which closures can be applied. Insert identity let-expressions and do binding-time analysis under the assumption that x is dynamic. Annotate the program accordingly. Analyse the number of occurrences of dynamic let-bound variables, and annotate the let expressions accordingly.

```
(define (f x)
  (if (zero? x)
      (+ (h (lambda (y) (+ y 1))) 42)
      (+ (h (lambda (y) (+ y 1))) (h (lambda (y) (+ y x))))))
(define (h g)
  (+ (g 17) (g 42)))
```

□

Exercise 10.2 Execute the preprocess phase for the following program, and specialize f1 under the assumption that x is dynamic. Repeat the process with x static and specialize with respect to x = 25.

```
(define (f1 x)
  (f2 (lambda (y) (if (< x y) x y))))
(define (f2 g)
  (+ (g 17) (g 42)))
```

□

Exercise 10.3 Specialize f in the following program with x dynamic without inserting identity let-expression. Then specialize again now with the identity let-expressions inserted. What is gained by inserting identity let-expression?

```
(define (f x)
  (g (fak x) (fak (+ x 5)) (power 2 8)))
(define (g x y z)
  (+ x x y y z z))
(define (fak x)
  (if (equal? x 1) 1 (* x (fak (- x 1)))))
(define (power x n)
  (if (equal? n 0) x (* x (power x (- n 1)))))
```

□

Exercise 10.4 Consider the append function below and assume that truth values and conditionals are encoded as described in Section 10.4, that is, (null? xs) returns either (lambda (x) (lambda (y) x)) or (lambda (x) (lambda (y) y)). Try specializing (while doing call unfolding on the fly) with respect to xs dynamic and ys static without inserting specialization points for dynamic lambdas. Why does the strategy for call unfolding on the fly fail?

```
(define (append xs ys)
  ((((null? xs)
     (lambda (z) ys))
    (lambda (z) (cons (car xs) (append (cdr xs) ys)))) '()))
```

□

Exercise 10.5 Consider the following program, where n (which is dynamic) is indexed in a static environment (ns holds the names and vs holds the values). For simplicity we have assumed that the indexing always succeeds. Since the static ns decreases for every recursive call to lookup it is safe to unfold completely; termination is guaranteed. Thus it is not necessary to insert a specialization point at the dynamic if. Execute the preprocess phase, without inserting a specialization point for the dynamic if, and specialize f using the direct style specializer. Specialize again using the CPS style specializer. What is gained by using the CPS style specializer?

```
(define (f n)
  (+ 1 (lookup n '(a b c) '(1 2 3))))
(define (lookup n ns vs)
  (if (null? (cdr ns))
      (car vs)
      (if (equal? n (car ns))
          (car vs)
          (lookup n (cdr ns) (cdr vs)))))
```

□

Exercise 10.6 Write a program to perform bubble sort. The input parameters must be an array a and its length n. Use Similix to specialize the program with respect to a known n. Comment on the length and efficiency (complexity) of the residual program.

□

Exercise 10.7 Consider the following program to find a path of length n from node x to node y in the directed graph G.

```
(define (sons G a) (cdr (assoc a G)))
(define (path G n x y)
  (if (< n 0)
      '#f
      (if (= n 0)
          (if (equal? x y)
              (list y)
              '#f)
          (let ((p (path* G (- n 1) y (sons G x))))
            (if (null? p)
                '#f
                (cons x p))))))
(define (path* G n y xs)
  (if (null? xs)
      '#f
      (let ((p (path G n (car xs) y)))
        (if (null? p)
            (path* G n y (cdr xs))
            '()))))
```

Using Similix, try specializing `path` to y dynamic, x = 1, n = 1, and

```
G = ((a . (b c))        ;; edges from a to b and c
     (b . (d))          ;; edge from b to d
     (c . (d))          ;; edge from c to d
     (d . (e))          ;; edge from d to e
     (e . ()))          ;; no edges from e
```

Specialize again now with n = 3. Notation: $a \to_n b$ means that there exists a path from a to b of length n. A better algorithm can be based on the following observation: $a \to_m b$ if and only if either $m = 0$ and $a = b$, or $m > 0$ and there exists a node c with $a \to_{m\ div\ 2} c$ and $c \to_{m-(m\ div\ 2)} b$. Implement the better algorithm in Scheme, and specialize it to various combinations of known arguments.   □

Exercise 10.8 Implement the interpreter for the call-by-value lambda calculus in Figure 3.1 in Scheme. Use Similix to specialize the interpreter to various lambda expressions, thereby compiling them to Scheme. Specialize Similix to the interpreter, thereby generating a lambda-to-Scheme compiler. Use the generated compiler on the same lambda-expressions as before. Which is the most efficient way to compile? Why?   □

Exercise 10.9 Elimination of type checking by partial evaluation. Assume that a hypothetical, very advanced partial evaluator `supermix` is available. It is the intention to use `supermix` to compile a statically typed (like Pascal, C, ML, Miranda) language S to L given an interpreter `sint` for that language S.

1. Apply `supermix` to the interpreter `sint`, an S-program p, and the type of the input to p. How much type checking will be left in the residual program?

2. Same question, but for a dynamically typed (like Lisp, Scheme) language D.

□

Chapter 11

Partial Evaluation for the C Language

Lars Ole Andersen

This chapter describes offline partial evaluation for a subset of the pragmatically oriented C programming language. C is a widely used imperative language with several features not available in the languages studied in the previous chapters. There are data structures such as structs, multidimensional arrays, and pointers; a rich variety of statements and expressions; and functions.

Partial evaluation for large-scale imperative languages is currently an active research area. Here we present principles suitable for automatic specialization of a substantial subset of C, but the techniques carry over to related languages such as Pascal and Fortran. The chapter ends with a description of the kernel of a C specializer.

11.1 Introduction

The goal of partial evaluation is *efficiency*: by specializing a program to parts of its input, a faster *specialized* version can often be constructed. The aim of this chapter is to describe partial evaluation applied to a realistic large-scale imperative programming language. We shall see that several of the basic techniques from the previous chapters can be employed, but new aspects must be considered because of the more complicated semantics of C. These include, in particular, specialization of functions with side-effects, and pointers and dynamic memory allocation.

We shall consider only offline partial evaluation where the specialization is performed in two stages: first the program is *binding-time analysed*, and subsequently it is *specialized*. We argue that the explicit separation of the binding times is an important stepping stone for successfully processing programs that exploit pointers and addresses. Without a prior binding-time analysis, the partial evaluator must be overly conservative, reducing the potential gain of a specialization.

Some knowledge and experience with the C programming language is expected, e.g. corresponding to Kernighan and Ritchie [147].

11.1.1   What is partial evaluation for C?

The language we consider is a substantial subset of the C programming language
[124,147], including global variables, functions with both parameters and local
variables, the usual statements and expressions, and data structures such as structs,
multidimensional arrays, and pointers.

Given only partial input, not all statements can be executed during the specialization. Those that can be executed are called *static* and those that cannot are
called *dynamic*, and similar for expressions. The goal of the binding-time analysis
is to mark all statements as either static or dynamic. Given an annotated program, specialization proceeds by a *symbolic execution* where static statements are
executed and code is generated for the dynamic ones.

Example 11.1 Consider a mini-version of the formatted print function `printf()`[1]
where for simplicity we assume that only integers can be printed out.

```
void mini_printf(char *fmt, int *value)
{
    int i;
    for (i = 0; *fmt != '\0'; fmt++)
        if (*fmt != '%') putchar(*fmt);
        else switch (*++fmt) {
                case 'd': printf("%d", value[i++]); break;
                case '%': putchar('%'); break;
                default:  abort(); /* Error */
            }
}
```

The function could for instance be found in a program implementing scientific
computation, where there would be several calls such as `mini_printf("Result is
%d\n", v)`. Since the format string is given (static) it makes sense to specialize
`mini_printf()` with respect to a static `fmt`.

Consider each statement of `mini_printf()`. Clearly, the `for` loop is entirely
controlled by the `fmt` string and so are the `if` and `switch`. These can thus be
classified as static. On the other hand, the output functions must be deemed
dynamic since output is supposed to be delivered at run time.

Suppose a non-standard symbolic execution given as input the value `"n = %d"`
of the format string `fmt` but no value for `value`. Static statements are executed as
usual, and code is generated for dynamic statements. Static expressions, that is,
expressions depending solely on static values, are evaluated, and dynamic expressions are reduced. This results in the following residual program.

---

[1]This example can be found in Kernighan and Ritchie [147], and has also been demonstrated
in the Scheme language [58]

```
/*  Computes mini_printf("n% = %d", v) for all v  */
void mini_printf_fmt(int *value)
{
    putchar('n');
    putchar(' ');
    putchar('=');
    putchar(' ');
    printf("%d", value[0]);
}
```

The cost of run time interpretation of the format string is often named the *interpretation overhead*. By specialization the interpretation overhead is completely eliminated. Evidently, the specialized version will be faster than the general version.   □

Automatic binding-time analysis of C is a major problem which we briefly consider in Section 11.6. The focus of this chapter, however, will mainly be on the specialization phase, so we henceforth simply assume for the most part that binding-time annotations are present in the programs we consider. In Section 11.2 the specialization of statements and expressions is described. Function specialization is problematic due to side-effects and global data structures — it is important that the order of side-effects is preserved, and sharing of residual functions is complex due to 'hidden' side-effects. This is the subject of Section 11.3. Next, in Section 11.4 we address the treatment of data structures and in particular pointers. We describe specialization of structs to static fields, dynamic memory allocation via malloc(), and how the binding-time separation can be improved by the means of pointer information.

11.1.2   The C language

The standard of C imposes only a few restrictions upon its users. We are solely interested in automatic methods, and clearly this restricts the kind of 'nasty' features that can be allowed. For example, it is difficult to handle programs exploiting uninitialized pointers that the programmer happens to know will point to something sensible. Thus a certain 'clean' programming style is required.

We reject programs using features such as casting void pointers to different types. The recurring problem is binding-time analysis, which must then be overly conservative and in the worst case assume that a pointer can point to any dynamic object in a program. Naturally, one cannot expect good results when this is the case. On the other hand, if the goal is to process programs written in a larger subset of C, this can be done by our methods, the risk being that the benefit from specialization may be limited.

In general, a C program can be seen as a set of modules: there are files with the `main()` function, functions for opening and reading files, functions implementing computation, etc. We propose to apply partial evaluation to the latter functions, and for simplicity we assume that all static input is through the parameters of a goal function. In practice, reading of input from files is convenient and possible, but it requires additional attention.[2]

11.2   Specialization of control flow

The statements making up the body of a function can by simple transformations be brought into a form resembling the flowchart language of Chapter 4. For example, a `while` loop can be transformed into `L: if () ... goto L`. The abstract syntax of a `mix` language is defined in Section 11.5; for now, though, we leave the convertion implicit. Suppose that all statements are consistently marked as being either static or dynamic.

11.2.1   Polyvariant program-point specialization

Consider first specialization of statements where the control flow is entirely static. This implies that test expressions can be evaluated and branches performed.

Example 11.2 The well-known function `power()`[3] computes `base` to the n'th.

```
int power(int base, int n)
{
    int pow;
    for (pow = 1; n; n--)
        pow *= base;
    return pow;
}
```

Assume that `power` is to be specialized with respect to n. Then the `for` loop can be executed during the specialization since it solely depends on the static n. The local variable `pow` must be dynamic due to the assignment `pow *= base`, forcing the initialization `pow = 1` to be suspended as well.

Let n be equal to 3 and suppose that `power` is symbolically executed on this input. The test in the `for` loop is determined by the static n, so the loop can be unrolled three times. In the body of the loop, the dynamic assignment to `pow` gives rise to generation of a residual statement, as shown below.

---

[2]For example, to avoid a stream being read repeatedly whereas normal execution only would read it once.

[3]See Kernighan and Ritchie, Chapter 1 [147].

```
/*  This program computes  base to the 3'rd. */
int power_3(int base)
{
    int pow;
    pow = 1;
    pow *= base;
    pow *= base;
    pow *= base;
    return pow;
}
```

□

This program can, of course, be further optimized via traditional optimizations such as folding and constant propagation, but this can be accomplished by a good optimizing C compiler. On the other hand, since C compilers lack binding-time information, it is unreasonable to expect a compiler to execute static statements. The example also illustrates the typical tradeoff between speed and size. The size of the residual program grows with the size of the static input n, and for huge n specialization may be undesirable.

Consider now the processing of a dynamic control flow statement, e.g. an if where the test expression is dynamic. The branch cannot be determined at specialization time and hence *both* branches must be specialized with respect to the values of the static variables.

Example 11.3 The strcmp() function returns 0 if two strings are equal.

```
int strcmp(int *s, int *t)
{
    for (; *s == *t; s++, t++) if (*s == '\0') return 0;
    return *s - *t;
}
```

The for loop can be considered as syntax for the equivalent:

```
L: if (*s == *t) {
        if (*s == '\0') return 0;
        s++; t++;
        goto L;
    }
    else return *s - *t;
```

Assume that the string s is static ('ab') but t is dynamic. Then the if inevitably must be annotated dynamic, and thus both branches of it must be specialized just like a compile compiles both branches even though only one will be executed at run time. The inner if is completely static, but note that both return statements must be dynamic since the function is supposed to return at run time.

```
int strcmp_s(int *t)
{
  L_0: if ('a' == *t)
        { t++; L_1: if ('b' == *t)
                      { t++; L_2: if ('\0' == *t) return 0;
                                  else return '\0' - *t;
                      }
                      else return 'b' - *t;
        }
        else return 'a' - *t;
}
```

In this particular example, the specialization is nothing more than loop unrolling. In other cases some static computations could appear in the branches and thus disappear. □

In general, a dynamic if (e) S_1 else S_2 is specialized as follows. The expression e is reduced as far as possible using the values of the static variables. Then copies of the static values are made (one for each branch), and both S_1 and S_2 are specialized with respect to these. Finally a residual statement if (e') S'_1 else S'_2 is generated. Notice the similarities with the specialization algorithm for the flowchart language given in Chapter 4. An algorithm for C is given in Section 11.5.

11.2.2   Managing a mutable memory

As described above, every time a specialization point is processed, a copy of the memory, or the store, has to be made. The presence of pointers complicates this process since these must be adjusted to reflect possibly new locations of the objects they originally pointed to, and cyclic data structures must be taken into account.

In order to implement sharing of specialization points, i.e. to detect that a certain program point already has been specialized with respect to particular values of static values, it must be possible to 'compare' different copies of the store against each other [6]. We consider this again below.

11.3   Function specialization

By *function specialization* we mean the generation of a function f_s, specialized with respect to static data s. For example, in Section 11.1 the power() function was specialized to 3 yielding power_3(). In the previous section we considered specialization of the body of a function. In this section we address issues such as side-effects, sharing, and specialization strategy. Due to the semantics of C this is considerably more involved than seen in the foregoing chapters.

11.3.1 Function specialization, pointers, and sharing

Functions must naturally be specialized with respect to both static parameters and static global variables.[4] Since the only way to refer to heap-allocated objects is via pointer variables, no special action needs to be taken. What, however, does it mean to specialize with respect to a pointer?

Suppose a function `foo(int *p)` has a static formal parameter of pointer type, and is to be specialized due to a call `foo(e)` giving the residual function `foo'()`. The specialization must be with respect to both the *address* (of e) and the *indirection*, that is, the content of all the locations that p legally can point to when the actual parameter expression is e. For example, if e is a where a is a static array `int a[10]`, then p can refer to `a[0]`,...,`a[9]`.

Suppose another call of `foo()` in the program. If the *call signatures* of the two calls are equal, that is, the values of the static variables at the call are equal to those to which `foo()` was specialized, then seemingly `foo'()` can be *shared*. To decide this, the specialization time stores have to be compared. Notice that in general it can first be determined at specialization time which locations that must be compared — consider for example the difference between two calls `foo(a)` and `foo(&x)` — and thus information about the size of static objects must thus be present during the specialization. One way to achieve this is to maintain a table of the start and end addresses of all objects allocated at specialization time.

11.3.2 Functions and non-local side-effects

Functional languages are characterized by *referential transparency*, meaning that two calls to a function with the same arguments always yield the same result. As is well known, this property is not valid in C due to global variables and nonlocal side-effects.

Example 11.4 Assume a global integer stack `int stack[STACK_SIZE]` and an integer stack pointer sp.

```
int main(void)                    void push(int v)
{                                 {
    int x;                            stack[++sp] = v;
    push(e1);                     }
    push(e2);                     int pop(void)
    x = pop() + pop();            {
    push(x);                          return stack[sp--];
                                  }
}
```

In many situations the content of the stack is dynamic while the stack pointer is static. Suppose we want to specialize the push() and pop() functions.

---

[4]Much of the discussion in this subsection carries over to specialization of control flow.

First observe that function specialization must be *depth-first* in order to preserve the order of side-effects. This means that a function must be specialized before the statements following the call. In this example, when the dynamic call to push(e_1) is met, push() must be specialized before the remaining statements in main(). Thus sp will be incremented properly before the next push() is considered. Since the value of sp now differs from the first call, push() must be specialized again.

However, at the third call, it seems that the first residual version of push() can simply be shared since sp possesses the same value as originally. By doing so, though, the static value of sp will not be incremented, which is semantically wrong. To remedy this, it is necessary to *update* the value of static variables after sharing a residual function.

```
int main(void)                    void push_0(int v)
{  int x;                         { stack[4] = v; }
   /*   sp = 3 */
   push_0(e'_1);                   void push_1(int v)
   push_1(e'_2);                   { stack[5] = v; }
   x = pop_0() + pop_1();
   push_0(x)                       int pop_0(void)
   /*   sp = 4 */                  { return stack[5]; }
}
                                   int pop_1(void)
                                   { return stack[4]; }
```

At specialization time, after the last call to push_0() the static value of sp has been updated to 4.

In practice the calls to push() and pop() would, of course, be unfolded. Furthermore, as described in the next section, the array representing the stack could be split. □

Without a mechanism for updating the static values of variables after sharing a call, every dynamic call must either cause the function to be specialized again (or at least the static part to be re-executed) with consequent risk of non-termination; or all non-local side-effects must be suspended.

11.3.3 Non-local static side-effects under dynamic control

In the previous subsection problems with static (non-local) side-effects in residual functions were illustrated. However, the side-effects can even be under dynamic control, as shown below. The scenario is that in a function, a non-local variable is assigned static values *under* a dynamic if. At specialization time, the if cannot be executed and hence both the branches are specialized. This means that eventually both the static assignments will be evaluated.

Example 11.5 Suppose `global` is classified as static and the function `foo()` below is specialized.

```
int global;
int main(...)                    int foo(...)
{                                {
    global = 0;                      if ( dyn) global = 1;
    foo(...);                        else global = -1;
    S                                return  dyn;
                                 }
}
```

where *dyn* represents a dynamic expression. Observe that even though `global` is assigned static values in each branch of the dynamic `if` in `foo()`, the *concrete* value is unknown (at specialization time) after the call. □

This is called non-local *static side-effects* under *dynamic control*. The problem is that after processing a residual call, i.e. specializing a function, seemingly static variables becomes dynamic. When specializing a sequence of statements

if (*e*) S_1 else S_2; S,

where *e* is dynamic, the problem is solved by unfolding the remaining statements S into the branches, but this solution is not immediately applicable here since the `if` is hidden in another function. Either the power of the specializer must be strengthened to handle such situations, or non-local variables under dynamic control must be classified dynamic.

Suspension of side-effects under dynamic control
The immediate solution is to suspend all (non-local) side-effects under dynamic control. Thus specialization can proceed as normal after a call, since possibly side-effected static variables can at most assume one value after a call. The reader should be aware that heap-allocated data structures are in the same category as global variables, so this strategy may have a major impact on the results gained by specialization.

A slightly improved strategy is to change the binding time of variables under dynamic control from static to dynamic by insertion of so-called *explicators* [85], i.e. assignments `global = 1`. This is, however, in conflict with the monovariant division of variables into static and dynamic, and we shall not pursue this idea any further.

Unfolding of functions with side-effects under dynamic control
Suppose that all calls to a function containing static side-effects under dynamic control are unfolded. Then we can unfold the statements after the call into the now revealed dynamic `if`, and specialize these with respect to the different values of side-effected variables.

Example 11.6 Reconsider Example 11.5. By unfolding foo() into main(), the following residual program could be generated:

```
int main(...)
{
    if ( dyn' )    /* global = 1 */    S'
    else           /* global = -1 */   S''
}
```

where an attached prime indicates 'specialized'. Notice in particular that the remaining statements S have been specialized with respect to global being 1 and -1, respectively.   □

The unfolding strategy fails when the candidate function is recursive and the recursion is under dynamic control, and even when the recursion is statically controlled, termination problems can occur. Moreover, unrestricted unfolding may lead to code size explosion since no sharing of functions occurs.

Online function unfolding is addressed in Section 11.5.

Handling static side-effects under dynamic control by specialization
Observe that if specialization terminates, a static variable can assume only finitely many values. A tempting idea is to specialize the statements following a function call with respect to the finitely many *different* values, but without unfolding the function. For instance, in the running example, we would specialize S with respect to global being 1 and -1. We then need some machinery in the residual program which, at run time, can lead the control flow to the right specialized version of S. Notice that the decision to execute a particular version is determined by return statements in the called function, leading to a simple idea: to introduce the C equivalent of a *continuation* variable, to be set to a unique value before each return.

Example 11.7 Following is an example of a residual program using a continuation variable.

```
int endconf; /*  Continuation variable */
int main(...)                        int foo_0(...)
{                                    {
    foo_0(...);                          if ( dyn' )
    switch (endconf) {                       endconf = 1; return dyn';
    case 1: /* global = 1 */             else
        S'; break;                           endconf = 2; return dyn';
    case 2: /* global = -1 */        }
        S''; break;
    }
}
```

In the specialized version of `foo()`, the continuation variable `endconf` is set to a unique value before every return. After the call, a branch is made to the code corresponding to the path through `foo_0()` actually taken. Note that this allows sharing of residual functions. □

More generally, the idea is to record the values of non-local static variables immediately after every `return`. For instance, in the example we would record `global` to be 1 at return statement 1, and -1 at return statement 2.

Then, after processing a call, we specialize the remaining statements to the stores obtained by updating the store active before the call with respect to the accumulated end-configurations. For example, `global` would be updated to 1, since this is the value it has when the called function returns. In the residual program, we generate an assignment to a continuation variable before every `return` statement, and after the call, we generate code to branch on the continuation variable to the various specialized versions.

The end-configuration can also be used to update the static store after sharing a residual function (cf. Section 11.3.1). We just have to omit the function specialization.

Similar to the unfolding strategy, this method fails to handle recursive functions. The reason is that in order to specialize a function call, the called function must have been completely processed. Moreover, an extra call overhead is introduced in the residual program. In most cases, though, the overhead will be compensated for by other savings. More problematic is the copying of possibly huge static data structures which are side-effected under dynamic control. Pragmatic reasons may require such structures to be suspended.

11.4 Data structures and their binding-time separation

In this section we consider specialization of data structures and in particular pointers. Pointers are central to C: they occur in connection with arrays, the address operator &, and dynamically allocated memory can only be referred to by means of pointers.

The main problem is the binding-time separation. Consider for example a program which dynamically allocates a list `p = malloc(sizeof(struct Node))` where `Node` is a struct with a 'next' pointer field. If all pointers assigned to the next field are static, then we can allocate the list at specialization time and use it. However, suppose an assignment `p->next = `*dynamic-value* occurs later in the program. This implies that the structure of the list becomes dynamic and thus all the allocation calls must be suspended. Without a global analysis this cannot be determined when looking at the `malloc()` call in isolation. However, a binding-time analysis can, prior to the specialization, mark all those allocation calls that can be evaluated and those which must be suspended.

11.4.1   Partially static arrays

Consider a program containing an array a[n+1] whose elements are dynamic, but where all of a's subscript expressions are static. It is then, under some restrictions, possible to split a into separate variables a_0,...,a_n. The objective is to eliminate subscript calculations and an indirection, enable register allocation, etc.

Example 11.8 Consider the following code fragment implementing addition of two numbers using a stack.

```
stack[++sp] = 2;
stack[++sp] = 3;
sp--;
stack[sp] = stack[sp+1] + stack[sp];
```

It is often the case that the content of the stack is dynamic but the stack pointer itself is static. This means that the stack can be split into separate variables as illustrated below.

```
stack_13 = 2;
stack_14 = 3;
stack_13 = stack_14 + stack_13;
```

During partial evaluation, all the operations on the stack pointer have been performed and the stack has been split into separate variables.[5]

□

It is crucial that *every* index expression e in a[e] in the program is static, otherwise a[e] cannot be replaced by a_3 (assuming that e evaluates to 3). This is not sufficient, though. Assume that there is a dynamic pointer p. Unless it can be established that p newer will point to a, the array cannot be split since an expression *p cannot be replaced by the proper variable, say, a_7.

Next, recall that arrays are passed by reference in C. Suppose that a is passed to a residual function f and it is split. If, in the residual program, it is passed as f(a_1,...,a_n), there is a change in the passing semantics from call-by-reference to call-by-value which in general is unsound.[6] Thus, it seems reasonable to prohibit splitting of arrays which are passed to functions.

The decision whether or not to split an array depends on global information, and is thus hard to make online during the specialization. The binding-time analysis can, however, reveal the needed information and mark those arrays that can be split safely.

---

[5]Furthermore, applying constant folding in another postphase would give $3 + 2 = 5$.

[6]Passing pointers to the variables are not desirable either, since it increases the call overhead.

11.4.2 Struct specialization

Consider a word count program counting the number of occurrences of words in an input stream.[7] A natural data representation is an array of structs

```
struct key { char *word; int count; } keytab[NKEYS];
```

Suppose that the words are static but the number of occurrences is dynamic. If the **struct** **key** is treated as a single entity, the staticness of **word** will be lost, and we thus have to split the data structure into two separate arrays:

```
char *keyword[NKEYS];   int keycount[NKEYS];
```

in order to recover the static information.[8]

To avoid this it seems desirable to assign to each field in a struct an individual binding time, and then to specialize the *struct type* to the static fields. References to static fields are evaluated during partial evaluation, while all others are suspended to run time.

Example 11.9 Assume that we employ a binary search routine to look up the index of a word in the **keytab**.

```
struct key { char *word; int count; };
struct key keytab[NKEYS];
/*  Update word with count and return count */
int update(char *word, int count)
{
    int n = binsearch(word); /*  Find index of word */
    return keytab[n].count = count;
}
```

When specializing the **update()** function to a static word, the call to **binsearch()** can be fully evaluated since it depends on nothing but the static **word** in **keytab**. Only references to the dynamic **count** field appear in residual program.

```
struct key_word { int count; } keytab[NKEYS];
int update_word(int count)
{ return keytab[13].count = count;  }
```

□

Postprocessing can remove singleton structs such as **struct** { int count; }. Another strategy is to *split* structs into separate variables. Notice, however, that it is in general unsound to perform online splitting of structs that encapsulate arrays, since this may change the parameter passing semantics from call-by-value to call-by-reference.

---

[7]See Kernighan and Ritchie, Section 6.3 [147].

[8]Recall the two-list representation of the environment in the flowchart **mix**, Chapter 4.

11.4.3   The taming of pointers

A pointer is classified as *static* if it solely points to objects with a specialization time known location. Otherwise a pointer is said to be *dynamic*. For example, if x is a local variable, then p in p = &x can be classified as static, even though x may be dynamic. Let all dynamic objects contain their *symbolic address*, for instance, x could contain the symbolic address (or run time address) *loc-x*. Consider partial evaluation of the following lines of code:

```
int x, *p;
p = &x;    /*  Take address of dynamic x */
*p = 2;    /*  Assign constant to x */
```

The first expression can be evaluated completely, and thus p can be bound to the specialization time address of x. Dereferencing p subsequently yields the symbolic run time address *loc-x* which can be used to generate the residual expression x = 2 as expected.

Example 11.10 In the program fragment below the pointer p must necessarily be classified as dynamic.

```
int a[10], *p;
p = &a[ dynamic expression]
```

Even though a exists during specialization, the assignment cannot be evaluated statically.   □

   Similarly, objects of struct type contain their symbolic run time addresses. For example, a variable **struct key** s can be bound to *loc-s*. The expression s.word can be evaluated completely at specialization time since **word** is static. In the case of a selector expression s.count, a residual expression s.count can be generated from the symbolic address *loc-s* and **count**.[9]
   The same technique carries over to pointers. Let static p be a pointer to a **struct key** with symbolic address *loc-s1*. The expression p->count, which is semantically equivalent to (*p).count, can then be reduced to s1.count. First *p is evaluated to the struct object *loc-s1*, and then the residual struct indexing expression is generated.

Example 11.11 Pointers to non-local objects must be treated with care. Suppose that a global pointer p is assigned the address of a local dynamic variable x, and then a function foo() is called. In foo(), any dereferencing of p will evaluate to *loc-x* and thus x will appear in the residual version of foo(), which is clearly wrong. Similar problems occur when partially static variables are passed using call-by-reference. Hence pointers to variables otherwise out of scope must be suspended, and name clashes must be avoided.   □

---

[9]Recall that a partially static struct is not split but specialized.

As we have seen, *when* pointers have been classified as either static or dynamic, the specialization is straightforward, provided no pointer can point to objects with different binding times, and that the specializer simulates the runtime memory management. The real problem is to *obtain* a safe binding-time separation. For example, when must a pointer be suspended due to (possibly) non-local references, and when is it safe to split an array?[10]

Consider an analysis that can say which objects a pointer may point to during program execution. If the analysis says that no dynamic pointers can point to an array a, the array can be marked to be split. Similarly, if the analysis says that a pointer may reference a non-local variable, this variable can be classified as dynamic if needed. Without detailed information about pointers, the binding-time analysis must conservatively assume that any pointer can point to all objects and thus most pointer operations would be suspended.

11.4.4 Replacing dynamic memory allocation by static allocation

In C dynamic memory allocation is performed, directly or indirectly, via calls to the library function `malloc()`. Since the heap management must be known to the specializer, we shall, for simplicity, assume that all memory allocation is achieved through a `mix` function `alloc(S)`, where S is the name of the desired struct.[11]

Example 11.12 The following program dynamically allocates a list of n elements. Suppose the key and next fields are static but data is dynamic.

```
struct Node { int key, data; struct Node *next; } *p, *list;
/* Built a list */
for (list = p = alloc(Node); n--; )
    { p = p->next = alloc(Node); p->key = n; p->data = ...; }
list = list->next;
/* Look up the N element */
for (p = list; p != NULL && p->key != N; p = p->next);
printf("Key = %d\n", p != NULL ? p->data : -1);
```

The key observation is that even though struct Node is a partially static struct, eventually the *whole* list will be allocated and built at specialization time. This allow us to replace *dynamic* allocation by *static* allocation:

```
struct Node_key { int data; } alloc_0, ..., alloc_n;
alloc_0.data = ...;
...
alloc_n.data = ...;
printf("Key = %d\n", alloc_N.data);
```

---

[10]Recall that an array cannot be split if it is addressed by a dynamic pointer.

[11]The discussion carries over to dynamic allocation of base type and array objects.

During specialization the list has been allocated and in the residual program the nodes appear as separate variables. Moreover, `struct Node` has been specialized to the static `key` and `next` fields. All pointer chaining has been resolved, so the desired node can be referred to directly.   □

The benefit of the optimization is two fold. The expensive calls to `alloc()` are replaced by cheaper static allocation, and all pointer indirections are performed during specialization.

If the result of an `alloc()` is assigned a dynamic pointer, the call is suspended. For example, suppose that a `next` field is assigned a dynamic pointer. Then the allocation of the whole list would be suspended. This is reasonable because then the list cannot be traversed at specialization time.

11.4.5   Improving the separation of binding times

Without detailed knowledge of pointer usage, binding-time analysis must implement the most conservative assumption — that any pointer potentially can point to all objects of its type. For example, consider variable declarations `struct key k, l, *p`. If the `word` field in `k` is dynamic then also the `word` field in `l` must be classified as dynamic, as it could be that `p` might point to either of the two variables. However, if it can be revealed that `p` at most can point to one of them, for example `k`, then `word` in `l` can be classified as static.

As a variable can be characterized by its name, a heap-allocated object can be named from the `alloc()` from which it originates.

Let all `alloc()` calls be labelled uniquely. A call $\text{alloc}_l(S)$ is said to be the l'th *birthplace* of an S object. Generalizer such that the birthplace of a statically allocated variable is its (unique) name.

Example 11.13 Let $\mathcal{P}(\text{p})$ mean the set of objects, identified by their birthplaces, that pointer variable p *may* point to during program execution. We have: $\mathcal{P}(\text{p}) = \mathcal{P}(\text{list}) \supseteq \{0,1\}$, $\mathcal{P}(\text{q}) \supseteq \{2\}$, $\mathcal{P}(\text{1.next}) \supseteq \{1\}$,

```
list = p = alloc₀(Node);
for (; n--; ) { p = p->next = alloc₁(Node); ...; }
list = list->next;
q = alloc₂(Node);
```

where `1.next` means `next` in 1-objects.   □

The binding-time congruence principle can then be refined to read: for all pointer variables p it holds that any variable in $\mathcal{P}(\text{p})$ possesses the same binding time.[12] A analysis in which pointer analysis and binding-time analysis are partly intermingled is outlined in Section 11.6.

---

[12]This is similar to the use of closure analysis in higher-order partial evaluation (Chapter 10).

$$
\begin{array}{lll}
\textit{id, fid, eid} & \in & \text{Identifiers} \\
\textit{lab} & \in & \text{Labels} \\
\textit{const} & \in & \text{Constants (int, char, double, \ldots)} \\
\textit{uop, bop} & \in & \text{Unary and binary operators} \\
\textit{base} & \in & \text{Base types (\texttt{int}, \texttt{char}, \texttt{double}, \ldots)} \\
\end{array}
$$

⟨CC⟩	::=	⟨decl⟩* ⟨fundef⟩⁺	*Core C*
⟨decl⟩	::=	⟨type⟩ *id* ⟨typespec⟩	*Declarations*
⟨type⟩	::=	*base* │ ⟨type⟩ * │ struct *id* { ⟨decl⟩⁺ }	
⟨typespec⟩	::=	ϵ │ ⟨typespec⟩ [*const*]	
⟨fundef⟩	::=	⟨type⟩ *fid* (⟨decl⟩*) { ⟨decl⟩* ⟨stmt⟩⁺ }	*Functions*
⟨stmt⟩	::=	*lab* : expr ⟨exp⟩	*Statements*
	│	*lab* : return ⟨exp⟩	
	│	*lab* : goto *lab*	
	│	*lab* : if (⟨exp⟩) *lab lab*	
	│	*lab* : call *id* = *fid* (⟨exp⟩*)	
⟨exp⟩	::=	cst *const* │ var *id*	*Expressions*
	│	struct ⟨exp⟩ . *id*	
	│	index ⟨exp⟩ [⟨exp⟩] │ indr ⟨exp⟩	
	│	addr ⟨exp⟩	
	│	unary *uop* ⟨exp⟩ │ binary ⟨exp⟩ *bop* ⟨exp⟩	
	│	ecall *eid* (⟨exp⟩*) │ alloc (*id*)	
	│	assign ⟨exp⟩ = ⟨exp⟩	

Figure 11.1: Abstract syntax of Core C.

11.5   Partial evaluation for C by two-level execution

In this section we illustrate partial evaluation for C by means of a two-level execution of Core C. First we define a *kernel language* Core C and extend it to a *two-level* Core C language with explicit binding-time separation. Then we state *well-annotatedness* requirements and finally we present the specialization kernel.

The subset of C we consider in this section excludes function pointers and unions.

11.5.1   The Core C kernel language

A good way to partially evaluate a large-scale language is by 'syntactic desugaring': to translate it into a smaller *kernel language* capturing the essential constructs of the subject language. The abstract syntax of Core C is displayed in Figure 11.1. All syntactic matters such as type name declarations, scoping, nested declarations, etc. are assumed to be solved during transformation from C to Core C. Obviously, most Ansi C conforming programs can automatically be transformed into an equivalent Core C representation, and even so that the structure of the program is preserved.

A Core C program consists of an optional number of global variable declarations followed by at least one function definition. Functions can declare both parameters and local variables, but further nesting of scopes is not possible. A variable can be of base or struct type, a multidimensional array, or a pointer. The semantics of Core C is as expected [6].

The body of a function is a sequence of labelled statements. A statement can be an expression (`expr`), a conditional jump (`if`), an unconditional jump (`goto`), a function return (`return`), or a function call (`call`). In contrast to ordinary C, calls to user defined functions are all at the statement level rather than at the expression level. This has been done in order to separate the control flow from the evaluation of expressions. Clearly, the 'lifting' of calls out of expressions can be done automatically by introduction of new local variables.

An expression can be a constant, a variable, a struct or array indexing, a pointer dereferencing, an application of the address operator, an application of a unary or binary operator, a call to an **external** function, the memory allocation call `alloc()`, or an assignment.

Example 11.14 The `power()` function from Example 11.2 can be represented as a Core C program as follows.

```
int power(int base int n)
{
    int pow
    1: expr assign var pow = cst 1
    2: if (var n) 3 6
    3:    expr assign var pow = binary var pow * var base
    4:    expr assign var n = binary var n - cst 1
    5: goto 2
    6: return var pow
}
```

□

11.5.2   Binding time made explicit

Aiming at making binding times explicit, we extend the Core C language into a two-level version where dynamic constructs are annotated by an underline. The abstract syntax of two-level Core C is depicted in Figure 11.2.

Underlined versions of statements and expressions have been added to the Core C syntax. Intuitively, in the two-level language, the semantics of non-underlined constructs is the standard semantics, while the meaning of underlined constructs is 'generate code'.

Suppose a two-level Core C program is given. An `assign` is evaluated in the normal way, while a residual assignment is generated in case of an <u>assign</u>, where both the subexpressions have been reduced.

⟨2CC⟩	::= ⟨2decl⟩* ⟨2fundef⟩⁺	*2-level Core C*
⟨2decl⟩	::= ⟨2type⟩ *id* ⟨2typespec⟩ | decl	*2-level declarations*
⟨2type⟩	::= *base* | ⟨2type⟩ <u>*</u> | <u>struct</u> *id* { ⟨2decl⟩⁺ }	
	| type	
⟨2typespec⟩	::= ⟨2typespec⟩ [*const*] | typespec	
⟨2fundef⟩	::= ⟨2type⟩ *fid*(⟨2decl⟩*) {⟨2decl⟩*⟨2stmt⟩⁺}	*2-level functions*
⟨2stmt⟩	::= ⟨stmt⟩	*2-level statements*
	| *lab* : <u>expr</u> ⟨2exp⟩	
	| *lab* : <u>return</u> ⟨2exp⟩	
	| *lab* : <u>goto</u> *lab*	
	| *lab* : <u>if</u> (⟨2exp⟩) *lab lab*	
	| *lab* : <u>call</u> *id* = *fid* (⟨2exp⟩*)	
⟨2exp⟩	::= ⟨exp⟩ | <u>lift</u> ⟨exp⟩	*2-level expressions*
	| <u>struct</u> ⟨2exp⟩ . *id*	
	| <u>index</u> ⟨2exp⟩ [⟨2exp⟩] | <u>indr</u> ⟨2exp⟩	
	| <u>addr</u> ⟨2exp⟩	
	| <u>unary</u> *uop* ⟨2exp⟩ | <u>binary</u> ⟨2exp⟩ *bop* ⟨2exp⟩	
	| <u>ecall</u> *eid* (⟨2exp⟩*) | <u>alloc</u> (*id*)	
	| <u>assign</u> ⟨2exp⟩ = ⟨2exp⟩	

Figure 11.2: Abstract syntax of two-level Core C.

A `lift` operator has been added to the set of two-level expressions. Its purpose is to indicate static values appearing in dynamic contexts. The two-level meaning is: evaluate the expression and generate a residual constant. There is no underlined `var` since all dynamic variables are supposed to be bound to their symbolic addresses, and thus can be evaluated.

Example 11.15 The Core C version of the `power()` function from Example 11.14 is below shown in a two-level version.

```
int power(int base int n)
{
    int pow
    1: expr assign var pow = lift cst 1
    2: if (var n) 3 6
    3:     expr assign var pow = binary var pow * var base
    4:     expr assign var n = binary var n - cst 1
    5: goto 2
    6: return pow
}
```

Notice that a `lift` has been inserted in the first statement since the static constant 1 appears in a dynamic context. ☐

The meaning of a jump is to continue (two-level) program execution at the target label. The meaning of a <u>goto</u> is to generate a residual goto and to specialize the target statements to the current values of the static variables. The meaning of a <u>call</u> statement is to execute the function (which must be completely static), and the meaning of a <u>call</u> is to specialize the call.

To indicate the desired processing of function calls, the two-level language is furthermore extended with the forms:

<u>rcall</u> and <u>ucall</u>.

In the former case, the function is specialized under the assumption that *no* static side-effects under dynamic control occur in the called function (cf. Section 11.3).[13] The <u>ucall</u> form indicates that the function is to be unfolded.

11.5.3   Well-annotated two-level Core C

Not all two-level Core C program specialize well. The indispensable congruence requirement, that static computation must be independent of dynamic values, is not captured by the purely syntactic definition of the two-level language. A program fulfilling this principle is said to be *well-annotated*. A set of rules is needed such that if a program satisfies them, then no binding time error can occur during specialization.

Binding times can be seen as types in the two-level language. For instance, a constant has type static S, an expression depending on a dynamic value has type dynamic D. This can be formalized by the means of a *two-level binding-time* type system. A binding-time type (BTT) $\mathcal{T}$ is given inductively by the grammar:

$$\mathcal{T} ::= S \mid D \mid \mathcal{T} \times \cdots \times \mathcal{T} \mid *\mathcal{T}$$

where S and D are *ground types*. The constructor $\times$ describes the components of a value of struct type. For example, a <code>struct { int x, y; }</code> could be assigned the binding time $S \times D$ meaning that <code>x</code> is static but <code>y</code> dynamic. Finally, the star constructor $*\mathcal{T}$ denotes a *static* pointer to an object of binding time $\mathcal{T}$.

Example 11.16 Consider the <code>struct Node</code> defined in Section 11.4, and suppose that <code>key</code> and <code>next</code> are static fields but <code>data</code> dynamic. Thus the type T_{Node} is

$$T_{Node} = S \times D \times *T_{Node}$$

where the recursive definition is due to the fact that the <code>struct Node</code> is recursively defined. Formally we would have to add a fixed-point operator μ to the two-level type system, defined by $\mu T.\mathcal{T} = \mathcal{T}[\mu T.\mathcal{T}/T]$, but this is omitted for simplicity. □

---

[13]This is an example of a *well-annotatedness* requirement which is treated in the next subsection.

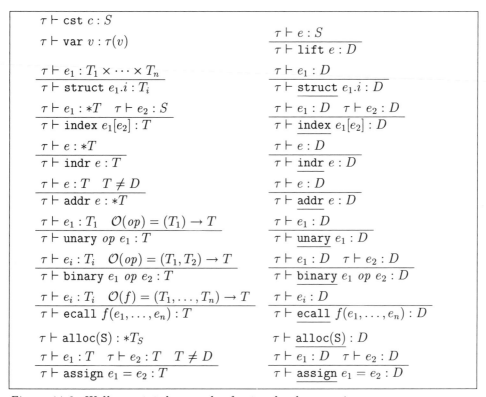

$$\tau \vdash \texttt{cst } c : S$$

$$\tau \vdash \texttt{var } v : \tau(v)$$

$$\dfrac{\tau \vdash e : S}{\tau \vdash \texttt{lift } e : D}$$

$$\dfrac{\tau \vdash e_1 : T_1 \times \cdots \times T_n}{\tau \vdash \texttt{struct } e_1.i : T_i}$$

$$\dfrac{\tau \vdash e_1 : D}{\tau \vdash \underline{\texttt{struct }} e_1.i : D}$$

$$\dfrac{\tau \vdash e_1 : *T \quad \tau \vdash e_2 : S}{\tau \vdash \texttt{index } e_1[e_2] : T}$$

$$\dfrac{\tau \vdash e_1 : D \quad \tau \vdash e_2 : D}{\tau \vdash \underline{\texttt{index }} e_1[e_2] : D}$$

$$\dfrac{\tau \vdash e : *T}{\tau \vdash \texttt{indr } e : T}$$

$$\dfrac{\tau \vdash e : D}{\tau \vdash \underline{\texttt{indr }} e : D}$$

$$\dfrac{\tau \vdash e : T \quad T \neq D}{\tau \vdash \texttt{addr } e : *T}$$

$$\dfrac{\tau \vdash e : D}{\tau \vdash \underline{\texttt{addr }} e : D}$$

$$\dfrac{\tau \vdash e_1 : T_1 \quad \mathcal{O}(op) = (T_1) \to T}{\tau \vdash \texttt{unary } op \; e_1 : T}$$

$$\dfrac{\tau \vdash e_1 : D}{\tau \vdash \underline{\texttt{unary }} e_1 : D}$$

$$\dfrac{\tau \vdash e_i : T_i \quad \mathcal{O}(op) = (T_1, T_2) \to T}{\tau \vdash \texttt{binary } e_1 \; op \; e_2 : T}$$

$$\dfrac{\tau \vdash e_1 : D \quad \tau \vdash e_2 : D}{\tau \vdash \underline{\texttt{binary }} e_1 \; op \; e_2 : D}$$

$$\dfrac{\tau \vdash e_i : T_i \quad \mathcal{O}(f) = (T_1, \dots, T_n) \to T}{\tau \vdash \texttt{ecall } f(e_1, \dots, e_n) : T}$$

$$\dfrac{\tau \vdash e_i : D}{\tau \vdash \underline{\texttt{ecall }} f(e_1, \dots, e_n) : D}$$

$$\tau \vdash \texttt{alloc(S)} : *T_S$$

$$\tau \vdash \underline{\texttt{alloc(S)}} : D$$

$$\dfrac{\tau \vdash e_1 : T \quad \tau \vdash e_2 : T \quad T \neq D}{\tau \vdash \texttt{assign } e_1 = e_2 : T}$$

$$\dfrac{\tau \vdash e_1 : D \quad \tau \vdash e_2 : D}{\tau \vdash \underline{\texttt{assign }} e_1 = e_2 : D}$$

Figure 11.3: Well-annotatedness rules for two-level expressions.

Let $\tau : \text{Id} \to \text{BTT}$ be a type assignment mapping identifiers to binding-time types. For example, $\tau(\texttt{base}) = D$ in case of the $\texttt{power()}$ function. Moreover, let $\mathcal{O} : \text{OId} \to \text{BTT}^* \to \text{BTT}$ map operators and external functions to their static binding-time types. For example, '+' maps static base values to a static base value: $\mathcal{O}(+) = (S, S) \to S$.

Suppose that e is a two-level expression and that all identifiers in e are in the domain of τ. Then e is *well-annotated* iff there exists a binding-time type T such that $\tau \vdash e : T$ where the relation $\vdash$ is defined in Figure 11.3.

A constant is static and the binding-time type of a variable is given by the environment τ. The $\texttt{lift}$ operator converts a static base value to a dynamic constant.[14]

In any indexing of a dynamic struct, the subexpression must be dynamic. Otherwise the type of the result is given by the corresponding field. An index expression is static if its left expression is of static pointer type and the index expression is static. Otherwise both the subexpressions must be dynamic and the indexing suspended. In the case of a deference operator, the subexpression must be of static

---

[14]Notice that values of struct or pointer type are not allowed to be lifted.

pointer type for the application to be non-underlined.

The cases for application of unary and binary operators and external functions are all similar. Either the arguments are static as given by the type assignment, or all the arguments are dynamic and the application is suspended. The `alloc` call returns a static pointer, and an assignment is non-underlined if both the subexpressions are non-dynamic.

The rules for structs are more liberal than assumed in the previous sections. Recall that we do not want to split structs but to specialize their static fields. We could therefore additionally require any struct expression whose relevant field is non-static to be underlined.

Given the definition of well-annotatedness of expressions, well-annotatedness of statements can be defined. For example, an `if` is static if the test expression is static. A function definition is static if it does not contain a dynamic statement. In a dynamic function, every **return** must be dynamic since a residual function is supposed to return a value at run time — not at specialization time. The last step is to impose conditions regarding the treatment of recursive functions and non-local side-effects: e.g. to make all assignments to non-local variables dynamic [6,10]. To this end the output of a pointer analysis is useful to detect whether and — in the affirmative case — which non-local variables a function may refer to.

11.5.4   Two-level execution of Core C

In this section we present the core of a specializer for two-level Core C. It comes in two parts: the two-level execution of statements, and the surrounding kernel for polyvariant specialization of program points.

Two-level execution of statements
Let the value of parameters, local variables, and global variables be represented by three separate arrays `pstore`, `lstore`, and `gstore` respectively. The heap is represented by an array `heap`, which `alloc()` administrates.

The program representation is assumed to be encapsulated via external functions. An example is `stmt_kind()`, which returns the tag of a particular statement in a function. The whole program is represented by the variable `pgm`.

The residual code is generated by external library functions such as `gen_()`, which adds a statement to the residual function currently being made.

The two-level execution of two-level statements is given in Figure 11.4. The variable `pp` is the current program point, and **func** the current function index. Given the label of a statement, all following statements up to the next dynamic control statement (`goto`, `if`, `call`, `return`) are specialized.

The function `eval()` evaluates an expression yielding a value, and the function `reduce()` reduces an expression giving a residual expression.[15]

---

[15]We assume that suitable data types for representation of expressions and values exist.

```
while (pp != HALT)                          /*  Two-level execution of statements/ */
    switch (stmt_kind(func,pp,pgm))
      {
      case EXPR:                                        /*  Static expression  */
        eval( exp, pstore, lstore, gstore);
        pp += 1; break;
      case _EXPR_:                                      /*  Dynamic expression  */
        gen_expr(reduce( exp, pstore, lstore, gstore));
        pp += 1; break;
      case GOTO:                                          /*  Static jump  */
        pp = target-label; break;
      case _GOTO_:                                      /*  Dynamic jump  */
        lab = seenB4( target-label, pstore, lstore, gstore);
        if (!lab) lab = insert_pending( target-label, pstore, lstore, gstore);
        gen_goto(lab);
        pp = HALT; break;
      case IF:                                          /*  Static conditional  */
        if (eval( test-exp, pstore, lstore, gstore)) pp = then-lab;
        else pp = else-lab;
        break;
      case _IF_:                                        /*  Dynamic conditional  */
        lab1 = seenB4( then-lab, pstore, lstore, gstore);
        if (!lab1) lab1 = insert_pending( then-lab, pstore, lstore, gstore);
        lab2 = seenB4( else-lab, pstore, lstore, gstore);
        if (!lab2) lab2 = insert_pending( else-lab, pstore, lstore, gstore);
        gen_if(reduce( test-exp, pstore, lstore, gstore), lab1, lab2);
        pp = HALT; break;
      case CALL:                                        /*  Static function call  */
        store = eval_param( parameters, pstore, lstore, gstore);
        *eval_lexp( var, pstore, lstore, gstore) =  exec_func( fun, store);
        pp += 1; break;              ˻
      case _CALL_:                                      /*  Residual call: specialize  */
        store = eval_param( parameters, pstore, lstore, gstore);
        if (!(lab = seen_call( fun, store, gstore)))
            { code_new_fun(); spec_func( fun,store); code_restore_fun(); }
        gen_call( var, fun, store);
        for (n = 0; n < # endconfigurations; n++) {
            update( n'th endconf, pstore, lstore, gstore);
            insert_pending(pp+1, pstore, lstore, gstore);
            }
        gen_callbranch();
        pp = HALT; break;
      case _RCALL_:                                     /*  Recursive residual call: specialize  */
        store = eval_param( parameters, pstore, lstore, gstore);
        if (!(lab = seen_call( fun, store, gstore)))
            { code_new_fun(); spec_func( fun, store); code_restore_fun(); }
        update( end-conf, pstore, lstore, gstore);
        gen_call( var, fun, store);
        pp += 1; break;
      case _UCALL_:                                     /*  Residual call: unfold  */
        store = eval_param( parameters, pstore, lstore, gstore);
        gen_param_assign(store);
        spec_func( fun, store);
        pp = HALT; break;
      case _RETURN_:                                    /*  Dynamic return  */
        n = gen_endconf_assign();
        gen_return(reduce( exp, pstore, lstore, gstore));
        save_endconf(n, func, pstore, gstore);
        pp = HALT;

      }
```

Figure 11.4: Two-level execution of statements.

Static expressions are evaluated and dynamic expressions are reduced.

In the case of a dynamic `goto`, the target program point is specialized. If it has not already been specialized with respect to the current values of static variables, it is inserted into a pending list (`insert_pending()`). A residual jump to the residual target point is finally generated.

Dynamic `if` is treated in a similar way. Both branches are checked to see whether they have been specialized before, and a residual `if` is added to the residual code.

Consider function specialization. First it is checked to see whether the function already has been specialized with respect to the static values. If so, the residual function is shared, otherwised it is specialized via a recursive call to `spec_fun` (defined below). Next the end-configuration branch is generated (`gen_callbranch()`), and the following program point is inserted into the pending list to be specialized with respect to each of the static stores obtained by an updating according to the saved end-configurations (`update'()`).

To generate a new residual function corresponding to the called function, a library function `code_new_fun()` is used. This causes the output of the `gen(_)` to be accumulated. When the function has been specialized, the code generation process is returned to the previous function by calling (`code_restore_fun()`).

Online function unfolding can be accomplished as follows. First, assignments of the dynamic actual parameters to the formal parameters (`gen_param_assign()`) is made. Next, the called function is specialized but such that residual statements are added to the current function. By treating `returns` in the called as `goto` to the statement following the call, the remaining statements will be specialized accordingly. In practice, though, the process is more involved since care must be taken to avoid name clashes and the static store must be updated to cope with side-effects.

In case of a `return`, the expression is reduced and a residual `return` made. Furthermore, the values of static variables are saved (`save_endconf()`) as part of the residual function.

The pending loop

The pending loop driving the polyvariant specialization is outlined in Figure 11.5. As parameter it takes the index of a function to be specialized and the parameter store. It then allocates storage for local variables and initializes the specialization by inserting the first program point into the pending list.

Let $\langle p, s \rangle$ be a specialization point in the pending list, where p is a program point and s a copy of the static store. To specialize p with respect to s, pp is initialized to p, and the values of static variables restored according to s (`pending_restore()`). Finally, the specialization point is marked as 'processed' (`pending_processed()`) such that later specializations of the same program point are shared.

The actual specialization is done by a two-level execution (see Figure 11.4). This is repeated until all pending specialization points have been processed, i.e. until the pending list is empty.

```
Value *gstore;                                    /*  Global store */
Value heap[HEAP]                                      /*  Heap */

int spec_func(int func, Value *store)
{
    int pp;                                       /*  Program point */
    Value *store;                       /*  Store for actual parameters */
                                                 /*  Initialize */
    lstore = alloc_store(func);
    pending_insert(1, pstore, lstore, gstore);
                            /*  Specialize all reachable program points */
    while (!pending_empty())
        {                  /*  Restore configuration according to pending */
            pending_restore(pstore, lstore, gstore);
            pp = pending_pp();
            pending_processed(pp);
                                             /*  Two-level execution */
            ⟨Figure 11.4⟩
        }
    return  function index;
}
```

Figure 11.5: Function specialization.

11.6   Separation of the binding times

In this section we briefly consider binding-time analysis of C with emphasis on basic principles rather than details [10]. Due to the semantics of C, and the involved well-annotatedness conditions, the analysis is considerably more complicated than of the lambda calculus (for example), but nevertheless the same basic principles can be employed. The analysis consists of three main steps:

1. Call-graph analysis: find (possibly) recursive functions.

2. Pointer analysis: approximixate the usage of pointers.

3. Binding-time analysis: compute the binding times of all variables, expressions, statements, and functions.

11.6.1   Call-graph analysis

The aim of the call-graph analysis is to annotate calls to possibly recursive functions by `rcall`. This information is needed to suspend non-local side-effects in residual recursive functions. The analysis can be implemented as a fixed-point analysis.

The analysis records for every function which other functions it calls, directly or indirectly. Initially the description is empty. At each iteration the description is updated according to the calls until a fixed point is reached [4]. Clearly the analysis will terminate since there are only finitely many functions.

11.6.2 Pointer analysis

The aim of the pointer analysis is for every pointer variable to approximate the set of objects it *may* point to, as introduced in Section 11.4.

The pointer analysis can be implemented as an abstract interpretation over the program, where (pointer) variables are mapped to a set of object identifiers [121]. In every iteration, the abstract store is updated according to the assignments, e.g. in case of a p = &x, 'x' is included in the map for p. This is repeated until a fixed-point is reached.

11.6.3 Binding-time analysis

The binding-time analysis can be realized using the ideas from Chapter 8 where the type inference rules for the lambda calculus were transformed into a constraint set which subsequently was solved.

The analysis proceeds in three phases. Initially, a set of constraints is collected. The constraints capture the requirements stated in Figure 11.3 and the additional conditions imposed by the handling of recursive functions with non-local side-effects. Next, the constraints are normalized by applying a number of rewriting steps exhaustively. Finally, a solution to the normalized constraint set is found. The output is a program where every expression is mapped to its binding time.

We introduce five syntactic constraints between binding time types:

$$T_1 = T_2 \quad T_1 \preceq T_2 \quad *T_1 \sqsubseteq T_2 \quad T_1 \times \cdots \times T_n \sqsubseteq T \quad T_1 \trianglelefteq T_2 \quad T_1 \vartriangleright T_2$$

which are defined as follows. The '$\preceq$' represents lift: $S \prec D$. The '$\sqsubseteq$' represents splitting of dynamic arrays: $*D \sqsubseteq D$. Furthermore, it captures completely dynamic structs: $D \times \cdots \times D \sqsubseteq D$. The '$\trianglelefteq$' is for expressing the binding time of operators. Its definition is given by $T_1 \trianglelefteq T_2$ iff $T_1 = T_2$ or $T_2 = D$. The last constraint '$\vartriangleright$' introduces a dependency: given $T_1 \vartriangleright T_2$, if $T_1 = D$ then $T_2 = D$.

The constraints for an expressions e are inductively defined in Figure 11.6.

The constraints capture the dependencies between the expression itself and its subexpressions. A unique type variable is assigned to each variable[16], expression node, statement node and function.

A constant e is static, captured by the constraint $T_e = S$. The binding time of a variable reference e is given by a unique type variable for every variable v, thus $T_e = T_v$.

Consider the two-level typing of an index expression $e_1[e_2]$. Either the left expression is a static pointer and the index is static, or both subexpressions are dynamic. This is contained in the constraint $*T_e \sqsubseteq T_{e_1}$, and the constraint $T_{e_2} \vartriangleright T_{e_1}$ assures that if e_2 is dynamic then so is e_1.

---

[16]Contrary to the analysis for the lambda calculus (Chapter 8), we only assign one variable T_e to each expression e. Instead we introduce a 'lifted' variable $\overline{T}_e$ when needed.

$$\mathcal{C}_{exp}(e) = \text{case } e \text{ of}$$

$[\![\texttt{cst } c]\!]$	$\Rightarrow \{S = T_e\}$
$[\![\texttt{var } v]\!]$	$\Rightarrow \{T_v = T_e\}$
$[\![\texttt{struct } e_1.i]\!]$	$\Rightarrow \{T_1 \times \cdots \times T_e \times \cdots \times T_n \sqsubseteq T_{e_1}\} \cup \mathcal{C}_{exp}(e_1)$
$[\![\texttt{index } e_1[e_2]]\!]$	$\Rightarrow \{*T_e \sqsubseteq T_{e_1}, T_{e_2} \triangleright T_{e_1}\} \cup \mathcal{C}_{exp}(e_i)$
$[\![\texttt{indr } e_1]\!]$	$\Rightarrow \{*T_e \sqsubseteq T_{e_1}\} \cup \mathcal{C}_{exp}(e_1)$
$[\![\texttt{addr } e_1]\!]$	$\Rightarrow \{*T_{e_1} \sqsubseteq T_e, T_{e_1} \triangleright T_e\} \cup \mathcal{C}_{exp}(e_1)$
$[\![\texttt{unary } op\ e_1]\!]$	$\Rightarrow \{T_{op_1} \trianglelefteq \overline{T}_{e_1}, T_{e_1} \preceq \overline{T}_{e_1}, \overline{T}_{e_1} \triangleright T_e, T_{op} \trianglelefteq T_e, T_e \triangleright \overline{T}_{e_1}\} \cup \mathcal{C}_{exp}(e_1)$
$[\![\texttt{binary } e_1\ op\ e_2]\!]$	$\Rightarrow \{T_{op_i} \trianglelefteq \overline{T}_{e_i}, T_{e_i} \preceq \overline{T}_{e_i}, \overline{T}_{e_i} \triangleright T_e, T_{op} \trianglelefteq T_e, T_e \triangleright \overline{T}_{e_i}\} \cup \mathcal{C}_{exp}(e_i)$
$[\![\texttt{ecall } f(e_1, \ldots, e_n)]\!]$	$\Rightarrow \{T_{f_i} \trianglelefteq \overline{T}_{e_i}, T_{e_i} \preceq \overline{T}_{e_i}, \overline{T}_{e_i} \triangleright T_e, T_f \trianglelefteq T_e, T_e \triangleright \overline{T}_{e_i}\} \cup \mathcal{C}_{exp}(e_i)$
$[\![\texttt{alloc(S)}]\!]$	$\Rightarrow \{*T_s \sqsubseteq T_e\}$
$[\![\texttt{assign } e_1 = e_2]\!]$	$\Rightarrow \{T_e = T_{e_1}, T_{e_2} \preceq T_{e_1}\} \cup \mathcal{C}_{exp}(e_i)$

Figure 11.6: Constraints for expressions.

The constraints generated for applications of unary, binary and external functions are analogous. Consider the case for `ecall`. In the typing rule it is defined that either the arguments are all static or they are all dynamic. In the latter case it may be desired to insert a `lift` to avoid forcing a static computation dynamic. We introduce n 'lifted' variables $\overline{T}_{e_i}$ corresponding to possibly lifted arguments. The are constrained by the static binding time type of the called function $T_{f_i} \trianglelefteq \overline{T}_{e_i}$, cf. the use of $\mathcal{O}$ map in the well-annotatedness rules. Next, via lift constraints $T_{e_i} \preceq \overline{T}_{e_i}$ capture the fact that the actual parameters can be lifted. Finally, dependency constraints are added to assure that if one argument is dynamic, then the application is suspended.

In the case of assignments, it is captured that a static right expression can be lifted if the left expression is dynamic, by $T_{e_2} \preceq T_{e_1}$.

The constraints for statements are given in Figure 11.7. For all statements, a dependency between the binding time of the function T_f and the statement is made. This is to guarantee that a function is made residual if it contains a dynamic statement.

$$\mathcal{C}_{stmt}(s) = \text{case } s \text{ of}$$

$[\![\texttt{expr } e]\!]$	$\Rightarrow \{T_e \triangleright T_f\} \cup \mathcal{C}_{exp}(e)$
$[\![\texttt{goto } m]\!]$	$\Rightarrow \{\}$
$[\![\texttt{if } (e)\ m\ n]\!]$	$\Rightarrow \{T_e \triangleright T_f\} \cup \mathcal{C}_{exp}(e)$
$[\![\texttt{return } e]\!]$	$\Rightarrow \{T_e \preceq \overline{T}_e, \overline{T}_e \triangleright T_f, T_{f_s} \trianglelefteq \overline{T}_e, T_f \triangleright \overline{T}_e\} \cup \mathcal{C}_{exp}(e)$
$[\![\texttt{call } x = f'(e_1, \ldots, e_n)]\!]$	$\Rightarrow \{T_{e_i} \preceq T_{f'_i}, T_{f'} = T_x, T_x \triangleright T_f\} \cup \mathcal{C}_{exp}(x) \cup \bigcup_i \mathcal{C}_{exp}(e_i)$

Figure 11.7: Constraints for statements.

Using the information collected by the call graph analysis and the pointer analysis, additional constraints can be added to assure, for example, suspension of non-local side-effects in recursive functions. For example, if a pointer p is set to point to a global variable v in a recursive function, a constraint $T_v = D$ must be added.

Given a multiset of constraints, a solution is looked for. A solution is a substitution mapping type variables into binding time types which satisfies all the constraints (Chapter 8) [10]. From this it is easy to derive a well-annotated two-level program.

11.7   Self-application, types, and double encoding

So far we have not considered self-application. Contrary to the languages studied previously, C has typed data structures, and this interferes with self-application.

A partial evaluator is a general program expected to work on programs taking all kinds of input, for example integers and characters. To fulfil this, it is necessary to *encode* the static input into a single uniform data type Value. In C, Value could be a huge struct with fields for int, char, doubles, etc. Let the notation $\overline{d}^t$ denote an unspecified representation of a datum d (of some type) in a data structure of type t. The proper extensional type of mix (ignoring annotations for simplicity) can then be written as follows:

$$\llbracket\texttt{mix}\rrbracket_C(\overline{p}^{\text{Pgm}}, \overline{s}^{\text{Value}}) = \overline{p_s}^{\text{Pgm}}$$

where the result is a representation of the residual program, and the subscripts indicate the languages in use.

Consider self-application $\llbracket\texttt{mix}\rrbracket_C(\texttt{mix}, \texttt{int})$, where int is an interpreter. As input to mix, int must of course be encoded into the program representation $\overline{\texttt{int}}^{\text{Pgm}}$. As for any program input to the running mix, this must be encoded into the Value type. The result may be a huge data structure slowing self-application down and causing memory problems.

This is also seen in the Futamura projections, which can be restated as follows.

1. Futamura $\llbracket\texttt{mix}\rrbracket_C(\overline{\texttt{int}}^{\text{Pgm}}, \overline{\overline{p}^{\text{Pgm}}}^{\text{Value}})$ $= \overline{\texttt{target}}^{\text{Pgm}}$

2. Futamura $\llbracket\texttt{mix}\rrbracket_C(\overline{\texttt{mix}}^{\text{Pgm}}, \overline{\overline{\texttt{int}}^{\text{Pgm}}}^{\text{Value}})$ $= \overline{\texttt{compiler}}^{\text{Pgm}}$

3. Futamura $\llbracket\texttt{mix}\rrbracket_C(\overline{\texttt{mix}}^{\text{Pgm}}, \overline{\overline{\texttt{mix}}^{\text{Pgm}}}^{\text{Value}})$ $= \overline{\texttt{cogen}}^{\text{Pgm}}$

Notice the double encoding of the second argument to mix, and in particular the speculative double encoding of programs. To overcome the problem, the type of the program representation can be added as a new base type. Hereby a level of encoding can be eliminated, a technique also used elsewhere [6,69,169].

11.8   C-mix: a partial evaluator for C programs

C-mix is a self-applicable partial evaluator based on the techniques described in this chapter [6,9,10]. It can handle a substantial subset of the Ansi C programming language, and is fully automatic. In this section we report some benchmarks. The specialization kernel, described in Section 11.5, takes up 500 lines of code. The whole specializer including library functions consists of approximately 2500 lines of C code.

11.8.1 Benchmarks

All experiments have been run on a Sun Sparc II work station with 64M internal memory. No exceptionally large memory usage has been observed. The reported times (cpu seconds) include parsing of Core C, specialization, and dumping of the residual program, but not preprocessing.

Specialization of general programs

The program least_square implements approximation of function values by orthogonal polynomials. Input is the degree m of the approximating polynomial, the vector of x-values, and the corresponding function values. It is specialized with respect to fixed m and x-values. The program scanner is a general lexical analyser which as input takes a definition of a token set and a stream of characters. Output is the recognized tokens. It is specialized to a fixed token set.

Program run	Run time		Code size	
	time	ratio	size	ratio
$[\![\text{least\_square}]\!](m, \textit{Input})$	6.3		82	
$[\![\text{least\_square}_m]\!](\textit{Input})$	3.7	1.9	1146	0.07
$[\![\text{scanner}]\!](\textit{Table}, \textit{Input})$	1.9		65	
$[\![\text{scanner}_{\textit{Table}}]\!](\textit{Input})$	0.7	2.7	1090	0.06

The least_square program was specialized to degree 3 and 100 fixed x-values. The speedup obtained was 1.9.[17] It is rather surprising that specialization to the innocent looking parameters of the least-square algorithm can give such a speedup. Furthermore, it should be noted that the so-called 'weight-function', which determines the allowed error, is completely static. Thus, more involved weight-functions give larger speedup. The price paid is the size of the residual program which grows linearly with the number of static x-values.

The scanner was specialized to a subset of the C keywords, and applied to a stream with 100 000 tokens. The speedup was 2.7. This is also rather satisfactory, and it shows that efficient lexers can be generated automatically from general scanners. The residual program is rather large, but is comparable to a lex-generated lexical analyser for the same language.[18]

---

[17]The programs were run 100 times on the input.

[18]This example was also used in Chapter 6, where the scanner was specialized to two-character tokens.

Compiler generation by self-application

The C mix specializer kernel is self-applicable. Compiler generation is demonstrated by specialization of spec to an interpreter int for an assembly language. This example is taken from Pagan who by hand makes a generating extension of the interpreter [213]. The interpreted program Primes computes the first n'th primes.

Program run	Run time		Code size	
	time	ratio	size	ratio
$[\![\text{Int}]\!](\text{Primes}, 500)$	61.9		123	
$[\![\text{Int}_{\text{Primes}}]\!](500)$	8.9	7.0	118	1.0
$[\![\text{spec}]\!](\text{Int}, \text{Primes})$	0.6		474	
$[\![\text{spec}_{\text{Int}}]\!](\text{Primes})$	0.5	1.2	760	0.6
$[\![\text{spec}]\!](\text{spec}, \text{Int})$	2.2		474	
$[\![\text{cogen}]\!](\text{Int})$	0.7	3.1	2049	0.2

The compiled primes program (in C) is approximately 7 times faster than the interpreted version. Compiler generation using cogen compared to self-application is 3 times faster. The compiler generator cogen is 2000 lines of code plus library routines.

11.9   Towards partial evaluation for full Ansi C

In this chapter we have described partial evaluation for a substantial subset of C, including most of its syntactical constructs. This does not mean, however, that an arbitrary C program can be specialized well. There are two main reasons for this.

Some C programs are simply not suited for specialization. If partial evaluation is applied to programs not especially written with specialization in mind, it is often necessary to rewrite the program in order to obtain a clean separation of binding times so as much as possible can be done at specialization time. Various tricks which can be employed by the binding-time engineer are described in Chapter 12, and most of these carry over to C. Such transformations should preferably be automated, but this is still an open research area.

A more serious problem is due to the semantics of the language. In C, programmers are allowed to do almost all (im)possible things provided they know what they are doing. By developing stronger analyses it may become possible to handle features such as void pointers without being overly conservative, but obviously programs relying on a particular implementation of integers or the like cannot be handled safely. The recurring problem is that the rather open-ended C semantics is not a sufficiently firm base when *meaning-preserving* transformations are to be performed automatically.

11.10   Exercises

Exercise 11.1 Specialize the mini_printf() in Example 11.1 using the methods described in this chapter, i.e. transform to Core C, binding-time analyse to obtain a two-level Core C program, and specialize it.   □

Exercise 11.2 In the two-level Core C language, both a static and a dynamic goto exists, even though a goto can always be kept static. Find an example program in which it is useful to annotate a goto dynamic   □

Exercise 11.3 In the Core C language, all loops are represented as L: if () ... goto L;. Consider an extension of the Core C language and the two-level algorithm in Figure 11.4 to include while. Discuss advantages and disadvantages.   □

Exercise 11.4 Consider the binary search function binsearch().

```
#define N 10
int binsearch(int n)
{
    int low, high;
    low = 0; high = N - 1;
    while (low <= high) {
        mid = (low + high) / 2;
        if (table[mid] < n)
            high = mid - 1;
        else if (table[mid] > n)
            low = mid + 1;
        else
            return mid;
    }
}
```

Assume that the array table[N] of integer is static. Specialize with respect to a dynamic n. Predict the speedup. Is the size of the program related to N?   □

Exercise 11.5 The Speedup Theorem in Chapter 6 states that mix can at most accomplish *linear speedup*. Does the theorem hold for partial evaluation of C? Extend to speedup analysis in Chapter 6 to cope with functions.   □

Exercise 11.6 Consider the inference rule for the address operator in Figure 11.3. Notice that if the expression evaluates to a dynamic value, then the application is suspended. This is desirable in the case of an expression &a[e] where e is dynamic, but not in case of &x where x is dynamic. Find ways to remedy this problem.   □

Exercise 11.7 Formalize the well-annotatedness requirements for statements, functions, and Core C programs.   □

Exercise 11.8 Develop the call-graph analysis as described in Section 11.6. Develop the pointer analysis.   □

Part IV

Partial Evaluation in Practice

Chapter 12

Binding-Time Improvements

Two programs that are semantically, and even operationally, equivalent with respect to time or space usage may specialize very differently, giving residual programs with large differences in efficiency, size, or runtime memory usage. Thus partial evaluator users must employ a good programming style to make their programs specialize well. The purpose of this chapter is to give some hints about 'good style', based on examples and experience.

Good style depends on the particular partial evaluator being used, but it is a common pattern that binding times should be mixed as little as possible: partially static items are harder to handle than fully static, a dynamic choice between static items is harder to use than a static choice, etc. A simple example (in SML):

```
fun f1 x y = (x+1)+y;
fun f2 x y = (x+y)+1;
```

If x is static and y is dynamic, a partial evaluator will typically manage to reduce x+1 in f1 but be unable to reduce the body of f2. To do the latter, commutative and associative laws for addition must be applied, either during partial evaluation or in a prepass. A suitable prepass could, for example, transform function definition f2 into f1, semantically equivalent but more amenable to partial evaluation.

A program transformation that preserves semantics but makes the program more suited for partial evaluation is called a *binding-time improvement*. Binding-time improvements are transformations applied, automatically or by hand, to a source program prior to the specialization phase. We do not, however, consider transformations such as car(cons E1 E2) ⇒ E1 that may change program semantics (E2 could loop, assuming call-by-value).

For one example, we outlined in Section 4.9.3 how a simple program transformation could make a simple partial evaluator mimic the use of polyvariant divisions. This is a natural example of a binding-time improvement which is often applied manually, and occurs automatically in the Schism system [60].

Binding-time improvements are rapidly being automated and incorporated into systems (Similix and Schism in particular), so there are floating boundaries among hand improvements; automated improvements achieved by preprocessing; and automated improvements that are incorporated into the specialization algorithm itself. For instance, the introduction of a binding-time improvement prepass provides a very modular way to squeeze more power out of a simple specializer. Thus just which binding-time improvements can make programs run faster depends critically on the strength of the specializer and its BTA.

This complicates objective discussion, since the same example may specialize differently on different systems. In order to clarify the problems involved and their solution, we assume the *improvements are applied by hand*, and that a *very simple specializer* is used.

Below we describe several strategies. All the examples presented are in Scheme and have been run with Similix[1]. When residual programs or fragments thereof are presented, these are shown exactly as they were produced by Similix.

The role of binding-time analysis
Binding-time improvements are of course relevant to both online and offline specializers. Binding-time analysis is especially helpful for seeing *global* improvements, since the information it provides is visible (in the form of annotations) and can help determine *where* changes really do a difference in binding times. One strategy could be to obtain good offline binding-time separation with the aid of BTA, and then specialize the same program by online methods to get still better results.

12.1   A case study: Knuth, Morris, Pratt string matching

This section shows how partial evaluation and binding-time improvements can generate Knuth, Morris, and Pratt's pattern matching algorithm [150] from a naive pattern matcher. The original version of this much-referenced example of binding-time improvements is due to Consel and Danvy [54]. We present a simpler version which produces the same result.

The Scheme program of Figure 12.1 implements the first (very) naive attempt. It takes a pattern p and a subject string d and returns yes if the pattern occurs inside the subject string, otherwise no. The variable pp is a copy of the original pattern and dd a copy of the rest of the string from the point where the current attempt to match started. Its time is $O(m \cdot n)$, where m is the length of the pattern and n is the length of the subject string.

If the function kmp is specialized with respect to some static pattern p and dynamic string d, the result still takes time $O(m \cdot n)$. A better result can be obtained by exploiting the information that when matching fails, the characters up to the mismatch point in d and p are identical. The trick is to collect this information, i.e. the common static prefix of p and d that is known at a given

---

[1]Version 5.0

```
(define (kmp p d)    (loop p d p d))

(define (loop p d pp dd)
  (cond
   ((null? p) 'yes)
   ((null? d) 'no)
   ((equal? (car p) (car d))
    (loop (cdr p) (cdr d) pp dd))
   (else (kmp pp (cdr dd))))))
```

Figure 12.1: Naive string matcher.

time, and to first compare the pattern against this prefix, switching over to the
rest of d only when the prefix is exhausted. Improvement is possible because the
test against the prefix is static.

In the improved version of Figure 12.2, prefix ff is clearly of bounded static
variation. The variable f plays the same role in relation to ff as d in relation to
dd. The function snoc adds an element to the end of a list and is not shown.

```
(define (kmp p d)    (loop p d p '() '()))

(define (loop p d pp f ff)
  (cond
   ((null? p) 'yes)
   ((null? f)
    (cond
     ((null? d) 'no)
     ((equal? (car p) (car d))
      (loop (cdr p) (cdr d) pp '() (snoc ff (car p))))
     ((null? ff)
      (kmp pp (cdr d)))
     (else
      (loop pp d pp (cdr ff) (cdr ff)))))
   ((equal? (car p) (car f))
    (loop (cdr p) d pp (cdr f) ff))
   (else
    (loop pp d pp (cdr ff) (cdr ff)))))
```

Figure 12.2: String matcher good for specialization.

Because the character causing the mismatch is ignored we can expect some
redundant tests in the residual program. These can be eliminated by a minor
change in loop, making it possible to exploit this 'negative' information as well, i.e.
that a certain character is definitely not equal to a known static value. Figure 12.3
shows a program that does this, where variable neg is a list of symbols that the

```
(define (kmp p d)
  (loop p d p '() '() '()))

(define (loop p d pp f ff neg)
  (cond
    ((null? p) 'yes)
    ((null? f)
     (cond
       ((and (not (null? neg)) (member (car p) neg))
        (if (null? ff)
            (kmp pp (cdr d))
            (loop pp d pp (cdr ff) (cdr ff) neg)))
       ((and (null? neg) (null? d)) 'no)
       ((equal? (car p) (car d))
        (loop (cdr p) (cdr d) pp '() (snoc ff (car p)) '()))
       ((null? ff)
        (kmp pp (cdr d)))
       (else
        (loop pp d pp (cdr ff) (cdr ff) (cons (car p) neg)))))
    ((equal? (car p) (car f))
     (loop (cdr p) d pp (cdr f) ff neg))
    (else
     (loop pp d pp (cdr ff) (cdr ff) neg))))
```

Figure 12.3: Matcher with negative information.

first symbol of d cannot match.

Figure 12.4 shows the result of specializing the matcher with negative information to p = (a b a b). The residual program is identical in structure to that yielded by Knuth, Morris, and Pratt's clever technique [150]. The complexity of the specialized algorithm is $O(n)$, where n is the length of the string. The naive algorithm has complexity $O(m \cdot n)$, where m is the length of the pattern. Perhaps counterintuitively, this speedup is considered linear since for each static m it is constantly faster than the naive algorithm (see Section 6.2).

This example is particularly interesting because a clever algorithm is generated automatically from a naive one using binding-time improvements and partial evaluation. This is thought-provoking even though such binding-time improvements may be hard to automate.

12.2   Bounded static variation

A more easily systematized technique was applied in earlier chapters to both flow chart and Scheme0 programs (Sections 4.8.3 and 5.4.3 respectively). The

```
(define (kmp-0 d_0)
  (define (loop-0-1 d_0)
    (cond ((null? d_0) 'no)
          ((equal? 'a (car d_0)) (loop-0-2 (cdr d_0)))
          (else (loop-0-1 (cdr d_0)))))
  (define (loop-0-2 d_0)
    (cond ((null? d_0) 'no)
          ((equal? 'b (car d_0))
           (let ((d_1 (cdr d_0)))
             (cond ((null? d_1) 'no)
                   ((equal? 'a (car d_1))
                    (let ((d_2 (cdr d_1)))
                      (cond ((null? d_2) 'no)
                            ((equal? 'b (car d_2))
                             (begin (cdr d_2) 'yes))
                            (else (loop-0-5 d_2)))))
                   (else (loop-0-1 (cdr d_1))))))
          (else (loop-0-5 d_0))))
  (define (loop-0-5 d_0)
    (if (equal? 'a (car d_0))
        (loop-0-2 (cdr d_0))
        (loop-0-1 (cdr d_0))))
  (loop-0-1 d_0)))
```

Figure 12.4: Specialized matcher to pattern 'abab'.

technique[2] can be employed when a dynamic variable d is known to assume one of a finite set F of statically computable values. To see how it works, consider an expression context $C[d]$ containing d. Assuming F has already been computed, the idea is to replace $C[d]$ by

1. code that compares d with all the elements of F, certain to yield a successful match $d = d1 \in F$; followed by

2. code to apply the context $C[\_]$ to static d1.

We shall see later (Section 12.3) that the same effect can sometimes be realized by conversion to continuation passing style.

As an example of its use we show how a general regular expression matcher can be specialized with respect to a specific regular expression to obtain a dedicated matcher in the form of a DFA (deterministic finite automaton). The example from Bondorf's PhD thesis [27] was developed by Mogensen, Jørgensen, and Bondorf, and appears in Prolog in Section 9.1.

---

[2]So popular among partial evaluation users that it is sometimes called 'The Trick'.

Regular expressions are built up as in [4] from symbols, and the empty string ε using concatenation, union and the Kleene star *. For example, the regular expression $a\varepsilon(b^*|c)$ will generate the strings abb and ac, but not the string aa.

The programs below work on a concrete Scheme representation of regular expressions. The concrete representation is less readable than the abstract one, so in the descriptions of regular expression operations we use the abstract form. Symbol r denotes a regular expression in abstract syntax whereas r (used in program texts) denotes a regular expression in concrete syntax. The same distinction is made between sym and sym. Dually, any operation Op working on the abstract forms r or sym corresponds to a concrete operation Op working on the concrete forms r or sym. Op is used in the descriptions, Op in program texts.

The Scheme program below interprets regular expressions. It takes a regular expression r and a string s as input and returns the boolean true (#t) if the regular expression generates the string, otherwise false (#f).

```
(define (match r s)
  (if (null? s)
      (generate-empty? r)
      (let ((sym (car s)))
        (and (member sym (first r))
             (match (next r sym) (cdr s))))))
```

We assume that certain functions are available without including their definition: generate-empty?, first, and next. Function generate-empty? checks whether a regular expression generates the empty string. Function first computes the list of all symbols that appear as the first of some string generated by the regular expression. Given a regular expression r and a symbol sym that is the first in some generable string, (next r a_0) computes a regular expression r1 which generates all strings $a_1 a_2 \ldots a_n$ such that r generates $a_0 a_1 a_2 \ldots a_n$.

Some examples of the use of these functions (in the abstract notation):

$$
\begin{aligned}
generate\text{-}empty?\ a^* &= true \\
generate\text{-}empty?\ (a\mid c) &= false \\
first\ ((a\mid \varepsilon)\ (c\ d)^*) &= \{a,c\} \\
next\ ((a\mid \varepsilon)\ (c\ d)^*)\ c &= d\ (c\ d)^*
\end{aligned}
$$

If we specialize the match program above with respect to some static regular expression r and dynamic string s, the resulting target program is not very good. The problem is that sym is a dynamic value because it is computed from s. Therefore, the regular expression (next r sym) cannot be computed at partial evaluation time, and all static information is 'lost'.

We therefore wish to improve the binding times of match. Observe that sym is a member of the statically computable (first r). Applying 'the trick', the program is rewritten as:

```
(define (match r s)
  (if (null? s)
      (generate-empty? r)
      (let ((f (first r)))
        (and (not (null? f))
             (let ((sym (car s)))
               (let loop ((f f))
                 (and (not (null? f))
                      (let ((A (car f)))
                        (if (equal? A sym)
                            (match (next r A) (cdr s))
                            (loop (cdr f)))))))))))
```

Now the static A is used instead of the dynamic sym. We have sneaked in another very common improvement into this program. If one can statically determine not to perform some dynamic computation, this can be used to improve the size and speed of the residual program. If the list f is empty, there is clearly no need to perform the operation (car s), explaining the first test of (not (null? f)) in match.

Let us take, as an example, the regular expression $(ab|bab)^*$. When specializing the binding-time improved interpreter just given with respect to this regular expression, the target program of Figure 12.5 is generated by Similix.

```
(define (match-0 s_0)
  (define (match-0-1 s_0)
    (if (null? s_0)
        #t
        (let ((sym_1 (car s_0)))
          (cond ((equal? 'a sym_1) (match-0-3 (cdr s_0)))
                ((equal? 'b sym_1) (let ((s_2 (cdr s_0)))
                                     (and (not (null? s_2))
                                          (equal? 'a (car s_2))
                                          (match-0-3 (cdr s_2)))))
                (else #f)))))
  (define (match-0-3 s_0)
    (and (not (null? s_0))
         (equal? 'b (car s_0))
         (match-0-1 (cdr s_0))))
  (match-0-1 s_0))
```

Figure 12.5: Specialized matching program.

There are no r variables in the target program since r was static and has vanished at partial evaluation time. The specialized versions of match correspond to different values of the static r. All operations on r have been reduced, so the target program contains no generate-empty?, first, or next operations.

The target program corresponds *exactly* to a three-state deterministic finite[3] automaton as derived by standard methods [4]. There are, however, only two procedures (besides the start procedure) in the target program, not three. This is because the procedure representing the state with only one in-going arrow is unfolded.

12.3   Conversion into continuation passing style

A simple method that often improves a program's binding-time separation is to convert it into *continuation passing style* [219,68], introduced in Section 10.5 and from now on abbreviated to CPS. Although indiscriminate CPS conversion is to be avoided (see a counterexample below), it is more easily automated than many other binding-time improvements.

CPS conversion has the effect of linearizing program execution, and can bring together parts of a computation that are far apart in its direct (non–continuation) form. Further, continuation style has practical advantages for functions that return multiple values, as these can be programmed without the need to package their results together before return, just to be unpackaged by the caller.

We mentioned earlier that the relevance of a given binding-time improvement depends on the partial evaluator being used. As explained in Section 10.5 Similix implicitly performs some CPS conversion during specialization (see Section 10.5), so not all the improvements discussed in this section are relevant for Similix.

Plotkin describes a general CPS transformation for lambda expressions, and Danvy and Filinski do it for Scheme [219,68]. Other work includes a simple first-order CPS transformation for binding-time improvements by Holst and Gomard and a detailed discussion of CPS for binding-time improvements by Consel and Danvy [118,56].

A very simple example.   Consider the expression

```
(+ 7 (if (= x 0) 9 13))
```

where x is dynamic. As the expression stands, the + operation is dynamic. Conversion into CPS yields:

```
(let ((k (lambda (temp) (+ 7 temp))))
   (if (= x 0)    (k 9)    (k 13)))
```

Using Lambdamix notation, the continuation k has binding time $S \rightarrow S$ and the + operation is now static. Partial evaluation yields the residual expression:

```
(if (= x 0) 16 20)
```

---

[3]Finiteness follows from the fact that any regular expression has only finitely many different 'derivatives', where a derivative is either r itself, or an expression obtained from a given derivative r' by computing (next r' a).

An example involving function calls. Consider the problem encountered in Section 5.4.3 where a dynamic function name f was looked up in a static program by the call (lookup f program). Assuming for simplicity that the search is always successful, lookup can be programmed:

```
(define (lookup f p)
   (cond
     ((null? (cdr p)) (take-first-body p))
     ((is-first-function? f p) (take-first-body p))
     (else (lookup f (remove-first-definition p)))))
```

Unless we use 'the trick', all computations depending on the result returned by the lookup call will be dynamic because n is dynamic. This may be circumvented by introducing a continuation parameter to lookup, yielding lookup1:

```
(define (lookup1 f p k)
   (cond
     ((null? (cdr p)) (k (take-first-body p)))
     ((is-first-function? f p) (k (take-first-body p)))
     (else (lookup1 f (remove-first-definition p) k))))
```

A call (C (lookup f program)) in context C is transformed into (lookup1 f program (lambda (val) (C val))). Again, k gets binding time $S \to S$, so C is called with a static argument — and the problem is solved by automatic CPS conversion *without* smart reprogramming.

Functions returning partially static structures. CPS transformation is also very useful for handling functions returning partically static structures; say, a pair (s, d) consisting of a static and dynamic item. We introduce a continuation k defined by (lambda (s d) ...) where s is to be bound to the static component of the answer and d to the dynamic component.

Example 12.1 Suppose an expression e is either the variable x or a sum of two expressions. Then we can write a function eval, which, given an expression and the value of x, returns the size of the expression and its value.

```
(define (eval e v)
   (cond
     ((equal? e 'x) (cons 1 v))
     (else
       (let ((t1 (eval (cadr e) v)) (t2 (eval (caddr e) v)))
         (cons (+ 1 (car t1) (car t2)) (+ (cdr t1) (cdr t2)))))))
```

Here the binding times are mixed and it will not specialize well. In the following example we have introduced a continuation k, which is applied to the size of the expression and its value. To get the ball rolling eval1 must be called with the continuation (lambda (s v) (cons s v)).

```
(define (eval1 e v k)
  (cond
    ((equal? e 'x) (k 1 v)) ; Apply k to size 1 and value v
    (else (eval1 (cadr e)    ; Evaluate 1st subexpression
                 v
                 (lambda (s1 v1)     ; Name its two results
                   (eval1 (caddr e)  ; Evaluate 2nd subexpression
                          v
                          (lambda (s2 v2)
                            (k (+ 1 s1 s2) (+ v1 v2)))))))))
```

We assume e static but the value v of x to be dynamic. Then continuation k gets binding time $S \times D \to D$, so a call to eval1 with expression (+ x (+ x x)) will specialize to (cons 5 (+ v (+ v v))). Note that the size computation has been done statically even though intermixed with dynamic operations.   □

Larger-scale applications.   Jørgensen has used the CPS transformation and self-application of Similix to generate a pattern-matching compiler producing better code than that by methods of Peyton Jones [137,138]. Danvy uses CPS to compile non-linear patterns [66]. Another experiment by Jørgensen using CPS led to the generation of a compiler for a lazy functional language. The speed of compiled code equalled that of a commercially available compiler [140].

12.3.1   Advantages and disadvantages

Transformation into CPS is not always desirable. The resulting programs are of higher-order than the original ones and higher-order facilities are generally harder to manipulate by partial evaluation. A worse problem is that the CPS conversion can affect termination properties of partial evaluation. A call to the append function (append xs ys) is transformed into (append1 xs ys (lambda (t) t)), where the transformed append1 is defined by:

```
(define (append1 xs ys k)
  (if (null? xs)
      (k ys)
      (append1 (cdr xs) ys (lambda (t) (k (cons (car xs) t))))))
```

If xs is dynamic and ys is static then partial evaluation will loop infinitely because the lambdas in the continuation parameter will become more deeply nested for each recursive call, yielding an infinite residual program. This is an accumulating parameter under dynamic control.

12.4 Eta conversion

In the lambda calculus community one often uses *η-conversion:* λx.Mx ⇔ M, if x is not free in M. Although in a certain sense computationally trivial (no operations are performed), it can in some cases improve binding-time separation.

Consider an expression

```
(let ((f (lambda (x) ...)))
  (+ (f ...) (g f)))
```

where g is dynamic and hence the application (g f) is dynamic. The occurrence of f in the application (g f) is known as a *residual code context*[4] in [28]: f becomes dynamic and the lambda expression also becomes dynamic. Consequently no *β*-reduction of the application (f ...) will take place either. This problem can be overcome by *η*-conversion:

```
(let ((f (lambda (x) ...)))
  (+ (f ...) (g (lambda (z) (f z)))))
```

As f no longer occurs in a residual code context both (f ...) and (f z) can be *β*-reduced during specialization. Hence the lambda expression (lambda (x) ...) becomes reducible. Note that the new lambda expression inserted by *η*-conversion becomes dynamic.

Eta conversion can also be used for another kind of binding-time improvement. Consider the following expression:

```
((if (equal? a 2) x y) 3)
```

Now suppose x and y are higher-order values with x being a static closure and y dynamic. Furthermore suppose that a is static. The conditional will be classified as dynamic, because one of the branches is dynamic. This means that we will not be able to reduce the application, not even if a is equal to 2. Using eta conversion the expression can be rewritten into

```
((if (equal? a 2) x (lambda (z) (y z))) 3)
```

Now both branches of the condition will be classified as static closures, and so will the conditional. Hence we are now able to reduce the application: if a = 2 then specializing the expression will be the result of evaluating (x 3), otherwise if a ≠ 2 specializing the expression will result in (y 3).

The two examples demonstrate two different kinds of binding-time improvements. In the first example we had a static closure (f). We encapsulated it with a lambda, which was classified as dynamic. In this case eta conversion was used to *protect* the binding-time of an expression from being classified as dynamic. In the second example we had something dynamic (y) in a context where we would like something with the binding-time static closure. In this case eta conversion

---

[4]Also known as dynamic code context

was used to *hide* the fact that an expression was dynamic. Note that we cannot change the binding time of an expression, which is dynamic for other reasons: y is still dynamic after the transformation.

12.5   Improvements derived from 'free theorems'

From a function's polymorphic type, a 'free theorem' may be derived [222,275]. Holst and Hughes have proposed deriving binding-time improvements from these theorems. Here we show how their technique applies to the standard problem of dynamic lookup in a static list (using ML syntax):

For any natural number i, let `select i` be the function that selects the ith element of a list. Then `select` has the type:

$$\forall \alpha . \mathcal{N} \rightarrow List(\alpha) \rightarrow \alpha$$

Holst and Hughes show that the free theorem for functions of this type is:

```
f (select i xs)  = select i (map f xs)
```

for any function $f : \alpha \rightarrow \beta$. If i is dynamic and xs is static, a binding-time improvement is obtained by replacing the left hand side by the right hand side. The 'improved' version appears to be the less efficient, since it applies f to all the elements of the static list, while the original version only applies f to the selected element. A partial evaluator would indeed apply f to all the elements of the static list, but this computation is now entirely static and performed during partial evaluation. The residual program would contain a precalculated list of results f x for all x in xs and a residual selection of the needed result(s).

See papers by Holst and Hughes, and Nielson and Nielson, for more examples and details [119,203,204].

12.6   Exercises

Exercise 12.1 Consider the following Scheme expression, where e1 is a static expression and e2 is a dynamic expression.

```
(if (and e1 e2) e3 e4)
```

If e1 evaluates to false, the test can be determined statically (at specialization time) since e2 need not be evaluated. Suppose your partial evaluator classifies the entire test (and e1 e2) (and thereby also the conditional) as dynamic. Suggest a transformation that will lead to a better residual program in case e1 evaluates to false. Note that the transformation must not lead to code duplication, and it must leave the strictness properties of the original expression unchanged.
Now consider the following expression:

```
(if (or e1 e2) e3 e4)
```

As above, if e1 evaluates to true, the test can be determined statically. Suppose as above that the entire test will be classified as dynamic. Suggest a transformation to solve the problem. Again you must avoid code duplication and leave the strictness properties unchanged. □

The following exercises require Similix. Hint: use some of Similix's utility functions to show the binding times of the program, e.g. (showpall) shows all binding times in the current program.

Exercise 12.2 Consider the following Scheme program, where you wish to specialize f with respect to some known list xs and unknown n.

```
(define (f n xs)
   (if (equal? (nth n xs) 42) 'yes 'no))

(define (nth n xs)
   (if (null? xs)
       'error
       (if (equal? n 0)
           (car xs)
           (nth (- n 1) (cdr xs)))))
```

The binding-time analysis performed in Similix will classify the equal? operation in f as dynamic. Because we know (nth n xs) will evaluate to one of the elements of xs, we can apply The Trick to make the equal? operation static. Do this by introducing a continuation. □

Exercise 12.3 Consider the following Scheme program where you wish to specialize f with respect to some known x and unknown y. Then z will be marked as dynamic and none of the branches in the if-statement can be reduced.

```
(define (f x y)
   (g (h x y)))

(define (h x y)
   (cons (* x x) y))

(define (g z)
   (if (equal? (cdr z) 0)
       (+ (car z) 2)
       (- (car z) 2)))
```

Introduce a continuation so the branches in the if-statement can be reduced. □

Exercise 12.4 Extend the final version of the pattern matcher to handle wildcards in patterns, e.g. * can match any symbol. In what way does this affect the binding times? □

Exercise 12.5 Consider the following interpreter (written in CPS style) for a version of the lambda calculus. The function **run** takes a lambda expression E and a value **w**. The evaluation function **ev** takes an expression E, an environment **env**, and a continuation **k**. An example of a lambda expression could be

```
(apply (apply (lambda x (lambda y
                (+ (var x) (var y)))) (cst 2)) (cst 3))
```

Identify the place where the continuation **k** appears in a residual code context and perform an eta conversion (this is the same kind of binding-time improvement as in the first example in Section 12.4). Identify the place where **ev** is called with a dynamic continuation and perform an eta conversion (this is the same kind of binding-time improvement as in the second example in Section 12.4).

Try specializing **run** (with both the initial version and the improved version) with respect to the lambda expression above and **w** dynamic. The effect of specializing the improved version should be a conversion of the lambda expression into CPS-style (the style of the interpreter), besides a translation to Scheme.

```
; E ::= (cst C) | (var V) | (+ E1 E2)
;     | (lambda V E) | (apply E1 E2)

(define (run E w) (ev E (lambda (V) w) (lambda (x) x)))

(define (ev E env k)
  (cond
    ((equal? (car E) 'cst) (k (cadr E)))
    ((equal? (car E) 'var) (k (env (cadr E))))
    ((equal? (car E) '+)
     (ev (cadr E)
         env
         (lambda (w1)
           (ev (caddr E)
               env
               (lambda (w2) (k (+ w1 w2)))))))
    ((equal? (car E) 'lambda)
     (k (lambda (w1 c1)
          (ev (caddr E)
              (lambda (V1)
                (if (equal? (cadr E) V1)
                    w1
                    (env V1)))
              c1))))
    ((equal? (car E) 'apply)
     (ev (cadr E)
         env
         (lambda (w1)
           (ev (caddr E) env (lambda (w2) (w1 w2 k))))))
    (else
     (error 'ev "unknown syntactic form: ~s" E))))
```

□

Exercise 12.6 * Discuss the problems involved with automating the process of applying binding-time improvements. Which binding-time improvements can be automated and which can not?

□

Chapter 13

Applications of Partial Evaluation

The purpose of this chapter is to show that a wide spectrum of apparently problem-specific optimizations can be seen as instances of partial evaluation, and that partial evaluation gives a systematic way to devise new optimizations. We shall not, however, attempt a comprehensive coverage of applications to date since the full potential of partial evaluation for solving various practical problems is as yet far from realized, and the distribution of the examples we know of is quite uneven.

In the first section a selection of problem types that are well suited to optimization by partial evaluation is described, with the hope that the reader may see analogies in his or her own sphere of interest. The second section discusses in more general terms circumstances under which partial evaluation can be of benefit, and points out some pitfalls and ways to overcome them.

Video games. First, an amusing small-scale example of program specialization by hand [224]. The *Nevryon* game driver needed very fast execution for satisfactory playing speed on an Archimedes personal computer. General code to display a 'sprite' in various sizes and motions, and to flip a sprite horizontally and vertically, was found to be too slow. The solution adopted was to write about 20 separate sprite routines, each displaying sprites in slightly different ways (moving up, flipped and moving left, etc.). Similar ideas were applied to scrolling and to plotting the backdrop.

13.1 Types of problems susceptible to partial evaluation

13.1.1 Modularity and related issues

Modular programming is a 'good thing' for many reasons. Small modules, each with clearly defined goals, allow a separation of concerns that increases program portability and eases program reuse and adaptation. This is especially important if programs are frequently changed or replaced, for instance in a scientific modelling situation where several people or groups, possibly from different disciplines, are trying to find adequate computational models for an external phenomenon.

Modules are often highly parametrized to make them more flexible. Similarly, functional programmers use high-level combining constructs such as `map`, `fold`, and `reduce` as 'glue' to combine modules in a variety of ways. Modules are often computationally trivial, for example containing only the values of certain key parameters used by other parts of the system, and few or no commands.

There is a cost for a modular, parametrized, high-level programming style: efficiency. Such programs can spend quite a lot of computation time calling modules, transporting data, perhaps converting data across module interfaces, and creating and invoking closures for functional objects.

Partial evaluation, even with no static data input at all, can speed up such programs. The effect is to compress modules by merging groups of them together, expanding intermodular calls in place, propagating constants from modules where they are defined into those where they are used, and precomputing wherever possible. The result is a smaller set of more complex modules, quite likely *unsuited* for human reading, understanding and modification, but significantly more efficient[1].

13.1.2   Parameters with different rates of variation

Partial evaluation can help in the following frequently occurring situation:

- a function $f(x, y)$ is to be computed for many different pairs (x, y),

- x is changed less frequently than y, and

- a significant part of f's computation depends only on x.

Following are a few examples of a non-interpretive nature to illustrate that these conditions are often satisfied; some interpretive examples appear in the next section.

Computer graphics
Mogensen did an experiment at Copenhagen with the 'ray-tracing' method of computer graphics [186]. The method is known to give good picture rendition, but is rather slow since it involves tracing the paths of thousands of light rays between various points in a scene to be displayed.

The usual implementation is by a general algorithm which, given a scene and a light ray, performs computations to follow its path. The scene (a collection of 3-dimensional objects) does not change while tracing the light rays, which makes partial evaluation highly relevant.

---

[1]One might expect a good compiler to do 'constant propagation' at compile time. While true

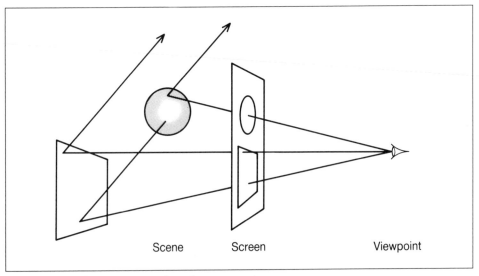

Scene   Screen   Viewpoint

Figure 13.1: Computer graphics by ray tracing.

One algorithm has the following overall structure (see Figure 13.1). Variable `Point` ranges over pixels on a viewing screen, and `Viewpoint` is the location of the observer's eye. `Ray` is the line from eye to screen point, extended into the scene being drawn. For any object in the scene, `intersect(Object,Ray)` finds its intersection point (if any) with the given ray, and variable `Intersections` is the set of all such intersection points.

The algorithm finds the nearest intersection point `Obpoint`, i.e. the only point visible to the observer along the current ray, and the object that the ray hits. Finally the light intensity at `Obpoint` can be calculated using the object's properties such as colour and reflectivity, and this is plotted.

```
ray-trace(Scene, Screen, Viewpoint):
    for Point in Screen do
        plot(Point, colour(Scene, Viewpoint, Point));

colour(Scene, Viewpoint, Point) =
    let Ray = line(Viewpoint, Point) in
    let Intersections =
            {intersect(Object, Ray) | Object in Scene} in
    let (Object, Obpoint) = closest(Viewpoint, Intersections) in
        shade(Object, Obpoint)
```

Mogensen optimized this general ray-tracing program by specializing it to a single, fixed scene. Concretely, variables `Scene` and `Object` were classified as static. The

---

for a single function or procedure, few compilers if any do interprocedural constant propagation, and even fewer do loop unrolling based on the values of constant data.

result was a new program, only good for tracing rays through that particular scene. In experiments the specialized ray tracer was from 8 to 12 times faster than the original. Analysis of the results indicate speedups of about 2.5 from specializing the intersection point computations, and of about 4 from specializing the colour functions.

Sparse systems of linear equations

An early example of problem solving by program generation that amounts to specializing a general program is from 1970 by Gustavson and others [107]. They described a program (called GNSO) which takes as input a sparse system $Ax = b$ of linear equations where A is an $N \times N$ matrix.

The novelty of their approach is that GNSO generates a program SOLVE from A, which is then executed on input b. It has the form of a long loop-free sequence of Fortran statements. If the input matrix is sparse, the generated program is small and so quite fast. The method works for arbitrary sparsity structures, e.g. it is not restricted to matrices with non-zero elements on a band along the diagonal.

This approach can clearly be thought of as specializing a general Crout algorithm to a particular matrix, and then executing the resulting program. The following is a shortened quote from the article:

> In many instances we must solve the system with a fixed sparseness structure but with varying numerical values of the elements of A ... for example (1) linear systems where A depends on parameters which vary from case to case, (2) a system of nonlinear equations by iteration with Newton's method, (3) an initial value problem for partial differential equations or for a system of ordinary differential equations by an implicit numerical integration method. ... The gain is even greater if only b changes from system to system. In this case the factorization of A is done only once, and we just repeat the back substitutions.

Experimental modelling

We believe partial evaluation can substantially increase human and computer efficiency in experimental modelling over a range of sciences. This section should be taken with a grain of salt, as preliminary studies are under way but results and evaluations have not yet been published.

Computational modelling has some common characteristics:

- a natural system is being studied, e.g. oceanographic, meteorological, or ecological processes;

- mathematical models are developed to account for evolution of the system's state variables over time and space; and

- repeated computer simulation of the model on various initial state conditions is done to compare real-world observations of interesting state variables with the values predicted by the model.

Applications include real-world predictions (weather, pollution, etc.), and obtaining information to identify where to make further observations, so as to gain a more complete and faithful system description.

Such a computational model is often quite large, and is developed by several researchers and/or groups from different disciplines. Model building is a long lasting and usually continuous process. If the model computes results disagreeing with observed values, a natural first step is to 'tune' critical parameters such as exchange rates or conversion efficiencies, and then rerun the simulation in the hope of obtaining a better fit. (This is defensible since critical parameters are often physically unobservable.)

If this fails, parts of the mathematical model may have to be changed, for instance by modifying the differential equations to give a more sophisticated description of the phenomenon, or adding new equations to model processes not accounted for before. These are programmed, and the whole process is repeated.

This scenario offers many opportunities to exploit partial evaluation. First, such a system must necessarily be programmed in a modular way to separate scientific concerns and to allow different workers to concentrate on their specialities. As argued above, partial evaluation can gain efficiency.

Second, parts of the model and its parameters may change much less rapidly than others, so it may be worthwhile to specialize the model with respect to them. One example is the number and forms of the topographical cells used to model an ocean basin. This is naturally a user-definable parameter, refinable when more precise simulations are needed; but *not* a parameter that is changed often. Thus specializing a program suite with respect to the number and dimensions of topographical cells could increase efficiency by unfolding loops, and precomputing values that do not change when doing repeated runs to tune boundary conditions or exchange rates.

13.1.3   Improving recursive programs

The *divide and conquer* paradigm is used in constructing algorithms in a wide range of areas. A problem instance is classified as atomic or composite, and atomic problems are solved at once. A composite problem is decomposed into subproblems, each is solved separately, and their results are combined to yield the entire problem's solution.

The approach naturally leads to recursive algorithms. Efficiency is often obtained by decomposing composite problems into subproblems of nearly equal size, so binary decompositions often lead to a near-balanced binary tree of subproblems.

Atomic instances are usually solved quite quickly, so the time spent at the lower tree levels in calling functions, transmitting parameters, and related stack manipulation can be large relative to the amount of computation actually done. Further, in a binary tree half the nodes are leaves, and 15/16 are within distance 3 of a leaf.

A consequence is that an optimizing computation at the bottom-most levels will, in some cases, *speed up the entire computation* by a significant factor. Just when this occurs will depend on the recurrence equations describing the algorithm's running time.

One strategy to exploit this phenomenon, assuming for simplicity that subproblems form a balanced binary tree, is to let the program maintain a counter measuring distance to the frontier. This code can be transformed by total call unfolding for sufficiently small values of the counter by partial evaluation. For a simple example, begin by rewriting definition

```
f(x)    = if atomic?(x) then  Base case code else
              g(f(part1(x)),f(part2(x)))
g(u,v) = ...
```

by adding a level counter, assumed 0 for atomic subproblems:

```
f(x,k) = if k=0 then  Base case code else
              g(f(part1(x),k-1),f(part2(x),k-1))
g(u,v) = ...
```

Then add a new function f1, identical to f but called when k becomes 2 or less:

```
f(x,k)   = if k=2 then f1(x,2) else
              if k=1 then f1(x,1) else
              if k=0 then  Base case code else
                g(f(part1(x),k-1),f(part2(x),k-1))
g(u,v)   = ...

f1(x,k1) = if k=0 then  Base case code else
              g(f1(part1(x),k-1),f1(part2(x),k-1))
```

Argument k1 of f1 is constant and so static, giving the partial evaluator opportunity for complete unfolding and simplification and thus reducing call overhead.

Suppose that solving an atomic problem takes time a, that a composite problem of size $n > 1$ involves two subproblems of size $n/2$, and that combining two subproblem solutions takes constant[2] time b. This leads to a recurrence equation whose solution is of the form $(a + b) \cdot n + \ldots$ with coefficient additively dependent on a. The strategy above in effect reduces a and n since more subproblems are solved without recursive calls, and problems for small n are solved faster.

13.1.4   Problems of an interpretive nature

It has become clear that partial evaluation is well suited to applications based on programming language interpreters. It is perhaps less clear that many problem solutions *outside* programming languages are also essentially interpretive in nature, and so susceptible to automatic optimization using our methods. A few examples

---

[2]This is a correct assumption for some problems but not, for example, for sorting.

follow, with some overlap with Sections 13.1.1 and 13.1.2 since the concepts of modularity, varying rates of parameter variation, and interpretation are hard to separate and often appear in the same program.

Interpretation evolves naturally in the quest for generality and modifiability of large-scale programming problems. We outline a common scenario. Once several related problems in an applications area have been understood and solved individually, the next step is often to write a *single general* program able to solve any one of a family of related problems. This leads to a program with parameters, sometimes numerous, to specify problem instances.

Use of the program for new applications and by new user groups make it desirable to devise a *user-oriented language*, to specify such parameters in a way more related to the problems being solved than to the programming language or the algorithms used to solve them. The existing general program will thus be modified to accept problem descriptions that are more user-oriented. The result is a flexible and problem-oriented tool which may, in comparison with the time spent on the underlying computational methods, spend relatively much of its time testing and/or computing on parameters, and deciphering commands in the user-oriented language. In other words it is an *interpreter*, and as such subject to optimization by our methods.

Circuit simulation

Circuit simulators take as input an electrical circuit description, construct differential equations describing its behaviour, and solve these by numerical methods. This can be thought of as interpreting the circuit description. Berlin and Weise [21] cite large speedups resulting from specializing a general circuit simulator written in Scheme to a fixed circuit.

Neural networks

Training a neural network typically uses much computer time. Partial evaluation has been applied to a simulator written in C for training neural networks by backpropagation [126]. The resulting generator transforms a given network into a faster simulator, specialized to the fixed network topology. Observed speedups were from 25% to 50% — not dramatic but significant given the amount of computer time that neural net training takes.

Computing in networks

Consider a problem to be solved by a MIMD (multiple instruction, multiple data) network of processors connected together for communication along some topological configuration. This models some physical phenomena directly, e.g. solution of heat equations or fluid dynamics, and is also a standard framework for general parallel processing not directed towards particular concrete problems.

What code is to be stored in each processor? A complicating factor is that not all processors appear in identical contexts, for example those modelling boundary situations may have fewer neighbours than those more centrally in the network[3].

A simple approach is to write *one* piece of code which is given the processor's network location as a parameter, and which can compute as required for processors anywhere in the network. In our context it is natural use partial evaluation to specialize this code to its location parameter, obtaining as many programs as there are differing network environments. Pingali and Rogers report significant efficiency gains using exactly this technique [225,217].

Table-directed input

Given a source program character sequence, it is well known that token scanning (or lexical analysis) can be done using a state transition table that associates with each pair (`state`, `input-character-class`) a *transition*, which is another pair (`action`, `next-state`).

For example, a scanner might go into state `Number` when a sign or digit is seen and, as long as are read, remain in that state, performing actions to accumulate the number's value; with similar state and action transitions for other token types such as identifiers or strings. To illustrate, suppose numerical tokens have syntax:

$$\langle\text{Integer}\rangle \quad ::= \quad \langle\text{Space}\rangle^* \; [\; + \; | \; -] \; (\langle\text{Digit}\rangle \; | \; \langle\text{Space}\rangle)^*$$
$$\langle\text{Digit}\rangle \quad ::= \quad 0 \; | \; 1 \; | \; \ldots | \; 9$$

Following is a state transition table for numbers.

State	⟨Space⟩	+	-	⟨Digit⟩	End-of-line
0	no action	`sign := 1;` `sum := 0`	`sign := -1;` `sum := 0`	`sign := 1;` `sum :=` ⟨Digit⟩	
next:	0	1	1	2	0
1	no action	error	error	`sum :=` ⟨Digit⟩	`result :=` `sign*sum`
next:	1	0	0	2	0
2	no action	error	error	`sum := 10*sum` + ⟨Digit⟩	`result :=` `sign*sum`
next:	2	0	0	2	0

In practice the transition table approach is useful as it ensures *completeness*, since all combinations of state and input character must be accounted for; and *ease of modification*, since many corrections involve only a single table entry or a single action routine.

This scheme is usually implemented by storing the transition table in memory as data, and writing a small interpreter to follow its directives (an instance by Oliver uses microprogramming [206]). Alternatively, one may 'compile' the transition table directly into code, for example with one label for each state, and with a state transition being realized by a '`goto`'. The result is usually faster, but the program

---

[3]An exception is the hypercube, where every processor has an identical environment; but even here asymmetry problems arise if some processors develop faults.

structure and logic may be more complex and so hard to modify.

Partial evaluation allows an automatic transformation of the first data-directed program into the more efficient alternate form. Experience shows a substantial speedup (unless masked by input/outout operations).

A related example showing quite significant speedup is due to Penello. His 'very fast LR parsing' method takes as starting point a parsing table as produced by the Yacc parser generator [216]. The method compiles the table into assembly code, yielding a specialized parser that runs 6 to 10 times faster than table interpretation.

Pattern matching

Section 12.2 showed that partial evaluation of a general regular expression matcher with respect to a fixed regular expression R gave very efficient residual programs. All parts of R were 'compiled' away and the residual program was essentially a deterministic finite automaton.

Logical meta-systems

As seen in Chapter 6, partial evaluation can be of considerable use when one uses a high-level metalanguage to describe other systems or languages.

There are good reasons to believe that similar benefits will accrue from mechanical treatment of other high-level specification languages. For example, the Edinburgh/Carnegie-Mellon/Gothenburg Logical Framework activity involves a combined theorem prover and reduction engine which might be much improved in efficiency by specialization to particular theories.

13.2   When can partial evaluation be of benefit?

We now take another tack, trying to explore reasons for success or failure of partial evaluation for automatic program improvement.

Suppose program p computes function $f(s, d)$, where input s is static, i.e. known at specialization time, and d is dynamic. Termination of partial evaluation, and the size and efficiency of the specialized program p_s, depends critically on the way p uses its static and dynamic inputs.

We now analyse these. A first case is that p has no static inputs. Even in this case partial evaluation can be of benefit, as discussed in Sections 13.1.1 and 13.2.1. A second case generalizes an idea from complexity theory to see when partial evaluation can give predictably good results. An *oblivious* Turing machine is one whose read head motion depends only on the length of the machine's input tape, and is independent of its contents.

Oblivious algorithms.   We call program p *oblivious* (with respect to its input division) if its control flow depends only on the values of static inputs, i.e. if it never tests dynamic data[4]. Such programs are common and are discussed further in Section 13.2.2.

The absence of dynamic tests implies that partial evaluation of an oblivious program exactly parallels normal execution; just one thread of code is to be accounted for. An important consequence is that termination depends on the values static data assume in a *single computation* and not on many possible combinations of static values, the choice among which will be determined by dynamic input.

The size *and* run time of p_s are both proportional to the number of times code in p containing dynamic commands or expressions is encountered. Specialization time is proportional to the time to perform p's static computations plus the time to generate p_s.

Henceforth we shall assume offline partial evaluation, where every command or expression in p has been annotated as static or dynamic. Predicting time and size of p_s appears to be harder when using online partial evaluation, since non-obliviousness manifests itself only during specialization and not before.

Non-oblivious algorithms. A non-oblivious program may follow many possible computation threads, depending on the values of dynamic inputs. A partial evaluator must account for all such possibilities, generalizing specialized code for each combination (concretely it must specialize code for *both* branches of all dynamic tests). This can result in large specialized programs p_s, even though they are likely to be faster than p.

Interpreters are non-oblivious due to their need to implement tests in the program being interpreted. In later sections we shall discuss both non-oblivious programs as well as 'weakly oblivious' ones.

13.2.1   Partial evaluation without static data

Partial evaluation can be of use even when there is no static program input at all. One example: its utility for improving modularly written, parametrized high-level programs was described at the beginning of this chapter. Another is that partial evaluation encompasses a number of traditional compiler optimizations, as explained by A.P. Ershov [79].

Constant propagation is a familiar optimization, and arises in practical situations beyond user control. It is needed to generate efficient code for array accesses, e.g. intermediate code for `A[I,1] := B[2,3] + A[I,1]` will have many operations involving only constants. Constant folding is clearly an instance of partial evaluation, as are several other low-level optimizations.

Partial evaluation also realizes 'interprocedural optimizations', in some cases entirely eliminating procedures or functions. Finally, the technique of 'procedure cloning' is clearly function specialization, and Appel's 're-opening closures' [61,13]

---

[4]Alternative terms are 'data independent' or 'static' [21,173].

is another example of partial evaluation without static input data.

13.2.2 Oblivious algorithms

The natural program to compute the matrix product $prod(p, A, B)$ where A, B are $p \times p$ matrices is oblivious in dimension p.

```
prod(p,A,B):
   for i := 1 to p do
   for j := 1 to p do [
      C[i,j] := 0;
      for k := 1 to p do C[i,j] := C[i,j] + A[i,k] * B[k,j];
      write C[i,j]    ]
```

A sufficient test for obliviousness. First do a binding-time analysis. Then p is oblivious if $\mathbf{p}^{ann}$ contains no tests on dynamic variables.

Consequences of obliviousness. Let $\mathbf{p_s}$ be the result of specializing program p to static s. If p is oblivious then $\mathbf{p_s}$ will contain no control transfers, since all tests are static and thus done at specialization time. In general $\mathbf{p}_n$ has size and running time $O(n^3)$. For instance, $\mathbf{p_2}$ could be

```
prod_2(A,B):
   write A[1,1] * B[1,1] + A[1,2] * B[2,1];
   write A[1,1] * B[1,2] + A[1,2] * B[2,2];
   write A[2,1] * B[1,1] + A[2,2] * B[2,1];
   write A[2,1] * B[1,2] + A[2,2] * B[2,2]
```

Compiling. Partial evaluation of oblivious programs (or functions) gives long sequences of straight line code in an imperative language, or large expressions without conditionals in a functional language. This gives large 'basic blocks', and for these there are well-developed compiling and optimization techniques [4].

In particular good code can be generated for *pipelined* architectures due to the absence of tests and jumps. Basic blocks can also be much more efficiently implemented on *parallel architectures* than code with loops. Both points are mentioned by Berlin and Lisper [21,173]. Further, exploitation of distributive laws can lead to very short parallel computing times, for example $\log(n)$ time algorithms for multiplying matrices of fixed dimension n.

An example in scientific computing. Oblivious programs are quite common, for example numerical algorithms are often oblivious in dimensional parameters, and otherwise contain large oblivious parts. This makes them very suitable for improvement by partial evaluation. For a concrete example, consider a general Runge-

Kutta program for approximate integration of ordinary differential equations[5] of form

$$\frac{dy_i(t)}{dt} = f_i'(t, y_1, \ldots, y_n). \qquad i = 1, \ldots, n$$

where $f_i'(t, y_1, \ldots, y_n)$ is the derivative of f_i with respect to t. Functions $y_i(t)$ are often called state variables.

The goal is to tabulate the values of $y_i(t), y_i(t + \Delta), y_i(t + 2\Delta), \ldots$ for a series of t values and $i = 1, \ldots, n$, given initial values of the state variables and t. One step of the commonly used fourth-order Runge-Kutta method involves computing $f_i'(t, y_1, \ldots, y_n)$ for four different argument tuples, and for each $i = 1, \ldots, n$. The inputs to an integration program Int might thus be

1. Eqns, the system of equations to be solved;

2. Coeffs, numerical coefficients used in the equations;

3. Step, the step size to be used for integration (called Δ above) and M, the number of steps to be performed; and

4. Init, initial values for the state variables and t.

Among the inputs, Eqns varies least frequently, and will either be interpreted, or represented by calls to a user-defined function, say Fprime(I,Ys), where Ys is the array of state variables and I indicates which function is to be called. If interpretation is used, as has been seen in, for example, circuit simulators, specialization with respect to Eqns and Coeffs will remove the often substantial overhead.

If a user-defined Fprime(I,Ys) is used, two improvements can be realized automatically. The first is *splitting*: specialization can automatically transform the 'bundled' code for Fprime(I,Ys) into n separate function definitions. Further, splitting array Ys into n separate variables can reduce computation time. The second improvement is that the code for $f_i'(t, y_1, \ldots, y_n)$ can be inserted inline in the integrator, avoiding function call, parameter passing, and return time.

It often happens that the same equations are to be integrated, but with different coefficients, e.g. for experimental modelling. The generating extension of Int with respect to Eqns yields a program that, when given Coeffs, will produce a specialized integrator and precompute what is possible using the known coefficient values. Here optimizations such as $x \cdot 0 = 0$ done at specialization time can give significant speedups.

---

[5]Runge-Kutta integration is also used as an example in [21].

13.2.3   Weakly oblivious programs

We call p *weakly oblivious* if changes in dynamic inputs cannot effect changes in the *sequences of values* bound to static variables — a weaker condition than obliviousness since p is allowed to contain dynamic tests.

A 'bubble sort' program Bsort is weakly oblivious in the length n of the list to be sorted since, even though dynamic comparison and exchange operations exist, they do not affect the values assigned to any static variables. A specialized program $Bsort_n$ is a linear sequence of comparisons and conditional element swaps, with size and running time $O(n^2)$.

Partial evaluation of a weakly oblivious program p terminates on s if and only if p terminates on this s and any d, since dynamic tests do not affect the value sequences assigned to static variables. As before the size of p_s is proportional to the number of times code in p containing dynamic commands or expressions is encountered. Its run time may be larger, though, due to the presence of dynamic loops.

Weakly oblivious programs have much in common with oblivious ones. For example, although not yielding straightline code, p_s still tends to have large basic blocks suitable for pipelined or parallel architectures; and its size is much more predictable than for non-oblivious programs.

A simple program that is *not* weakly oblivious is

```
double(x) = f(x,0)
f(x,y)    = if x = 0 then y else f(x-1, y+2)
```

where x is dynamic. The values of variable y are initially zero and thereafter incremented by a constant, so a naive binding time analysis would classify y as static (though less naive analyses as in Chapter 14 would classify it as dynamic).

Even though y does not directly depend on x, the *sequence* of values it assumes is in fact determined by x. This is dynamic, so a partial evaluator will have to account for both possibilities of the test outcome, leading to specialization with infinitely many values of y.

For another example let program p perform binary search in table $T_0, \ldots, T_{2^n-1}$, with initial call Find(T, 0, m, x) and $m = 2^{n-1}$. The program is weakly oblivious if we assume delta is static and i is dynamic, since the comparison with x does not affect the value assigned to delta.

```
Find(T, i, delta, x) =
   Loop: if delta = 0 then
              if x = T[i] then return(i) else return(NOTFOUND);
          if x >= T[i+delta] then i := i + delta;
          delta := delta/2;
          goto Loop]
```

Specializing with respect to static delta = 4 and dynamic i gives

```
if x >= T[i+4] then i := i+4;
if x >= T[i+2] then i := i+2;
if x >= T[i+1] then i := i+1;
if x = T[i] then return(i) else return(NOTFOUND)
```

In general p_n runs in time $O(\log(n))$, and with a better constant coefficient than the general program. Moreover, it has size $O(\log(n))$.

13.2.4   Non-oblivious algorithms

Many programs are not oblivious in either sense, and this can lead to unpredictable results in partial evaluation. We have seen that p_s can become enormous or infinite since all possible combinations of static variable values must be accounted for, even though few of these may occur in any one computation of $[\![p]\!]$ [s,d] for any one value of d.

To illustrate the problems that can occor, reconsider the binary search program above with n static. One may certainly classify i as static since it ranges over $0, 1, \ldots, n-1$. The resulting program is, however, not oblivious since the test on x affects the value of static i.

Specialization with respect to static delta $= 4$ and $i = 0$ now gives

```
if x >= T[4] then
  if x >= T[6] then
    if x >= T[7] then
    [if x = T[7] then return(7) else return(NOTFOUND)] else
    [if x = T[6] then return(6) else return(NOTFOUND)] else
    if x >= T[5] then
    [if x = T[5] then return(5) else return(NOTFOUND)]
    [if x = T[4] then return(4) else return(NOTFOUND)] else
  if x >= T[2] then
    if x >= T[3] then
    [if x = T[3] then return(3) else return(NOTFOUND)] else
    [if x = T[2] then return(2) else return(NOTFOUND)] else
    if x >= T[1] then
    [if x = T[1] then return(1) else return(NOTFOUND)] ·
    [if x = T[0] then return(0) else return(NOTFOUND)]
```

The specialized program again runs in time $O(\log(n))$, and with a yet better constant coefficient than above. On the other hand it has size $O(n)$ — exponentially larger than the weakly oblivious version!

However, the consequences are not always negative. Following are two case studies illustrating some problems and ways to overcome them.

Path finding in a graph

Suppose one is given a program p to compute $Find(G, A, B)$, where G is a graph and A, B are a source and target node. The result is to be some path from A to B if one exists, and an error report otherwise. The result of specializing p with respect to statically known G and B is a program good for finding paths from the various A to B. This could be useful, for example, for finding routes between various cities and one's home.

Naively specializing p would probably give a slow algorithm since for example Dijkstra's algorithm would trace all paths starting at dynamic A until static B was encountered. Alternatively, one can use the fact that A is of bounded static variation to get better results. The idea is to embed p in a program that calls the Find function only on fully static arguments:

```
function Paths-to(G, A, B) =
    let nodes = Node-list(G) in
        forall A1 ∈ nodes do
            if A = A1 then Find(G, A1, B)
    function Find(G, A, B) = ...
```

Note that nodes and so A1 are static. The result of specializing to G, A could thus be a program of form

```
function Paths-to-Copenhagen(A) =
    if A = Hamburg then [Hamburg, C1, ..., Copenhagen] else
    if A = London  then [London, D1, ..., Copenhagen]  else
    ...                                                 else
    if A = Paris   then [Paris, E1, ..., Copenhagen]   else NOPATH
```

in which all path traversal has been done at specialization time. In fact most partial evaluators, for example Similix, would share the list-building code, resulting in a specialized program with size proportional to the length of a shortest-path spanning tree beginning at A.

Sorting

Consider specializing a sorting algorithm with respect to the number of elements to be sorted. This can be profitable when sorting variable numbers of elements. One can use traditional methods, e.g. merge sort, until the number of elements to be sorted becomes less than, say, 100, at which point a specialized sorter is called. Figure 13.2 contains an example, run on Similix (syntax rewritten for clarity), resulting from specializing merge sort to $n = 4$.

The first program version used a function merge to merge two lists. This had only dynamic arguments, so very little speedup resulted. To gain speedup, the lengths of the two lists were added as statically computable parameters, giving code like

```
function merge-sort-4(A);   A,B:array[0..3] of integer;

if A0 <= A1 then [B0:=A0; B1:=A1] else [B0:=A1; B1:=A0];
if A2 <= A3 then [B2:=A2; B3:=A3] else [B2:=A3; B3:=A2];
if B0 <= B2 then
    [A0:=B0;
     if B1<=B2 then [A1:=B1; A2:=B2; A3:=B3]
               else [A1:=B2; merge-4(B,A)]]   else
    [A0:=B2;
     if B0<=B3 then [A1:=B0; merge-4(B,A)]
               else [A1:=B3; A2:=B0; A3:=B1]];
merge-sort-4:=A
end


procedure merge-4(A,B);
if A1<=A3 then [B2:=A1; B3:=A3] else [B2:=A3; B3:=A1]
end
```

Figure 13.2: Specialized merge sorting program.

```
procedure merge(A, Alength, B, Blength);
merge :=
    if Alength = 0 then B else
    if Blength = 0 then A else
    if first(A) < first(B) then
        cons(first(A), merge(rest(A), Alength - 1, B, Blength) else
        cons(first(B), merge(A, Alength, rest(B), Blength - 1)
    end
```

The length arguments of **merge** are static so all calls can be unfolded, resulting in essentially the specialized code seen in Figure 13.2.

The good news is that this program is between 3 and 4 times faster than the recursive version. The bad news is that specializing to successively larger values of n gives program size growing as $O(n^2)$, making the approach useless in practice.

What went wrong? In general the question of *which* of **Alength** or **Blength** is decreased depends on a dynamic test, so **mix** must account for all possible outcomes. Each length can range from 0 to n. There are $O(n^2)$ possible outcomes, so the specialized program will have size $O(n^2)$. (Its run time will still be of order $n \cdot \log(n)$ but with a smaller constant, so something has been gained.)

This problem is entirely due to non-obliviousness of the sorting algorithm. It leads directly to the question: does there exist a comparison-optimal weakly oblivious sorting algorithm?

Batcher's sorting algorithm [17] is both weakly oblivious and near optimal. It runs in time time $O(n \cdot \log^2 n)$, and so yields specialized programs with size and speed $O(n \cdot \log^2 n)$. Ajtai's sorting algorithm [5] is in principle still better, achieving the lower bound of $n \cdot \log(n)$. Unfortunately it is not usable in practice due to an enormous constant factor, yielding extremely large specialized sorters or sorting networks.

Interpreters

Interpreters are necessarily non-oblivious if the interpreted language contains tests, but we have seen that interpreters as a rule specialize quite well. This is at least partly because much experience has shown us how to write them so they give good results. Following are a few characteristics that seem important.

First, interpreters are usually written in a nearly *compositional* way, so the actions performed on a composite source language construction are a combination of the actions performed on its subconstructions. Compositionality is a key assumption for denotational semantics, where its main motivation is to make possible proofs based on structural induction over source language syntax.

From our viewpoint, compositionality implies that an interpreter manipulates only pieces of the original program. Since there is a fixed number of these they can be used for function specialization.

In fact, compositionality may relaxed, as long as all static data is of bounded static variation, meaning that for any fixed static interpreter program input, all variables classified as static can only take on finitely many values, thus guaranteeing termination. A typical example is the list of names appearing an environment binding source variables to values which for any given source program can grow, but not unboundedly in a language with static name binding (false for Lisp).

Interpreters written in other ways, for example ones which construct new bits of source code on the fly, can be difficult or impossible to specialize with good speedup.

Second, well-written interpreters do not contain call duplication. An example problem concerns implementation of `while E do Command`. A poorly written interpreter might contain two calls to evaluate `E` or to perform `Command`, giving target code duplication (especially bad for nested while commands).

13.3 Exercises

Exercise 13.1 Suggest three applications of partial evaluation to problems *not* discussed in this book.

$\square$

Exercise 13.2 The following program `p` stores the smallest among $A_i, \ldots, A_j$ in A_i, and the largest in A_j, assuming for simplicity that $j - i + 1$ is a power of 2. It uses $3n/2 - 2$ comparisons, provably the least number of comparisons that is sufficient to find both minimum and maximum among n elements.

```
procedure Minmax(i,j);
  if j - i = 1 then
    [ if A[i] > A[j] then
      [tem := A[i]; A[i] := A[j]; A[j] := tem]  ]
  else
    [ i1 := (i+j-1)/2; j1 := (i+j+1)/2;
      Minmax(i,i1); Minmax(j1,j);
      A[i] := Min(A[i],A[j1]); A[j] := Max(A[i1],A[j]); ]
```

1. Hand specialize p to $i = 0, j = 7$, unfolding all calls, to obtain program p_{07}.

2. Compare the run time of p with that of p_{0n} for $n = 2^m - 1$, as a function of n, including a constant time c to perform one procedure call.

3. How large is program p_{0n} for $n = 2^m - 1$, as a function of n? Given your conclusion, under what circumstances would specialization of p be worth while?

4. Let p_{ij}^k be p specialized to $j - i + 1 \leq 2^k$ as in Section 13.1.3. Note that for each k, program p_{ij}^k has a fixed size independent of i, j. Compare the run time for p_{0n}^k with those of p and p_{ij}. Does the speedup for fixed k 'propagate' to arrays of arbitrarily large size?

5. Does a similar speedup propagation occur when specializing a merge sort program to fixed array size?

□

Exercise 13.3 The 'table-directed input' of Section 13.1.4 can be implemented by at least three methods:

1. by a general interpreter, taking as parameters the table, its dimensions, and an array of action routine addresses;

2. by an interpreter tailored to a fixed table with known dimensions and known action routines; or

3. by a 'compiled' version of the table, realized by tests and goto's with inline code for the actions.

Compare the run time of these three approaches. Which method is used by scanner generators such as Yacc?

□

Exercise 13.4 Residual program size explosions as seen in Section 13.2.4 can make partial evaluation unprofitable. Can the size explosion problem always be solved by choosing a more conservative binding-time analysis (i.e. one with fewer static variables)? Suggest a BTA tactic for avoiding such size explosions.

□

Part V

Advanced Topics

Chapter 14

Termination of Partial Evaluation

Many partial evaluators have imperfect termination properties, the most serious being that they are not guaranteed to terminate on all static input. Partial evaluators do speculative evaluation on the basis of incomplete information, giving them a tendency to loop infinitely more often than a standard evaluator would. For example, a non-trivial partial evaluator reduces both branches of a conditional when they cannot resolve the guarding condition. Another way to put this is that partial evaluation is more eager than standard evaluation.

Non-termination is a most unfortunate behaviour from an automatic tool to improve programs. The problem is exacerbated if a compiler generated from the partial evaluator inherits its dubious termination properties. Such a compiler would be close to worthless: a non-expert user would be without a clue as how to revise the source program that made the compiler loop. An objection: some languages, e.g. PL/I, may have static semantics that open up for compile-time looping, but in this chapter our concern will be to *ban* non-termination of partial evaluation. In another setting, one could imagine that a cognizant user could be allowed to override the conservative assumptions of a specializer to obtain extra static computation.

After briefly describing termination strategies used in online partial evaluators, we analyse the problem of non-terminating partial evaluation in the offline framework of Chapter 4. We then develop a binding-time analysis that solves termination problems.

14.1 Termination of online partial evaluators

Online partial evaluators employ a number of techniques to ensure termination. Most consult some form of computational history, maintained during the specialization process, to make folding and unfolding decisions. When a call is encountered during specialization the decisions are: should this call be unfolded; and if not, *how specialized* a residual call should be generated?

There are several well-known tradeoffs. Unfolding too liberally can cause infinite specialization-time loops, even without generating any residual code. Generating residual calls that are too specialized (i.e. contain too much static data) can lead to an infinitely large residual program; while the other extreme of generating too general residual calls can lead to little or no speedup.

A variety of heuristics have been devised to steer online call unfolding, beginning with the very first partial evaluation articles. Infinite unfolding cannot occur without recursion; so specializers often compare the sizes and/or structures of arguments encountered in a function or procedure call with those of its predecessors, and use the outcome to decide whether to unfold and, if not, how much to generalize the call. A variety of strategies, some rather sophisticated, have been described [19,75,112,158,178,230,235,267,269,281].

14.2   Termination of offline partial evaluators

In offline partial evaluation, essentially the same decisions have to be taken, with the same tradeoffs. A difference is that this is preprocessing work, done by the BTA (binding-time analysis). BTA computes a division for *all* program variables on the basis of a division of the *input* variables. At specialization time this classification of variables (and thereby computations) as static or dynamic is blindly obeyed — so all-important decisions of when to specialize are encapsulated within the computed division.

In the literature on termination of offline partial evaluation, including this chapter, emphasis is on the distinction between increasing and decreasing static variables [117,130,246]. (An exception is Holst's *poor man's generalization*, which generalizes all variables which do not have control decisions depending on them. This does not *guarantee* termination, but the heuristic might have some practical merit.)

14.2.1   Problem formulation

How much freedom is there in the choice of division? An indispensable requirement is that it must be *congruent*: any variable that depends on a dynamic variable must itself be classified as dynamic. (Without this, code generation is impossible.) Further, some congruent divisions are bad in that they lead to infinite residual programs, as seen in the example of Section 4.4.5.

The division may also be used to make annotations indicating when it is safe to compress transitions (unfold) without causing code duplication or computation duplication. Usefulness is also practically relevant: if a variable is dead, i.e. if no computation depends on it, then it should be classified as dynamic. This principle was found to be crucial for specialization of larger, imperative programs in Chapter 4.

Since ensuring finite specialization is by far the hardest problem, we shall concentrate exclusively on it, and ignore the other problems. Recall from Chapter 4 that the specialized program will be finite if and only if its set of specialized program points *poly* is finite. We thus ignore questions of code generation and transition compression. Consequently we have reduced the problem to the following:

Given a division of the program inputs, find a division of all variables that

1. is congruent;

2. is finite, so for all input data, the set *poly* of reachable specialized program points will be finite; and in which

3. as many variables as possible are classified as 'static'.

A congruent finite division is an achievable goal, since classifying *all* variables as dynamic is congruent and will indeed ensure termination (a trivial solution that yields no specialization at all.) The main problem is thus to classify 'just' enough variables as dynamic to ensure congruence and finiteness. Point 3 ensures performance of a maximal amount of computation by the specializer, thus increasing residual program efficiency and avoiding the trivial solution when possible.

14.2.2   Problem analysis

Given a program p, a division, and static program input vs_0, the set *poly* of all reachable specialized program points was defined in Chapter 4 to be the smallest set such that

- (pp_0, vs_0) is in *poly*, where pp_0 is p's initial program point; and

- if $(pp, vs) \in poly$, then *successors*$((pp, vs))$ is a subset of *poly*

where *successors*$((pp, vs)) = \{(pp_1, vs'), \ldots, (pp_n, vs')\}$ is the set of static parts of program points reachable in computations beginning at (pp, vs) and continuing to the end of the basic block begun by pp. Clearly, *poly* is finite if and only if all static variables assume only finitely many different values.

Bounded static variation
Certain source program variables can only assume finitely many different values. One example is a static program input that is never changed. Another is a variable that can change during execution, but always assumes values that are substructures of a static input. The idea can be formalized as follows.

The binding-time analysis algorithm in Section 4.4.6 constructs a division *div* which is congruent but not always finite. Let us say that a variable x_k is of *bounded static variation* if (1) it is classified as static by *div*; and (2) for any static program input vs_0, the following set is finite:

$$\{v_k \mid (pp, (v_1 \dots v_k \dots v_n)) \in poly\}$$

Our goal is thus a program analysis to construct a better division by recognizing certain variables as of bounded static variation, classifying them as 'static', and classifying all other variables as 'dynamic'.

Example 14.1 Consider the following program and assume that x is known to be static. How should y be classified?

```
      y := 0;
loop: x := x-1;
      y := y+2;
      if x≠0 goto loop else exit;
exit: ...
```

Classifying y as static violates neither congruence nor finiteness as the assignment y:=y+2 is only performed n times if n is the initial value of x. The value of y throughout the computation is thus bounded by $2n$. Observe that though for any one value for x there is a bound for y, there exists no uniform bound for y.

Things look different if x is dynamic: we lose the bound on the number of iterations. Thus y is unbounded, even though the binding-time analysis in Section 4.4.6 would call it static. Hence to comply with the finiteness criterion, y should be classified as dynamic.   □

Finite downwards closure
How can we choose the division to make *poly* finite? A program analysis to recognize such properties as bounded static variation can be done using the fact that many value domains used in practice are are finitely downwards closed.

Definition 14.1 A set D with partial ordering $<$ is *finitely downwards closed* iff $\forall x \in D : \{y \mid y < x\}$ is finite.   □

A trivial consequence is that there exists no infinite descending chain, that is, a sequence $v_1, v_2, v_3, \dots$ with $v_i \in D$ and $v_i > v_{i+1}$ for $i \geq 1$.

Examples

- The set of natural numbers $\mathcal{N}$ with the usual ordering $<$ is finitely downwards closed.

- The set of integers $\mathcal{Z}$ with the usual ordering $<$ is *not* finitely downwards closed since $\forall x \in \mathcal{Z} : \{y \mid y < x\}$ is *infinite*.

- Defining $x < y$ to mean *x is a substructure of y*, the set of finite trees is finitely downwards closed. So are the sets of finite lists and S-expressions, together with other common finite algebraic structures.

Since a variable can only have its value decreased finitely many times, we get a bound on the number of iterations in a loop where a static variable is decreased at every iteration. As seen in the first part of Example 14.1, this can bound the number of times other variables can be increased in that loop.

The finite downwards closure property is crucial for this reasoning, which means that our methods do not work for, say, integer types. Therefore we assume all numerals in the rest of this chapter to be natural numbers.

14.3 Binding-time analysis ensuring termination

In this section we develop a new algorithm that yields a congruent and always finite division, in contrast to that of Section 4.4.6. Variables will be classified in one of three categories: *static*, meaning that it is guaranteed to assume only finitely many values, and can be computed at partial evaluation time (congruence); or *dubious*, meaning that it is not dependent on dynamic variables, but is not (yet) known to be of bounded static variation; or *dynamic*.

(Note that previous chapters have taken a more relaxed attitude towards the term 'static'.) Our definition does not mean that a static variable cannot grow, only that all variation must be bounded for any static program input.

To ensure finiteness it may be necessary to reclassify some dubious variables as dynamic, and this may lead to yet more reclassifications to re-establish congruence. For example, a variable is dubious if it is increased inside a loop. If a bounded static variable is properly decreased in the same loop, then its growth is limited; if not, it must be classified as dynamic.

Below we present an analysis that collects information about dependencies and size relations among variables in a program. From the result of this analysis, a division ensuring termination will be found roughly in the following manner:

1. Classify all variables that depend on dynamic input variables as dynamic. Classify all non-dynamic variables as dubious.

2. A dubious variable x that only depends on itself and on static variables is reclassified as static if

   whenever x is increased in a loop, some static variable is decreased. (Special case: x is never increased in a loop.)

3. When step 2 is no longer applicable, reclassify remaining dubious variables as dynamic.

14.3.1   Important concepts

Syntax and semantics

Recall that a flow chart program with input variables $x_1 \ldots x_k$ consists of a read statement read $x_1 \ldots x_k$; followed by a sequence of labelled basic blocks: $l_0:bb_0$ $l_1:bb_1 \ldots l_n:bb_n$. If the program has variables $x_1, \ldots, x_m$ ($m \geq k$) then a *store* $\bar{v}$ is represented by an m-tuple of values $\bar{v} = (v_1, \ldots, v_m)$. Below we shall use the mathematical semantics for flow chart programs shown in Section 3.3.3.

Dependency

Variable x *depends* on variable y over the one-assignment sequence $x := e$ if y occurs in e. Further, x depends on y over sequence seq_1; seq_2 if one of the following conditions holds:

1. z depends on y over seq_1 and x depends on z over seq_2;

2. x depends on y over seq_1 and x is not assigned in seq_2.

Variable x *depends* on variable y along a path of labels $l_1, l_2, \ldots, l_i$ in the flow chart iff x depends on y over the concatenation of the assignments at $l_1, \ldots$.

Loops

A *loop* is a sequence of labels $l_1, l_2, \ldots, l_i$ where $l_1 = l_i$. Note that we do not disallow $l_j = l_1$ for $1 \leq j \leq i$. A variable y is *increased* in a loop when y depends on y along the loop *and* its value grows for each iteration. Similarly, x is *decreased* in a loop if x depends on x along the loop and its value diminishes for each iteration. In Example 14.1, y is increased and x is decreased in the loop.

Example 14.2 Consider the following program fragment:

```
a: x := x-1;
   y := y+2;
   if e₁ goto a else b;
b: x := x+2;
   y := y-1;
   if e₂ goto a else b;
```

x is decreased and y is increased in the loop a, a. Note that both variables are increased in the loop a, b, a. Both variables should be classified as dynamic no matter what the rest of program looks like.   □

14.3.2   Size and dependency analysis

In this section we analyse the dependencies and size variances among the program variables $x_1 \ldots x_m$ along various program control paths $pp_i, pp_{i+1}, \ldots, pp_j$ in the flow chart. A *flow description* is of form $(pp_i, pp_j) : (d_1, \ldots, d_m)$. Each d_k describes the dependency of the value of variable x_k at the end of the path on the variables $x_1 \ldots x_m$ at the beginning of the path.

Variable descriptions

A variable description has one of three forms: $d = I(V)$, $d = E(V)$, or $d = D(V)$, where $V \subseteq \text{VarIndex} = \{1, \ldots, m\}$. VDesc is the set of all variable descriptions.

When a variable x_i is described by d, then it depends on those variables x_j for which $j \in V$. The letter I, E, or D describes the relation between the size of x_i and the x_j's: D denotes *strictly Decreasing*, E denotes *non-increasing = less than or Equal*, and I denotes *(possibly) Increasing*. Also, when a value is both increased and decreased we classify it as increasing.

Given a flow description of form $(pp_i, pp_j):\bar{d}$, the table below summarizes how to interpret the elements of $\bar{d}$ (recall that $\bar{v} \downarrow k$ selects the k'th component of $\bar{v}$):

$$
\begin{aligned}
d_k &= D(V) \quad \text{means} \quad \bar{v}_j \downarrow k < \bar{v}_i \downarrow s, && \text{for all } s \in V \\
d_k &= E(V) \quad \text{means} \quad \bar{v}_j \downarrow k \leq \bar{v}_i \downarrow s, && \text{for all } s \in V \\
d_k &= I(V) \quad \text{means} \quad \bar{v}_j \downarrow k \text{ depends on } \bar{v}_i \downarrow s, && \text{for all } s \in V
\end{aligned}
$$

We take $?(V)$ to mean either $I(V)$, $E(V)$, or $D(V)$. Note the special case $V = \{\}$. This implies that x_i depends on *no* variables and thus is constant. Any description $?(\{\})$ would correctly describe the effect of an assignment of constant value such as $x_i := 42$.

Flow descriptions

Associate with any two program points, pp_i and pp_j, a description of the variables to get a *flow description* of form $(pp_i, pp_j) : \bar{d}$, where $\bar{d} = (d_1, \ldots, d_m)$. The type of a flow description is thus $\text{PPoint} \times \text{PPoint} \times \text{Vdesc}^m$. A flow description of this form means that in one possible computation

$$(pp_i, \bar{v}_i) \rightarrow \cdots \rightarrow (pp_j, \bar{v}_j)$$

the dependency of $\bar{v}_j$ on $\bar{v}_i$ is described by $(d_1, \ldots, d_m)$. Note that we also include computations that do not start at the initial program point.

14.3.3 Flow description of all possible computations

We shall now define a set of flow descriptions *FD*: $\wp(\text{PPoint} \times \text{PPoint} \times \text{Vdesc}^m)$ that captures all possible computations. *FD* will be a set of triples $(pp_i, pp_j) : \bar{d}$, where $\bar{d}$ describes the dependency relations between program variables at the end of one possible path from pp_i to pp_j, and the variables' values at the start of that same path.

Note that *FD* is finite since there are only finitely many different triples (even though there are infinitely many paths). We approximate the control function c_i

by ac_i (independent of the store), defined by:

$$
\begin{array}{lll}
ac_i & = & \{\mathrm{l}_j, \mathrm{l}_k\} \quad \text{if } \mathrm{bb}_i = \ldots; \text{ if e then goto } \mathrm{l}_j \text{ else goto } \mathrm{l}_k \\
ac_i & = & \{\mathrm{l}_j\} \qquad \text{if } \mathrm{bb}_i = \ldots; \text{ goto } \mathrm{l}_j \\
ac_i & = & \{\} \qquad\ \ \text{if } \mathrm{bb}_i = \ldots; \text{ return e}
\end{array}
$$

and define *FD* inductively by the following two rules:

1. For all program points pp_i, $(\mathrm{pp}_i, \mathrm{pp}_i) : (E(\{1\}), \ldots, E(\{m\})) \in FD$

2. If $(\mathrm{pp}_i, \mathrm{pp}_j) : \bar{\mathrm{d}} \in FD$, $\mathrm{pp}_q \in ac_j$, and $\bar{\mathrm{d}}' = BlockDesc[\![\mathrm{bb}_j]\!]\bar{\mathrm{d}}$ then $(\mathrm{pp}_i, \mathrm{pp}_q) :$ $\bar{\mathrm{d}}' \in FD$.

The function *BlockDesc* which is defined below computes the effect of a basic block on a store description $\bar{\mathrm{d}}$.

$$
\begin{array}{ll}
BlockDesc[\![\mathrm{a}_1; \ \ldots; \ \mathrm{a}_n]\!]\bar{\mathrm{d}} = (AsgDesc[\![\mathrm{a}_n]\!] \circ \ldots \circ AsgDesc[\![\mathrm{a}_1]\!])\ \bar{\mathrm{d}} \\[4pt]
AsgDesc[\![\mathrm{x}_k := \mathrm{e}]\!]\ \bar{\mathrm{d}} = (\mathrm{d}_1, \ \ldots, \ \mathrm{d}_{k-1},\ ExpDesc[\![\mathrm{e}]\!]\bar{\mathrm{d}},\ \mathrm{d}_{k+1},\ \ldots,\ \mathrm{d}_m) \\
\qquad\qquad\qquad\qquad \text{where } \bar{\mathrm{d}} = (\mathrm{d}_1, \ \ldots, \ \mathrm{d}_m)
\end{array}
$$

$$
\begin{array}{ll}
ExpDesc[\![\mathrm{e}_1 + \mathrm{e}_2]\!]\bar{\mathrm{d}} & = I(V_1 \cup V_2) \\
& \text{where } ?(V_1) = ExpDesc[\![\mathrm{e}_1]\!]\bar{\mathrm{d}} \\
& \qquad\ \ ?(V_2) = ExpDesc[\![\mathrm{e}_2]\!]\bar{\mathrm{d}} \\
ExpDesc[\![\mathrm{sub1}\ \mathrm{e}]\!]\bar{\mathrm{d}} & = decrease(ExpDesc[\![\mathrm{e}]\!]\bar{\mathrm{d}}) \\
ExpDesc[\![\mathrm{cons}\ \mathrm{e}_1\ \mathrm{e}_2]\!]\bar{\mathrm{d}} & = ExpDesc[\![\mathrm{e}_1 + \mathrm{e}_2]\!]\bar{\mathrm{d}} \\
ExpDesc[\![\mathrm{hd}\ \mathrm{e}]\!]\bar{\mathrm{d}} & = ExpDesc[\![\mathrm{sub1}\ \mathrm{e}]\!]\bar{\mathrm{d}} \\
ExpDesc[\![\mathrm{x}_p]\!]\bar{\mathrm{d}} & = \bar{\mathrm{d}}{\downarrow}p \\
ExpDesc[\![\texttt{<constant>}]\!]\bar{\mathrm{d}} & = ?(\{\})\ (\text{choice of } I,\ E,\ \text{or } D \text{ immaterial})
\end{array}
$$

d	$I(V)$	$E(V)$	$D(V)$
$decrease(\mathrm{d})$	$I(V)$	$D(V)$	$D(V)$

The `cons` case is typical of increasing functions, and the `hd` case is typical of decreasing functions.

14.3.4   Binding-time analysis algorithm

Let a program with basic blocks $\mathrm{pp}_0 : \mathrm{bb}_{pp_0}\ \mathrm{pp}_1 : \mathrm{bb}_{pp_1}\ \ldots\ \mathrm{pp}_n : \mathrm{bb}_{pp_n}$ be given. Input variables are $\mathrm{x}_1 \ldots \mathrm{x}_k$ of which $\mathrm{x}_1 \ldots \mathrm{x}_s$, $s \leq k$, are *dubious*. (We carefully avoid the word static until the boundedness has been shown.) The algorithm below computes a division that guarantees termination of partial evaluation.

1. Compute *FD* as described in the previous section.

2. Classify as dynamic $\mathrm{x}_{s+1} \ldots \mathrm{x}_k$ as well as all variables x_j for which there exist $q \in \{0, \ldots, n\}$ and $i \in \{s+1, \ldots, k\}$ such that

$$(pp_0, pp_q):(d_1, \ldots, d_{j-1}, ?(V), d_{j+1}, \ldots, d_m) \in FD, i \in S$$

3. Classify all yet unclassified variables as dubious.

4. Reclassify as static, any set W of dubious variables fulfilling both of the following conditions:

   (a) $\forall x_j \in W, \forall (pp_p, pp_q):(d_1, \ldots, d_{j-1}, ?(V), d_{j+1}, \ldots, d_m) \in FD$, $\forall i \in V$:

   $$x_i \text{ dubious implies } x_i \in W$$

   (b) $\exists g \in \{1, \ldots, m\}$, such that:[1]
   $$\forall (pp_q, pp_q):(d_1, \ldots, d_{j-1}, I(V), d_{j+1}, \ldots, d_m) \in FD:$$

   $$(j \in V \text{ and } x_j \in W) \text{ implies } (x_g \text{ is static and } d_g = D(T) \text{ and } g \in T)$$

5. When step 4 can no longer be used to reclassify dubious variables as static, reclassify remaining dubious variables as dynamic.

Note that step 4 can reclassify a *set* of dubious variables at a time. This is useful when dubious variables are mutually dependent and cannot be reclassified 'one at a time'.

14.4 Safety of BTA algorithm

What needs to be proven about the above algorithm is that an application of step 4 does not classify any variable that can assume infinitely many values as static. Assume that the division obtained by reclassifying all dubious variables as dynamic guarantees finiteness of *poly* and prove that one application of step 4 does not destroy this property.

Suppose the algorithm classifies $x_1 \ldots x_s$ as static and $x_{s+1} \ldots x_m$ as dynamic. Let div_s: Value^m → Value^s be the function that selects the static part vs of a store $\bar{v}$. Define $(pp_i, vs_i) \Rightarrow (pp_j, vs_j)$ to hold, iff

1. $pp_j \in ac_i$

2. $\exists \bar{v}: vs_i = div_s(\bar{v}), vs_j = div_s(w_i(\bar{v}))$

The relation $\Rightarrow$ approximates the notion of being a 'successor' as defined in Chapter 4 since both branches are followed for static conditionals. Let a program and static input vs_0 be given. We shall demonstrate the finiteness of *poly* by showing the following superset to be finite:

---

[1] See Exercise 14.8 for a generalization of this step.

$$\{(\texttt{pp}, \texttt{vs}) \mid (\texttt{pp}_0, \texttt{vs}_0) \Rightarrow^* (\texttt{pp}, \texttt{vs})\}$$

where $(\texttt{pp}_0, \texttt{vs}_0)$ is the initial specialized program point.

The proof is by contradiction, so assume conversely that $\{(\texttt{pp}, \texttt{vs}) \mid (\texttt{pp}_0, \texttt{vs}_0) \Rightarrow^* (\texttt{pp}, \texttt{vs})\}$ is infinite. Then there must exist an infinite chain where all $(\texttt{pp}_i, \texttt{vs}_i)$ are different:[2]

$$(\texttt{pp}_0, \texttt{vs}_0) \Rightarrow (\texttt{pp}_1, \texttt{vs}_1) \Rightarrow \ldots$$

We shall refer to this infinite chain as $(*)$.

A *dependency chain* is a sequence of pairs of natural numbers $(i_1, k_1) \rhd (i_2, k_2) \rhd \ldots$ satisfying:

1. $(\texttt{pp}_{i_1}, \texttt{vs}_{i_1}) \Rightarrow^+ (\texttt{pp}_{i_2}, \texttt{vs}_{i_2}) \Rightarrow^+ \ldots$

2. For $j = 1, 2, \ldots$:

    $(\texttt{pp}_{i_j}, \texttt{pp}_{i_{j+1}}){:}\bar{\texttt{d}} \in FD, \bar{\texttt{d}} = (\texttt{d}_1, \ldots, \texttt{d}_{k_{j+1}-1}, I(V), \texttt{d}_{k_{j+1}+1}, \ldots, \texttt{d}_m), k_j \in V$

In the definition of dependency chains the *i*s are indexes into $(*)$. For each j, $\texttt{x}_{k_{j+1}}$ depends on and is larger than $\texttt{x}_{k_j}$. Observe that any subchain of a dependency chain is itself a dependency chain.

There are arbitrarily long dependency chains. Justification: suppose they had a maximum length K. Variables are assigned constant values a finite number of places (initial binding of input variables and (possibly) assignments to constant expressions). Also, a finite number of store transformations are defined by the basic blocks. By the finite downwards closure property of the value domains, applying at most K consecutive increasing store transformations can only lead to a finite number of different values.[3]

From the existence of arbitrarily long dependency chains, we may conclude the existence of arbitrarily long *self-dependency* chains of form $(i_1, k) \rhd (i_2, k) \rhd \ldots$ with $\texttt{pp}_{i_1} = \texttt{pp}_{i_2} = \ldots$, as there are only finitely many different program points and variables. For a two-element self-dependency chain $(i_1, k) \rhd (i_2, k)$ we have (by the definition of dependency chains) an element in FD of form $(\texttt{pp}_i, \texttt{pp}_i){:}\bar{\texttt{d}}$, where $\bar{\texttt{d}} = (\texttt{d}_1, \ldots, \texttt{d}_{k-1}, I(V), \texttt{d}_{k+1}, \ldots, \texttt{d}_m), k \in V$, and for such k step 4b in the BTA provides a g such that $\texttt{d}_g = D(T), g \in T, \texttt{x}_g$ static.

This fact yields arbitrarily long chains

$$\texttt{vs}_{i_1}{\downarrow}g > \texttt{vs}_{i_2}{\downarrow}g > \ldots$$

of unbounded length which contradicts the finite downwards closure property and concludes the proof.

---

[2]Not hard to show (König's Lemma).
[3]See Exercise 14.6.

14.5 Exercises

Exercise 14.1 Execute the binding-time analysis algorithm of Section 14.3.4 on the programs in Example 14.1 and 14.2. □

Exercise 14.2 In Section 4.4.5 it is claimed that there is no computable BTA that always guarantees termination and never generalizes unnecessarily. Prove this by reduction from the halting problem. Show that lifting any one of the two requirements renders the problem computable. □

Exercise 14.3 Consider the mix equation (Definition 4.2). Assuming mix is the partial evaluator described in Chapter 4, does there exist a program for which the left hand side loops and the right hand side terminates? □

Exercise 14.4 Prove that the 91 function and Ackermann's function terminate for any input. The 91 function:

$$f(x) = \begin{cases} x - 10 & \text{if } x > 100 \\ f(f(x + 11)) & \text{otherwise} \end{cases}$$

Ackermann's function:

$$ack(m, n) = \begin{cases} n + 1 & \text{if } m = 0 \\ ack(m - 1, 1) & \text{if } m \neq 0 \land n = 0 \\ ack(m - 1, ack(m, n - 1)) & \text{if } m \neq 0 \land n \neq 0 \end{cases}$$

□

Exercise 14.5 Construct a program and a finite division such that reclassifying a static variable as dynamic renders poly infinite. □

Exercise 14.6 Find a program and a division such that poly is infinite but no there is no infinite dependency chain. □

Exercise 14.7 Let B_1 and B_2 be divisions, let $B_1 \sqcup B_2$ be the division that classifies variable x_i as static if and only if x_i is static by both B_1 and B_2, and let $B_1 \sqcap B_2$ be the division that classifies x_i as static if x_i is static by at least one of B_1 and B_2. Assume that both B_1 and B_2 are congruent and finite.

1. Is $B_1 \sqcap B_2$ congruent? Is it finite?

2. Is $B_1 \sqcup B_2$ congruent? Is it finite?

□

Exercise 14.8 In the BTA algorithm, step 4b can be relaxed to:

$\forall\,(\text{pp}_q,\text{pp}_q):\bar{\text{d}} \in FD,\ \bar{\text{d}} = (\text{d}_1,\ \ldots,\ \text{d}_{j-1},\ I(V),\ \text{d}_{j+1},\ \ldots,\ \text{d}_m),\ j \in V$
implies $\exists g \in \{1,\ldots,m\} : \text{d}_g = D(T), g \in T,\ \text{x}_g$ static

1. Find programs for which the relaxed algorithm produces a different result than the original algorithm.

2. Prove that the relaxed algorithm is still safe.

□

Chapter 15

Program Analysis

The purpose of automatic *program analysis* is to obtain some information about the execution of a program without actually executing it, and without using its input. Typical examples of such information are: 'the value of variable y will always be an even integer' and 'the value of variable g will never be the lambda abstraction $\lambda x^{\ell}.e$'. The information must be valid for all possible executions of the program.

This chapter explains the program analysis methodology called *abstract interpretation*, and discusses some program analyses relevant to partial evaluation: the binding-time analysis for Scheme0 programs (Section 5.2) is revisited, and a closure analysis for higher-order languages is presented. We show how to combine these analyses to obtain a binding-time analysis for the higher-order language Scheme1. Finally, we present Launchbury's projection-based binding-time analysis of partially static structures.

15.1 Abstract interpretation

Consider an arithmetic expression such as 8 + 3 and suppose we want to know whether its result is even or odd. We may evaluate it concretely, obtaining the concrete number 11, which is odd. However, we may also *abstract* the values 8 and 3 by their parity (that is, *even* and *odd*), and consider instead the problem *even + odd*. This may be evaluated abstractly, giving the abstract result *odd*.

Clearly, one could consider other abstractions instead to obtain different information about the expression, such as its sign. For this we would abstractly evaluate *positive + positive* yielding *positive*.

The important observation is that we have abstract versions of the *values* (such as 8) as well as of the *operations* on them (such as '+'). The following tables define abstract addition and multiplication on {*even, odd*}:

+	*even*	*odd*
even	*even*	*odd*
odd	*odd*	*even*

×	*even*	*odd*
even	*even*	*even*
odd	*even*	*odd*

Applying the idea of abstract evaluation to programs, we arrive at *abstract interpretation*: programs may be interpreted concretely or abstractly. Abstract interpretation of imperative programs was introduced by Sintzoff [251] and studied in depth by Cousot and Cousot [65,64] and Nielson [198,200]. Here we outline the abstract interpretation of functional programs, which was pioneered by Mycroft [197].

15.1.1   Variables, conditionals, and functions

An expression may contain variables: x * 3 + 7. Ordinary evaluation of this expression relies on an environment to supply a (concrete) value for x, say 8, and evaluates the expression using this value. Abstract evaluation of this expression naturally relies on an *abstract environment* to supply an abstract value for x, say *even*.

Continuing the parity example, we let *EvenOdd* denote the set of abstract parities. So far we have *even*, *odd* ∈ *EvenOdd*, but we shall see that *EvenOdd* must have two more elements: one because of conditionals (this section), and one because of recursive definitions (next section).

Consider a conditional expression, such as if e then 3 else 2. Clearly the abstract value of the first branch is *odd* and that of the second branch is *even*, but what is the abstract value of the entire expression? If we could decide whether the condition e is true or false, there would be no problem, but in general we cannot.

Thus the best description we can give is 'it is either *even* or *odd*': we know nothing, but so far we lack a way of saying this. We are forced to introduce a new abstract value ⊤ ∈ *EvenOdd* (pronounced 'top') to represent the absence of knowledge.

We also provide {*even*, *odd*, ⊤} ⊆ *EvenOdd* with an ordering ⊑, such that *even* ⊑ ⊤ and *odd* ⊑ ⊤. When $s ⊑ t$, that is, when s is less than or equal to t, then clearly s is more precise (or more informative) than t. The relation between the three abstract values can be shown as follows, with the smaller (or more informative) values below the larger (or less informative) one:

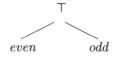

Let s, t be two abstract values. Then they have a *least upper bound*, denoted by $s \sqcup t$. This is the least element which is greater than or equal to both s and t. Now $s \sqsubseteq t$ means that s is more precise (or more informative) than t, so $s \sqcup t$ is the best (or most informative) joint description of s and t. This allows us to abstractly interpret the conditional expression `if e then 3 else 2` by considering its branches in isolation, obtaining the abstract values *odd* and *even*, then compute $odd \sqcup even$ to obtain the abstract value $\top$ of the entire conditional.

The least upper bound $s \sqcup t$ is also called the *lub* or *join* of s and t.

Finally, consider a function definition `f(x) = x + 1`. When abstractly interpreting a program involving this function, we simply use the corresponding *abstract function*, written $f^\#$. In this case, $f^\#(X) = X + odd$, so

$$f^\#(X) \quad = \quad odd \quad \text{if } X = even$$
$$= \quad even \quad \text{if } X = odd$$

In summary, we find the abstract value of an expression by first replacing each operation (such as $+$ or $\times$) by its abstract version, and each conditional by the least upper bound of its branches, then evaluate the resulting abstract expression. If the expression involves a function application, we just apply the corresponding abstract function, obtained by making its body into an abstract expression.

15.1.2 Recursively defined functions

This approach works even for recursively defined functions such as

```
g(x) = if x > 17 then x else 8 + g(3*x)
```

Since `g` is recursively defined, so is its abstract function $g^\#$:

$$g^\#(X) \quad = \quad X \sqcup (even + g^\#(odd \times X))$$

We now have a recursive equation describing the abstract function $g^\#$. Does it have any solutions? The answer turns out to be 'yes', if only we introduce yet a new abstract value $\bot \in EvenOdd$ (pronounced 'bottom') to stand for 'not defined' or 'no value'. Putting $\bot \sqsubseteq s$ for all other abstract values $s \in EvenOdd$, the full set $EvenOdd = \{\bot, even, odd, \top\}$ of abstract values is:

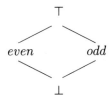

That is, *EvenOdd* is a complete lattice: every set S of elements from *EvenOdd* has a least upper bound $\bigsqcup S$ and a greatest lower bound $\bigsqcap S$. Provided that the abstract operations $+$ and $\times$ are monotonic (and they are), there is therefore a least solution to the equation defining $g^\#$ (and indeed any abstract function) [261]. Recall that least means most informative. Since the lattice has finite height, this solution can even be found in finite time, which is important since program analyses should always terminate. For this reason the abstract values are usually required to form a lattice of finite height.

In the case of $g^\#$ above, a tabulation of the (argument, result) pairs for the four possible argument values shows that $g^\#$ is the identity on *EvenOdd*:

$$
\begin{aligned}
g^\#(X) \;&=\; \top \quad &&\text{if } X = \top\\
&=\; even \quad &&\text{if } X = even\\
&=\; odd \quad &&\text{if } X = odd\\
&=\; \bot \quad &&\text{if } X = \bot
\end{aligned}
$$

Abstract addition and multiplication on *EvenOdd* $= \{\bot, even, odd, \top\}$ is defined by the tables below. Notice that these are extensions of the tables given at the beginning of the section.

$+$	$\bot$	$even$	odd	$\top$
$\bot$	$\bot$	$\bot$	$\bot$	$\bot$
$even$	$\bot$	$even$	odd	$\top$
odd	$\bot$	odd	$even$	$\top$
$\top$	$\bot$	$\top$	$\top$	$\top$

$\times$	$\bot$	$even$	odd	$\top$
$\bot$	$\bot$	$\bot$	$\bot$	$\bot$
$even$	$\bot$	$even$	$even$	$even$
odd	$\bot$	$even$	odd	$\top$
$\top$	$\bot$	$even$	$\top$	$\top$

In summary, we have seen that expressions can be evaluated abstractly, for instance to know whether the result of ordinary evaluation will be *even* or *odd*. We have also seen that because of conditional expressions and recursively defined functions, we need two more abstract values $\top$ and $\bot$, which correspond to 'no information' and 'not defined'.

15.1.3   Abstraction and concretization mappings

Informally, the abstract value *even* represents all even numbers, *odd* represents all odd numbers, $\top$ represents all numbers, and $\bot$ represents no numbers. Also, if a number is represented by some abstract value $s \in EvenOdd$, then also by every abstract value t which is greater than s, that is, which is less precise than s.

These notions can be formalized using an *abstraction function* α and a *concretization function* γ. Let $\mathcal{N} = \{0, 1, \ldots\}$ be the set of natural numbers, and let $\wp(\mathcal{N})$ be the powerset of $\mathcal{N}$, that is, the set of subsets of $\mathcal{N}$, partially ordered by set inclusion $\subseteq$.

Then the concretization function $\gamma : EvenOdd \to \wp(\mathcal{N})$ maps an abstract value s to the set $\gamma(s)$ of concrete numbers represented by s. Conversely, the abstraction function $\alpha : \wp(\mathcal{N}) \to EvenOdd$ maps a set V of numbers to the (smallest) abstract value $\alpha(V)$ representing all numbers in the set.

The abstraction and concretization functions must (1) be monotonic, and further satisfy the following requirements:

(2) $\forall s \in EvenOdd. \ \alpha(\gamma(s)) = s$
(3) $\forall V \in \wp(\mathcal{N}). \ \gamma(\alpha(V)) \supseteq V$

The monotonicity requirement (1) means that a larger abstract value represents a larger set of concrete values. Requirement (2) means that every abstract value represents something; there are no superfluous abstract values. Requirement (3) means that abstracting and then concretizing a set V of concrete values gives a set containing V. In other words, the abstraction of V safely represents all elements of V.

In the *EvenOdd* example, the concretization function γ is

$$
\begin{array}{lll}
\gamma(\bot) & = \ \{\} & \text{the empty set} \\
\gamma(even) & = \ \{0, 2, \ldots\} & \text{the set of even numbers} \\
\gamma(odd) & = \ \{1, 3, \ldots\} & \text{the set of odd numbers} \\
\gamma(\top) & = \ \{0, 1, 2, 3, \ldots\} & \text{the set of all numbers}
\end{array}
$$

Using α and γ we can now define what it means for an abstract function $f^\# : EvenOdd \to EvenOdd$ to safely abstract a concrete function $f : \mathcal{N} \to \mathcal{N}$. Namely, let $n \in \mathcal{N}$ be a concrete number; it is described by the abstract value $\alpha(\{n\})$. The requirement on $f^\#$ is that the concrete result $f(n)$ is safely represented by the abstract result $f^\#(\alpha(\{n\}))$:

$$\forall n \in \mathcal{N}. \ f(n) \in \gamma(f^\#(\alpha(\{n\})))$$

15.1.4 The Scheme0 binding-time analysis as an abstract interpretation

Looking back on the binding-time analysis for Scheme0 presented in Section 5.2, we find that it is a very simple abstract interpretation. Consider the expression x+8 and assume x is dynamic (clearly the constant 8 is static). That is, x has binding time D and 8 has binding time S, so the entire expression has binding time $D + S$ which is D.

In Scheme0, every expression having a dynamic subexpression is itself dynamic, so all abstract operators are very simple: the abstract value of an expression is the least upper bound of the abstract values of all subexpressions. In particular, the abstract evaluation of a function application (f e) does not use any abstraction of f, only the binding time of e. Although the analysis is very simple, it gives reasonably good results because Scheme0 is a first-order language and has no partially static structures: a value is either fully static or dynamic. Thus if e is dynamic, then (f e) will be dynamic (unless the function f always ignores its argument). The set $BindingTime = \{S, D\}$ of abstract values form the simple lattice

Another particular feature of the Scheme0 binding-time analysis is that the abstract values do not represent the values used in standard evaluation, but the 'values' used during partial evaluation.

For a rough formalization of this, let Scheme0Val denote the set of (first-order) values used during an ordinary Scheme0 computation: numbers such as 1, symbols such as a, pairs such as (1 . a), lists such as (a b), and so on. Let SchemeExpr denote the set of (Scheme0) expressions: numerals such as 1, constant expressions such as (quote a) and (quote (1 . a)), expressions, and so on. Further assume that the two sets are disjoint, so we can distinguish their elements. Then the set of values used during partial evaluation is

$$\text{PEValue0} \quad = \quad \text{Scheme0Val} \cup \text{SchemeExpr}$$

The binding time S describes an expression which must evaluate to an ordinary value, and D describes an expression which may reduce to a residual expression or an ordinary value. That is, S represents values in Scheme0Val and D represents all specialization-time values, including residual expressions. Thus the abstraction and concretization maps are

$$\gamma\colon \text{BindingTime} \to \wp(\text{PEValue0})$$
$$\gamma(S) \quad = \quad \text{Scheme0Val}$$
$$\gamma(D) \quad = \quad \text{PEValue0}$$

$$\alpha\colon \wp(\text{PEValue0}) \to \text{BindingTime}$$
$$\alpha(V) \quad = \quad S \qquad\qquad \text{if } V \cap \text{SchemeExpr} = \{\}$$
$$\qquad\quad = \quad D \qquad\qquad \text{if } V \cap \text{SchemeExpr} \neq \{\}$$

These functions satisfy the three requirements in Section 15.1.3 above. Namely, (1) they are monotonic, and (2) $\alpha(\gamma(S)) = \alpha(\text{Scheme0Val}) = S$ and $\alpha(\gamma(D)) = \alpha(\text{PEValue0}) = D$. Requirement (3) is proved similarly.

15.2   Closure analysis

In a first-order language it is always clear which function is applied in an application such as (f e). In a higher-order language this is not the case. What function is applied in an application $(e_1\ e_2)$ is determined only when e_1 is evaluated.

The purpose of a *closure analysis* is to compute this information without actually executing the program. That is, a closure analysis computes an approximation to the set of functions that e_1 may evaluate to [247].

First we present the components of the closure analysis, then we see how it can be seen as an abstract interpretation.

15.2.1 The higher-order language Scheme1

We describe a closure analysis for the higher-order functional language Scheme1 used in Chapter 10. Recall that a Scheme1 program pgm has the form:

```
(define (f₁ x₁₁ ... x₁ₐ₁)  body₁)
        ⋮
(define (fₙ xₙ₁ ... xₙₐₙ) bodyₙ)
```

Each function body body$_i$ is a Scheme1 expression. The syntax of expressions is shown in Figure 10.1 on page 206. All lambda abstractions and the corresponding lambda-bound variables are *labelled* by a superscript ℓ. For brevity we say 'lambda' instead of 'lambda abstraction', and write $(\lambda x^\ell . e)$ instead of $(\text{lambda}^\ell \ (x) \ e)$ in this chapter.

We distinguish three kinds of variables: *function variables* x_{ij}, *lambda variables* x^ℓ, and let variables x. A function variable x_{ij} is a formal parameter of a named function, a lambda variable x^ℓ is bound by a lambda abstraction, and a let variable is bound in a let expression. All variable names must be distinct. The arguments and results of the goal function and of base functions must be base values.

15.2.2 Closure analysis functions

Assume that a Scheme1 program pgm, of the form shown above, is given. We want to know which lambdas can be applied in an application $(e_1 \ e_2)$. Therefore we need to know which lambdas e_1 can evaluate to. An important step in that direction is to find the set of lambdas that variables and applications can evaluate to. The closure analysis is based on two maps ϕ and ρ giving these two kinds of information, where we identify a lambda expression $\lambda x^\ell . e$ with its *label* ℓ. Formally, let

$$
\begin{array}{rcll}
y & \in & \text{Var} & = \ \{ \text{ variables in pgm } \} \\
\ell & \in & \text{Label} & = \ \{ \text{ labels in pgm } \} \\
L & \in & \text{LabelSet} & = \ \wp(\text{Label}) \\
 & & \text{Names} & = \ \{f_1, \ldots, f_n\} \cup \text{Label} \\
\phi & \in & \text{ResEnv} & = \ \text{Names} \rightarrow \text{LabelSet} \\
\rho & \in & \text{VarEnv} & = \ \text{Var} \rightarrow \text{LabelSet}
\end{array}
$$

The intended meanings of ϕ and ρ are

$\phi\mathtt{f}_i$ = the set of lambdas that the body $\mathtt{body}_i$ of $\mathtt{f}_i$ can evaluate to.

$\phi\ell$ = the set of lambdas that the body $\mathtt{e}$ of $\lambda\mathtt{x}^\ell.\mathtt{e}$ can evaluate to.

$\rho\mathtt{x}_{ij}$ = the set of lambdas that function variable $\mathtt{x}_{ij}$ can get bound to.

$\rho\mathtt{x}^\ell$ = the set of lambdas that lambda variable $\mathtt{x}^\ell$ can get bound to.

$\rho\mathtt{x}$ = the set of lambdas that $\mathtt{let}$ variable $\mathtt{x}$ can get bound to.

As before, we must satisfy ourselves with *approximate* information, so we actually just require that the set $\phi\mathtt{f}_i$ *contains* all the lambdas that $\mathtt{e}_i$ can evaluate to, and similarly for the ρ. Thus the *safety requirement* is: closure analysis of expression $\mathtt{e}_1$ must tell us at least all lambdas that $\mathtt{e}_1$ can evaluate to (and possibly some more). Note that by the restrictions the goal function, $\phi\mathtt{f}_1 = \{\}$ and $\rho\mathtt{f}_1 = \{\}$.

In the analysis, the label ℓ abstracts the set of all the closures that can be built (at run time) from the expression $\lambda\mathtt{x}^\ell.\mathtt{e}$.

Example 15.1 Consider the following program (the superscript ℓ is a lambda label):

```
(define (f x n) ((λk^{ℓ₁}.k x) (if (even n) (λy^{ℓ₂}.y*y) (λz^{ℓ₃}.2*z))))
```

We have $\rho\mathtt{k} = \{\ell_2, \ell_3\}$ since the expression $(\mathtt{if} \ \ldots)$ can evaluate to $\lambda\mathtt{y}^{\ell_2}.\mathtt{y}*\mathtt{y}$ as well as $\lambda\mathtt{z}^{\ell_3}.\mathtt{2}*\mathtt{z}$. Also, $\rho\mathtt{v} = \{\}$ for all other variables $\mathtt{v}$, $\phi\mathtt{f} = \{\}$, and $\phi\ell = \{\}$ for all labels ℓ.

Now consider the equivalent but more complicated program:

```
(define (f x n)    (g ((λx1^{ℓ₁}.λk^{ℓ₂}.k x1) x)
                       (h (even n) (λx3^{ℓ₃}.x3*x3) (λx4^{ℓ₄}.2*x4))))
(define (g k1 z)   (k1 z))
(define (h b c a)  (if b c a))
```

Here we have $\rho\mathtt{k1} = \phi\ell_1 = \{\ell_2\}$, $\rho\mathtt{z} = \phi\mathtt{h} = \{\ell_3, \ell_4\}$, $\rho\mathtt{c} = \{\ell_3\}$, $\rho\mathtt{a} = \{\ell_4\}$, $\rho\mathtt{v} = \{\}$ for all other variables $\mathtt{v}$, $\phi\ell = \{\}$ for all other labels ℓ, and $\phi\mathtt{f} = \phi\mathtt{g} = \{\}$. $\square$

To compute ϕ and ρ in general, we define two analysis functions $\mathcal{P}_e$ and $\mathcal{P}_v$, where $\mathcal{P}_e$ is called the *closure analysis function* and $\mathcal{P}_v$ is called the *closure propagation function*. The closure analysis function $\mathcal{P}_e$ is defined in Figure 15.1.

The intention is that $\mathcal{P}_e[\![\mathtt{e}]\!]\phi\rho$ is (a superset of) the set of lambdas that $\mathtt{e}$ may evaluate to. The variable environment ρ is defined using the analysis function $\mathcal{P}_v$, to be shown shortly.

The equations defining $\mathcal{P}_e$ in Figure 15.1 are justified as follows. A constant can evaluate to no lambda. A variable $\mathtt{x}$ can evaluate only to those lambdas it can be bound to, that is, $(\rho \ \mathtt{x})$. A conditional can evaluate only to those lambdas that the two branches can evaluate to. An application of a named function $\mathtt{f}_i$ can evaluate to those lambdas that the function's body can evaluate to, that is, $(\phi\mathtt{f}_i)$. A base function must return a base value and so cannot evaluate to a lambda. The lambda expression labelled ℓ can evaluate only to itself. The application $(\mathtt{e}_1 \ \mathtt{e}_2)$ can evaluate to those lambdas which an application of lambda ℓ can, when $\lambda\mathtt{x}^\ell.\ldots$ is a possible value of $\mathtt{e}_1$. A let expression can evaluate to those lambdas that its body can evaluate to.

$$
\begin{aligned}
\mathcal{P}_e[\![c]\!]\phi\rho &= \{\} \\
\mathcal{P}_e[\![x]\!]\phi\rho &= \rho\ \mathtt{x} \\
\mathcal{P}_e[\![\texttt{if } e_1\ e_2\ e_3]\!]\phi\rho &= \mathcal{P}_e[\![e_2]\!]\phi\rho \cup \mathcal{P}_e[\![e_3]\!]\phi\rho \\
\mathcal{P}_e[\![(\texttt{call } f_i\ e_1\ \dots\ e_a)]\!]\phi\rho &= \phi f_i \\
\mathcal{P}_e[\![(\texttt{op } e_1\ \dots\ e_a)]\!]\phi\rho &= \{\} \\
\mathcal{P}_e[\![(\lambda \mathtt{x}^\ell.e)]\!]\phi\rho &= \{\ \ell\ \} \\
\mathcal{P}_e[\![(e_1\ e_2)]\!]\phi\rho &= \bigcup\{\ \phi\ \ell \mid \ell \in \mathcal{P}_e[\![e_1]\!]\phi\rho\ \} \\
\mathcal{P}_e[\![(\texttt{let } (\mathtt{x}\ e_1)\ e)]\!]\phi\rho &= \mathcal{P}_e[\![e]\!]\phi\rho
\end{aligned}
$$

Figure 15.1: The closure analysis function $\mathcal{P}_e$.

The closure propagation function $\mathcal{P}_v$ is shown in Figure 15.2. The application $\mathcal{P}_v[\![e]\!]\phi\rho\mathtt{y}$ is (a superset of) the set of lambdas that variable $\mathtt{y}$ can be bound to in an evaluation of e. If $\mathtt{y}$ is a function variable $\mathtt{x}_{ij}$, it can be bound to a lambda only in an application of function f_i. Similarly, if $\mathtt{y}$ is a lambda variable $\mathtt{x}^\ell$, it can be bound to a lambda only in an application of the lambda expression $\lambda \mathtt{x}^\ell\dots$ labelled ℓ. If $\mathtt{y}$ is a let variable, it can get bound only in the corresponding let.

$$
\begin{aligned}
\mathcal{P}_v[\![c]\!]\phi\rho\mathtt{y} &= \{\} \\
\mathcal{P}_v[\![x]\!]\phi\rho\mathtt{y} &= \{\} \\
\mathcal{P}_v[\![\texttt{if } e_1\ e_2\ e_3]\!]\phi\rho\mathtt{y} &= \mathcal{P}_v[\![e_1]\!]\phi\rho\mathtt{y} \cup \mathcal{P}_v[\![e_2]\!]\phi\rho\mathtt{y} \cup \mathcal{P}_v[\![e_3]\!]\phi\rho\mathtt{y} \\
\mathcal{P}_v[\![(\texttt{call } f_i\ e_1\ \dots\ e_a)]\!]\phi\rho\mathtt{y} &= L \cup \mathcal{P}_e[\![e_j]\!]\phi\rho \text{ if } \mathtt{y} \text{ is } \mathtt{x}_{ij} \\
&= L \qquad\qquad\quad \text{otherwise} \\
& \text{where } L = \bigcup_{j=1}^a \mathcal{P}_v[\![e_j]\!]\phi\rho\mathtt{y} \\
\mathcal{P}_v[\![(\texttt{op } e_1\ \dots\ e_a)]\!]\phi\rho\mathtt{y} &= \bigcup_{j=1}^a \mathcal{P}_v[\![e_j]\!]\phi\rho\mathtt{y} \\
\mathcal{P}_v[\![(\lambda \mathtt{x}^\ell.e)]\!]\phi\rho\mathtt{y} &= \mathcal{P}_v[\![e]\!]\phi\rho\mathtt{y} \\
\mathcal{P}_v[\![(e_1\ e_2)]\!]\phi\rho\mathtt{y} &= L \cup \mathcal{P}_e[\![e_2]\!]\phi\rho \text{ if } \mathtt{y} \text{ is } \mathtt{x}^\ell \text{ and } \ell \in \mathcal{P}_e[\![e_1]\!]\phi\rho \\
&= L \qquad\qquad\quad \text{otherwise} \\
& \text{where } L = \mathcal{P}_v[\![e_1]\!]\phi\rho\mathtt{y} \cup \mathcal{P}_v[\![e_2]\!]\phi\rho\mathtt{y} \\
\mathcal{P}_v[\![(\texttt{let } (\mathtt{x}\ e_1)\ e)]\!]\phi\rho\mathtt{y} &= L \cup \mathcal{P}_e[\![e_1]\!]\phi\rho \text{ if } \mathtt{y} \text{ is } \mathtt{x} \\
&= L \qquad\qquad\quad \text{otherwise} \\
& \text{where } L = \mathcal{P}_v[\![e_1]\!]\phi\rho\mathtt{y} \cup \mathcal{P}_v[\![e]\!]\phi\rho\mathtt{y}
\end{aligned}
$$

Figure 15.2: The closure propagation function $\mathcal{P}_v$.

The equations defining function $\mathcal{P}_v$ in Figure 15.2 are therefore justified as follows. Evaluating a constant or a variable cannot bind variable $\mathtt{y}$. Evaluating a conditional can do those bindings that any of the three subexpressions can do. Applying a named function f_i binds $\mathtt{y}$ if it is one of the parameters $\mathtt{x}_{ij}$ of f_i. In this case, y can get bound to whatever lambdas the argument e_j can evaluate to. Moreover, y can get bound by evaluating any of the argument expressions. In a lambda abstraction, y can get bound in the body e. A lambda application (e_1 e_2) binds y if it is a lambda variable x^ℓ and e_1 can evaluate to the lambda labelled ℓ. In this case, y can get bound to whatever lambdas the argument e_2 can evaluate to. Finally, a let expression binds y if y is the same as the variable x being bound.

15.2.3 Closure analysis of a program

Closure analysis of a program should produce a safe description (ϕ,ρ) which is as precise as possible. The description is obtained as the least solution to a set of equations specifying the safety requirement.

As described above, ϕ should map a named function f_i to the set of lambdas that its body can evaluate to, that is, $\mathcal{P}_e[\![\text{body}_i]\!]\phi\rho$. Similarly, it should map a lambda label ℓ to the set of lambdas that the body e of $\lambda x^\ell.e$ can evaluate to, that is, $\mathcal{P}_e[\![e]\!]\phi\rho$.

The map ρ should map a function variable x to the set of lambdas that it can be bound to, that is, the union of $\mathcal{P}_v[\![\text{body}_i]\!]\phi\rho x$ over all function bodies body_i. Similarly, ρ should map a lambda variable x^ℓ to the set of lambdas it can be bound to, that is, the union of $\mathcal{P}_v[\![\text{body}_i]\!]\phi\rho x^\ell$ over all function bodies body_i; and likewise for the let-variables.

These requirements are summarized by the equations below:

$$
\begin{aligned}
\phi f_i &= \mathcal{P}_e[\![\text{body}_i]\!]\phi\rho \\
\phi\ell &= \mathcal{P}_e[\![e]\!]\phi\rho && \text{where e is the body of } \lambda x^\ell.e \\
\rho x &= \textstyle\bigcup_{i=1}^{n} \mathcal{P}_v[\![\text{body}_i]\!]\phi\rho x && \text{for every function variable x} \\
\rho x^\ell &= \textstyle\bigcup_{i=1}^{n} \mathcal{P}_v[\![\text{body}_i]\!]\phi\rho x^\ell && \text{for every lambda variable } x^\ell \\
\rho x &= \textstyle\bigcup_{i=1}^{n} \mathcal{P}_v[\![\text{body}_i]\!]\phi\rho x && \text{for every let-variable x}
\end{aligned}
$$

Any solution to these equations is a safe analysis result. The least solution is the most precise, safe solution.

15.2.4 Closure analysis as an abstract interpretation

The closure analysis as described above can be understood as an abstract interpretation. An abstract value $L \in \text{LabelSet}$ is a set of labels. The abstract values are ordered by inclusion: L_1 is smaller than L_2 if and only if $L_1 \subseteq L_2$. This makes LabelSet a lattice and is very reasonable, intuitively: a smaller lambda label set is more informative, since it says: *only* these lambdas are possible.

Abstract interpretation of a program produces a description $(\phi,\rho) \in \text{ResEnv} \times \text{VarEnv}$. Recall that ResEnv and VarEnv are mappings (from function and variable names) to label sets, so the set ResEnv $\times$ VarEnv of descriptions can be ordered by pointwise inclusion, which makes it a lattice.

To roughly formalize the abstraction and concretization functions, we must define the set Scheme1Val of values that can appear in an *ordinary* Scheme1 evaluation. This is the set of (first-order) Scheme0 values, extended with closure objects:

Scheme1Val = Scheme0Val $\cup$ Closure

Closure = { (closure ℓ vv) | $\ell \in$ Label, vv $\in$ Scheme1Val* }

With this definition, the abstraction and concretization functions are

γ: LabelSet $\rightarrow$ $\wp$(Scheme1Val)

$\gamma(\{\ell\})$ = { (closure ℓ vv) | vv $\in$ Scheme1Val* }
$\cup$ Scheme0Val

$\gamma(\bigcup_i L_i)$ = $\bigcup_i \gamma(L_i)$

α: $\wp$(Scheme1Val) $\rightarrow$ LabelSet

$\alpha(\{v\})$ = {}   when v $\in$ Scheme0Val

$\alpha(\{(\text{closure } \ell \text{ vv})\})$ = $\{\ell\}$

$\alpha(\bigcup_i C_i)$ = $\bigcup_i \alpha(C_i)$

It is clear that γ and α are monotonic, and not hard to see that they also satisfy requirements (2) and (3) on abstraction and concretization functions.

15.3   Higher-order binding-time analysis

Using the closure analysis, the first-order Scheme0 binding-time analysis from Section 5.2 can be extended to a higher-order binding-time analysis for Scheme1. This gives a monovariant binding-time analysis without partially static structures.

In Section 10.1.4 we discussed three problems with binding-time analysis for Scheme1. Problem (1) is the handling of lambda applications (e$_1$ e$_2$). To solve this we use the closure analysis from Section 15.2 and let $\mathcal{P}_e[\![e_1]\!]$, simply, stand for the set of lambdas that e$_1$ may evaluate to.

Problem (2) is the detection of lambdas in dynamic contexts. If a lambda λx^ℓ. e may appear in a dynamic context, then code must be generated for the lambda, so x^ℓ must be dynamic and its body e is in a dynamic context. To detect lambdas in dynamic contexts we introduce a new map δ and a new analysis function $\mathcal{B}_d$ (in addition to the maps ψ and τ and functions $\mathcal{B}_e$ and $\mathcal{B}_v$ known from the Scheme0 binding-time analysis).

Problem (3) is the binding-time analysis of let. In this presentation we use the conservative rule suggested in Section 10.1.4. This is unavoidable if the specializer does not use continuation-based reduction (Section 10.5). If the specializer uses continuation-based reduction, then we might use instead the more liberal rule in Section 10.5.5.

15.3.1   Binding-time analysis maps

As in the Scheme0 binding-time analysis, the binding-time domain is BindingTime $= \{S, D\}$ with $S < D$. The analysis uses three maps ψ, τ, and δ, whose intended meanings are

$$
\begin{aligned}
\psi\mathbf{f}_i &= \text{the binding time of the body of } \mathbf{f}_i \\
\psi\mathbf{x}^\ell &= \text{the binding time of the body } \mathbf{e} \text{ of } \lambda\mathbf{x}^\ell.\mathbf{e} \\[4pt]
\tau\mathbf{x}_{ij} &= \text{the binding time of function variable } \mathbf{x}_{ij} \\
\tau\mathbf{x}^\ell &= \text{the binding time of lambda } \mathbf{x}^\ell \\
\tau\mathbf{x} &= \text{the binding time of } \mathtt{let}\text{-variable } \mathbf{x} \\[4pt]
\delta\ell &= D \text{ if } \lambda\mathbf{x}^\ell.\mathbf{e} \text{ needs to be lifted, } S \text{ otherwise}
\end{aligned}
$$

Thus ψ maps a lambda to the binding time of the result of applying it, and τ is a *binding-time environment* that maps a variable (whether bound by a named function, a lambda, or a $\mathtt{let}$), to its binding time. The use of these maps is similar to that of ϕ and ρ in the closure analysis above. The map δ is used to record the lambdas that may appear in dynamic contexts.

15.3.2   Binding-time analysis functions

The analysis consists of a binding-time analysis function $\mathcal{B}_e$ and a binding-time propagation function $\mathcal{B}_v$, akin to the functions $\mathcal{B}_e$ and $\mathcal{B}_v$ in the Scheme0 binding-time analysis. In addition, there is a context propagation function $\mathcal{B}_d$ for detection of lambdas in dynamic contexts.

An application $\mathcal{B}_e[\![\mathbf{e}]\!]\psi\tau\delta$ of the $\mathcal{B}_e$ function finds the binding time of expression $\mathbf{e}$ in binding-time environment τ. The $\mathcal{B}_e$ function is defined in Figure 15.3. Equations one, two, three and five are explained as for Scheme0. Equation four (function call) states that the result of a function call is dynamic if the called function's body is. The binding time can no longer be determined from the arguments, since a static argument may be a partially static lambda containing free dynamic variables. Equation six states that a lambda expression is dynamic if it may appear in a dynamic context, and static otherwise. Equation seven says that the binding time of a higher-order application $(\mathbf{e}_1\ \mathbf{e}_2)$ is dynamic if $\mathbf{e}_1$ is, or if any lambda that $\mathbf{e}_1$ can evaluate to gives a dynamic result when applied. Equation eight says that the binding time of a $\mathtt{let}$ expression is dynamic if the bound expression $\mathbf{e}_1$ or the body $\mathbf{e}$ is.

An application $\mathcal{B}_v[\![\mathbf{e}]\!]\psi\tau\delta\mathbf{y}$ finds the binding time of the values assigned to variable $\mathbf{y}$ during evaluation of expression $\mathbf{e}$, where $\mathbf{y}$ may be a function variable $\mathbf{x}_{ij}$, a lambda variable $\mathbf{x}^\ell$, or a $\mathtt{let}$ variable $\mathbf{x}$. The $\mathcal{B}_v$ function is defined in Figure 15.4 and is very similar in structure and purpose to function $\mathcal{P}_v$ in the closure analysis.

An application $\mathcal{B}_{dd}[\![\mathbf{e}]\!]\psi\tau\delta\ell t$ returns the context (S or D) of lambda $\lambda\mathbf{x}^\ell.\ldots$.

$$
\begin{aligned}
\mathcal{B}_e[\![\mathtt{c}]\!]\psi\tau\delta &= S \\
\mathcal{B}_e[\![\mathtt{x}]\!]\psi\tau\delta &= \tau\mathtt{x} \\
\mathcal{B}_e[\![\mathtt{if}\ e_1\ e_2\ e_3]\!]\psi\tau\delta &= \mathcal{B}_e[\![e_1]\!]\psi\tau\delta \sqcup \mathcal{B}_e[\![e_2]\!]\psi\tau\delta \sqcup \mathcal{B}_e[\![e_3]\!]\psi\tau\delta \\
\mathcal{B}_e[\![(\mathtt{call}\ f_i\ e_1\ \ldots\ e_a)]\!]\psi\tau\delta &= \psi f_i \\
\mathcal{B}_e[\![(\mathtt{op}\ e_1\ \ldots\ e_a)]\!]\psi\tau\delta &= \bigsqcup_{j=1}^{a} \mathcal{B}_e[\![e_j]\!]\psi\tau\delta \\
\mathcal{B}_e[\![(\lambda\mathtt{x}^\ell.e)]\!]\psi\tau\delta &= \delta\ell \\
\mathcal{B}_e[\![(e_1\ e_2)]\!]\psi\tau\delta &= \mathcal{B}_e[\![e_1]\!]\psi\tau\delta \sqcup (\bigsqcup\{\ \psi\ell\ |\ \ell \in \mathcal{P}_e[\![e_1]\!]\ \}) \\
\mathcal{B}_e[\![(\mathtt{let}\ (\mathtt{x}\ e_1)\ e)]\!]\psi\tau\delta &= \mathcal{B}_e[\![e_1]\!]\psi\tau\delta \sqcup \mathcal{B}_e[\![e]\!]\psi\tau\delta
\end{aligned}
$$

Figure 15.3: The Scheme1 binding-time analysis function $\mathcal{B}_e$.

$$
\begin{aligned}
\mathcal{B}_v[\![\mathtt{c}]\!]\psi\tau\delta\mathtt{y} &= S \\
\mathcal{B}_v[\![\mathtt{x}]\!]\psi\tau\delta\mathtt{y} &= S \\
\mathcal{B}_v[\![\mathtt{if}\ e_1\ e_2\ e_3]\!]\psi\tau\delta\mathtt{y} &= \mathcal{B}_v[\![e_1]\!]\psi\tau\delta\mathtt{y} \sqcup \mathcal{B}_v[\![e_2]\!]\psi\tau\delta\mathtt{y} \sqcup \mathcal{B}_v[\![e_3]\!]\psi\tau\delta\mathtt{y} \\
\mathcal{B}_v[\![(\mathtt{call}\ f_i\ e_1\ \ldots\ e_a)]\!]\psi\tau\delta\mathtt{y} &= t \sqcup \mathcal{B}_e[\![e_j]\!]\psi\tau\delta\ \text{if y is } \mathtt{x}_{ij} \\
&= t\ \qquad\qquad \text{otherwise} \\
&\quad \text{where } t = \bigsqcup_{j=1}^{a} \mathcal{B}_v[\![e_j]\!]\psi\tau\delta\mathtt{y} \\
\mathcal{B}_v[\![(\mathtt{op}\ e_1\ \ldots\ e_a)]\!]\psi\tau\delta\mathtt{y} &= \bigsqcup_{j=1}^{a} \mathcal{B}_v[\![e_j]\!]\psi\tau\delta\mathtt{y} \\
\mathcal{B}_v[\![(\lambda\mathtt{x}^\ell.e)]\!]\psi\tau\delta\mathtt{y} &= \mathcal{B}_v[\![e]\!]\psi\tau\delta\mathtt{y} \\
\mathcal{B}_v[\![(e_1\ e_2)]\!]\psi\tau\delta\mathtt{y} &= t \sqcup \mathcal{B}_e[\![e_2]\!]\psi\tau\delta\ \text{if y is } \mathtt{x}^\ell \text{ and } \ell \in \mathcal{P}_e[\![e_1]\!] \\
&= t\ \qquad\qquad \text{otherwise} \\
&\quad \text{where } t = \mathcal{B}_v[\![e_1]\!]\psi\tau\delta\mathtt{y} \sqcup \mathcal{B}_v[\![e_2]\!]\psi\tau\delta\mathtt{y} \\
\mathcal{B}_v[\![(\mathtt{let}\ (\mathtt{x}\ e_1)\ e)]\!]\psi\tau\delta\mathtt{y} &= t \sqcup \mathcal{B}_e[\![e_1]\!]\psi\tau\delta\ \text{if y is x} \\
&= t\ \qquad\qquad \text{otherwise} \\
&\quad \text{where } t = \mathcal{B}_v[\![e_1]\!]\psi\tau\delta\mathtt{y} \sqcup \mathcal{B}_v[\![e_2]\!]\psi\tau\delta\mathtt{y}
\end{aligned}
$$

Figure 15.4: The Scheme1 binding-time propagation function $\mathcal{B}_v$.

in e, where t is the context of e. An application $\mathcal{B}_d[\![e]\!]\psi\tau\delta\ell$ returns the context (S or D) of lambda $\lambda\mathtt{x}^\ell\ldots$ in e, where e is in a static context, so $\mathcal{B}_d[\![e]\!]\psi\tau\delta\ell = \mathcal{B}_{dd}[\![e]\!]\psi\tau\delta\ell S$.

Except for the complications due to lifting of lambda abstractions (see Section 10.1.4), the binding-time analysis functions $\mathcal{B}_e$ and $\mathcal{B}_v$ for Scheme1 are rather similar to those for Scheme0. Also, the results of the closure analysis $\mathcal{P}_e[\![e]\!]$ are used only in the higher-order applications $(e_1\ e_2)$. Closure analysis gives a very simple, essentially first-order, extension of analyses to higher-order languages. This approach works reasonably well for monovariant binding-time analysis, as in Similix, but may be very imprecise for other program analyses.

$$
\begin{array}{lll}
\mathcal{B}_d[\![\mathtt{c}]\!]\psi\tau\delta\ell & = S \\
\mathcal{B}_d[\![\mathtt{x}]\!]\psi\tau\delta\ell & = S \\
\mathcal{B}_d[\![\mathtt{if}\ e_1\ e_2\ e_3]\!]\psi\tau\delta\ell & = \mathcal{B}_d[\![e_1]\!]\psi\tau\delta\ell \sqcup \mathcal{B}_d[\![e_2]\!]\psi\tau\delta\ell \sqcup \mathcal{B}_d[\![e_3]\!]\psi\tau\delta\ell \\
\mathcal{B}_d[\![(\mathtt{call}\ f_i\ e_1\ \ldots\ e_a)]\!]\psi\tau\delta\ell & = \bigsqcup_{j=1}^{a} \mathcal{B}_{dd}[\![e_j]\!]\psi\tau\delta\ell(\tau\mathtt{x}_{ij}) \\
\mathcal{B}_d[\![(\mathtt{op}\ e_1\ \ldots\ e_a)]\!]\psi\tau\delta\ell & = \bigsqcup_{j=1}^{a} \mathcal{B}_d[\![e_j]\!]\psi\tau\delta\ell \\
\mathcal{B}_d[\![(\lambda\mathtt{x}^{\ell'}.e)]\!]\psi\tau\delta\ell & = \mathcal{B}_{dd}[\![e]\!]\psi\tau\delta\ell(\delta\ell') \\
\mathcal{B}_d[\![(e_1\ e_2)]\!]\psi\tau\delta\ell & = \mathcal{B}_{dd}[\![e_1]\!]\psi\tau\delta\ell(\mathcal{B}_e[\![e_1]\!]\psi\tau\delta) \sqcup \mathcal{B}_{dd}[\![e_2]\!]\psi\tau\delta\ell t \\
& \quad\text{where } t = \bigsqcup\{\tau\mathtt{x}^\ell | \ell \in \mathcal{P}_e[\![e_1]\!]\} \\
\mathcal{B}_d[\![(\mathtt{let}\ (\mathtt{x}\ e_1)\ e)]\!]\psi\tau\delta\ell & = \mathcal{B}_{dd}[\![e_1]\!]\psi\tau\delta\ell(\tau\mathtt{x}) \sqcup \mathcal{B}_d[\![e_2]\!]\psi\tau\delta\ell \\
\\
\mathcal{B}_{dd}[\![e]\!]\psi\tau\delta\ell t & = D & \text{if } t = D \text{ and } \ell \in \mathcal{P}_e[\![e]\!] \\
& = \mathcal{B}_d[\![e]\!]\psi\tau\delta\ell & \text{otherwise}
\end{array}
$$

Figure 15.5: The Scheme1 dynamic context function $\mathcal{B}_d$.

15.3.3   Comparison with the real Similix

The present binding-time lattice is $\{S, D\}$ with S as least element. The binding-time lattice used in Similix is $\{\bot, S, Cl, D\}$, which distinguishes static first-order values from static closure values [27, Section 5.7]. The new bottom element $\bot$, which describes non-terminating expressions, is needed because the elements S and Cl are incomparable.

However, Cl plays the role of a type rather than a binding time in Similix. It allows the specializer to distinguish static closures from other static data without using type tags during specialization. Thus the distinction between S and Cl is not important for pure binding-time reasons and has been left out here. Indeed, in a binding-time analysis for Similix developed recently, the type and binding-time aspects have been separated into two different analyses.

15.3.4   Binding-time analysis of a Scheme1 program

Binding-time analysis of a program should produce a safe description (ψ, τ, δ) which is as precise as possible. This is obtained as the least solution to a set of equations specifying the safety requirement.

First, ψ must map a lambda label ℓ to the binding time $\mathcal{B}_e[\![e]\!]\psi\tau$ of the body of $\lambda\mathtt{x}^\ell.e$.

Secondly, τ should map a function variable $\mathtt{x}$ to its binding time, that is, the least upper bound (lub) of the binding times of the values that it can be bound to. But this is the lub of $\mathcal{B}_v[\![e]\!]\psi\tau\delta\mathtt{x}$ over all function bodies $\mathbf{body}_i$ in the program. Also, τ should map a lambda variable $\mathtt{x}^\ell$ to its binding time, that is, the lub of

$\mathcal{B}_v[\![\text{body}_i]\!]\psi\tau\delta\mathbf{x}^\ell$ over all function bodies body_i. Third, δ should map a lambda label ℓ to D if the lambda $\lambda\mathbf{x}^\ell.\mathbf{e}$ is in a dynamic context, that is, the lub of $\mathcal{B}_d[\![\text{body}_i]\!]\psi\tau\delta\ell$ over all function bodies body_i in the program.

These requirements are embodied in the equations below:

$$\psi\mathbf{f}_i = \mathcal{B}_e[\![\text{body}_i]\!]\psi\tau\delta \qquad \text{where } \text{body}_i \text{ is the body of } \mathbf{f}_i$$
$$\psi\ell = \mathcal{B}_e[\![\mathbf{e}]\!]\psi\tau\delta \qquad \text{where } \mathbf{e} \text{ is the body of } \lambda\mathbf{x}^\ell.\mathbf{e}$$

$$\tau\mathbf{x} = \bigsqcup_{i=1}^n \mathcal{B}_v[\![\text{body}_i]\!]\psi\tau\delta\mathbf{x} \qquad \text{for every function variable } \mathbf{x}$$
$$\tau\mathbf{x}^\ell = \delta\ell \sqcup (\bigsqcup_{i=1}^n \mathcal{B}_v[\![\text{body}_i]\!]\psi\tau\delta\mathbf{x}^\ell) \qquad \text{for every lambda variable } \mathbf{x}^\ell$$
$$\tau\mathbf{x} = \bigsqcup_{i=1}^n \mathcal{B}_v[\![\text{body}_i]\!]\psi\tau\delta\mathbf{x} \qquad \text{for every } \texttt{let}\text{-variable } \mathbf{x}$$

$$\delta\ell = \bigsqcup_{i=1}^n \mathcal{B}_d[\![\text{body}_i]\!]\psi\tau\delta\ell$$

Note that if lambda ℓ is dynamic ($\delta\ell = D$), then so is its variable $\mathbf{x}^\ell$ (that is $\tau\mathbf{x}^\ell = D$), by virtue of the second τ equation.

Any solution to these simultaneous equations is a safe analysis result. The least solution is the most precise one.

15.4 Projections and partially static data

In the binding-time analyses shown so far, only functional values have been partially static, whereas first-order values have been considered either completely static, or else dynamic. However, as outlined in Section 10.6, it is possible to allow *partially* static first-order data structures also.

For instance, a value may be a pair whose first component is static and whose second component is dynamic. Another typical case is an association list used to represent the environment in an interpreter. This is a list of (name, value)-pairs, each with static left component and dynamic right component.

Below we explain a projection-based approach to binding-time analysis of partially static data structures in strongly typed languages. The method is due to Launchbury, and this description is based on his thesis and book [167]. Essentially we shall *exemplify* Launchbury's approach, and for simplicity our rendering will be less precise than his.

15.4.1 Static projections

Let X be a domain of values, equipped with an ordering $\sqsubseteq$ and a least element $\bot$ (meaning 'undefined' or 'not available'). A *projection* γ on X is a function $\gamma : X \to X$ such that for $x, y \in X$ the following three conditions are satisfied: (1) $\gamma x \sqsubseteq x$, (2) $\gamma(\gamma x) = \gamma x$, and (3) $x \sqsubseteq y$ implies $(\gamma x) \sqsubseteq (\gamma y)$.

If we read $y \sqsubseteq x$ as 'y is a part of x' (where $\bot$ is the 'empty' or 'void' part), then requirement (1) says that γ maps a value x to a part of x.

Now think of γx as the *static part* of x. Then requirement (1) says that the static part of x must indeed be a part of x, requirement (2) says that the static part of the static part γx of x is precisely the static part of x, and requirement (3) says that when x is a part of y, then the static part of x is a part of the static part of y. These are all intuitively reasonable requirements.

In this case, we call γ a *static projection*: the projection picking out the static part of a value.

15.4.2   Projections on atomic type domains

First consider a type of atomic data, such as int or bool. If X is the domain of values of type int, then $X = \{\bot, 0, 1, -1, \ldots\}$. The ordering on X is very simple: $y \sqsubseteq x$ if and only if $y = \bot$ or $y = x$, so the static part y of an integer x must either be void or else x itself. This reflects the fact that integers are *atomic values*.

There are infinitely many projections on X. For instance, for each integer i, there is a projection which maps i to itself and everything else to $\bot$.

However, for binding-time analysis, only two projections on X are particularly useful: ABS and ID, where for all $x \in X$,

$$ABS\ x\ =\ \bot$$
$$ID\ x\ =\ x$$

The *absent* projection ABS says that no part of x is static, and the *identity* projection ID says that the whole of x is static. It is clear that ABS and ID are precisely the binding-times D and S from the Scheme0 binding-time analysis (Section 5.2).

It is conventional to define the ordering on projections pointwise, as for other functions. Thus $ABS \sqsubseteq ID$, which is just the *opposite* of the ordering $S < D$ on $\{S, D\}$, and also contrasts with the usual situation in abstract interpretation, where the smaller abstract values are the more informative. This difference is purely a formality, though. We just have to remember that a *larger* static projection is *better* (more informative) than a smaller one.

Usually, only a few of the projections on a domain, such as ABS and ID above, are useful for binding-time analysis. These 'useful' projections are here called the *admissible* static projections. We shall define the set of admissible static projections as we proceed, by induction on the structure of the types they work on (hence the requirement of strong typing).

We define: an admissible static projection on an atomic type domain is ABS or ID. Thus it corresponds to one of the binding times D and S previously used.

15.4.3   Projections on product type domains

The above example shows that projections can describe binding times of atomic values, but their real utility is with composite data, such as pairs, which can be partially static.

Consider a *product type*, such as `int * bool`. If X and Y are the value domains corresponding to `int` and `bool`, then the domain of values of type `int * bool` is

$$X \times Y = \{(x,y) | x \in X, y \in Y\}$$

A value v in product domain $X \times Y$ has form $v = (x, y)$, and the values are ordered componentwise, so $(\bot, \bot)$ is the least element. The following four projections on the domain are particularly useful:

$v =$	(x, y)
$\gamma_a(v) =$	$(\bot, \bot)$
$\gamma_b(v) =$	$(x, \bot)$
$\gamma_c(v) =$	$(\bot, y)$
$\gamma_d(v) =$	(x, y)

Projection γ_a says that none of the components is static; γ_b says that the left component is static; γ_c the right component; and γ_d that both are static. The four projections could be given the more telling names ABS, $LEFT$, $RIGHT$, and ID.

The static projections on $X \times Y$ can often be written as *products* of projections on X and Y. Namely, whenever γ_1 is a projection on X and γ_2 is a projection on Y, their product $\gamma_1 \times \gamma_2$ is a projection on $X \times Y$, defined by

$$(\gamma_1 \times \gamma_2)(x, y) = (\gamma_1\ x, \gamma_2\ y)$$

In particular, the four projections listed above are

$$\begin{aligned}
\gamma_a &= ABS \times ABS \\
\gamma_b &= ID \times ABS \\
\gamma_c &= ABS \times ID \\
\gamma_d &= ID \times ID
\end{aligned}$$

We define: an admissible static projection on a product type is the *product* of admissible projections on the components.

15.4.4 Projections on data type domains

Consider the non-recursive data type

```
datatype union = Int of int | Bl of bool
```

where `Int` and `Bl` are the *constructors* or *tags* of the data type. If X and Y are the value domains corresponding to types `int` and `bool`, then the value domain corresponding to `union` is the tagged sum domain

$$Int\ X + Bl\ Y = \{\bot\} \cup \{Int(x) | x \in X\} \cup \{Bl(y) | y \in Y\}$$

A value v of the sum domain either is $\bot$ or has one of the forms $v = Int(x)$ and $v = Bl(y)$. The new value $\bot$ is less than all others, two values of the same form are compared by the second component, and values of different forms are incomparable. There are five particularly useful projections on the sum domain:

$v =$	$\bot$	$Int(x)$	$Bl(y)$
$\gamma_a(v) =$	$\bot$	$\bot$	$\bot$
$\gamma_b(v) =$	$\bot$	$Int(\bot)$	$Bl(\bot)$
$\gamma_c(v) =$	$\bot$	$Int(x)$	$Bl(\bot)$
$\gamma_d(v) =$	$\bot$	$Int(\bot)$	$Bl(y)$
$\gamma_e(v) =$	$\bot$	$Int(x)$	$Bl(y)$

Projection γ_a says that no part of the value is static; γ_b says that the tags are static but nothing else is; γ_c says that the tags are static, and if the tag is Int, then the argument is static too; γ_d says the tags are static, and if the tag is Bl, then the argument is static; and γ_e says that the entire value is static. Thus γ_a and γ_e really are ABS and ID on the sum domain, and a suitable name for γ_b would be TAG.

Note that there exist other projections on the union type, for instance γ'_b with $\gamma'_b(Int(x)) = Int(\bot)$ and $\gamma'_b(Bl(y)) = \bot$. However, such projections are unlikely to be useful as binding times, since a specializer cannot easily exploit a static tag such as Int unless *all* tags are static.

Some of the projections on $Int\ X + Bl\ Y$ can be written as *sums* of projections in X and Y. Whenever γ_1 is a projection on X and γ_2 is a projection on Y, their tagged sum $Int\ \gamma_1 + Bl\ \gamma_2$ is a projection on $Int\ X + Bl\ Y$, defined by

$$
\begin{aligned}
(Int\ \gamma_1 + Bl\ \gamma_2)(\bot) &= \bot \\
(Int\ \gamma_1 + Bl\ \gamma_2)(Int(x)) &= Int\ (\gamma_1\ x) \\
(Int\ \gamma_1 + Bl\ \gamma_2)(Bl(y)) &= Bl\ (\gamma_2\ y)
\end{aligned}
$$

Projection γ_a above cannot be written as a sum of projections, but the other four can:

$$
\begin{aligned}
\gamma_a &= ABS \\
\gamma_b &= Int\ ABS + Bl\ ABS \\
\gamma_c &= Int\ ID + Bl\ ABS \\
\gamma_d &= Int\ ABS + Bl\ ID \\
\gamma_e &= Int\ ID + Bl\ ID
\end{aligned}
$$

We define: an admissible static projection on a data type is ABS, or the *sum* of admissible projections on the constructor argument types.

The sum of projections $\gamma_1, \ldots, \gamma_n$ over constructors $c_1, \ldots, c_n$ is written $\sum_{i=1}^{n} c_i \gamma_i$.

15.4.5 Projections on recursive data type domains

Consider the *recursive data type*

```
datatype intlist = Nil | Cons of (int * intlist)
```

defining the type of lists of integers. It is rather similar to the datatype definition in the preceding section, except for the recursion: the fact that `intlist` is used to define itself.

Writing instead `datatype intlist = `μ`T. Nil | Cons of (int * T)`, we can emphasize the recursion, using the recursion operator μ. If X is the value domain corresponding to `Int`, then the value domain corresponding to `intlist` is the recursively defined domain

$$\mu V.Nil + Cons\ (X \times V) = \bigcup_{k=0}^{\infty} F^k(\{\bot\})$$

where $F(V) = Nil + Cons\ (X \times V)$. That is, the values of this type are $\{\bot, Nil, Cons(\bot, \bot), Cons(1, \bot), Cons(1, Nil), Cons(1, Cons(2, Nil)), \ldots\}$, namely the finite and partial lists of values of type `int`.

There are three particularly useful projections on the recursively defined domain:

$v =$	$\bot$	Nil	$Cons(x, v')$
$\gamma_a(v) =$	$\bot$	$\bot$	$\bot$
$\gamma_b(v) =$	$\bot$	Nil	$Cons(\bot, \gamma_b v')$
$\gamma_c(v) =$	$\bot$	Nil	$Cons(x, \gamma_c v')$

Projection γ_a says that no part of the value is static; γ_b says that the tags are static and that γ_b much of the list tail is static; and γ_c says that the tags, the list head, and γ_c much of the list tail are static. Thus γ_a is ABS on the recursively defined domain. Projection γ_b says that the tags are static and that the same holds for the list tail, so the *structure* of the entire list must be known. An appropriate name for γ_b therefore is $STRUCT$. Note that when the structure is static, in particular the *length* of the list will be known during partial evaluation. Projection γ_c says that the tags and the list head are static and that the same holds for the list tail, so everything is static. Formally, $\gamma_c = ID$, the identity on the recursively defined domain.

When considering projections over recursively defined datatypes, we require them to be *uniform projection* in the same manner as γ_b and γ_c above. They must treat the recursive component of type `intlist` the same as the entire list — we want to consider only binding-time properties which are the same at every level of recursion in the data structure.

A non-ABS uniform projection over `intlist` has form $\mu\gamma.Nil + Cons(\gamma' \times \gamma)$, defined by

$$\mu\gamma.Nil + Cons(\gamma' \times \gamma) = \bigsqcup_{k=0}^{\infty} G(ABS)$$

where $G(\gamma) = Nil + Cons\ (\gamma' \times \gamma)$ and where γ' is a projection over type `int`.
The projections γ_b and γ_c above do have this form:

$$\begin{aligned}
\gamma_a &= ABS \\
\gamma_b &= \mu\gamma.Nil + Cons\ (ABS \times \gamma) \\
\gamma_c &= \mu\gamma.Nil + Cons\ (ID \times \gamma)
\end{aligned}$$

Note that ABS and ID are precisely the admissible static projections on the component type `int`.

We define: an admissible static projection on a recursive datatype is ABS, or the *uniform sum* of admissible projections on the components. This completes the inductive definition of admissible projections.

15.4.6   An example: Association lists

In Section 10.5.5 we considered a Scheme function `mkenv` building an association list: a list of (name, value)-pairs. We also saw how one could use grammars to say that all the name components were static and that the value components were not. In a typed language the association list would belong to a recursive datatype

```
datatype assoc = End | More of ((name * value) * assoc)
```

where `name` and `value` are the types of names and values, assumed to be atomic. The admissible projections on these component types (`name` and `value`) are ABS and ID, and the admissible projections on `name * value` are ABS, $RIGHT$, $LEFT$, and ID shown in Section 15.4.3.

Following the section on recursive datatypes, we use the following five uniform projections on the `assoc` type:

$$\begin{aligned}
\gamma_a &= ABS \\
\gamma_b &= \mu\gamma.End + More\ (ABS \times \gamma) \\
\gamma_c &= \mu\gamma.End + More\ (LEFT \times \gamma) \\
\gamma_d &= \mu\gamma.End + More\ (RIGHT \times \gamma) \\
\gamma_e &= \mu\gamma.End + More\ (ID \times \gamma)
\end{aligned}$$

Projection $\gamma_a = ABS$ says that nothing is static; γ_b says the structure is static; γ_c says the structure and all the `name` (that is, left) components are static; γ_d says the structure and all the `value` (that is, right) components are static; and $\gamma_e = ID$ says everything is static. Suitable names for γ_b, γ_c, and γ_d would be $STRUCT$, $STRUCT(RIGHT)$, and $STRUCT(LEFT)$.

The binding time of `mkenv`'s result, which was described by a grammar in Section 10.5.5, can now be described simply as $STRUCT(RIGHT)$.

15.5   Projection-based binding-time analysis

We have introduced projections and have shown how they describe the binding times of partially static data in a typed language. Now we outline a monovariant projection-based binding-time analysis for such a language. This analysis should be compared to the Scheme0 binding-time analysis in Section 5.2.

15.5.1 The example language PEL

The example language is Launchbury's PEL ('partial evaluation language'). A program consists of datatype definitions and simply typed first-order function definitions. Each function has exactly one argument (which may be a tuple):

```
datatype T₁ = ...
...
datatype Tₘ = ...

fun f₁ x₁ = e₁
...
and fₙ xₙ = eₙ
```

The syntax of expressions is given in Figure 15.6.

⟨Expr⟩	::=	⟨Var⟩	Variable
	|	(⟨Expr⟩, ..., ⟨Expr⟩)	Tuple
	|	⟨Constr⟩ ⟨Expr⟩	Constructor applic.
	|	⟨FuncName⟩ ⟨Expr⟩	Function application
	|	case ⟨Expr⟩ of ⟨Match⟩...⟨Match⟩	Case expression
⟨Match⟩	::=	⟨Constr⟩ ⟨Var⟩ => ⟨Expr⟩	Case match

Figure 15.6: Syntax of PEL, a typed first-order functional language.

15.5.2 Binding-time analysis maps

Let FuncName be the set of function names, Var the set of variable names, and Proj the set of admissible projections (on all types). The binding-time analysis uses two maps ψ and τ to compute a third, namely the monovariant division σ, where

$$\begin{array}{llll} \psi & : & \text{FunEnv} & = & \text{Fun} \to (\text{Proj} \to \text{Proj}) \\ \tau & : & \text{BTEnv} & = & \text{Var} \to \text{Proj} \\ \sigma & : & \text{Monodivision} & = & \text{Fun} \to \text{Proj} \end{array}$$

When projection γ describes how much of f's argument is static, then $(\psi f)\gamma$ is a projection describing how much of f's result is static; τx describes how much of the value of variable x is static; and (σf) describes how much of f's argument is static.

Compare this with the Scheme0 binding-time analysis. The role of τ is the same: describing the binding time of variables. The Scheme0 binding-time analysis needs no ψ map, since the binding time of the result of f may safely be equated to that of its argument. If the argument is static, then surely the result is static too, and if the argument is dynamic, then the result may safely be assumed to be dynamic too.

On the other hand, the Scheme1 binding-time analysis (Section 15.3) does use a ψ map. This is because in Scheme1 the result of a function may be dynamic although its arguments are static. The reason is that Scheme1 allows *partially static functions*: an argument may be a (partially) static lambda with dynamic free variables.

15.5.3   Binding-time analysis functions

The projection-based binding-time analysis for PEL consists of two functions $\mathcal{B}_{pe}$ and $\mathcal{B}_{pv}$, analogous to $\mathcal{B}_e$ and $\mathcal{B}_v$ in the Scheme0 binding-time analysis. That is, $\mathcal{B}_{pe}[\![e]\!]\psi\tau$ is a projection describing how much of e's value is static, and $\mathcal{B}_{pv}[\![e]\!]\psi\tau g$ is a projection describing how much of g's argument is static in the applications of g found in e. Function $\mathcal{B}_{pe}$ is shown in Figure 15.7 and $\mathcal{B}_{pv}$ is shown in Figure 15.8.

In the figures, $[x \mapsto \gamma] \in$ BTEnv maps x to γ and everything else to ABS, and $\tau[x \mapsto \gamma]$ denotes τ updated to map x to γ.

$$
\begin{array}{ll}
\mathcal{B}_{pe}[\![e]\!]: \text{FunEnv} \rightarrow \text{BTEnv} \rightarrow \text{Proj} \\[4pt]
\mathcal{B}_{pe}[\![x]\!]\psi\tau & = \quad \tau x \\[4pt]
\mathcal{B}_{pe}[\![(e_1,\ldots,e_m)]\!]\psi\tau & = \quad \mathcal{B}_{pe}[\![e_1]\!]\psi\tau \times \cdots \times \mathcal{B}_{pe}[\![e_m]\!]\psi\tau \\[4pt]
\mathcal{B}_{pe}[\![c_i\ e]\!]\psi\tau & = \quad c_1\ ID + \cdots + c_i\ (\mathcal{B}_{pe}[\![e]\!]\psi\tau) + \cdots + c_m\ ID \\[4pt]
\mathcal{B}_{pe}[\![f\ e]\!]\psi\tau & = \quad (\psi f)\ (\mathcal{B}_{pe}[\![e]\!]\psi\tau) \\[4pt]
\mathcal{B}_{pe}[\![\text{case } e \text{ of } c_1\ x_1 \texttt{=>} e_1 \mid \ldots \mid c_n\ x_n \texttt{=>} e_n]\!]\psi\tau = \\
\qquad \text{case } \mathcal{B}_{pe}[\![e]\!]\psi\tau \text{ of} \\
\qquad\qquad \sum_{i=1}^{n} c_i\gamma_i \quad \texttt{=>} \quad \sqcap_{i=1}^{n}\ \mathcal{B}_{pe}[\![e_i]\!]\psi(\tau[x_i \mapsto \gamma_i]) \\
\qquad\quad \mid \quad ABS \qquad \texttt{=>} \quad ABS
\end{array}
$$

Figure 15.7: The PEL binding-time analysis function $\mathcal{B}_{pe}$.

15.5.4   Safety

When e is an expression with free variable x, let $\mathcal{E}[\![e]\!][x \mapsto v]$ denote the (standard) result of evaluating e with x bound to the value v. Also, recall that when σ is a division, then (σf) denotes the static part of f's formal parameter.

$$\mathcal{B}_{pv}[\![e]\!]: \text{FunEnv} \rightarrow \text{BTEnv} \rightarrow \text{FuncName} \rightarrow \text{Proj}$$

$$\mathcal{B}_{pv}[\![x]\!]\psi\tau g \quad = \quad ID$$

$$\mathcal{B}_{pv}[\![(e_1,\dots,e_m)]\!]\psi\tau g \quad = \quad \mathcal{B}_{pv}[\![e_1]\!]\psi\tau g \sqcap \dots \sqcap \mathcal{B}_{pv}[\![e_m]\!]\psi\tau g$$

$$\mathcal{B}_{pv}[\![c_i\ e]\!]\psi\tau g \quad = \quad \mathcal{B}_{pv}[\![e]\!]\psi\tau g$$

$$\mathcal{B}_{pv}[\![f\ e]\!]\psi\tau g \quad = \quad \mathcal{B}_{pe}[\![e]\!]\psi\tau \sqcap \mathcal{B}_{pv}[\![e]\!]\psi\tau g$$

$$\mathcal{B}_{pv}[\![\text{case } e \text{ of } c_1\ x_1\text{=>}e_1 \mid \dots \mid c_n\ x_n\text{=>}e_n]\!]\psi\tau g =$$
$$\text{case } \mathcal{B}_{pe}[\![e]\!]\psi\tau \text{ of}$$
$$\sum_{i=1}^{n} c_i\gamma_i \quad \Rightarrow \quad \mathcal{B}_{pv}[\![e]\!]\psi\tau g \sqcap (\sqcap_{i=1}^n \mathcal{B}_{pv}[\![e_i]\!]\psi(\tau[x_i \mapsto \gamma_i]))$$
$$\mid \quad ABS \quad \Rightarrow \quad \mathcal{B}_{pv}[\![e]\!]\psi\tau g \sqcap (\sqcap_{i=1}^n \mathcal{B}_{pv}[\![e_i]\!]\psi(\tau[x_i \mapsto ABS]))$$

Figure 15.8: The PEL binding-time propagation function $\mathcal{B}_{pv}$.

We define that σ is a *safe division* if whenever the body of function f contains a function call (g e),

```
fun f x = ... (g e) ...
```

it holds for every value v that

$$(\sigma g)\ (\mathcal{E}[\![e]\!]\ [x \mapsto (\sigma f)v]) = (\sigma g)\ (\mathcal{E}[\![e]\!]\ [x \mapsto v])$$

The equation says: to compute the static part (σg) of g's argument e, we need only the static part $(\sigma f)v$ of the value of f's parameter x.

Launchbury shows that his projection-based analysis is safe, and that safety is equivalent to *uniform congruence* (see Section 4.4.1).

15.5.5 Binding-time analysis of a PEL program

The purpose of the analysis is to determine a division σ mapping each function to a static projection for its argument. To be safe, the division σ must satisfy the equations

$$(\psi f)\gamma \quad = \quad \mathcal{B}_{pe}[\![\text{body}]\!]\psi([x \mapsto \gamma]) \qquad \text{for each function f x = body}$$
$$\sigma f \quad = \quad \sqcap_{i=1}^n \mathcal{B}_{pv}[\![\text{body}_i]\!]\psi([x_i \mapsto \sigma f_i]) \quad \text{for each function f x = body}$$

Any solution to these equations is a safe division. Recall that larger static projections are the more informative, which implies that the greatest solution is the most informative. This explains the use of greatest lower bound $\sqcap$ above.

15.6   Describing the dynamic data

A static projection describes the static part of a value, but what then is the dynamic part? During partial evaluation we *use* the static part, and *leave* the dynamic in the residual program. At first it seems that *projection complements* provide the right mechanism for describing dynamic data.

Let $\gamma, \gamma' : X \to X$ be projections on X. If $\gamma x \sqcup \gamma' x = x$ for all $x \in X$, then γ' is a *complement* of γ (and vice versa).

When γ is a static projection describing the static part of x, its complement γ' is supposed to describe the dynamic part of x. Between them, they describe the whole of x as expected. The complement γ' is not uniquely defined. To have as little dynamic data as possible, the complement should be as small as possible. Requiring the complement to be an admissible projection (as for the static projections in Section 15.4.1) ensures that there is a least complement.

To illustrate how the least complement describes the dynamic data, consider again the assoc example (Section 15.4.6), and assume the static projection is $STRUCT(LEFT)$, which says that the structure is static and all the name components are static. The least complement is the projection $STRUCT(RIGHT)$, which maps a list of (name,value)-pairs to a list containing only the value components. This complement says that the structure and the value components are dynamic. This is a useful result: it means that only the value list, not the name components, will appear in data structures handled by the residual program.

However, for the datatype union from Section 15.4.4 the result is not so good. Assume the static projection is TAG, saying that the tags are known. Then the least complement is ID, saying that the whole value is dynamic, which means that the tags Int and Bl will still be present in the residual program.

A closer look at the assoc example shows that it too is less than perfect. Namely, when the static projection is $STRUCT(LEFT)$, the structure and thus the length of the list is known, but the complement $STRUCT(RIGHT)$ says that the structure and length are dynamic. This prevents replacing the list by a tuple of its components in the residual program.

In summary, a static projection and its complement give a useful but not optimal factorization of a value into its static and dynamic components.

To improve on this, Launchbury describes dynamic data not by the complement, but rather by the *inverse images* or *fibres* of the static projection. This allows an exact factorization in the form of a *dependent sum* (over possible static values) of the domains of dynamic data. Moreover, this gives a characterization of the types of residual functions and a systematic approach to arity raising, since it allows variable splitting and tag removal in residual programs [167, Chapter 5].

15.7 Summary

The theme of this chapter was automatic program analysis: how to obtain information about the execution of a program, *without* actually executing it. We presented abstract interpretation: a systematic technique for program analysis, and reconsidered the Scheme0 binding-time analysis (from Section 5.2) as an abstract interpretation. We presented a closure analysis, which produces information about function applications in higher-order languages, and used this to extend the first-order Scheme0 binding-time analysis to a higher-order Scheme1 binding-time analysis. Finally, we presented Launchbury's projection-based binding-time analysis for partially static data.

15.8 Exercises

Exercise 15.1 Construct a program analysis that detects duplicable and discardable variables (the concept of duplicability and discardability can be used to control unfolding, see Chapter 5). □

Exercise 15.2 Modify the binding-time analysis presented in Section 5.2 to compute polyvariant divisions. Indicate the necessary changes (if any) to the domains, the analysis functions $\mathcal{B}_e$ and $\mathcal{B}_v$, the congruence requirement, the strategy for finding the best division, etc. □

Exercise 15.3 Consider the program

```
(define (f xs)
  (sum (map (lambda (x) (+ x 1)) xs)))
(define (sum ys)
  (if (null? ys) 0 (+ (car ys) (sum (cdr ys)))))
(define (map g zs)
  (if (null? zs)
      '()
      (cons (g (car zs)) (map g (cdr zs)))))
```

1. Do closure analysis and binding-time analysis of the function f, assuming that xs is static.

2. Now assume the program also contains the function definition

   ```
   (define (h ws) (map (lambda (w) w) ws))
   ```

   where ws is dynamic. Redo the closure analysis and the binding-time analysis of f and comment on the results.

□

Exercise 15.4 Apply the closure analysis to the Y combinator. □

Exercise 15.5 Apply the closure analysis to the lambda calculus interpreter in Chapter 8. □

Exercise 15.6 For monovariant binding-time analysis without partially static structures, the domain of abstract values containing just S and D is the obvious choice. Explain why there is no 'obvious choice' when partially static structures also must be handled. □

Chapter 16

Larger Perspectives

The possibility of program specialization, under the name of the *s-m-n property*, is one of the cornerstones of computability (or recursive function) theory as developed by Kleene, Rogers, and others [149,226]. We begin by relating the fundamental assumptions of recursive function theory to programming language concepts as studied in this book.

An alternative perspective is to see partial evaluation as an operation *on program texts* that realizes the *mathematical* operation of 'freezing' some of a multi-argument function's arguments to fixed values. This leads to a more general discussion of symbolic operations, and to the development of a novel type system able to describe the types of interpreters, compilers, and partial evaluators.

16.1   Relations to recursive function theory

The partial recursive functions have been studied extensively, using a framework very similar to our own but usually with function arguments, results and program encodings drawn from the natural numbers $\mathcal{N} = \{0, 1, 2, ...\}$.

A wide variety of formalizations proposed in the 1930s as candidates to define the class of all computable partial functions have turned out to be equivalent. This led to the famous *Church-Turing thesis*. Let p_i be the ith Turing machine in a standard enumeration p_0, p_1, p_2,... of all Turing machines. For each $i \geq 0$, let $\varphi_i : \mathcal{N} \to \mathcal{N}$ be the partial function that p_i computes. The thesis: a partial function $f : \mathcal{N} \to \mathcal{N}$ is computable *if and only if* it equals φ_i for some i.

Recursive function theory begins more abstractly: instead of an enumeration p_0, p_1, p_2,... of programs, one only assumes for each $i \geq 0$ there is given a partial function $\varphi_i : \mathcal{N} \to \mathcal{N}$ which satisfies the natural conditions given below.

The first similarity with our framework is immediate, if we identify the ith Turing machine 'program' with its numerical index i. Then the given enumeration of Turing machines defines a programming language with data domain $D = \mathcal{N}$ and semantic function $[\![\_]\!]_L : \mathcal{N} \to \mathcal{N} \to \mathcal{N}$ where $[\![p_i]\!]_L d = \varphi_i(d)$. This is extended to multi-argument functions by defining the partial n-ary function $\phi_i^n : \mathcal{N}^n \to \mathcal{N}$ to be

$$\varphi_i^n(x_1, \ldots, x_n) = \varphi_i(<x_1, \ldots x_n>)$$

where $<\_, \ldots, \_>$ is a one-to-one 'tupling function' that assigns a unique natural number to each n-tuple of natural numbers[1]. The superscript of φ_i^n is dropped when the number of arguments is clear from context.

Actually, pairing is enough since tuples can be formed by repeated pairing: define $<x_1, x_2, \ldots, x_n>$ to be $<x_1, <x_2, \ldots, <x_{n-1}, x_n> \ldots >>$.

We now revert to using D to denote the set of Lisp lists. D is certainly closed under formation of pairs, and any pair in D can be uniquely decomposed into its constituents, giving the effect of pairing functions. Further, programs *are* elements of D, so the need to enumerate programs by assigning each one a numerical index by an often complex Gödel numbering scheme is completely circumvented.

The following definition by Rogers captures properties sufficient for a development of computability theory independent of any particular model of computation [226]. Our version differs only in the use of D instead of the traditional $\mathcal{N}$.

The programming language $\varphi = [\![\_]\!]$ is said to be an *acceptable programming system* if it satisfies the following:

1. *Completeness property*: for any effectively computable partial function $\psi : D \to D$ there exists a program $p \in D$ such that $\varphi_p = \psi$.

2. *Universal function property*: there is a *universal program* $\mathrm{up} \in D$ such that for any program $p \in D$, $\varphi_{\mathrm{up}}(p, x) = \varphi_p(x)$ for all $x \in D$.

3. *s-m-n function property*: for any natural numbers m, n there exists a computable function $s_n^m \in D$ such that for any program $p \in D$ and any input $(x_1, \ldots, x_m, y_1, \ldots, y_n) \in D$

$$\varphi_p^{m+n}(x_1, \ldots, x_m, y_1, \ldots, y_n) = \varphi_{s_n^m(p, x_1, \ldots, x_m)}^n(y_1, \ldots, y_n)$$

These properties correspond to quite familiar programming concepts. Completeness says that the language is 'Turing powerful' and so is at least as strong as any other computing formalism. The universal function property amounts to the existence of a self- or meta-circular interpreter of the language, and the s-m-n function property simply asserts the possibility of partial evaluation.

To see this, let $m = n = 1$. Since s_1^1 is computable, by property 1 there must be a program mix that computes it, so $s_1^1 = [\![\mathrm{mix}]\!]$. The last equation above becomes, after omitting sub- and superscripts:

---

[1] An example 2-tupling or pairing function is $<x, y> = 2^x \cdot (2 \cdot y + 1)$. This is obviously computable, and it is easy to see that x and y may be computably extracted from $z = <x, y>$.

$$\varphi_{\mathbf{p}}(\mathbf{x}, \mathbf{y}) = \varphi_{\varphi_{\mathtt{mix}}(\mathbf{p}, \mathbf{x})}(\mathbf{y})$$

which is just the 'mix equation' in another guise.

The standard proof of the s-m-n property for Turing machines in essence uses a trivial construction that *never* gains efficiency, but this suffices for the purposes of recursive function theory. Efficiency is very important in applications though, so partial evaluation may be regarded as the quest for efficient implementations of the s-m-n theorem.

Clearly each of the languages we have studied in earlier chapters is an acceptable programming system.

The traditional usage of natural numbers in recursive function theory is simple, abstract and elegant, but involves a high computational price: all program structures and non-numeric data must be encoded by means of Gödel numbers, and operations must be done on encoded values. Letting *programs and data* have the same form allows the theory to be developed without the trick of Gödel numbering. This is a substantial advantage when doing recursion theoretic constructions such as needed to prove Kleene's s-m-n and Second Recursion theorems, and leads to faster constructed programs.

16.2 Types for interpreters, compilers, and partial evaluators

High-level operations in programming languages
Programming languages of higher and higher abstraction levels have evolved since the first years of computing, when programming languages were just symbolic codes reflecting the computer's architecture. Due to higher level basic operations, modern functional languages allow a mathematical style of thinking while programming, for example using function composition, partial function application, set comprehension, and pattern matching. This is possible since these operations are all in the so-called 'constructable' part of mathematics, known to give computable results when applied to computable arguments.

Many operations on mathematical objects can be faithfully realized by corresponding operations on symbolic expressions. Classically, algebraic manipulation is used to organize arithmetic computations more efficiently — possible because algebra abstractly but correctly describes concrete operations on numbers. On digital computers, symbolic operations are specified by textual objects, i.e. programs and their subexpressions. The term 'symbolic computation' often refers to algebraic manipulations when realized on the computer, but can be interpreted more broadly to describe the entire theme of this book[2].

---

[2]Much of this material is from [132].

Operations on functions and programs

Two useful operations on (mathematical) functions are:

- *Composition* of f with g as in Chapter 2, written as $f; g$ or $g \circ f$.

- *Function specialization* of $f(x, y)$, obtaining for example a one-argument function $f_{|x=a}(y) = f(a, y)$ by 'freezing' x to a fixed value a.

Corresponding symbolic operations on programs (assuming for concreteness that they are written in the λ-calculus):

Symbolic composition. The *symbolic composition* of expressions e_f and g could be expression $\lambda x.e_g(e_f(x))$.

Partial evaluation. The specialization of function f to $x = a$ can be realized symbolically as the program $\lambda y.e_f(a, y)$. In the context of recursive function theory this is Kleene's s-m-n theorem [149,226], and its efficient realization is of course the theme of this book.

Efficient operations on programs

The symbolic operations above, while computable, do not lead to particularly efficient programs. For example, the program above realizing function composition, $\lambda x.e_g(e_f(x))$, is no faster than just running the two programs from which it is constructed, one after the other. A main theme of this book is the *efficient* implementation of program operations that realize mathematical operations.

Deforestation as in Chapter 17 symbolically realizes function composition, and partial evaluation is of course a symbolic realization of function specialization.

Data and program types

How can one describe the types of operations on symbolic expressions? A symbolic composition operator (for example) takes programs p_f, p_g computing $f : A \to B$ and $g : B \to C$ (respectively) into a program q computing $f; g : A \to C$. The same symbolic composer works, *independently* of A, B, C. Thus a symbolic operation should in some sense be polymorphic [185] in the types of its arguments.

A more subtle problem is the 'level shift' that occurs when going from a program text p to the function $[\![p]\!]_X$ it denotes when regarded as a program in language X. To describe this symbolically we assume assume given a fixed collection of programming languages generically called X, and extend the usual concept of type according to the following syntax:

$$t : type ::= \underline{t}_X \mid firstorder \mid t \times t \mid t \to t$$

Type *firstorder* describes values in D, for example S-expressions, and function types and products are as usual. For each language X and type t we have a type $\underline{t}_X$,

$$\frac{exp : \underline{t}_\mathsf{X}}{[\![exp]\!]_\mathsf{X} : t} \qquad\qquad \frac{exp_1 : t_2 \to t_1, \quad exp_2 : t_2}{exp_1(exp_2) : t_1}$$

$$\frac{}{firstordervalue : firstorder} \qquad \frac{exp : \underline{t}_\mathsf{X}}{exp : firstorder}$$

Figure 16.1: Some type inference rules for closed expressions.

meaning the type of all X-programs which denote values of type t. For example, atom 1066 has type *firstorder*, and Scheme program (quote 1066) has type $\underline{firstorder}_{\mathsf{Scheme}}$.

The subscript X will often be dropped when the language being discussed is the standard implementation language, always called L.

Semantics of types. The meaning of type expression t is a set $\mathcal{T}(t)$ defined as follows, where $[A \to B]$ is the set of all functions from A to B:

$$
\begin{aligned}
\mathcal{T}(firstorder) &= \mathsf{D} \\
\mathcal{T}(t_1 {\to} t_2) &= [\mathcal{T}(t_1) \to \mathcal{T}(t_2)] \\
\mathcal{T}(t_1 \times t_2) &= \{(v_1, v_2) \mid v_1 \in \mathcal{T}(t_1), v_2 \in \mathcal{T}(t_2)\} \\
\mathcal{T}(\underline{t}_\mathsf{X}) &= \{\mathsf{p} \in \mathsf{D} \mid [\![\mathsf{p}]\!]_\mathsf{X} \in \mathcal{T}(t)\}
\end{aligned}
$$

Polymorphism. We shall also allow *polymorphic* type expressions to be written containing *type variables* $\alpha, \beta, \gamma, \ldots$. Such a polymorphic type will always be understood as standing for the set of all the *monomorphic instances* obtained from it by consistently replacing type variables by variable-free type expressions. To emphasize this, we will often (informally) quantify type variables universally, e.g. $\forall \alpha.(\alpha \to \alpha)$. The result of replacing type variables is called an *instance* of the polymorphic type.

Type inference rules. Figure 16.1 contains some rules sufficient to infer the types involved in program runs, i.e. evaluations of closed expressions. Note that an object p of type $\underline{t}_\mathsf{X}$ is a program text and thus *in itself* a value in D, i.e. $\underline{t}_\mathsf{X}$ denotes a subset of D. On the other hand, p's meaning $[\![\mathsf{p}]\!]_\mathsf{X}$ may be any value, for example a higher-order function.

Program equivalence. It is important to be able to say when two programs p, $\mathsf{q} \in D$ are computationally equivalent. In recent years two views have developed, *semantic equivalence* and *observational equivalence* [244,219][3]. Both concepts make sense in our framework, defined as follows. Let p, $\mathsf{q} \in D$. Then p and q are

---

[3]A denotational semantics is said to be *fully abstract* with respect to an operational semantics if observational and semantic equivalence are the same.

semantically equivalent   if $[\![\mathrm{p}]\!] = [\![\mathrm{q}]\!]$

observationally equivalent   if $[\![\mathrm{p}]\!] \approx [\![\mathrm{q}]\!]$, where we define $f \approx g$ to mean that for all $n \geq 0$ and for all $\mathrm{d}_1, \ldots, \mathrm{d}_n \in D$ and $\mathrm{d} \in D$,

$$(f\mathrm{d}_1 \ldots \mathrm{d}_n = \mathrm{d}) \text{ if and only if } (g\mathrm{d}_1 \ldots \mathrm{d}_n = \mathrm{d})$$

The first definition is the easier to formulate, but a case can be made that the second is more relevant in practice. The reason is that establishing the first requires verifying equality between two elements of a semantic function domain. This can be a tricky task, and computationally speaking too strict if the semantic function $[\![\_]\!]$ is not fully abstract.

The second definition is a version of the observational equivalence studied by Plotkin, Milner, and others, limited to first-order applicative contexts. It only involves assertions that can in principle be verified by running the program on first-order inputs and observing its first-order outputs or nontermination behaviour.

16.2.1   Efficient symbolic composition

Symbolic composition can be described as commutativity of the diagram in Figure 16.2, where α, β, γ range over all types. We now list some examples of symbolic composition, and discuss what is saved computationally.

Vector spaces and matrix multiplication.   Suppose M, N are $n \times n$ matrices over (for example) the real numbers $\mathcal{R}$. Each determines a linear transformation, e.g. $[\![M]\!] : \mathcal{R}^n \to \mathcal{R}^n$. If $M \cdot N$ is their matrix product, then

$$[\![M \cdot N]\!](\vec{w}) = [\![M]\!]([\![N]\!](\vec{w}))$$

The composite linear transformation can be computed in either of two ways:

- by applying first N and then M to $\vec{w}$, taking time $2n^2$; or

- by first multiplying M and N (time n^3 by the usual algorithm), and applying the result to $\vec{w}$ (time n^2)

It may be asked: what if anything has been saved? The answer is: nothing, if the goal is only to transform a single vector, since the second time always exceeds the first. There is, however, a net saving if more than n vectors are to be transformed since the matrix product need only be computed once.

The moral: an operation so familiar as matrix multiplication can be thought of as symbolic composition, and composition can save computational time.

Other examples of efficient symbolic composition include the fact that two *finite state transducers* can be combined into one with no intermediate symbols; *deforestation*, seen in Chapter 17; and composition of *derivors* or of *attribute coupled grammars*. The latter two can be used automatically to combine multipass compiler phases into a single phase.

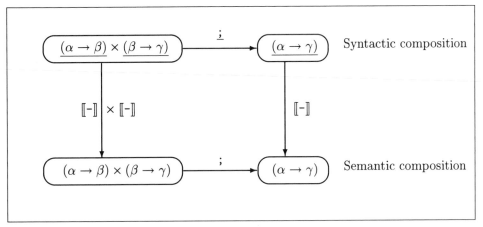

Figure 16.2: Symbolic composition.

16.2.2   Symbolic function specialization = partial evaluation

Specializing (also called *restricting*) a two-argument function $f(x, y) : \alpha \times \beta \rightarrow \gamma$ to $x = a$ gives the function $f_{|x=a}(y) = f(a, y)$. Function specialization thus has polymorphic type

$$\texttt{fs} : (\alpha \times \beta \rightarrow \gamma) \times \alpha \rightarrow (\beta \rightarrow \gamma)$$

Partial evaluation is the symbolic operation corresponding to function specialization. Using $\texttt{peval} = [\![\texttt{mix}]\!]$ to denote the partial evaluation function, its correctness is expressed by commutativity of the diagram in Figure 16.3. Partial evaluation has polymorphic type

$$\texttt{peval} : \underline{(\alpha \times \beta \rightarrow \gamma) \times \alpha \rightarrow (\beta \rightarrow \gamma)}$$

Redefinition of partial evaluation
The description of $\texttt{peval}$ can be both simplified and generalized by writing the functions involved in *curried* form[4]. This gives $\texttt{peval}$ a new polymorphic type:

$$\texttt{peval} : \underline{\alpha \rightarrow (\beta \rightarrow \gamma) \rightarrow \alpha \rightarrow \beta \rightarrow \gamma}$$

which is an instance of a more general polymorphic type:

$$\texttt{peval} : \underline{\rho \rightarrow \sigma \rightarrow \rho \rightarrow \sigma}$$

Maintaining our emphasis on observable values, we will require ρ to be a first-order type (i.e. *base* or a type $\underline{t}_{\text{L}}$).

---

[4]The well-known 'curry' isomorphism on functions is $(\alpha \rightarrow (\beta \rightarrow \gamma)) \simeq (\alpha \times \beta \rightarrow \gamma)$.

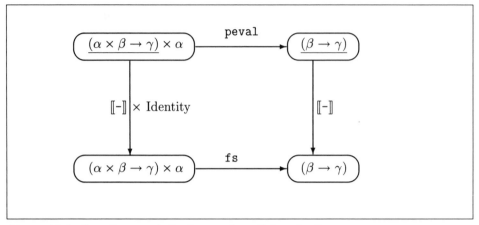

Figure 16.3: Function specialization and partial evaluation.

Remark. The second input to `peval` is a *value* of type ρ, and not *representation* of a value. In practice, especially if `peval` is programmed in a strongly typed language, one may need to work with representations rather than directly with values. We ignore this aspect partly because of notational complexity, and partly because the use of representations leads quickly to problems of size explosion when dealing with representations of representations of .... This problem has been addressed by Launchbury [169], and appears in Chapter 11.

The mix equation revisited.   `mix` $\in D$ is a *partial evaluator* if for all p, a $\in D$,

$$[\![\mathrm{p}]\!] \; \mathrm{a} \approx [\![[\![\mathrm{mix}]\!] \; \mathrm{p\,a}]\!]$$

Thus for any $n+1$ first-order values d, $d_1,\ldots,d_n$, we have $[\![\mathrm{p}]\!] \, \mathrm{a}\,d_1\ldots d_n = d$ if and only if $[\![[\![\mathrm{mix}]\!] \; \mathrm{p\,a}]\!] \, d_1\ldots d_n = d$.

16.2.3   Compiler and interpreter types

Similarly, the definitions of interpreter and compiler of Section 3.1.1 may be elegantly restated, a little more generally than before:

$$\boxed{\begin{array}{c} \mathrm{S} \\ \mathrm{L} \end{array}} \;=\; \{\mathrm{int} \mid [\![\mathrm{s}]\!]_{\mathrm{S}} \approx [\![\mathrm{int}]\!]_{\mathrm{L}}\mathrm{s}\}$$

and

$$\boxed{\begin{array}{c} \text{S} \longrightarrow \text{T} \\ \hline \text{L} \end{array}} = \{\ \text{comp}\ |\ [\![\text{s}]\!]_\text{S} \approx [\![[\![\text{comp}]\!]_\text{L}\text{s}]\!]_\text{T}\ \}$$

Can an interpreter be typed?

Suppose we have an interpreter up for language L, and written in the same language — a universal program or self-interpreter. By definition up must satisfy $[\![\text{p}]\!] \approx [\![\text{up}]\!]$ p for any L-program p. Consequently as p ranges over all L-programs, $[\![\text{up}]\!]$ p can take on *any* program-expressible type. A difficult question arises: is it possible to define the type of up non-trivially[5]?

A traditional response to this problem has been to write an interpreter in an *untyped* language, e.g. Scheme. This has the disadvantage that it is hard to verify that the interpreter correctly implements the type system of its input language (if any). The reason is that there are two classes of possible errors: those caused by errors in the program being interpreted, and those caused by a badly written interpreter. Without a type system it is difficult to distinguish the one class of interpret-time errors from the other.

Well-typed language processors

Given a source S-program denoting a value of some type t, an S-interpreter should return a value whose type is t. From the same source program, a compiler should yield a target language program whose T-denotation is identical to its source program's S-denotation. This agrees with daily experience—a compiler is a meaning-preserving program transformation, insensitive to the type of its input program (provided only that it *is* well-typed). Analogous requirements apply to partial evaluators.

A well-typed interpreter is required to have many types: one for every possible input program type. Thus to satisfy these definitions we must dispense with type *unicity*, and allow the type of the interpreting program not to be uniquely determined by its syntax.

Compilers must satisfy an analogous demand. One example: $\lambda\text{x}.\text{x}$ has type $t_\text{L} \rightarrow t_\text{L}$ for all types t. It is thus a trivial but well-typed compiling function from L to L. (Henceforth we omit the subscript L.)

A well-typed partial evaluator can be applied to any program p accepting at least one first-order input, together with a value a for p's first input. Suppose p has type $\rho \rightarrow \sigma$ where ρ is first-order and a $\in [\![\rho]\!]$. Then $[\![\text{mix}]\!]$ p a is a program p_a whose result type is σ, the type of $[\![\text{p}]\!]$a. Thus p_a has type $\underline{\sigma}$.

---

[5]This question does not arise at all in classical computability theory since there is only one data type, the natural numbers, and all programs denote functions on them. On the other hand, computer scientists are unwilling to code all data as numbers and so demand programs with varying input, output and data types.

1. Interpreter int $\in$ $\boxed{\begin{smallmatrix} S \\ L \end{smallmatrix}}$ is *well-typed* if it has type[6] $\forall \alpha . \underline{\alpha}_S \to \alpha$.

2. Compiler comp $\in$ $\boxed{\begin{smallmatrix} S & \to & T \\ & L & \end{smallmatrix}}$ is *well-typed* if it has type
$\forall \alpha . \underline{\alpha}_S \to \underline{\alpha}_T$.

3. A partial evaluator mix is *well-typed* if it has type
$\forall \rho . \forall \sigma . \underline{\rho \to \sigma \to \rho \to \sigma}$, where ρ ranges over first-order types.

Remark. The definition of a well-typed interpreter assumes that all observable S-types are also L-types. Thus it does not take into account the possibility of encoding S-values.

16.2.4   Self-application and types

Definitions involving self-application often (and rightly) cause concern as to their well-typedness. We show here that natural types for mix-generated compilers and target programs (and even cogen as well) can be deduced from the few type rules of Figure 16.1. Let   source: $\underline{\alpha}_S$ be an S-program denoting a value of type α.

First Futamura projection
We wish to find the type of target $= [\![$mix$]\!]$ int source. The following inference concludes that the target program has type $\underline{\alpha} = \underline{\alpha}_L$, i.e. that it is an L program of the same type as the source program. The inference uses only the rules of Figure 16.1 and instantiation of polymorphic variables.

$$\frac{\dfrac{\dfrac{\text{mix} : \underline{\rho \to \sigma \to \rho \to \sigma}}{[\![\text{mix}]\!] : \underline{\rho \to \sigma \to \rho \to \sigma}}}{[\![\text{mix}]\!] : \underline{\alpha}_S \to \alpha \to \underline{\alpha}_S \to \underline{\alpha}} \quad \dfrac{\text{int} : \underline{\alpha}_S \to \alpha}{[\![\text{mix}]\!] \,\text{int} : \underline{\alpha}_S \to \alpha}}{\dfrac{[\![\text{mix}]\!] \,\text{int} : \underline{\alpha}_S \to \alpha \quad \text{source} : \underline{\alpha}_S}{[\![\text{mix}]\!] \,\text{int source} : \underline{\alpha}}}$$

Second Futamura projection
The previous inference showed that $[\![$mix$]\!]$ int has the type of a compiling *function*, though it is not a compiler *program*. We now wish to find the type of compiler $=$

---

[6]As a consequence, $[\![$int$]\!]_L$ has type $\forall \alpha . \underline{\alpha}_S \to \alpha$, that is to say type $\underline{t}_S \to t$ for every type t.

$[\![\mathtt{mix}]\!]\,\mathtt{mix}\,\mathtt{int}$. It turns out to be notationally simpler to begin with a program p of more general type $\alpha \to \beta$ than that of $\mathtt{int}$.

$$\cfrac{\cfrac{\cfrac{\mathtt{mix} : \underline{\rho \to \sigma \to \rho \to \sigma}}{[\![\mathtt{mix}]\!] : \underline{\rho \to \sigma \to \rho \to \sigma}}}{[\![\mathtt{mix}]\!] : \underline{\alpha \to \beta \to \alpha \to \beta \to \alpha \to \beta \to \alpha \to \beta}} \quad \cfrac{\mathtt{mix} : \underline{\underline{\alpha \to \beta \to \alpha \to \beta}}}{[\![\mathtt{mix}]\!]\,\mathtt{mix} : \underline{\alpha \to \beta \to \alpha \to \beta}}}{\cfrac{[\![\mathtt{mix}]\!]\,\mathtt{mix} : \underline{\alpha \to \beta \to \alpha \to \beta}}{[\![\mathtt{mix}]\!]\,\mathtt{mix}\,\mathrm{p} : \underline{\alpha \to \beta}}} \quad \mathrm{p} : \underline{\alpha \to \beta}$$

Some interesting substitution instances. Compilers can be generated by the second Futamura projection: $\mathtt{compiler} = [\![\mathtt{mix}]\!]\,\mathtt{mix}\,\mathtt{int}$. The type of $\mathtt{int}$ is $\underline{\delta_{\mathrm{S}} \to \delta}$, an instance of the type assigned to p above. By the same substitution we have $\mathtt{compiler} : \underline{\delta_{\mathrm{S}} \to \delta}$. Moreover, δ was chosen arbitrarily, so $[\![\mathtt{compiler}]\!] : \forall \delta . \underline{\delta_{\mathrm{S}} \to \delta}$ as desired.

The type of a compiler generator. Even $\mathtt{cogen}$ can be given a type, namely $\underline{\alpha \to \beta \to \alpha \to \beta}$ by exactly the same technique; but the tree is rather complex. One substitution instance of $\mathtt{cogen}$'s type is the conversion of an interpreter's type into that of a compiler.

The type of $[\![\mathtt{cogen}]\!]$ is thus $\underline{\alpha \to \beta \to \alpha \to \beta}$, which looks like the type of the identity function(!) but with some underlining. It is substantially different, however, in that it describes program generation. Specifically

1. $[\![\mathtt{cogen}]\!]$ transforms a two-input program p into another program p-gen, such that for any $a \in D$

2. $\mathrm{p}' = [\![\mathrm{p\text{-}gen}]\!]a$ is a program which

3. for any $\mathrm{d}_1, \ldots, \mathrm{d}_n \in D$ computes

$$[\![\mathrm{p}']\!]\mathrm{d}_1 \ldots \mathrm{d}_n \approx [\![\mathrm{p}]\!]a\,\mathrm{d}_1 \ldots \mathrm{d}_n$$

One could even describe the function $[\![\mathtt{cogen}]\!]$ as an *intensional version of currying*, one that works on program texts instead of on functions. To follow this, the type of $[\![\mathtt{cogen}]\!]$ has as a substitution instance

$$[\![\mathtt{cogen}]\!] : \underline{\alpha \to (\beta \to \gamma) \to \alpha \to \beta \to \gamma}$$

In most higher-order languages it requires only a trivial modification of a program text with type $(\alpha \times \beta \rightarrow \gamma)$ to obtain a variant with type $(\alpha \rightarrow (\beta \rightarrow \gamma))$, and with the same (or better) computational complexity. So a variant cogen' could be easily constructed that would first carry out this modification on its program input, and then run cogen on the result. The function computed by cogen' would be of type:

$$[\![\text{cogen}']\!] : \underline{\alpha \times \beta \rightarrow \gamma} \rightarrow \underline{\alpha \rightarrow \beta \rightarrow \gamma}$$

which is just the type of the curry transformation, plus some underlining.

16.3   Some research problems

Exercise 16.1 Informally verify type correctness of a simple interpreter with integer and boolean data □

Exercise 16.2 Figure 16.1 contains no *introduction* rules for deducing that any programs at all have types of form $\underline{t}_L$. Problem: for a fixed programming language, find type inference rules appropriate for showing that given programs have given types. □

Exercise 16.3 For a familiar language, e.g. the λ-calculus, formulate a set of type inference rules that is sufficiently general to verify type correctness of a range of compilers, interpreters and partial evaluators. □

Exercise 16.4 Find a suitable model theory for these types (domains, ideals, etc.). The type semantics given earlier uses ordinary sets, but for computational purposes it is desirable that the domains be ω-algebraic, and that the values manipulated by programs should only range over computable elements. □

Chapter 17

Program Transformation

Program transformation has been studied for many years since John McCarthy's groundbreaking paper [180]. Burstall and Darlington devised a widely cited approach [43], and they and many others have developed computer-aided transformation systems. Their method can achieve asymptotic (superlinear) speedups, in contrast to the constant speedups we have seen in partial evaluation. A recurring problem with such systems is incomplete automation, resulting in the need for a user to read (and evaluate the efficiency of!) incompletely transformed programs.

Partial evaluation can be seen as an automated instance of Burstall and Darlington's 'fold/unfold' methodology. We describe their framework, and express a simple and automatic online partial evaluator using their methodology. We also describe Wadler's 'treeless transformer'. This is an application of Turchin's 'supercompilation', and is another automated instance of fold/unfold transformations.

17.1 A language with pattern matching

For simplicity and elegance of presentation we use a program form based on pattern matching, assuming all data are structured. Figure 17.1 shows the syntax, and Figure 17.2 the semantics of the language. Here a program is a collection of *rewrite rules* of form L -> R used to transform tree-structured values.

Additional syntactic restrictions: that function names, constructor names, and variable names are pairwise disjoint; that every variable in the right side of rule L -> R must also appear in its left side L; and *left linearity:* no variable appears twice in the same left side.

Pgm :	Program	::=	$Defn_1 \ldots Defn_n$	
Defn :	Functionrule	::=	L -> R	
L :	Leftside	::=	$f\ P_1 \ldots P_n$	
P :	Pattern	::=	$x \mid c\ P_1 \ldots P_n$	
t,s,R :	Term	::=	x	
			$f\ t_1 \ldots t_n$	Function call
			$c\ t_1 \ldots t_n$	Construct term
f,g,... :	Fcnname			
x,y,... :	Variable			
c,... :	Constructor			

Figure 17.1: Syntax of pattern-matching language.

17.1.1   Semantics

Informally the semantics may be stated as follows: suppose one is given a program p and a *ground term* t, i.e. a term containing constructors and function names but no variables. First pick any function call $f\ t_1 \ldots t_n$ in t, together with a function rule $f\ P_1 \ldots P_n$-> R in p whose patterns match $t_1 \ldots t_n$. The call $f\ t_1 \ldots t_n$ in t is then replaced by the right side R of the chosen rule, after substituting the appropriate terms for f's pattern variables. This may be done as long as any function calls remain in the term.

To make this idea concrete, we introduce a few concepts. A *substitution* θ is a mapping from variables to ground terms. Term θt denotes the result of replacing every variable X in term t by θX. (This is very simple since terms have no local scope-defining operators such as λ.) Term θt is called an *instance* of t. Alternatively one may say that t' *matches* t if it is an instance of t.

A *context* is a term t[] with exactly one occurrence of [] (a 'hole') at a place where another term could legally occur, for instance (f (g [] Nil) Nil). As a special case, [] by itself is also a context. Further, we let t[t'] denote the result of replacing the occurrence of [] in t[] by t'. So writing u = t[t'] points out a particular occurrence of t' in u, and t[t''] is the result of replacing that t' in u by t''.

Figure 17.2 defines assertion t $\Rightarrow$ t', meaning that t can be rewritten to t' as described informally above.

Determinacy. Term t'' in t = t'[t''] is called a *redex* if it can be rewritten by the 'function call' semantic rule 3. Further, t is said to be in *normal form* if it contains no redex. Reduction t $\Rightarrow$ ... can be non-deterministic in two respects:

1. term t may contain several redexes; or

2. a redex may be reducible by more than one program rewrite rule.

As for (1), the *confluence property* of the lambda calculus and many functional languages ensures that no two terminating computation sequences yield different results. Nonetheless, some deterministic strategy must still be taken in a computer implementation. A common approach is to select an 'attention point' by restricting applicability of Rule 1 to certain contexts, i.e. to redefine the notion of context to select at most one decomposition of a term t into form t′[t″] where t″ is a redex.

As for (2), many implementations apply program rules in the sequence they are written until a match at the attention point is found. Another approach is only to accept a program as well-formed if the left sides of no two rules L->R and L′->R′ have a common instance $\theta L = \theta' L'$.

We adopt the latter, to avoid tricky discussions concerning the order in which rules can be applied when only partial data is available.

1. Context	$\dfrac{t' \Rightarrow t''}{t[t'] \Rightarrow t[t'']}$
2. Transitivity	$\dfrac{t \Rightarrow t', \ t' \Rightarrow t''}{t \Rightarrow t''}$
3. Function call	$\dfrac{L \ \text{->} \ R \in \text{Pgm}}{\theta L \Rightarrow \theta R}$

Figure 17.2: Rewriting semantics.

Call-by-value semantics. This can be defined by restricting the context rule to

$$(\text{Value context}) \quad \frac{t' \Rightarrow t''}{t[t']^{in} \Rightarrow t[t'']^{in}}$$

Here $t[t']^{in}$ denotes a *leftmost innermost* context, meaning that t' is a call containing no subcall, and that there is no complete call to its left. Thus calls within constructor subterms are evaluated, and function arguments are fully evaluated before substitutions are performed. Clearly any term containing a redex (i.e. not in normal form) also contains a redex in a value context.

Lazy evaluation. This is a variant of call-by-name much used in functional languages. Its characteristic is that neither user-defined functions *nor data constructors* evaluate their arguments unless needed, e.g. to perform a match or to print the program's final output. It is defined by restricting the context rule as follows.

$$(\text{Lazy context}) \quad \frac{t' \Rightarrow t''}{t[t']^{lazy} \Rightarrow t[t'']^{lazy}}$$

where $t[t']^{lazy}$ denotes a term with subterm t' which is not contained in any constructor, and that there is no call beginning to its left. Note that a term may contain one or more redexes and still have no redexes in a lazy context (as in the next example).

Consequently, evaluation is outside-in as much as possible. Constructor components of c $E_1 \dots E_n$ are not evaluated at all, and function arguments are not evaluated before substitutions are performed[1]. Further reductions will occur only if there is a demand (e.g. by the printer) for more output. Following is an example. The calls in the last line will not be not further evaluated unless externally demanded.

```
append [append (Cons A Nil) (Cons B Nil)]^lazy (Cons C Nil) ⇒
[append (Cons A (append Nil (Cons B Nil)))]^lazy (Cons C Nil) ⇒
Cons A (append (append Nil (Cons B Nil)) (Cons C Nil))
```

The following example illustrates that lazy semantics assigns meaningful results to programs which would loop using call-by-value. Here, ones is intuitively an infinite list of 1's, and take u v returns the first n elements of v, where n is the length of list u.

```
f n   -> take n ones
ones -> Cons 1 ones

take Nil ys  -> Nil
take (Cons x xs) (Cons y ys) -> Cons y (take xs ys)
```

In the following example, lazy evaluation stops after the first line. For illustration we assume that the printer demands the entire output, repeatedly forcing evaluation of constructor argments:

```
f (Cons A (Cons B Nil)) ⇒ Cons 1 (take (Cons B Nil) ones)
                        ⇒ Cons 1 (Cons 1 (take Nil ones))
                        ⇒ Cons 1 (Cons 1 Nil).
```

17.2   Fold/unfold transformations

Transformations as used by Burstall and Darlington [43] are shown in Figure 17.3, which shows how one adds new rules to·a given set Pgm. Transformation 'define' allows a new function rule to be introduced, or it may extend an existing definition and so cause the program to be defined on more inputs than before. 'Instantiate' allows an existing rule to be specialized. 'Unfold', like the 'function call' semantic rule, replaces a call of a function definition by its right side, after performing the needed substitutions. 'Fold' does the converse.

Restrictions. If used too freely, the transformations of Figure 17.3 could lead to inconsistent or badly formed programs. The 'Define' restriction ensures that newly defined function values cannot conflict with old ones. Instantiation will *always* lead

---

[1]In practice implementations use 'call-by-need' to avoid repeated subcomputations. This does not change program meanings, just their efficiency.

to overlap, but not in conflict with existing definitions. A transformed program may thus contain many overlapping rules so a final pass may be performed to remove unneeded or unreachable rules to obtain a complete and minimal set.

Finally, we restrict the 'Instantiate' and 'Fold' transformations to be applied *only in case* the conclusion is a rule as defined in Figure 17.1. In particular one disallows introduction in a left side of repeated variables or nested function calls, or introduction in a right side of variables not found on the left.

(Define)	$\dfrac{\text{Pgm contains no rule L -> R where L overlaps L}'}{\text{L}' \text{ -> R}' \in \text{Pgm}}$
(Instantiate)	$\dfrac{\text{L->R} \ \in \ \text{Pgm}}{\theta\text{L -> } \theta\text{R} \in \text{Pgm}}$
(Unfold)	$\dfrac{\text{L->R} \in \text{Pgm and L}' \text{ -> R}'[\theta\text{L}] \in \text{Pgm}}{\text{L}' \text{ -> R}'[\theta\text{R}] \in \text{Pgm}}$
(Fold)	$\dfrac{\text{L->R} \in \text{Pgm and L}' \text{ -> R}'[\theta\text{R}] \in \text{Pgm}}{\text{L}' \text{ -> R}'[\theta\text{L}] \in \text{Pgm}}$

Figure 17.3: Program transformations.

17.2.1 Examples

Figure 17.3 adds rules in a completely free way, so before discussing ways to automate the transformations we give some examples. A common usage pattern:

1. devise a new *definition*, and

2. *instantiate* it so as to enable

3. *unfolding* at various places, followed by

4. *folding* the resulting rules into earlier ones.

Devising new definitions requires the most creativity, whence it is sometimes called a 'eureka' step. The cycle may be repeated, followed by a final phase to remove redundant or unreachable rules to obtain a complete and non-overlapping set.

Double append
The following program with pattern matching defines h:

```
1. h us vs ws      -> append (append us vs) ws
2. append Nil ys           ->  ys
3. append (Cons x xs) ys  ->  Cons x (append xs ys)
```

and traverses its first argument us twice. To transform it into a more efficient one pass program, we instantiate h's definition twice, followed by some unfolding and finally folding, as follows.

```
4. h Nil vs ws            -> append (append Nil vs) ws        (1,2)
5. h (Cons u us) vs ws -> append(append (Cons u us)vs) ws (1,3)
```

Unfolding the innermost append calls gives

```
6. h Nil vs ws            -> append vs ws                     (4,2)
7. h (Cons u us) vs ws -> append (Cons u(append us vs)) ws (5,3)
```

and unfolding the outermost call in this gives

```
8. h (Cons u us) vs ws -> Cons u (append(append us vs) ws) (7,3)
```

Finally, folding with the original definition of h gives

```
9. h (Cons u us) vs ws -> Cons u (h us vs ws)                (8,1)
```

Selecting a minimal complete set gives the desired program, which traverses the first argument of h only once:

```
6.   h Nil vs ws           -> append vs ws
9.   h (Cons u us) vs ws   -> Cons u (h us vs ws)
2.   append Nil ys         -> ys
3.   append (Cons x xs) ys -> Cons x (append xs ys)
```

First thoughts towards automation

The example above follows the cycle 'define, instantiate, unfold, fold,' and some characteristics suggest how the process may be more fully automated. Suppose we think of the transformation process as beginning with a program and a 'rule of interest' $L_{initial}$ -> $R_{initial}$, and that we separate the original program from the newly constructed rules.

In the example we began with rule of interest and added new rules which were then processed in turn. It is natural to describe this by a set *Pending*, of rules that have been selected for attention, together with a set *Out*, of finished rules that have been added to the transformed program. In the example just seen, initially Pending = {h us vs ws -> append(append us vs)ws} and Out = { } .

Transformation processes the rules in Pending. Some lead to new definitions that are added to Pending for further processing, and others are added to Out at once, to appear in the final transformed program. We have not yet described the core problem: how new definitions are devised. Two special transformation algorithms, one for partial evaluation and one for deforestation, and each with its own definition strategy, will be seen in later sections. To our knowledge, however, no one has successfully automated the full fold/unfold paradigm.

Fibonacci

Applying the same approach to an exponential time program to compute the nth Fibonacci number yields a more dramatic speedup. For simplicity n is represented using constructors as 0+1+1...+1, writing the binary constructor + in infix notation. This example follows the cycle 'define, instantiate, unfold, fold,' but a bit more inventively.

```
1.  fib x    -> f x
2.  f 0      -> 0
3.  f 0+1    -> 0+1
4.  f n+1+1 -> f(n+1) + f(n)
```

First introduce a new rule 5 by a so-called 'eureka!' step, instantiate it twice, and then unfold some f calls. Here (_,_) is a pair constructor, written in 'outfix' notation.

```
5.  g x   ->  (f(x+1),f(x))
6.  g 0   ->  (f(0+1),f(0))  -> (0+1,0)
7.  g x+1 ->  (f(x+1+1),f(x+1))
8.  g x+1 ->  (f(x+1) + f(x), f(x+1))
```

Call f(x+1) occurs twice, suggesting a new definition to eliminate the common subexpression:

```
9.  h (u,v) -> (u + v, u)
```

Folding with definitions of h and then the original g gives:

```
10.  g x+1 -> h(f(x+1), f(x))
11.  g x+1 -> h(g(x))
```

The last transformation is to express fib in terms of g:

```
12.  snd (u, v)          -> v
13.  snd (f(x+1),f(x)) ->  f(x)
14.  snd (g(x))          -> f(x)
15.  fib x -> snd(g(x))
```

Selecting a minimal complete set gives the transformed program:

```
15.  fib x    ->  snd(g(x))
 6.  g 0      ->  (0+1,0)
11.  g x+1    ->  h(g(x))
 9.  h (u,v) ->  (u + v, u)
```

A major improvement has occurred since the transformed program's running time has been reduced from exponential to linear, assuming either call-by-value or call-by-need evaluation.

17.2.2   Correctness

For general optimization the rule of interest is just a call to the program's main function, as in the examples above. For partial evaluation we are interested in *function specialization,* so the rule of interest is a call giving values to some static inputs, e.g. $f_{5,7}$ y z -> f 5 7 y z.

Correctness means that any call to $L_{initial}$ in the original program gives exactly the same results in the transformed program. For some purposes this may be relaxed so a transformed program is acceptable if it terminates on *at least* all the inputs on which the original program terminates, and gives the same answers on them. It is less acceptable that a transformed program terminates *less often* than the original, and quite unacceptable if it gives different answers.

A full discussion of correctness is beyond the scope of this book; see Kott and Courcelle for formal treatments [154,63]. Intuitively, unfolding is correct since it follows execution as described in the rewriting rules, and definition and instantiation cannot go wrong. On the other hand, folding in effect 'runs the program backwards' which can in some cases cause a loss of termination. To see this, consider rule f x -> x+1. Here term x+1 can be folded into the same rule's left side, yielding f x -> f x. This is a trivially complete and non-overlapping program, but never terminates.

Unfolding can increase termination under call-by-value, an example being

```
f x   ->  g x (h x)
g u v ->  u+1
h y   ->  h y
```

where unfolding the g call yields f x -> x+1. This terminates for all x, though the original program *never* terminates under call-by-value.

17.2.3   Steering program transformation

The rules of Figure 17.3 are highly non-deterministic, particularly with regard to making new definitions and instantiation. We saw that one must take care to avoid changing program termination properties. On the other hand substantial payoff can be realized, for instance improving the Fibonacci program from exponential to linear time.

In this section we describe a general goal-directed transformation method. It will first be specialized to yield a simple online partial evaluator, and will later give a way to remove intermediate data structures, e.g. as in 'double append' of Section 17.2.1.

An approach to deterministic transformation
The method uses two sets of rules in addition to the original program: *Out,* the rules that so far have been added to the transformed program; and *Pending,* a

set of rules that have not yet been processed. Initially Pending has only one goal rule, representing a call to the program on unspecified input. Each rule in Pending is of form L -> R where term R has as an instance some term obtained while symbolically executing the original program. (This is essentially the same as to Turchin's *basic configurations* [263].) L defines a new function, to appear in the transformed program.

Rules in Pending are processed one at a time, sometimes causing new rules to be added to Out or Pending. The algorithm stops when no unprocessed rules remain. An informal algorithm invariant: the rule set Out ∪ Pending is consistent with the meaning of the original program Pgm. When finished, Out is the transformed program.

We implicitly assume *variable name standardization* so Pending and Out will never contain rules L -> R and L' -> R' differing only in the names of left side variables. The general method is as follows:

1. Simulate the program's computation, using variables for unknown values. Allow for all possible program inputs.

2. At each stage look for a *potential redex*. If variables are insufficient to continue the simulation, instantiate them in all possibly relevant ways.

3. Unfold a redex whenever possible. Rationale: computation done at transformation time need not be done in the transformed program.

4. Reasons *not* to unfold:

   - The chosen semantics would not unfold.

   - The current call configuration has been seen before. Unfolding too liberally could cause looping at transformation time. An appropriate response is to *specialize* or *memoize*, i.e. to generate code to call the configuration seen before (a fold step)[2].

   - There is insufficient information to decide which rule would be applied to the redex. Response: make a new function definition f $P_1 \ldots P_n$ -> B; fold the potential redex into a call to f; and instantiate the new rule as in 2 to account for all possible rule matches.

17.3   Partial evaluation by fold/unfold

Following is a sketch of a simple online partial evaluator for the current language with a control strategy used earlier: unfold as long as no dynamic tests occur, and specialize calls to configurations seen before. We assume a call-by-value semantics, as in the partial evaluators of earlier chapters.

---

[2]This could be called a *déjà vu* tactic.

A partial evaluation algorithm

The algorithm is shown in Figure 17.4. It begins with an initial goal rule L_0 ->
R_0, where R_0 would typically be a function name applied to some constants and
some ground terms. Attention points are leftmost innermost calls, and the rules
added to Pending have form ... -> f $P_1 \ldots P_n$, where in the right side basic
configurations, each P_i is either a variable or a ground term.

In a call f $t_1 \ldots t_n$, if argument t_i contains no variables, then it will be reduced
until its value t_i' is known (it could be or contain a call). This paves the way for
definition to create a specialized version of f, in case some t_i's evaluate to ground
terms. Instantiation is done to ensure completeness — that all possibly applicable
rules will also be processed.

Main program
Out := {};
Pending := {$L_{initial}$ -> $T_{initial}$};
while ∃ an unmarked rule L_0->R_0 ∈ Pending **do**
   Mark it;
   forall L -> R ∈ Program and θ, θ_0 **such that** $\theta L = \theta_0 R_0$ **do**
      Add $\theta_0 L_0$ -> $T[\![\theta R]\!]$ to Out;

Definition of T
$T[\![x]\!]$ = x
$T[\![c\ t_1 \ldots t_n]\!]$ = c $T[\![t_1]\!] \ldots T[\![t_n]\!]$

$T[\![f\ t_1 \ldots t_n]\!]$ =
      let $u_1 = T[\![t_1]\!], \ldots, u_n = T[\![t_n]\!]$ in
      let $(\theta_0, L_0$->$R_0) = \text{Make\_new}(f\ u_1 \ldots u_n)$ in
      if L_0 -> R_0 ∈ Pending then $\theta_0 L_0$ else
      if ∃ rule L -> R ∈ Pgm and θ with $\theta L = f\ u_1 \ldots u_n$ then $T[\![\theta R]\!]$ else
         Add L_0 -> R_0 to Pending;
         result is $\theta_0 L_0$

Definition of Make_new
$\text{Make\_new}(f\ t_1 \ldots t_n) = (\theta, g\ x_{i1} \ldots x_{im}$->$f\ s_1 \ldots s_n)$ **where**
    s_i = if t_i is ground then t_i else x_i
    $\theta(f\ s_1 \ldots s_n) = f\ t_1 \ldots t_n$
    g is a new function name, depending only on f and the ground s_i's
    $\{i_1, \ldots i_m\}$ = $\{i \mid t_i$ is non $-$ ground$\}$

Figure 17.4: Partial evaluation by fold/unfold.

Explanation. In partial evaluation terms, we assume the initial call configuration
contains some arguments which are ground terms and some variables. Variables

that have not been rewritten as a result of unfolding remain unchanged, and arguments of constructors are transformed.

Function $\mathcal{T}[\![\_]\!]$ unfolds a call whenever the statically available information is sufficient to see which rule is to be applied. When dynamic information is needed, no left side will match at partial evaluation time, and so a new rule is created. The effect of 'Make_new' is to create a new function, specialized to all those arguments of the current call which are ground terms. Thus new functions are created whenever a dynamic test is encountered, a strategy we have seen before.

In fold/unfold terms, Pending contains only definitions L_0 -> R_0 of new functions, either the initial one or ones devised in $\mathcal{T}[\![\_]\!]$ when no left side matched the current configuration.

In the main program, the condition that L -> R $\in$ Program and $\theta L = \theta_0 R_0$ implies that rule $\theta_0 L_0$ -> θR can be obtained by instantiation and unfolding.

The rules added to Out are obtained from $\theta_0 L_0$ -> θR by applying function $\mathcal{T}[\![\_]\!]$, which either unfolds further, or folds with a function whose definition has been placed in Pending.

Thus each step follows one of Burstall and Darlington's rules. It can be seen that Out will be a complete and non-overlapping set, provided the original program was.

Example
We specialize Ackermann's function `ack m n` to static values of m, writing $1,2,\ldots$ instead of $0+1, 0+1+1, \ldots$. The initial rule is a_2 x -> `ack 2 x`, and the original program is

```
ack 0 n      ->   n+1
ack m+1 0    ->   ack m 1
ack m+1 n+1  ->   ack m (ack m+1 n)
```

Applying the algorithm above constructs in turn

Pending = { a_2 x -> ack 2 x}	Initial
Out = { a_2 0 -> 3}	Match x to 0, evaluate completely
Pending = { a_1 y -> ack 1 y,...}	Match x to n+1, add fcn. a_1
Out = { a_2 n+1 -> a_1 (a_2 n), ...}	Call the new function
Out = { a_1 0 -> 2, ...}	Match x to 0, evaluate completely
Out = { a_1 n+1 -> (a_1 n)+1, ...}	By a_1 n+1 -> ack 0 (ack 1 n)

Final remarks. Thus at least one partial evaluation algorithm can be expressed using fold/unfold transformations. We hope the reader can see that the more complex offline algorithms of earlier chapters can also be seen as instances of Burstall and Darlington's approach.

This scheme is deterministic, and folding is done in a sufficiently disciplined way to avoid losing termination. On the other hand, it suffers from three weaknesses seen in earlier partial evaluators:

- It can increase termination, since some unfolding is done when the call-by-value semantics would not do it.

- Partial evaluation can produce infinitely many residual rules, or can loop non-productively while computing on ground values.

- Subcomputations can be repeated.

17.4   Supercompilation and deforestation

Supercompilation (in the sense of 'supervised compilation') is a program transformation technique developed in the USSR in the 1970s by Valentin Turchin. It is of interest in this book for several reasons:

- Historical: it appears that Turchin and, independently, Beckman *et. al.* were the first to realize that the third Futamura projection would yield a generator of program generators (Futamura described only the first two) [263,92,19].

- Philosophical: supercompilation is a concrete manifestation of the very general concept of 'metasystem transition' [266,98].

- Power: supercompilation can both do partial evaluation and remove intermediate data structures as seen in the 'double append' example of Section 17.2.1.

On the other hand, supercompilation in its full generality has not yet been self-applied without hand annotations, partly due to problems concerning termination.

Turchin's work has only become appreciated in the West in recent years [267]. His earlier papers were in Russian, and expressed in terms of a functional language Refal not familiar to western readers. Many important ideas and insights go back to the 1970's, but that work has some loose ends, e.g. semantics is not always preserved exactly.

Wadler's 'deforestation' [274], with a more solid semantic foundation, can be regarded as a limited application of supercompilation to a lazy language. In this section we shall present what in our conception is the essence of Turchin and Wadler's ideas, also using a lazy functional language.

An example

The earlier program using infinite lists with initial rule f n -> take n ones has a call which cannot immediately be unfolded. Instantiating n and unfolding ones yields rules that can be rewritten:

```
f Nil          -> take Nil ones
f (Cons x xs)  -> take (Cons x xs) (Cons 1 ones)
```

Unfolding the `take` calls yields:

```
f Nil          -> Nil
f (Cons x xs)  -> Cons 1 (take xs ones)
```

containing the configuration `take xs ones`, which has already been seen. This can be folded back into `f` to yield a simpler and faster program:

```
f Nil          -> Nil
f (Cons x xs)  -> Cons 1 (f xs)
```

Informal explanation. Computations are simulated to allow for all constructors in `f n` for any n. To find the outermost constructor, it is necessary to find the outermost constructor of `take n ones`. The first `take` rule requires instantiating n to `Nil`, and the second requires instantiating n to `Cons x xs` plus a single unfolding of `ones`. Further unfolding of `ones` is not done, since this would not faithfully model lazy evaluation.

A syntactic restriction

The program transformation algorithm is easier to express if we assume there are only two function definition forms, either h-functions or g-functions. The 'generic' letter `f` will stand for either form.

$$h\ x_1 \ldots x_n\ \rightarrow R_h \qquad \text{One rule, no pattern matching}$$

$$g\ P_1\ x_1 \ldots x_n\ \rightarrow R_{g1} \qquad \text{A rule set, with pattern matching}$$
$$\ldots \qquad \qquad \text{on the first argument only}$$
$$g\ P_m\ x_1 \ldots x_n\ \rightarrow R_{gm}$$

where each $P_i = c_i\ y_1 \ldots y_{p_i}$ is a *simple pattern* only one constructor deep. Augustsson describes how an arbitrary program may be put into this form without changing its semantics, even when overlapping rules are resolved by top-to-bottom rule application [15].

Note that `append` has g-form. The program using infinite lists needs a little rewriting to fit the two forms (where `f` and `ones` are functions of form h):

```
f n  -> take n ones
ones -> Cons 1 ones

take Nil ys          -> Nil
take (Cons x xs) ys  -> u ys xs

u (Cons y ys) xs     -> Cons y (take xs ys)
```

Lazy contexts.   These, as defined before, can only take on the following forms. For use in transformation we add a clause for terms with free variables.

1. $g_1(g_2 \ldots (g_n \; [h \; t_1 \ldots t_m] \; t_1^n \ldots t_{m_n}^n) \ldots) t_1^1 \ldots t_{m_1}^1 \quad (n \geq 0)$, or

2. $g_1(g_2 \ldots [g_n \; (c \; t_1 \ldots t_m) \; t_1^n \ldots t_{m_n}^n] \ldots) t_1^1 \ldots t_{m_1}^1 \quad (n \geq 1)$, or

3. $g_1(g_2 \ldots [g_n \; v \; t_1^n \ldots t_{m_n}^n]) \ldots) t_1^1 \ldots t_{m_1}^1 \quad (n \geq 0)$

Explanations.   A call $h \; t_1 \ldots t_n$ can be rewritten at once, while a call $g \; t_0 t_1 \ldots t_n$ forces evaluation of t_0 to bring its outermost constructor 'to the surface' before rewriting can be done. The 'attention point' can thus appear inside a nest of g calls, as seen in all three cases.

For program transformation, cases 1 and 2 can be unfolded at once. Case 3 cannot, but one may define a new function with 3 as its right side, and instantiate v to allow the g_n call to be rewritten.

Short form.   We write $e[f \; t_0 t_1 \ldots t_n]$ to indicate all three context forms, so $e[]$ $= g_1(g_2 \ldots [] \ldots) \ldots) \ldots)$.

17.4.1   A transformation algorithm

By the following strategy intermediate data structures produced in one part of a program and consumed in another part may be eliminated entirely. This pattern was seen in 'double append' of Section 17.2.1, which illustrates combining phases of a multipass algorithm. In other words, the discipline is good for *symbolic function composition.*

The process is automatic and preserves lazy semantics, but in its first version will not terminate on all programs. After illustrating how (and why) it works, we discuss ways to guarantee termination.

Deforestation
Rule sets Pending and Out are used in Figure 17.5 as in the partial evaluation algorithm. We now argue that the algorithm preserves the lazy semantics, with the following assumptions:

1. Global: that any part of the program's output on any input can possibly be demanded; and

2. Local: that evaluation proceeds only until a value's outermost constructor is known.

The global assumptions ensure the transformed program will cover all possible run-time situations. The program is processed systematically, generating new rules to

Main program
Out := {};
Pending := $\{L_{initial}$ -> $T_{initial}\}$;
while ∃ an unmarked rule g' v $x_1 \ldots x_m$ -> e[g v $t_1 \ldots t_n$] ∈ Pending **do**
   Mark it;
     forall g P $v_1 \ldots v_n$ -> R ∈ Program **do**
       Add g' P $x_1 \ldots x_m$ -> $T[\![(e[g P t_1 \ldots t_n])]\!]$ to Out;

Definition of T
$T[\![x]\!]$ = x
$T[\![c\ t_1 \ldots t_n]\!]$ = c $T[\![t_1]\!] \ldots T[\![t_n]\!]$

$T[\![e[h\ t_1 \ldots t_n]]\!]$ =
   let rule L -> R ∈ Pgm with $\theta L = h\ t_1 \ldots t_n$ in $T[\![e[\theta R]]\!]$

$T[\![e[g(c\ t'_1 \ldots t'_m)t_1 \ldots t_n]]\!]$ =
   let rule L -> R ∈ Pgm with $\theta L = e[g(c\ t'_1 \ldots t'_m)t_1 \ldots t_n]$ in $T[\![e[\theta R]]\!]$

$T[\![e[g\ v\ t_1 \ldots t_n]]\!]$ =
     let L_0->R_0 = make_new(e[g v $t_1 \ldots t_n$]) in
     if L_0->R_0 ∈ Pending **then** L_0 **else**
       Add L_0->R_0 to Pending;
      result is L_0

Definition of Make_new
Make_new(e[g v $t_1 \ldots t_n$]) = g' v $x_1 \ldots x_m$ -> e[g v $t_1 \ldots t_n$] **where**
   g' is a new function name, depending only on e[g v $t_1 \ldots t_n$], and
   $\{x_1, \ldots, x_m\}$ = FreeVariables(e[g v $t_1 \ldots t_n$])\{v}

Figure 17.5: Deforestation by fold/unfold.

cover computations on all possible inputs. By 1, one instantiates variable v in a lazy context e[g v ...] for all possibly matching g rules. Components of a construction c $t_1 \ldots t_n$ so obtained may be processed further since the values of $t_1 \ldots t_n$ can possibly be demanded.

Assumption 2 implies that unfolding and instantiation may *only* be done if forced by lazy evaluation. By 1, a call not inside another call may be unfolded, even if inside a constructor term. For an outermost g call (g (h...)...), the value of h will be needed in order to determine which g rule can be applied. Thus the h call may be unfolded at transformation time.

Summing up, when outermost call unfolding is impossible the algorithm instantiates or unfolds calls in a first g argument as needed to be able to continue. The result is a program with call configurations e[g v $t_1 \ldots t_n$], perhaps nested. New function definitions are made for each for appropriate instantiations of v, and the program is folded to refer to the new functions. Termination requires the number of these to be finite — which often occurs in practice.

17.4.2   Achieving finiteness

The algorithm above often improves programs significantly. Careful attention has been paid to preserving the language's lazy semantics, but there are problems: it loops infinitely on some source programs, and can slow programs down because of duplicated computations. We briefly discuss the problems and some approaches to solving them.

Finiteness by syntactic restrictions
Wadler's 'deforestation' algorithm resembles the one above, and has been proven both to terminate and not decrease execution speed when applied to *treeless* programs [274,86], defined by some restrictive syntactic conditions. Non-degradation of run time further requires rules to be *right linear*, meaning that no pattern variable is used more than once on a rule's right side.

Wadler's transformation rules, and the algorithm above as well, succeed on some non-treeless programs, and improve some non-linear programs. A result recently proven (not yet published) is that the algorithm above terminates and yields the same result whenever applied to a treeless program.

In the literature, relaxation of the syntactic conditions has been done in two ways. Wadler defines 'blazing', a way to recognize parts of a program dealing with non-treelike data, for instance integers, and only requires that the non-blazed parts be treeless and linear. Chin has a 'variables only' requirement somewhat more liberal than Wadler's conditions [45]. Further, he devises a type system to extend 'blazing' to arbitrary programs, so that every term in a program is annotated as treeless or non-treeless. The result is that any program may be handled; but the annotation scheme is rather conservative, leaving untransformed many terms that the algorithm above can optimize.

Finiteness by generalization
The algorithm of Figure 17.5 'can go wrong' by adding rules g' v $x_1 \ldots x_m$ -> t to Pending or Out for infinitely many t. In general the right side has the form

$$t = g_1(\ldots (g_n [g \ v \ t_1 \ldots t_n] \ldots) \ldots)$$

so the problem is unboundedly deep call nesting. A concrete example to illustrate the problem is the 'flatten' program (a is 'append' from before):

```
g (Leaf x)            ->   Cons x Nil
g (Branch t₁ t₂)      ->   a (g t₁) (g t₂)
a Nil ys                   ->   ys
a (Cons x xs)         ->   Cons x (a xs ys)
```

which returns a list of all leaves of a binary tree. The algorithm of Figure 17.5 begins by constructing

$$
\begin{aligned}
\text{Pending} &= \{g_0 \ x \ \text{->} \ g \ x\} \\
\text{Out} &= \{g_0(\text{Leaf } x) && \text{-> Cons x Nil}\} \\
\text{Pending} &= \{g_1 \ t_1 \ t_2 && \text{-> a (g } t_1) \ (g \ t_2), \ldots\} \\
\text{Out} &= \{g_0(\text{Branch } t_1 \ t_2) && \text{-> } g_1 \ t_1 \ t_2, \ldots\} \\
\text{Out} &= \{g_1(\text{Leaf } x) t_2 && \text{-> Cons x } (g_0 \ t_2), \ldots\} \\
\text{Out} &= \{g_1(\text{Branch } t_1 \ t_2) t_3 && \text{-> } g_2 \ t_1 \ t_2 \ t_3, \ldots\} \\
\text{Pending} &= \{g_2 \ t_1 \ t_2 \ t_3 && \text{-> a(a(g } t_1)(g \ t_2)) \ (g \ t_3), \ldots\}
\end{aligned}
$$

Function g_0 has one argument, g_1 has two, g_2 has three, etc., so transformation fails to terminate.

A natural solution to this is to *generalize*, i.e. to add fewer and more general new definitions. One way is to extend syntax to include 'Term ::= gen(t)'. (gen is not a constructor, and should be ignored in the standard semantics.) In the example above, t_1 would not be instantiated to Leaf x and Branch t_1 t_2.

To illustrate suppose we annotate the program as

```
g (Leaf x)            ->   Cons x Nil
g (Branch t₁ t₂)      ->   a gen(g t₁) (g t₂)
a Nil ys                   ->   ys
a (Cons x xs)         ->   Cons x (a xs ys)
```

Applying Figure 17.5 with generalization proceeds as follows:

$$
\begin{aligned}
\text{Pending} &= \{g_0 \ x \ \text{->} \ g \ x\} \\
\text{Out} &= \{g_0(\text{Leaf } x) && \text{-> Cons x Nil}\} \\
\text{Pending} &= \{g_1 \ t_1 \ t_2 && \text{-> a gen(g } t_1) \ (g \ t_2), \ldots\} \\
\text{Out} &= \{g_0(\text{Branch } t_1 \ t_2) && \text{-> } g_1 \ (g_0 \ t_1) \ t_2, \ldots\} \\
\text{Out} &= \{g_1 \ \text{Nil } t_2 && \text{-> } g_0 \ t_2, \ldots\} \\
\text{Out} &= \{g_1(\text{Cons x xs}) \ t_2 && \text{-> Cons x } (g_1 \ xs \ t_2), \ldots\}
\end{aligned}
$$

The transformed program is thus:

```
g₀ (Leaf x)            ->   Cons x Nil
g₀ (Branch t₁ t₂)      ->   g₁ (g₀ t₁) t₂
g₁ Nil t₂                   ->   g₀ t₂
g₁ (Cons x xs) t₂      ->   Cons x (g₁ xs t₂)
```

How can one generalize?

There is no definitive answer to this question as yet. Turchin has a sophisticated online approach which is rather complex, partly due to the language Refal being transformed [269].

Current research involves an offline approach, preprocessing a program to find out where to place generalization annotations. The idea is to construct a grammar able to generate all configurations that could ever arise in transformation by the algorithm above. The grammar will be finite even if transformation would continue infinitely. Once the grammar is constructed it may be analysed to recognize the sources of infinity, to see where to place gen(_) annotations, and how to interpret them so transformation will create only finitely many configurations.

17.5   Exercises

Exercise 17.1 Use the algorithm described in Figure 17.4 to partially evaluate the power-program with respect to n = 5 and unknown x. The initial rule is power₅ x -> power 5 x, and the original program is

```
1. power 0 x    -> 1
2. power n+1 x -> x * power n x
```

□

Exercise 17.2 Use the same algorithm to partially evaluate the following program. This time with respect to xs = [a,b], zs = [c,d], and unknown ys. The initial rule is aa_abcd ys -> append (append [a,b] ys) [c,d], and the original program is

```
1. append Nil ys         -> ys
2. append (Cons x xs) ys -> Cons x (append xs ys)
```

□

Exercise 17.3 Apply Burstall and Darlington's method (as in Section 17.2.1) to improve the following program:

```
1. f xs -> rev (db xs) Nil

2. db Nil           -> Nil
3. db (Cons y ys) -> Cons (2*y) (db ys)

4. rev Nil ws           -> ws
5. rev (Cons v vs) ws -> rev vs (Cons v ws)
```

□

Exercise 17.4 Apply the deforestation algorithm described in Figure 17.5 to the following expressions: flip (flip tree) and (sum (map square (upto 1 n))), with the following definitions:

```
1. flip (Leaf a)     -> (Leaf a)
2. flip (Branch x y) -> Branch (flip x) (flip y)

3. upto m n -> if (m > n) then Nil else (Cons m (upto m+1 n))

4. sum Nil          -> 0
5. sum (Cons x xs) -> x + (sum xs)

6. square Nil          -> Nil
7. square (Cons x xs) -> Cons (x*x) (square xs)

8. map f Nil          -> Nil
9. map f (Cons x xs) -> Cons (f x) (map f xs)
```

□

,uide to the Literature

This chapter gives an overview of the current literature on partial evaluation. We first sketch the history from 1952 to 1984. Then we give an overview of the literature grouped by subject language (imperative, functional, logical), by the techniques used in partial evaluation (including binding-time analysis), and by applications. Finally, we mention some related topics.

The bibliography file is available for anonymous ftp from `ftp.diku.dk` as file `pub/diku/dists/jones-book/partial-eval.bib.Z`. See page 123 of this book.

18.1 A brief historical overview

18.1.1 The classics

Kleene's *s-m-n theorem* (1952) essentially asserts the feasibility of partial evaluation [149]. Kleene proved that for any given program (Turing machine) for a general $m + n$-argument function f, and given values $a_1, \ldots, a_m$ of the first m arguments, there exists a program (a Turing machine) for the specialized function $g = f_{a_1, \ldots, a_m}$ which satisfies $g(b_1, \ldots, b_n) = f(a_1, \ldots, a_m, b_1, \ldots, b_n)$ for all $b_1, \ldots, b_n$. Moreover, there is a program (a Turing machine) which effectively constructs the specialized program from the general one and the inputs. Thus Kleene's constructive proof provides the design for a partial evaluator.

However, his design did not, and was not intended to, provide any improvement of the specialized program. Such improvement, by symbolic reductions or similar, has been the goal in all subsequent work in partial evaluation.

Lombardi (Italy and the USA, 1964) is probably the first use to the term 'partial evaluation', when discussing the use of Lisp for incremental computation, or computation with incomplete information [175,176]. Landin (UK) also mentions partial evaluation, but does not define it, in a discussion on evaluation of lambda calculus expressions [161, p. 318].

Futamura (Japan, 1971) is the first researcher to consider a partial evaluator as a *program* as well as a transformer, and thus to consider the application of the partial evaluator to itself [92]. Futamura's paper gives the equations for compilation and compiler generation (single self-application) using partial evaluation, but not that for compiler generator generation (double self-application). The three equations were called *Futamura projections* by Andrei Ershov [80]. Futamura's early ideas were not implemented.

Around 1975, Beckman, Haraldsson, Oskarsson, and Sandewall (Sweden) developed a partial evaluator called *Redfun* for a substantial subset of Lisp, and described the possibilities for compilation, compiler generation, and compiler generator generation by single and double self-application [19]. This is probably the first published description of the possibility of compiler generator generation by double self-application.

Turchin and his group in Moscow (USSR) also discovered the idea of partial evaluation in the early 1970s, while working with symbolic computation in the functional language *Refal*. A description of self-application and double self-application is found in [263] (in Russian). The history of that work is briefly summarized in English in [264].

Andrei Ershov in Novosibirsk (USSR) worked with imperative languages also, and used the term *mixed computation* to mean roughly the same as partial evaluation [76,77]. Ershov gave two comprehensive surveys of the activities in the field of partial evaluation and mixed computation, including overviews of the literature up until that time [78,79]. Futamura gave another overview of the literature [93].

18.1.2   Renewed interest

However, until 1984 neither single nor double self-application had been carried out in practice. At that time Jones, Sestoft, and Søndergaard (Denmark) constructed the first self-applicable partial evaluator. It was written in a language of first-order recursion equations (or first-order statically scoped pure Lisp), and was used to generate toy compilers and compiler generators [135,136,245].

At the same time the interest in partial evaluation in logic programming and other areas was increasing. This was the background for the first Workshop on Partial Evaluation and Mixed Computation (PEMC) held in October 1987 in Denmark. The workshop was organized by Dines Bjørner (Denmark), Andrei P. Ershov (USSR), and Neil D. Jones (Denmark), and was the first to bring together a substantial number of partial evaluation researchers from all over the world.

The papers from the workshop have been published in a book [24] and in a special issue of the journal New Generation Computing [84]. Both contain Andrei Ershov's personal account of the history of mixed computation and partial evaluation [82, 83], and a bibliography of all known papers on partial evaluation [248,249]. The bibliography includes a substantial number of papers published in Russian and largely unknown to western researchers.

An ACM Sigplan Symposium on Partial Evaluation and Semantics-Based Program Manipulation (PEPM) was held June 1991 in the USA and was organized by Charles Consel (USA) and Olivier Danvy (USA) [1]. An ACM Sigplan Workshop on the same theme was held June 1992 in the USA [2], and another ACM Sigplan PEPM Symposium was held June 1993 in Denmark.

18.2   Partial evaluation literature by subject language

18.2.1   Imperative languages

Ershov and his group worked primarily on imperative languages [76,78,79]. In 1985 Bulyonkov and Ershov constructed their first self-applicable partial evaluator (for a flow chart language), reported in [42].

Gomard and Jones reported a self-applicable partial evaluator for a flow chart language in [103].

Jacobsen constructed a partial evaluator for a small subset of C [126]. Meyer studies procedure specialization in an imperative language [182,183]. Nirkhe and Pugh report a similar partial evaluator, but it cannot produce recursive residual procedures [205]. Andersen's partial evaluator for a C subset handles procedures as well as pointers and arrays, and is self-applicable [7,8,9]. See Chapter 11 of this book.

18.2.2   Functional languages

Beckman, Haraldsson, Oskarsson, and Sandewall constructed the first major partial evaluator, called Redfun for a substantial subset of Lisp [19,112,113].

Later partial evaluators for Lisp and Scheme have been reported by Kahn [143], Schooler [243], and Guzowski [108]. Weise *et al.* constructed a fully automatic online partial evaluator for a subset of Scheme [281].

Jones, Sestoft, and Søndergaard constructed the first self-applicable partial evaluator for first-order recursion equations. It was called *mix*, following Ershov's terminology. The first version required user supplied annotations [135,245], but a later version was fully automatic [136,246]. Sergei Romanenko improved on that work in various respects [227]. Chapter 5 of this book presents a self-applicable partial evaluator for a first-order functional language.

Consel constructed a self-applicable partial evaluator called *Schism* for a user-extensible first-order Scheme subset, handling partially static structures and polyvariant binding times [51,52,60]. Later he extended it to handle higher-order functions also [53].

Bondorf and Danvy constructed a self-applicable partial evaluator *Similix* for a user-extensible first-order subset of Scheme [32]. Subsequently Bondorf constructed a series of extensions, which handle a higher-order subset of Scheme, including restricted side effects [28,27,29]. See Chapter 10 of this book.

Recently, Sergei Romanenko has developed a Similix-like system, called *Semilux*, for use on personal computers.

Gomard and Jones described a self-applicable partial evaluator for an applied untyped call-by-value lambda calculus [102,106]. See Chapter 8 of this book.

Mogensen developed a self-applicable partial evaluator for the pure untyped lambda calculus, not restricted to call-by-value reduction [191]. Bondorf, Danvy, Gomard, Jones, and Mogensen gave a joint discussion on self-applicable partial evaluation of higher-order languages [133].

18.2.3 Refal, supercompilation, and term-rewriting systems

Turchin's *Refal* language is designed for symbolic manipulation of programs, and a Refal program is a kind of term-rewriting system. By the operation of *driving*, a Refal program with partial inputs can be unfolded to a graph of *configurations* (terms) and transitions, where the transitions are marked with *assignments* (substitutions) and *contractions* (matchings). The purpose of *supercompilation* is to control the driving process so that the resulting graph is finite. This is done by selecting a finite set of *basic configurations*, and *generalizing* all configurations to match on the basic configurations [264,267,268,269,270]. Thus supercompilation and generalization in Refal are strongly related to partial evaluation, and supercompilation has been used to specialize and transform algorithms by e.g. Glück and Turchin [100]. See Section 17.4 of this book.

Bondorf constructed a partial evaluator for term-rewriting systems using methods more similar to those previously used for functional languages [26].

18.2.4 Prolog and logic programming languages

Komorowski pioneered partial evaluation of *Prolog* [151,152]. Venken showed that a partial evaluator can be developed from a Prolog meta-interpreter [272,273],

This approach has been taken in much of the subsequent work on partial evaluation of various subsets of Prolog. This includes Takeuchi and Furukawa [260], Fujita [88], Fuller [89,90,91], Gallagher [95,96], Kursawe [157], Chan and Wallace [44], Lakhotia and Sterling [159], Bugliesi, Rossi, Lamma, and Mello [38,39], Bossi, Cocco, and Dulli [35], and Benkerimi and Lloyd [20].

Sahlin constructed a practical (but not self-applicable) partial evaluator for full Prolog [235,236].

A report by Lam and Kusalik compares five partial evaluators for pure Prolog, constructed by Fujita, Kursawe, Lakhotia, Levi and Sardu, and Takeuchi [160].

Komorowski suggested the term *partial deduction* for partial evaluation of pure logic programming languages [153]. Lloyd and Shepherdson gave a formal definition for the declarative as well as procedural semantics [174]. Sahlin suggests the term *partial evaluation* for the processing of Prolog programs, which may have non-logical features and side effects, and gives a definition [236].

Bondorf, Frauendorf, and Richter described the first automatic self-applicable partial evaluator, including a binding-time analysis, for a Prolog subset [33]. Bondorf and Mogensen subsequently constructed a stronger self-applicable partial evaluator for a more substantial subset of Prolog, but without an automatic binding-time analysis [34]. See Chapter 9 of this book.

18.2.5   Object oriented languages

Steensgaard and Marquard constructed a partial evaluator for an object oriented imperative language [178].

Khoo and Sundaresh used Consel's partial evaluator Schism to compile inheritance in an object oriented language, thus eliminating all method lookups [148].

18.3   Principles and techniques

18.3.1   Polyvariant specialization

A specialization technique in which several program points in the specialized program may correspond to one program point in the original program is called *polyvariant specialization*. The term is due to Itkin [125] according to Bulyonkov [40,41]. Polyvariant specialization is discussed also by Ershov [81] and Jones [130]. It is usually implemented sequentially by computing the set of specialized program points reachable from the initial one. Consel and Danvy show how this can be done on a parallel architecture with shared memory [55].

18.3.2   Binding-time analysis

The first *binding-time analysis* in partial evaluation (for a first-order language with atomic binding-time values) was developed in 1984 by Jones, Sestoft, and Søndergaard [135] and is described by Sestoft in [245]. Section 5.2 of this book presents essentially that binding-time analysis.

Mogensen devised methods for binding-time analysis of *partially static* data structures [187] and for polymorphically typed higher-order languages [188,189].

Launchbury studied binding-time analysis (for a first-order language) for data structures using domain projections, which gives a very natural formalism for partially static structures [164,165,166,167,168]. See Section 15.4 of this book.

Hunt and Sands formalize binding-time analysis for partially static data structures and higher-order functions, using partial equivalence relations ('pers') instead of projections [122].

Bondorf used a closure analysis to construct a binding-time analysis for (higher-order dynamically typed) Scheme in the Similix partial evaluator [28]. Consel describes a binding-time analysis for partially static structures in (higher-order dynamically typed pure) Scheme, which does not require a separate closure analysis [53]. Rytz and Gengler describe a polyvariant binding-time analysis for Similix [233].

Type systems for binding-time analysis of variants of the lambda calculus are described by Nielson and Nielson [199,202] and by Schmidt [242]. Gomard gives a simpler type system and an inference algorithm for binding-time analysis of the lambda calculus [102,104]. Andersen and Mossin investigated the (somewhat complicated) extension of Gomard's type system needed for Bondorf's Similix [12]. Henglein gave an efficient inference algorithm for Gomard's type system [114].

18.3.3 Automatic arity raising

Arity raising is the replacement of one variable by several variables, each holding a certain component of the original variable. Handmade annotations for arity raising were suggested in [245] where this process was called *variable splitting*.

Automatic arity raising was achieved in Mogensen's work on partially static structures [187].

Sergei Romanenko coined the term 'arity raising' [227], and described analyses and a transformation for arity raising in a first-order functional language in [228]. Steensgaard and Marquard extended Romanenko's method to a higher-order functional language using a closure analysis [253].

18.3.4 Call unfolding

Most papers on automatic partial evaluators discuss how to control unfolding of calls during partial evaluation. Sestoft gave a discussion of call unfolding in a functional setting [246], and Bondorf and Danvy improved on this [32, Section 5]. Fuller [89], Lakhotia [158], and Bruynooghe, de Schreye and Martens [37] discuss how to avoid infinite unfolding during partial evaluation of logic programs.

18.3.5 Binding-time improvements

Various techniques for binding-time improvement are discussed by Nielson and Nielson [203,204], Holst and Hughes [119], Holst and Gomard [118], and Jørgensen [139].

Consel and Danvy show that transforming the subject program to continuation passing style (before partial evaluation) gives a better separation between static and dynamic data (during partial evaluation) [56]. Subsequent work by Bondorf on the Similix partial evaluator achieves some of the same effect without a preceding transformation of the subject program [31]. See Section 10.5 of this book.

18.3.6   Effectiveness of partial evaluation

Nielson suggests ranking partial evaluators by the 'reducedness' of their residual programs [199]. Hansen gives another framework for reasoning about efficiency improvements [111], and Malmkjær shows how to predict the form of residual programs [177]. Andersen and Gomard give a simple way to estimate the speed-up achieved by partial evaluation [11]. See Chapter 6 of this book.

18.3.7   Online and offline partial evaluation

Most of the self-applicable partial evaluators mentioned above use offline techniques, but Glück shows that it is possible to construct a self-applicable partial evaluator which does not need binding-time analysis [98, Section 3].

In contrast, online techniques have been favoured when efficiency, simplicity, or maximal use of static data were considered more important than self-application.

Several reports and papers by Ruf and Weise [230,231,232], and Ruf's thesis [229], discuss the merits of online and offline partial evaluation. See also Chapter 7 of this book.

18.4   Applications

18.4.1   Parsers and pattern matching

Dybkjær used the partial evaluator 'mix' to specialize Earley's general context-free parser [72] to given context-free grammars [70].

Ershov and Ostrovski use partial evaluation to specialize (semi-automatically) a general parser to specific parsers for real programming languages [85,207]. Pagan studies the effect of (hand-) specializing parsers in [212].

Emanuelson specializes a general pattern-matching algorithm to an efficient one for a given pattern [73,74]. Danvy [66] and Jørgensen [138] independently obtained very efficient matching of alternative patterns, by partial evaluation of a general pattern matcher.

Consel and Danvy derive the efficient Knuth–Morris–Pratt pattern matching algorithm from a naive one, using partial evaluation [54]. Smith extends that work to matching in other domains [252].

18.4.2 Transformation and derivation of programs

The *staging transformations* of Jørring and Scherlis, which divide computations into stages based on the availability of data, are closely related to partial evaluation [141]. Similar techniques are used in the derivation of compilers and abstract machines (or, run time systems) by Kröger [155], Kursawe [156], and Hannan [109]. Another example of such staging is Consel and Danvy's derivation of a compile time type checker from a type checking interpreter [57].

Partial evaluation is used for transformation of logic programs by Gallagher [94], Codish and Shapiro [50], and Sakama and Itoh [237].

18.4.3 Compilation and compiler generation

Many of the works on partial evaluation already mentioned emphasize its use in compilation and compiler generation.

Kahn and Carlsson actually applied this technique to compile Prolog into Lisp by partial evaluation of a Prolog interpreter written in Lisp [145]. Whereas Kahn and Carlsson generate target programs only, Consel and Khoo take one more step and generate a stand-alone compiler from Prolog to Scheme [59]. Similarly, Jørgensen generates a compiler from a Miranda subset to Scheme [139,140].

A special case occurs when a (meta-)interpreter is used to extend a programming language with a so-called embedded language. Partial evaluation of the meta-interpreter achieves compilation of the embedded language, and removes the meta-interpretation overhead. This has been used in the Lisp world by Emanuelson and Haraldsson [75,113].

In the logic programming community, the use of meta-interpreters is very popular, and partial evaluation of many kinds of meta-interpreters has been investigated by Safra and Shapiro [234], Sterling and Beer [254,255], Takeuchi and Furukawa [259,260], Levi and Sardu [172], Coscia [62], Venken [272], Huntbach [123], Owen [208], and Glück [99].

18.4.4 Incremental computation

Lombardi's work on incremental computation [175,176] from the 1960s has been taken up recently by Sundaresh and Hudak [257,258].

18.4.5 Artificial intelligence

The relations between partial evaluation and artificial intelligence are discussed by Kahn [144] and Van Harmelen and Bundy [271].

18.4.6   Program specialization in scientific computation

Early examples of work in automatic program specialization are provided by Gustavson *et al.* [107] and Goad [101]. These authors do not associate themselves with the partial evaluation paradigm, however.

Specializing general scientific computation algorithms by partial evaluation may give substantial savings. This has been used by Mogensen for ray tracing [186], by Berlin and Weise for calculation of planet trajectories [21,22], and by Jacobsen for neural network training [126].

18.5   Other topics related to partial evaluation

18.5.1   Program transformation

Program transformation by hand, or symbolic evaluation using rewrite systems, has been used in program optimization or improvement for many years. In contrast to these methods, partial evaluation involves an automatic *strategy* for applying the transformations.

McCarthy is probably the first to give program transformation rules, in the form of provable equivalences between program phrases [180].

Boyer and Moore work the other way round: they prove program equivalences essentially by using valid transformations or 'partial evaluations' (such as unfolding and simplification) [36].

Burstall and Darlington classify transformation rules as *definition, instantiation, unfolding, folding, abstraction,* and *laws* (such as associativity) [43].

Bird's hand derivation of the Knuth–Morris–Pratt pattern matching algorithm from a naive one is a precursor to the derivations using partial evaluation [23].

Using another set of transformation rules, Scherlis improve programs by specialization and by elimination of unneeded computations [238,239]. An as example, Scherlis systematically develops Earley's parsing algorithm from the 'derives' relation of context-free grammars.

Wand [276] and Wegbreit [280] discuss methods to make program transformation more automatic and systematic.

18.5.2   Compilation by program transformation

The first hand derivation of a compiler from an interpreter is probably that given by F. Lockwood Morris [193]. Such derivations have been studied also by Pagan [209,210,213], Wand [277,278], and Mazaher and Berry [179]. Pagan suggested using compiler derivation as a teaching aid in compiler courses [211].

18.5.3 Parser generator systems

There are several systems for automatic generation of parsers from grammars. What happens in these generators could be seen as the specialization of a general parser to a given concrete grammar, but this is usually not the way their authors view them. Johnson's Yacc (for 'Yet Another Compiler-Compiler') is probably the most well-known LALR(1) parser generator [3,128] and [4, Section 4.9].

Parser generator systems leave it to the user to design and code the 'semantic actions' which are executed at certain points during parsing. The semantic actions take care of symbol table manipulation, code generation, and similar compile time tasks. Compiler generation from attribute grammars presents a step towards automatic generation of semantic actions. Kastens and his group constructed a system for generating specialized parsers and attribute evaluators from attribute grammars [146].

18.5.4 Compiler generation systems

Further integration of parsing and semantic actions leads to true compiler generators, where the user specifies the semantics of a programming language in some definition language. The compiler generator constructs a parser and semantic actions from the specification without assistance from the user. This comes closer to the kind of compiler generation done with partial evaluation. A collection of papers on *semantics-directed compiler generation* is found in [129].

Several systems for compiler generation from various kinds of language specifications have been proposed. Mosses constructed a system called 'Semantics Implementation System' or '*SIS*', for turning denotational semantics specifications into compilers [194,195]. A program is compiled by building the symbolic composition of the language definition (in the style of denotational semantics) and the source program, then reducing this to a lambda term, which is the target program. The compiled programs are, however, very slow.

Gaudel's system *Perluette* takes care mainly of the syntactic aspects of compilation [97]. Jones and Schmidt's compiler generator is (like Mosses's SIS) based on automatic symbolic composition. A definition (in terms of the lambda calculus) of a specific language is composed with a general compilation of the lambda calculus into machine code; the result is then simplified by symbolic reductions [134,240].

Christiansen and Jones constructed a system called *CERES* which further developed the idea of symbolic composition of language definitions [46]. Tofte noted that compiler generation could be seen as a special case of compilation, and made CERES self-generating [262].

Paulson's system can compile and execute languages defined by a so-called semantic grammar, an attribute grammar which specifies the static and dynamic aspects of the language [214,215]. More recent work includes that of Pleban [218] and Lee [170,171].

The Self-Applicable Scheme0 Specializer

This appendix describes a simple self-applicable specializer for Scheme0, the first-order pure subset of Scheme presented in Chapter 5. The files can be obtained electronically as explained in Section 5.6.

The Scheme0 specializer has been tested with Chez Scheme, xscheme, Yale T Scheme, and TI PC Scheme 2.0. Moreover, it is supposed to work for any Scheme system (such as MIT Scheme and elk) which roughly conforms with the IEEE Scheme standard, and in addition has an `eval` function. For Yale T Scheme and MIT Scheme you may have to redefine the function s0eval in file "scheme0.ss".

A.1 Using the Scheme0 specializer

A.1.1 To load the specializer,

- start your Scheme system

- type (load "scheme0.ss")

- type (create)

A.1.2 Main functions in the Scheme0 specializer

We use the following notation:

program	is a plain Scheme0 program
annprogram	is an annotated (two-level) Scheme0 program
sdpattern	is a tuple of argument binding times S and D
division	is a (possibly polyvariant) division
staticinputs	is a tuple of static argument values.

376

The effect and use of the main functions defined by loading `scheme0.ss` and doing (`create`) is described below. The precise syntax of plain and annotated Scheme0 programs is described in Section A.2.

(`monodiv program sdpattern`) Does a monovariant binding time analysis of the subject program `program`, given the binding times `sdpattern` of its goal function. Returns the resulting (monovariant) division.

(`polydiv program sdpattern`) Similar to `monodiv`, but does a polyvariant binding time analysis. Returns the resulting (polyvariant) division.

(`annotate program division`) Annotates the Scheme0 `program` according to the (monovariant or polyvariant) `division`. May make several copies of each function for a polyvariant division. Returns the annotated (two-level) Scheme0 program or reports that `division` is not congruent.

(`monotate program sdpattern`) Does monovariant binding time analysis and annotation of `program` given the binding times `sdpattern` of its goal function. Returns the annotated (two-level) Scheme0 program.

(`polytate program sdpattern`) Similar to `monotate` but performs polyvariant binding time analysis and annotation. Returns the annotated (two-level) Scheme0 program.

(`spec annprogram staticinputs`) Specializes the annotated `annprogram` with respect to the list `staticinputs` of static argument values. Returns the residual Scheme0 program.

(`monope program sdpattern staticinputs`) Does a monovariant binding time analysis and annotation of `program`, then specializes it with respect to the given static inputs `staticinputs`. Returns the residual Scheme0 program.

(`polype program sdpattern staticinputs`) Similar to `monope` but does polyvariant binding time analysis and annotation. Returns the residual Scheme0 program.

(`make f program`) Converts `program` from Scheme0 to Scheme and defines a Scheme function `f` to invoke the converted program. Returns the name `f`. Side effect: Defines function `f`. This is for executing (residual) Scheme0 programs.

(`scheme program`) Converts `program` from Scheme0 to Scheme, possibly renaming functions. Returns a list of Scheme function definitions. This is for studying residual Scheme0 programs.

`onlineunfolding` Global Boolean variable. If `#t`, then `annotate` gives on the fly call unfolding as shown in Section 5.5; if `#f`, then only calls without dynamic arguments will be unfolded. The default value is `#t`.

A.1.3   Hints, and requirements on the input

The goal function must never be called (by another function in the program) with other binding time patterns than that specified at binding time analysis. This can be relaxed for monovariant analysis: it must not be called with binding times which are not smaller than the given one. For polyvariant analysis: it must not be called with binding times which *are* smaller than the given one.

   Note that all residual programs take exactly one input: the list of dynamic argument values.

A.2   Data structures in the Scheme0 specializer

A.2.1   Representation of Scheme0 programs

The syntax closely follows that given in Figure 5.1, so a program must have at least one definition, and function definitions may have zero or more arguments.

```
program ::= (def ... def)
def     ::= (define (funcname var ... var) exp)
exp     ::= ()
          | number
          | var
          | (quote S-expression)
          | (if exp exp exp)
          | (call funcname exp ... exp)
          | (op basefunction exp ... exp)
```

Variables are Scheme symbols, that is, non-numeric atoms different from (). Function names may also be simple Scheme symbols, but in residual programs, a function name is a pair (`annotatedname . staticvalues`) of an annotated function name and the values of the function's static arguments for this variant. Annotated function names are those found in the annotated subject programs given to the specializer (see below).

A.2.2   Representation of two-level Scheme0 programs

The syntax of annotated (or, two-level) Scheme0 programs is very close to that given in Figure 5.5.

```
program ::= (def ... def)
def     ::= (define (funcname (var ... var) (var ... var)) exp)
exp     ::= ()
          | number
          | var
          | (quote S-expression)
          | (ifs exp exp exp)
          | (ifd exp exp exp)
          | (calls funcname (exp ... exp) (exp ... exp))
          | (calld funcname (exp ... exp) (exp ... exp))
          | (ops basefunction exp ... exp)
          | (opd basefunction exp ... exp)
          | (lift exp)
```

A variable is a Scheme symbol as above, but a function name must have the form:

```
((f . dynvaroccs) . sdpattern)
```

Here f is a function name from the Scheme0 subject program; dynvaroccs is a list of the number of occurrences of f's dynamic parameters; and sdpattern describes the binding times of the parameters of (this variant of) f. Thus f is a Scheme symbol; dynvaroccs is a list of 0, 1, or 2, where 2 represents any number greater than 1; and sdpattern is a list of S and D.

The sdpattern component is used to distinguish the binding time variants of f (and is present also in monovariantly annotated programs). The dynvaroccs component is used to avoid unfolding static calls to f when this may cause duplication of a non-trivial (non-variable) dynamic argument expression. This component could in principle be computed during specialization (in which case it need not be part of the function name), but this would incur unnecessary recomputation, so we choose to compute it when annotating the program.

A.2.3 Representation of divisions

A division is a list $((\text{fun}_1 \ . \ \text{sdpatterns}_1) \ ... \ (\text{fun}_n \ ... \ \text{sdpatterns}_n))$, associating with each function a list of sdpatterns. Each list of sdpatterns is sorted in non-decreasing order (the ordering is partial).

This format caters for polyvariant as well as monovariant divisions: in a monovariant division the list sdpatterns has just one element. The list may also be empty if the corresponding function is never called.

A.3   The components of the Scheme0 specializer

The file `scheme0.ss` defines syntactic shorthands and the main functions used for experiments.

```
; File "scheme0.ss" -- Global definitions and syntactic shorthands
; Partial evaluator for first order functional language

; Syntactic sugar for Scheme0.  Format: list of triples (abbrev var term),
; meaning: expand (abbrev e) into  term  with  e  substituted for  var .

(define sugars '(
; Select from e == (tag e1 e2 e3 ...)
    (tag e (hd e))
    (e1 e   (hd (tl e)))
    (e2 e   (hd (tl (tl e))))
    (e3 e   (hd (tl (tl (tl e))))))
; Select from e == (call funname sfunargs dfunargs)
    (funname  e (hd (tl e)))
    (sfunargs e (hd (tl (tl e))))
    (dfunargs e (hd (tl (tl (tl e))))))
; Select from e == (call/op funname . callargs)
    (callargs e (tl (tl e)))
; Select from def == (define (name svar dvar) body)
    (name def (hd (hd (tl def))))
    (svar def (hd (tl (hd (tl def)))))
    (dvar def (hd (tl (tl (hd (tl def))))))
    (body def (hd (tl (tl def))))
; Select from def == (define (name . var) body)
    (var def (tl (hd (tl def))))
; Introducing Scheme0 base operation shorthands
    (hd e (op car e))
    (tl e (op cdr e))
))


; Desugar: From sugared Scheme0 to plain Scheme0, using the "sugars" table

(define (desugar program)
  (define (desug e sub)
    (if (or (null? e) (number? e)) e
    (if (atom? e) (let ((var-term (assoc e sub)))
                    (if var-term (cdr var-term) e))
    (if (equal? (car e) 'quote) e
    (if (equal? (car e) 'if)
        (cons 'if (desug* (cdr e) sub))
    (if (member (car e) '(call op))
        (cons (car e) (cons (funname e) (desug* (callargs e) sub)))
    (if (equal? (car e) '::)
        (list 'op 'cons (desug (e1 e) sub) (desug (e2 e) sub))
    (if (equal? (car e) 'list)                ; (list e1 e2 ... en)
        (foldr (lambda (e lst) (list 'op 'cons (desug e sub) lst))
               () (cdr e))
    (if (equal? (car e) 'slet)                ; (slet (var exp) body)
        (desug (caddr e)
               (cons (cons (caadr e) (desug (cadadr e) sub)) sub))
    ; else it must be an abbreviation
        (let ((expansion (assoc (car e) sugars)))
          (if expansion
              (let ((var (cadr expansion))
                    (term (caddr expansion)))
                (desug (desug term (cons (cons var (cadr e)) sub)) sub))
              (error 'desugar "Unknown operator or macro: ~s" (car e))
```

```
                  ))))))))))))
      (define (desug* es sub) (map (lambda (e) (desug e sub)) es))
      (define (desugardef def)
          (list 'define (cons (name def) (var def)) (desug (body def) ()))
      (map desugardef program)
  )

  ; Define Scheme functions corresponding to abbreviations
  (define (sugartoscheme abbrevtriple)
      (let ((abbrev (car   abbrevtriple))
            (var    (cadr  abbrevtriple))
            (term   (caddr abbrevtriple)))
          (list 'define (list abbrev var)
                (if (and (pair? term) (equal? (car term) 'op)) (cdr term) term)
  )))

  ; Convert plain Scheme0 programs to Scheme, possibly renaming functions

  (define (scheme program)
    (define (rename fn)
        (define (variant f)
            (let ((original (car (car f))) (btvariant (cdr f)))
                (foldl string-append ""
                       (map symbol->string (cons original (cons '* btvariant))))))
        (define (gi f vs defs)
            (if defs
                (let ((fvs (name (car defs))))
                    (if (equal? f (car fvs))
                        (if (equal? vs (cdr fvs))
                            1
                            (+ 1 (gi f vs (cdr defs))))
                        (gi f vs (cdr defs))))
                (error 'rename "Unknown function: ~s" (cons f vs))))
        (if (atom? fn)
            fn
            (let ((f (car fn)) (vs (cdr fn)))
                (string->symbol
                    (string-append (variant f) "-"
                                   (number->string (gi f vs program)))))))
    (define (schdef def)
        (list 'define
              (cons (rename (name def)) (var def))
              (schexp (body def))))
    (define (schexp e)
        (if (null? e)    e
        (if (number? e) e
        (if (atom? e)    e
        (if (equal? (tag e) 'quote) e
        (if (equal? (tag e) 'if)
            (list 'if (schexp (e1 e)) (schexp (e2 e)) (schexp (e3 e)))
        (if (equal? (tag e) 'call)
            (cons (rename (funname e)) (map schexp (callargs e)))
        (if (equal? (tag e) 'op)
            (cons (funname e) (map schexp (callargs e)))
            (error 'scheme "Illegal Scheme0 expression: ~s" e)))))))))
    (map schdef program)
  )

  (define (reorder parameters sdpattern)
    (if parameters
        (let ((pspd (reorder (cdr parameters) (cdr sdpattern))))
            (if (equal? (car sdpattern) 'S)
                (cons (cons (car parameters) (car pspd)) (cdr pspd))
                (cons (car pspd) (cons (car parameters) (cdr pspd)))))
        (cons () ())))
```

```scheme
))

; General auxiliary functions

(define (foldl f a bs) (if bs (foldl f (f a (car bs)) (cdr bs)) a))
(define (foldr f a bs) (if bs (f (car bs) (foldr f a (cdr bs))) a))
(define (all bs) (if bs (and (car bs) (all (cdr bs))) 't))

(define (s0sort leq? xs)
   (define (insert x xs)
      (if xs
          (if (leq? x (car xs))
              (cons x xs)
              (cons (car xs) (insert x (cdr xs))))
          (list x)))
   (foldr insert () xs)
)

(define (number->string n)       ; Works only for strictly positive n
   (define (num->str n digits)
      (if (equal? n 0)
          digits
          (num->str (quotient n 10)
                    (cons (integer->char (+ 48 (remainder n 10))) digits))))
   (list->string (num->str n ()))
)

; *** Eval is not standard Scheme.  Redefine to suit your Scheme version ***

; For Chez Scheme, xscheme, TI PC Scheme, and elk:
 (define (s0eval schemeexpression) (eval schemeexpression))
; For Yale T Scheme:
; (define (s0eval schemeexpression) (eval schemeexpression scheme-env))

; Main variables and functions for experiments

(define onlineunfolding 't)

(define (create)
   (map s0eval (map sugartoscheme sugars))
   (load "spec.ss")
   (make 'spec specializer)
   (load "annotate.ss")
   (load "analyse.ss")
   (load "subject.ss")
)

(define (polytate program sdpat) (annotate program (polydiv program sdpat)))
(define (monotate program sdpat) (annotate program (monodiv program sdpat)))
(define (polype program sdpat vs0) (specialize (polytate program sdpat) vs0))
(define (monope program sdpat vs0) (specialize (monotate program sdpat) vs0))

(define (make nam residual)
   (let ((schemeprogram (scheme residual)))
   (let ((f (name (car schemeprogram))))
      (s0eval (cons 'define
               (cons (cons nam 'args)
                     (append schemeprogram (list (list 'apply f 'args)))
))))))
```

The file `analyse.ss` defines the binding time analysis functions, and functions for handling `divisions` and `sdpatterns`.

```
; File "analyse.ss" -- Binding time analysis of Scheme0 programs
; Partial evaluator for first order functional language

; General (monovariant or polyvariant) binding time analysis

(define (finddivision program sdpattern update)
  (define (bv e vn vt division)
    (if (null? e)   division
    (if (number? e) division
    (if (atom? e)   division
    (if (equal? (tag e) 'quote) division
    (if (equal? (tag e) 'if)
        (bv (e1 e) vn vt (bv (e2 e) vn vt (bv (e3 e) vn vt division)))
    (if (equal? (tag e) 'call)
        (let ((argsdpat (map (lambda (e) (be e vn vt)) (callargs e))))
          (foldl (lambda (d e) (bv e vn vt d))
                 (update (funname e) argsdpat division bv)
                 (callargs e)))
    (if (equal? (tag e) 'op)
        (foldl (lambda (d e) (bv e vn vt d)) division (callargs e))
        (error 'bv '"Illegal Scheme0 expression: ~s" e)
        ))))))))
  (let ((def (car program)))
    (let ((division0 (list (cons (name def) (list sdpattern)))))
      (bv (body def) (var def) sdpattern division0)
)))

; Monovariant binding time analysis

(define (monodiv program sdpattern)
  (define (monoupdate f sdpat div0 bv)
    (define (monoupd div0)
      (if div0
          (let ((d1 (car div0)))
            (if (equal? f (car d1))
                (let ((oldsdpattern (car (cdr d1))))
                  (cons (cons f (list (lub* sdpat oldsdpattern)))
                        (cdr div0)))
                (cons d1 (monoupd (cdr div0)))))
          (list (cons f (list sdpat)))))
    (let ((div1 (monoupd div0)))
      (if (equal? div0 div1)
          div0
          (let ((def (lookupfun f program)))
            (bv (body def) (var def) (car (getsdpatterns f div1)) div1)
            ))))
  (finddivision program sdpattern monoupdate)
)

; Polyvariant binding time analysis

(define (polydiv program sdpattern)
  (define (polyupdate f sdpat div0 bv)
    (define (polyupd div0)
      (if div0
          (let ((d1 (car div0)))
            (if (equal? f (car d1))
                (let ((oldsdpatterns (cdr d1)))
                  (if (member sdpat oldsdpatterns)
                      div0
                      (cons (cons f (append oldsdpatterns (list sdpat)))
                            (cdr div0))))
                (cons d1 (polyupd (cdr div0)))))
          (list (cons f (list sdpat)))))
```

```
        (let ((div1 (polyupd div0)))
          (if (equal? div0 div1)
              div0
              (let ((def (lookupfun f program)))
                (bv (body def) (var def) sdpat div1)
                ))))
    (sortdivision (finddivision program sdpattern polyupdate))
)

; Returns S if e is static, D if e is dynamic.
; vn = variable names, vt = variable binding times

(define (be e vn vt)
   (if (null? e)     'S
   (if (number? e)   'S
   (if (atom? e)  (lookupbt e vn vt)
   (if (equal? (tag e) 'quote) 'S
   (if (equal? (tag e) 'if)
       (lub (be (e1 e) vn vt)
            (lub (be (e2 e) vn vt) (be (e3 e) vn vt)))
   (if (equal? (tag e) 'call)
       (foldl lub 'S (map (lambda (e) (be e vn vt)) (callargs e)))
   (if (equal? (tag e) 'op)
       (foldl lub 'S (map (lambda (e) (be e vn vt)) (callargs e)))
       (error 'be '"Illegal Scheme0 expression: ~s" e)
)))))))))

(define (lub t1 t2) (if (equal? t1 'D) 'D t2))

(define (lub* t1s t2s)
  (if t1s
      (cons (lub (car t1s) (car t2s))
            (lub* (cdr t1s) (cdr t2s)))
      ()
))

(define (sdpattern-leq sdpat1 sdpat2) (equal? sdpat2 (lub* sdpat1 sdpat2)))

(define (sortdivision division)
   (map (lambda (fun-sdpats)
          (cons (car fun-sdpats) (s0sort sdpattern-leq (cdr fun-sdpats))))
        division
))

(define (getsdpatterns f division)
  (let ((binding (assoc f division)))
    (if binding (cdr binding) ())
))

(define (lookupbt x xs vs)
  (if xs
      (if (equal? x (car xs))
          (car vs)
          (lookupbt x (cdr xs) (cdr vs)))
      (error 'lookupbt '"Unknown variable: ~s" x)
))
```

The file `annotate.ss` defines the annotation functions and occurrence counting functions.

```
; File "annotate.ss" -- Annotation (mono- or polyvariant) of Scheme0 programs
```

```
; Partial evaluator for first order functional language

; Takes a Scheme0 program and a (possibly polyvariant) division; returns
; an annotated Scheme0 program or reports non-congruence of the division.

(define (annotate program division)
   (foldl append ()
          (map (lambda (def) (anndef def program division)) program)
))

(define (anndef def program division)
   (define (anndefversion sdpattern)
       (let ((xsxd (reorder (var def) sdpattern)))
          (list 'define
                (list (cons (cons (name def)
                                  (dynoccs (name def) sdpattern program))
                            sdpattern)
                      (car xsxd)
                      (cdr xsxd))
                ((if (cdr xsxd) lift exp)
                 (annexp (body def) (var def) sdpattern onlineunfolding)))))
   (define (annexp e vn vt unf)
     (if (null? e)    (cons e 'S)
     (if (number? e) (cons e 'S)
     (if (atom? e)    (cons e (lookupbt e vn vt))
     (if (equal? (tag e) 'quote) (cons e 'S)
     (if (equal? (tag e) 'if)
         (let ((ae1 (annexp (e1 e) vn vt unf)))
         (let ((ae2 (annexp (e2 e) vn vt (and unf (static ae1))))
               (ae3 (annexp (e3 e) vn vt (and unf (static ae1)))))
            (if (static ae1)
                (if (and (static ae2) (static ae3))
                    (cons (list 'ifs (exp ae1) (exp ae2) (exp ae3)) 'S)
                    (cons (list 'ifs (exp ae1) (lift ae2) (lift ae3)) 'D))
                (cons (list 'ifd (exp ae1) (lift ae2) (lift ae3)) 'D))))
     (if (equal? (tag e) 'call)
         (let ((aes (map (lambda (e) (annexp e vn vt unf)) (callargs e)))
               (f (funname e)))
         (let ((argsdpat (map cdr aes)))
         (let ((sdpattern (getleast argsdpat (getsdpatterns f division) f)))
         (let ((esed (reorder aes sdpattern))
               (dynvaroccs (dynoccs f sdpattern program)))
         (let ((es (car esed)) (ed (cdr esed)))
         (let ((staticcall (or (null? ed)
                               (and unf (nodup dynvaroccs (map exp ed))))))
            (cons (list (if staticcall 'calls 'calld)
                        (cons (cons f dynvaroccs) sdpattern)
                        (map exp es)
                        (map lift ed))
                  (if (null? ed) 'S 'D)))))))))
     (if (equal? (tag e) 'op)
         (let ((aes (map (lambda (e) (annexp e vn vt unf)) (callargs e))))
            (if (all (map static aes))
                (cons (cons 'ops (cons (funname e) (map exp aes))) 'S)
                (cons (cons 'opd (cons (funname e) (map lift aes))) 'D)))
     (error 'annotate "Illegal Scheme0 expression: ~s" e)
     )))))))))
   (map anndefversion (getsdpatterns (name def) division)))
)

(define (dynoccs f sdpattern program)
   (let ((def (lookupfun f program)))
   (let ((vn (var def)))
   (let ((occs (count (body def) vn sdpattern (map (lambda (v) 0) vn))))
      (cdr (reorder occs sdpattern))
```

```
))))

; Count occurrences of all variables vn in e, giving a list of 0, 1, or 2,
; (meaning 0, 1, or >= 2) occurrences of the corresponding variable in vn.

(define (count e vn vt occurrences)
   (if (null? e) occurrences
   (if (number? e) occurrences
   (if (atom? e) (incvar e vn occurrences)
   (if (equal? (tag e) 'quote) occurrences
   (if (equal? (tag e) 'if)
        (if (equal? (be (e1 e) vn vt) 'S)
            (count (e1 e) vn vt (maxoccs (count (e2 e) vn vt occurrences)
                                         (count (e3 e) vn vt occurrences)))
            (count (e1 e) vn vt (count (e2 e) vn vt
                                       (count (e3 e) vn vt occurrences))))
   (if (or (equal? (tag e) 'call) (equal? (tag e) 'op))
        (foldl (lambda (occs e)(count e vn vt occs)) occurrences (callargs e))
        (error 'count "Illegal Scheme0 expression: ~s" e)
))))))))

(define (incvar x vn occurrences)
   (if vn
       (if (equal? x (car vn))
           (cons (if (equal? (car occurrences) 0) 1 2)
                 (cdr occurrences))
           (cons (car occurrences) (incvar x (cdr vn) (cdr occurrences))))
       (error 'incvar "Unknown variable: ~s" x)
))

(define (maxoccs occs1 occs2)
   (if occs1 (cons (max (car occs1) (car occs2))
                   (maxoccs (cdr occs1) (cdr occs2)))
        ()
))

(define (static ae) (equal? (cdr ae) 'S))

(define (exp ae) (car ae))

(define (lift ae) (if (static ae) (list 'lift (car ae)) (car ae)))

; Find least sdpattern in sdpatterns which is compatible with sdpat

(define (getleast sdpat sdpatterns f)
   (if sdpatterns
       (if (sdpattern-leq sdpat (car sdpatterns))
           (car sdpatterns)
           (getleast sdpat (cdr sdpatterns) f))
       (error 'annotate "Incongruent division ~s at function ~s" sdpat f)
))
```

The file `specialize.ss` defines the specializer itself and its auxiliary functions
(successors, diff, lookupfun, ...).

```
; File "spec.ss" -- The specializer written in Scheme0
; Partial evaluator for first order functional language

; The specializer itself, written in Scheme0.  Inputs: annotated Scheme0
; program and values of the static parameters.  Output: a Scheme0 program.
```

```
(define specializer (desugar '(

(define (specialize program vs0)
  (call complete (list (:: (name (hd program)) vs0)) () program)
)

(define (complete pending marked program)
  (if pending
      (call generate (hd pending) program pending marked program)
      ()
))

(define (generate fvs defs pending marked program)
  (if defs
      (slet (def (hd defs))
        (if (op equal? (name def) (hd fvs))
            (slet (evs  (call reduce (body def) (svar def) (tl fvs)
                                     (dvar def) (dvar def) program))
              (slet (newmarked (:: fvs marked))
                (call gen1 def evs fvs pending newmarked program)))
            (call generate fvs (tl defs) pending marked program)))
      (op error 'generate '"Undefined function: ~s" (hd fvs))
))

(define (gen1 def evs fvs pending newmarked program)
  (slet (newpending (op diff (op successors evs pending) newmarked))
  (slet (newdef     (list 'define (:: fvs (dvar def)) evs))
    (:: newdef (call complete newpending newmarked program))
)))

(define (reduce e xs vs xd vd p)
  (if (op null? e)    e
  (if (op number? e)  e
  (if (op atom? e)        (call lookupvar e xs vs xd vd)
  (if (op equal? (tag e) 'quote) (e1 e)
  (if (op equal? (tag e) 'ifs)
      (if (call reduce (e1 e) xs vs xd vd p)
          (call reduce (e2 e) xs vs xd vd p)
          (call reduce (e3 e) xs vs xd vd p))
  (if (op equal? (tag e) 'ifd)
      (list 'if (call reduce (e1 e) xs vs xd vd p)
                (call reduce (e2 e) xs vs xd vd p)
                (call reduce (e3 e) xs vs xd vd p))
  (if (op equal? (tag e) 'calls)
      (call docalls (op lookupfun (funname e) p) p
            (call reduce* (sfunargs e) xs vs xd vd p)
            (call reduce* (dfunargs e) xs vs xd vd p))
  (if (op equal? (tag e) 'calld)
      (:: 'call
          (:: (:: (funname e) (call reduce* (sfunargs e) xs vs xd vd p))
              (call reduce* (dfunargs e) xs vs xd vd p)))
  (if (op equal? (tag e) 'ops)
      (op evalbase (funname e) (call reduce* (callargs e) xs vs xd vd p))
  (if (op equal? (tag e) 'opd)
      (:: 'op  (:: (funname e) (call reduce* (callargs e) xs vs xd vd p)))
  (if (op equal? (tag e) 'lift)
      (list 'quote (call reduce (e1 e) xs vs xd vd p))
      (op error 'reduce '"Illegal annotated Scheme0 expression: ~s" e)
)))))))))))

(define (reduce* es xs vs xd vd p)
  (if es
      (:: (call reduce (hd es) xs vs xd vd p)
          (call reduce* (tl es) xs vs xd vd p))
      '()
```

```
))

(define (docalls def p args argd)
   (if (op nodup (tl (hd (name def))) argd)
       (call reduce (body def) (svar def) args (dvar def) argd p)
       (:: 'call (:: (:: (name def) args) argd))
))

(define (lookupvar x xs vs xd vd)
  (if xs
      (if (op equal? x (hd xs))
          (hd vs)
          (call lookupvar x (tl xs) (tl vs) xd vd))
      (call lookupvar x xd vd 'slam 'slam)
))
)))

; Auxiliary base functions for the specializer
(define (successors e s)
  (if (null? e)   s
  (if (number? e) s
  (if (atom? e)   s
  (if (equal? (tag e) 'quote) s
  (if (equal? (tag e) 'if)
      (successors (e1 e) (successors (e2 e) (successors (e3 e) s)))
  (if (equal? (tag e) 'call)
      (successors* (callargs e) (cons (funname e) s))
  (if (equal? (tag e) 'op)
      (successors* (callargs e) s)
  (error 'successors '"Illegal Scheme0 expression: ~s" e)
))))))))

(define (successors* es s) (foldl (lambda (s e) (successors e s)) s es))

(define (diff set1 set2)
  (if set1
      (if (member (car set1) set2)
          (diff (cdr set1) set2)
          (cons (car set1) (diff (cdr set1) set2)))
      ()
))

(define (nodup occs exps)
   (if occs
       (and (or (atom? (car exps)) (< (car occs) 2))
            (nodup (cdr occs) (cdr exps)))
       't
))

(define (lookupfun f program)
  (if program
      (if (equal? f (name (car program)))
          (car program)
          (lookupfun f (cdr program)))
      (error 'lookupfun '"Undefined function: ~s" f)
))

(define (evalbase f args) (apply (s0eval f) args))
```

Bibliography

[1] ACM, *Partial Evaluation and Semantics-Based Program Manipulation, New Haven, Connecticut (Sigplan Notices, vol. 26, no. 9, September 1991)*, New York: ACM, 1991.

[2] ACM, *Partial Evaluation and Semantics-Based Program Manipulation, San Francisco, California, June 1992 (Technical Report YALEU/DCS/RR-909)*, New Haven, CT: Yale University, 1992.

[3] A.V. Aho and S.C. Johnson, 'LR parsing', *Computing Surveys*, 6(2):99–124, 1974.

[4] A.V. Aho, R. Sethi, and J.D. Ullman, *Compilers: Principles, Techniques, and Tools*, Reading, MA: Addison-Wesley, 1986.

[5] M. Ajtai, J. Komlos, and E. Szemeredi, 'Sorting in $c \log n$ parallel steps', *Combinatorica*, 3:1–19, 1983.

[6] L.O. Andersen, 'C program specialization', Master's thesis, DIKU, University of Copenhagen, Denmark, December 1991. Student Project 91-12-17.

[7] L.O. Andersen, *C Program Specialization*, Technical Report 92/14, DIKU, University of Copenhagen, Denmark, May 1992.

[8] L.O. Andersen, 'Partial evaluation of C and automatic compiler generation (extended abstract)', in U. Kastens and P. Pfahler (eds.), *Compiler Construction, Paderborn, Germany, October 1992 (Lecture Notes in Computer Science, vol. 641)*, pp. 251–257, Berlin: Springer-Verlag, 1992.

[9] L.O. Andersen, 'Self-applicable C program specialization', in *Partial Evaluation and Semantics-Based Program Manipulation, San Francisco, California, June 1992 (Technical Report YALEU/DCS/RR-909)*, pp. 54–61, New Haven, CT: Yale University, June 1992.

[10] L.O. Andersen, 'Binding-time analysis and the taming of C pointers', in *Partial Evaluation and Semantics-Based Program Manipulation, Copenhagen, Denmark, June 1993*, New York: ACM, 1993. To appear.

[11] L.O. Andersen and C.K. Gomard, 'Speedup analysis in partial evaluation (preliminary results)', in *Partial Evaluation and Semantics-Based Program Manipulation, San Francisco, California, June 1992 (Technical Report YALEU/DCS/RR-909)*, pp. 1–7, New Haven, CT: Yale University, 1992.

[12] L.O. Andersen and C. Mossin, 'Binding time analysis via type inference'. Student Project 90-10-12, DIKU, University of Copenhagen, Denmark, October 1990.

389

[13] A. Appel, 'Reopening closures'. Personal communication, January 1988.

[14] W.-Y. Au, D. Weise, and S. Seligman, 'Generating compiled simulations using partial evaluation', in *28th Design Automation Conference*, pp. 205–210, New York: IEEE, June 1991.

[15] L. Augustsson, 'Compiling pattern matching', in J.-P. Jouannaud (ed.), *Functional Programming Languages and Computer Architecture, Nancy, France, 1985 (Lecture Notes in Computer Science, vol. 201)*, pp. 368–381, Berlin: Springer-Verlag, 1985.

[16] H.P. Barendregt, *The Lambda Calculus: Its Syntax and Semantics*, Amsterdam: North-Holland, second edition, 1984.

[17] K.E. Batcher, 'Sorting networks and their applications', in *Proceedings AFIPS Spring Joint Computer Conference*, pp. 307–314, American Federation of Information Processing Societies, 1968.

[18] D. Bechet, 'Partial evaluation of interaction nets', in M. Billaud *et al.* (eds.), *WSA '92, Static Analysis, Bordeaux, France, September 1992. Bigre vols 81–82, 1992*, pp. 331–338, Rennes: IRISA, 1992.

[19] L. Beckman *et al.*, 'A partial evaluator, and its use as a programming tool', *Artificial Intelligence*, 7(4):319–357, 1976.

[20] K. Benkerimi and J.W. Lloyd, 'A partial evaluation procedure for logic programs', in S. Debray and M. Hermenegildo (eds.), *Logic Programming: Proceedings of the 1990 North American Conference, Austin, Texas, October 1990*, pp. 343–358, Cambridge, MA: MIT Press, 1990.

[21] A. Berlin and D. Weise, 'Compiling scientific code using partial evaluation', *IEEE Computer*, 23(12):25–37, December 1990.

[22] A.A. Berlin, 'Partial evaluation applied to numerical computation', in *1990 ACM Conference on Lisp and Functional Programming, Nice, France*, pp. 139–150, New York: ACM, 1990.

[23] R.S. Bird, 'Improving programs by the introduction of recursion', *Communications of the ACM*, 20(11):856–863, 1977.

[24] D. Bjørner, A.P. Ershov, and N.D. Jones (eds.), *Partial Evaluation and Mixed Computation. Proceedings of the IFIP TC2 Workshop, Gammel Avernæs, Denmark, October 1987*, Amsterdam: North-Holland, 1988.

[25] D. Bjørner and C.B. Jones, *Formal Specification and Software Development*, Englewood Cliffs, NJ: Prentice Hall, 1982.

[26] A. Bondorf, 'Towards a self-applicable partial evaluator for term rewriting systems', in D. Bjørner, A.P. Ershov, and N.D. Jones (eds.), *Partial Evaluation and Mixed Computation*, pp. 27–50, Amsterdam: North-Holland, 1988.

[27] A. Bondorf, 'Self-applicable partial evaluation', Ph.D. thesis, DIKU, University of Copenhagen, Denmark, 1990. Revised version: DIKU Report 90/17.

[28] A. Bondorf, 'Automatic autoprojection of higher order recursive equations', *Science of Computer Programming*, 17:3–34, 1991.

[29] A. Bondorf, *Similix Manual, System Version 3.0*, Technical Report 91/9, DIKU, University of Copenhagen, Denmark, 1991.

[30] A. Bondorf, *Similix Manual, System Version 4.0*, technical report, DIKU, University of Copenhagen, Denmark, 1991.

[31] A. Bondorf, 'Improving binding times without explicit cps-conversion', in *1992 ACM Conference in Lisp and Functional Programming, San Francisco, California (Lisp Pointers, vol. V, no. 1, 1992)*, pp. 1–10, New York: ACM, 1992.

[32] A. Bondorf and O. Danvy, 'Automatic autoprojection of recursive equations with global variables and abstract data types', *Science of Computer Programming*, 16:151–195, 1991.

[33] A. Bondorf, F. Frauendorf, and M. Richter, *An Experiment in Automatic Self-Applicable Partial Evaluation of Prolog*, Technical Report 335, Lehrstuhl Informatik V, University of Dortmund, Germany, 1990.

[34] A. Bondorf and T. Mogensen, 'Logimix: A self-applicable partial evaluator for Prolog'. DIKU, University of Copenhagen, Denmark, May 1990.

[35] A. Bossi, N. Cocco, and S. Dulli, 'A method for specializing logic programs', *ACM Transactions on Programming Languages and Systems*, 12(2):253–302, April 1990.

[36] R.S. Boyer and J.S. Moore, 'Proving theorems about Lisp functions', *Journal of the ACM*, 22(1):129–144, January 1975.

[37] M. Bruynooghe, D. de Schreye, and B. Martens, 'A general criterion for avoiding infinite unfolding during partial deduction of logic programs', in V. Saraswat and K. Ueda (eds.), *Logic Programming: International Symposium*, pp. 117–131, Cambridge, MA: MIT Press, 1991.

[38] M. Bugliesi, E. Lamma, and P. Mello, 'Partial evaluation for hierarchies of logic theories', in S. Debray and M. Hermenegildo (eds.), *Logic Programming: Proceedings of the 1990 North American Conference, Austin, Texas, October 1990*, pp. 359–376, Cambridge, MA: MIT Press, 1990.

[39] M. Bugliesi and F. Rossi, 'Partial evaluation in Prolog: Some improvements about cut', in E.L. Lusk and R.A. Overbeek (eds.), *Logic Programming: Proceedings of the North American Conference 1989, Cleveland, Ohio, October 1989*, pp. 645–660, Cambridge, MA: MIT Press, 1989.

[40] M.A. Bulyonkov, 'Polyvariant mixed computation for analyzer programs', *Acta Informatica*, 21:473–484, 1984.

[41] M.A. Bulyonkov, 'A theoretical approach to polyvariant mixed computation', in D. Bjørner, A.P. Ershov, and N.D. Jones (eds.), *Partial Evaluation and Mixed Computation*, pp. 51–64, Amsterdam: North-Holland, 1988.

[42] M.A. Bulyonkov and A.P. Ershov, 'How do ad-hoc compiler constructs appear in universal mixed computation processes?', in D. Bjørner, A.P. Ershov, and N.D. Jones (eds.), *Partial Evaluation and Mixed Computation*, pp. 65–81, Amsterdam: North-Holland, 1988.

[43] R.M. Burstall and J. Darlington, 'A transformation system for developing recursive programs', *Journal of the ACM*, 24(1):44–67, January 1977.

[44] D. Chan and M. Wallace, 'A treatment of negation during partial evaluation', in H. Abramson and M.H. Rogers (eds.), *Meta-Programming in Logic Programming*, pp. 299–318, Cambridge, MA: MIT Press, 1989.

[45] W.N. Chin, 'Automatic methods for program transformation', Ph.D. thesis, Department of Computing, Imperial College, London, England, March 1990.

[46] H. Christiansen and N. Jones, 'Control flow treatment in a simple semantics-directed compiler generator', in D. Bjørner (ed.), *Formal Description of Programming Concepts — II, Garmisch-Partenkirchen, Germany, June 1982*, pp. 73–97, Amsterdam: North-Holland, 1983.

[47] A. Church, 'A note on the Entscheidungsproblem', *Journal of Symbolic Logic*, 1:40–41 and 101–102, 1936.

[48] A. Church, *The Calculi of Lambda-Conversion*, volume 6 of *Annals of Mathematics Studies*, Princeton, NJ: Princeton University Press, 1941.

[49] W. Clinger and J. Rees (editors), 'Revised[4] report on the algorithmic language Scheme', *Lisp Pointers*, IV(3):1–55, 1991.

[50] M. Codish and E. Shapiro, 'Compiling or-parallelism into and-parallelism', in E. Shapiro (ed.), *Third International Conference on Logic Programming, London, United Kingdom (Lecture Notes in Computer Science, vol. 225)*, pp. 283–297, Berlin: Springer-Verlag, 1986. Also in New Generation Computing 5 (1987) 45-61.

[51] C. Consel, 'New insights into partial evaluation: The Schism experiment', in H. Ganzinger (ed.), *ESOP '88, 2nd European Symposium on Programming, Nancy, France, March 1988 (Lecture Notes in Computer Science, vol. 300)*, pp. 236–246, Berlin: Springer-Verlag, 1988.

[52] C. Consel, 'Analyse de programmes, evaluation partielle et génération de compilateurs', Ph.D. thesis, Université de Paris 6, Paris, France, June 1989. (In French).

[53] C. Consel, 'Binding time analysis for higher order untyped functional languages', in *1990 ACM Conference on Lisp and Functional Programming, Nice, France*, pp. 264–272, New York: ACM, 1990.

[54] C. Consel and O. Danvy, 'Partial evaluation of pattern matching in strings', *Information Processing Letters*, 30:79–86, January 1989.

[55] C. Consel and O. Danvy, *Partial Evaluation in Parallel (Detailed Abstract)*, Research Report 820, Computer Science Department, Yale University, 1990.

[56] C. Consel and O. Danvy, 'For a better support of static data flow', in J. Hughes (ed.), *Functional Programming Languages and Computer Architecture, Cambridge, Massachusetts, August 1991 (Lecture Notes in Computer Science, vol. 523)*, pp. 496–519, ACM, Berlin: Springer-Verlag, 1991.

[57] C. Consel and O. Danvy, 'Static and dynamic semantics processing', in *Eighteenth Annual ACM Symposium on Principles of Programming Languages, Orlando, Florida*, pp. 14–24, New York: ACM, January 1991.

[58] C. Consel and O. Danvy, 'Tutorial notes on partial evaluation', in *Twentieth ACM Symposium on Principles of Programming Languages, Charleston, South Carolina, January 1993*, pp. 493–501, ACM, New York: ACM, 1993.

[59] C. Consel and S.C. Khoo, 'Semantics-directed generation of a Prolog compiler', in J. Maluszyński and M. Wirsing (eds.), *Programming Language Implementation and Logic Programming, 3rd International Symposium, PLILP '91, Passau, Germany, August 1991 (Lecture Notes in Computer Science, vol. 528)*, pp. 135–146, Berlin: Springer-Verlag, 1991.

[60] Charles Consel, *The Schism Manual, Version 1.0*, Yale University, New Haven, Connecticut, December 1990.

[61] K.D. Cooper, M.W. Hall, and K. Kennedy, 'Procedure cloning', in *Fourth IEEE International Conference on Computer Languages*, pp. 96–105, Oakland, California, April 1992.

[62] P. Coscia *et al.*, 'Object level reflection of inference rules by partial evaluation', in P. Maes and D. Nardi (eds.), *Meta-Level Architectures and Reflection, Sardinia, Italy, October 1986*, pp. 313–327, Amsterdam: North-Holland, 1988.

[63] B. Courcelle, 'Equivalences and transformations of regular systems – applications to recursive program schemes and grammars', *Theoretical Computer Science*, 42:1–122, 1986.

[64] P. Cousot, 'Semantic foundations of program analysis', in S.S. Muchnick and N.D. Jones (eds.), *Program Flow Analysis: Theory and Applications*, chapter 10, pp. 303–342, Englewood Cliffs, NJ: Prentice Hall, 1981.

[65] P. Cousot and R. Cousot, 'Abstract interpretation: A unified lattice model for static analysis of programs by construction or approximation of fixpoints', in *Fourth ACM Symposium on Principles on Programming Languages, Los Angeles, California, January 1977*, pp. 238–252, New York: ACM, 1977.

[66] O. Danvy, 'Semantics-directed compilation of nonlinear patterns', *Information Processing Letters*, 37(6):315–322, March 1991.

[67] O. Danvy, 'Back to direct style', *Science of Computer Programming*, 1993. To appear.

[68] O. Danvy and A. Filinski, 'Representing control: A study of the cps transformation', *Mathematical Structures in Computer Science*, 2(4):361–391, 1992.

[69] A. De Niel, E. Bevers, and K. De Vlaminck, 'Partial evaluation of polymorphically typed functional languages: The representation problem', in M. Billaud *et al.* (eds.), *Analyse Statique en Programmation Équationnelle, Fonctionnelle, et Logique, Bordeaux, France, Octobre 1991 (Bigre, vol. 74)*, pp. 90–97, Rennes: IRISA, 1991.

[70] H. Dybkjær, 'Parsers and partial evaluation: An experiment'. Student Project 85-7-15, DIKU, University of Copenhagen, Denmark, July 1985.

[71] H. Dybkjær, 'Category theory, types, and programming languages', Ph.D. thesis, DIKU, University of Copenhagen, Denmark, 1991. Also DIKU Report 91/11.

[72] J. Earley, 'An efficient context-free parsing algorithm', *Communications of the ACM*, 13(2):94–102, February 1970.

[73] P. Emanuelson, 'Performance enhancement in a well-structured pattern matcher through partial evaluation', Ph.D. thesis, Linköping University, Sweden, 1980. Linköping Studies in Science and Technology Dissertations 55.

[74] P. Emanuelson, 'From abstract model to efficient compilation of patterns', in M. Dezani-Ciancaglini and U. Montanari (eds.), *International Symposium on Programming, 5th Colloquium, Turin, Italy (Lecture Notes in Computer Science, vol. 137)*, pp. 91–104, Berlin: Springer-Verlag, 1982.

[75] P. Emanuelson and A. Haraldsson, 'On compiling embedded languages in Lisp', in *1980 Lisp Conference, Stanford, California*, pp. 208–215, New York: ACM, 1980.

[76] A.P. Ershov, 'On the partial computation principle', *Information Processing Letters*, 6(2):38–41, April 1977.

[77] A.P. Ershov, 'Mixed computation in the class of recursive program schemata', *Acta Cybernetica*, 4(1):19–23, 1978.

[78] A.P. Ershov, 'On the essence of compilation', in E.J. Neuhold (ed.), *Formal Description of Programming Concepts*, pp. 391–420, Amsterdam: North-Holland, 1978.

[79] A.P. Ershov, 'Mixed computation: Potential applications and problems for study', *Theoretical Computer Science*, 18:41–67, 1982.

[80] A.P. Ershov, 'On Futamura projections', *BIT (Japan)*, 12(14):4–5, 1982. (In Japanese).

[81] A.P. Ershov, 'On mixed computation: Informal account of the strict and polyvariant computational schemes', in M. Broy (ed.), *Control Flow and Data Flow: Concepts of Distributed Programming. NATO ASI Series F: Computer and System Sciences, vol. 14*, pp. 107–120, Berlin: Springer-Verlag, 1985.

[82] A.P. Ershov, 'Opening key-note speech', *New Generation Computing*, 6(2,3):79–86, 1988.

[83] A.P. Ershov, 'Opening key-note speech', in D. Bjørner, A.P. Ershov, and N.D. Jones (eds.), *Partial Evaluation and Mixed Computation*, pp. xxiii–xxix, Amsterdam: North-Holland, 1988.

[84] A.P. Ershov, D. Bjørner, Y. Futamura, K. Furukawa, A. Haraldson, and W. Scherlis (eds.), *Special Issue: Selected Papers from the Workshop on Partial Evaluation and Mixed Computation, 1987 (New Generation Computing, vol. 6, nos. 2,3)*, Tokyo: Ohmsha Ltd. and Berlin: Springer-Verlag, 1988.

[85] A.P. Ershov and B.N. Ostrovsky, 'Controlled mixed computation and its application to systematic development of language-oriented parsers', in L.G.L.T. Meertens (ed.), *Program Specification and Transformation. Proc. IFIP TC2/WG 2.1 Working Conference on Program Specification and Transformation*, pp. 31–48, Amsterdam: North-Holland, 1987.

[86] A.K. Ferguson and P. Wadler, 'When will deforestation stop?', in C. Hall, J. Hughes, and M. O'Donnell (eds.), *Draft Proceedings, 1988 Glasgow Workshop on Functional Programming, Bute, Scotland*, pp. 39–56, Glasgow University, 1988.

[87] M.J. Fischer, 'Lambda calculus schemata', in *ACM Conference on Proving Assertions about Programs (Sigplan Notices, vol. 7, no. 1, January 1972)*, pp. 104–109, New York: ACM, 1972.

[88] H. Fujita and K. Furukawa, 'A self-applicable partial evaluator and its use in incremental compilation', *New Generation Computing*, 6(2,3):91–118, 1988.

[89] D.A. Fuller, 'Partial evaluation and mix computation in logic programming', Ph.D. thesis, Imperial College, London, England, February 1989.

[90] D.A. Fuller and S. Abramsky, 'Mixed computation of Prolog programs', *New Generation Computing*, 6(2,3):119–141, 1988.

[91] D.A. Fuller and S.A. Bocic, 'Extending partial evaluation in logic programming', in *Proceedings of the XI International Conference of the Chilean Computer Science Society, Santiago, Chile, October 1991*, New York: Plenum Press, 1991.

[92] Y. Futamura, 'Partial evaluation of computation process – an approach to a compiler-compiler', *Systems, Computers, Controls*, 2(5):45–50, 1971.

[93] Y. Futamura, 'Partial computation of programs', in E. Goto *et al.* (eds.), *RIMS Symposia on Software Science and Engineering, Kyoto, Japan, 1982 (Lecture Notes in Computer Science, vol. 147)*, pp. 1–35, Berlin: Springer-Verlag, 1983.

[94] J. Gallagher, 'Transforming logic programs by specialising interpreters', in *ECAI-86. 7th European Conference on Artificial Intelligence, Brighton Centre, United Kingdom*, pp. 109–122, Brighton: European Coordinating Committee for Artificial Intelligence, 1986.

[95] J. Gallagher and M. Bruynooghe, 'Some low-level source transformations for logic programs', in M. Bruynooghe (ed.), *Proceedings of the Second Workshop on Meta-Programming in Logic, April 1990, Leuven, Belgium*, pp. 229–246, Department of Computer Science, KU Leuven, Belgium, 1990.

[96] J. Gallagher, M. Codish, and E. Shapiro, 'Specialisation of Prolog and FCP programs using abstract interpretation', *New Generation Computing*, 6(2,3):159–186, 1988.

[97] M.C. Gaudel, 'Specification of compilers as abstract data type representations', in N.D. Jones (ed.), *Semantics-Directed Compiler Generation, Aarhus, Denmark, January 1980 (Lecture Notes in Computer Science, vol. 94)*, pp. 140–164, Berlin: Springer-Verlag, 1980.

[98] R. Glück, 'Towards multiple self-application', in *Partial Evaluation and Semantics-Based Program Manipulation, New Haven, Connecticut (Sigplan Notices, vol. 26, no. 9, September 1991)*, pp. 309–320, New York: ACM, 1991.

[99] R. Glück, 'Projections for knowledge based systems', in R. Trappl (ed.), *Cybernetics and Systems Research '92. Vol. 1*, pp. 535–542, Singapore: World Scientific, 1992.

[100] R. Glück and V.F. Turchin, 'Application of metasystem transition to function inversion and transformation', in *International Symposium on Symbolic and Algebraic Computation, ISSAC '90, Tokyo, Japan*, pp. 286–287, New York: ACM, 1990.

[101] C. Goad, 'Automatic construction of special purpose programs', in D.W. Loveland (ed.), *6th Conference on Automated Deduction, New York, USA (Lecture Notes in Computer Science, vol. 138)*, pp. 194–208, Berlin: Springer-Verlag, 1982.

[102] C. K. Gomard, 'Higher order partial evaluation – HOPE for the lambda calculus', Master's thesis, DIKU, University of Copenhagen, Denmark, September 1989.

[103] C. K. Gomard and N. D. Jones, 'Compiler generation by partial evaluation', in G. X. Ritter (ed.), *Information Processing '89. Proceedings of the IFIP 11th World Computer Congress*, pp. 1139–1144, IFIP, Amsterdam: North-Holland, 1989.

[104] C.K. Gomard, 'Partial type inference for untyped functional programs', in *1990 ACM Conference on Lisp and Functional Programming, Nice, France*, pp. 282–287, New York: ACM, 1990.

[105] C.K. Gomard, 'A self-applicable partial evaluator for the lambda calculus: Correctness and pragmatics', *ACM Transactions on Programming Languages and Systems*, 14(2):147–172, April 1992.

[106] C.K. Gomard and N.D. Jones, 'A partial evaluator for the untyped lambda-calculus', *Journal of Functional Programming*, 1(1):21–69, January 1991.

[107] F.G. Gustavson, W. Liniger, and R. Willoughby, 'Symbolic generation of an optimal Crout algorithm for sparse systems of linear equations', *Journal of the ACM*, 17(1):87–109, January 1970.

[108] M.A. Guzowski, 'Towards developing a reflexive partial evaluator for an interesting subset of Lisp', Master's thesis, Dept. of Computer Engineering and Science, Case Western Reserve University, Cleveland, Ohio, January 1988.

[109] J. Hannan, 'Staging transformations for abstract machines', in *Partial Evaluation and Semantics-Based Program Manipulation, New Haven, Connecticut (Sigplan Notices, vol. 26, no. 9, September 1991)*, pp. 130–141, New York: ACM, 1991.

[110] J. Hannan and D. Miller, 'From operational semantics to abstract machines', in *1990 ACM Conference on Lisp and Functional Programming, Nice, France*, pp. 323–332, New York: ACM, June 1990.

[111] T.A. Hansen, 'Properties of unfolding-based meta-level systems', in *Partial Evaluation and Semantics-Based Program Manipulation, New Haven, Connecticut (Sigplan Notices, vol. 26, no. 9, September 1991)*, pp. 243–254, New York: ACM, 1991.

[112] A. Haraldsson, 'A program manipulation system based on partial evaluation', Ph.D. thesis, Linköping University, Sweden, 1977. Linköping Studies in Science and Technology Dissertations 14.

[113] A. Haraldsson, 'A partial evaluator, and its use for compiling iterative statements in Lisp', in *Fifth ACM Symposium on Principles of Programming Languages, Tucson, Arizona*, pp. 195–202, New York: ACM, 1978.

[114] F. Henglein, 'Efficient type inference for higher-order binding-time analysis', in J. Hughes (ed.), *Functional Programming Languages and Computer Architecture, Cambridge, Massachusetts, August 1991 (Lecture Notes in Computer Science, vol. 523)*, pp. 448–472, ACM, Berlin: Springer-Verlag, 1991.

[115] J.R. Hindley, B. Lercher, and J.P. Seldin, *Introduction to Combinatory Logic*, Cambridge: Cambridge University Press, 1972.

[116] C.K. Holst, 'Poor man's generalization'. DIKU, University of Copenhagen, Denmark, 1988.

[117] C.K. Holst, 'Finiteness analysis', in J. Hughes (ed.), *Functional Programming Languages and Computer Architecture, Cambridge, Massachusetts, August 1991 (Lecture Notes in Computer Science, vol. 523)*, pp. 473–495, ACM, Berlin: Springer-Verlag, 1991.

[118] C.K. Holst and C.K. Gomard, 'Partial evaluation is fuller laziness', in *Partial Evaluation and Semantics-Based Program Manipulation, New Haven, Connecticut (Sigplan Notices, vol. 26, no. 9, September 1991)*, pp. 223–233, New York: ACM, 1991.

[119] C.K. Holst and J. Hughes, 'Towards binding-time improvement for free', in S.L. Peyton Jones, G. Hutton, and C. Kehler Holst (eds.), *Functional Programming, Glasgow 1990*, pp. 83–100, Berlin: Springer-Verlag, 1991.

[120] N.C.K. Holst, 'Language triplets: The AMIX approach', in D. Bjørner, A.P. Ershov, and N.D. Jones (eds.), *Partial Evaluation and Mixed Computation*, pp. 167–185, Amsterdam: North-Holland, 1988.

[121] P. Hudak, 'Collecting interpretation of expressions', *ACM Transactions on Programming Languages and Systems*, 13(2):269–290, April 1991.

[122] S. Hunt and D. Sands, 'Binding time analysis: A new PERspective', in *Partial Evaluation and Semantics-Based Program Manipulation, New Haven, Connecticut (Sigplan Notices, vol. 26, no. 9, September 1991)*, pp. 154–165, New York: ACM, 1991.

[123] M. Huntbach, 'Meta-interpreters and partial evaluation of Prolog', *Formal Aspects of Computing*, 1(2):193–211, 1989.

[124] ISO/IEC 9899:1990 International Standard, *Programming Languages — C*, 1990.

[125] V.E. Itkin, 'On partial and mixed program execution', in *Program Optimization and Transformation*, pp. 17–30, Novosibirsk: Computing Center, 1983. (In Russian).

[126] H.F. Jacobsen, 'Speeding up the back-propagation algorithm by partial evaluation'. Student Project 90-10-13, DIKU, University of Copenhagen, Denmark. (In Danish), October 1990.

[127] K. Jensen and N. Wirth, *Pascal. User Manual and Report*, Berlin: Springer-Verlag, second edition, 1978.

[128] S.C. Johnson, *Yacc — Yet Another Compiler Compiler*, Computing Science Technical Report 32, AT&T Bell Laboratories, New Jersey, USA, 1976.

[129] N.D. Jones (ed.), *Semantics-Directed Compiler Generation, Aarhus, Denmark, January 1980 (Lecture Notes in Computer Science, vol. 94)*, Berlin: Springer-Verlag, 1980.

[130] N.D. Jones, 'Automatic program specialization: A re-examination from basic principles', in D. Bjørner, A.P. Ershov, and N.D. Jones (eds.), *Partial Evaluation and Mixed Computation*, pp. 225–282, Amsterdam: North-Holland, 1988.

[131] N.D. Jones, 'Partial evaluation, self-application and types', in M.S. Paterson (ed.), *Automata, Languages and Programming. 17th International Colloquium, Warwick, England (Lecture Notes in Computer Science, vol. 443)*, pp. 639–659, Berlin: Springer-Verlag, 1990.

[132] N.D. Jones, 'Efficient algebraic operations on programs', in *AMAST: Algebraic Methodology and Software Technology*, pp. 245–267, University of Iowa, USA, May 1991.

[133] N.D. Jones, C.K. Gomard, A. Bondorf, O. Danvy, and T. Mogensen, 'A self-applicable partial evaluator for the lambda calculus', in *1990 International Conference on Computer Languages, New Orleans, Louisiana, March 1990*, pp. 49–58, New York: IEEE Computer Society, 1990.

[134] N.D. Jones and D.A. Schmidt, 'Compiler generation from denotational semantics', in N.D. Jones (ed.), *Semantics-Directed Compiler Generation, Aarhus, Denmark (Lecture Notes in Computer Science, vol. 94)*, pp. 70–93, Berlin: Springer-Verlag, 1980.

[135] N.D. Jones, P. Sestoft, and H. Søndergaard, 'An experiment in partial evaluation: The generation of a compiler generator', in J.-P. Jouannaud (ed.), *Rewriting Techniques and Applications, Dijon, France. (Lecture Notes in Computer Science, vol. 202)*, pp. 124–140, Berlin: Springer-Verlag, 1985.

[136] N.D. Jones, P. Sestoft, and H. Søndergaard, 'Mix: A self-applicable partial evaluator for experiments in compiler generation', *Lisp and Symbolic Computation*, 2(1):9–50, 1989.

[137] S.L. Peyton Jones, *The Implementation of Functional Programming Languages*, Englewood Cliffs, NJ: Prentice Hall, 1987.

[138] J. Jørgensen, 'Generating a pattern matching compiler by partial evaluation', in S.L. Peyton Jones, G. Hutton, and C. Kehler Holst (eds.), *Functional Programming, Glasgow 1990*, pp. 177–195, Berlin: Springer-Verlag, 1991.

[139] J. Jørgensen, 'Compiler generation by partial evaluation', Master's thesis, DIKU, University of Copenhagen, Denmark, 1992. Student Project 92-1-4.

[140] J. Jørgensen, 'Generating a compiler for a lazy language by partial evaluation', in *Nineteenth ACM Symposium on Principles of Programming Languages, Albuquerque, New Mexico, January 1992*, pp. 258–268, New York: ACM, 1992.

[141] U. Jørring and W.L. Scherlis, 'Compilers and staging transformations', in *Thirteenth ACM Symposium on Principles of Programming Languages, St. Petersburg, Florida*, pp. 86–96, New York: ACM, 1986.

[142] G. Kahn, 'Natural semantics', in F.J. Brandenburg, G. Vidal-Naquet, and M. Wirsing (eds.), *STACS 87. 4th Annual Symposium on Theoretical Aspects of Computer Science, Passau, Germany (Lecture Notes in Computer Science, vol. 247)*, pp. 22–39, Berlin: Springer-Verlag, 1987.

[143] K.M. Kahn, 'A partial evaluator of Lisp programs written in Prolog', in M. Van Caneghem (ed.), *First International Logic Programming Conference, Marseille, France*, pp. 19–25, Marseille: Association pour la Diffusion et le Développement de Prolog, 1982.

[144] K.M. Kahn, 'Partial evaluation, programming methodology, and artificial intelligence', *The AI Magazine*, 5(1):53–57, 1984.

[145] K.M. Kahn and M. Carlsson, 'The compilation of Prolog programs without the use of a Prolog compiler', in *International Conference on Fifth Generation Computer Systems, Tokyo, Japan*, pp. 348–355, Tokyo: Ohmsha and Amsterdam: North-Holland, 1984.

[146] U. Kastens, B. Hut, and E. Zimmermann, *GAG: A Practical Compiler Generator (Lecture Notes in Computer Science, vol. 141)*, Berlin: Springer-Verlag, 1982.

[147] B.W. Kernighan and D.M. Ritchie, *The C Programming Language*, Englewood Cliffs, NJ: Prentice Hall, second edition, 1988.

[148] S.C. Khoo and R.S. Sundaresh, 'Compiling inheritance using partial evaluation', in *Partial Evaluation and Semantics-Based Program Manipulation, New Haven, Connecticut (Sigplan Notices, vol. 26, no. 9, September 1991)*, pp. 211–222, New York: ACM, 1991.

[149] S.C. Kleene, *Introduction to Metamathematics*, Princeton, NJ: D. van Nostrand, 1952.

[150] D.E. Knuth, J.H. Morris, and V.R. Pratt, 'Fast pattern matching in strings', *SIAM Journal of Computation*, 6(2):323–350, 1977.

[151] H.J. Komorowski, 'A specification of an abstract Prolog machine and its application to partial evaluation', Ph.D. thesis, Linköping University, Sweden, 1981. Linköping Studies in Science and Technology Dissertations 69.

[152] H.J. Komorowski, 'Partial evaluation as a means for inferencing data structures in an applicative language: A theory and implementation in the case of Prolog', in *Ninth ACM Symposium on Principles of Programming Languages, Albuquerque, New Mexico*, pp. 255–267, 1982.

[153] J. Komorowski, *Synthesis of Programs in the Framework of Partial Deduction*, Reports on Computer Science and Mathematics, Ser. A 81, Department of Computer Science, Åbo Akademi, Finland, 1989.

[154] L. Kott, 'Unfold/fold program transformations', in M. Nivat and J. Reynolds (eds.), *Algebraic Methods in Semantics*, pp. 411–434, Cambridge: Cambridge University Press, 1985.

[155] H. Kröger, 'Static-scope-Lisp: Splitting an interpreter into compiler and run-time system', in W. Brauer (ed.), *GI-11. Jahrestagung, München, Germany, Informatik-Fachberichte 50*, pp. 20–31, Berlin: Springer-Verlag, 1981. (In German).

[156] P. Kursawe, 'How to invent a Prolog machine', *New Generation Computing*, 5:97–114, 1987.

[157] P. Kursawe, 'Pure partial evaluation and instantiation', in D. Bjørner, A.P. Ershov, and N.D. Jones (eds.), *Partial Evaluation and Mixed Computation*, pp. 283–298, Amsterdam: North-Holland, 1988.

[158] A. Lakhotia and L. Sterling, 'How to control unfolding when specializing interpreters', *New Generation Computing*, 8(1):61–70, 1990.

[159] A. Lakhotia and L. Sterling, 'ProMiX: A Prolog partial evaluation system', in L. Sterling (ed.), *The Practice of Prolog*, chapter 5, pp. 137–179, Cambridge, MA: MIT Press, 1991.

[160] J. Lam and A. Kusalik, *A Partial Evaluation of Partial Evaluators for Pure Prolog*, Technical Report TR 90-9, Department of Computational Science, University of Saskatchewan, Canada, November 1990.

[161] P.J. Landin, 'The mechanical evaluation of expressions', *Computer Journal*, 6(4):308–320, January 1964.

[162] P.J. Landin, 'A correspondence between Algol 60 and Church's lambda-notation', *Communications of the ACM*, 8:89–101 and 158–165, 1965.

[163] J. Lassez, M.J. Maher, and K. Marriott, 'Unification revisited', in J. Minker (ed.), *Foundations of Deductive Databases and Logic Programming*, chapter 15, pp. 587–625, Los Altos, CA: Morgan Kauffman, 1988.

[164] J. Launchbury, 'Projections for specialisation', in D. Bjørner, A.P. Ershov, and N.D. Jones (eds.), *Partial Evaluation and Mixed Computation*, pp. 299–315, Amsterdam: North-Holland, 1988.

[165] J. Launchbury, 'Projection factorisations in partial evaluation', Ph.D. thesis, Department of Computing, University of Glasgow, November 1989. Revised version in [167].

[166] J. Launchbury, 'Dependent sums express separation of binding times', in K. Davis and J. Hughes (eds.), *Functional Programming, Glasgow, Scotland, 1989*, pp. 238–253, Berlin: Springer-Verlag, 1990.

[167] J. Launchbury, *Projection Factorisations in Partial Evaluation*, Cambridge: Cambridge University Press, 1991.

[168] J. Launchbury, 'Strictness and binding-time analyses: Two for the price of one', in *SIGPLAN '91 Conference on Programming Language Design and Implementation, June 1991, Toronto, Canada (Sigplan Notices, vol. 26, no. 6, June 1991)*, pp. 80–91, New York: ACM, 1991.

[169] J. Launchbury, 'A strongly-typed self-applicable partial evaluator', in J. Hughes (ed.), *Functional Programming Languages and Computer Architecture, Cambridge, Massachusetts, August 1991 (Lecture Notes in Computer Science, vol. 523)*, pp. 145–164, ACM, Berlin: Springer-Verlag, 1991.

[170] P. Lee, *Realistic Compiler Generation*, Cambridge, MA: MIT Press, 1989.

[171] P. Lee and U. Pleban, 'A realistic compiler generator based on high-level semantics', in *Fourteenth Symposium on Principles of Programming Languages, Munich, Germany, January 1987*, pp. 284–295, New York: ACM, 1987.

[172] G. Levi and G. Sardu, 'Partial evaluation of metaprograms in a multiple worlds logic language', *New Generation Computing*, 6(2,3):227–247, 1988.

[173] B. Lisper, 'Detecting static algorithms by partial evaluation', in *Partial Evaluation and Semantics-Based Program Manipulation, New Haven, Connecticut (Sigplan Notices, vol. 26, no. 9, September 1991)*, pp. 31–42, New York: ACM, 1991.

[174] J.W. Lloyd and J.C. Shepherdson, 'Partial evaluation in logic programming', *Journal of Logic Programming*, 11:217–242, 1991.

[175] L.A. Lombardi, 'Incremental computation', in F.L. Alt and M. Rubinoff (eds.), *Advances in Computers, vol. 8*, pp. 247–333, New York: Academic Press, 1967.

[176] L.A. Lombardi and B. Raphael, 'Lisp as the language for an incremental computer', in E.C. Berkeley and D.G. Bobrow (eds.), *The Programming Language Lisp: Its Operation and Applications*, pp. 204–219, Cambridge, MA: MIT Press, 1964.

[177] K. Malmkjær, 'Predicting properties of residual programs', in *Partial Evaluation and Semantics-Based Program Manipulation, San Francisco, California, June 1992 (Technical Report YALEU/DCS/RR-909)*, pp. 8–13, New Haven, CT: Yale University, 1992.

[178] M. Marquard and B. Steensgaard, 'Partial evaluation of an object-oriented imperative language', Master's thesis, DIKU, University of Copenhagen, Denmark, 1992.

[179] S. Mazaher and D.M. Berry, 'Deriving a compiler from an operational semantics written in VDL', *Computer Languages*, 10(2):147–164, 1985.

[180] J. McCarthy, 'A basis for a mathematical theory of computation', in P. Brafford and D. Hirschberg (eds.), *Computer Programming and Formal Systems*, pp. 33–70, Amsterdam: North-Holland, 1964.

[181] J. McCarthy *et al.*, *LISP 1.5 Programmer's Manual*, MIT Computation Center and Research Laboratory of Electronics, 1962.

[182] U. Meyer, 'Techniques for partial evaluation of imperative languages', in *Partial Evaluation and Semantics-Based Program Manipulation, New Haven, Connecticut (Sigplan Notices, vol. 26, no. 9, September 1991)*, pp. 94–105, New York: ACM, 1991.

[183] U. Meyer, 'Partial evaluation of imperative languages', Ph.D. thesis, Justus-Liebig-Universität, Giessen, Germany, 1992. (In German).

[184] R. Milner, 'A theory of type polymorphism in programming', *Journal of Computer and System Sciences*, 17:348–375, 1978.

[185] R. Milner, M. Tofte, and R. Harper, *The Definition of Standard ML*, Cambridge, MA: MIT Press, 1990.

[186] T. Mogensen, 'The application of partial evaluation to ray-tracing', Master's thesis, DIKU, University of Copenhagen, Denmark, 1986.

[187] T. Mogensen, 'Partially static structures in a self-applicable partial evaluator', in D. Bjørner, A.P. Ershov, and N.D. Jones (eds.), *Partial Evaluation and Mixed Computation*, pp. 325–347, Amsterdam: North-Holland, 1988.

[188] T. Mogensen, 'Binding time analysis for polymorphically typed higher order languages', in J. Diaz and F. Orejas (eds.), *TAPSOFT '89. Proc. Int. Conf. Theory and Practice of Software Development, Barcelona, Spain, March 1989 (Lecture Notes in Computer Science, vol. 352)*, pp. 298–312, Berlin: Springer-Verlag, 1989.

[189] T. Mogensen, 'Binding time aspects of partial evaluation', Ph.D. thesis, DIKU, University of Copenhagen, Denmark, March 1989.

[190] T. Mogensen, 'Separating binding times in language specifications', in *Fourth International Conference on Functional Programming Languages and Computer Architecture, London, England, September 1989*, pp. 14–25, Reading, MA: Addison-Wesley, 1989.

[191] T. Mogensen, 'Self-applicable partial evaluation for pure lambda calculus', in *Partial Evaluation and Semantics-Based Program Manipulation, San Francisco, California, June 1992 (Technical Report YALEU/DCS/RR-909)*, pp. 116–121, New Haven, CT: Yale University, 1992.

[192] T. Mogensen and A. Bondorf, 'Logimix: A self-applicable partial evaluator for Prolog', in K.-K. Lau and T. Clement (eds.), *LOPSTR 92. Workshops in Computing*, Berlin: Springer-Verlag, January 1993.

[193] F.L. Morris, 'The next 700 formal language descriptions'. (Stanford University, California), November 1970.

[194] P. Mosses, 'Mathematical semantics and compiler generation', Ph.D. thesis, Oxford University, England, 1975.

[195] P. Mosses, *SIS — Semantics Implementation System, Reference Manual and User Guide*, DAIMI Report MD-30, DAIMI, University of Århus, Denmark, 1979.

[196] C. Mossin, 'Similix binding time debugger manual, system version 4.0', Included in Similix distribution, September 1991.

[197] A. Mycroft, 'Abstract interpretation and optimising transformations for applicative programs', Ph.D. thesis, Department of Computer Science, University of Edinburgh, Scotland, 1981. Also report CST-15-81.

[198] F. Nielson, 'A denotational framework for data flow analysis', *Acta Informatica*, 18:265–287, 1982.

[199] F. Nielson, 'A formal type system for comparing partial evaluators', in D. Bjørner, A.P. Ershov, and N.D. Jones (eds.), *Partial Evaluation and Mixed Computation*, pp. 349–384, Amsterdam: North-Holland, 1988.

[200] F. Nielson, 'Two-level semantics and abstract interpretation', *Theoretical Computer Science – Fundamental Studies*, 69:117–242, 1989.

[201] F. Nielson and H.R. Nielson, *Two-Level Functional Languages*, volume 34 of *Tracts in Theoretical Computer Science*, Cambridge: Cambridge University Press, 1992.

[202] H.R. Nielson and F. Nielson, 'Automatic binding time analysis for a typed λ-calculus', *Science of Computer Programming*, 10:139–176, 1988.

[203] H.R. Nielson and F. Nielson, 'Transformations on higher-order functions', in *Fourth International Conference on Functional Programming Languages and Computer Architecture, London, England, September 1989*, pp. 129–143, Reading, MA: Addison-Wesley, 1989.

[204] H.R. Nielson and F. Nielson, 'Using transformation in the implementation of higher-order functions', *Journal of Functional Programming*, 1(4):459–494, 1991.

[205] V. Nirkhe and W. Pugh, 'Partial evaluation and high-level imperative programming languages with applications in hard real-time systems', in *Nineteenth ACM Symposium on Principles of Programming Languages, Albuquerque, New Mexico, January 1992*, pp. 269–280, New York: ACM, 1992.

[206] S. Oliver and N. D. Jones, 'Interpreting transition matrices - a novel application of microprogramming', in *ACM SIGMINI-SIGPLAN Interface Meeting on the Small Processor Environment*, pp. 70–77, New York: ACM, 1976.

[207] B.N. Ostrovski, 'Implementation of controlled mixed computation in system for automatic development of language-oriented parsers', in D. Bjørner, A.P. Ershov, and N.D. Jones (eds.), *Partial Evaluation and Mixed Computation*, pp. 385–403, Amsterdam: North-Holland, 1988.

[208] S. Owen, 'Issues in the partial evaluation of meta-interpreters', in H. Abramson and M.H. Rogers (eds.), *Meta-Programming in Logic Programming*, pp. 319–340, Cambridge, MA: MIT Press, 1989.

[209] F.G. Pagan, 'On the generation of compilers from language definitions', *Information Processing Letters*, 10(2):104–107, March 1980.

[210] F.G. Pagan, 'Converting interpreters into compilers', *Software — Practice and Experience*, 18(6):509–527, June 1988.

[211] F.G. Pagan, 'Partial computation as a practical aid in the compiler construction course', *SIGCSE Bulletin*, 21(2):2–8, June 1989.

[212] F.G. Pagan, 'Comparative efficiency of general and residual parsers', *Sigplan Notices*, 25(4):59–65, April 1990.

[213] F.G. Pagan, *Partial Computation and the Construction of Language Processors*, Englewood Cliffs, NJ: Prentice Hall, 1991.

[214] L. Paulson, 'A semantics-directed compiler generator', in *Ninth ACM Symposium on Principles of Programming Languages*, pp. 224–233, New York: ACM, 1982.

[215] L. Paulson, 'Compiler generation from denotational semantics', in B. Lorho (ed.), *Methods and Tools for Compiler Construction*, pp. 219–250, Cambridge: Cambridge University Press, 1984.

[216] T.J. Penello, 'Very fast LR parsing', in *Sigplan '86 Conference on Compiler Construction, Palo Alto, California (Sigplan Notices, vol. 21, no. 7, July 1986)*, pp. 145–151, ACM, 1986.

[217] K. Pingali and A. Rogers, 'Compiler parallelization of simple for a distributed memory machine', in *International Conference on Parallel Programming, St. Charles IL, August 1990*, 1990.

[218] U.F. Pleban, 'Compiler prototyping using formal semantics', in *Symposium on Compiler Construction (Sigplan Notices, vol. 19, no. 6, June 1984)*, pp. 94–105, New York: ACM, 1984.

[219] G. Plotkin, 'Call-by-name, call-by-value and the lambda-calculus', *Theoretical Computer Science*, 1:125–159, 1975.

[220] G.D. Plotkin, *A Structural Approach to Operational Semantics*, Technical Report FN-19, DAIMI, Aarhus University, Denmark, 1981.

[221] C. Pu, H. Massalin, and J. Ioannidis, 'The synthesis kernel', *Computing Systems*, 1(1):11–32, 1988.

[222] J. C. Reynolds, 'Types, abstraction, and parametric polymorphism', in R. E. A. Mason (ed.), *Information Processing '83. Proceedings of the IFIP 9th World Computer Congress*, pp. 513–523, IFIP, Amsterdam: North-Holland, 1983.

[223] J.C. Reynolds, 'Definitional interpreters for higher-order programming languages', in *ACM Annual Conference, Boston, MA, August 1972*, pp. 717–740, New York: ACM, 1972.

[224] G. Richardson, 'The realm of Nevryon', *Micro User*, June 1991.

[225] A. Rogers and K. Pingali, 'Process decomposition through locality of reference', in *1989 SIGPLAN Conference on Programming Language Design and Implementation, Portland OR, June 1989*, pp. 69–80, New York: ACM, 1989.

[226] H. Rogers, *Theory of Recursive Functions and Effective Computability*, New York: McGraw-Hill, 1967.

[227] S.A. Romanenko, 'A compiler generator produced by a self-applicable specializer can have a surprisingly natural and understandable structure', in D. Bjørner, A.P. Ershov, and N.D. Jones (eds.), *Partial Evaluation and Mixed Computation*, pp. 445–463, Amsterdam: North-Holland, 1988.

[228] S.A. Romanenko, 'Arity raiser and its use in program specialization', in N. Jones (ed.), *ESOP '90. 3rd European Symposium on Programming, Copenhagen, Denmark, May 1990 (Lecture Notes in Computer Science, vol. 432)*, pp. 341–360, Berlin: Springer-Verlag, 1990.

[229] E. Ruf, 'Topics in online partial evaluation', Ph.D. thesis, Stanford University, California, February 1993. Published as technical report CSL-TR-93-563.

[230] E. Ruf and D. Weise, *Opportunities for Online Partial Evaluation*, Technical Report CSL-TR-92-516, Computer Systems Laboratory, Stanford University, Stanford, CA, April 1992.

[231] E. Ruf and D. Weise, *Preserving Information during Online Partial Evaluation*, Technical Report CSL-TR-92-517, Computer Systems Laboratory, Stanford University, Stanford, CA, April 1992.

[232] E. Ruf and D. Weise, 'On the specialization of online program specializers', *Journal of Functional Programming*, 1993. To appear.

[233] B. Rytz and M. Gengler, 'A polyvariant binding time analysis', in *Partial Evaluation and Semantics-Based Program Manipulation, San Francisco, California, June 1992 (Technical Report YALEU/DCS/RR-909)*, pp. 21–28, New Haven, CT: Yale University, 1992.

[234] S. Safra and E. Shapiro, 'Meta interpreters for real', in H.-J. Kugler (ed.), *Information Processing 86, Dublin, Ireland*, pp. 271–278, Amsterdam: North-Holland, 1986.

[235] D. Sahlin, 'The Mixtus approach to automatic partial evaluation of full Prolog', in S. Debray and M. Hermenegildo (eds.), *Logic Programming: Proceedings of the 1990 North American Conference, Austin, Texas, October 1990*, pp. 377–398, Cambridge, MA: MIT Press, 1990.

[236] D. Sahlin, 'An automatic partial evaluator for full prolog', Ph.D. thesis, Kungliga Tekniska Högskolan, Stockholm, Sweden, 1991. Report TRITA-TCS-9101.

[237] C. Sakama and H. Itoh, 'Partial evaluation of queries in deductive databases', *New Generation Computing*, 6(2,3):249–258, 1988.

[238] W.L. Scherlis, 'Expression procedures and program derivation', Ph.D. thesis, Stanford University, California, August 1980. Stanford Computer Science Report STAN-CS-80-818.

[239] W.L. Scherlis, 'Program improvement by internal specialization', in *Eighth ACM Symposium on Principles of Programming Languages, Williamsburg, Virginia, January 1981*, pp. 41–49, New York: ACM, 1981.

[240] D.A. Schmidt, 'Compiler generation from lambda calculus definitions of programming languages', Ph.D. thesis, Kansas State University, Kansas, USA, 1981.

[241] D.A. Schmidt, *Denotational Semantics*, Boston, MA: Allyn and Bacon, 1986.

[242] D.A. Schmidt, 'Static properties of partial evaluation', in D. Bjørner, A.P. Ershov, and N.D. Jones (eds.), *Partial Evaluation and Mixed Computation*, pp. 465–483, Amsterdam: North-Holland, 1988.

[243] R. Schooler, 'Partial evaluation as a means of language extensibility', Master's thesis, MIT/LCS/TR-324, Laboratory for Computer Science, MIT, Cambridge, Massachusetts, August 1984.

[244] D.S. Scott, *Lectures on a Mathematical Theory of Computation*, Technical Report PRG-19, Programming Research Group, Oxford University, 1981.

[245] P. Sestoft, 'The structure of a self-applicable partial evaluator', in H. Ganzinger and N.D. Jones (eds.), *Programs as Data Objects, Copenhagen, Denmark, 1985 (Lecture Notes in Computer Science, vol. 217)*, pp. 236–256, Berlin: Springer-Verlag, 1986.

[246] P. Sestoft, 'Automatic call unfolding in a partial evaluator', in D. Bjørner, A.P. Ershov, and N.D. Jones (eds.), *Partial Evaluation and Mixed Computation*, pp. 485–506, Amsterdam: North-Holland, 1988.

[247] P. Sestoft, 'Replacing function parameters by global variables', Master's thesis, DIKU, University of Copenhagen, Denmark, October 1988.

[248] P. Sestoft and A.V. Zamulin, 'Annotated bibliography on partial evaluation and mixed computation', *New Generation Computing*, 6(2, 3):309–354, 1988.

[249] P. Sestoft and A.V. Zamulin, 'Annotated bibliography on partial evaluation and mixed computation', in D. Bjørner, A.P. Ershov, and N.D. Jones (eds.), *Partial Evaluation and Mixed Computation*, pp. 589–622, Amsterdam: North-Holland, 1988.

[250] D. Sherman, R. Strandh, and I. Durand, 'Optimization of equational programs using partial evaluation', in *Partial Evaluation and Semantics-Based Program Manipulation, New Haven, Connecticut (Sigplan Notices, vol. 26, no. 9, September 1991)*, pp. 72–82, New York: ACM, 1991.

[251] M. Sintzoff, 'Calculating properties of programs by valuations on specific models', in *ACM Conference on Proving Assertions about Programs, Las Cruces, Mexico (Sigplan Notices, vol. 7. no. 1, January 1972)*, pp. 203–207, New York: ACM, 1972.

[252] D.A. Smith, 'Partial evaluation of pattern matching in constraint logic programming languages', in *Partial Evaluation and Semantics-Based Program Manipulation, New Haven, Connecticut (Sigplan Notices, vol. 26, no. 9, September 1991)*, pp. 62–71, New York: ACM, 1991.

[253] B. Steensgaard and M. Marquard, 'Parameter splitting in a higher order functional language'. Student Project 90-7-1, DIKU, University of Copenhagen, Denmark, August 1990.

[254] L. Sterling and R.D. Beer, 'Incremental flavor-mixing of meta-interpreters for expert system construction', in *Proc. 3rd Symposium on Logic Programming, Salt Lake City, Utah*, pp. 20–27, New York: IEEE Computer Society, 1986.

[255] L. Sterling and R.D. Beer, 'Metainterpreters for expert system construction', *Journal of Logic Programming*, 6:163–178, 1989.

[256] J.E. Stoy, *Denotational Semantics: The Scott-Strachey Approach to Programming Language Theory*, Cambridge, MA: MIT Press, 1977.

[257] R.S. Sundaresh, 'Building incremental programs using partial evaluation', in *Partial Evaluation and Semantics-Based Program Manipulation, New Haven, Connecticut (Sigplan Notices, vol. 26, no. 9, September 1991)*, pp. 83–93, New York: ACM, 1991.

[258] R.S. Sundaresh and P. Hudak, 'Incremental computation via partial evaluation', in *Eighteenth Annual ACM Symposium on Principles of Programming Languages, Orlando, Florida*, pp. 1–13, New York: ACM, January 1991.

[259] A. Takeuchi, 'Affinity between meta interpreters and partial evaluation', in H.-J. Kugler (ed.), *Information Processing 86, Dublin, Ireland*, pp. 279–282, Amsterdam: North-Holland, 1986.

[260] A. Takeuchi and K. Furukawa, 'Partial evaluation of Prolog programs and its application to meta programming', in H.-J. Kugler (ed.), *Information Processing 86, Dublin, Ireland*, pp. 415–420, Amsterdam: North-Holland, 1986.

[261] A. Tarski, 'A lattice-theoretical fixpoint theorem and its applications', *Pacific Journal of Mathematics*, 5:285–309, 1955.

[262] M. Tofte, *Compiler Generators. What They Can Do, What They Might Do, and What They Will Probably Never Do*, volume 19 of *EATCS Monographs on Theoretical Computer Science*, Berlin: Springer-Verlag, 1990. Earlier version: DIKU Report 84/8, DIKU, University of Copenhagen, Denmark, 1984.

[263] V.F. Turchin (ed.), *Basic Refal and Its Implementation on Computers*, Moscow: GOS-STROI SSSR, TsNIPIASS, 1977. (In Russian).

[264] V.F. Turchin, 'A supercompiler system based on the language Refal', *SIGPLAN Notices*, 14(2):46–54, February 1979.

[265] V.F. Turchin, 'Semantic definitions in Refal and automatic production of compilers', in N.D. Jones (ed.), *Semantics-Directed Compiler Generation, Aarhus, Denmark (Lecture Notes in Computer Science, vol. 94)*, pp. 441–474, Berlin: Springer-Verlag, 1980.

[266] V.F. Turchin, 'The use of metasystem transition in theorem proving and program optimization', in J. De Bakker and J. van Leeuven (eds.), *Automata, Languages and Programming. Seventh ICALP, Noordwijkerhout, The Netherlands (Lecture Notes in Computer Science, vol. 85)*, pp. 645–657, Berlin: Springer-Verlag, 1980.

[267] V.F. Turchin, 'The concept of a supercompiler', *ACM Transactions on Programming Languages and Systems*, 8(3):292–325, July 1986.

[268] V.F. Turchin, 'Program transformation by supercompilation', in H. Ganzinger and N.D. Jones (eds.), *Programs as Data Objects, Copenhagen, Denmark, 1985 (Lecture Notes in Computer Science, vol. 217)*, pp. 257–281, Berlin: Springer-Verlag, 1986.

[269] V.F. Turchin, 'The algorithm of generalization in the supercompiler', in D. Bjørner, A.P. Ershov, and N.D. Jones (eds.), *Partial Evaluation and Mixed Computation*, pp. 531–549, Amsterdam: North-Holland, 1988.

[270] V.F. Turchin, R.M. Nirenberg, and D.V. Turchin, 'Experiments with a supercompiler', in *1982 ACM Symposium on Lisp and Functional Programming, Pittsburgh, Pennsylvania*, pp. 47–55, New York: ACM, 1982.

[271] F. van Harmelen and A. Bundy, 'Explanation-based generalisation = partial evaluation', *Artificial Intelligence*, 36:401–412, 1988.

[272] R. Venken, 'A Prolog meta-interpreter for partial evaluation and its application to source to source transformation and query-optimisation', in T. O'Shea (ed.), *ECAI-84, Advances in Artificial Intelligence, Pisa, Italy*, pp. 91–100, Amsterdam: North-Holland, 1984.

[273] R. Venken and B. Demoen, 'A partial evaluation system for Prolog: Some practical considerations', *New Generation Computing*, 6(2,3):279–290, 1988.

[274] P. Wadler, 'Deforestation: Transforming programs to eliminate trees', in H. Ganzinger (ed.), *ESOP'88. 2nd European Symposium on Programming, Nancy, France, March 1988 (Lecture Notes in Computer Science, vol. 300)*, pp. 344–358, Berlin: Springer-Verlag, 1988.

[275] P. Wadler, 'Theorems for free!', in *Fourth International Conference on Functional Programming Languages and Computer Architecture, London, England, September 1989*, pp. 347–359, Reading, MA: Addison-Wesley, 1989.

[276] M. Wand, 'Continuation-based program transformation strategies', *Journal of the ACM*, 27(1):164–180, January 1980.

[277] M. Wand, 'Deriving target code as a representation of continuation semantics', *ACM Transactions on Programming Languages and Systems*, 4(3):496–517, July 1982.

[278] M. Wand, 'From interpreter to compiler: A representational derivation', in H. Ganzinger and N.D. Jones (eds.), *Programs as Data Objects, Copenhagen, Denmark, 1985 (Lecture Notes in Computer Science, vol. 217)*, pp. 306–324, Berlin: Springer-Verlag, 1986.

[279] M. Wand, 'Specifying the correctness of binding-time analysis', in *Twentieth ACM Symposium on Principles of Programming Languages, Charleston, South Carolina, January 1993*, pp. 137–143, ACM, New York: ACM, 1993.

[280] B. Wegbreit, 'Goal-directed program transformation', *IEEE Transactions on Software Engineering*, SE-2(2):69–80, June 1976.

[281] D. Weise, R. Conybeare, E. Ruf, and S. Seligman, 'Automatic online partial evaluation', in J. Hughes (ed.), *Functional Programming Languages and Computer Architecture, Cambridge, Massachusetts, August 1991 (Lecture Notes in Computer Science, vol. 523)*, pp. 165–191, Berlin: Springer-Verlag, 1991.

Index